London's Necropolis

A Guide to Brookwood Cemetery

JOHN M. CLARKE

FOREWORD BY
JULIAN W.S. LITTEN

MODERN PHOTOGRAPHS BY
ANTHONY MONTAN

SUTTON PUBLISHING

First published in 2004 by
Sutton Publishing Limited · Phoenix Mill
Thrupp · Stroud · Gloucestershire · GL5 2BU

Reprinted 2006

British Library Cataloguing in Publication Data
A catalogue record for this book is available from the British Library.

ISBN 0-7509-3513-8

In Memory of my Father
George Edward Clarke
1912–1996
Londoner

Typeset in 10/12 pt Baskerville.
Typesetting and origination by
Sutton Publishing Limited.
Printed and bound in England by
J.H. Haynes & Co. Ltd, Sparkford.

CONTENTS

LIST OF MAPS

LIST OF ILLUSTRATIONS

Where appropriate, reference numbers refer to entries in the main sections of this guide.

ABBREVIATIONS

BEF	British Expeditionary Force
CTC	Cyclists Touring Club
CWGC	Commonwealth War Graves Commission
GER	Great Eastern Railway
GWR	Great Western Railway
IWGC	Imperial War Graves Commission
LNC	London Necropolis [& National Mausoleum] Company
LSWR	London & South Western Railway
LTSR	London Tilbury & Southend Railway
RAF	Royal Air Force
VAD	Voluntary Aid Detachment

FOREWORD

Every historian of the Anglo-Catholic movement will be aware of Fr Mackonochie, Fr Stanton and Fr Dolling, and it was the result of a pilgrimage to the graves of these venerable divines that I took myself to the St Alban's, Holborn, plot at Brookwood Cemetery in the summer of 1972. I was aware of the London Necropolis Company's association with Waterloo Station, and hoped that Brookwood Station would deposit me close to the cemetery. I was not to be disappointed, and was able to walk off the down-line platform and straight into the Necropolis and the Actors' Acre, acquired in 1858 by the Dramatic, Equestrian and Musical Sick Fund.

I had arrived on the late morning of a warm July day. The trees were at their very best, and rhododendron could be seen in profusion. There were no signposts, and I felt both lost and lonely. Walking from the Roman Catholic Chapel to the distant Non-Conformist Chapel I crossed what appeared to be a disused railway track. Deciding to follow it I turned right and was soon traversing a sunken avenue, passing the buildings of the abandoned Masonry Works on my left and then on and up to the two Anglican chapels and then to South station, the siding's terminus. The wooden buildings were deserted, neglected and sad. There was an almost tangible eeriness about the place; the gents' lavatory was still working, but all the other station doors were locked. Looking in through one of the windows I was surprised to see what looked like a pub bar. To this day I wonder if they served 'spirits'.

However, the cemetery did not disappoint. My principle objective was the St Alban's plot, but there was no one to ask directions of. Having looked at the outsides of the two Anglican chapels I took myself off down St Augustine's Avenue and on to the outer circle of St George's Avenue. And, suddenly, there it was: a little ivy-clad lych-gate, with neat rows of tombs. The laity with their feet addressed to the east, the clergy – including my heroes – at the far end of the plot, with their feet addressed to the west, as if to face their long-dead congregation when all will stand up at the Last Day. It was a glad meeting, and the result of much research on my behalf to discover where they might be.

Coming out of the St Alban's plot I continued my journey round St George's Avenue. To my left was an overgrown expanse, full of graves, but too much of a wilderness to explore. I was soon back on the disused railway track, so I retraced my steps to Brookwood station, turning left by the site of North station, and down Long Avenue to the military cemeteries. The American chapel came as a great surprise. It looked like a private mausoleum in Greenwood Cemetery, New York; the interior was neat and tidy, and not even the flags had been vandalised. I was fascinated by the Czechoslovakian plot, with its enormous rampant bronze lion, a most robust statement when compared to the adjacent RAF ground with its regulation Commonwealth War Graves Commission headstones.

What I had not been prepared for was the wealth of mausoleums. The massive Scottish granite Dudgeon mausoleum, the huge structure entombing the Wood family, the delicate Italianate loggia of the Drake mausoleum, the Gothic structure for the Keith family, the pink granite Egyptian tomb of the Hughes family and the brick columbarium for the Phipson family, to mention but a few. However, the best structures were to be found in the Parsee section, opened in 1862, and the massive mausoleums of the Tata and Wadia familes, arguably amongst the best – and best-kept – mausoleums in Great Britain.

My second visit to Brookwood, in the late 1980s, gave me more time to explore off the main avenues. It was then that I came across the burial grounds established by various religious communities, such as those of the Sisterhood of St John the Divine and of the Order of Reparation to Jesus in the Blessed Sacrament, both opened in 1872, of the Community of the Holy Name (1887) and of St Mary's Convent, Wantage (1920). More unusual were the burial grounds of the Ancient Order of Foresters (1863), the London & South Western Railway (1865), the Independent Order of Oddfellows (1869) and the Corps of Commissionaires (c. 1870).

One way whereby the Cemetery served the burial needs of the metropolis was by offering space for those churches without burial provision or whose churchyards were deemed 'full'. In addition to St Alban's, Holborn (1863), other parishes that acquired extensive plots at Brookwood include St Saviour, Southwark, in 1854, the three parishes of St Anne, Soho, St Margaret, Westminster, and St John, Westminster, in 1855 and St Stephen, Gloucester Road, in 1910. The Royal Hospital, Chelsea, acquired a plot in 1894.

Brookwood was also empowered under its original Act not only to accept but also to manage the disinterment and transfer of remains from redundant City churches, churchyards and burial grounds. The first parish to take up this opportunity was St Margaret, Westminster, in 1866. Between 1875 and 1900 Brookwood received the disinterred remains from twelve more churches,[1] including its oldest burial: a coffin of 1559 from the vaults of St Michael, Wood Street, City of London. Twentieth-century removals include those from St George, Botolph Lane (1902), Holy Trinity, Kingsway (1909), St Olave, Southwark (1928), St George, Southwark (1940), St Swithin, Cannon Street (1958), and St Marylebone and St Michael, Fish Street Hill, as recently as 1987.

The coin that John Clarke has minted is one of much worth. His story is one of great beginnings and sad endings, of a cemetery dogged with indecision at all stages of its history, of an inability to accept modern trends and an erosion of the consecrated and non-conformist sections by the intrusion of other faith burials in an attempt to keep the cemetery alive. In the 1870s one of the cemetery's greatest advocates, Sir Francis Seymour Haden, railed against cremation, issuing the prophetic words that the process was 'wasteful, costly and would unnecessarily pollute the atmosphere'. This was followed up in 1946 with an observation from Edward White, the distinguished landscape architect, that most cremation gardens were primitive and featureless. Rightly or wrongly, Brookwood resisted building a crematorium. And that was almost certainly the beginning of its decline as a place of burial.

What I had not been prepared for in 1972 was the sheer size of the cemetery. Four hundred acres, with so much space between the plots that one could scarcely believe that it contained the remains of a quarter of a million people. What I did not know then was that the cemetery is only a fifth of the size of the original purchase and that its quarter of a million occupants represents the Company's hopes of potential occupation in 1879 rather than 1972.

John Clarke is to be congratulated for bringing the story of Brookwood to life. It is a tribute to one of the greatest unsung enterprises of the nineteenth century: to establish a single cemetery for Great Britain, utilising the efficiency of the railway system, and affording large parochial and community plots. That it failed was due to the multiplicity of public and private cemeteries throughout the country, indecision within the London Necropolis Company itself, and lack of central government support to promote Brookwood as England's Valhalla.

Julian W.S. Litten Ph.D. FSA
Walthamstow, January 2004

PREFACE

Brookwood Cemetery is the largest burial ground in the United Kingdom. Opened in 1854 by the London Necropolis & National Mausoleum Company (LNC) and at that time, the largest cemetery in the world, it was intended to become London's only cemetery, big enough to serve the capital for ever. Even today Brookwood is vast and quite unlike any of the other cemeteries it was designed to surpass and replace. The bold, imaginative planting, which includes several avenues of giant sequoia, has now matured. The grounds include some major pieces of architecture, as well as areas of conservation and natural beauty. Brookwood Cemetery is a national treasure, a 'star of England', ours to enjoy and to cherish. But few seem to know of it, and fewer still care about Brookwood. It is one of Surrey's (and the south's) best-kept secrets. I hope this guide will prove that Brookwood deserves to be recognised as a site of national historical importance.

There is an enormous indifference to most of our country's cemeteries and burial grounds. These largely Victorian showpieces are still sadly misunderstood and disregarded, and therein lies the major threat to their future. The neglect that is only too apparent in these burial grounds arises from many factors: burial is not as common as it was; many families no longer visit or tend loved ones' graves; no longer do families invest in the maintenance of graves, should visiting be difficult;[1] the dead are rarely respected or remembered, as persistent vandalism reveals; and cemetery managers are left with the problem of trying to maintain grounds against static or falling incomes, while being condemned for neglecting their charges by those who misunderstand the perilous economics of modern burial ground management. It is a remarkable paradox that despite the affluence of modern society modern man neglects his past.[2] Too few people realise that cemeteries may be interpreted and enjoyed in many ways: they were and are guides to architecture, sculpture, landscape gardening, history, education, arboriculture, botany, wildlife and general gardening, and provide valuable public open spaces.

Despite the enormous importance of Brookwood Cemetery in the funerary history of Britain, as an attempt to solve London's burial problem once and for all time, its significance has still to be acknowledged, recognised and supported by bodies such as the Department of National Heritage, English Heritage, Surrey County Council or Woking Borough Council. Consequently it has yet to attract any major funding or grants for restoration, repairs and maintenance. Woking Borough Council has until very recently remained remarkably indifferent to this historic gem set within its western wards. And unfortunately, as this guide makes clear, the council is responsible for one of the worst planning decisions regarding Brookwood Cemetery, by allowing the intrusive redevelopment of the former superintendent's offices.

No general guide to those buried at Brookwood was ever produced by the LNC. Brochures of the time alluded to 'renowned Actors and Artists, Doctors and Divines, Laymen and Lawyers, Servants and Statesmen, Soldiers and Sailors', yet were curiously reticent about naming names.[3]

This book is designed to fill this enormous omission by listing over 800 items or individuals of interest. The range of people buried here is astonishingly broad and reflects virtually all levels of a lost society. That Brookwood was originally conceived as *the* cemetery for London should not be regarded as imposing any geographical (or social) limitation on those represented in its spacious grounds. At one extreme are the humble pauper burial areas, with their anonymous depressions in the ground; at the other the grave of a Master of the Household of Queen Victoria, with its fantastic statuary memorial. Here are the graves of four women executed at Holloway Prison; elsewhere are the relics of a saint. Brookwood incorporates burials from Finchley to Fiji, from Beer to Bombay.

Prior to the publication of this guide the only one available was *An Introduction to Brookwood Cemetery*, which was originally compiled for the launch of the Brookwood Cemetery Society in April 1992.[4] This listed just sixty-two separate items, although the Society promised a more definitive guide within two years. Unfortunately this target could not be met, while ongoing and continuing research resulted in many new discoveries within the cemetery grounds. Therefore it was decided to wait a little longer before a more comprehensive guide was compiled. Meanwhile the Society produced a series of 'trails', or mini-guides, describing routes through various parts of the cemetery grounds. So far eight trail leaflets have been produced which, together with the *Introduction*, describe over 180 items within the cemetery grounds. However, the scale of selection used in the trail guides is illustrated by the size and scope of this new guide, which describes a total of over 800 items within the cemetery. Even so, this guide remains incomplete. In order to be truly comprehensive, it would have to list all those contained in the cemetery's burial registers, a total of about 235,000 names, which is outside the scope of this publication. The guide is therefore necessarily selective in its approach, but seeks to include a much broader range of individuals, from humble paupers to the aristocracy, than was possible in the original *Introduction* and trail guides.

Brookwood Cemetery is partly known for its railway funeral service. This operated from a private station just outside Waterloo and trains actually ran through the cemetery grounds. The service all but ceased in April 1941 when the station in London was bombed. The railway does not feature as a major factor in this guide, although the location of the cemetery stations and parts of the route are noted in the relevant sections. Readers requiring further details of the service should obtain my book *The Brookwood Necropolis Railway*, originally published in 1983 and still in print.[5]

Despite the research undertaken by members of the Society a number of graves of individuals known to be buried in the cemetery have so far evaded location. These 'missing persons' – missing because they cannot be included in any of the chapters – are listed, with brief biographical notes, in Appendix A. The author would welcome details of the location of the graves concerned (assuming they survive), or indeed for any graves that may have been unfortunately overlooked for inclusion in this guide. Such discoveries and rediscoveries will be included in any subsequent edition of this guide.

In listing the great and good, the rich and poor, the famous and infamous, the otherwise forgotten heroes and heroines, slaves and sultans with stories to tell, this guide is designed to encourage interested readers to visit Brookwood and so discover this unique cemetery for themselves. It really is a 'fine and private place', as many visitors to Brookwood have discovered. The cemetery provides a window on to the world of our Victorian and Edwardian forebears as effective as any study of the art, architecture or literature of these periods. The ancient Egyptians believed that 'to speak the name of the dead is to make them live again'. Through reading these pages, and perhaps by visiting their graves, a special sort of immortality will be granted to those who lie in London's greatest cemetery.

During the twenty-seven years or so that I have come to know Brookwood Cemetery I have visited it at all times of the day (and night), and at all seasons of the year. It never fails to fascinate and inspire me. It truly represents the extraordinary boldness and vision of our Victorian forefathers. James Stevens Curl, in his *Victorian Celebration of Death*, states that 'the Victorians did things in a big way, and their cemeteries echo that grandeur of vision and hope for a future which vanished in 1914'.[6] All this is true. I hope this guide will encourage you to visit the cemetery and become convinced of its charm, beauty and importance in the history of the Victorian celebration of death.

John Clarke
Surbiton, Surrey
April 2003

OTHER BOOKS BY THE SAME AUTHOR

The Brookwood Necropolis Railway
An Introduction to Brookwood Cemetery

ACKNOWLEDGEMENTS

Many people have helped me gather information on Brookwood Cemetery over
number of years. My principal debts rest with Mark Wealthy, the source of muc.
precious information and material; George Lambert, an ex-Superintendent of th
London Necropolis; and the staff at the Brookwood Cemetery Office: Mr Ramadan Guney an
Mrs Diane Guney. In the past I have received assistance from the previous owner of the cemeter
Mr D.J. Dally, and his secretaries, Miss E.M. Iggulden (later Mrs Maeder) and Mrs Jackson.

I am very grateful to Dr Julian Litten for agreeing to write a foreword especially for this book. Als
many thanks to Brian Parsons, who read the entire manuscript and made many valuable suggestion
additions and improvements to the text. Any remaining errors or omissions are my own.

I am indebted to the following for their help in particular areas: Father Alexis and othe
members of the St Edward Brotherhood, Ian Alvey, Mrs S. Argyropoulo, the Revd Bria
Arscott, Claire Aston, Sheila and Tim Baker, David and Sian Barber, Mr C.J.S. Bartlett, Luc
Baxter, Mrs T. Beal, Mr A. Bisset, Jennie Bisset, Mr and Mrs Blanks, James and Susan Brazie
Mr D. Brooks, Joyce Brown, Mrs V. Brown, Mrs T. Bullen, Mr and Miss Charlton, Mr
Clifford, Tina Cockett, Mrs M. Cockram, Ms R. Coombes, Mr B. Copper, David and Lynr
Cowley, Mrs G. Dalgleish, Mr M. Darling, Mr L. Davies, Mr and Mrs Dendy, Kevin and Mar
Desmond, Mr I. Devine, Amanda Devonshire, Edward Evans, Sir B. Falkiner, Mrs B.A. Farris
Mr D. Finnegan, Mrs A. Fisk, Bob Flanagan, Mr R. Ford, Mr D. Frith, Nick Gilman, Mrs
Graveson, Leslie Grout, David Harvey, Mr H. Haydon, Mr A. Hayhurst, Paul Hetheringto
Lindsay Hewitt, Margaret Hobbs, Mr C. Hobson, Mr H. Holwell, Derek Hoodless, Lisa-Jar
Howe, John and Karen Humpage, His Excellency Mr F. Jitoko, Mr S. Johnson, Sarah and Col
Kellam, Maurice C. Lawson, Dr Julian Litten, Mrs D. Lowes, Mary Lucas, Charl
McLauchlan, Mr John McLaughlin, Sir E.I.R. Moir, Mr R. Molock, Anthony Montan, Mrs
Mukerji, Mr J.P.A. Mullinger, Andrew and Julia Nicholson, Mrs M. Parrett, Brian Parson
Daphne and Rick Pendrill, Joan Pollard, Mr and Mrs Powney, Ms B. Prest, Mrs E.M. Rainfor
John Robertson, Mr R. Rowley, Peter Salter, Mrs J. Shea, Geoff Simpson, Peter Sleath, Robe
Stephenson, Laura Stevens, Mrs E.L. Svoboda, Mr P. Temple, Joanna Toogood, Mr S. Rumb
Mr S. Verrinder, Mr J. Vince, Miss S. Walker, Professor René Weis, Mr Carl Wheeling, Mr
White, Mr D.S. Whitelegge, Mrs M. Wilkins and Dr Robert Wilkins.

I would like to thank the staff at the following libraries and institutions for their unfailing he
the Bodleian Library, Oxford, the British Library, Farnborough Library, the Guildford Institu
the Guildford Muniments Room, Lambeth Library, the Public Record Office (Kew), the Surr
History Centre, the University Library Cambridge, the Westminster Central Reference Libra
and Woking Library.

Images credited to 'Lyndon Davies, Past Images collection' are from a private collecti
marketed as 'Past Images' by retired headteacher and writer Lyndon Davies. The collection
based in Woking and may be contacted via pastimages@hotmail.com.

NOTES ON USING THIS GUIDE

This section describes how to get the most out of using this book. The Introduction gives a history of the LNC and the cemetery. It is followed by the main body of the text, divided into nine chapters, which list the key memorials and structures to be found throughout the cemetery grounds.

Any guide to Brookwood is complicated by the sheer size of the cemetery. The approach taken here is to divide the cemetery grounds into manageable portions, starting first with the natural division provided by Cemetery Pales, which separates the Church of England sections (covered in Chapters 1–6) from the Dissenters (covered in Chapters 7–9). This method has another advantage in that the size and complexity of the cemetery are immediately apparent: that the old Anglican sections form by far the greater part of the grounds. All this is reflected in the structure of the guide.

Each chapter covers a self-contained route through part of the cemetery grounds. There is a key map for each chapter, providing an outline of the route through each section. Monuments or other points of interest are shown as items on these plans, and refer to the appropriate numbered section within the text. Where a portion of the grounds deserves greater attention (for instance, the burial ground of **St Alban the Martyr, Holborn**) a more detailed plan of that area is provided. Each chapter opens with a brief description of the area to be covered, and each grave or item of interest is linked with notes on how to move from one memorial to another. A brief description of the memorial is usually given, while many of the more interesting or obscure ones are illustrated.

Any text printed in **bold type** indicates there is an entry for that person or feature within this guide. Refer to the Index to identify the section where the item is described in more detail. The reference numbers in the Index refer to the chapter number followed by the entry number within that chapter. For instance, an index entry for 2.15 indicates the main entry may be found in Chapter 2, under item 15.

MEMORIAL STYLES

The usual descriptions of memorial styles are as follows:

Body stone
A coffin-shaped stone with a rounded top. The stone is usually the length of the grave space and may be incorporated between a headstone and footstone. This type is uncommon at Brookwood.

Cenotaph
An empty tomb or monument, usually erected to commemorate someone buried elsewhere.

Cross memorials

The cross, as a memorial style, became popular only towards the latter part of the nineteenth century. It has proved very popular, partly because it is relatively cheap to make. There are many styles, including:

- *Calvary cross* – a cross set on top of three stepped bases. Each base may represent faith, hope and charity.
- *Canopied cross* – a cross with a gable top or roof over its top arms.
- *Celtic cross* – a cross where the arms are connected by arcs of a circle (sometimes called a wheel cross), often elaborately carved with Celtic (or other) symbols. Celtic crosses in modern cemeteries are rare before 1890.
- *Cross of Lorraine* – this has two bars, the first (top) being shorter than the second. It was adopted as the emblem of the Free French during the Second World War.
- *Latin cross* – is probably the most common form of memorial design.
- *Maltese cross* – based on the badge of the Knights of Malta, formed of four barbed arrowheads with their points meeting in the centre of the cross.
- *Russian cross* – a cross with three bars, the lowest being set at an angle.

Chest (or table) tomb

A stone or brick box rectangle raised over the grave space. The box or 'tomb' is empty, the coffins being buried below ground. The 'tomb' is often built on a ledger stone, while the main inscription(s) may be on the top or sides of the 'tomb'.

Footstone

The footstone is a small 'headstone' but placed at the foot of the grave space. Usually they mirror the same design as the headstone. At Brookwood the footstone usually includes the name(s) or initials of the deceased, along with the grave number.

Graveboard

A wooden board running the length of the grave and supported at each end by an upright post.

Headstone

Headstones were the usual style for memorials well into the nineteenth century. They are reminders of wall tablets within churches. Headstones were made in a variety of shapes, some symbolic of classical Greek or Roman tombs. The inscription is usually carved on the front face of the stone. Sometimes this can also continue on the rear face, while some headstones may include metal or terracotta inserts. The grave numbers at Brookwood occasionally may be found on the front or rear face of headstones.

Kerb

The edging stones around a grave, usually in the same material as the main memorial. However, some graves are just kerbed, therefore these stones would record the inscription(s). The grave number typically appears on the front left (or right) of any kerbing at Brookwood.

Ledger stone

A large horizontal slab placed directly over the grave. It may cover the entrance to the shaft of a brick grave, otherwise the entrance to an underground vault. The ledger stone may be very thick and typically has the inscription on the top face. Ledgers may be shaped in various ways: for instance, an angled top (to allow moisture to run off) running with the length or width of the stone. A cross ledger has a cross as part of the design.

Mausoleum
A tomb house which may look like a small chapel, often magnificently decorated. The bodies may be buried within the structure or in a vault beneath. Often the family of the deceased used the mausoleum as a private chapel.

Pedestal tomb
An upright memorial where the height of the design is greater than its length. Pedestals may be surmounted by angel figures, obelisks, draped urns and similar symbolic design elements. Pedestal tombs are usually built on a square podium and capped by a pediment of Greek or Roman architecture.

SYMBOLISM

There are many symbols that can be found on memorials. Some of these are referred to in the main text, but you will see many examples as you explore the cemetery grounds. Some memorials may include more than one emblem, and many have biblical significance. The following is a list of the more common symbols that can be seen:

Anchor – hope (see Hebrews 6: 19), at rest, security.
Angel – agents of God and the guardians of the dead. Often depicted pointing towards heaven.
Book – the open book symbolises the book of life (see Philippians 4: 3, Revelation 3: 5); with a cross it symbolises faith (i.e. the Bible).
Butterfly – resurrection, rebirth, the symbol of the soul.
Circle – eternity; it may appear in several guises, for instance as a circular wreath or other design element. Otherwise as part of a Celtic cross; cf. snake.
Column – the broken column symbolises death.
Crown – used as an emblem of the Christian martyr who may expect reward in heaven (see Revelation 2: 10, James 1: 12).
Dove – peace, the symbol of the Holy Ghost (sometimes with seven rays representing the seven gifts of the Holy Spirit), the soul, innocence, love.
Fish – used as a symbol of Christ by the early Christians on account of the feeding of the five thousand.
Hands – usually shown as clasped and depicting farewell.
Heart – love, devotion.
Hourglass – symbol of the passage of time, mortality and death (the sands of time are running out); cf. sundial.
IHS – represents the first two and last letters of the Greek for Jesus. In 1424 St Bernadine of Sienna applied them to *Iesus Hominum Salvator* ('Jesus, Saviour of men'). Other explanations include *In Hac Salus* ('in this [cross] salvation') and *In Hoc Signo* ('in this sign [ye shall conquer]').
Ivy – as an evergreen, ivy represents everlasting life (hence the use of evergreen planting in cemeteries and burial grounds).
Lamb – the lamb may represent innocence, or the Redeemer (see John 1: 29, Revelation 5: 6–14).
Lamp – immortality, knowledge of God ('lighten my darkness' see 2 Samuel 22: 29, Psalm 119: 105). The moon is sometimes referred to as the 'lamp of heaven'.
Laurel – peace, victory, or fame (especially in literature and the arts).
Lily – chastity, innocence and purity.
Lion – courage, strength, the resurrection (tradition dictates that the lion's whelp is born dead and remains so for three days until its father breathes on it). The lion is also the symbol of St Mark.

Obelisk – taken from ancient Egypt, the obelisk was part of their sun worship and was usually placed as a pair in front of temples. It represents eternal life.

Passion flower – sacrifice and redemption, Christ's passion. Some of the symbols of the passion flower are as follows: the five petals and sepals represent the ten apostles (Peter and Judas are omitted), the five anthers represent the wounds of Christ, the tendrils represent the scourges, the stamens represent the hammers, the three stigmas represent the nails and the filaments within the flower represent the crown of thorns.

Pelican – charity or piety, also the emblem of Christ. St Jerome described the pelican restoring its young by the blood of Christ. The popular myth of pelicans feeding their young with their blood comes from the parent transferring macerated food from its large bill to its young. The 'pelican in her piety' is the term used for the heraldic form.

Rock or rocks – the Church or Christian steadfastness, solidity and strength. 'Rock of Ages' is Christ as the unshakeable foundation of the Church (see Isaiah 26: 4; 2 Samuel 22: 2–3). The symbolism of the rock is the most universal in any cemetery or burial ground since any stone used for a memorial may be perceived as 'rock' in the sense of permanence and solidity.

Rose – innocence, a paragon, one without peer. It is usually associated with the Virgin Mary.

Ship – the Christian Church, carrying the faith throughout the world.

Skull – death, mortality.

Snake – a serpent eating its own tail symbolises eternity; cf. circle.

Sundial – the passage of time; cf. hourglass.

Sword – justice, constancy, fortitude. Also the Holy Spirit as part of the 'armour of God' (see Ephesians 6: 10–18).

Torch – an upturned torch means life extinguished.

Urn – death. The urn is empty and draped, and this is derived from cinerary urns of classical civilisation.

Wheat – represents the divine harvest (fruitfulness gathered in); the grain (seed) may symbolise the growth of faith or the kingdom of heaven.

TYPICAL STONE TYPES

By its very nature, stone or rock is symbolic of permanence and eternity. Many different types of stone may be found within a cemetery for a variety of reasons. This was made possible by the development of the railways which allowed materials from other parts of the country (or from overseas) to be transported more easily and cheaply than ever before. The colour of stone might be important. White marble might be chosen to represent purity, black stone could be a reminder of mourning, while other colours may have a special significance to the departed or their religious beliefs. Sometimes stones might be chosen for their attractiveness, or because the rock came from an area important to the person being commemorated.

The typical stones found in cemeteries are:

Granite

Granite is a hard stone comprising quartz, felspar and mica. It is a coarse or medium-grained intrusive igneous rock that is the most common plutonic rock of the earth's crust. Granite is formed by the cooling of magma (silicate melt) at depth. The mixture of quartz and felspar can give either a silver, grey, grey-green or pink appearance to the stone. Granite is a very hard stone, and although it may be highly polished it can be difficult to carve and cut in high relief. Granite may occur in dikes or sills (tabular bodies injected in fissures and inserted between other rocks), but more characteristically it forms irregular masses of extremely variable size.

Limestone

Limestone is a sedimentary rock composed mainly of calcium carbonate, often in the form of calcite or aragonite. It may contain considerable amounts of magnesium carbonate (dolomite) as well. Most limestones have a granular texture. Their constituent grains range in size from 0.00004in to visible particles. In many cases, the grains are microscopic fragments of fossil animal shells, other types may be rich in animal and vegetable fossil remains (e.g. Purbeck stone or marble).

Marble

Marble is a granular limestone or dolomite (composed of calcium-magnesium carbonate) that has been recrystallised under the influence of heat, pressure and aqueous solutions. Commercially it includes all decorative calcium-rich rocks that can be polished. It often occurs interbedded with such metamorphic rocks as mica schists, phyllites, gneisses, and granulites. The change from limestones rich in fossils into true marbles in metamorphic regions is a common phenomenon. Occasionally, as at Carrara (Italy), recrystallisation of the rock has not completely obliterated the organic structures. Marble has been favoured by sculptors throughout the ages and is commonly used for statues and angels. Angel figures are often made from Italian marbles, mass-produced and imported to a variety of catalogue designs.

Metamorphic rocks

Metamorphic rocks are derived from igneous or sedimentary rocks that have altered their form (recrystallised) as a result of changes in their physical environment, changes in pressure, temperature and the composition of fluids percolating through them. Metamorphism changes both the mineralogy and fabric of the original rock. These are often quite attractive rocks since some have streams or bands of colour (otherwise called gneissic rock), caused by changes in heat and pressure as the rock is formed.

Sandstone

Sandstone consists of two components: a framework composed of sand-sized grains, and interstitial volume between grains, which may be empty or filled with either a chemical cement of silica or calcium carbonate or a fine-grained matrix. Sandstones come with a variety of textures which are based on the size of the grains which formed the rock. The coarser grains make sandstones known as 'gritstone'. Sandstone is the second most common sedimentary rock after shale, constituting about 10 to 20 per cent of the sedimentary rocks in the earth's crust. Because of their abundance, diverse textures and mineralogy, sandstones are important indicators of erosion and depositional processes. Sandstones also have a wide range of colour, depending on the grains of sand that went to form the rock.

Slate

Slate is a fine-grained, clayey metamorphic rock that cleaves, or splits, readily into thin slabs with great strength and durability. Slate was formed under relatively low temperature and pressure. The original material was a fine clay, sometimes with sand or volcanic dust, usually in the form of a sedimentary rock (e.g. a mudstone or shale). Slates may be black, blue, purple, red, green, or grey. Dark slates usually owe their colour to carbonaceous material or to finely divided iron sulphide. Reddish and purple varieties owe their colour to the presence of hematite (iron oxide), and green varieties owe theirs to the presence of much chlorite, a green micaceous clay mineral. Slate can be very finely carved and may be highly polished. It is also relatively light for its size and therefore may be more easily transported. Despite these advantages, slate is not commonly used at Brookwood.

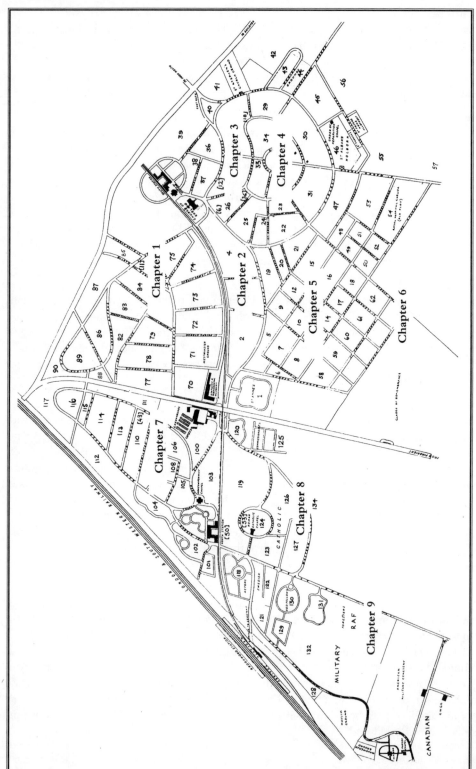

Brookwood Cemetery.

INTRODUCTION

A BRIEF HISTORY OF THE
LONDON NECROPOLIS COMPANY
AND BROOKWOOD CEMETERY

B rookwood Cemetery was established in 1854 to solve London's burial problem, which was caused by a chronic lack of land amid a rapidly growing population. The metropolitan community had more than doubled in the first half of the nineteenth century, from just under one million people in 1801 to over two and a quarter million by 1851; and there was a corresponding increase in annual burials, from 49,900 in 1838 to 55,500 in 1851. But in spite of London's growth, from 44,800 acres in 1838 to 78,000 acres by 1851, the total area of burying grounds remained relatively stable at under 300 acres, resulting in acute burial congestion.[1]

The consequences of this situation were horrific. The sanctity and permanence of burial spaces were rarely respected, and graves were continually reused, the contents broken through, unearthed and scattered over the ground. Alternatively, vast pits were excavated, involving the desecration of many previously buried corpses, into which any number of new bodies would be ruthlessly crammed. Debris from the previous occupants' graves was either burned or collected for the second-hand 'coffin furniture' market. Scraps of coffin wood were used for household fuel in poor neighbourhoods, while many tons of human bones were shipped from London to the north each year, to be crushed and used as fertiliser.

Many contemporary medical experts believed that these repugnant modes of interment affected public health. They thought that exhalations from the improperly and inadequately buried dead poisoned the air, rendering it harmful to life. Those living adjacent to graveyards, usually the poorest classes, were especially at risk. Decomposition also led to the contamination of drinking wells, springs and watercourses.[2]

No radical, comprehensive or worthwhile solution was attempted until the cholera epidemic of 1848–9, which resulted in 14,601 deaths in London alone and exacerbated the interments problem to saturation point. Two main schemes, both designed to relieve this intolerable pressure on the burying grounds, evolved from this crisis of congestion. One was an unsuccessful Government enterprise which attempted to place the administration of all metropolitan burials under the supervision of a public burial board. Two 'national' cemeteries would be opened (one based on an enlarged Kensal Green Cemetery and to be called the Great Western Metropolitan Cemetery, the other to be opened near Abbey Wood and called the Great Eastern Metropolitan Cemetery) and managed by this board. Thenceforth all the overcrowded burying grounds would be closed and all interments channelled into the two public cemeteries.[3] This project failed to mature because of flaws in the Metropolitan Interments Act (1850),[4] its dependence on a central monopoly for success, the scepticism of the Treasury concerning its financial viability and the resentment engendered by its interference with private enterprise. All this, and the rise of the second scheme, led the Government to reconsider the propriety of the measure in 1852.[5]

The other plan was the London Necropolis, devised by Sir Richard Broun[6] and Mr Richard Sprye[7] at the end of 1849.[8] This project was intended to solve the burials problem by itself. The cemetery, to be situated beyond any possible future extension of London, at Woking in Surrey, could never endanger the public health of the capital, while its vast area would provide ample capacity for the anticipated volume of metropolitan dead for many years to come. This scheme transcended all the disadvantages of intramural burial: a site that would not become engulfed by London; cheap, common land; and inexpensive, rapid rail transit from central London to the cemetery. In his original prospectus for the plan Sir Richard Broun explained:

> The object of this Company, as the name implies, is to furnish London with that which is at length felt by all classes to be a great and crying desideratum – namely, a 'City for the Dead', at such a distance from the Metropolis as public health requires; upon a scale of magnitude commensurate with a population rapidly increasing . . . at such charges as shall be consistent with the utmost possible economy; and at a site which will admit of spacious sepulchral structures, a National Mausoleum Church, and variously-decorated grounds, such as become not only the capital of the largest and wealthiest nation in Christendom, but a people who, for religious feeling, education, and general habits of life, hold the first rank among the believers of the Christian faith.
>
> A grand and complete system of extramural metropolitan sepulture ought to embrace the following features: – 1st. An area of ground so distant as to be beyond any possible future extension of the Capital, sufficiently large to allow of its sub-division, not only into

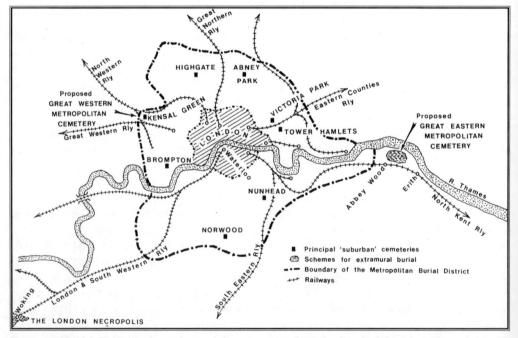

Extramural burial. This map shows the two schemes proposed to solve London's burial problem, along with the eight major private cemeteries. All these cemeteries lay within the proposed Metropolitan Burial District. Note how the site of the London Necropolis is well beyond its boundary.

spacious distinct portions for the burial of each sect of the Christian Public, but also, if desired and deemed expedient, into as many separate compartments as there are parishes within London and its suburbs. 2nd. The administration of the Company's affairs upon liberal principles. . . . And 3rd. A Mausoleum Church, with funereal chapels, private mausolea, vaults, and catacombs, large enough to contain, not only the thousands of coffins now lying within our numerous Metropolitan Churches, but also the coffins of all such dying in London, in this and future generations.[9]

After the public inauguration of the plan Broun and Sprye nominated four 'provisional trustees'[10] to help establish the projected company. Under a 'deed of agreement', ironically dated 1 April 1851, Broun and Sprye were to obtain considerable benefits – amounting to at least £20,000 – from the sale of their scheme to the trustees.[11] However, the trustees went on to appoint their own officers[12] and directors at the end of 1850, without further reference to the two founders. Moreover, they issued their own prospectus and took the initiative in the negotiations with Lord Onslow (for acquiring much of Woking Common)[13] and the LSWR, all without the consent of Broun and Sprye and against the spirit of the deed of agreement. Worse followed. On 3 October 1851 a 'deed of settlement'[14] for the projected company was signed which clearly stated that 'the said several Persons [the trustees] . . . had agreed to form a Joint Stock Company . . .'.[15] This document ignored the role of Broun and Sprye and the deed of agreement, and sealed the independence of the nascent necropolis company. Broun used this affront to confront the promoters in public. He poured scorn and criticism on the 'spurious and substituted' company prospectus, which he claimed was 'full of misrepresentations and ambiguous assertions', and he continued to bombard the company with letters, tracts and pamphlets in order to regain control of his company.[16]

THE 1852 ACT

The bill to incorporate the London Necropolis & National Mausoleum Company was introduced into the 1852 session of Parliament. Broun and Sprye objected on the grounds that it contained no protection of their rights under the deed of agreement, and because the bill departed from their original plans.[17] One major difference was clause XI, which allowed the LNC to sell surplus land. Henry Drummond,[18] MP for West Surrey, asserted in the House of Commons that the LNC 'contemplated a direct fraud on the public' by intending to use only 400 acres for the cemetery, while selling the remainder for building leases.[19] Broun and Sprye objected to the compensation set aside for the commoners of Woking. They considered £1,000 sufficient for the loss of turbary rights, but the LNC had reserved £22,000 for this purpose.[20] Even so, Henry Drummond believed the commoners were not being properly consulted, nor their interests considered. James Mangles, the MP for Guildford, opposed the bill as he feared the loss of 'every acre' of common land to the people of Woking. Since the opponents to the bill were humble men, it was futile to expect them to bear the costs of opposing the bill in its committee stages.[21] Broun and Sprye also questioned the high railway fares cited in the bill, along with the proposed clergy fees, arguing that both charges would add £47,000 to the funeral expenses of those Londoners being buried at Brookwood.[22]

However, Broun and Sprye failed to petition against the bill in time for their case to be considered by the House of Commons. The LNC could argue that clause XI was a saving clause should the company fail to attract the number of burials anticipated, and was in fact a fairly standard clause inserted into many railway companies' bills.[23] Henry Robert Abraham,[24] the LNC's architect, had prepared detailed plans for use of the whole site as a burial ground, which were explained to the satisfaction of the Parliamentary Select Committee. Nevertheless a clause was inserted into the bill that forbade the sale of land for building purposes.[25] Regarding the commoners, the Select Committee's objective was 'to prevent the poor people having their cottages taken away from them' and to forestall an 'Irish clearance' of two-thirds of the parish of Woking.[26] Therefore a protecting clause was introduced into the bill allowing landholders listed in the first schedule to exchange their lands for others on the company's estate.[27] The railway fares also remained modest, since it was clearly in the railway company's interests to attract as much custom as possible. The LSWR expected to make some £40,000 a year from this additional traffic, estimated at 10,000 bodies a year, plus mourners and visitors, and handled by two or three funeral trains in each direction each day.[28] The clergy fees were required by the Cemetery Clauses Act (1847), while the suggested charge of 6s 2d was lower than in many other cemeteries closer to London. It was also a useful way to rally clerical support for the bill.[29]

The House of Commons was largely satisfied by the bill, which obtained its third reading on 21 May 1852. One of its main advantages was the intention to remove the practice of burial within London without undue interference with the existing Metropolitan Interments Act. Henry Drummond was by now content with the clauses preventing land sales and protecting the commoners' rights, and only Viscount Ebrington complained that the bill ought to be delayed until the Government's policy on metropolitan burials had been clarified.[30]

By the time the bill had reached the House of Lords, Broun and Sprye were able to have their petition heard. This resulted in a saving clause being added, intended to protect their rights and interests, but it proved to be of little practical value.[31] Generally the Lords, like the Commons, were sympathetic to a private company undertaking its own solution to the metropolitan burials problem. Only Lord Ashley really objected to the bill, believing it to be subversive to the principles of the 1850 Act, which aimed to put an end to private speculation in the burial of London's dead. He deplored the idea of conveying thousands of corpses across London to Waterloo station, where they would be stored close to dwelling houses while awaiting transport down to Woking. Moreover, if the company failed to attain the anticipated number of interments it would be unable to meet the preliminary expenses of establishing its new cemetery. But these prophetic words were ignored, and the bill moved on.[32]

COMPANY POLITICS 1852–4

The LNC's private Act of Parliament received the Royal Assent on 30 June 1852.[33] This Act incorporated the company and outlined the requirements for setting up this huge metropolitan necropolis. But there followed a period of one and a half years during which the scheme stagnated: money raised from shareholders was – according to Broun – 'squandered' and 'wasted' to the sum of £20,000 or more; valuable time was lost; public confidence in the company collapsed; and at one point it seemed that the London Necropolis would never be opened.

Broun was incensed at the delay, which he felt was due to the 'pseudo board' of directors and their wasting an alleged sum of £86,620 out of the £125,000 share capital, while the residue was clearly inadequate for establishing the enterprise.[34] Yet if the LNC was so keen to open a cemetery, what caused the delay? Abraham's surveys of the estate proved inadequate, since they were not based on 'accurate trigonometrical measurements' and had to be redone.[35] The Board of Directors was not seen as representative, since there was some dubious electioneering, with directors using 'faggot' votes (votes allocated illegally to make someone eligible to vote) and abusing proxies. Supposed 'committees' were attended by only one director, while the complete lack of shareholders and capital was widely reported in the press. Behind all this was Mr Voules, acting chairman of the LNC, who became the scapegoat for all these misdeeds.[36]

The case of *Harris* v. *Thompson* further damaged the company's tarnished reputation. Harris was auditor to the LNC, and Charles R. Thompson was one of its directors and a trustee. Both men were on the board of an assurance company. After Harris had been dismissed as a director of the assurance company, through 'gross misconduct and for obtaining money under false pretences', Thompson accused him of being unfit to serve on the board of the LNC. He was therefore dismissed from the LNC on the basis of Thompson's privileged information. Three separate court hearings were widely reported in the press, and served to reinforce the lack of public confidence in the company.[37]

Matters deteriorated so much that a group of shareholders determined that the fortunes of the LNC be reversed. At an Extraordinary Special Meeting of shareholders held on 17 May 1853 two men, John Stirling Taylor and Charles R. Thompson, moved that 'a committee of 5 shareholders be appointed to investigate the affairs of the Company with full power over all Books, Deeds, Documents and Papers'. But this motion was defeated by 164 votes to 136.[38] Eventually, however, the company bowed to pressure from its shareholders. At a general meeting held on 19 July 1853 a 'committee of enquiry' was formed to investigate 'the affairs of the company and report thereon'. Its objectives were:

1st – To enquire how far the Directors have fulfilled the duties entrusted to them.
2nd – To ascertain the present state of the Company, and also its future prospects; and
3rd – To decide whether an entire change of the executive body is necessary, and to frame a report to the Shareholders, recommending a course for their adoption.[39]

Under the chairmanship of **Henry C. Rothery**, all accusations of fraud and mismanagement were considered, and a report was issued to the shareholders on 27 September 1853. Broun had criticised this committee from the start, especially since two of the 'usurping directors' sat on it. He derided their 'slow and unbusinesslike' deliberations, which only inflicted more harm on the LNC. However, the shareholders unanimously approved the committee's report. This resulted in the removal of all four trustees, and Mr Voules had to forego his 'award' of 100 shares and 'fees' of £2,000 for 'services' to the company.[40] The committee also recommended an immediate settlement of the commoners' claims, and for the committee to 'confer with such Gentlemen as may be willing to form a powerful and influential Board'.[41]

THE FOUNDATION OF THE LONDON NECROPOLIS

Henceforth a new spirit of confidence was instilled into the LNC. Its true financial state was ascertained, and a list of 'competent' shareholders – those who had paid calls of £3 per share – was drawn up. New officers were appointed,[42] and twelve new directors were also properly elected and appointed.[43] The surveys of the company's estate recommenced and a new prospectus was issued. Sir William Cubitt's[44] report to the Chairman and Board of Directors outlined the progress to date:

I received from Capt. Moorsom, your late Engineer, the Plans and papers relative to the surveys of the estate then in progress, and had some personal interviews with that gentleman on the subject . . . [he turned] over to my directions his principal Engineer-Surveyor, Mr Bridge of Kingston-on-Thames, who was then carrying on the surveys under the direction of Capt. Moorsom himself, and is now, with Mr Lofthouse, an experienced Land Surveyor sent by me to assist, busily engaged in completing the plan of the whole property – Lithographed copies of which I trust in a few weeks to have ready for the Members of the Board, in particular, and soon after, with the proposed disposition of the land laid down, for the use of the Proprietors generally.

Having put the survey of the property in course of completion, my next objective was to make a personal examination of the same, with a view to determine what portion or portions of the Land it would be advisable in the first instance to enclose with proper fences and connect with the London and South Western Railway – but being unfortunately much indisposed at the time, I engaged my son, Mr [Joseph] Cubitt C.E. (the Chief Engineer of the Great Northern Railway) to accompany a few of the Directors to the ground, and examine as to the most suitable portion of the property for that purpose – and he (Mr Cubitt) advised, that a piece of land containing about 400 acres, lying at the Western end of the estate and on the South side of and adjoining to the Railway, was the best fitted so to enclose &c – inasmuch as it was capable of being easily and inexpensively connected with the Railway, and had the advantage of two public roads, branching off to Guildford and Purbright [sic] respectively, already passing through it, which would so much facilitate funeral operations.

The Engineering expenses of fencing in this 400 acres of land as required by law, and laying down a single line of Railway Branch with a junction and sidings at each, exclusive of all Architectural works, such as Reception Rooms, Chapels, &c – would probably amount to £3,000 or thereabouts, if performed in the most economical manner. The designs and costs of such Buildings as would suffice for a commencement your Architect Mr Sydney Smirke will be able in due time to inform you of.[45]

This spirit of optimism was reflected in the LNC's first annual report, which was issued on 7 February 1854:

At the time of the election of the new members of the Board in November last they found the prospects of the Company very gloomy, with pressing Creditors and an empty Exchequer. They are now gratified by being able to report that the affairs of the Company present a very different aspect – the pressing liabilities of the Company are in course of arrangement, able and distinguished Officers have been appointed, and steps have been taken . . . to carry out the necessary works to enable the Company to commence operations.

. . . The appointment of Auditors by the Shareholders has hitherto been neglected but the Directors, feeling the importance of an Audit of the Accounts take place previously to their being presented to the consideration of the Shareholders, have appointed Alfred Hudson Shadwell Esquire and William Wing Esquire Auditors on their behalf [and] have submitted the Accounts to these Gentlemen and thus audited have caused them to be printed and circulated among the Shareholders.

By this account the disbursements of the Company to the 31st January are £21,860 12s 1d. The balance at the Bankers is £4,428 7s 7d. Accounting for the total receipts of £26,288 19s 8d.

These receipts are upon a Share List numbering 9,219 to which additions are being constantly made. This represents a Capital of £92,190 from which, if the payments of £21,860 12s 1d be deducted, an available balance of £70,329 7s 11d for the discharge of the liabilities of the Company and for the prosecution of the works necessary for the commencement of operations.

. . . The Directors have also to report that they have been in frequent communication with many of the Metropolitan Vestries and that there is every reason to believe that as soon as this Company is in a position to place facilities at their disposal the greater number of these will not only send the funerals over which they have absolute control to Woking, but will also use their powerful influence over the remaining portion of their parishioners in favor [sic] of the Necropolis Company.[46]

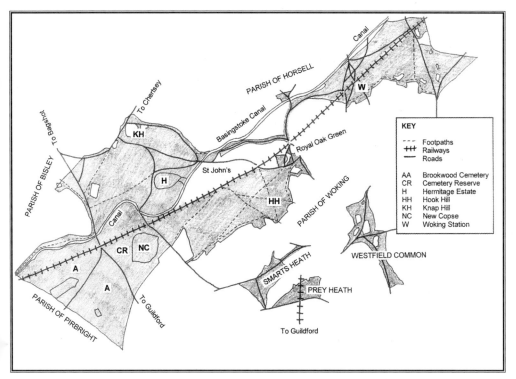

The LNC estate in 1854. It shows the (largely) common land acquired by the LNC under the terms of its 1852 Act. Virtually all the land shown here was previously owned by Lord Onslow.

The scheme sped forward during 1854. Arrangements were made for the rental of land from the LSWR, located between the Westminster Bridge Road and York Street (now Leake Street), for the site of the private station. Despite opposition from local people, who feared the deposition of corpses in large numbers next to their homes, this unique station was constructed and completed by October 1854. It occupied the space immediately adjacent to the LSWR's viaduct into Waterloo station, and was designed by William Tite[47] in consultation with Cubitt, the LNC's consulting engineer. The designs were approved during the period May–June 1854, and Messrs Nicholsons were awarded the contract to build the new station. It was completed at a cost of £23,231 14s 4d.[48]

At Woking some 2,200 acres of common land were acquired from the Lord of the Manor, Lord Onslow. About 500 acres[49] were initially laid out and planted for the London Necropolis (as Brookwood was originally called) and opened from 13 November 1854. As the cemetery was over twenty-five miles from central London the LSWR was engaged to convey coffins and mourners from the private station just outside London Waterloo down the main line and into the cemetery grounds. Here two stations were provided to serve each part of the cemetery: one for Dissenters ('North') and one for Anglicans ('South'). These were adjacent to the two chapels where the funeral services were conducted.

The areas of common land acquired from Lord Onslow had been referred to as the 'waste of Woking' in the eighteenth century. It comprised the eastern sections of the huge heaths and commons that at the time stretched westwards into Hampshire and Berkshire, and southwards into Sussex – vast, windswept and desolate expanses of sandy soil, with furze (gorse), heather, bracken and isolated clumps of pine and silver birch. Paradoxically areas like these are now *un*common, but parts of Chobham Common, or the area within the present Brookwood Cemetery called '**Brookwood Heath**', give an impression of what the land looked like when the LNC first obtained most of Lord Onslow's wasteland.[50] The local writer George Sturt remembered these areas as a small boy and later described them as 'the wide heaths of Hampshire and Surrey. Modern England has broken up the heaths: their desolation has gone; their silence, their savagery, their impressive beauty . . . As late as 1870 or thereabouts they stretched, almost unbroken, east to west from Woking to Heath End beyond Aldershot; and, north to south, from Hartford Bridge Flats to Hindhead.'[51]

LANDSCAPE AND PLANTING

The transformation of this waste into an area of charm and beauty took many years to achieve; only much later did the planting mature to give Brookwood its special and unique funerary landscape. In March 1854 Murray Marshall was awarded the contract to fence in the area set aside for the initial site of the London Necropolis. This work was completed in May, comprising about 2 miles of earthworks surmounted by a wooden fence or paling, at a cost of £1,561 9s 4d.[52] The initial plan for cemetery roads or avenues was entrusted to William Elliott, and the contract for making these was awarded to Charles Hawkes in July 1854, with payments amounting to £160 2s 0d being made by August. The original network of paths was completed in the following summer, when a maximum of £150 for gravel was authorised by the Board of Directors.[53]

At this date the pattern of avenues and pathways was not what we see today. An engraving of the London Necropolis published in 1856 shows St Cyprian's, St Andrew's, St Chad's and St George's avenues on the Anglican side; and Eastern, Western, Chapel and Long avenues in the Nonconformist section. However, it also shows a 'long' St Luke's Avenue that stretches from St Cyprian's Avenue, crossing the line of the private railway, extending up to St Andrew's Avenue, and lined throughout with redwoods. This engraving is also of interest because it shows the **pauper burial grounds** as distinct and distant areas located on the cemetery boundary closest to Pirbright. The 1888 1-inch Ordnance Survey shows St Cyprian's, St Andrew's, St Chad's, St George's and St Mark's avenues on the Anglican side; and just Eastern, Western, Chapel, Long and Pine avenues in the Nonconformist sections.

A cemetery map published in an LNC brochure of about 1890 shows a different network of paths from that seen today in the Anglican section, with the 'long' St Luke's Avenue truncated slightly at the St Andrew's end and no longer crossing the cemetery railway. It also shows a series of straight avenues dividing the areas beyond the '**Gridiron**', presumably to facilitate access to the pauper burial grounds. By contrast the Nonconformist section is very similar to the present-day layout. Other pathways may have existed, but were either just grassed tracks or unofficial routes through the grounds. Today's network of roads was first formalised into large-scale plans of the cemetery grounds sometime in the years before the First World War.[54]

The matter of draining the area assigned for the cemetery was addressed at a board meeting in July 1854, when various tenders were considered. That submitted by Mr R.J. Carlisle for £1,711 was accepted, and the same gentleman was awarded the contract to form the railway embankment into the cemetery. Carlisle's contract appears to have covered just the Nonconformist section, and by October 1854 work on this had advanced sufficiently for the directors to consider drainage for the rest of the cemetery. Once again Carlisle was given the contract, although his official tender for £2,442 13s 7d was dated 31 January 1855. This implies that the work was not started until after the cemetery had opened.[55]

The responsibility for the landscape and planting at Brookwood is not entirely clear. Although it has been widely attributed to William Tite, there is no evidence for this in the LNC's Minute Books. It seems to have been shared between Sydney Smirke[56] (the LNC's architect),

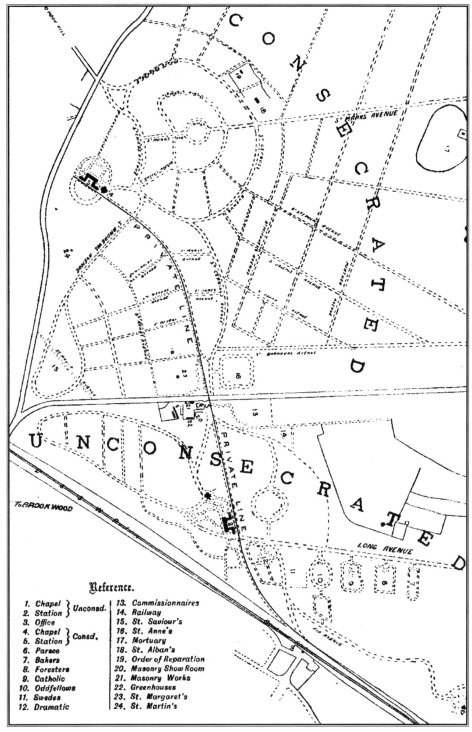

Brookwood Cemetery *c.* 1890. Of particular interest is the network of straight avenues beyond the 'Gridiron' to facilitate access to the extensive pauper burial grounds on the cemetery boundary. *(Author's collection)*

Mr Thomas and Robert Donald. Abraham, who was the original architect to the LNC (1851–3), certainly produced plans for the new necropolis (including suggestions for planting) at the committee stages of the LNC's private Act of Parliament in 1852.[57] However, Abraham ceased to be architect to the company during the spring of 1853 when the committee of enquiry was set up. He was replaced by Sydney Smirke in December 1853. It is quite possible that Smirke sought advice from Tite – whose designs include the South Metropolitan Cemetery at West Norwood – but it seems he had little or no direct involvement with the designs for Brookwood. A letter from Smirke to the secretary of the LNC suggests the overall plan at Brookwood was Smirke's, including the general layout of the cemetery, along with the planting:

> I beg to forward you a plan of the ground [at Woking] shewing the positions which I would suggest for the Reception Rooms and Chapels.
>
> That marked A, in the portion of ground North of the Purbright Road [sic], which I would set apart as a Dissenter's Cemetery, offers a very advantageous site, being on high ground and not far removed from the Railway.
>
> The other site, marked B, in the portion of ground lying between the Guildford and Purbright Roads, which I would appropriate as the Episcopal Cemetery, is farther removed from the Railway, but being on the summit of rising ground, the Chapel would form a conspicuous object, in every direction, and from considerable distances.
>
> Both sites are favourable for drainage and while they would of course be kept contiguous to the intended Branch Railway, they would at the same time be readily accessible from the public roads.
>
> In the plan herewith sent I have marked with red color [sic] the temporary Chapels which it is determined now to erect; the other suggestions shew the permanent and larger Chapels which it may be deemed, at some future time, desirable to erect. I have also indicated other works, which it may possibly be hereafter expedient to undertake.
>
> Adjoining the Episcopal Chapel I have imagined a spacious cloistered Enclosure containing 2 or 3 acres of land, which would afford a sheltered walk, and the open arcade surrounding it would afford a suitable position for mural monuments, brasses, and other sepulchral works which it may be desired to protect from the weather. . . .
>
> Adjoining the Chapels I have shewn a range of low buildings to serve as public and private reception rooms for corpses, and for the mourners' waiting rooms &c.
>
> Some of these buildings it will be necessary to erect at once; keeping them at first of minimum size, and expense.
>
> I am proceeding to prepare Plans for the two temporary Chapels, and I hope that about next week I shall be in a position to invite builders to tender for the works.[58]
>
> I am preparing also for the consideration of the board, a scheme for the ornamental planting and laying out of the ground; I need not remind the board that the season is at hand when planting can no longer be advantageously undertaken.[59]

Subsequently the LNC formed a 'planting committee' which consulted with Smirke later in March 1854. It initially agreed to set aside £500 for this task. In April 1854 'Mr Thomas, the Landscape Gardener[60] had been engaged to prepare a plan for the ornamental laying out and planting of the cemetery which plan was submitted to the Board & Mr S. Smirke and approved'.[61] In May Mr Donald tendered for planting in the cemetery amounting to £100. Robert Donald (c. 1826–66) was the son of Robert Donald (c. 1769–1854), owner of the Goldsworth Nursery, Woking, and friend of the important landscape gardener and horticultural writer John Claudius Loudon. Donald junior trained at Kew and became a partner in his father's nursery in 1842, which traded as Donald & Son. By 1848 he was running the entire business. Using his various contacts Donald established a profitable business as a specialist supplier of rare and exotic trees and shrubs for fashionable residences, using the arboretum he and his father had established at Goldsworth. By 1861 the nurseries occupied about 200 acres, and employed over forty men.[62] Being based locally, Donald was in the best position to supply most of the LNC's needs for landscaping and planting, and thus he became almost solely responsible for the planting at Brookwood in its early years:

> the company's landscape gardener, Mr Donald, of Woking, has laid out future avenues, terraces, lawns, grassy knolls, and fringing belts of woodland, with admirable effect, as may already be seen. Fully aware that in this part of Surrey the class of American evergreens flourishes with surprising luxuriance, and that a garden dedicated to such a solemn purpose as that of enshrining the ashes of the dead should bloom with *ver perpetuum* – perpetual spring – these have been largely planted. Here magnolias, andromedas, azaleas, and rhododendrons will thrive as in their native forests, and, at their time of bloom, spread their honied scent for miles.[63]

In October 1854 Donald was paid a further £500 for planting, another £500 in April 1855 and a further £250 in August 1855.[64] The planting committee continued its work until June 1857 under the guidance of one of the LNC directors, Francis Dobinson.[65] Planting by the LNC continued from time to time, although it is rarely formally noted by the Minute Books.

At this time the principal plan of planting involved the first large-scale use of giant sequoia (*sequoiadendron giganteum*) in Britain. Sequoia trees were first reported by the botanist and explorer James Bidwell in 1842, but it was William Lobb who appears to have introduced these trees into Europe, having sent seeds to Messrs Veitch in 1853.[66] These noble trees – which dominate parts of the grounds to this day – are the largest known to man.[67] Their use at Brookwood, then the largest cemetery in the world, was therefore fitting and appropriate. The sequoias were planted in several avenues flanking the main routes through the cemetery grounds. The 1856 engraving of the cemetery appears to show sequoias planted on an extended St Luke's Avenue (running from St Cyprian's Avenue to St Andrew's Avenue), along part of St Agnes's Avenue (from St Luke's to Cemetery Pales), and along some of the paths radiating out from St Margaret's Avenue to St George's Avenue. Perhaps some of these trees were subsequently moved elsewhere, or perhaps it is just artistic licence; we may never know for certain. However, at some stage the major cemetery avenues were lined with sequoias: the route of the railway, St Andrew's Avenue, and parts of St Mark's and Long Avenues. Elsewhere individual specimens were planted, along with solitary coastal redwoods (*sequoia sempervirens*), although there is a small grove of these trees behind the **Drake mausoleum**.

Monkey puzzles (Chilean pine or *araucaria araucana*) appear to have been another favourite. These were planted adjacent to the Nonconformist chapel (apparently the two largest specimens at Brookwood), as a circle in the area later developed as the 'Ring' (as shown in the 1856 engraving), and scattered elsewhere. The parish of **St Saviour's**, **Southwark**, appears to have been partial to these trees, since the boundaries of its two burial areas were each planted with a line of these fascinating pines. In order to improve the appearance of the area around each station and chapel, cedars of Lebanon (*cedrus libani*), bay trees, Portugal laurels (*prunus lusitanica*) and rhododendrons were planted. The cedar opposite the site of South station, and now within the **St Edward Brotherhood**'s ground, is one of the most impressive in the cemetery and was certainly planted for the service of consecration in November 1854.[68]

Later, as funds permitted, other trees would be introduced into the landscape: a wide variety of pine, cedar, cypress, holly, beech and yew, supplemented by trees, shrubs and plants chosen by relatives of the deceased and planted adjacent to family graves and mausolea. These changes reveal that the landscape at Brookwood was able to develop beyond Loudon's ideas, for, in time, the emphasis on conifer planting was seen to be out of date. Thus parts of Brookwood Cemetery may be seen to reflect the American 'park-like cemetery', with less formal landscaping and greater use of deciduous trees and extensive flowerbeds. This reflects the important influence of the American 'rural cemetery' movement as exemplified by Mount Auburn Cemetery, Cambridge, Massachusetts. Mount Auburn was a pioneering funerary landscape. Opened in 1831, the cemetery became a major point of interest in the Boston area. The beauty of its landscape was an enormous attraction, being variously described as 'a pleasure garden instead of a place of graves', or 'really perfect'. One Swedish visitor commented that 'a glance at this beautiful cemetery almost excites a wish to die'.[69] Compare this with the following description of a visit to Brookwood Cemetery in 1856:

> The first impression gained of the Cemetery is that of some such noble garden as the gorgeous fancy of Bacon loved to picture; for one passes clumps of young woodland, wide plots of heather, whole groves of American plants . . . [The] grave may lie where the falling blooms of azalea or magnolia may cover it with perfume and beauty; or where acacia, or purple beech, or Irish yew, lend shade; or, dug amidst the native heather, may in summer have a myriad little humming visitants – the bees.[70]

The **military cemeteries**, developed at the end of the First World War, reflect a further change in cemetery style and layout. Here there is a uniform treatment not only in the headstones but also in the extensive use of lawns and the restrained use of trees and shrubs, all designed for ease of maintenance. The idea of the 'lawn cemetery' for the Imperial War Graves Commission (IWGC) cemeteries was outlined in the Kenyon Report of 1918.[71] It was otherwise described as follows:

> The most perfect, the noblest, the most classically beautiful memorial that any loving heart or any proud nation could desire to their heroes fallen in a foreign land. Picture this strangely stirring place. A lawn enclosed of close clipped turf, banded across with line on line of flowers, and linked by these bands of flowers, uncrowded, at stately intervals stand in soldierly ranks the white headstones. And while they form as perfect, as orderly a whole as any regiment on parade, yet they do not shoulder each other. Each one is set apart in flowers, every one casts its shade upon a gracious space of green. Each one, so stern in outline, is most rich in surface, for the crest of the regiment stands out with bold and arresting distinction above the strongly incised names. . . . It is the simplest, it is the grandest place I ever saw.[72]

After the Second World War the **Glades of Remembrance** may be seen as a further landscape development, that of the 'forest cemetery', with its low density of burial and mature woodland setting. The Glades were planned from September 1945 by Messrs Milner, White & Sons as the LNC's landscape consultants.[73] **Edward White**, who designed several memorial gardens, described his rules for their design as follows:

> The Garden of Rest or Remembrance, as a crematorium garden is usually called, is in a category of its own. . . . The Garden of Rest constitutes an important feature of special concern: it is a kind of public park, incorporating an indefinite number of small private memorials, and as an idealistic affair it is deserving of the best artistic treatment, involving delicate psychological problems. Gardening is a popular source of pleasure which offers a favourite symbol of remembrance of those with whom its enjoyment was previously shared.

The association of a beautiful garden with the principle of cremation is therefore a strong inducement for many who, otherwise, might hesitate to approve it. . . . Casual arrangements of cremation gardens fail to impress, and conventional advertisements about lovely gardens of rest that are neither lovely nor restful do no good to the cause of Cremation.[74]

Taken as a whole, these developments have resulted in a cemetery landscape of great variety, spaciousness and grandeur. Indeed, Pevsner described this mature scenery, with its impressive trees, as 'a sombre complex landscape unlike anything anywhere else in the country'.[75]

THE LONDON NECROPOLIS OPENS

The original intention was that Brookwood would be sufficiently large to contain all of London's dead for ever. In the opinion of Dr Sutherland[76] of the Home Office, 1,200 acres would be sufficient for all of London's dead (averaging 60,000 deaths a year in 1856) in perpetuity. The arithmetic behind this assumed one body per grave, with the power to reopen the grave after ten years. A cemetery of this size would also permit a large area to be set aside for ornamental purposes.[77] Therefore the LNC deliberately set out to make Brookwood beautiful and attractive: a 'cemetery beautiful' or 'God's acre'. In 1854 the cemetery was by far and away the largest anywhere in the world. As *The Times* declared on its opening, 'It was fitting enough that the largest city in the world should have the largest cemetery in the world.'[78] Its size, although designed primarily to allow sufficient burial space for the capital, was also strongly symbolic: it suggested infinity, the afterlife and the unknown.

The cemetery was consecrated by the Lord Bishop of Winchester, the Right Revd Charles Sumner,[79] at a special service in the Anglican chapel on Tuesday, 7 November 1854. A special train, carrying shareholders and directors of the LNC along with directors of the LSWR, left Waterloo at 12.30 p.m. for the cemetery, which was reached in three-quarters of an hour. The train, with driver **Joseph Porter** in charge, then travelled through the grounds to South station. At a few moments before 2 p.m. the Bishop, attended by his Commissary, Dr Haggard, and the Registrar of the Diocese, Mr Rothery, arrived in the grounds, and were received by the Chairman of the LNC (**Thomas Dakin**), the directors and the local clergy. The Revd L. Humbert, Curate of St Olave's, Southwark, officiated as chaplain. On arriving outside the Anglican chapel, Dr Haggard and Mr Rothery presented the Bishop with a petition and the plans of the cemetery, requesting him to consecrate the chapel and ground. The Bishop entered the chapel and, standing in the centre, repeated prayers and the 49th Psalm. The sentence of consecration was then read by the Commissary and signed by the Bishop, who gave it to his Registrar requesting him to enrol and preserve it in the Registry. Parts of the 39th Psalm were sung, followed by further prayers. The Bishop then left the chapel, thereby ending the service. There was time to view the extensive grounds only briefly, after which followed a light lunch in the station. The directors and shareholders then returned to London by train.[80]

The cemetery was opened a week later on Monday, 13 November 1854.[81] There was a staff of twenty: two gatekeepers and eighteen porters.[82] The very first burial to take place on that morning, was of the stillborn male twins of a **Mr and Mrs Hore** of 74 Ewer Street, Borough. This burial took place at the expense of the parish of St Saviour's, Southwark (then still part of the Diocese of Winchester), in what is now an unmarked grave in the unconsecrated ground set aside for the parish (plot 116 or 117). Of the four burials that took place on that morning, three were pauper burials from St Saviour's, the other being a burial from St Luke's, Chelsea.

The very first private grave at Brookwood, with the right to erect a permanent memorial, was that of **Lieutenant General Sir Henry Goldfinch** KCB, who died aged 73 at his home, 11 Upper Wimpole Street, on 21 November 1854. His funeral took place on Saturday,

25 November, the only burial service that day. It was conducted by the LNC's Anglican chaplain, the Revd Henry Atcheson. Goldfinch's grave may still be seen today, close to the former Anglican chapel in plot 27. In the burial registers Goldfinch appears as entry 26, and this burial number may be seen on the footstone to his grave. The earliest memorial in the Nonconformist section commemorates **Charles Milligan Hogg**, the infant son of **Robert Hogg**, a botanist. Charles died at 13 Gilson Road, Brompton, on 6 December 1854, aged just 2 years and 4 months. His funeral took place on Tuesday, 12 December, and was the only private burial that day (although nine pauper burials also took place). The service was conducted by the Revd Thomas Alexander MA. In the registers Charles appears as entry 76, although this does not appear on the surviving memorial in plot 105. Somewhat curiously, Charles is recorded as being 2 years 3 months in the registers, although the memorial states 2 years 4 months.

Apart from St Saviour's, the following London parishes started using Brookwood for the burial of their dead from the early years: Bermondsey; Chiswick; **St Anne's**, **Soho**; St George's, Bloomsbury; St Giles-in-the-fields; **St John's**, **Westminster**; **St Luke's**, **Chelsea**; **St Margaret's**, **Westminster**; St Nicholas', Deptford; and St Paul's, Deptford. Under the terms of the Metropolitan Interments Amendment Act (1852),[83] the Government was empowered to close down the overcrowded London burial grounds, and enabled the parishes affected to elect burial boards to arrange for the burial of their dead. **St Anne's**, **Soho** reckoned to be the very first London parish to elect a burial board under the terms of this Act. Using funds raised from the poor rate, burial boards could arrange with a cemetery company for the burial of their dead; otherwise they could open and maintain their own cemeteries. The LNC anticipated that most metropolitan parishes would make arrangements with them, but most chose to open or use cemeteries closer to London. This decision obviously limited the potential number of burials that might otherwise have taken place at Brookwood. From the number of enquiries from various vestries referred to in the Minute Books, it is clear that had the cemetery opened in 1853 (or earlier in 1854) more London parishes would have chosen Brookwood for the burial of their dead.[84]

THE 1855 ACT AND LAND SALES

The LNC began to draft an amending Act at the end of 1854. Its main purpose was to abandon the powers of compulsory purchase granted in 1852. The cost of establishing the cemetery and associated works had virtually bankrupted the company, and it could not afford to buy all the land listed in the first schedule to the 1852 Act. The evidence for financial hardship is not hard to find. In order to pay Lord Onslow for his estate, the LNC was obliged to borrow £26,000 from Messrs Overend & Company to purchase the land it was already transforming into a cemetery before its consecration. Another example is the £15,000 paid to the Woking Commoners, which was likewise paid from a bank loan. Similarly economy governed the designs of the buildings erected in the cemetery, almost all of which were considered temporary structures to be replaced by more flamboyant and permanent designs in due course. Moreover, since the Metropolitan Interments Amendment Act (1852) had paved the way for parishes to open burial grounds closer to London, the LNC saw little respite in the immediate future.[85]

These facts were stated very clearly in the various submissions the LNC drafted for petitions and memorials to support its case for the new bill. In one, the sum of £150,000 is mentioned as the cost of establishing 'this much required national undertaking', which had so far proved 'wholly unremunerative'.[86] Only 15,000 out of 25,000 shares had so far been subscribed to, necessarily limiting the available funds. The LNC also reminded the Government that it had established the cemetery 'upon the supposition that the condemned practice of burial in populated districts would cease'. Moreover, the Home Secretary, Lord Palmerston, had imposed regulations on new cemeteries (including Brookwood) of one body to each grave and a surface allotment of 9ft × 4ft for each adult, without extending the same requirements to existing burial grounds.[87]

The LNC's new bill was initiated in the House of Lords in May 1855 and extinguished the company's powers of compulsory purchase. It also proposed to allow the sale of certain land for a period of ten years. The lands included the Hermitage estate, the 400 acres or thereabouts surrounding Woking station, and land at Maybury, Knaphill and St John's. This part of the bill provoked comment from several peers concerned at this apparent change of intention so soon after the passage of the 1852 Act. Nevertheless the bill received its Royal Assent on 23 July 1855.[88]

It should be noted that the land eligible to be sold was still limited by Parliament and, as the LNC quickly found out, just because it was free to sell certain parts of its estate it did not mean that there were eager and ready buyers. Of the 2,200 acres of common land purchased from Lord Onslow about 900 acres were reserved for various purposes. Of this, 500 acres were used for the London Necropolis, about 200 acres formed the adjacent 'cemetery reserve', while another 200 acres formed the outlying areas of Prey Heath, Smarts Heath and Westfield Common – which could not be discommoned and would remain untouched by building developments. The remaining 1,300 acres took a considerable time to sell off and never provided the quick profits that some authorities have alleged was the main reason behind the Necropolis venture. Although a total of 346 acres had been sold by 1865, much of this was from Government purchases for the Woking prisons (64 acres in 1858) and the County Lunatic Asylum (150 acres in 1860), along with the unusually large private sales to the Rastrick family (40 acres, also in 1860) and to Mr Lyon (the 27-acre Hermitage estate, 1857). No large purchases of this scale took place after 1865, and most of the remaining land sales were piecemeal. Even the special sale of land immediately surrounding Woking station in 1860 only resulted in 49 acres being sold, most of it to the Rastrick family. On average surplus land was sold at the rate of just 12½ acres a year.[89]

In 1856 the cemetery was described in the following terms:

> The whole scene is most varied and extensive, though a succession of encircling hills bound this extent and tend the charm of peacefulness and solitude. To the west and south these hills are very striking. Those towards Hants lie as we can see, amid wilds and solitary heaths, and bear to their summits traces of rugged nature; whilst those to the south are fringed by woodlands, and softened, in some degree, by cultivation. . . . [The LNC's] pre-vision in purchasing so vast a tract of land as shall meet the needs of generations yet unborn, and of the liberality and earnestness with which it has commenced the work of making this vast graveyard for London the most beautiful garden in the world – thus asso-ciating the solemnities of death with nature in her loveliest and purest aspects – must be commended by all those who see the foundations on which social progress and public morality truly rest. As we take our way amidst winding walks and future avenues; as we pause upon beautifully-preserved patches of the ancient heather, listen to the murmur of countless bees . . . if we breathe – if it be May or June – the accumulated, almost overpow-ering scent of countless American plants, then in all the luxuriance of leaf and blossom . . . we can but rejoice that our lot is cast in the age of ameliorations, and that countless gener-ations shall rest here – honoured in their dust – when their varied work be done.[90]

The LNC was able to attract burials from an astonishingly wide range of other churches, guilds, societies, communities and similar associations. The idea behind this was that those who had been united in life would not be separated in death. A select list published by the LNC in about 1895 included the **Ancient Order of Foresters**, the **Bakers**, the **Chelsea Hospital**, the **Corps of Commissionaires**, the **Dramatic Equestrian & Musical Sick Fund**, the **London & South Western Railway**, the Metropolitan Asylums Board, the **Oddfellows**, the **Order of Reparation**, the **Parsees**, St John's House, **St Joseph's Hospital** and the **Sisterhood of St John**. In virtually all cases separate grounds were allotted and laid out for the exclusive use of these groups. In many cases these grounds may still be explored today, and those that have been traced in the cemetery are listed within this guide. Some of these sections date back to the earliest years of the cemetery's existence. For instance, the plot for the **Swedish Church in London** (plot 122) was opened in 1857; the '**Actors' Acre**' (plot 118) dates back to June 1858; the **Oddfellows**' ground (plots 129 and 130) was inaugurated in 1861; and the earliest use of the **London & South Western Railway** ground (plot 47) appears to be 1863.

Throughout the nineteenth century a mainstay of the LNC's business was the burial of paupers from various London parishes. It was usual for cemetery companies to tender for the burial of paupers with appropriate parishes or Guardians of the Poor. It is estimated that some 80 per cent of the total burials at Brookwood are of paupers. The usual charge made to the parish for burial at Brookwood was 10s for a child's burial and 14s for an adult. These fees included the return railway fare for one mourner (in the case of a child) and two mourners for an adult funeral. The ticket(s) could be claimed by the mourner(s) at the LNC's private station on presentation of an appropriate warrant that was issued to the family by the parish authorities. However, for much of the nineteenth century the LNC performed a great service to paupers, since every grave at Brookwood – irrespective of class or cost – was 'private' in the sense of being shared with no one else, save next of kin. For many years the LNC was the only metropolitan burial ground to observe this practice. The better classes of graves included the right to erect a memorial, to perpetuate the memory of the departed. Pauper graves remained anonymous and without a name (unless the family subsequently managed to 'purchase' the grave space as a private '2nd-class' or '1st-class' grave, although this rarely happened);[91] nevertheless the deceased pauper was buried decently and with the dignity of an individual 9ft × 4ft grave space. Brookwood Cemetery also provided a striking contrast to the bereaved poor families and their London homes. What must they have thought when they first saw the carefully laid out gardens and grounds at Brookwood?

> Who knows how the poor and lowly might go back to their lives of struggle and labour soothed, comforted, braced to new endeavour, by the thought that they have left their beloved dead in a place so beautiful and cared for! Who knows what feeling may be awakened in the ignorant or hardened by this their first impression of the peaceful and beautiful in connexion with death and the grave![92]

In its earliest years the LNC used London undertakers to assist with the funeral arrangements. In November 1854 the firms of Barnard, Bedford and Dottridge Brothers[93] were used to facilitate the company's business. From 1886, however, the LNC formally expanded its activities and eventually conducted all its own undertaking, including coffin making, statuary and masonry work.[94]

FUNERALS BY RAILWAY

How were funerals by railway conducted? The arrangements for a funeral at Brookwood were not that different from any other arranged in London, except that a railway journey rather than the traditional hearse and carriage procession transported coffins and mourners to Brookwood. The corpse was usually left at home until the funeral arrangements were concluded; sometimes the body might be taken to the LNC's private station and placed in a mortuary there. If required, invitations to attend funerals could be sent out from the LNC's offices. These letters eventually included details of the waiting room(s) allocated to the funeral party, the departure time of the train, and the expected time of arrival back in London. Then the customary hearse and carriage procession took place on the appointed day, from the deceased person's house to the local parish church (if the funeral service was to take place in London) and then proceeded to the LNC's private station; otherwise the procession went directly to the LNC's private station (assuming that the funeral service was to take place at Brookwood). Upon arrival the mourners were led to a private waiting room during the brief interval wherein the final preparations were made for the departure to Brookwood. Separate waiting rooms were provided for those attending a better class funeral (available in 1st or 2nd class), while those accompanying the cheapest (3rd or pauper class) funerals were escorted to one large communal waiting room. Meanwhile the coffin was unloaded from the hearse in the LNC's private driveway and sent up to platform level by lift. Then one party at a time was summoned from its waiting room and escorted to a compartment in the train. Small cards, with the name of each funeral party, were placed on the relevant waiting room doors and on the corresponding compartment doors of the passenger and hearse carriages, to prevent any embarrassing errors. This process continued until all funeral parties were in the train.

Alternatively the LNC's 'reformed funeral' could be adopted. Under these arrangements the corpse was brought to the company's private station and placed either in one of the private mortuaries, in the communal mortuary (used for the cheaper funerals) or in the private chapel of rest at platform level. Whatever the option, there the coffin remained until the day of the funeral, when the mourners would arrange to meet at the LNC's station and the procedure would revert to that described above. This arrangement was usually adopted by those Guardians of the Poor of the metropolitan parishes that had contracted with the LNC for the burial of paupers under their jurisdiction. It also appealed to those who preferred to meet at the Necropolis station and avoid the conventional funeral procession through crowded streets, and proved invaluable to those friends or family who might be unable to accompany the body to Brookwood for the final rites, in which case the first part of the funeral service would take place in the private chapel within the station.

The railway journey to Brookwood followed. On arrival at the cemetery the train was propelled through the cemetery grounds to North station (for Roman Catholics, Jews, Parsees and other Dissenters). The train was met by staff of the LNC, who escorted the mourners to the nearby chapel. The relevant hearse vans were carefully stopped opposite the peculiar 'dip' in the platform face, which helped the attendants unload the coffins from the lowest 'shelf' in the vans. The coffins were carefully placed on to a special hand-bier, drawn by the LNC's attendants, and taken to the relevant chapel.

It was left to the family of the deceased to decide what kind of service they desired and could afford. Usually each party had a brief service in the chapel (pauper funeral services were conducted *en masse* in the appropriate chapel), after which the coffin was taken to the graveside, attended by the mourners and the chaplain or minister who would perform the last rites. Sometimes a more elaborate and expensive private service was held in the chapel, for the wealthy or famous, followed by the graveside ceremony. In some cases the main part of the funeral service may already have taken place in London – either in the deceased's parish church or in the LNC's private chapel – so that only the brief graveside ceremony took place. A good impression of the funeral arrangements at Brookwood can be obtained from an account of an actress's funeral, as described in the *Era*:

> The writer was much impressed at Miss Goodwin's funeral. . . . Everything worked smoothly and in perfect decorum. Particularly was this noticeable at the graveside, where, in place of the old and often rather distressing method of lowering the coffin by ropes, a device called the 'National Burial Device' was in use, and, controlled by the funeral director, acted automatically when the time for committal arrived.[95]

On arrival at the station the mourners were shown to their private waiting room or communal room (for the cheapest funerals). All necessary conveniences were provided at each station, including a refreshment room where light luncheons could be obtained at a moderate charge – along with a wide selection of alcoholic beverages! As the correspondent from the *Era* explained:

> In a hundred other ways those who use the Brookwood Necropolis will find their convenience studied by the company. . . . [It] extends to everything that pertains to the burial of the dead, from embalming, cremation, the making of coffins, the provision of mortuary chambers and *chapelle ardente*, conveyance with hearse and carriages, to the interment and the very gravestone itself.[96]

A similar procedure to that described above was followed when the train reached South station, in the Anglican section of the cemetery. The Necropolis Train usually left South station for the return journey to London at 2.15 p.m., and left Necropolis Junction at 2.30 p.m. For most of the duration of the service the return trip took up to an hour; by the 1920s the journey time had been reduced to about forty minutes.[97]

CREMATION *v*. 'EARTH TO EARTH'

Brookwood Cemetery was intimately involved in the early history of the Cremation Society in Britain. The Cremation Society was established by Sir Henry Thompson in April 1874.[98] One of its first objectives was to construct a crematorium. Having been denied permission by the Bishop of Rochester to erect one in the grounds of the Great Northern Cemetery, the Society turned its attention to Woking. In 1878 an acre of secluded freehold land was acquired off Hermitage Road, and towards the end of the year work began on constructing the furnace. The land had previously formed part of the LNC's estate. It was not sold directly to the Cremation Society but to a third party apparently for a totally different purpose, in order to avoid undue attention. Whether the LNC was a willing or innocent party to this transaction will probably never be known. Owing to the hostility aroused by the construction of the furnace, the LNC was quick to disassociate itself from the project, which its secretary, **Julian Larkman**, undertook through a letter to *The Times*:

> The Necropolis Company in no degree favour such preparations as are now being made in the vicinity of Woking for incinerating the dead. They regard cremation as the residents of the parish regard it – namely, with abhorrence. . . . It is true the land now in possession of the Cremation Society of London originally belonged to the company, but it was purchased from them in the ordinary way, and they never once anticipated that by a second purchase it would pass into the hands of the Cremation Society or be used for a funeral pyre. Had the company had the faintest idea that the ground would be conveyed to its present possessors, no inducement would have caused them to part with it.[99]

Mr Larkman also took part in the deputation by the residents of Woking to the Home Secretary and testified that the land had originally been purchased for the purpose of constructing a convalescent hospital.[100] But the furnace was completed in 1879. Because of difficulties with the Home Office, it remained unused for its intended purpose. It was finally used for the cremation of Mrs Jeanette Pickersgill on 26 March 1885.[101]

In the wake of the foundation of the Cremation Society another surgeon, **Sir Francis Seymour Haden**, published a series of letters to *The Times* strongly opposing cremation. He pointed out that the process was wasteful, costly and would unnecessarily pollute the atmosphere. He also described cremation as an 'incentive to crime', since incineration would remove all evidence of poisoning or other methods of murder. Crime could be concealed. Haden argued that bodies should continue to be buried but in disposable or 'Earth-to-Earth' coffins,[102] whereby the body would be naturally and quickly broken down by the 'resolvent action of the earth upon human remains'. The grave space might then be reused some years after burial. These views are still relevant today. Haden's original correspondence was subsequently printed in pamphlet form as *Earth to Earth: An Answer to a Pamphlet on 'Cremation'*, *Reprinted from* The Times (London, Macmillan, 1875).[103]

In January 1876 it was reported that Mr Larkman (the secretary) and Mr Diprose (a shareholder) had taken out a patent for such a coffin 'suitable for the object often discussed at this Board & advocated by Mr Haden'. Both had acted without the Board's sanction, but agreed to 'assign the patent & stock in hand . . . and profits already made . . . for £278 18s. 11d.'.[104] The cause was taken up with relish by the LNC. The company had already published (in 1875) a leaflet on *The Patent Necropolis Earth-to-Earth Coffins*. Sample coffins were sent to many sanitary and trade exhibitions. In 1878 it was agreed to donate an 'Earth-to-Earth' coffin to Parkes's Museum of Hygiene, as requested by its curator. The LNC shortly relinquished its patent rights, believing that these coffins should be made as widely available as possible. The enormous interest aroused by these coffins promoted Haden's ideas, provided a sanitary alternative to cremation, allowed for the reuse of graves (hence perpetuity of burial revenues) and promoted burial at Brookwood (where the soil was especially suitable for these coffins). The LNC continued to promote the 'Earth-to-Earth' system as an alternative to cremation:

> The mode of interment, now widely known as the 'Earth-to-Earth' system, strongly rec-ommended some years since by **Mr Seymour Haden** in eloquent letters to *The Times* is that which the London Necropolis Company endeavour to carry out. The company can-not countenance the disposal of the dead either by burning or subjection to the action of quicklime. They have full faith in the drying and congealing power of the earth itself, when the ground is of a suitable nature, and thus chemically calculated to facilitate 'innocuous resolution' in opposition to 'destructive putrefaction' engendered by solid coffins and satu-rated and 'choked' soils.[105]

Ultimately the LNC, along with the residents of St John's, Woking, failed to prevent the Cremation Society from opening and operating its first crematorium. As we shall see, by 1890 the LNC was already considering constructing its own crematory within the cemetery. Later still the company passed two private Acts of Parliament in similar attempts to open and operate a crematorium in Brookwood Cemetery.

LATE NINETEENTH-CENTURY DEVELOPMENTS

Brookwood Cemetery was described in the following terms in one of the LNC's brochures of 1887:

> Travellers on the South-Western line must have noticed the vast expanse of undulating com-mon land, carpeted with heather, studded profusely with evergreens and shrubs, and dotted here and there with picturesque ivy-clad chapels, and mausoleums embowered in greenery that stretches away out of sight to the left of the line beyond Woking Station. This is the LONDON NECROPOLIS, a site unequalled in the country, and as pleasing a picture of repose and rural scenery as can well be desired. . . . The site of the London Necropolis is of singular beauty. Placed in the midst of an elevated and extensive plateau, in the picturesque county of Surrey, it presents to the eye on every side one of the grandest and most varied panoramas in England. In the laying out of this ground, an equal regard has been had to convenience, completeness of arrangement, and beauty of effect – trees, flowers, plants, and winding walks diversifying the scene, and breaking the monotony of the ordinary grave ground.[106]

In December 1887 **Cyril Tubbs** was appointed (initially) as an assistant to supervise the LNC's buildings and estates, and generally to 'advance the company's interests'. His initial duties were described as:

> the management and disposal of surplus land; circularizing and advertising; arranging prices for all purchases [of land]; superintendence and surveying of buildings and stations, and Cemetery generally; communication with [the] South-Western Railway when requested by the Board . . . the preparation of advertisements, estimates, plans and surveys; [and] all such matters as may be specially confided to or required of him.[107]

This resulted in several important improvements in the cemetery. For it was Tubbs who originated the plan for 'how the cemetery may be laid out to advantage, a scheme for the classification of districts of the cemetery so that any grave may be found with ease, and to propose names for such districts . . .'. From this resulted an expanded network of avenues and roadways that largely remain intact at Brookwood today. Tubbs named the cemetery avenues and arranged for signposts to be erected to identify each one for visitors. He also appears to have been responsible for recommending the establishment of a nursery within the cemetery for the sale of plants, shrubs and wreaths; and for a **Masonry Works** in the cemetery grounds.[108]

Tubbs was very forward thinking, for in July 1891 he suggested the LNC consider 'erecting a Crematorium and a Mausoleum for ashes in the Cemetery'.[109] Yet this was at a time when very few cremations had taken place, partly because the Cremation Society's crematorium at St John's, Woking, was (until 1892) the only crematorium in the country. Furthermore it was the only crematorium serving London until Golders Green opened in 1902. Tubbs therefore perceived a new market for the LNC to exploit, using its private funeral train to accommodate cremations within the metropolitan area. Therefore in 1890 correspondence was started with the Cremation Society with a view to work jointly for this trade, and to seek a reduction of the Cremation Society's fees for funerals introduced to them by the LNC:

> it was most probable that the negotiations would end in a substantial reduction of fees. A statement of costs was submitted, and it was found that, allowing a good margin for profit this Company, taking bodies from London by their Train, could supply Coffin and undertake all arrangements for £12 to the Trade and £15 to private individuals. The present trade price charged by Messrs Dotteridge Bros. [*sic*] was shewn to be £15 15s. 0d.[110]

Ultimately the LNC hoped to undertake all funeral arrangements for the Cremation Society and to open its own crematorium within the cemetery. Although this never happened, the Cremation Society was aware of the LNC's intentions and, since it did not wish to see another crematorium opened so close to its own, it sought to accommodate the LNC as far as possible.[111] However, it should be remembered that for many years to come cremation remained the exception to the LNC's funeral business. The first cremated remains to be buried at Brookwood appear to be those of **Arthur Jackman**, who died in 1890.[112]

So successful was the LNC in attracting selected customers that Brookwood Cemetery was dubbed the 'Westminster Abbey of the middle classes'. This may be illustrated by one example of an important funeral service that took place in August 1892, that of Viscount Sherbrooke. Sherbrooke, as **Robert Lowe**, is best remembered for his opposition to the Second Reform Bill (1866–7). He became Chancellor of the Exchequer in Gladstone's first Ministry, was subsequently Home Secretary, but thereafter was elevated to the peerage and held no further major political post. Sherbrooke died at his home in Warlingham, Surrey, on 27 July 1892. The funeral was held a few days later on 3 August. That morning, at 8.30 a.m., the cortège left his house for the local station. A detachment of police acted as escort, while the papier-mâché 'Earth-to-Earth' coffin,[113] covered in violet velvet and embellished with a silver cross and tablet, was followed by his widow and other relatives and members of his household in carriages. A large number of villagers and tenants followed on foot. Warlingham station was on the South Eastern Railway, and lay but a few hundred yards from Sherbrooke's home. Prior arrangements had been made with the railway company for the journey to London. The coffin was placed in a carriage (possibly a horsebox or milk van), while the mourners were provided with two saloon coaches. All these vehicles were attached to the 9 a.m. ordinary up train. The extra carriages were detached from the rest of the train upon arrival at Waterloo Junction. From there an LSWR locomotive hauled the coaches over the single line connecting Waterloo Junction with Waterloo proper, and thence to the LNC's private station. On arrival it was connected to other carriages that contained relatives, friends and other mourners who had chosen to join the train in London. Details of the locomotive that took this train to Brookwood are not known; because it was a special train, an express engine may well have hauled it. The train left the Necropolis station shortly afterwards, and arrived at South station in the cemetery at about 11.30 a.m.

Preceded by the Revd Neville Sherbrooke, who read the service, the coffin was removed from the train and carried into the Anglican chapel, where the first part of the burial service was conducted. Thence it was borne through the cemetery grounds to St Mark's Avenue, where the remains of Viscount Sherbrooke's first wife lay. *The Times* suggested that 'no more beautiful burial-place could have been selected'. Here an ordinary earth grave had been prepared, the sides of which were concealed by bracken leaves and knots of white dahlias, lilies, roses, chrysanthemums and geraniums. Beside this grave the burial service was concluded. Among the large number of floral tributes was a beautiful wreath of delicate violet-coloured orchids from Lady Sherbrooke. Shortly before noon the mourners and friends were leaving the cemetery in the special train.[114]

As the nineteenth century progressed more plots were planted with graves, trees, shrubs and flowers. The LNC skilfully exploited the growing beauty of its cemetery, especially to the middle classes and better off. Brochures were produced promoting the benefits of burial at Woking in almost overpowering language:

> though trees have been planted in profusion, no mere turfing has been allowed to blot out the rich purple of the native heather, and the gorgeous masses of rhododendrons that make such a brave show in the early summer are in perfect harmony with the surrounding scene. Here indeed it seems impossible to realise that London is within 40 minutes by train, where only the glorious stretch of the Surrey Hills lies before our eyes. There is no crowding here; in many parts one comes on a grave with almost the same surprise as if it were in some private park, and there are quiet spots, shaded by trees and undergrowth, where none have yet been buried. Truly, it is just such a spot as mourners seek to lay to rest the one most dear to them; a place beautiful, 'far from the madding crowd'. . . . Trees of every kind flourish here; silver birches and copper beeches add beauty with their contrasting foliage, cypress trees and shrubs galore give warm shelter when the winds are cold, and stately wellingtonias stand like giant sentries keeping vigil over the sleepers till the great awakening. In addition the visitor will not fail to note the splendid show of flowers on every side, many of the graves being a mass of glowing bloom. Indeed, there is not a more beautiful cemetery in the whole world. In this respect it is safe to say that Brookwood Cemetery is unapproached, so that the whole effect produced is veritably a 'Garden of Sleep'.[115]

Until the end of the nineteenth century the Nonconformist chapel was used for all funeral services in the unconsecrated parts of Brookwood Cemetery. All the funeral services for those buried in this part of the necropolis would have taken place here. Only in 1899 was a second chapel provided. This formed the centrepiece of the new Roman Catholic grounds (now plots 119, 123, 124 and 126). It was constructed by Harris & Company, and the architect was probably **Cyril Tubbs**. The new chapel was dedicated to the Holy Souls and consecrated by the Bishop of Southwark, as the foremost Roman Catholic in England, on 6 November 1899.

THE 1864 AND 1869 ACTS

Up to the mid-1860s land sales had proved disappointing for the LNC. Therefore a third private Act was passed in 1864 as the ten-year limit on land sales imposed by the 1855 Act was about to expire. The new Act granted a five-year extension for the sale of land.[116] However, as the LNC's financial problems remained unresolved, many shareholders pressed for the complete removal of restrictions on land sales. This was partly prompted by outstanding debts. For instance, the undertakers Dottridge Brothers were 'insisting upon payment of [their] account and threatening to discontinue the business with the [LNC]'. One of the LNC's directors agreed to advance £2,000 to settle this account, which was repayable with 6 per cent interest with monies from land sales.[117] The financial problems that faced the LNC in 1854–5 remained ten years later, with burials in the cemetery nowhere near the anticipated 10,000 bodies a year.

Unfortunately the cemetery never attracted the number of dead it was designed to accommodate. Although the LNC had probably anticipated 10,000 burials a year, during the first twenty years of operation (1854–74) the total number of annual burials never exceeded 4,100, and averaged only 3,200 a year. This average declined further over time. By November 1954 total burials amounted to 216,390 (an average of 2,163 burials a year), while by November 1994 total burials had reached only 231,730 (an average of 1,655 burials a year). Clearly Brookwood Cemetery had failed as a single solution to London's burial problem. The graph shows that half the total burials at Brookwood had taken place by April 1891, and that three-quarters of the total had taken place by April 1914.[118]

By 1869 the company's situation was little changed, and a further Act of Parliament was promoted. The financial position of the LNC was the chief reason behind this Act.[119] It removed the restrictions on land sales by repealing clause XVI of the 1852 Act. But section 2 of the 1869 Act guaranteed that the cemetery, and the land lying between the Bagshot Road and Blackhorse Road, could not be sold without further parliamentary authority. The area next to the cemetery was for many years called the 'cemetery reserve' and remained as such until the 1956 Act allowed it to be sold. The rest of the company's estate could now be sold at any time and at any price. The reason for this was simple: the LNC had entailed great expense in opening its cemetery; it had not attracted the anticipated level of burials, and the limited income from undertaking was insufficient to pay an attractive dividend; therefore the company hoped for a solution through land sales. Lord Ashley's prophetic comments during the closing stages of the 1852 Act had proved correct.[120]

Initially land sales did not materialise. In 1870 the directors admitted that 'sales of land this year have not produced the same average price as hitherto. This result is caused by the sale of a plot of 20 acres of outlying and inferior land, fit only for making a plantation, and which the Directors were glad to dispose of at £35 per acre.' Similarly in 1887: 'land sold amounts to only 38 perches'.[121] Between 1876 and 1885 the average sale per year was just over 8 acres, so that, by 1887, less than half the company's estate (570 acres) had been sold. The appointment of **Cyril Tubbs** as surveyor and land agent saw several improvements in the way in which the LNC dealt with its estate.

Upon his appointment Tubbs advised that the company's estate be divided into three areas: (1) Woking station, including Goldsworth and Mayford; (2) Knaphill, including Brookwood and Hermitage Woods; and (3) Hook Heath and Royal Oak Green. Within each area Tubbs recommended separate estate agents be appointed to oversee sales, subject to the order and control of the Board of Directors. Two such agents were appointed: Mr Nicholas of Reading and Mr Drewitt of Guildford were assigned areas (1) and (2) respectively. Yet an auction arranged by Nicholas for part of the 'Maybury estate' proved a failure, since no plots reached their reserve price. However, twelve lots were subsequently sold at the reserve and a further thirteen lots at just below, resulting in an out-of-auction sale of 7 acres for £2,557, or £365 an acre. Clearly at this time there was no immediate market for land even near to Woking station, but Tubbs had proved a point by improving considerably on the average price per acre. He felt this should be between £250 and £450 depending on location.

For Tubbs's third estate, Hook Heath, no estate agent was found, therefore the area was retained under the control of the Board of Directors. During the 1890s Tubbs developed this estate, with its attractive views to the south, generously sized plots for substantial detached houses and the added attraction of a golf course for residents on the estate. This area was carefully advertised as follows:

> Hook Heath . . . represents the cream of the property [of the LNC]. . . . Approached by a gentle hill from Woking station, the Heath stands high and dry, covered with a glorious carpet of white and purple heather, and sheltered with picturesque clusters of pines, commanding such a view of hill and dale as only Surrey can present. Right before us lie the famous Hog's Back and Leith Hill, forming a panorama of exquisite charm, while on every side are masses of golden gorse, broom, and bracken which must delight every lover of Nature.[122]

The writer might have been describing Brookwood Cemetery! Using the motto 'Midst Surrey Pines' the LNC offered the discerning buyer a property of quality and distinction, with its own golf club and the option of an equally attractive permanent home in the cemetery. Moreover, at this time New Copse, an extensive plantation of pine trees, formed a natural screen between Hook Heath and the cemetery. All this activity resulted in some improvement in sales, which averaged over 11 acres a year from 1890 to 1905. Thereafter sales fell back considerably, to little more than 6 acres a year or rather less.[123] In February 1906 the Chairman of the LNC, **Edward Ford North**, purchased 10 acres of the company's land at Hook Heath for £3,000. North subsequently built a house there. At the next AGM North stated that he and his family intended to live there, thereby showing their faith in the company's estate. Another director, **William Austin**, felt it was advantageous to have the Chairman holding land that belonged to the company, as he would be able to see what was going on in the neighbourhood of Brookwood and Woking.[124]

EARLY TWENTIETH-CENTURY DEVELOPMENTS

Other building developments continued into the new century. A new London terminus was opened at 121 Westminster Bridge Road in February 1902. This replaced the original station, located between York Street and the Westminster Bridge Road, which had been opened in November 1854. The site of this station, along with All Saints' Church, Lambeth, which stood opposite one of the private station entrances, was required by the LSWR for the complete reconstruction of Waterloo station. (Interestingly, the very last vicar of All Saints, **Revd Frederick Lee**, is buried at Brookwood.) The railway company built the new station at their own expense and also gave the LNC £12,000 for the inconvenience caused to its business. Part of this sum was used to repair and maintain the various cemetery buildings. More importantly, the original wooden fence or paling that had been erected all around the cemetery in 1854 was replaced by a more substantial brick and pebble-dashed wall, which largely survives intact to this day. This wall was erected in the early years of the twentieth century.

About this time, the LNC's **Masonry Works** was considerably improved. The original 'works' was located adjacent to the Cemetery Superintendent's offices, and its showroom was in fact a greenhouse. All this was replaced by completely new premises located directly opposite, just inside the Anglican section of the cemetery. An L-shaped single-storey building contained the various workshops and machinery, while a private siding and yard was provided adjacent to **Cemetery Pales**. The Masonry Works became the centre of the LNC's statuary and masonry business, for designs were made and erected for use not only at Brookwood but also in cemeteries and churchyards anywhere within the United Kingdom, or indeed anywhere in the world. The railway siding meant that blocks of stone and marble could be easily transported into the works, while completed memorials, suitably packed and crated, could be moved out of the cemetery grounds and off to their final destination.

Perhaps the grandest building to be completed was the new **Anglican chapel**. This was constructed in 1908–10 to designs by **Cyril Tubbs** and **Arthur Messer**. It was presumably provided because of the need for a more spacious chapel than the original design by Sydney Smirke. It is in an 'Arts and Crafts' style, and is certainly reminiscent of the architects' domestic designs on the Hook Heath estate, and on similar estates at Weybridge and elsewhere. The interior features massive timbers supporting the roof, along with stained-glass and other memorial windows.[125]

Shortly afterwards the **Columbarium** was created from Lord Cadogan's private mausoleum, thereby fulfilling part of **Cyril Tubbs**'s scheme of 1891. The building had been constructed for Lord Cadogan in about 1878–80, and was the largest family mausoleum within the cemetery. However, in the summer of 1910 Lord Cadogan decided that he no longer wished to use it, and he sold it to the LNC for £200. Thereafter the interior was altered, and 'COLUMBARIUM' was cut into the stone pediment above the entrance. Inside, a number of shelves or niches were provided around the walls at entrance level and also in the underground vault, to provide many *loculi* for the reception of cinerary urns. The LNC soon advertised this new service, which complemented the crematory facilities at nearby St John's.

THE MILITARY CEMETERIES

The First World War led to the development of the Brookwood Military Cemeteries. Many people think only of this section when Brookwood Cemetery is mentioned, but although the military areas now comprise about 37 acres, making it the largest military burial ground in the United Kingdom, this is only a small proportion of the total area of Brookwood. The LNC originally offered the War Office one acre of land 'for the free interment of soldiers and sailors who have returned from the front wounded and may subsequently die' in August 1914. However, the original **British Military Cemetery** was set aside only in 1917 under an agreement between the War Office and the LNC. This area is the oldest part of the military burial ground and was used for the burial of soldiers, sailors, airmen and nurses who died in hospitals within the London Military District. The burials in this section cover most of the dominions and colonies of the British Empire, and the whole section is laid out in the typical style of the War Graves Commission. The overall layout appears to have been the work of Captain Goulden RE and Colonel B.R. Ward as Chief Engineer to the London District.[126]

The American Military Cemetery (later renamed the **Brookwood American Cemetery**) was laid out adjacent to this. It is still important, since it remains the only military burial ground in this country for American soldiers and sailors who lost their lives in Great Britain, or in its surrounding waters, during the First World War. The ground contains the bodies of 468 servicemen, while the Memorial Chapel at the far end of the plot commemorates a further

563 casualties, all of whom were either lost or buried at sea. It was designed by Egerton Swartwout,[127] John Russell Pope[128] and Harry B. Creswell.[129] At present the Memorial Chapel, the flagstaff and entrance walls are the only listed structures anywhere in Brookwood Cemetery. Although the chapel was largely completed in 1929, the special service of dedication did not take place until 15 August 1937, twenty years to the day when American troops first marched through London. The service was scheduled to fall within the same fortnight as dedication services held at the seven other American memorial chapels in France and Belgium. The service at Brookwood should have been presided over by General Pershing, Chairman of the American Battle Monuments Commission, but ill health meant he was unable to attend. The service was extensively covered in the press: *The Times* even devoted a leading article to the event.[130]

After the war the railway service continued to be available for those who desired burial at Brookwood from London and elsewhere. However, the funeral trains ran less frequently, usually operating twice weekly at most, unless the number of burials demanded extra trains. Nevertheless Brookwood was still a popular choice of burial ground for the discerning customer. An example of this patronage was the internationally famous portrait artist **John Singer Sargent**, who died at his London home in April 1925. He was subsequently laid to rest in his family's allotment in the centre of the 'Ring', although his headstone is remarkably modest for an artist of his stature and reputation.

THE INTER-WAR YEARS

In February 1925 Lieutenant-Colonel Henry George Ricardo[131] succeeded **Edward F. North** as Chairman. Ricardo had been a director of the LNC since 1904. After his death, in December 1940, he was succeeded by **John B. Walker**. In 1927 the LNC officially changed its name to the shorter form, The London Necropolis Company. One of the main reasons for this change was that numerous people dealing with the company objected to the words 'National Mausoleum' and, as the LNC was generally known by its shorter form, these words could be omitted. This resolution was passed at extraordinary general meetings of the LNC that took place at 121 Westminster Bridge Road on 16 June and 14 July 1927. The notice of change of name was subsequently published in the *London Gazette* on 25 November 1927.[132]

In another way 1927 was a grim time for the LNC, since three of its sterling servants, **Cyril Tubbs**, **Edward Ford North** and **George Barratt**, died during the course of the year. Between them they represented some 140 years' service to the company. Tubbs's death was formally recorded at the Board Meeting on 13 April: 'Resolved that they [the Directors] desire to express and record their sincere regret at the death of their valued colleague and to place on record their deep sense of the important services rendered by him to the Company during his 40 years' connection with its affairs as its Surveyor, General Manager and later as one of its Directors.'[133] The LNC's Chairman, Edward North, had been suffering from ill health for some months, and his death in October 1927 was not entirely unexpected. In December George Barratt's loss was again recorded at the subsequent Board Meeting: 'Mr Barratt's death on 28 December was reported and the Directors recorded their deep regret at the loss of such an old and valued servant who entered the Company's service 63 years ago and was for 41 years Superintendent at the Cemetery.'[134]

The LNC was still trading successfully within and without Brookwood Cemetery during the 1930s and well beyond. The incomplete set of Ledger Books that is now held at the Surrey History Centre provides a valuable record of the extraordinary range of work undertaken by the company between 1932 and 1956. The following sample entries refer to various work undertaken within the cemetery at this time:[135]

15 November 1932
<u>194665 9ft x 10ft Kidson</u>
To S[upply] & P[lant] Daffodils, Blue Hyacinths & Scillas (as before)   £1–10–6

21 April 1933
<u>Newly born child unknown (female)</u>
To Child's Coffin & removal etc.   15–0
To Parish Interment   7–6
       £1–2–6

9 March 1934
<u>197413 (Hodson)</u>
To eighteen unmounted photographs P[ost] C[ard] size of open grave   10/6*d*

6 May 1936
<u>190675 **Tiller**</u>
To Engraving 74 lead letters of Add[itional] Insc[ription] @ 12/- per dozen
       £3–14–0

30 September 1936
<u>168832 **Moir**</u>
To Thoroughly cleaning Bronze Memorial Figure   £3–5–0

4 January 1938
Braine Mausoleum
To supplying cut flowers in 2 Vases each Weds. For one year @ 3/- weekly.
       £7–16–0

27 March 1941
<u>202619 **Painter**</u>
To Portland Stone Headstone & Kerbing with corner posts, f[itting] & f[ixing]
       £26–0–0
Engraving 268 lead letters of Ins[cription] @ 8/- doz.   £8–18–8
Carving RAF badge   £3–5–0
       £38–3–8

During the same period, no fewer than four new mausoleums were constructed in the cemetery grounds, three in the Anglican sections and one in the Nonconformist area.[136] The following entries refer to work undertaken outside the cemetery. Note that this included funerals of the famous who chose the LNC to undertake the arrangements for their final journey even if they did not wish to be buried at Brookwood:[137]

10 February 1933
<u>George Sydenham Clarke deceased, Lord Sydenham of Coombe</u>[138]
To Cremation Shell covered violet, silk tassells, upholstered, etc, Conveyance to house, Superintendents & Assistants, Motor Hearse, Superintendent & Assistants to remove to Golder's Green Crematorium & Cinerary Urn with engraved plate of inscription
       £23–3–0
Paid fee for Incinerator   £6–6–0
       £29–9–0

2 February 1934
Edward Stuart Talbot, Bishop[139]
To Special Earth to Earth Coffin & removal to Southwark Cathedral & removal to
Winchester Cathedral etc £40–0–0
Trunk phone calls etc. 8–6
£40–8–6

16 March 1934
Kingston Cemetery
To Rustic Grey Cornish Granite Cross & Kerbing to enclose 3 spaces f[itting] & f[ixing]
£38–0–0
Eng[raving] 75 lead letters of ins[cription] @ 1/6 doz. £5–12–6
Fee paid at Kingston £3–0–0
£43–15–6

11 December 1956
Portsmouth Generating station: St Mary's Churchyard & Site
Clearance of site of Human Remains inc[luding] transport to & re-interment in Milton
Cemetery Portsmouth in accordance with terms of contract S/11/1 dated 20 July 1956
£2,750–0–0

By this time Brookwood Cemetery often featured in county guides as well worth visiting.
The following extract may be taken as typical for the 1930s excursionist:

> On the other side of the railway spreads a great Camp of the Dead, which Londoners will
> style *Woking* Cemetery, to the indignation of that lively young town, three or four miles
> away. The Brookwood burying-ground . . . is the largest in the country, and in beauty
> grows in competition with some of the elaborate cemeteries of American cities. Laid out
> half a century ago [*sic*] . . . it encloses 500 acres of sandy land, which, among its native turf
> and heather, has been planted with flower-beds, clumps of wood, banks of rhododendrons
> and other shrubs, that go to disguise the gloomy shadows of the grave. Apart from the divi-
> sion between those who have and have not the right to sleep in consecrated earth, certain
> areas are allotted to London parishes, or to communities . . . so that the associations of life
> are not lost in death . . . fellow-countrymen too, can lie side by side, and fellow-believers of
> many a creed: a notable feature, for instance, is the Parsees' resting-place, so far from their
> Eastern Towers of Silence.[140]

In addition to the service of dedication for the American Memorial Chapel, 1937 also saw a
similar service for the **Royal Hospital Chelsea** plot. A large memorial was constructed in the
centre of this burial ground and was unveiled and dedicated on 27 April 1937. It serves as a
general memorial to all those pensioners buried here. The ceremony was performed by the
Governor of the Royal Hospital, and was attended by over 300 pensioners in uniform. The
service of dedication was conducted by the Hospital's chaplain, after which a wreath was laid by
the senior captain of invalids.[141]

THE SECOND WORLD WAR AND ITS AFTERMATH

The Second World War had dramatic results on the LNC and its cemetery. On the worst night
of the Blitz to date – 16–17 April 1941 – the private London station was largely destroyed.

Henceforth a limited number of railway funerals were catered for from Waterloo station, but this attack effectively spelt the end of the LNC's railway funeral service. In 1943 there was the loss of another highly respected member of the Board, **John B. Walker**, who had been associated with the LNC since 1889. The directors recorded their 'desire to place on record the great loss the Company has sustained by the death of their esteemed colleague. Under his very capable Management and by his unfailing endeavours the affairs of the Company have shown great progress.'[142]

After the war the LNC decided that its private station would be too expensive to rebuild, especially since demand for railway funerals had continued to decline during the 1930s. Therefore the site of the London station at 121 Westminster Bridge Road was sold. Under the terms of the original lease the railway company could retain the land and buildings at platform level, and it agreed that the LNC should be free to sell or let the ground site that fronted the Westminster Bridge Road. An agreement was signed in December 1946 and the ground site was subsequently sold to the British Humane Association for £21,000. The headquarters of the LNC was transferred to the **Superintendent's office** in the cemetery with effect from 29 July 1946. This move necessarily resulted in weakening its links with the metropolis, although the LNC retained a number of local offices in central London and the suburbs. These included a lease on the premises at 123 Westminster Bridge Road, which was converted into a branch office. In December 1947 this became the LNC's official registered office.[143]

The entrances into the cemetery were also remodelled at this time. Traditionally the main 'gateways' had been the two cemetery stations. However, it was felt that, with the removal of the railway track in 1946–7, better road access should be provided off **Cemetery Pales**. This resulted in the semi-circular access road on the Nonconformist side, and the creation of a new avenue on the former railway line leading up towards North station. The entrance to the Anglican section was hardly altered. It was also intended that new entrances for cars should be created opposite the West Hill Golf Course (on the A322), and by the East Gate, opposite Heath House Lane. Neither proposal was ever acted upon.[144]

The military sections were considerably extended after the Second World War. This included the formation of the **RAF** section and shelter, and areas set aside for **Belgians**, the **Free French**, **Poles**, **Czechs**, **Canadians** and **Italians**. All these allotments include a national memorial of varying size and importance. The Queen officially inaugurated one of the most important war memorials in the United Kingdom when the **Brookwood Memorial** was unveiled in October 1958. It commemorates 3,500 men and women of the land forces of the British Commonwealth to whom the fortunes of war denied a known and honoured grave. During the special service the Queen said: 'Had it not been for their courage and that of others like them, the war on land could not have been won and final victory would not have been achieved.'[145]

THE GLADES OF REMEMBRANCE

The LNC twice obtained parliamentary authority to erect a crematorium within Brookwood Cemetery, but these powers were never exploited. Under the terms of the London Necropolis Act (1946),[146] the LNC was empowered to erect and maintain a crematorium. An area of land in the Nonconformist section and measuring 400ft × 200ft was set aside for this purpose. This land had been previously used for **pauper burials**, and is located opposite today's entrance to the **Glades of Remembrance**. But a crematorium was never built there. Instead, in May 1950 the LNC opened the Glades of Remembrance, with a service of dedication led by the Bishop of Guildford. This ceremony took place nearly three years after the first burial of ashes in the grounds. The Glades were planned from September 1945 using Messrs Milner, White & Sons as the LNC's landscape consultants to advise on the layout. Set amid semi-woodland, the Glades were designed purely for the reception of cremated remains.[147] No obtrusive memorials

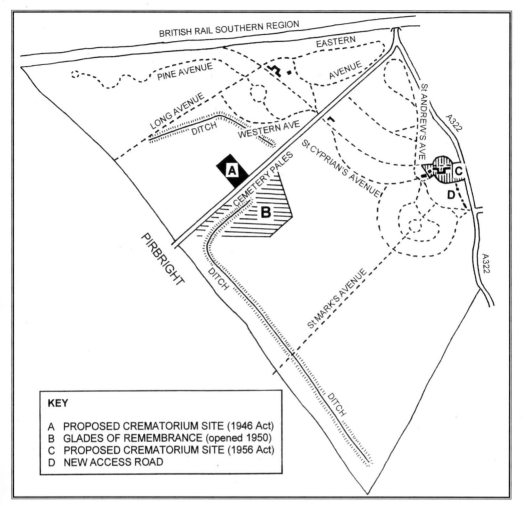

The Brookwood Cemetery crematorium. The map shows the locations referred to in the private Acts of 1946 and 1956.

were allowed. The setting was designed to be informal and unsentimental, with none of the usual features of a cemetery or graveyard; it was entirely unmonumental. The writer Bernard Darwin described the Glades as follows:

> Till quite lately there was nothing here but a tract of almost impenetrable woodland, and its old character has been most wonderfully retained. Here may be seen landscape gardening at its simplest and so most inconspicuous best. . . . The casket or urn that holds the Ashes is placed just below ground level and all that marks its site is a small stone two or three inches high . . . and these little stones lie for the most part so inconspicuously among their green surroundings as almost to escape notice. . . . The visitor feels himself to be in the wildest of wild gardens, lonely and tranquil and cut off from the noisy outer world.[148]

The earliest plans for the Glades refer to the 'memorial garden' or 'garden of remembrance'. The very first burial of cremated remains in the Glades was that of **Ann Isabella**

Stonebridge on 19 July 1947.[149] Once opened, it was felt little further work was required: 'with the erection of the Lodge, the Bridge, and the clearing of the Stream no further developments in the Glades of Remembrance are considered necessary for some long time . . . the maintenance of the existing lay-out will ensure an adequate choice for all enquiries.'[150]

The LNC also tried to build its crematorium under another private Act of 1956.[151] This time the powers were extended to include about 2½ acres of largely unused land adjacent to the site of **South station** which would be deconsecrated under clause 5 of the Act. Access to the crematorium would have been via a new entrance into the cemetery by the East Gate on the A322, or otherwise by a new gateway leading directly on to this road. The intention was to convert the original – and by now long-disused – Anglican chapel into the crematorium, thus saving some expense and without having to construct a completely new structure. The larger adjacent chapel would have been used for burial and crematory services. South station would have continued in use as a refreshment room, and might also have provided accommodation for coffins prior to cremation. All this would have ensured the longer-term future of this unique trinity of funerary buildings.[152] But once again the crematorium failed to materialise owing to the lack of funds, and almost certainly because of the serious distractions caused by a series of hostile takeover bids that began in 1955 and are described below. Never again would the LNC attempt to construct its own crematorium. Never again would two opportunities to do so present themselves to the company. It is interesting to speculate what might have happened to the subsequent fortunes of the LNC had it succeeded in doing so. The post-war preference for cremation strongly suggests the LNC might have enjoyed greater commercial success than it did, rather than depending entirely on income generated by selling burial plots in an increasingly old-fashioned Victorian cemetery of enormous expanse.

The LNC was also busy in expanding its network of branches. During 1946 it acquired the business and lease of the premises of Messrs C.G. Hatt, Funeral Directors. This firm was based at 82 Kensington High Street, and the LNC purchased it in October 1946. In 1947 the trustees of Frederick W. Paine approached the LNC regarding offers to acquire the business. Paine's was an established, extensive, well-equipped and well-respected family-run undertaking business. It had nineteen branches operating in the Kingston-upon-Thames area. This network of branches in south-west London complemented the LNC's funeral work now that its main base was outside central London; indeed the company saw Paine's as providing a link between London and Brookwood. The purchase was completed in early 1947 for £108,500.[153] Although these acquisitions strengthened the LNC's business, because of the company's unique nature – still retaining property assets in a fast expanding part of Surrey – it became increasingly vulnerable to acquisition by other companies. These speculators were interested only in the areas of land, ripe for property development, that the LNC still owned. These companies were not interested in the preservation and promotion of Brookwood Cemetery.[154]

THE LAST YEARS OF THE LNC

During the 1950s the LNC's Board of Directors fought a long battle to prevent any hostile takeover, but the battle was lost in 1959. The first bid came from the Alliance Property Company Ltd in May 1955. It was forced to raise its offer to the LNC's shareholders, without effect. But the LNC bowed to the pressure of this bid by establishing the Brookwood Estates Realisation Company during the course of the year. This new division was set up to realise the value of the remaining surplus lands of the LNC and distribute the proceeds to its shareholders through the issue of debenture stock issued by Brookwood Estates.[155] Land still owned by the LNC included parts of Connaught Road, Brookwood; Bagshot Road, Knaphill; the Broadway, Knaphill; Golf Club Road; Mile Path; Brook Farm; Blackhorse Road; Folks Orchard; Maybury; Brookwood Lye; Hermitage Wood; and land north of Hermitage Road. The LNC also retained the lease for the 186-acre Woking Golf Club on Hook Heath, established in 1893.[156] Another major area of land still owned by the LNC was that occupied by the West Hill Golf Club, and otherwise known as the 'cemetery reserve'. But this land could not be sold except with parliamentary sanction, since the company was prevented from doing so under the terms of the LNC's Act of 1869.[157]

This was the main reason for the promotion of the private London Necropolis Act (1956), which, in addition to new powers for constructing a crematorium, also allowed the sale of two main plots of land. By selling this land the LNC effectively admitted that its existing cemetery would be sufficient for burial purposes for the foreseeable future. The 'cemetery reserve' comprised about 160 acres and had been leased to the West Hill Golf Club for many years. Now the club would be free to purchase this land outright,[158] while Brookwood Estates could distribute the sales proceeds as debenture issue to its shareholders.[159] The logical conclusion to this policy was the loss of potential rental income to subsidise the cemetery. The move towards the accelerated sale of remaining land, while of short-term benefit to the shareholders, ultimately threatened the future viability of Brookwood Cemetery. Yet this policy was to be pursued by all its owners from 1959 to 1985. In addition there were the considerable investments made by the LNC over many years from the charges made for the maintenance of graves. The dividends from these securities were used to pay for all types of maintenance, repairs and planting within the cemetery, the loss of which would also threaten the future of Brookwood Cemetery.

The foundation of Brookwood Estates merely fuelled other companies' interest in the LNC and its new subsidiary, especially since the group paid 11s net per £1 share from the surplus land account in October 1955. In December the Board of Brookwood Estates was recommending the refusal of an offer from George Brodie & Company, while in January 1956 interest in both the LNC and Brookwood Estates came from the New Centurion Trust Ltd, and yet another offer came from the Franco-British and General Trust in November 1957.[160] In December 1957 the Alliance Property Company Ltd announced that, having acquired over 63 per cent of the share capital of Brookwood Estates, the Board would be reconstituted. Having secured Brookwood Estates, Alliance was able to disclose in January 1959 its successful bid for the balance of ordinary shares in the LNC. After 107 years it had effectively ceased to exist as an independent company, since shortly afterwards two key board members – Sir Harold Kenyon[161] and George B. Geen – resigned;[162] however, the name London Necropolis Company Ltd appears to have been retained for the undertaking sector of Alliance Property. When in September 1960 Alliance Property announced a £300,000 investment in property, it was clear its main priority was not going to be the effective promotion and maintenance of Brookwood Cemetery; nor would Brookwood's proposed crematorium ever be built.[163]

FURTHER CHANGES IN OWNERSHIP AND THE 1975 ACT

By the 1960s Brookwood Cemetery was simply failing to attract sufficient burials to generate enough income to maintain its grounds and encourage further burials. Earth burial by this time was probably at its twentieth-century nadir. But Brookwood's case was made worse by its vast size and its distinctive Victorian character. Cremation was believed to be more hygienic, convenient and appropriate to the 1960s. Slowly but surely Brookwood was left to revert to wilderness and woodland. The problem was exacerbated by Alliance Property's main interest in accelerating the sale of remaining surplus lands owned by the LNC, yet failing to promote burial (even of cremated remains) in the cemetery it had acquired along with the land it saw so ripe for sale and profit. During the next twenty-five years a succession of new owners followed a similar policy, each one neglecting the cemetery. These businesses saw the cemetery as a wasting asset, and one important consequence was that rationalisation of operations took place. In 1970 London Necropolis Company Ltd was acquired by Cornwall Property (Holdings) Limited.

By this time most undertaking work had ceased at Brookwood: the **Masonry Works** were leased to Messrs Clements, and the major tasks retained were those of digging graves, and selling and maintaining burial plots. Funeral direction was concentrated in the Frederick Paine sector. Yet while the overall group structure of London Necropolis Company Ltd was retained, a policy of cross-subsidisation was possible. With Alliance Property having previously divested the old LNC of the majority of its non-cemetery estate, there was little attraction in this acquisition. Therefore Cornwall Property was keen to sell London Necropolis Company Ltd.

The Great Southern Group acquired Brookwood Cemetery from Cornwall Property in August 1972, at a time when it was actively expanding in the funeral directing market. The Great Southern Group was previously called the Great Southern Cemetery, Crematorium and Land Company Ltd and had opened Streatham Park Cemetery in 1907 and the South London Crematorium in 1936. It also owned the funeral business of Messrs Bedford Sons and Slater in Farringdon Street and Blackfriars Road. Brookwood Cemetery was purchased along with Frederick W. Paine Ltd, under its generic title London Necropolis Company Ltd, and Great Southern paid £435,000 for the package.[164] This gave Great Southern a total of twenty branches in south-west London, Surrey and Berkshire and 'a platform for a vigorous programme of expansion'.[165] During its brief ownership by Great Southern it was decided that Brookwood Cemetery should become separated from the more successful parts of London Necropolis Company Ltd. This meant the branches of Frederick W. Paine Ltd were retained, along with the Necropolis Company. This confusingly named division (subsequently renamed Necropolis) specialised in the exhumation and reburial of human remains from disused churches and burial grounds in preparation for redevelopment of the site. In taking this course of action the cemetery was totally divorced from the more profitable sectors of London Necropolis Company Ltd, and was deemed a financial liability. By this time virtually all the LNC's surplus land had been disposed of, along with its portfolio of investments.[166] Brookwood Cemetery was effectively bankrupt. Therefore in July 1973 Great Southern sold it to Maximillian Investments for about £400,000.[167]

What was the attraction of Brookwood for yet another property company? This question was answered by the promotion of a new private Act of Parliament. Only by identifying land actually within the cemetery boundary could Maximillian Investments hope to make a profit out of this acquisition. Under the terms of the Brookwood Cemetery Act (1975), the new owners were permitted to sell off parts of the cemetery. Entitled 'An Act to empower Brookwood Cemetery Limited [i.e. a subsidiary of Maximillian Investments] to dispose of certain lands belonging to the said Company not required for cemetery purposes free from restrictions', it identified about 117 acres of land for disposal.[168] At the time local residents were alarmed at what 'redevelopment' might mean once the Act became law. Max Lewinsohn, the Chairman of Maximillian Investments, was quoted as saying: 'We have no plans to redevelop the surplus land at the moment. . . . But it makes sound economic sense to remove the statutory bar to selling our surplus land or putting it to some other use. If we decided to develop, we should consult local residents and other interested parties about how to put this land to other use without spoiling the environment of the cemetery.'[169]

Unfortunately Mr Lewinsohn could give assurances only that *his* company had no intention of developing this land, although this would not prevent another corporation from doing so. Other property developers might come forward with plans to erect large, exclusive and expensive houses, and would have only limited burial areas to clear. Maximillian Investments also sought an application to fell 10,000 trees within the cemetery on the grounds of 'good husbandry' and 'fire safety'. The company alleged that unless considerably thinned the trees were a considerable fire risk; however, the corporation promised that 'at least' 1,800 trees would remain.[170]

As a direct consequence of the 1975 Act the site of the former **Superintendent's office**

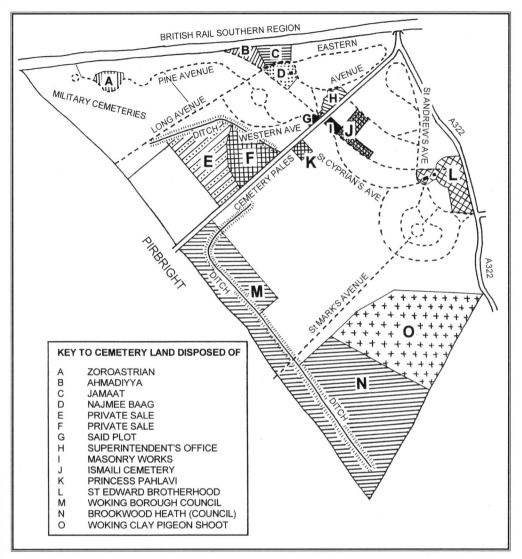

The Brookwood Cemetery Act (1975). The map shows the several areas of cemetery land disposed of under the terms of this private legislation.

and its associated outbuildings was sold. The cemetery office was transferred down the road to **Glades House**, the old caretaker's lodge at the entrance to the **Glades of Remembrance**. As space was severely restricted in the new premises, someone decided that the vast majority of the surviving records of the LNC should be destroyed rather than donated to the Surrey Records Office. The new owners of the site leased the old offices to the firm of Wootton Jeffreys, transport consultants, who occupied the site until August 1994.[171]

The relocation of the cemetery offices coincided with a new management under Brookwood Cemetery Ltd, based in Cheam, Surrey. This change in ownership was purely nominal, since a number of directors remained unchanged. Brookwood Cemetery was 'acquired' by the Stockport Borough Cemetery Company Ltd, a wholly owned subsidiary of Dundonian Ltd. Two of Dundonian's five directors were none other than Mr Lewinsohn and a Mr Neville, and the four directors of Brookwood Cemetery Ltd were also directors of Dundonian. The Stockport company paid £228,000 for the cemetery in March 1976.[172] One of its priorities was precisely that behind the 1975 Brookwood Cemetery Act: to maximise the income generated by selling off discrete portions of the cemetery. This included the **Superintendent's office**, and its adjacent greenhouses and outbuildings. Other cemetery land sold included the old cottages and surrounding land off **Long Avenue**, the land now maintained as **Brookwood Heath** at the end of St Mark's Avenue, areas adjacent to this and bordering the parish boundary with Pirbright, and the area that was subsequently acquired by the Woking Clay Pigeon Club, also off St Mark's Avenue. Subsequent sales included several large plots to particular groups or individuals, although these were for uses more appropriate for the cemetery. They included the private **Said family plot**, the **Nagmee Baag** burial ground, the **Ismaili Cemetery** and the **St Edward Brotherhood**. Under the terms of the 1975 Act at least some of the profits from these land sales were supposed to be used for the restoration and improvement of the rest of the cemetery.

While all these developments were going on the cemetery sank into a period of further neglect. The tiny workforce was entirely inadequate for the demands of maintaining upwards of 400 acres of cemetery. Mechanisation would have helped, but this was something that Brookwood Cemetery Ltd was unwilling to invest in. It seems that the company was interested only in selling cemetery land at whatever price it could get and for whatever purpose. At the same time the company was content to leave vast areas of the cemetery to revert to woodland. All this contravened the provisions of the 1975 Act, which clearly stated that 'the Company should have power to dispose of such lands to enable the Company to provide a proper standard of maintenance and to continue its programme of restoration and improvement of the cemetery'.[173]

Summer students who were employed to assist with maintenance remember they were armed only with hand tools while they cut their way towards the suspected locations of graves so that a further burial might take place in a family plot. Apart from this, only the major avenues on each side of the cemetery were adequately maintained. Everything else was left to grow like the forest around Sleeping Beauty's castle. Although this might add to the gothic drama of a visit to the cemetery, it did little to help those trying to locate graves or memorials; nor had the cemetery ever been intended to appear like this.

The neglected and overgrown cemetery was more prone to vandalism. This was partly because of the general appearance of the cemetery, and was encouraged also by the limited number of visitors to the grounds. The former cemetery chapels were rarely used and were left to rot and decay; nothing was done to repair or restore them. Both cemetery stations had disappeared by 1972. North station was demolished in the late 1960s because of dry rot, while South station was burned down in September 1972. Precious and semi-precious metal decorations were ruthlessly removed from the more visible and accessible memorials. The future of Brookwood Cemetery looked bleak indeed.

MODERN TIMES

There have been at least five positive developments in recent years. The first of these was the acquisition of the two former Anglican chapels, the site of South station and plot 39 by the **St Edward Brotherhood**. This Orthodox monastic community moved into its site in March 1982 having paid £28,000 for 5 acres of land.[174] Both chapels were derelict, and the original and smaller structure was on the verge of collapsing. Over the years the Brotherhood has repaired and restored both buildings. The larger chapel now houses the relics of **St Edward the Martyr**, and serves as the church for this small parish. The smaller chapel, happily retaining many of its original features, is used for accommodation by members of the Brotherhood. Both buildings are therefore preserved for posterity, while the relics of St Edward form a valuable focus for parishioners and visitors alike.

In March 1985 Mr D.J.T. Dally, previously the cemetery manager under Brookwood Cemetery Ltd, but by now the owner of the cemetery, sold it on to Mr Ramadan Guney, and at a similar price to that paid by Maximillian Investments in 1973. It appears that Mr Guney became interested through his desire to purchase a family plot at Brookwood, and subsequently through his links with the London Mosque and its need to identify new burial areas for worshippers there. However, instead of acquiring a portion of the cemetery he purchased the entire site. It is true that Mr Guney subsequently cleared some areas of the cemetery of trees and undergrowth, but this was partly an attempt to correct the problem of a rising water table[175] and partly to create new burial areas. It should also be considered in the context of the neglected cemetery described above. Brookwood was never designed to be dense woodland but a managed landscape. It is very easy to criticise cemetery management, but over the years Mr Guney has tried to maintain the neglected and overgrown ground as far as burial receipts will allow. This has proved to be a slow and frustrating process, and has also been undertaken without any external funding whatsoever. Mr Guney has also invested heavily in the computerisation of the cemetery's surviving burial records.[176]

The contrast between the well-maintained Muslim and Catholic sections at Brookwood and the former Church of England areas is symbolic of where most burials are taking place today; these communities tend to visit and remember their dear departed relatives. The neglect apparent in parts of the former Church of England sections is a sad indication that much of modern society has already forgotten its dead. Mr Guney is now second only to the LNC in his period of continuous ownership, something the cemetery has lacked since 1959; he is also the first owner of the cemetery since the LNC to be *acquiring* land previously sold off under the terms of the 1975 Brookwood Cemetery Act. So far this has included the outlying areas adjacent to the parish boundary with Pirbright, subsequently repurchased from Woking Borough Council. Unfortunately, with most of these former cemetery lands having been sold off as freehold properties, the scope for further acquisitions remains distinctly limited.[177]

The third major development was the formation of the Brookwood Cemetery Society in April 1992. The Society's aim is to promote a wider interest in the cemetery as a means to ensure its long-term future. This is done through guided walks, an annual open day, by lectures, through publications, and the Society's website. Further information about the Society may be found in **Appendix C**.[178]

The Society has worked with Mr Guney to improve parts of the cemetery. One of its more visible projects is to place avenue signposts throughout the grounds, replacing many old or illegible ones, but also placing new ones as appropriate. The design of these signs is based on a surviving example that was found off St John's Avenue.[179] The Society has also worked with various groups to restore certain memorials. One example is the restoration of the **De Morgan** memorial, paid for entirely by the De Morgan Foundation,[180] which was previously unaware of this important headstone. In other cases the Society has paid for the repair of memorials itself. Pride of place must go to the first project, the repair and restoration of the magnificent statue commemorating **Elaine Falkiner**, which was pushed off its pedestal in May 1995. It was fully restored in October 1996. This is the first of many other memorials that deserve attention so they may continue to be enjoyed by visitors to the cemetery. A more recent restoration project has been to repair, restore and tidy memorials along St David's Avenue and in the 'Ring'. But despite the enormous importance of Brookwood Cemetery in the funerary history of Britain, its significance has still to be acknowledged and recognised and supported by bodies such as Woking Borough Council, Surrey County Council, the Department of National Heritage and English Heritage; consequently it has yet to attract any major funding or grants for restoration, repairs and maintenance.[181] The admittedly modest achievements to date have been accomplished with the support and interest of Mr and Mrs Guney and the limited funds raised by the determined but purely voluntary efforts of the Brookwood Cemetery Society.

The fourth major development has been the publication of the House of Commons Select Committee on the Environment, Transport & Regional Affairs report on cemetery provision in the United Kingdom.[182] This wide-ranging report is the first of its kind for 150 years and covers important issues such as the value of cemeteries, cemeteries in decline, causes for concern, halting decline and reviewing current legislation. In doing so the report addresses the cultural value of cemeteries, their value to the environment and local community and their role in urban renaissance. It also makes valuable comments on and recommendations about the ways in which cemeteries may be better funded and maintained, principally via English Heritage, the Heritage Lottery Fund or the New Opportunities Fund, along with support from local authorities and cemetery preservation groups. Moreover, these recommendations cover both local authority and privately owned cemeteries. Therefore ways have been identified by Parliament for the future funding of restoration and maintenance of many of our hitherto neglected cemeteries, and the Government is committed to making formal proposals in the near future. Yet Woking Borough Council remains remarkably indifferent to this historic gem, set within its western wards, and gives little support to this unique cemetery. In fact, as will shortly be described, the council has been directly responsible for one of the worst planning decisions regarding Brookwood Cemetery.

The Government's response to the Select Committee was published in October 2001.[183] It provides for a preliminary survey of the number, condition and operational liability of cemeteries in the United Kingdom. The work on this cemetery survey has already begun. The Government also accepts that cemeteries should be properly maintained and managed, and that local authorities should pay more attention to the cultural significance of their burial grounds. It recommends that the Quality of Life Capital methodology (published jointly by English Heritage, English Nature, the Countryside Agency and the Environment Agency[184]) should be applied to cemeteries throughout the country, along with the provisions of the Urban White Paper *Our Towns and Cities the Future: Delivering an Urban Renaissance*.[185] The Home Office will establish an advisory group of relevant organisations which will provide advice to the Government as required, make appropriate expertise and advice available to cemetery managers, coordinate the cemetery survey exercise and evaluate the outcome of the project, and provide a framework for which standards for burial grounds can be set and monitored. The report is less open about funding solutions, partly because this will depend on the outcome of the national survey. However, it does make several suggestions for funding bodies – principally the Heritage Lottery Fund and the New Opportunities Fund – that should be more proactive in supporting bids from cemeteries, and notes that the new advisory body will be in a position to give appropriate guidance to these funding bodies. Overall the Government's response is very positive, particularly regarding the national survey and the creation of what may become an inspectorate for cemeteries.

Brookwood Cemetery was selected as an early case study for the Home Office research into British cemeteries and their management. The initial report by Brenda Wilson, an independent consultant, was compiled in 2002. It covers the background to the cemetery, its maintenance and capacity, management practice, local issues and national priorities. The case summary is clearly stated as:

A site of extreme importance as a cemetery, as a cultural, historical and architectural record for this and many other nations. The sheer scale of the site is a serious undertaking for a family business. Despite the strong dedication and commitment of the owner to bringing the site fully back to its former glory, it is difficult to see how this can be achieved without aid from the various funding streams that exist, such as the Heritage Lottery Fund. The site has the potential to become a World Heritage Site, and the owners would like to share their enthusiasm and enjoyment of a unique site to the full with others.[186]

Clearly there are a number of major national and local initiatives taking place that means the future of cemeteries in Britain, and Brookwood Cemetery in particular, seems more assured. One outcome of Mr Guney's clearance work described above was that Woking Borough Council designated the entire cemetery a conservation area in June 1989.[187] This means the council has in theory recognised the historic importance of the cemetery, and has greater official control over any demolition, alterations, tree felling or new building within the grounds. The cemetery has subsequently been declared a site of special scientific interest (SSSI), and it is situated within the green belt. One might have supposed these measures would have helped preserve the cemetery's historic landscape. Instead the council allowed the site of the former **Superintendent's office** to be dramatically redeveloped with a devastating impact on the landscape beside the entrance to the former Nonconformist section.[188] Incredibly, the Deputy Borough Planning Officer stated publicly that 'the proposed new office building . . . was appropriately designed and would considerably enhance the appearance of the Brookwood Cemetery Conservation Area'.[189] Therefore, despite the supposed safeguards of the green belt, the conservation area, and SSSI status, Woking Borough Council is pursuing a contradictory and conflicting policy. Either the cemetery *is* a conservation area and an SSSI, or it is not. Over this office development the council ignored the advice of the County Archaeologist (who insisted the development would destroy 'an important historic landscape'); the council ignored its own published local plan for Brookwood (which is meant to ensure that 'any development preserves the historic character of the cemetery both as a conservation area and as an historic park and garden'); and the council ignored its own planning restrictions supposedly imposed by the Brookwood Cemetery Conservation Area – a device created entirely by itself! The council could and should have refused planning consent.

The final major development has occurred within the past year. This has seen the beginnings of a dialogue with Woking Borough Council that the Brookwood Cemetery Society is keen to see develop further. Discussions to date have covered tree management, restoration and the availability of local grants. Unfortunately the funds available are strictly limited to £8,000 per year, and the maximum grant given for any project is £600. However, it may be possible to bid for the restoration of selected memorials of local interest, for providing site interpretation boards, tree planting and seating. In addition the Principal Planning Officer, Barry Williams, submitted a formal request to the Department of Culture, Media and Sport to have certain memorials statutorily listed. The twenty memorials selected for their architectural and historic importance are: the **Bent memorial**, **Alfred Bestall**, the **Brookwood Memorial**, the **Columbarium**, the **De Morgan memorial**, the **Drake mausoleum**, **Elaine Falkiner**, **Sir Luke Fildes**, **Freshfield family memorial**, **Arthur Hacker**, **Dr Robert Knox**, **Dr G.W. Leitner**, **Sir E.W. Moir**, the **Nicols mausoleum**, the **Parsee ground**, **Lord Edward Pelham-Clinton**, **G. Salviati**, **John S. Sargent**, **Henri van Laun** and the **Vickers family memorial**. Having monuments listed will assist their protection and help attract funding for repairs to safeguard their future. At the time of writing representatives from English Heritage have made a preliminary visit to Brookwood Cemetery, and one can but hope that the council's important recommendation will be accepted.

It is astonishing that the significance of Brookwood Cemetery has been almost totally ignored by architectural and social historians, Woking Borough Council, Surrey County Council, English Heritage and the Department of Culture, Media and Sport. Through the efforts of the Brookwood Cemetery Society over a decade and more, perceptions may be changing at last. Perhaps the last word should rest with Simon Ashall, a local journalist, who wrote the following editorial for the *Woking News & Mail*:

> Brookwood Cemetery opened in 1854 and triggered a rapid increase in Woking's size and significance, leading it from small market town to Surrey's second transport hub within

120 years. Yet Surrey County Council, Woking Borough Council and the Department of Culture, Media and Sport have largely ignored it and made little attempt to seriously fund or communicate its importance. Even English Heritage, which professes to be interested in such things, only gives a minimal grade II designation to the cemetery as an historic park and garden. Government excuses that Brookwood is a private cemetery and no business of public authorities are a gross abdication of responsibility. This is Woking's – and Surrey's – monument as well as a place of rest. We all have a stake in its upkeep and preservation.

We owe a debt of gratitude to the volunteers of the Brookwood Cemetery Society. They give their time and money to help maintain the cemetery for the benefit of everyone and carry out notable repairs and restoration work. But the Society is comparatively small. Brookwood Cemetery is huge and dedication can only go so far without cash. If the authorities showed half as much commitment to the cemetery as the Society, its funding problems could be resolved. Failing that, Woking can be the Surrey borough that presides over a decaying and shameful 400 acre monument to our indifference.[190]

Chapter One

THE EASTERN PART OF THE FORMER ANGLICAN SECTION

The former Anglican sections cover the greater part of the cemetery grounds. Altogether they comprise about 300 acres, some two-thirds of the total acreage at Brookwood. Originally this section of the cemetery was reserved for Church of England funerals only. If any other burial service was required, then burials would have been in the unconsecrated sections that are discussed in Chapters 7 to 9. This difference is underlined by the naming of the avenues. On this side of the cemetery all are named after saints, whereas in the Nonconformist sections the road names are purely descriptive.

This chapter covers a roughly triangular area to the east of the route of the cemetery railway. Two main avenues proceed across this area: St Andrew's, running from the **St Edward Brotherhood**; and All Souls', which branches off St Andrew's Avenue. Both offer good views of the plots in these areas. St Andrew's is flanked by a fine avenue of giant sequoias, while All Souls' is very picturesque when the heather is in bloom.

The graves and memorials covered by this chapter still show strong links with London. The first parish to use Brookwood Cemetery, St Saviour's, Southwark, has three of its plots in this area. Elsewhere are the several allotments covering the reinterments of human remains from many famous City churches and churchyards. In some cases the churches were subsequently demolished, or destroyed during the Blitz; so these memorials and plots at Brookwood are the remaining evidence of a once teeming parochial life.

1.1. The St Edward Brotherhood [former Anglican chapels and plot 39]

The Brotherhood is a small Orthodox monastic community that maintains the shrine and church dedicated to **St Edward the Martyr** and tends an Orthodox Christian cemetery (plot 39). The history of each building will be described in turn.

The smaller religious building in this area, the Brotherhood House, was the original **Anglican chapel**, designed by Sydney Smirke (1798–1877) for the opening of the cemetery in 1854. As constructed, it was described as 'built in the Tudor style of architecture, and remarkable for [its] singularly neat appearance . . . [with a] small tower and spire, loop windows, open pointed roofs, open stained pewing and neat Gothic pulpit. . . . The floors are paved with blue and red Staffordshire tiles, and bear a resemblance to tessellated pavement.'[1]

The service of consecration took place in this chapel on the afternoon of 7 November 1854, led by the Bishop of Winchester. Over the years this chapel proved inadequate for funeral services and therefore the second, larger chapel was provided. Under the terms of the London Necropolis Act 1956,[2] this chapel would have been converted into a crematorium (see

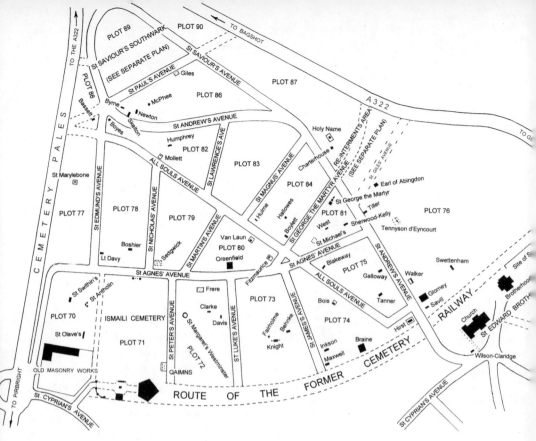

The eastern part of the former Anglican section.

Introduction). The chapel has now been converted for parochial purposes and living quarters for members of the St Edward Brotherhood.

The larger building was originally built as the second Anglican chapel between 1908 and 1910. It was designed by **Cyril Tubbs** and **Arthur Messer** and constructed by Mr E.C. Hughes for £1,507 7s 4d, exclusive of internal decoration.[3] The arrangements for 'linen, altar cloths, vases, candlesticks, credence table, hassocks, etc.' were prepared by **John B. Walker** and **Canon Skelton**.[4] Subsequently it was agreed that memorial tablets would be allowed subject to the position, design and lettering being approved by the LNC. Later still memorial windows were authorised.[5] The chapel was without its own organ, that from the old chapel being used. This proved inadequate, however, and a new organ was ordered from Messrs Bishop & Sons for £643 17s 6d in December 1926.[6] Under the terms of the London Necropolis Act 1956 it was intended to de-consecrate this area and convert the original Anglican chapel into a crematorium. The larger chapel would have been used for services, while South station would have served as a refreshment room and a reception area for coffins prior to cremation. Road access would have been either via the East Gate, or by a new entrance on to the A322 adjacent to the station platform. In more recent times this church was virtually derelict until the St Edward Brotherhood was established in the cemetery from 1982. Regular church services are now held here. The members of the monastic community run a small bookstall in the church, and sell items such as hand-dipped candles, incense and honey. Further details may be obtained by writing to St Edward Brotherhood, St Cyprian's Avenue, Brookwood, Woking, Surrey, GU24 OBL.

Beyond the Brotherhood House is the site of **South station**, the terminus of the cemetery railway. The stations were described as follows in 1854:

The stations are constructed with peculiar neatness, and are situated at a very convenient distance from the chapels. They comprise first class and general reception rooms, apartments for the officials, and first and second class refreshment rooms. The latter have semicircular counters formed of marble. Attached to each station is a courtyard of small dimensions for the conveniences of the *attachés* of the company. The south, or Church of England station, is situated about half a mile from the South-Western main line. . . .[7]

In 1854 the station was occupied by the Superintendent for the Anglican section, George Bupell, who had accommodation adjacent to the refreshment rooms. Later the station was used as living quarters for one of the cemetery porters, **Stephen Bassett**, and his wife **Catherine**. After she was widowed in 1880 Catherine remained in the station with her niece Annah Meetens until her death the following year. Subsequently Walter Parker and his wife Mary lived here, but Parker was dismissed in October 1892.[8] **Robert Spooner** then moved here from **North station**. The subsequent occupants are not known, although Mr and Mrs Wilkins lived there in the 1930s. After the cemetery railway was closed, the refreshment rooms remained open as the 'South Bar', providing food and drinks for funeral parties. The South Bar was latterly run by Mr and Mrs Ladd, the last known occupants of these premises. After they retired in the late 1960s, the building was used as a store until it was burned down in September 1972, in what was almost certainly an act of vandalism. About half the station was destroyed. There were some attempts to preserve the buildings as a unique example of Victorian railway architecture, but the site was cleared shortly after the fire. The remains of the platform, which is longer than that at **North station**, may be seen, and it is still possible to find some of the foundations of the station buildings.

St Edward the Martyr (*c.* 959–978/9), whose relics lie in the church, was the son of King Edgar (*c.* 944–75) by his first wife Ethelfleda (died *c.* 963/4). King Edgar reigned from 959 to 975 and on his death Edward became king. The succession was disputed because King Edgar's second wife, Aelfthryth (*c.* 945–1000) wished her son Ethelred to be king. (Ethelred is known to history as Ethelred the Unready or 'the Redeless'.) Two or three years later, on 18 March 978 or 979, Edward was murdered near the site of Corfe Castle, Dorset, almost certainly the victim of his stepmother's intrigues. His initial burial was hurried. Soon miraculous cures were attributed to him by visitors to the site of his grave. In 980 his body was removed to Shaftesbury Abbey, where it was translated to a splendid shrine within the Abbey Church in 1001. St Edward was officially canonised in 1008. This shrine survived until the Dissolution of the Monasteries, but St Edward's remains had previously been removed and hidden in the Abbey Church. In 1931 a crude casket was unearthed during an archaeological investigation of the site. The remains were studied and pronounced consistent with the injuries received by St Edward. The Director of Excavations, **John Wilson-Claridge**, whose family then owned the site, began years of painstaking negotiations with all the major Churches in order to find a suitable resting place for the relics. He imposed three conditions: that they were recognised as the relics of a saint, that a shrine would be established for their reception and that St Edward's feast days would be celebrated. These conditions were met only by the Russian Orthodox Church in Exile, which entered into detailed negotiations in the late 1970s. At the same time the Orthodox Church purchased the site at Brookwood with the intention of using the larger of the two mortuary chapels for the reception of St Edward's bones.

The formal ceremony of enshrinement took place during 15–16 September 1984. The service was led by Bishop Gregory of Washington, assisted by Father Alexis, Archpriest John Sorochka of Mayfield, Pennsylvania, Archpriest Michael Malakov of the Orthodox Church of St Nicholas in Rome and Father David Hritcko of the Endicott, New York parish. Father Deacon Christopher officiated.

Just before two-thirty, the Mayor and Mayoress of Woking, Cllr and Mrs John Jewson, were met at the entrance to the church and introduced to the Bishop and to Mr Wilson-Claridge. The clergy and the faithful then made their way to the far end of the Brotherhood property, where, inside the East Gate, Mr Wilson-Claridge formally handed over the sacred relics to His Grace Bishop Gregory. Immediately the deacon asked the Bishop's blessing for the beginning of the service of Supplication to Saint Edward, and this service was chanted as the clergy and faithful made their way back to the church along the new path cut through the Orthodox cemetery. Thus the sacred relics were brought through the whole of our land; they were carried under a golden canopy and the procession was accompanied by the chanting of hymns to the saint. . . . Having re-entered the church, the sacred relics were placed on a small table in the centre, and the service continued as the faithful . . . approached to venerate and kiss the sacred relics . . . so many came that the choir had to sing many of the hymns over and over again, before Bishop Gregory could take up the sacred relics and place them in the casket that had been prepared for them. . . . In the evening . . . we began the Vigil Service, combining hymns for the Resurrection with those appointed in the service to Saint Edward. At the *litya*, at the end of Vespers, a procession was made around the outside of the church with the sacred relics. The deacon intoned petitions at each of the points of the compass, and then the sacred relics were brought back into the church and taken into the sanctuary, where they were placed on the Holy Table. At the *polyeleos* in Mattins, they were brought forth and placed on a table in the centre of the church. . . . On the Sunday morning, 16 September, the day set aside for the celebration of the translation of the relics, the . . . Bishop preached on the Gospel of the day . . . and he linked the Gospel message with the special celebration of St Edward . . . and to establishing an Orthodox Christian mission in England dedicated to one of the saints of England.[9]

Thus for the first time in nearly 450 years the remains of St Edward have a fitting resting place within a church whose doctrine is closest to that which he knew in his lifetime. On the outside wall of the shrine there is a fine icon of St Edward that was carved by Keith Newstead for the Brotherhood.

John Wilson-Claridge (1905–93) was Director of Excavations at Shaftesbury Abbey in the 1930s at the time the relics of **St Edward** were rediscovered (see above). His grave, a ledger stone of grey granite, is just outside the entrance to the church.

From the church, turn right along St Andrew's Avenue. The next tomb-style grave may be found to the right of the road.

1.2. Rosette Savill (1899–1983) [plot 76]

Founder of the Paddock Wood School, Camberley. Mrs Savill was born in Monaco and lived in Paris until the late 1930s. During the Second World War she and her husband worked tirelessly for the **Free French** cause by converting their home (Paddock Wood) into a haven for Resistance fighters recuperating from injuries. After the war the house remained open for French families recovering from imprisonment in German concentration camps. Later she started a summer school for overseas pupils: girls spent six weeks at the school, learning English and enjoying the local countryside. From this developed the Paddock Wood Finishing School, which became internationally famous. Unfortunately, because of various international problems the number of students fell, and the school closed in 1982.

The mausoleum is just beyond.

1.3. Glorney family mausoleum [plot 76]

This mausoleum is located opposite the junction between St Andrew's Avenue and All Souls' Avenue. It was built on a site measuring 13ft x 21ft which cost £288 8s 0d. Constructed of Cornish granite, it is unusual in having a rusticated finish. Unfortunately further particulars of this mausoleum have not survived.[10] It appears to have been built in 1934–5 for **Corlette Glorney** (dates not known), but it has not been possible to trace if anyone was ever buried within. Regrettably the 1930s stained glass, possibly by Tiffany,[11] has not survived. The doorway has been bricked up, like all mausoleums at Brookwood, in an attempt to prevent further vandalism.

The next chest tomb memorial is directly opposite.

1.4. Hirst family grave [plot 74]

Hugo Hirst, 1st Baron Hirst of Witton (1863–1943), was an industrial engineer and founder of the General Electric Company (GEC). He moved to England in about 1880 and was naturalised in 1883. His own electrical firm became GEC in 1889. The company became a leader in the manufacture and supply of electric equipment. Hirst was Managing Director (1900–43), and Chairman (1910–43) of GEC. Hirst was also President of the Radio Manufacturers Association, an Honorary Member of the Institution of Electrical Engineers, Master of the Worshipful Company of Glaziers (1929–30), and Honorary Treasurer of the Empire Industries Association. He was a member of the Board of Trade Advisory Council (1922–5, 1929–32 and 1936–9), of the Committee on Unemployment Insurance (1925–6), of the British Economic Mission to Australia (1928–9), and a representative of HM Government on the League of Nations Subcommittee of Experts for Scientific Property. He was created a Baronet (1925) and Baron (1934).

    Harold Hugh Hirst (1893–1919), his only son, died in July 1919 of an illness contracted after four years' service on various fronts during the First World War. He was a Lieutenant in the 21st Manchester Regiment. Although commemorated on this memorial, he is actually buried in Earley churchyard, Berkshire.

    Pilot Officer Hugh Harold Hirst (1919–41), Baron Hirst's grandson, died on operational duties with the RAF on 7 May 1941. He is also commemorated on panel 30 of the RAF Runnymede Memorial. It is interesting to note that Baron Hirst's son and grandson fought in wars against his native Germany, and that he outlived them both.

    Also buried here is Baron Hirst's eldest daughter, **Muriel Elsie, Lady Gamage** (1894–1969), who married **Sir Leslie Gamage** (1887–1972) in 1919. She was sometime Chairman of the National Society for the Prevention of Cruelty to Children, and was killed in a car accident. Her husband was the second son of A.W. Gamage, the founder of Gamage's toyshop. He was educated at Marlborough and Exeter College, Oxford. Gamage originally intended to go into law, but on the outbreak of the First World War he joined the Army. He served as Captain and Adjutant to the 24th London Regiment, was twice wounded, and was awarded the Military Cross before being taken prisoner. Afterwards he joined GEC, where his legal knowledge was a great asset. He became successively General Manager, Joint Managing Director and ultimately Chairman and Managing Director (1957–60). For some years he was President of the Institution of Exporters.

From here, turn left into All Souls' Avenue. As you turn the second corner it is worth pausing to admire the view along the avenue that stretches away in front of you. Further to the left, in plot 74, is another family mausoleum.

1.5. Braine family mausoleum [plot 74]

This attractive mausoleum off St James's Avenue has a green pantiled roof and 1930s-style door, now bricked up. The mausoleum was designed and constructed by the LNC and is built on a plot measuring 12ft 6in x 12ft 6in. It is built of Portland stone, with interior marble decorations, and was designed to accommodate up to six coffins. It cost £850 to build. The walls are 9in thick and include Portland stone pilasters of 1½in relief depth on all four elevations. The interior linings are of white Carrara marble, with an air passage between the main walls and linings. The floor and roof are made of 6in reinforced concrete. The ceiling was treated with Portland stone dust. At the back is a bull's-eye stained-glass window, and an altar and kneeling block in white Carrara marble.[12] The mausoleum was built for **Fanny Braine**, **née Robertson** (*c*. 1872–1934). Her husband, Robertson Braine, is apparently not buried here.

The next two graves (both headstones with kerbing) may be found on the right-hand side of St James's Avenue.

1.6. General Sir George Vaughan Maxwell (1818–1892) [plot 74]

Maxwell entered the Army as an Ensign in the 88th Regiment in 1838. He served in the Crimean War (1854–5) and was present at the battles of the Alma, Inkerman and Sebastopol. During the Indian Mutiny (1857–8) he took part in the campaign at Oudh, the operations at Cawnpore and the siege of Lucknow. He commanded a brigade at Mooltan, Bengal (1864), and at Rawalpindi (1865–9). Maxwell commanded the 3rd Infantry Brigade at Aldershot (1870–3), and was Colonel of the 1st Battalion, East Lancashire Regiment (1881–92). He was promoted to General (1881).

1.7. Colonel Edgar Thomas Inkson, VC (1872–1947) [plot 74]

Born at Naini Tal, India, Inkson was educated at the Edinburgh Collegiate School and at University College London. He joined the Royal Army Medical Corps as a Lieutenant in 1899, and served in South Africa (1899–1904). He was a Regimental Medical Officer with three batteries of the Royal Field Artillery. On 24 February 1900 Inkson was present at the battle of Colenso where he was awarded his VC. This was for his bravery in carrying 2nd Lieutenant Devenish, who was severely wounded and unable to walk, for 300–400 yards and under very heavy fire to a place of safety. With the 27th Royal Inniskilling Fusiliers Inkson also saw action at Vaalrantz, Spion Kop, Pieter's Hill, the relief of Ladysmith and the Battle of Roydam. He served also during the First World War (DSO 1917) and retired in 1926.

Cross St James's Avenue into plot 73 to locate the next headstone with kerbing that is adjacent to a mass of rhododendrons.

1.8. Emil Behnke (1836–1892) [plot 73]

Expert on voice training and teacher of voice production to singers and speakers. Behnke lectured on the mechanism of the voice from 1866, and was employed by the main musical and scientific societies. He pioneered the education of voice production and the treatment of stammering and other voice defects, and founded an entirely new profession. Latterly Behnke devoted himself to the education and treatment of stammering and other defects of speech. He published many books and papers on speech and the voice including *The Mechanism of the Human Voice* (London, J. Curwen, 1881), *Voice, Song and Speech: A Practical Guide for Singers and Speakers* (London, Low, Marston, 1883), *The Child's Voice* (London, Sampson Low, 1885), and *Stammering, its Nature & Treatment* (London, T. Fisher Unwin, 1891). Behnke died at Ostend, and his headstone records that it was erected as part of a memorial fund contributed by a few firm friends and pupils 'in affectionate remembrance of the deceased'.

The next barrel-topped granite ledger stone is located between two cypress trees.

1.9. Isabella Hirst Knight (*c.* 1845–1891) [plot 73]

This memorial commemorates the wife of **Walter Knight** (died 1903). The inscription records that she was cremated on 14 February 1891, and this is the first memorial in Brookwood Cemetery to do so.[13] At that time cremation was still a radical choice for the disposal of the dead. The first cremation at St John's, near Woking, had taken place only six years previously; yet up to the beginning of 1891 only 177 cremations had taken place.[14]

Immediately behind this is a cross on a low pink granite base, leaning precariously to the right.

1.10. Fairholme family grave [plot 73]

Charles Fairholme (1829–91) served throughout the Crimean War, first as a Lieutenant in HMS *Agamemnon* under Lord Lyons[15] at the attack on Fort Constantine, then as Naval ADC to the General Commander-in-Chief during the siege and capture of Sebastopol, and lastly in HMS *Medusa* under Commodore Sherard Osborn during the final operations in the Sea of Azof. For these services Fairholme was awarded the Crimean and Turkish medals and the Sebastopol clasp. He commanded the gunboat HMS *Havoc* at the capture of the Peiho forts and other operations in China (1860), for which he was awarded the Chinese War medal. His wife, **Julie Charlotte Fairholme** (1831–95), was born Baroness Poellnitz Frankenberg.

Cross over St Luke's Avenue. The next headstone with kerbing is about halfway along the plot, and faces towards the path.

1.11. P. H. Davis (*c.* 1852–1899) [plot 72]

This grave is a reminder of a maritime tragedy. The inscription records that Davis 'lost his life on the ill-fated *Stella*, March 30th 1899'. The SS *Stella* was completed in about 1896 and was one of three twin-screw vessels constructed for the LSWR and its Channel Islands traffic. The *Stella*, with her sister ships the *Frederica* and *Lydia*, was purpose-built to compete with the GWR steamship services to the Islands, and was expected to reach 19 knots. The *Stella* struck the Casquet rocks near Guernsey on the morning of 30 March 1899 in dense fog. She sank with great loss of life, although the LSWR's ship *Vera* and the GWR's ship *Lynx* were able to rescue some of the survivors. A stewardess who gave her lifebelt to a passenger and went down with the ship has her own memorial in Southampton. Strangely, the *Stella*'s sister ship *Lydia* had previously struck rocks off Guernsey in fog on 6 May 1891, but the vessel survived.[16]

At the end of the path turn left into St Agnes's Avenue. The next kerbed memorial, with crosses set into the ground, is to the left of the road.

1.12. Mary Eliza Isabella Frere (1845–1911) [plot 72]

Author. The eldest child of the colonial administrator Sir Henry Bartle Frere.[17] Educated privately at Wimbledon, she accompanied her father on his appointments abroad (e.g. Bombay in 1865 and South Africa in 1877). Particularly interested in India, she went on many tours of that country, gathering a large number of folk stories from her *ayah* (maid). Frere published twenty-four of these tales as *Old Deccan Days: Hindoo Fairy Legends Current in Southern India* (London, John Murray, 1868). The introduction to the book was written by her father, while the illustrations were completed by her sister, **Catherine Frere**. The book went through five impressions in thirty years. According to Sir George Birdwood[18] the book opened up an entirely new field of scientific research, and gave fresh impetus to the study of folklore in the United Kingdom and throughout Europe and the Americas. The book was translated into several languages. Frere also travelled extensively in Europe, Egypt and Palestine.

Also buried here is **Catherine Frances Frere** (1848–1921), who illustrated *Old Deccan Days*. She also wrote books on cooking and cookery, such as *The Cookery Book of Lady Clark of Tillypronie* (London, Constable & Co., 1909), and edited *A Proper Newe Booke of Cokerye* (Cambridge, W. Heffer, 1913), which includes an account of the domestic life, cookery and feasts in Tudor times, and notes on the first owners of the book, Matthew Parker, Archbishop of Canterbury, and his wife.[19]

Sir Bartle Compton Arthur Frere (1854–1933), 2nd Baronet, was the only son of Sir Henry Bartle Frere. Educated at Eton and Trinity College, Cambridge, he then joined the Rifle Brigade. He served in the Zulu War (1879), the Bechuanaland Expedition (1884–5), and in Burma (1886–8). He succeeded his father in 1884 but had no heir, so the baronetcy died with him in 1933.

Further into the same plot and facing towards St Agnes's Avenue is the next headstone with kerbing.

1.13. George Clarke (1818–1891) [plot 72]

Chief Inspector at Scotland Yard. Clarke was born at Therfield and died in Westminster. He was described as 'a man of honour, of noble and generous nature'. Clarke was cremated at St John's, Woking.

On the other side of this section is a circular plot with railings.

1.14. St Margaret's, Westminster, reburials [plot 72]

This memorial comprises a small circular wall topped with cast-iron railings. The enclosure contains the remains of inhabitants of St Margaret's, Westminster, formerly buried in the churchyard and disinterred and removed here during the construction of the Metropolitan District Railway (1866). Memorials, presumably from the same churchyard, may be found lying flat in the ground between this memorial and stretching over to **George Clarke**'s grave. See also item 16 below.

Moving across St Peter's Avenue, the next kerbed allotment containing several graves is on the boundary of the Ismaili cemetery.

1.15. Queen Alexandra's Imperial Military Nursing Service [plot 71]

The Queen Alexandra's Imperial Military Nursing Service was founded in 1902 to provide service in military hospitals. Its formation was a direct result of the shortcomings of the existing Army nursing service which, during the Boer War (1899–1902), had proved less than satisfactory. In February 1901 Lord Roberts[20] wrote to Queen Alexandra asking her to support the idea and to give her name to the new service. It was renamed the Queen Alexandra's Royal Army Nursing Corps in 1949 and still exists. The ground includes a number of members of the service, one member of the Voluntary Aid Detachment (VAD) and one member of the Territorial Forces. The nurses represented here died of illness or wounds sustained while on active service in military hospitals overseas or in this country during the First World War. This section is maintained by the Commonwealth War Graves Commission. Here may be found the graves of **Sister Dorothy Helen Cole** (*c.* 1889–1918), who died in the London General Hospital on 21 October 1918 after four years' military nursing service, aged just 29, and **Sister Maude Ellen Hills** (died 1918), who was attached to the Territorial Forces Nursing Service. Hills worked in the 53rd General Hospital, BEF. She died on 22 July 1918 in the Queen Alexandra Military Hospital.

1.16. Ismaili cemetery [plot 71]

Established in about 1985 with the assistance of the Aga Khan.[21] The two mortuary buildings on the left-hand boundary of this ground occupy the trackbed of the former cemetery railway. Burials have commenced at the far side of the plot (by St Agnes's Avenue), with distinctive low stone markers.

The ground occupies much of the former parish plot of **St Margaret & St John**, **Westminster**. Like **St Anne's**, two plots were provided for this parish, one for Anglicans (plots 70–1) and one for Nonconformists (plot 110, see Chapter 7). Both allotments have pairs of fine granite obelisks that mark the burial grounds, and both pairs survive. They appear to have been erected in 1896, the date given on the side of the left-hand obelisk. Each one commemorates the members of the parish burial board in 1855 and 1896. It is interesting to note that only one member was still on the board in 1896, William Lewis Josephs. The plots came into use in April 1855. Part of the former Anglican plot is now used as the **Ismaili cemetery**. In plot 72 may be found another related burial site (see item 14 above). The plots appear to have fallen into disuse shortly after the First World War.

*Adjacent to these plots is a walled section that forms a boundary with the **Masonry Works**. The buildings are best seen from St Cyprian's Avenue, and it is possible to gain access to this road via the entrance to the Ismaili section.*

1.17. Masonry Works [adjacent to plots 2 & 70]

This range of red brick buildings is arranged in an L-shape plan. It formed the LNC's Statuary & Masonry Works, and was designed to replace the limited facilities available in the Company's original works situated adjacent to the **Superintendent's offices** off Cemetery Pales. Originally the LNC allowed independent masons to occupy land for statuary and masonry work, the first mason being Mr W. Boulton of Guildford. He was given permission to occupy sufficient land (presumably near the Superintendent's offices) for the exclusive purpose of his trade. Any buildings and workshops were to be erected at his expense and subject to the approval of the LNC.[22] This type of arrangement probably continued until about 1888 when the LNC decided to operate its own premises within the cemetery. Located beside the Superintendent's offices, a full range of work was undertaken, while the showroom appears to have comprised a greenhouse where various memorial designs could be inspected.[23] In the early twentieth century it was decided that these premises were too cramped, and therefore a new site was selected just across **Cemetery Pales**.

The new Masonry Works was constructed by Messrs Harris & Company, with the machinery being ordered from Wilcox & Son and Henderson & Company.[24] The works was provided with its own siding off the cemetery railway; this entrance is still marked by the two brick piers on the right-hand side of the plot (as viewed from St Cyprian's Avenue). The siding was constructed by the LSWR at a cost of £500, and the whole complex opened for business in about 1904–5. The area next to the siding was provided with a 5-ton derrick (or tripod) crane that was used to remove or load stone from railway wagons and into the yard. Here memorials would be designed and carved for erection within the cemetery. It should be remembered that the LNC also conducted funerals outside the cemetery, and therefore memorials from these works might be erected anywhere in the UK or indeed might be supplied for customers abroad.

At 2.03 p.m. on Friday 13 May 1938 the private funeral train collided with one of the LNC's lorries, registration number PL 6175, driven by Mr Cheeseman. This happened as the lorry was leaving the Masonry Works and, without making due observation, the train (which was being propelled) hit the lorry as it crossed the railway on the level crossing. Visibility was poor at this point as tall shrubs and trees flanked the track. The hearse carriage, which was leading, rode up over the lorry; the driver was lucky to escape without serious injury. No complaint was made by passengers on the train and arrangements were made for their conveyance by car to Brookwood station from whence they proceeded by ordinary train to Waterloo. Breakdown vehicles were requested from Guildford and they arrived in the cemetery at 3.40 p.m. The hearse van was re-railed at 4.35 p.m., and damage to the van amounted to £8 4s 0d. The LNC also had to purchase another lorry![25]

In November 1938 an accident occurred when the main timbers of the derrick crane were broken, presumably when trying to lift too much stone. **Mr Walker** obtained an estimate of £75 'from the Makers for carrying out the necessary repairs & replacements, but it was agreed to make enquiries for the purchase of a new or second-hand up-to-date crane'.[26] In June 1944 Mr A. Bolingbroke, 'the Company's letter-engraver', retired after sixty-two years' service. The LNC awarded him a cheque for £50 and a retirement allowance of £1 a week.[27]

Sometime in the early 1960s the Masonry Works was leased by the LNC to the firm of Messrs Clements, who continued their masonry business from here until the early 1980s. The area then became one of several sold off as a consequence of the 1975 Brookwood Cemetery Act.[28] Since then the site has been sold to a firm of architectural consultants who converted the former works into two office suites. The offices are now known as Stonemasons' Court.

Behind and beyond the Masonry Works is one of several areas in this section of the cemetery used for the reburial of human remains from churches and churchyards in London.

1.18. St Olave, Tooley Street, Southwark [plot 70]

This church was built by Henry Flitcroft in 1738 and was just a few hundred yards from old London Bridge. The church was demolished in 1926–8 at the instance of the Bishop of Southwark and Bermondsey Council. By 1928 only the tower remained, and a proposal to preserve this and create a small garden came to nothing, despite the opportunity to create a unique open space on Bermondsey's 3½-mile riverfront. The large memorial may be found behind a conifer screen, while the allotment contains the remains of 'generations of parishioners formerly buried within the precincts of the church'. It is possible that for the reburial of human remains in this area, the caskets were (unusually) unloaded from the funeral train using the low unloading platform beside the **Masonry Works**.[29] The memorial was designed by W.H. Randoll Blacking FRIBA,[30] and is constructed of Doulting stone. It cost £174 to complete and appears to have been constructed during 1934. The memorial includes three badges: the one in the centre is that of St Olave's, that on the left is of Southwark, while the right-hand one depicts Bermondsey. After the completion of the memorial eighty-four 15in high Lawson Cypresses (*Chamaecyparis lawsoniana*) were planted around the site.[31]

The site in London was sold and used for the head offices of Messrs Hay's Wharf Company, and was called St Olave's House (completed 1931). There is a carving on one corner of this building depicting St Olave. Part of the church tower survives as a disused water fountain in the recreation ground in nearby Tanner Street.

The next two memorials are hidden in the trees beyond the St Olave's allotment.

1.19. St Antholin, Budge Row (Watling Street) [plot 70]

This Wren church was built in 1678 to replace one gutted in the Great Fire. It was considered one of Wren's finest buildings, being in the form of an elongated octagon with oval dome and octagonal stone spire. The church was thoughtlessly demolished in 1874–5, and the human remains were transferred to this plot at Brookwood. The money raised by the sale of the church site was used partly to 'restore' the nearby church of St Mary, Aldermary (considered one of the most drastic Victorian restorations to any City church), and partly to build a new church in Nunhead Lane, Peckham. The memorial also records that the monumental tablets from St Antholin were re-erected in St Mary, Aldermary. The marker erected here is apparently incomplete. One section suggests it was erected here on 29 December 1880, and unveiled by Arthur Edward Taylor, Master of the Worshipful Company of Skinners. Other surviving sections list the churchwardens of St John the Baptist, Walbrook, along with those from St Antholin's. One of those listed for St Antholin's is **Thomas R. Pace**, who was churchwarden between 1869 and 1871.

A modern office block called Antholin House, now occupies the site of this church and its small churchyard. The upper part of the stone spire survives in Round Hill, Forest Hill, south London.

1.20. St Swithin, London Stone [plot 70]

This church was rebuilt by Wren (1677–85) but was destroyed during the 1940 Blitz. After the war it was decided not to rebuild this church, and so the site was cleared. The human remains, dating from the rebuilding of the church after the Great Fire to its destruction by enemy action, were transferred to Brookwood, presumably in February 1958, which is the date on the memorial.

The Bank of China, completed in 1961–2, now occupies the site of the church. The London Stone has been re-set into the front wall of the bank, as it used to be in the old church wall. Behind the bank part of the old churchyard survives as a small garden.

Cross St Agnes's Avenue and locate the next headstone with kerbing on the right-hand side of St Edmund's Avenue.

1.21. Lieutenant John Alfred Davy (*c.* 1898–1916) [plot 78]

Davy came from East Putney and was a First World War pilot who lost his life while training. He was flying a DH1 pusher biplane of No. 19 Reserve Squadron from Hounslow when he crashed at Didcot, Oxfordshire. He was buried in his mother's grave and did not have a separate memorial until the Commonwealth War Graves Commission set up one of its standard headstones over the grave in 1995.

On the opposite side of the path, note the large prominent white cross.

1.22. St Marylebone reburials [plot 77]

This large cross monument is a reminder that human remains are still removed to Brookwood from central London. The present church of St Marylebone was designed by Thomas Hardwicke and was consecrated in 1817. It was built over a large vaulted crypt that served as the parish burial ground until 1853, when the entrance was bricked up. In 1980 the church authorities decided to remove the dead and reuse the crypt for the living. Three years later, and with appropriate authority, over 850 coffins were reburied at Brookwood in the area surrounding this memorial. A complete list of those re-interred is held in the parish office of St Marylebone. In 1987 the crypt was opened as a Healing and Counselling Centre by the Prince of Wales.

Return to plot 78. The next kerbed grave with a low headstone may be found within a group of memorials at the St Agnes end of the plot.

1.23. Superintendent Ernest Boshier (*c.* 1874–1935) [plot 78]

Police chief and councillor. Boshier was born in Wokingham and joined the Surrey Constabulary at Guildford in 1893. He was a police constable at Chobham (1899), Addlestone (1899–1907) and Weybridge (1907–10). Boshier was promoted to sergeant and moved to Oxted (1910–19). He then moved to Leatherhead as Inspector (1920–1). Boshier was promoted to

Superintendent and moved to Woking in 1921. He was involved in several important cases including the arrest and prosecution of Monsieur Vaquier for the murder of Alfred Jones at the Blue Anchor Hotel, Byfleet, in March 1924; in the extended investigations surrounding the death of Mr Hilary Rougier at Nuthurst, Lower Knaphill, in August 1926; for the arrest of Mr Clarke, a notorious burglar; for the arrest of Anthony St George, otherwise known as the 'gentleman burglar'; and for the arrest and prosecution of Mr Honeybourne for the attempted murder of a domestic servant in 1928. Boshier retired in 1930. His conscientious and distinguished work resulted in his being awarded the Police Medal for Meritorious Service by King George V (1930). He was elected a councillor for the Maybury & Mount Hermon Ward of Woking Council (1932) and was a member of the Bisley Lodge of Freemasons. His funeral on 26 February 1935 was described as one of the largest in the locality. It took place at Christ Church, Woking. The pall bearers were all uniformed officers from the Surrey Constabulary and many of those who attended followed the funeral procession to Brookwood.

The next graves are in the plot opposite, screened by a conifer hedge.

1.24. Sedgwick family plot [plot 79]

Among those buried here are **Professor Adam Sedgwick** (1854–1913), zoologist and great-nephew of the geologist Adam Sedgwick (1785–1873). Born in Norwich, Sedgwick was educated at Marlborough College, King's College, London, and Trinity College, Cambridge. He was a Fellow of Trinity College (from 1880) and was made a Fellow of the Royal Society (1886). Sedgwick was appointed Reader in Animal Morphology at Cambridge in 1890. He was subsequently appointed Professor of Zoology, Cambridge (1907) and at Imperial College of Science & Technology, South Kensington (1909). His books include *A Student's Text-book of Zoology* (London, Swann Sonnenschein, 1898), and the section on peripatus in volume 5 of *The Cambridge Natural History* (London, Macmillan, 1905).

Also buried here is **Captain Francis Balfour Sedgwick** (*c.* 1896–1918), who served with the Suffolk Regiment before transferring to the RAF. He was killed in a Sopwith Camel at No. 54 Training Depot at Fairlop (Hainault Farm) in Essex when the aircraft stalled and spun into the ground. Note the carved emblem of the Royal Flying Corps at the top of the headstone.

At the rear of this plot is the grave of **Colonel Sir Andrew Muter John Ogilvie** (1858–1924). He was educated at University College London and was subsequently appointed Private Secretary to successive Postmasters General (1891–9). He was made Assistant Secretary to the Post Office (1903), and was a British delegate to the International Telegraph Conference held in Lisbon (1908). Ogilvie was appointed Third Secretary to the Post Office (1911–14), and Joint Second Secretary of the Post Office (1914–19). During the First World War he served also as Director of Army Signals (Home Defence). He was a member of the Council of the Institution of Electrical Engineers (1913–16 and 1921–4). He is described on his memorial as 'a very noble, modest gentleman'. Latterly he lived at Golf Cottage, St John's, Woking.

Continue along St Agnes's Avenue. The mausoleum is to the left of the path and stands facing St Luke's Avenue.

1.25. Greenfield family mausoleum [plot 80]

This building dates from 1891 when the body of **Leslie Kennard Greenfield** was transferred here from Kensal Green Cemetery. The family was charged £779 for the building, excluding the cost of the land. It was constructed by Mr Whitehead.[32] Seven other members of the family are also buried here: **William Bunce Greenfield** (*c.* 1823–1908), **Charles Bunce Greenfield** (*c.* 1856–1919), **Mary Jane Greenfield** (*c.* 1835–1921), **Herbert Bunce**

Greenfield (*c.* 1859–1925), **Henry Stanley Bunce Greenfield** (*c.* 1872–1954), and **Thomas Waring Bunce Greenfield** (*c.* 1866–1958). Bunce appears to have been a popular family name! The doors of the mausoleum were cleaned, restored and repainted in the summer of 1956 at a cost of £6 5s 0d.[33]

Continue following St Agnes's Avenue. The next memorial is a Celtic cross which stands in a kerbed allotment on the left, facing the junction with All Souls' Avenue.

1.26. Sir Maurice Fitzmaurice (1861–1924) [plot 80]

Civil engineer. Articled to Sir Benjamin Baker,[34] and engaged by Baker and Sir John Fowler[35] in the construction of the approach railways to the Forth Bridge (1885–88, opened 1890). He was involved in the construction of the Chignecto Ship Railway between Nova Scotia and New Brunswick (1888–91) and employed by the London Brighton & South Coast Railway (1891–2). Fitzmaurice was employed by the London County Council under **Sir Alexander R. Binnie** (1892). He was Chief Resident Engineer to the Egyptian Government (1898) and engaged in the construction of the Aswan Dam (1898–1901). Appointed Chief Engineer to the London County Council (1901–12), he was involved in the design and construction of the Rotherhithe Tunnel, Bermondsey (1904–8, and renovated 1979–81; 4,860ft long excluding the approaches), the Woolwich Foot Tunnel (1909–12 which completed an earlier attempted subway of 1876), improving the main drainage of London, the Kingsway and Aldwych road improvements, and the reconstruction of London's trams for electric traction. Fitzmaurice was knighted in 1912 and was elected a Fellow of the Royal Society in 1919. He advised Reginald Blomfield[36] on the foundations for the Menin Gate Memorial at Ypres. The proposed site had a poor sandy subsoil, and Fitzmaurice recommended the construction of a concrete platform resting on massive reinforced concrete piles some 36ft long extending down through the unstable ground.

Turn left into All Souls' Avenue. The next grave is a distinctive one in terracotta to the left of the path.

1.27. Henri van Laun (1819–1896) [plot 80]

Dutch academic. Van Laun settled in England from 1848. He became a journalist and then turned to teaching. He was French master at King William's College, Isle of Man, at Cheltenham College and the Edinburgh Academy. Van Laun moved to London and was appointed examiner in French for the Civil Service Commission. His many publications include *A Grammar of the French Language* (three vols, London, 1864), a *History of French Literature* (three vols, London, Smith, Elder, 1876–7), and his own translations of the dramatic works of Molière, *The Dramatic Works of J.B. Poquelin Molière, Rendered into English by Henri van Laun, with a Prefatory Memoir* (six vols, Edinburgh, William Paterson, 1875–6).

The unusual memorial was designed by **Emmeline Halse**. It comprises a terracotta square pedestal with a bas-relief portrait of van Laun on top. At each corner of the base are single-footed winged lions or leopards, with each wing extending along a side of the base. The muse of literature is depicted on the front of the pedestal, and copies of van Laun's books support his portrait. The 'marble book memorial' in front of the pedestal was added in 1932 at a cost of £17 5s 0d.[37] This memorial has been recommended for statutory listing by Woking Borough Council.

Continue walking along All Souls' Avenue. The next headstone is on the right-hand side, under a large pine tree.

1.28. Frederick Edward Hulme (1841–1909) [plot 84]

Botanist. The son of Frederick William Hulme,[38] a landscape painter, he was educated at the Western Grammar School and studied art at South Kensington. Hulme was sometime art master at Marlborough College, and in 1870 was appointed Professor of Geometrical Drawing at King's College, London. He was a lecturer to the Architectural Association, examiner to the London Chamber of Commerce and to the Science & Art Department. Hulme was keenly interested in the folklore of plants. He wrote many books on various aspects of art and botany, and these were mainly illustrated by coloured plates made from his own drawings. One of his most well-known works was *Familiar Wild Flowers* (five vols, London, Cassell, 1877–85), which went through several editions. Other books include *Principles of Ornamental Art* (London, Cassell, 1875), based on a series of articles he wrote for the *Art Journal* in 1873; *Wild Fruits of the Countryside* (London, Hutchinson, 1902); and *Butterflies and Moths of the Countryside* (London, Hutchinson, 1905), including thirty-five coloured plates by the author. He also illustrated books by other writers, for instance *Familiar Garden Flowers* by Shirley Hibberd[39] (five vols, London, 1879–87). Hulme was elected a Fellow of the Linnaean Society (1869) and of the Society of Antiquaries (1872). He was for several years Vice-President of the Selborne Society.

Continue walking along All Souls' Avenue. The next headstone with kerbing is at the top of the avenue.

1.29. Francis Mollett (*c.* 1859–1913) [plot 82]

Superintendent of Bisley Farm School, Surrey (*c.* 1893–1913). During his time at the school Mollett cared for over 1,000 boys. He was a lay reader of the Winchester Diocese and a Freemason of St Martin's Lodge, London. Mollett was keenly interested in Bisley village and was particularly associated with the cricket club and the new village hall. His preliminary funeral service was held in the Farm School chapel. About 175 boys from the Bisley and Shaftesbury Schools followed his coffin to Brookwood Cemetery. The main funeral service was held in the Anglican chapel, with an address given by the Revd H.N. Rodgers, Domestic Chaplain to the Bishop of Winchester.

The next grave is behind and to the right, adjacent to the Venables' pedestal memorial. Humphrey's grave is a low cross with a largely illegible inscription.

1.30. Thomas Humphrey (1839–1878) [plot 82]

Cricketer. Born at Mitcham and known as the 'pocket Hercules', since he was only 5ft 4in tall. Humphrey proved to be a splendid batsman and good bowler. In 1862 Humphrey was first engaged at the Oval as a bowler for Surrey. During 1865 he appeared in 44 matches and scored 1,728 runs. In 1867 he played in 34 matches, completed 56 innings and made 1,298 runs. Three of his brothers also played cricket. Humphrey was sometime landlord of the Cricketers' Inn at Westcott; and of the Ram Inn and Jolly Butchers' Inn, both in Dorking. He died in the **Brookwood Lunatic Asylum** on 3 September 1878. Although sadly unreadable now, his inscription recorded:

> BENEATH THIS CROSS LIES THE REMAINS OF THOMAS HUMPHREY WHO IN HIS DAY WAS ONE OF THE BEST CRICKETERS OF ENGLAND. BORN AT MITCHAM IN SURREY JANUARY 6TH 1839, DIED SEPTEMBER 3RD 1878. MEN OF ALL CLASSES AND ALL COUNTRIES WHO WISHED TO PERPETUATE HIS MEMORY VOLUNTEERED TO BEAR THE COST OF THIS TOMB, THE MAXIMUM SUBSCRIPTION BEING LIMITED TO ONE SHILLING FOR THE PURPOSE OF SHOWING HOW MANY THERE WERE.[40]

The next headstone memorial is off St Saviour's Avenue and faces on to St Paul's.

1.31. Bassett family grave [plot 82]

Employees of the LNC. **Catherine Bassett** (*c.* 1816–81) was for many years the 'female attendant' in the refreshment room of South station. Her husband, **Stephen Bassett** (*c.* 1820–80), was a general porter in the cemetery. After she was widowed in 1880 Catherine remained in the station with her niece, Annah Meetens, until her death the following year. Note the grave of **Katherine Meetens** (*c.* 1846–63) immediately to the right.

The next group of graves may be found off the top end of St Andrew's Avenue. The first is at the junction of the avenues. It is a fine obelisk in grey granite.

1.32. Lieutenant-Colonel Henry Cowell Boyes (1846–1900) [plot 82]

Senior officer in the London Rifle Brigade and one of its oldest officers. Boyes joined the Brigade after its formation in the early 1860s. He received his first commission in the Corps as Lieutenant in about 1872 and was promoted to Major, with the rank of Lieutenant-Colonel, in January 1896. The coat of arms of the London Rifle Brigade can be seen carved above the inscription. The memorial was erected 'by his comrades in the London Rifle Brigade which he served with devotion and distinction for over 36 years'.

Under the adjacent redwood is the next low headstone.

1.33. Sir Edmund Widdrington Byrne (1844–1904) [plot 86]

Judge. Born at Islington, he was educated at King's College, London, and entered as a student at Lincoln's Inn in 1863. He was called to the Bar in 1867. With family connections among solicitors, Byrne was able to establish a successful practice as a conveyancer and equity draftsman. Appointed QC (1888) and a bencher of Lincoln's Inn (1892), he attached himself to the court of **Justice Chitty** and obtained much work there. Byrne was Conservative MP for Walthamstow (1892–7). On the promotion of Chitty to the justiceship, Byrne was given the vacant judgeship in the Chancery Division (1897). Byrne has been described as an 'accurate and painstaking, but slow, judge'. He was knighted in 1897.

The next memorial is a cross with kerbing. It fronts St Andrew's Avenue.

1.34. Revd Charles Arthur Skelton (*c.* 1854–1913) [plot 86]

Rural Dean of Woking. Skelton's first appointment was as Deacon of Ripon (1880). He then became priest of St Mary's, Quarry Hill, Leeds (1880–1); of Earl's Heaton, Yorkshire (1881–3); and of St Thomas', Leeds (1883–8). Skelton was next appointed Chaplain of **Brookwood Asylum (Brookwood Hospital)** (1888–1913). During his time there he was instrumental in the provision of a church at the asylum, which was completed in about 1903. Skelton was Anglican Chaplain to the LNC (*c.* 1899–1913) and Honorary Canon of Winchester Cathedral (1905). He lived at The Meadows, Knaphill. His eldest son, Henry Skelton, also became a priest and was Bishop of Lincoln (1942–6).[41]

The next memorial is of similar design but further into the plot.

1.35. (Henry) Cecil Newton (1853–1915) [plot 86]

Railway administrator. Newton joined the GWR in 1869, working in the Goods Manager's office and then the General Manager's office. In 1875 he left the GWR and moved to Devon where he took charge of various minor railway companies. From 1878 he was also in charge of the Railway Department of the London Financial Association. In March 1881 he was appointed Secretary and Accountant to the London Tilbury & Southend Railway (LTSR). By 1896 his salary with the LTSR was £1,000 a year and was supplemented by his salaries with the Whitechapel & Bow Railway and the Tottenham & Forest Gate Railway. His LTSR post went in

1912 when the Midland Railway took over the line. He did not seek another post. On his death the Midland made a donation of £1,000 to his widow Catherine.

The next memorial is a prominent shrouded urn on a pedestal.

1.36. John Cameron McPhee (*c.* 1815–1880) [plot 86]

McPhee was surveyor of HM Customs, and sometime President of the Gaelic Society of London. His epitaph records that the memorial was erected by 'friends and brother officers of HM Customs as a mark of their affection and respect'.

The next memorial is a Calvary cross with kerbing. It is located about halfway along St Paul's Avenue and is on the right of the path.

1.37. Alfred Giles (1816–1895) [plot 86]

Civil engineer, second son of the engineer Francis Giles.[42] Educated at Charterhouse, Giles became a pupil in his father's firm. He then set up his own practice which was based at various London addresses. Giles specialised in the construction of railways and docks at home and abroad, and was Chief Engineer to the Southampton Docks Company for many years. He was MP for Southampton (1878–80 and 1883–92) and unsuccessfully contested the seat in 1880 and 1892. Giles was elected a member of the Institution of Civil Engineers (1846), and was its Vice-President (1889) and President (1893–4).

Sir Charles Tyrrell Giles (1850–1940), also buried here, was a lawyer and politician. Educated at Harrow and King's College, Cambridge. Giles qualified as a barrister in 1874, and was Chairman of the Wimbledon Petty Sessions (1904–17). Giles was Conservative MP for the Wisbech Division, Cambridgeshire (1895–1900), and contested his father's old seat of Southampton in 1910. Between 1907 and 1925 he served as Alderman of Surrey County Council, and was High Sheriff of Surrey (1915–16). Giles was President of the Wimbledon Parliamentary Borough Conservative and Unionist Association (1919–40) and was created Freeman of the Borough of Wimbledon (1937). He was Chairman of the Wimbledon and Putney Commons Conservators from 1892. His publications include *Skill with Rod and Gun* (London, Country Life, 1936) and editing *The Law Relating to Parliamentary & Municipal Elections and Petitions* (3rd edn, London, Sweet & Sons, 1885).

The St Saviour's plots occupy the rest of the ground up to the A322.

1.38. St Saviour's, Southwark [plots 88–90]

St Saviour's was the first metropolitan parish to use Brookwood as a burial ground. This was partly because the church was in the Diocese of Winchester, and partly because of the state of its existing burial grounds. St Saviour's is an ancient church, developed from one founded in 1106 and dedicated to St Mary Overie. In 1877 St Saviour's, along with other south London parishes, was transferred to the new Diocese of Rochester. In 1897 the church became a procathedral and was made the cathedral of the newly formed Diocese of Southwark in 1905.

St Saviour's had three burial grounds in London: the churchyard (which included vaults under the church and churchyard), the **Cross Bones burial ground**, and the old **Cure's College burial ground**. Only the latter was not in general use. The Vestry Minutes record a number of complaints from parishioners regarding the state of these overcrowded burial grounds, particularly during and after the cholera epidemic of 1848–9. In response to one letter signed by the inhabitants of High Street, Union Street and Red Cross Road, the Vestry reported on the current state of its burial grounds (17 November 1852). It subsequently met the LNC in

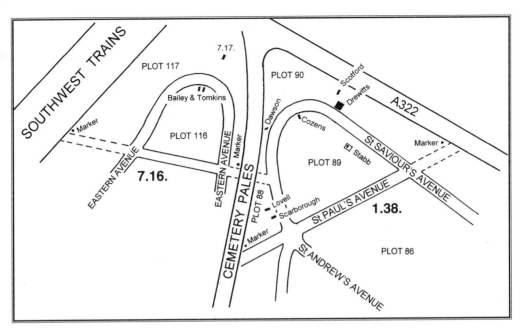

St Saviour's, Southwark, burial ground.

December 1852. Although the parish was keen to bury its dead at Brookwood, the LNC was in no position at that time to allocate land in the cemetery. It was only on 23 September 1853 that the LNC offered to set aside land for parish use for 999 years. This was a direct consequence of the parish having received notice of an Order in Council to close its existing burial grounds from 21 September 1853. As Brookwood Cemetery was still far from complete, St Saviour's used the Victoria Park Cemetery at Mile End as a temporary burial ground.[43]

In due course two areas were set aside for the use of the parish: plots 116–17 (just over 2 acres in the Nonconformist section, see Chapter 7), and plots 88–90 (just over 3 acres in the Anglican section). Gateways in the cemetery wall allowed pedestrian access between both plots. The boundaries of the allotments are still marked by pairs of cast-iron bollards, cast with the wording 'PARISH OF ST SAVIOUR'S SOUTHWARK', and by the line of monkey puzzle trees which were probably planted at the request of the parish burial board. The parish used these plots from November 1854 to about 1920, and it is estimated that upwards of 23,000 people are buried in these areas. Most of the ground is planted, but a number of memorials survive. The majority of those interred here were paupers, buried in unmarked graves.[44]

When someone died in a Southwark Union institution (a workhouse or infirmary) the relatives were informed. They could then arrange for a private burial at Brookwood (or elsewhere); otherwise the Borough arranged for a '3rd-class' or pauper burial here at Brookwood. There was no right to erect a permanent memorial, and the relatives received a 'travel warrant' that was exchanged for two 3rd-class mourner return tickets for use on the Necropolis train.[45]

Samuel Cozens (c. 1788–1869) [plot 89]. Cozens was for thirty-nine years Clerk of the Works at Guy's Hospital, London.

Cross Bones (Union Street) burial ground. This was one of three burial grounds within the parish and was located in Red Cross Street (off Union Street), Borough. It comprised an area of about 18,800 sq. ft and was otherwise referred to as the 'poor ground' since many of the Irish poor were buried there. It had been in use for about 100 years and was very full. Nevertheless two schools were built in it. After this burial ground was closed in October 1853 it was left untouched for many years. Mrs Holmes records that:

It has frequently been offered for sale as a building site, and has formed the subject of much litigation. It is made a partial use of by being let for fairs, swings, &c. It was sold as a building site in 1883, but, not having been used by 1884, the sale was declared (under the Disused Burial Grounds Act) null and void.[46]

At some time the site was rented to a showman who used it until the 1920s when the land was finally redeveloped. Human remains were discovered, even though it was assumed that they had previously been transferred to Brookwood! The bodies were removed to Brookwood Cemetery sometime in the late 1920s, although the precise location of these is unknown.

Cure's College burial ground. Another burial ground within the parish, next to almshouses in Park Street named after Thomas Cure, a local benefactor in the Tudor period. The site of this burial ground was purchased by the Charing Cross Railway Company and in 1862 the human remains of at least 270 former parishioners buried there were removed to Brookwood. Some seventy parishioners accompanied the remains to Brookwood where a special service took place. A few memorials in plots 88 and 90 can be identified as coming from Cure's College (e.g. James Dawson and Thomas Scarborough, below), but the reburials are not otherwise marked. The site became a builder's store yard over which the railway line passed on arches.[47]

James Dawson (c. 1795–1848) [plot 90]. One of several memorials in the St Saviour's ground which pre-date the opening of the cemetery. Dawson was 'of the George Inn in the Borough High Street'. The George Inn is the only galleried coaching inn remaining in London and is mentioned in Charles Dickens's Little Dorrit. Dawson's remains were removed from the old **Cure's College burial ground**.

Drewitt family grave [plot 90]. **Frederick Drewitt** (1820–94) was a son of **William Drewitt** (1782–1837) and **Ann Geary** (1788–1859), who are buried nearby. William was sexton to St Saviour's, while his wife was sextoness from his death until 1859. Frederick became an undertaker and helped form the company of Drewitt & Mummery. He was also Registrar to the parish of St Saviour's, based at 5 Church Street, Borough. He married **Mary Cowtan** (1820–99) in 1854. After Frederick's death his son (who was also called **Frederick Drewitt**, c. 1860–1912) carried on the undertaking business in the Borough High Street until his death in 1912. The **Cowtan family** also have graves nearby.

Emma Lovell (c. 1833–57) [plot 88]. This headstone records that Emma, mother of **Emma Jane Lovell**, 'died suddenly from the rupture of a blood vessel 18 May 1857'. She is buried with her daughter who died on 2 June 1856.

St George's Church, **Southwark**. Between February and June 1940 a total of forty-seven cases of human remains were removed from St George's Church and reburied at Brookwood. The total cost of this operation was £170 12s 0d. The precise location of these reburials is not known, but it has been assumed that they took place somewhere within this section.[48]

Scarborough family grave [plot 88]. The memorial records the names of this family 'who were removed from the College burial ground, St Saviour's Southwark, 1862'. **Thomas Scarborough** (c. 1803–76) was one of the original members of the St Saviour's Burial Board.

Henry Francis Scotford (c. 1859–61) [plot 90]. This memorial is behind the **Drewitt** allotment, and includes the following fine verse. It serves as a poignant reminder of the profound sense of grief and loss that resonates down the years:

Go to thy home the Lord hath need of thee
His glorious golden heaven was not complete
Without such gentle angel forms as thine
Go to thy home then fair and beautiful
Go to thy home O happy songful soul
Take all thy tender gentle music there
And for these broken songs and cries of earth
Lift up lift up beneath a fairer sky
The songs of heaven.

The next memorial may be found among the trees in plot 89. It comprises a massive block of pink granite with kerbing.

1.39. Sir Newton John Stabb (1868–1931) [plot 89]

Born at St John's, Newfoundland, Stabb entered the service of the Hong Kong & Shanghai Banking Corporation in 1886. He continued working with them until his death, latterly as Manager. His epitaph records:

HE WAS WISE IN THE WAYS OF NATIONS, STRONG IN THE AFFECTIONS AND RESPECT OF ALL HIS COLLEAGUES, A KINDLY HELPER AND COUNSELLOR, VERY HAPPY IN HIS FAMILY AND IN THE PATHS OF FRIENDSHIP.

Return to St Saviour's Avenue and continue walking in the direction of the church. At the next junction, the road becomes St Andrew's Avenue. Note the fine avenue of redwoods. The next two memorials are in the plot to your left.

1.40. Community of the Holy Name [plot 87]

This plot is marked by a Portland stone pentagonal cross with canopy on three octagonal bases that faces towards St Andrew's Avenue. The Community of the Holy Name was a religious order of sisters located at 141 Upper Kennington Lane, London. The first burial took place in 1887, that of **Ellen Johnstone** (died 1887) of the 'Sisterhood House'. The ground reserved for use by the community was extended in 1901 to include the cross memorial at the rear of the plot. The last burial appears to have been that of **Gwenllian Phillips** (*c.* 1872–1915). The original community subsequently moved from Upper Kennington to Malvern Link, since the Reverend Mother there paid £3 5s 0d for the cleaning of the memorial in 1934.[49]

The next memorial is a Latin cross on a large base, and is also on the left of the path.

1.41. The Charterhouse burial ground [plot 87]

The Charterhouse dates from a Carthusian Priory founded in 1370. In the early seventeenth century Thomas Sutton used the buildings as a school for forty poor boys and a hospital for eighty poor gentlemen pensioners. The Merchant Taylors' School took over the school premises in 1872 when the school moved to Godalming. This part of the Charterhouse became the Medical College of St Bartholomew's Hospital from 1933, and these buildings were much rebuilt after damage during the Blitz. The pensioners remained (and remain) in London. This small memorial commemorates nine officers and relatives of officers of Charterhouse whose remains were reburied here from the chapel of the Charterhouse in April 1898.

Just beyond this are a number of prominent memorials that mark the largest concentration of reburial of human remains at Brookwood. These will be dealt with in turn, starting with those in plot 87.

1.42. St John Clerkenwell [plot 87]

This allotment contains the human remains of about 325 bodies deceased between 1738 and 1853 from the 'ancient crypt' of the church. They were removed to this spot in 1894. The churchyard was subsequently laid out by the Metropolitan Public Gardens Association. The church lost its parish in 1929 and reverted to the new Order of St John of Jerusalem, a Church of England charitable and medical organisation founded in the nineteenth century. The church was damaged in the last war but was restored by 1958.

1.43. St Magnus the Martyr [plot 87]

St Magnus was built by Wren between 1671 and 1676, although the steeple was not finished until 1705. The church is now overshadowed by Adelaide House (1924–5) on the approach to London Bridge. St Magnus was the church of the United Parishes – a combination of parishes that included St Margaret, New Fish Street and St Michael, Crooked Lane. The obelisk marks

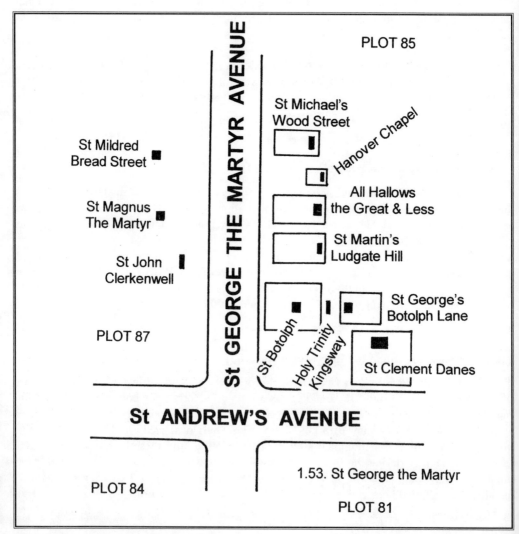

The reinterment plots off St Andrew's Avenue.

the resting place of the human remains removed from the vaults and places of burial under the church of St Magnus. The reinterments were prompted on sanitary grounds and took place in 1893–4.

1.44. St Mildred, Bread Street [plot 87]

This church was rebuilt by Wren between 1681 and 1687. Shelley was married in this church to Mary Wollstonecraft in 1816. The memorial records that human remains were removed from under the church and reburied here in 1898, presumably on sanitary grounds. Until the Second World War St Mildred's was generally considered one of the best preserved of Wren's churches, with its original pews and woodwork. Unfortunately the church was completely destroyed by enemy action in 1941.

At the end of this pathway note there was once a gateway in the cemetery wall. This was removed some years ago. The next sequence of memorials will be described in turn from the back of plot 85 and moving towards St Andrew's Avenue.

1.45. St Michael, Wood Street [plot 85]

This church was rebuilt by Wren between 1670 and 1675, although the steeple was replaced in 1804. The church was demolished in 1896–7 and the parish was united with that of St Alban, Wood Street. The inscription records that the remains of those buried during the years 1559–1853 are buried in the enclosure. Tradition had it that the severed head of King James IV of Scotland, who was killed at Flodden (1513), was buried in the church. But when the human remains were transferred to Brookwood no severed head was found.

1.46. The Hanover Chapel [plot 85]

This chapel was built under Nash's supervision by C.R. Cockerell between 1823 and 1825. Described as one of the most interesting churches of its time, it was demolished in 1896–7 as part of the remodelling of Regent Street. The small headstone records that human remains removed from the chapel during the course of its demolition were reburied here. **Charles Lucas** was organist there from 1839.

1.47. All Hallows the Great & Less [plot 85]

All Hallows the Great was rebuilt by Wren between 1677 and 1683. All Hallows the Less, which was also located in Upper Thames Street, was destroyed in the Great Fire and was not rebuilt. The parish was united with its sister church. Wren's design did not include a spire on the tower. In 1876 the north aisle and tower were demolished in order that Queen Victoria Street might be widened. The tower and a vestry were rebuilt on the south side. In 1893–6 the church was demolished except for the tower and vestry. This is why the human remains from the church were reburied here at Brookwood. The parish was united with St Michael, Paternoster Royal, and the site of the church was sold to an adjacent brewery, which paid for the construction of All Hallows, Gospel Oak. The tower and vestry were damaged during the Blitz. Part of the churchyard appears to have survived until 1969, although it is not known where these bodies were removed to.

1.48. St Martin's, Ludgate Hill [plot 85]

St Martin's was built by Wren between 1684 and 1687. This memorial marks the area where human remains, removed from under the church and its adjacent vaults, were reinterred here in 1893–4.

1.49. St Botolph Without, Aldersgate [plot 85]

The foundation of this church dates back to the thirteenth century. The church was rebuilt in 1788–91 by Nathaniel Wright. This large kerbed plot contains the remains of 'generations of parishioners' formerly buried within the church. The last burial within the church had taken place in 1852. Their removal appears to have been prompted by 'the offensive and obnoxious effluvia' from the church vaults, which made St Botolph's unfit for public worship. The exhumations took place in 1893–4, and involved the removal of human remains beneath the floor of the church to a depth of at least 6ft.

The next memorial is a small headstone directly behind the vast St Botolph's plot.

1.50. Holy Trinity, Kingsway [plot 85]

The original church was designed by Francis Bedford and was built in 1829–31. It was demolished in 1909 because its foundations were undermined by the construction of the Piccadilly Line. This memorial was placed over the human remains removed from the original church at this time. The new church was built by Belcher & Joass in 1909–11. It was closed in 1991. Despite Grade II listing permission for its demolition was granted in 1999, and only the frontage survives.

Behind the Holy Trinity memorial is the next.

1.51. St George's, Botolph Lane [plot 85]

A granite obelisk commemorates the removal of human remains from this church in 1902 when the parish was united with those of St Mary-at-Hill and St Andrew Hubbard in the City. The church was rebuilt by Wren between 1671 and 1674 using rubble from the old St Paul's Cathedral. The church was closed in 1891 and the structure was declared unsafe in 1903. It was demolished in 1904 and the parish was united with St Mary-at-Hill, Billingsgate. Here is a contemporary account of the last years of this church:

> The ancient church of St George, Botolph Lane, is sharing the fate that has befallen many of the City churches – demolition; and the site on which it stands will shortly be sold. The sum obtained for the site will be devoted to the erection of a new church in some populous suburb. Before the church was dismantled, the human remains buried in the building were reverently collected, and subsequently re-interred in the beautiful cemetery at Brookwood, under the direction of the churchwardens, the work of removal being carried out by the London Necropolis Company. When the official announcement appeared to the effect that the bodies beneath the church were to be removed, the churchwardens received a request to discover, if possible, the tomb of Sir William Cuddon, who was the Chamberlain of the City over two centuries ago. The burial register was found to contain a record of the fact that Sir William was buried within the Church, but all efforts to trace his remains failed. The pretty spot in Brookwood Cemetery where the bones of the old citizens have been re-interred is marked by a handsome obelisk of blue Aberdeen granite, the place of burial being also prettily laid out.[50]

The next allotment is adjacent to the St George's one and faces St Andrew's Avenue.

1.52. St Clement Danes [plot 85]

The foundation of this church may date back to Danish times. The medieval church was rebuilt by Wren between 1680 and 1682. It was destroyed by incendiary bombs during the night of 10 May 1941 and was restored between 1955 and 1958. St Clement Danes is now the

RAF church of London. A memorial in the church records the names of those members of the RAF who were awarded the George Cross, including **Forest Frederic Edward Yeo-Thomas**. This memorial at Brookwood records that the human remains of some 4,000 persons were removed here in 1900 from part of the churchyard required for road improvements in the Strand and Holborn.

Directly opposite is a sunken area of ground with the base of a large memorial.

1.53. St George the Martyr, Southwark [plot 81]

This church was built between 1734 and 1736 by John Price and replaced the old medieval church. St George's is referred to in Dickens's *Little Dorrit*. Here the heroine was christened, sought refuge and was married. Marshalsea Prison, where Dickens's father was imprisoned, adjoined the church. The large allotment in the cemetery was used for the reburial of human remains from the crypt of St George's in October 1899. The massive obelisk, which has since toppled, was a replica of one in St George's Circus, Southwark, and was erected here in 1900. The original obelisk in London survives and is dated 1771. For some years it stood in the grounds of the Imperial War Museum, but it was replaced in its original location in St George's Circus in 1998. A full list of the identifiable human remains that were removed here is available in the Southwark Local Studies Library.

From here, cross the road into plot 84. Towards the other side of the ground and diagonally in line with the memorial to Henri van Laun (item 27) is the next grave. It is a Celtic cross memorial on a base.

1.54. 2nd Lieutenant Rupert Price Hallowes, VC (*c.* 1881–1915) [plot 84]

Second Lieutenant Hallowes's VC was awarded during the fighting at Hooge in Belgium between 25 September and 1 October 1915. Hallowes, from the 4th Battalion of the Middlesex Regiment, showed unexampled bravery and energy throughout four heavy and protracted bombardments, heartening his men by his wonderful courage. On several occasions he climbed upon the parapet, heedless of danger, in order to put fresh courage into his men. Hallowes is also credited with a number of the most daring reconnaissances of the German positions, and when bombs were needed he went back and brought them up under heavy shell fire. Even when mortally wounded Hallowes continued to cheer those around him and to inspire them with fresh courage. Hallowes is only commemorated by the inscription on his family's grave; he is buried in Bedford House Cemetery at Zillebeke, Belgium (enclosure 4 XIV B 36).

The next memorial is a kerbed grave in pink granite that faces St George the Martyr Avenue.

1.55. Edmund Boylett (1858–1933) [plot 84]

Boylett worked for the LNC, the original owners of Brookwood Cemetery, for fifty-two years. He lived in the East Gate Cottage, a house provided by the LNC. Latterly Boylett was responsible for managing the greenhouses adjacent to the **Superintendent's offices**.

Nearby in plot 81 is a small allotment with a low headstone marking further reburials of human remains.

1.56. St Michael's, Fish Street Hill [plot 81]

A small memorial commemorating the removal of the remains of twenty-nine parishioners from this former City burial ground. The human remains were reburied here on 18 September 1987, because of construction work in the City.

The next headstone may be found adjacent to a screen of rhododendrons, and facing on to All Souls' Avenue.

1.57. Harry Blakeway (*c.* 1884–1919) [plot 75]

Surgeon. Born in Stourbridge, Blakeway studied medicine at St Bartholomew's Hospital, London between 1903 and 1908. He was awarded a large number of prizes and scholarships. Blakeway qualified in 1908 and was elected a Fellow of the Royal College of Surgeons in 1910. He became Demonstrator of Anatomy at Bart's, where he proved himself to be an excellent teacher. Blakeway worked also as a surgeon to the Victoria Hospital for Children and as Assistant Surgeon to the Truss Society. In 1913 he was appointed Surgical Registrar at Bart's, a post he held until his death. He died in February 1919, following an attack of influenza, aged just 35. A victim of the 'flu pandemic following the end of the First World War, he was described as 'one of the most promising of our young surgeons'. His wife, **Marjorie Campbell Blakeway** (*c.* 1892–1974), was born in Woking, which undoubtedly explains why he was buried at Brookwood.

Almost directly across All Souls' Avenue is the next grave, which includes an angel on a pedestal.

1.58. Sir Stanley Bois (1864–1938) [plot 74]

Director of tea and rubber companies. Educated at South Penge Park College, Bois originally worked in a shipbroker's office in London before travelling to the East. He arrived in Ceylon in 1882 and joined the staff of a firm he and his brother eventually acquired. Bois was a member of the Municipal Council of Colombo and Chairman of the Ceylon Chamber of Commerce. He was an acting member of the Legislative Council representing mercantile interests from 1903, a member representing European interests from 1906, and mercantile interests in 1910. Bois was President of the Ceylon Association in London and of the Rubber Growers Association.

Return to plot 81. The next headstone is to the right of the St Michael's, Fish Street Hill memorial (item 56).

1.59. Dame Rebecca West (1892–1983) [plot 81]

Author, reporter and literary critic. Born Cicily Fairfield, she began writing for *The Freewoman* under the pseudonym Rebecca West (one of Ibsen's characters) from 1912. Her life of Henry James (published in 1916) established her literary reputation. In 1913 she began a liaison with the writer H.G. Wells, which produced a son (Anthony West) in 1914. She subsequently married the banker Henry Maxwell Andrews in 1930. West's many novels include *The Fountain Overflows* (London, Macmillan, 1957), probably her best literary work from an artistic point of view. It was meant to be part of a trilogy, and is almost certainly based on her own youth. Her reportage includes *The Meaning of Treason, with Special Reference to the Trials of William Joyce and Others* (London, Macmillan, 1949), and *A Train of Powder* (London, Macmillan, 1955); both are brilliantly written. *A Train of Powder* is based on articles she published in newspapers and periodicals which together form an account of criminal cases including the Nuremberg trials. Her masterpiece is judged to be *Black Lamb and Grey Falcon* (two vols, London, Macmillan, 1941), drawn from the record of a journey through Yugoslavia in 1937. She was awarded the CBE in 1949 and DBE in 1959. In 1960 West advised Vyvyan Holland (the son of Oscar Wilde)[51] to publish all of his father's letters in full. After they appeared in 1962 she wrote to him that 'The impression left on me is that it was not just advisable that they were published, it was necessary. . . . I didn't think that anyone could read the volume without liking your father more than before.'[52]

In the same year West was a witness for the defence in the Lady Chatterley trial. which resulted in D.H. Lawrence's book becoming widely available in this country.[53] West selected this spot at Brookwood, which she visited many times. It reminded her of a private park. Her simple headstone records her three names.

The next memorial is a headstone with kerbing situated near St Andrew's Avenue.

1.60. Lieutenant-Colonel John Sherwood-Kelly, VC (1880–1931) [plot 81]

Educated at Grahamstown, South Africa, Sherwood-Kelly joined the Rhodesian Police in 1897. He served in the South African War (1899–1902) and in Somaliland (1902–4). During the First World War Sherwood-Kelly came to Britain and joined the Norfolk Regiment. On 20 November 1917 he was in charge of a party of men held up on one side of a canal bridge near Marcoing in France. Sherwood-Kelly ordered covering fire and personally led his leading company across the canal and reconnoitred the high ground held by the enemy. Using a Lewis gun team, Sherwood-Kelly forced his way through obstacles and covered the advance of his battalion, enabling them to capture the position. Later he took a number of pits, capturing five machine guns and forty-six prisoners. By 1918 he was Acting Lieutenant-Colonel with the Royal Inniskilling Fusiliers. In 1919 he commanded the 2nd Hampshire Regiment in Northern Russia. On 20 June 1919, in an attack on Troitsa, Sherwood-Kelly refused to attack because he felt his force would be cut off. He wrote home to a friend criticising the attack. He was relieved of his command. Sherwood-Kelly was subsequently court martialed (28 October 1919) with a severe reprimand. So ended his military career, and he was never allowed to rejoin the Army despite several attempts to do so. His memorial is one of only three at Brookwood that actually feature the VC medal. It includes the inscription 'One who never turned his back, but marched breast forward'.

Cross the road and enter plot 76, otherwise known as the 'lawn' or 'St Andrew's lawn'. Look for the small Calvary cross memorial to the right of the large Vaughan family allotment.

1.61. John Thomas Ibbotson Tiller (1854–1925) [plot 76]

Originator of military precision dancing and of the 'Tiller Girls'. Born in Blackburn, Tiller joined his uncle's cotton business, but all his spare time was devoted to music and dancing. In 1885 Tiller became director of the Comedy Theatre, Manchester. He also began teaching local children to dance, practising in one of his uncle's warehouses. The children performed tableaux and dances for pantomimes and church pageants. In 1890 Tiller was asked to present a quartet of girls at the Prince of Wales's Theatre, Liverpool. Tiller trained the girls to repeat every movement in perfect unison. He decided to become a professional manager, adding more songs and dances to his acts. The growing popularity of these acts meant Tiller had to train more girls and young ladies. Throughout his career Tiller produced hundreds of troupes with various names like the Tiller Quartette, the Tiller Ballet, the Forget-me-nots, and the Tiller Troubadours. Each one had its own speciality (small girls, tall girls, or talented acrobats, for example), but all could dance and sing. Tiller set high standards for his troupes and would not allow a public appearance until all the routines were impeccably performed. In the late 1890s Tiller opened his first training school in St James's Hall, Manchester (it later moved to Lime Grove). A London office and the Tiller Training School & Lyric Academy followed. By 1900 his troupes were showing all over England and also on the continent. At about this time he evolved a new routine, the Mystic Hussars, with twelve 'soldiers' and spectacular lighting and electrical effects. In 1910 he developed the kicking and linking routine that evolved from the Hussars, where the girls linked arms while performing high kicks. This routine made him world famous. Tiller's Palace Girls appeared in the first Royal Command Performance of 1912. During the First World War his troupes travelled widely to entertain the troops, while in the 1920s he began ciné-variety shows with alternating film and stage turns. Tiller travelled extensively to promote his shows, and died in New York. He married twice, first in 1873 Mary Carr (*c.* 1855–1905), and secondly in 1906 Jennie Walker (died 1936).[54]

Tiller died in the Lennox Hill Hospital, New York. His body was brought back to England for burial at Brookwood. At his funeral, fifty Tiller Girls, representing troupes from all over the country, met at the LNC's station in the Westminster Bridge Road. They travelled down on the Necropolis train, and gave way to hysterical giggling as they realised the train contained other mourners attending other funerals. A memorial window to Tiller was placed in St Stephen's-on-the-Cliff Church, Blackpool. The grave had marble chippings on a bed of concrete added in mid-1934.[55]

*The next headstone is near the **St Clement Danes** plot.*

1.62. Rt Hon. Montagu Henry Townley-Bertie, 8th Earl of Abingdon & 13th Earl of Lindsey (1887–1963) [plot 76]

The only son of Lord Norrys, the eldest son of the 7th Earl of Abingdon. Townley-Bertie served in the Grenadier Guards and in the Royal Naval Air Service (1914–18). He was wounded in action and subsequently posted to the Reserve Battalion at Chelsea Barracks. He succeeded his grandfather as 8th Earl of Abingdon in 1928, and his kinsman as 13th Earl of Lindsey in 1938. Townley-Bertie was High Steward of Abingdon and a Family Trustee of the British Museum. Sir Osbert Sitwell[56] described him as:

> That rare creature, a man-of-the-world who had formed his own opinions on most matters and could express them simply . . . thereby causing an effect like that of fresh air blowing through the platitudinous, slightly mephitic vapours of the Anteroom. He had no fear of expressing himself, indeed [he] seemed rather to enjoy it . . . and his views were always infused by an extreme common sense – if common sense can ever be extreme.[57]

Further over in the same plot is a tall cross memorial within a small group of three graves.

1.63. Sir Eustace Henry William Tennyson d'Eyncourt (1868–1951) [plot 76]

Naval architect. Apprenticed to Armstrong, Whitworth & Co., and subsequently employed in its design office, Tennyson d'Eyncourt was later placed in charge of the design office (1902–12), and was appointed Director of Naval Construction and Chief Technical Adviser at the Admiralty (1912–24). His designs included the 'Royal Sovereign' class of battleships, aircraft carriers, the battle cruiser HMS *Hood*, and the battleships HMS *Nelson* and HMS *Rodney*. Tennyson d'Eyncourt headed the Landships Committee which led to the production of tanks. When in 1915 Winston Churchill was replaced at the Admiralty by Arthur Balfour, Tennyson d'Eyncourt warned Churchill that the Landships Committee might be dissolved. Consequently Churchill convinced Balfour of the necessity of continuing the experimental prototypes. In 1919 the Royal Commission on War Inventions granted Tennyson d'Eyncourt £1,000, while Churchill refused any payment. Tennyson d'Eyncourt was appointed KCB in 1917 and a Fellow of the Royal Society in 1921. He resigned from the Admiralty in 1924, but remained as a Special Advisor. Tennyson d'Eyncourt was Managing Director of Armstrong Whitworth's shipyards at Newcastle (1924–8), and Director of the Parsons Marine Steam Turbine Company (1928–48). He was created a Baronet in 1930. Tennyson d'Eyncourt later published his memoirs, *A Shipbuilder's Yarn: the Record of a Naval Constructor* (London, Hutchinson, 1948).

The next tomb monument may be found adjacent to the screen of rhododendrons that form the boundary with the **St Edward Brotherhood.**

1.64. Sir Frank Athelstan(e) Swettenham (1850–1946) [plot 76]

Colonial administrator. Swettenham entered service in the Straits Settlements in 1871. He was adviser to the Sultan of Selangor (1874–5). Swettenham initiated the Federation of Perak, Selangor, Negri Sembilan and Pahang, and was Resident-General of the Federated States (1895–1901). He was High Commissioner of the Malay States and Governor of the Straits Settlements (1901–4), and Chairman of the Royal Commission on the Finances of Mauritius (1909). Swettenham was Joint-Director of the Press Bureau (1915–18). He was made KCMG (1897), GCMG (1909) and CH (1917). Swettenham published several books including *Malay Sketches* (London, John Lane, 1895), *Unaddressed Letters* (London, Bodley Head, 1898), and *The Real Malay* (London, John Lane, 1899). His book *British Malaya* (London, John Lane, 1907) is an account of the origin and progress of British influence in the region. Swettenham's Perak journals of 1874–6 were edited by Charles Cowan and published in the *Journal of the Malayan Branch of the Royal Asiatic Society* in 1952.

Two brilliant portraits of Swettenham by **John Singer Sargent** exist. The original version, commissioned by the Malay Straits Association of London, is still in Singapore. A replica was also made, which Sargent (unusually) largely painted. There are differences between the two since Swettenham agreed to give further sittings, so more Far Eastern accessories are used in the background and the pose is slightly different. The replica is now in the National Portrait Gallery.

The next memorial is a low headstone set at the rear of a large kerbed allotment. It fronts on to St Andrew's Avenue.

1.65. John Baker Walker (died 1943) [plot 76]

Director of the LNC, the original owners of Brookwood Cemetery. Walker joined the LNC in 1889 as a clerk. He was promoted to General Manager from 1897 and was Managing Director from 1919. Walker succeeded Henry G. Ricardo as Chairman of the Board of Directors (1941–3). He lived at The Cedars, Heath House Road. When he died, Walker had lived long enough to see the demise of the cemetery's railway service, as the LNC's private terminus was largely destroyed by bombs in April 1941. The directors recorded that '[They] desire to place on record the great loss the Company has sustained by the death of their esteemed colleague. Under his very capable Management and by his unfailing endeavours the affairs of the Company have shown great progress.'[58] He was succeeded as Chairman by **Frederick Green**.

Cross the path and look for the Celtic cross memorial in grey granite that faces towards the road.

1.66. Sir James Galloway (1862–1922) [plot 75]

Senior Physician and Lecturer in Medicine, Charing Cross Hospital. Born in Calcutta, but educated in Aberdeen, Galloway worked at the London Hospital from 1889 prior to his appointment as a pathologist at the Great Northern Hospital. While there he developed a particular interest in the microscopic investigation of malignant disease. In 1894 he moved to Charing Cross Hospital as physician to the skin department, where he worked until 1914. He was appointed successively Assistant Physician (1901), Physician (1906) and Senior Physician (1913). He was also a lecturer in the Medical School (1908–22). As a member of the Advisory Board for Army Medical Services, he was appointed Consulting Physician to the 1st and 2nd Armies in France, for which he was awarded the CB in 1917. He was later attached solely to the 2nd Army until recalled to serve with the Ministry of National Service (KBE, 1918). Galloway held high office within the Royal College of Physicians and the British Medical Association. He resigned his post at Charing Cross only shortly before his death. Galloway wrote many medical books and articles, yet he still found time to pursue interests outside his work. These included botany, geology and antiquarian studies. His interest in old London led to the publication of his *Historical Sketches of Old Charing* (London, Bale, Sons & Danielsson, 1914), a study of the old monastic institution of St Mary Roncevall (1219–1559) which stood on the site now occupied by Charing Cross station and Northumberland Avenue.

The last headstone in this section is further into plot 75.

1.67. James Tolman Tanner (1859–1915) [plot 75]

Author of many popular musical comedies. Tanner was born into great poverty, but his talents for writing libretti and attractive lyrics earned him great recognition and wealth. He lived for many years at Gravesend but, dogged by serious illness, he was not often seen in public. One of his most successful works was *The Quaker Girl* (1910), a 'new musical play' in three acts with lyrics by Adrian Ross[59] and Percy Greenbank[60] and music by Lionel Monckton.[61] It played for many years all over the world and was revised and revived in London in 1945 by Emile Littler;[62] it went on to tour England and Scotland right through to December 1948. Much of Tanner's writing was undertaken in his garden summerhouse.

Chapter Two

ST CYPRIAN'S AVENUE

T he next four chapters cover the richest sections of Brookwood Cemetery – richest in all senses of the word. The areas covered here perhaps above all others merit the description of Brookwood being the 'Westminster Abbey' of the middle classes. More selection has necessarily taken place for these chapters because of the number of important and interesting people buried within these sections. It includes the plots either side of the main driveway into this part of the cemetery (St Cyprian's Avenue), along with the attractive plots within the two main circular roadways, St George's and St Margaret's. Lastly the 'Gridiron' area is described. Owing to the size of the area covered it is difficult to suggest a straightforward route throughout. Therefore the plan followed is to start from St Cyprian's, then to continue along St George's and St Margaret's, finishing with the outlying areas to the right of St Cyprian's (the 'Gridiron'). The accompanying maps should help to clarify this approach.

The first section to explore is plot 1, opposite the former **Masonry Works**. *There are two cast-iron obelisks marking the entrance to this area.*

2.1. St Anne's, Westminster [plot 1]

This plot occupies the site of the former burial ground of **St Anne's, Westminster**. St Anne's church is situated off Wardour Street in Soho and was built in 1677–86 to the designs of either Wren or William Talman. King George II worshipped at this church when he was Prince of Wales. The original tower was replaced by S.P. Cockerell in 1801–3. The church, with the exception of the curious tower, was destroyed in 1940 during the Blitz. In recent years some rebuilding has taken place to provide accommodation for the Soho Housing Association and the Soho Society, along with a museum and chapel.

Under the terms of the Metropolitan Interments Amendment Act (1852)[1] the Government was empowered to close down overcrowded burial grounds in London, and metropolitan parishes were enabled to elect burial boards to arrange for the decent interment of their dead. St Anne's was the very first metropolitan parish to elect its own burial board. It received an Order in Council to close its churchyard on 25 August 1853. By this time it was estimated that some 10,000 burials had taken place there, and consequently the churchyard was some 6ft above the pavement level. The first meeting of the St Anne's burial board took place on 20 July 1854.[2] Eventually two areas at Brookwood were acquired for St Anne's: plot 120 in the former Nonconformist section (1 acre, see Chapter 8), and this one in the former Anglican section, comprising 2 acres. The agreement with the LNC was dated 26 April 1855 and was to last for 999 years. It is not known what burial ground the parish used during the intervening period 1853–5) but, like **St Saviour's, Southwark**, Victoria Park Cemetery may have been used.[3]

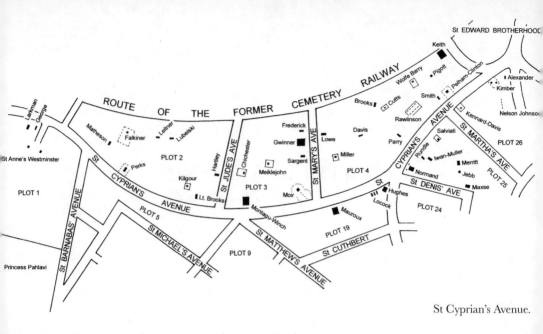

St Cyprian's Avenue.

Both plots at Brookwood had pairs of 10ft high cast-iron obelisks, but only this pair survives. They were made by Messrs Cottain & Hallow of Oxford Street for £54, and were painted to resemble stone. The boundaries of the plots were planted by Messrs Donald & Sons for £50.[4] Most of the burials here were of paupers, whose graves are unmarked. Burial at Brookwood was never popular with those parishioners who could afford to be buried elsewhere. The parish burial board inspected the plots annually until 1900, when the board was dissolved under the London Government Act (1899). Thereafter the Borough of Paddington maintained the plots until about 1921. Meanwhile in 1892 the churchyard in London was laid out as a garden by the Metropolitan Public Gardens Association and maintained by the Strand District Board of Works as a recreation ground. In 1903 part of the churchyard was cleared when Wardour Street was widened. The human remains were transferred to Brookwood in a large plot measuring 56ft by 20ft, but so far its location has not been traced.[5]

Dodi Fayed (1955–97), the friend of Diana, Princess of Wales (1961–97), was buried in the left-hand corner of this section for forty days. His body was then moved by his father, Mohammed Al Fayed, to the family estate at Oxted in Surrey, where a private mausoleum has since been erected.

At the entrance to the plot, and on the right-hand side, is a prominent headstone.

Joseph George (*c*. 1810–68) [plot 1]. George was a member of the St Anne's burial board and was instrumental in the selection of Brookwood for its burial ground. He was an ornamental leather manufacturer for cabinet and upholstery purposes. Examples of the firm's work could be seen in the Houses of Parliament (in the VR and portcullis decorations on the backs of the seats), and the gilt leather upon the library shelves at Longleat, Knebworth and many other country houses. George lived at 81 Dean Street, and actively campaigned for the better treatment of the poor, fighting for parochial and sanitary reform. He is buried with his wife and daughter in a prominent position just to the right of the entrance to this section. George chose to be buried here, in the cemetery which he did so much to secure for St Anne's. Yet even towards the end of the nineteenth century it was very little used by parishioners as a burying place.

Further to the right of this memorial is a headstone with kerbing that faces into the St Anne's ground.

Julian Chamberlin Larkman (*c*. 1826–1905) [plot 1]. Secretary of the LNC (1870–97). Larkman was originally employed as an office clerk to the nascent company in December 1850, working for its secretary, Richard Churchill. The LNC's new Board of Directors formally recorded his appointment as clerk in January 1854. Larkman succeeded Churchill, the company's first secretary (and apparently not buried at Brookwood), in May 1870. This arose from the death of Robert Donald and the collapse of his business. Since Donald owed the company money, it appears that Churchill had helped Donald using company funds.[6]

In January 1876 the Board of Directors noted that Mr Larkman and Mr Diprose (a shareholder) had taken out a patent for disposable 'Earth-to-Earth' coffins 'suitable for the object often discussed at this Board & advocated by **Mr [Francis S.] Haden**'. Both men had acted without the Board's sanction, but agreed to 'assign the patent & stock in hand . . . and profits already made . . . for £278 18*s* 11*d*'.[7] The company had already published (in 1875) a leaflet on *The Patent Necropolis Earth-to-Earth Coffins*, although the LNC shortly relinquished its patent rights, believing these coffins should be made as widely available as possible. The enormous interest aroused by these coffins promoted Haden's ideas, provided a sanitary alternative to cremation, allowed for the reuse of graves (hence perpetuity of burial revenues) and promoted burial at Brookwood (where the soil was especially suitable for these coffins).

Larkman was also involved in the controversy surrounding the construction of a crematorium at St John's, Woking, in 1878–9. A number of interesting issues came to light concerning the choice of this site. The land had previously formed part of the LNC's estate. It had been sold not directly to the Cremation Society but to a third party, and was originally for another purpose, to avoid undue attention. Whether the LNC was a willing or innocent party to this transaction will probably never be known. Because of the hostility aroused by the construction of the furnace the LNC was quick to disassociate itself from the project, which Larkman did through a letter to *The Times*:

> The Necropolis Company in no degree favour such preparations as are now being made in the vicinity of Woking for incinerating the dead. They regard cremation as the residents of the parish regard it – namely, with abhorrence. Some few years since application was sent to the Necropolis Company for a piece of land in their extensive burial-ground, with the view of setting up a crematory therein. I need scarcely say that the company rejected the proposition. It is true the land now in possession of the Cremation Society of London originally belonged to the company, but it was purchased from them in the ordinary way, and they never once anticipated that by a second purchase it would pass into the hands of the Cremation Society or be used for a funeral pyre. Had the company had the faintest idea that the ground would be conveyed to its present possessors, no inducement would have caused them to part with it.
>
> The mode of interment, now widely know as the 'Earth-to-Earth' system, strongly recommended some years since by **Mr Seymour Haden** in eloquent letters to *The Times* is that which the London Necropolis Company endeavour to carry out. The company cannot countenance the disposal of the dead either by burning or subjection to the action of quicklime. They have full faith in the drying and congealing power of the earth itself, when the ground is of a suitable nature, and thus chemically calculated to facilitate 'innocuous resolution' in opposition to 'destructive putrefaction' engendered by solid coffins and saturated and 'choked' soils.[8]

Larkman also took part in the deputation by the residents of Woking to the Home Secretary and testified that the land had originally been purchased for the purpose of constructing a convalescent hospital.[9]

In 1885 Larkman was offered the old **Parsonage House** as a residence at £25 per annum, but it is not clear if he actually moved in before **George Barratt** was appointed superintendent.[10] In 1888 the duties of the secretary were defined as:

> [Keeping] the accounts; receiving funeral orders and giving necessary directions; arranging sales of plots in the cemetery and giving orders to the Superintendent for digging graves; receiving and paying all monies for the Company, including rents; keeping the register of burials, transfers and all Registers required by the Act of Parliament; keeping Minutes and convening Board and Committee meetings; conducting correspondence; attending to all matters confided in him; [and] to assist other Officers of the Company as the Board may direct with information and give access to books and documents.[11]

During his long period of office, Larkman built up an unrivalled knowledge of the LNC. Latterly he lived in Brookwood Lodge, close to the cemetery. He was succeeded by **George Pole**.

Just beyond this area is a private plot reached by its own pathway off St Barnabas's Avenue.

2.2. Princess Shamdought Fatima Pahlavi (1917–1987) [plot 1]

The second and favourite daughter of Reza Khan, Shah of Iran between 1925 and 1941. Pahlavi was sister of Mohammad Reza Pahlavi, the late Shah of Iran.[12] She arranged the marriage of the Shah to Queen Soraya in 1951, although the marriage was dissolved in 1958. Pahlavi lived in Iran and Europe. Towards the end of her life she converted to Catholicism, which alienated many Muslims. She died of cancer in London. The inscription reads in part, 'In the name of Allah the forgiving [crown, and Pahlavi's name] 6th Khordad 1366 [i.e. July 1987]'. Then follow verses of poetry. The crown depicted on the headstone is the Pahlavi crown, symbolic of the Imperial dynasty.

Return to St Cyprian's Avenue and look for the large chest-style memorial within a private hedged allotment that faces the main path.

2.3. Sir Robert William Perks (1849–1934) [plot 2]

Methodist, contractor and politician. Perks was educated at Kingswood School, Bath, and King's College, London. He was a railway lawyer (1878–92). Perks was associated with the contractors T.A. Walker[13] in building the Barry Docks, Preston Docks, the Manchester Ship Canal, the Inner Circle railway, and other works. With Walker he assisted the construction of the Rio de Janeiro quays, harbour works for the Brazilian Government, the Buenos Aires Port extension for the Argentine Government, and the Transandine Railway from Chile to Argentina. Perks retired from Walker & Co. in 1912. In the same year he joined the firm of Macarthur, Perks & Company, which was responsible for large contracts in the Americas. Perks was Chairman of the Metropolitan District Railway during its conversion from steam to electric power (1902–6). He was Liberal MP for Louth Division (1892–1910) and founded the Nonconformist Parliamentary Committee. Perks organised the Methodist 'Million Guinea' Fund (otherwise known as the Wesleyan Methodist Twentieth Century Fund) in 1898. The purpose of this appeal ('one million guineas from one million Methodists') was partly to further develop Wesleyan Methodism, and partly to build a great memorial hall in London to mark the centenary of John Wesley's death (which had fallen in 1891). This resulted in the construction of Central Hall, Westminster, designed by Lanchester and Rickards and completed in 1911. Perks also worked successfully for Methodist union.

Further to the left of this grave, on the edge of the parking area, is a Celtic cross memorial with kerbing.

2.4. General Sir Torquhil George Matheson, 5th Baronet of Lochalsh (1871–1963) [plot 2]

Matheson served in the Coldstream Guards (1894–1919) in the South African War (1899–1902) and the First World War. He commanded the Waziristan force (1920–4). Matheson was General Officer Commander-in-Chief of the Western Command, India (1931–5). He retired in 1935. Matheson married **Lady Elizabeth Keppel** (1890–1986) in 1923. She was the only daughter of the 8th Earl of Albemarle, and niece of Mrs George Keppel, mistress of the Prince of Wales (later King Edward VII). She was a Lady of the Royal Red Cross and served as a Voluntary Aid Detachment nurse during the First World War.

Among the trees to the right of this grave is the next statue memorial.

2.5. Elaine Maynard Falkiner, née Farmer (1871–1900) [plot 2]

Largely hidden by trees, this large plot includes a splendid statue commemorating the first wife of Sir Leslie Falkiner (1866–1917).[14] Elaine, who was born in South Africa, married Sir Leslie in 1894. During the Boer War (1899–1902) her parents' house at Maynardville, Wynberg, was turned into a soldiers' hospital. Both Sir Leslie and Elaine assisted in its administration. She died in London on 28 December 1900 of 'enteric fever, 21 days'. Elaine was buried in a 'brick grave worked in cement £10 10s 0d' set within an enormous plot measuring 66ft × 26ft, which cost £858 for the land alone. The plot is enclosed by kerbing which used to support a cast-iron railing which surrounded this enclosure. Elaine's magnificent memorial statue, which is a life-size likeness, depicts her in Grecian dress. Note the attention to detail in the carving: the rose she holds in her left hand, the bracelet which includes a Star of David motif, the style of her hair and the folds of her dress. The inscription below the figure includes the line 'The silver cord was broken and her spirit returned to God who gave it.'[15] She is buried with her mother, **Anna Maria de Lorentz Farmer** (1842–1927), and her brother, **Henry H. Farmer** (c. 1882–1944).[16]

The statue suffered from brutal vandalism in May 1995, when it was forcibly removed from its pedestal. This resulted in damage to the left hand and rose. The Brookwood Cemetery Society successfully arranged for it to be restored and repaired, with the work being completed in October 1996 by Peter Sleath. The statue has been recommended for statutory listing by Woking Borough Council.

Beyond the grave of Elaine Falkiner is a large upright memorial in pink granite. It is located beneath the next redwood tree.

2.6. Dr Gottlieb William Leitner (1840–1899) [plot 2]

Leitner was responsible for making Woking a major centre for Islam. He was a noted linguist, being acquainted with over fifty languages and reputedly fluent in all of them. Leitner was lecturer in Arabic, Turkish and Modern Greek (1859–61), then Professor of Arabic (1861–4) and subsequently Fellow at King's College, London (1864–99); he founded the oriental section at the college. He became Principal of the Government college at Lahore and raised its status to that of a university in 1883. Leitner was appointed its first Registrar. He started six journals in English, Arabic and Urdu, one of which had the young Rudyard Kipling as assistant editor. During his many trips to India and elsewhere he founded over eighty institutions, mainly schools, literary associations and libraries. In 1881 he began to search for a suitable site for an

Oriental Institute in Europe, and eventually settled on the vacant **Royal Dramatic College** near Woking (1884). By the late 1890s Woking's Oriental Institute was awarding degrees under the auspices of the University of Lahore. Shah Jehan of Bhopal gave funds for the construction of a mosque, which was built in the grounds of the Oriental Institute and was completed in 1889. Leitner was co-editor of the *Arabic Quarterly Review*, published by the Oriental Institute in 1889. Leitner fell ill in late 1898 and died the following March in Bonn. The Oriental Institute closed for ever in the summer of 1899 and its priceless collections and artefacts were dispersed and sold.[17] Had the Institute survived, Woking would have become Surrey's first university town. The mosque closed along with the Institute, and remained deserted until 1912. Leitner's fine memorial includes a bust surrounded by the legend 'The learned are honoured in their work.' This memorial has been recommended for statutory listing by Woking Borough Council.

The next headstone memorial is immediately to the right.

2.7. Mieczyslaw Lubelski (1886–1965) [plot 2]

Polish sculptor. Born in Warsaw, Lubelski studied art at the Warsaw Academy (under Professor Dunikowski) and at the Imperial Academy of Fine Art, Berlin (1911–14), where he was awarded the silver medal. Lubelski was responsible for a number of major works in Poland between the two world wars. These include the Lancers' monument, Poznan; a monument to Kosciuszko in Lodz, which was destroyed during the Second World War but rebuilt afterwards under Lubelski's direction; and many decorative works in Warsaw. He moved to England in 1945. Lubelski designed and erected the Polish Air Force Memorial at Northolt (unveiled in 1948). He was awarded the Polish Air Force medal in 1949. His headstone includes a rendering of the Black Madonna of Warsaw at the top.

The next two memorials are closer to St Cyprian's Avenue. The first is a small obelisk in pink granite.

2.8. Captain Arthur Wilson Kilgour (*c.* 1892–1917) [plot 2]

Kilgour was an instructor-pilot based at Dover with No. 62 Training Squadron. He crashed while demonstrating aerobatics to a pupil in an Avro 504J trainer. Kilgour was admitted to Deal Road Hospital but was found to be dead on arrival; his pupil was luckier and survived, although badly injured. Kilgour was a Canadian and came from Toronto. He had married an English girl from St Margaret's Bay, a village near the airfield at Dover.

Immediately adjacent is a grey granite cross with a plaque set into the grave.

2.9. 2nd Lieutenant Francis Cyril Brooks (*c.* 1898–1917) [plot 2]

Brooks was a resident of Camberley. He joined the Royal Field Artillery in 1915 but later transferred to the Royal Flying Corps. Brooks was killed while flying a DH5 fighter of No. 45 Training Squadron at South Carlton airfield near the city of Lincoln. The aircraft's engine failed during take-off and Brooks made the classic mistake of turning back to try to reach the airfield instead of landing straight ahead into the wind. The aircraft stalled and spun into the ground, killing the pilot instantly.

At the extreme edge of this section and facing St Jude's Avenue is a low Celtic cross memorial in grey granite.

2.10. Colonel Edmund Baron Hartley, VC (1847–1919) [plot 2]

Hartley was born at Ivybridge, Devon, and educated privately and at St George's Hospital, London. He was a clerk in the Inland Revenue (1867–9), District Surgeon in Basutoland

(1874–7) and then moved to the Cape Colonial Forces. Hartley was Principal Medical Officer of the Cape Colonial Forces (1877–1903) and Principal Medical Officer of the Cape Mounted Riflemen. He was awarded the VC for conspicuous gallantry in attending the wounded under fire during the unsuccessful attack on Morosi's Mountain in Basutoland on 5 June 1879, and for having proceeded into the open ground under heavy fire and carried a wounded corporal to safety. He also saw active service in Tembuland and Basutoland (1880–1), Bechuanaland (1897) and South Africa (1899–1902).

Cross St Jude's Avenue into plot 3. The next grave has a cast-iron railing surrounding it.

2.11. Sir Alexander Palmer Bruce Chichester, 2nd Baronet (1842–1881) [plot 3]

Chichester succeeded to the title as a minor in 1851. He was a magistrate, a Captain in the North Devon Yeomanry and High Sheriff of Devon. Chichester's family seat was Arlington Court, near Barnstaple. This was not a large stately home, but a family house that was used and enjoyed by generations of the family. In 1851 the house was a simple Regency design; in 1864 Chichester added a servants' wing and made several changes within the main part of the house. He was a great yachtsman, owned the schooners *Zoe* and *Ermina*, and was a member of the Royal Yacht Squadron. During a cruise on the latter in the Mediterranean, Chichester contracted 'Maltese fever', from which he never fully recovered. There is a wall memorial to Chichester and his wife in the church of St James, adjacent to Arlington Court. His only child, Rosalie Chichester, took over the running of the estate after **Lady Rosalie Amelia Chichester** (*c.* 1843–1908, and also buried here) remarried in 1883. Rosalie remained in charge of Arlington Court until her death in 1949, when the house and the estate passed to the National Trust.

Beside St Cyprian's Avenue is a family mausoleum.

2.12. Montagu-Winch family mausoleum [plot 3]

This structure contains the body of **Henry Lewis William Winch** (*c.* 1882–1905). He was the son of Mr R. Winch of North Myons Park, Hatfield. Winch was the prospective Unionist candidate for South Norfolk and had recently married a daughter of the late **Captain Montagu**. Winch was killed in a motor car accident at Hook, Hampshire. On 10 August 1905 an obstacle obscured his view of the road and his car ran into the Crooked Billet Inn at Hook. The car overturned and Winch was pinned beneath it with a fractured skull. He subsequently died in hospital on 29 August. Winch appears to have been buried in a brick grave, perhaps until this mausoleum was completed. Also buried here is **Captain Philip Montagu** (*c.* 1852–98), presumed to be his father-in-law. Montagu was a Captain in the 12th Lancers. His coffin was subsequently placed here from its original brick grave situated in St Chad's Avenue.

Beyond the bank of rhododendrons towards the centre of this plot is a cross memorial set within a large kerbed grave.

2.13. Major Matthew Fontaine Maury Meiklejohn, VC (1870–1913) [plot 3]

Meiklejohn served with the Gordon Highlanders from 1891, and with the Chitral Relief Force (1895) and the Tirah Expedition (1897). He was promoted to Captain in 1899 and served in the South African War (1899–1902). Meiklejohn was awarded his VC on 21 October 1899 at the Battle of Elandslaagte. After the main Boer position had been captured some of the Gordon Highlanders were about to assault a kopje but were exposed to heavy fire. Meiklejohn rushed to the front and called on the Gordons to follow him. He rallied his men and led them against the enemy position where he fell, badly wounded. His right arm was amputated owing to the severity of his wounds. Meiklejohn was killed in Hyde Park when his horse was frightened by the salute during an OTC inspection. His horse galloped away towards some children. To avoid them he turned the horse against the railings of Rotten Row. Meiklejohn was thrown off and never regained consciousness. *The Times* reported that 'He thus gave his life for theirs and added one more to the long roll of his brave and unselfish acts.' A plaque was placed on the wall of Knightsbridge Barracks with details of the incident along with the words 'He gave his life to save others.'

Fronting St Cyprian's Avenue is a large private allotment with a splendid bronze angel.

2.14. Sir Ernest William Moir (1862–1933) [plot 3]

Civil engineer. Moir's works include the construction of the southern cantilevers of the Forth Bridge, the Hudson River tunnel, Blackwall Tunnel, the Surrey Commercial Docks, Seaham harbour, the Admiralty harbour, Dover, and Valparaiso harbour. During the First World War Moir served on the Council of the Ministry of Munitions. Lloyd George described him as 'a man of exceptional ability and tact'. Initially Moir was responsible to Eric Geddes[18] for machine gun production.[19] Later Lloyd George appointed Moir to the Inventions Department of the Ministry of Munitions. Announcing this appointment in the House of Commons on 28 July 1915, Lloyd George stated that:

I have appointed Mr E.W. Moir, a distinguished engineer who has already given valuable assistance to my department on a voluntary basis, to take charge of the new branch, and he will not only have an expert staff, but also a panel of scientific consultants on technical and scientific points.

But Moir soon discovered that the War Office was unwilling to cooperate fully with the Ministry. He wrote to Lloyd George about this in October 1915. Lloyd George reprinted his letter in full in his *War Memoirs*, using it as evidence of the difficulties that he was facing as Minister of Munitions.[20]

2nd Lieutenant Reginald (Rex) Moir (1898–1915), his son, is commemorated by a fine profile portrait in bronze. He was expecting to qualify as an engineer on the outbreak of war in 1914. Rex joined the Army instead. In 1915 he contracted meningitis and died in the Officers' Hospital, Park Lane. His epitaph records:

We dreamed great things for you
God intervened
And so the dreams came true.

The fine angel sculpture that surmounts the pedestal is by Lillian Wade. This memorial has been recommended for statutory listing by Woking Borough Council.

Turn left into St Mary's Avenue. The next Calvary cross memorial is before a family mausoleum.

2.15. Sir Charles Sargent (1821–1900) [plot 3]

Judge. Sargent was educated at King's College, London, and Trinity College, Cambridge. He was a Fellow of Trinity (1845–54). Sargent became a barrister at Lincoln's Inn in 1848. He was appointed a member of the Supreme Council of Justice of the Ionian Islands (1858–60) and was subsequently Chief Justice of the Ionian Islands (1860–6). Sargent became Puisne Judge of the High Court of Bombay (1866–82), and was Chief Justice of the High Court of Bombay (1882–95). He retired in 1895.

2.16. Gwinner Family Mausoleum [plot 3]

This mausoleum is identifiable by the initials H.E.G. carved over the door. It was built on a plot measuring 19ft × 12ft, which cost £119 14s 0d. It contains three members of this family who were removed here from the catacombs at Kensal Green Cemetery on 16 April 1920: **Rupert Gwinner** (died 1904 aged just 3 weeks), **Herman George Gwinner** (c. 1863–1907) and **Harry Ernest Gwinner** (c. 1866–1918), whose initials are carved above the door. In addition the ashes of **Muriel Beatrice Maud Gwinner** (died 1957) were later placed in the mausoleum. Immediately to the right of **Lieutenant-Colonel Frederick**'s grave is that of **Christopher Gwinner** (1937–91).

On the other side of the mausoleum is the next grave.

2.17. Lieutenant-Colonel Charles Arthur Frederick (1861–1913) [plot 3]

Frederick entered the Army in 1881 and served in the Sudan (1885). He was subsequently promoted to Captain (1891), Major (1898) and Lieutenant-Colonel of the Coldstream Guards (1903). He was appointed Deputy Master of the King's Household (1901–7), and Extra Equerry to King Edward VII (1902–10). In 1907 Frederick succeeded Lord Farquhar[21] as Master of the King's Household and he continued in this post until the King's death in 1910. King George V reappointed him Master of the King's Household in 1910. Because of failing health, caused by heart failure, he retired from this post in January 1913 and was succeeded by Sir Derek Keppel.[22] Frederick was created GCVO (1910) and KCB (1911). By express permission of King George V the first part of his funeral service took part in the Chapel Royal, St James' Palace, on Christmas Eve 1913. The King and Queen and other members of the royal family were represented at the service, which was led by Canon Edgar Sheppard, Sub-Dean of the Chapels Royal. Queen Alexandra sent a wreath with the following inscription written in her own hand: 'With deepest regret and sorrow, to our dear and devoted and never-to-be-forgotten friend Sir Charles Frederick, from Alexandra. Rest in peace.'

Cross over into plot 4. Look for the reddish stone cross memorial that faces St Mary's Avenue.

2.18. Dr John Lowe (1830–1902) [plot 4]

Lowe was born at the Old Place, Sleaford. He graduated from Edinburgh University and began to practise medicine in King's Lynn. Lowe was a skilled surgeon and was an early advocate of antiseptic treatment. He had become medical attendant to the Prince of Wales in 1871 and, together with Sir William Gull[23] and Dr William Jenner,[24] attended the Prince during his almost fatal attack of typhoid fever. Lowe was subsequently appointed Physician Extraordinary to King Edward VII. He was a keen scientific student and was especially interested in botany. Lowe wrote a considerable number of papers for scientific societies, and was the author of *Yew-Trees of Great Britain and Ireland* (London, Macmillan, 1897). He died at Oatlands Wood, Weybridge.

Further into the plot is a low greenish headstone.

2.19. Sydney Charles Houghton (Sammy) Davis (1887–1981) [plot 4]

Davis was actively involved in motor racing from 1919 to 1939, and for a short period after 1945. He was one of the most successful British all-round drivers, and first raced at Brooklands in 1921. His racing career effectively ended at Brooklands in 1931 after a serious accident in his 1½ litre Invicta. Although he continued to drive, Davis was able to devote more time to his equally successful career as a motoring journalist. Using the pen name Casque, he wrote every week for *The Autocar* right up until the 1950s, when he retired. He wrote a fascinating memoir of his racing days, *Motor Racing* (London, Iliffe & Sons, 1932); he later compiled *Memories of Men and Motor Cars* (London, Seeley, 1965). Davis was a fine engineer, having served his apprenticeship with Daimler. He was also an accomplished artist.

The next memorial is a Calvary cross with kerbing. It is nearer the main avenue.

2.20. Captain David Skinner Miller (1874–1909) [plot 4]

Miller was the only son of Mr D.S. Miller of The Hermitage, Troon, Ayrshire. He obtained a commission in the Gordon Highlanders in 1900 and served on the staff in the South African War (1900–2). Miller took part in the operations in the Transvaal, east of Pretoria, from July to November 1900. This included the actions at Belfast and Lydenberg. He also served on the staff in the Somaliland Campaign (1902–4), when he was employed as a Special Service Officer. Miller led the advance guard across the desert from Galadi to Bohottle in twenty-nine days, and was mentioned in dispatches.

Cross over St Cyprian's Avenue and find the modern mausoleum in plot 19.

2.21. Mauroux family mausoleum [plot 19]

This modern mausoleum is a striking contrast with the nineteenth- and early twentieth-century examples in this guide. Constructed of white marble, it contains the body of **Yvonne Mauroux** (*c*. 1913–82).

Further to the left is a line of six Calvary crosses facing the road.

2.22. Baronets Locock [plot 19]

Sir Charles Brodie Locock (1827–90), 2nd Baronet, was the eldest son of Sir Charles Locock, 1st Baronet, the eminent physician. Locock was educated at Trinity College, Cambridge, and was called to the Bar at Lincoln's Inn in 1853. He practised as an equity draftsman and conveyancer. His son, **Sir Charles Bird Locock** (1878–1965), 3rd Baronet, is also buried here.

At the end of plot 19 is another mausoleum.

2.23. Hughes family mausoleum [plot 19]

Largely obscured by the trees surrounding it is this fine family mausoleum made of polished pink granite. It is the only one in Egyptian style within the cemetery, with its lotus motifs flanking the doorway. The site was selected in 1907 and the ground alone cost £300. Buried within are the ashes of **Rosalind Ormond Hughes** (*c*. 1868–1907), **Sybil Ormonde Bell** (*c*. 1878–1911), **John Hughes** (*c*. 1844–1934) and **Major Otto Joseph Bell** (*c*. 1868–1939).

Cross over into plot 4 and look for a large family allotment with two lines of four headstones.

2.24. Rawlinson family grave [plot 4]

Sir Christopher Rawlinson (1806–88) was an Indian judge. He was educated at Charterhouse and Trinity College, Cambridge. He was called to the Bar at the Middle Temple in 1831 and worked on the Western Circuit. Rawlinson was Recorder of Portsmouth (1840–7) and Recorder of Prince of Wales Island, Singapore, and of Malacca (1847–50). He was appointed Chief Justice of the Supreme Court of Judicature at Madras in 1850 and retired in 1859. Rawlinson was the author of *Municipal Corporation Act 5 & 6 Will.IV.cap.76, and Acts Since*

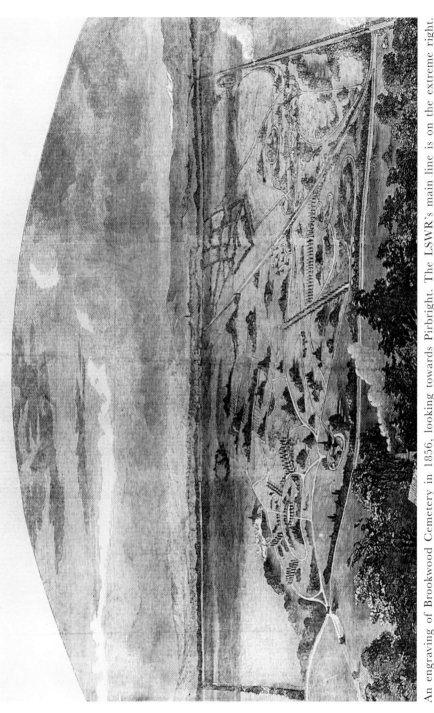

An engraving of Brookwood Cemetery in 1856, looking towards Pirbright. The LSWR's main line is on the extreme right. The Guildford–Bagshot road (now the A322) is in the foreground, and shows the original wooden fence or paling. *(Reproduced by permission of Surrey History Service)*

View of the Nonconformist section from Pine Avenue, early 1890s. Note the Nonconformist chapel on Chapel Hill, North station immediately below, and the roof of the Superintendent's office on the extreme right. *(Author's collection)*

THE LONDON NECROPOLIS, Brookwood Cemetery, Woking.

Telegrams: Tenebratio, London.

INCORPORATED BY SPECIAL ACT OF PARLIAMENT, 1852.

Telephone 839 Hop.

CHARGES AND FEES.

PRIVATE GRAVES.

* Private Grave in Perpetuity, 9 feet by 4 feet, including Conveyance of Body from the "Necropolis" Private Station, Westminster Bridge Road, Funeral Service and Interment .. £2 10 0 .. Subsequent Interments £2 2 0
* Ditto, Children .. .. 2 10 0 .. Do. do. 1 10 0
* Special Positions .. .. from £5 5 0 to 52 10 0 .. Do. do. 4 4 0

SECOND-CLASS GRAVE.

Grave space, including Conveyance of Body from the "Necropolis" Private Station, Westminster Bridge Road, Funeral Service and
Interment .. .. £1 0 0 .. Subsequent Interments £1 0 0
Children under 10 years of age .. .. 0 15 0 .. Do. do. 0 15 0
Privilege of placing Head and Foot Stones .. .. 10/- extra.

In case of the Erection of a Monument or Enclosure of Allotment, a margin of not less than 9 inches must be left on every side, thus only 7 feet 6 inches by 2 feet 6 inches may be enclosed of an ordinary grave space 9 feet by 4 feet.
The Cemetery is accessible in forty minutes by Special Train from the Westminster Bridge Road Station, or by the South-Western Railway to Brookwood, which station is at the Entrance to THE NECROPOLIS.

PRIVATE VAULTS.

	Area of Ground.	PURCHASE OF GROUND.		Brick Work, with York Landing.	Fees on Subsequent Interments.
		Special Positions.	Other Parts.		
		Per Foot.	£ s. d.	£ s. d.	£ s. d.
* Private Vault for Two Coffins ..	9 ft. × 6 ft.	5/- to 25/-	10 10 0	17 0 0	7 7 0
* Private Vault for Six Coffins ..	9 ft. × 9 ft.	5/- to 25/-	15 15 0	30 0 0	7 7 0
* Private Vault for Twelve Coffins ..	9 ft. × 9 ft.	5/- to 25/-	15 15 0	40 0 0	7 7 0

BRICK GRAVES.

	Area of Ground.	PURCHASE OF GROUND.		Brick Work, including Stone.	Fees on Subsequent Interments.
		Special Positions.	Other Parts.		
		Per Foot.	£ s. d.	£ s. d.	£ s. d.
* Single Grave for One Coffin ..	9 ft. × 5 ft.	5/- to 25/-	7 7 0	5 5 0	4 4 0
* Single Grave for Two Coffins ..	9 ft. × 5 ft.	5/- to 25/-	7 7 0	7 7 0	4 4 0
* Single Grave for Four Coffins ..	9 ft. × 5 ft.	5/- to 25/-	7 7 0	13 13 0	4 4 0
* Single Grave for Six Coffins ..	9 ft. × 5 ft.	5/- to 25/-	7 7 0	15 15 0	4 4 0
* Double Grave for Two Coffins ..	9 ft. × 7 ft.	5/- to 25/-	12 12 0	7 7 0	4 4 0
* Double Grave for Four Coffins ..	9 ft. × 7 ft.	5/- to 25/-	12 12 0	10 10 0	4 4 0
* Double Grave for Six Coffins ..	9 ft. × 7 ft.	5/- to 25/-	12 12 0	15 5 0	4 4 0

EXTRA DEPTH OF GRAVES.

From 6 to 10 feet .. .. £0 1 6 per foot. | From 14 to 17 feet .. .. £0 3 0 per foot.
„ 10 „ 14 „ .. .. 0 2 6 „ | „ 17 „ 20 „ .. .. 0 5 0 „

RETURN FARES TO BROOKWOOD *(per Necropolis Private Train).*

First-Class, Return .. .. 6/- | Second-Class, Return .. .. 3 6 | Third-Class, Return 2/-

ADDITIONAL CHARGES.

Consecration Fee .. .. £0 6 2 | Entry of Grant (Stamp Duty *Ad Val.*) £0 2 6
Turfing Grave, 9 ft. × 4 ft. .. .. .. 0 2 6 | Use of Shelter 0 10 6
Keeping Turf cut and in good order, 9 ft. × 4 ft., per annum 0 10 6 | Use of Tent for 25 persons 2 2 0
Ditto ditto and maintenance in perpetuity .. 10 10 0 | Certificate of Burial 0 2 7
Planting Grave with Spring Flowers .. .. 0 10 6 | Comparing and searching Register, one year .. 0 1 0
Planting, Turfing and Maintenance in perpetuity 9ft.×4ft. 21 0 0 | Ditto, every additional year 0 0 6
Lining Grave with evergreens .. .. .. 1 1 0 | Removing and Replacing Monuments and Grave { *According to*
Lining Grave with evergreens and flowers .. 2 2 0 | Stones .. .. { *Assessed Charge.*

Over which a Monument or Grave Stone, of a design to be approved by the Company, must be erected within 12 months.

OFFICES:—188, Westminster Bridge Road, S.E. ; 2, Lancaster Place, Strand.

16

WERTHEIMER, LEA & CO., PRINTERS, LONDON.

LNC scale of charges and fees, 1899. *(Author's collection)*

Lord Sherbrooke's grave, plot 31, *c.* 1906. Visible to the left are the graves of Susan Messiter (died 1900) and Lieutenant-Colonel Henry Sweet (died 1893) (3.51). *(Brian Parsons collection)*

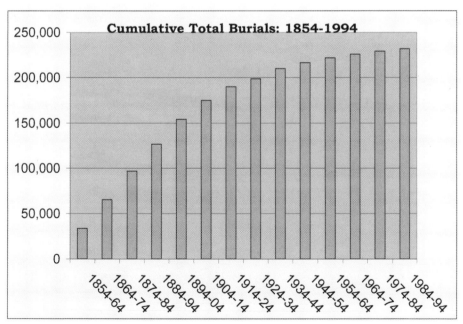

Graph showing the cumulative total burials in Brookwood Cemetery between 1854 and 1994. This shows that half the total burials had taken place by 1891 and three-quarters by 1914.

The original masonry showroom in the mid-1890s. Located near the Superintendent's office, it was opened in 1889 (7.2). *(Author's collection)*

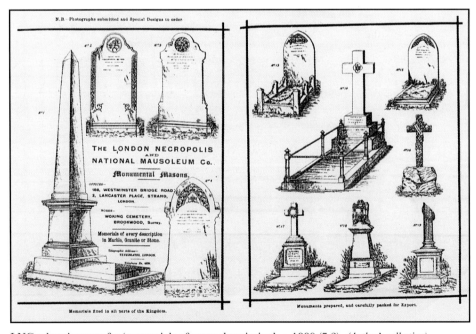

LNC advertisement for 'memorials of every description', *c.* 1889 (7.2). *(Author's collection)*

Brochure advertising the Columbarium, *c*. 1910. Originally constructed in about 1878–80 for Lord Cadogan, he sold it back to the LNC in 1910. Note that the lettering for 'Columbarium' has yet to be carved in the stone panel over the entrance (4.1). *(Author's collection)*

THE COLUMBARIUM,
BROOKWOOD CEMETERY.

PURCHASE OF NICHE.

A Niche may be purchased in this Columbarium in perpetuity from 7 guineas according to size and position.

INTERMENT AT BROOKWOOD CEMETERY.

Brookwood Cemetery is also an appropriate spot for interment of Urns. A Site in this lovely Cemetery, situated "Midst Surrey Pines," can be obtained from £5 5s. 0d.

The "Times" says: "No more beautiful spot could be selected"

The funeral train proceeding through the Anglican section, July 1938. Note the line is on a slight embankment, edged with laurel. *(Author's collection)*

The dedication of the Glades of Remembrance, 11 May 1950. The Bishop of Guildford leads the service by the 'pool of serenity' (6.1). *(Brian Parsons collection)*

The Brookwood Memorial, designed by Ralph Hobday and dedicated by HM the Queen on 25 October 1958 (9.14). *(J.P.A. Mullinger collection)*

The former Anglican chapels. The original chapel, designed by Sydney Smirke, is in the background. The larger chapel, designed by Cyril Tubbs and Arthur Messer, is now the church dedicated to St Edward the Martyr (1.1). *(Courtesy of the St Edward Brotherhood)*

South station, designed by Sydney Smirke, looking towards Cemetery Pales, *c.* 1904. Note how close the chapel is to the station. The building in the middle distance is the Keith family mausoleum of *c.* 1890 (1.1). *(Author's collection)*

An engraved view of the cemetery showing the Anglican chapel and the Bent family memorial, *c.* 1880. It appears to be drawn from St Mark's Avenue, by the Ring (plot 35). Part of South station may be seen beside the chapel. *(Author's collection)*

Glorney family mausoleum, plot 76, 1980. Massively constructed of rusticated Cornish granite, it was built in about 1934–5 (1.3). *(Author's collection)*

Braine family mausoleum, plot 74, 1979. It was constructed by the LNC in Portland stone, with a green pantiled roof, in about 1934–5. In this view the 1930s-style bronze door is intact (1.5). *(Author's collection)*

Isabella Hirst Knight (died 1891), plot 73. This is the first memorial at Brookwood to record that the deceased was cremated (1.9). *(Anthony Montan)*

The Masonry Works siding, *c.* 1910. This view is taken looking towards Cemetery Pales. The connection to the cemetery branch was to the right of the photograph (1.17). *(Author's collection)*

Inside the Masonry Works, *c.* 1950. Note the use of rails and trolleys to move stone through the workshops and from the yard outside. A substantial Celtic cross memorial awaits completion on the left (1.17). *(Author's collection)*

Right: Greenfield family mausoleum, plot 80, 1979. It was constructed in 1891 by Mr Whitehead (1.25). *(Author's collection)*

Far right: Henri van Laun (died 1896), plot 80. Designed by Emmeline Halse, this unusual memorial is made almost entirely of terracotta (1.27). *(Anthony Montan)*

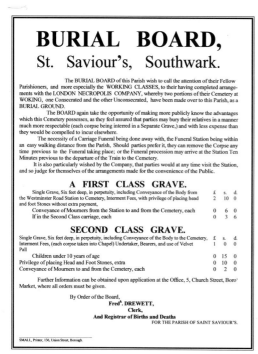

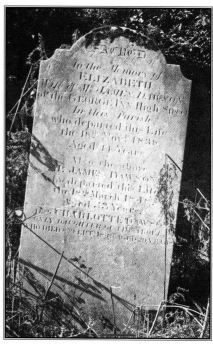

Above left: Facsimile of an advertisement produced by the St Saviour's Burial Board (1.38). *(Author's collection)*

Above right: James Dawson (died 1848), plot 90. One of several memorials that pre-date the opening of the cemetery in 1854 (1.38). *(Anthony Montan)*

2nd Lieutenant Rupert Price Hallowes, VC, MC (died 1915), plot 84. This is an example of a family adding a personal tribute on their own memorial. Hallowes is not buried here but in the Bedford House Cemetery, Zillebeke, Belgium (1.54). *(Anthony Montan)*

Right: Lieutenant-Colonel John Sherwood-Kelly, VC, CMG, DSO (died 1931), plot 81. The headstone incorporates his regimental badge and the Victoria Cross (1.60). *(Anthony Montan)*

Below: Gottlieb William Leitner (died 1899), plot 2. The founder of Woking's Oriental Institute and Mosque (2.6). *(Anthony Montan)*

Above: Elaine Maynard Falkiner (died 1900), plot 2. Vandalised in 1995, this was the first major restoration project undertaken by the Brookwood Cemetery Society (2.5). *(Sian Barber collection)*

Above: Montagu-Winch mausoleum, plot 3. Constructed in about 1906 for Captain Philip Montagu (died 1898) and Henry Lewis William Winch (died 1905) (2.12). *(Anthony Montan)*

Right: Moir family memorial, plot 3. The sculpture and profile portrait are by Lillian Wade (2.14). *(Sian Barber collection)*

Below: Major Matthew Fountaine Maury Meiklejohn, VC (died 1913), plot 3, *c.* 1914. This photograph shows the semi-wooded nature of this part of the cemetery at the beginning of the First World War (2.13). *(Lyndon Davies, Past Images collection)*

Gwinner family mausoleum, plot 3. Built in about 1919–20 for the reception of three members of the Gwinner family previously buried in the catacombs at Kensal Green Cemetery (2.16). *(Anthony Montan)*

Mauroux family mausoleum, plot 19. Built in about 1982, this is a striking example of a modern mausoleum at Brookwood (2.21). *(Anthony Montan)*

St Cyprian's Avenue, *c.* 1907. This postcard view looks towards the Anglican chapel and South station, near the junction with St George's Avenue (which can be seen beside the Normand family mausoleum to the right of the picture). *(J.P.A. Mullinger collection)*

Above left: Hughes family mausoleum, plot 19. This small mausoleum is constructed of polished pink granite in the Egyptian style. It contains only cinerary urns (2.23). *(Anthony Montan)*

Above right: Elaine Susan Brooks (died 1997), plot 4. A superb example of modern memorial design and craftsmanship, carved from Borrowdale volcanic stone. The reverse face (illustrated here) is visible from St Cyprian's Avenue (2.25). *(Anthony Montan)*

Sir John Wolfe Barry (died 1918), plot 4. The low laurel hedge behind the cross camouflages the route of the cemetery railway (2.28). *(Lyndon Davies, Past Images collection)*

Pelham-Clinton memorial, plot 4, *c.* 1900. This monument, with its magnificent bronze statuary, is probably the most important within Brookwood Cemetery. Note the original Anglican chapel; the second chapel is not yet built (2.30). *(Reproduced by permission of Surrey History Service)*

Keith family mausoleum, plot 4, 1981. This gothic-style mausoleum was completed *c.* 1890 and featured fine tracery and stained-glass windows. A curious feature about this mausoleum is that it faced the cemetery railway (2.32). *(Arthur Casey collection)*

Giulio Salviati (died 1898), plot 25. Another striking memorial with four separate mosaic panels forming the base to the monument, typical work of this famous Italian family of mosaic designers. The kneeling angel figure is an Italian imported design (2.37). *(Anthony Montan)*

Normand family mausoleum, plot 25, 1991. Another compact mausoleum adjacent to the junction with St George's Avenue. All the members of the family buried here were cremated. Part of the bronze doors can be seen in this photograph. Flanking the front of the mausoleum are two small *stelae*; the right-hand one commemorates the artists Ernest Normand (died 1923) and his wife Henrietta Rae (died 1928) (2.43). *(Author's collection)*

Passed for Amending the Same (London, 1842; it went through eight editions in his lifetime). The book is a commentary on the Municipal Corporation Act (1835), the first major reform of city and town government in this country.

The Rt Hon. John Frederick Peel Rawlinson (1860–1926) was his third and youngest son. Rawlinson was educated at Eton and Trinity College, Cambridge. He was called to the Bar at the Inner Temple in 1884, and worked on the South-Eastern Circuit. He represented the Treasury in the South African inquiry into the circumstances of the Jameson Raid (1896). Rawlinson became a QC in 1897. He was Recorder of Cambridge from 1898, Commissary of the University from 1900 and Deputy High Steward of the University from 1918 until his death. Rawlinson was Conservative MP for Cambridge University (1906–26). From 1916 he was one of the temporary Chairmen of Committees of the whole House, and was made a Privy Councillor in 1923. By the 1920s Rawlinson was one of very few MPs who adhered to the tradition of wearing a frock coat and top hat, and this, with his great height, made him a conspicuous figure in Parliament. He never married. Rawlinson edited the ninth and tenth editions of *The Municipal Corporations Acts and Other Enactments* (London, Sweet & Maxwell, 1903 and 1910). He died suddenly in his chambers in Crown Office Row, Temple. At the same time as his funeral at Brookwood a memorial service was held at Great St Mary's Church, Cambridge. On the following day a further memorial service was held at the Temple Church, at which the Master of the Temple officiated.

Edith Constance May Rawlinson, Countess Annesley (1897–1950) was the only daughter of **Major Albemarle Alexander Rawlinson** (1853–1930). She married Beresford Cecil Bingham, 8th Earl Annesley (1894–1957) in 1921, but they were divorced in 1940.

Behind this, near the back of the plot, is a striking modern slate headstone.

2.25. Elaine Susan Brooks (1953–1997) [plot 4]

This is a superb example of modern design and craftsmanship in the cemetery. The reverse of this headstone, made from slate and seen first approaching from St Cyprian's Avenue, depicts an angel figure. The angel's 'body' includes the following verse:

> May the choirs of angels come to greet you
> May they speed you to paradise
> May the Lord enfold you in his mercy
> May you find eternal life.

The memorial celebrates the life of Elaine Brooks, 'teacher, wife, mother'.

Diagonally in front of this is a wide kerbed plot with an unusual tall cross.

2.26. Edward Lewes Cutts (1824–1901) [plot 4]

Antiquary. Cutts was born in Sheffield and educated at the Sheffield Collegiate School and Queen's College, Cambridge. He was ordained in 1848 and was Curate of Ide Hill, Kent (1848–50), Coggeshall, Essex (1850–7), Kelvedon (1857–9) and of Billericay (1859–65). On leaving Billericay he became General Secretary of the Additional Curates Society in London (1865–71). In 1876 he was appointed to report on the state of the Syrian and Chaldean Churches, resulting in the Archbishops' Mission to the Assyrian Christians. Cutts later described these travels in his *Christians Under the Crescent in Asia* (London, SPCK, 1877). Cutts was also interested in archaeology and ecclesiastical history, and published many books on these topics. They include *A Manual for the Study of the Sepulchral Slabs and Crosses of the Middle Ages* (London,

J.H. Parker, 1849), *Colchester Castle not a Roman Temple* (London, George Bell, 1853), *A Dictionary of the Church of England* (London, SPCK, 1887), and *Colchester* (London, Longmans Green, 1888, in the 'Historic Towns' series).

Directly in front of this, and backing into a large rhododendron, is a Calvary cross with kerbing.

2.27. John Humffreys Parry (1816–1880) [plot 4]

Serjeant-at-law. Parry spent a short time in business before accepting a post in the department of printed books at the British Museum. He was engaged on the new catalogue (1839–43). While there he studied for the Bar, and joined the Middle Temple in 1843. He worked on the Home Circuit, largely at the Central Criminal Court and the Middlesex sessions. In 1856 he became serjeant-at-law when he moved into compensation cases, especially for the London Brighton & South Coast Railway. He became a Bencher of the Middle Temple in 1878. His best-known cases included the trial of Franz Muller for the murder of Thomas Briggs (1864),[25] the indictment of Arthur Orton, the Tichbourne Claimant (1873–4),[26] and the case of *Whistler* v. *Ruskin* (1878).[27] An advanced Liberal, Parry knew many of the Chartists, and was one of the founders of the Complete Suffrage Association in 1842. He contested the seats of Norwich (1847) and Finsbury (1857). His second wife, **Elizabeth Mead** (*c.* 1835–80), predeceased him by just a few hours.

Further across the plot, just in front of a redwood, is a large family grave with a fine granite Celtic cross.

2.28. Sir John Wolfe Barry (1836–1918)[28] [plot 4]

Civil engineer. Barry was the fifth and youngest son of Charles Barry, the famous architect who designed the Houses of Parliament. He was educated at Trinity College, Glenalmond, and King's College, London. Barry became a pupil of (Sir) John Hawkshaw[29] and was put in charge of several important undertakings. These included assistant resident engineer of the Charing Cross railway bridge and station, and resident engineer for the Cannon Street railway bridge and station (1865–6). Barry set up his own office in 1867. He specialised in the construction of railways, bridges and harbours. His major works include Earl's Court station and the extension of the Metropolitan District Railway to Ealing and Fulham (1877–80); the Lewes and East Grinstead Railway, part of which is now better known as the Bluebell Railway (1878–83); the completion of the Inner Circle line (1882–5); the subway at South Kensington for the Metropolitan District Railway (1884–5); Blackfriars railway bridge and station (1884–7, with H.M. Brunel), Tower Bridge (1886–94, with Sir Horace Jones); the Surrey Commercial Docks extension, including the Greenland Dock (1895–1906); and the King Edward VII road bridge at Kew (1898–1903, with Cuthbert Bereton). The main part of his funeral service took place in the church of **St Margaret's**, **Westminster**, prior to his burial here at Brookwood. The unusual length of the grave is down to the extension of the original allotment in 1936 when new sections of granite kerbing were added to create the present plot.[30]

His son, **Kenneth Alfred Wolfe Barry** (1879–1937), was educated at Winchester and Trinity College, Cambridge. He was articled to his father's firm and gained experience in civil engineering while working on various railway projects. He became a partner in the firm and was consulting engineer to the Bombay Port Trust, the Aden Port Trust, the Southern Punjab Railway, the Darjeeling & Himalayan Railway, the Bengal–Nagpur Railway, the Kowloon–Canton Railway and many other undertakings including docks.

Continue walking along St Cyprian's Avenue. The next memorial is a granite Celtic cross, located to the right of a cross with an anchor and chain.

2.29. Flying Officer Peter Granville Smith (*c.* 1903–1926) [plot 4]

Smith was a member of the Fleet Air Arm which during the 1920s came under the control of the RAF; therefore he was a Lieutenant in the Royal Navy as well as a Flying Officer in the RAF. He crashed in a Fairey Flycatcher fighter while flying at the Leuchars Training Base in Fifeshire and died the same day in Dundee Hospital.

Just beyond this grave is a splendid sculpture group set within mature conifers.

2.30. Pelham-Clinton memorial [plot 4]

This is probably the most important memorial in the cemetery, and has been recommended for statutory listing by Woking Borough Council. The statue group depicts a grief-stricken man crouching over the corpse of a woman, with one hand cupped behind her head; above them both her angelic form soars heavenwards, wings outspread and her face turned back with an expression of great sympathy. The sculpture is apparently unsigned, but is called *Into the Way of Peace*. It commemorates **Matilda Jane Pelham-Clinton** (1825–92) who was the third daughter of Sir William Cradock Hartopp, 3rd Baronet.[31] She married Lord Edward in 1865 and served in Queen Victoria's personal household.[32] Regrettably the bronze inscription plaque was stolen some years ago, but a partial record of its inscription survives through old photographs:

THY LOVE TO THEE WAS WONDERFUL
PASSING THE LOVE OF ONE
IN LOVING AND EVERLASTING REMEMBRANCE OF
TEEDIE
WIFE OF LORD EDWARD
PELHAM CLINTON
THIRD DAUGHTER OF SIR CRADDOCK HARTOPP
BORN 10 FEBRUARY 1825 DIED 2 AUGUST 1892
THIS MONUMENT WAS ERECTED BY . . .[33]

Lord Edward Pelham-Clinton (1836–1907) was the second son of the 5th Duke of Newcastle. In 1854 he was gazetted as an Ensign in the Duke of Connaught's Own Rifle Brigade. Lord Edward was promoted to Lieutenant in the same year and Captain in 1857. Between 1861 and 1865 he served in Canada. Lord Edward was MP for North Nottinghamshire (1865–8). He was promoted to Major (1872), and retired as Lieutenant-Colonel (1880). Lord Edward commanded the London Rifle Volunteer Brigade (1881–90). He joined Queen Victoria's household as Groom-in-Waiting (1881–94), and succeeded Sir John Cowell[34] as Master of the Queen's Household (1894). Lord Edward was involved with the domestic arrangements for foreign royalty visiting London for the Diamond Jubilee celebrations in 1897. He was at Osborne during the Queen's last illness, and was deeply involved in the arrangements for her funeral. At King Edward VII's express wish he was the only person who was not a member of the royal family present at the private interment of the Queen in the Royal Mausoleum at Frogmore (4 February 1901). During the service the King asked Lord Edward to scatter earth on the Queen's coffin: 'The last, the very last ceremony that can be performed', as Lord Edward recorded afterwards. He remained at court as Groom-in-Waiting to King Edward VII. Lord Edward's country residence was The Heights, Witley, Surrey. He died in London at 31 Eccleston Square on 8 July 1907.

Lord Edward's funeral took place at 3 p.m. on Saturday 13 July 1907. A special train left the Necropolis station in London at 1.50 p.m., returning from Brookwood at 3.55 p.m. The service was led by Canon Morris of St Gabriel's Church, Warwick Square. King Edward VII was represented by General Sir Godfrey Clerk,[35] and the Prince and Princess of Wales by Lieutenant-Colonel the Hon. Sir William Carington.[36] At the same time as his funeral at Brookwood a memorial service was held at St Gabriel's Church. The King and Queen and various members of the royal family sent messages of deep sympathy to his niece, Mrs Farnham.[37]

Almost directly behind the Pelham-Clinton memorial is a small obelisk in pink granite.

2.31. Mabel Piggott (1857–1949) and Eva Price (1860–1949) [plot 4]

The inscription on this memorial merits further study. Part of it reads:

> MABEL WALDRON, WIDOW OF SIR FRANCIS TAYLOR PIGGOTT, BORN JULY 11TH 1857. AND EVA MONTGOMERY, WIDOW OF SIR ROBERT JOHN PRICE, BORN OCTO-BER 17TH 1860. WHO WERE MARRIED TOGETHER ON APRIL 7TH 1881 AND DIED ON THE SAME DAY, MARCH 13TH 1949.

At the edge of the plot, fronting St Andrew's Avenue, is a gothic-style family mausoleum.

2.32. Keith family mausoleum [plot 4]

This gothic-style mausoleum was completed in about 1890, when an allotment of 18ft × 18ft was granted to the family for £140. The design includes Y-tracery stained-glass lancet windows on three elevations (three pairs on each side and one at the rear), and a similar design for the cast-iron door, where the family name also appeared. Those interred within include **Catherine Gertrude Keith** (*c.* 1816–89), widow of Lieutenant Colonel Keith, who was Deputy Adjutant General of the Bombay Army. Also buried here are **Emma Anne Keith** (*c.* 1843–89), and her husband **George Elphinstone Keith** (*c.* 1838–1900). The latter was sometime Sheriff of Calcutta, although other members of his family were doctors, with a successful practice in Mayfair. The family lived for many years in Hans Place, Chelsea.[38]

Locate the junction of St Cyprian's and St David's Avenues. The next headstone has a gable top with a small cross at the top, and faces St David's.

2.33. Alexander family grave [plot 26]

Sir Robert Alexander (1769–1859) was the 2nd Baronet. His son, **Sir William John Alexander**, 3rd Baronet (1797–1873), was a barrister. He was educated at Trinity College, Dublin, and Trinity College, Cambridge. Alexander was called to the Bar at the Middle Temple (1825) and worked on the Oxford Circuit. He was appointed QC (1844) and succeeded as 3rd Baronet (1859). Alexander was made Attorney General to the Prince of Wales in 1853 and was appointed one of the Prince's counsels in 1864. As he was a bachelor, on Alexander's death the baronetcy devolved to his brother, John Wallis Alexander (1812–88).

To the left of this grave is a line of four memorials, two with crosses flanking a pair of headstones.

2.34. Horatia Nelson Johnson (1832–1890) [plot 26]

Granddaughter of Lord Nelson. She married **William Johnson** (1827–91), and for many years they lived in Gower Street, London. Other relatives are buried in the adjacent graves.

Return to St Cyprian's Avenue. The next two memorials are set within a small enclosed allotment that fronts the main path. Both are pedestal memorials, one with an angel, the other with a cross on top.

2.35. Kimber family plot [plot 26]

Sir Henry Kimber, 1st Baronet (1834–1923), was a solicitor. He qualified in 1858 and founded the firm of Kimber & Ellis (later Kimbers, Williams & Co.). Kimber was the founder or reconstructor of several colonial and other undertakings; he enjoyed rescuing or reforming commercial enterprises. He was sometime solicitor to the LNC. Kimber was Vice-Chairman of the Capital & Counties Bank, and Chairman of the South Indian Railway Company. As Conservative MP for Wandsworth (1885–1913), Kimber contested this seat six times and was eight times elected (twice unopposed). He retired in favour of his sons in 1890. Kimber was one of the founders of New Rugby, Tennessee, and a founder of the City Carlton Club.

    Sir Henry Dixon Kimber, 2nd Baronet (1862–1950), was the eldest son of Sir Henry. He was educated at Oxford and became the senior partner in his father's firm of Kimbers, Williams, Sweetland, Stinson & Co.

*The next cross memorial is opposite the **Pelham-Clinton** statue.*

2.36. Pilot Officer Peter Kennard-Davis (*c.* 1920–1940) [plot 26]

Peter Kennard–Davis entered the RAF with a short service commission in May 1939, having already served two years with the Royal Navy. Following training and conversion to Spitfires at No. 7 Operational Training Unit at Hawarden, he joined No. 64 Squadron at Kenley on 3 August 1940. His operational career was tragically short, for just after midday on Thursday 8 August 1940 his Spitfire caught fire during a combat with Messerschmitt 109s over Dover. He baled out, seriously wounded, and was rushed to the Royal Victoria Hospital, Dover, where he died two days later, aged just 20. 'Called to higher service', he lies buried with his grandparents.

Cross into plot 25. The next memorial has mosaic decorations on the base.

2.37. Giulio Salviati (*c.* 1843–1898) [plot 25]

Venetian glass and mosaic merchant. Salviati was a member of the firm of Salviati, Jesuram & Co. of 213 Regent Street, London. This firm undertook a large number of mosaic commissions in this country, including decorations in the Albert Memorial Chapel, Windsor; the Albert Memorial, London; the Julius Beer mausoleum in Highgate Cemetery; the four prophets in the spandrels of the dome of St Paul's (1864–92); and in Westminster Abbey (reredos mosaic of the Last Supper, 1867). There is a link with **Sir William Drake** who was the founder and manager of Salviati & Company, re-formed in 1869 as the Venice & Murano Glass & Mosaic Company. On the evening of 4 March 1898 Salviati committed suicide in his shop after the last workman had left the premises. The inquest returned a verdict of 'suicide during temporary insanity', which accounts for his burial in consecrated ground. This memorial is one of the most striking in Brookwood Cemetery. The base has four separate mosaic panels executed by the firm. Each depicts flowers associated with remembrance and mourning: lilies, forget-me-nots, roses and laurel. This memorial has been recommended for statutory listing by Woking Borough Council.

Just beyond this is a cross memorial in polished grey granite.

2.38. Sir Henry Macleod Leslie Rundle (1856–1934) [plot 25]

Rundle was gazetted to the Royal Artillery in 1876. He served in the Zulu War at the battle of Ulundi (1879) and in the Boer War (1881), being wounded at Potchefstroom. In 1882 Rundle was present at the battle of Tel-el-Kebir. In the following year he joined the Egyptian Army and served in it from 1883 to 1898. Rundle took part in the Nile expedition (1884–5) under Lord

Kitchener and guarded the Nubian desert with a force of Ababdeh Arabs. He was promoted to Captain in 1885. Rundle was posted to the Sudan Frontier Field Force in 1885 and was awarded the DSO in 1887. He was next in the Sudan, and commanded the artillery in the decisive action at Toski in 1889. In 1891 he was engaged in the operations that resulted in the capture of Tokar. Between 1892 and 1896 he was largely based in Cairo. Rundle was Kitchener's Chief of Staff with the Dongola Expeditionary Force, and was present at the actions of Firket and Hafir (1896). He took part in the Battle of Omdurman (1898), after which he led a column up the Blue Nile to relieve Gedaref. Rundle commanded the South-Eastern District (1898–9) and the 8th Division of the South African Field Force (1900–2). He was in command at the battles of Biddulphsberg and Wittebergen. Rundle held the Northern Command (1905–7), he was Governor of Malta (1909–15) and succeeded Sir Ian Hamilton[39] as Commander-in-Chief, Central Force (1915–16).

Behind this grave is a cross of Calvary.

2.39. Ernest Bruce Iwan-Muller (1853–1910) [plot 25]

Journalist. Iwan-Muller was educated at Thurmanston Preparatory School, Leicestershire; King's College, London; and New College, Oxford. After graduating he became senior classics master at Brackenbury's School in Wimbledon. Between 1879 and 1884 Iwan-Muller was a private tutor in Oxford. From 1884 to 1893 he was editor of the *Manchester Courier*, where he did much to promote a great revival of Toryism in Lancashire. He was assistant editor of the *Pall Mall Gazette* (1893–6) before moving to the *Daily Telegraph* (1896–1910). During his time with the *Daily Telegraph* he undertook several special trips including a long spell in South Africa during the Boer War, a visit to Ireland (1907) and one to Paris (1908). Iwan-Muller also contributed many political articles to the *Quarterly Review*, the *Fortnightly Review* and other magazines. Iwan-Muller had an enormous knowledge of politics and enjoyed the confidence of many important political figures like Arthur Balfour and Lord Salisbury. His books include *Lord Milner and South Africa* (London, William Heinemann, 1902) and *Ireland To-day and To-morrow* (London, Chapman & Hall, 1907).

To the right of this grave is a grey granite obelisk beneath a redwood.

2.40. Sir Joshua Jebb (1793–1863) [plot 25]

Surveyor-General of Convict Prisons. Jebb entered the Royal Engineers and served in Canada and America (1813–20). He was appointed Surveyor-General of prisons from 1837. Jebb assisted in the construction of the 'model prison' at Pentonville with William Crawford[40] and Whitworth Russell[41]. It was used as the prototype for all English prisons until the 1870s. He also designed prisons at Portland, the convict prisons at Woking, Parkhurst (on the Isle of Wight) and the Broadmoor Asylum for mentally ill criminals at Crowthorne, Berkshire. Jebb was appointed Inspector-General of Military Prisons from 1844. As Chairman of Convict Prisons, Jebb developed the 'progressive' system. He retired from the Army in 1850 with the honorary rank of Major-General. Jebb was made a KCB in 1859. He published many works on prisons, artesian wells and fortifications, including *Modern Prisons: Their Construction and Ventilation* (London, J. Weale, 1844).[42]

Adjacent to this memorial is a large flat ledger stone.

2.41. Henry Merritt (1822–1877) [plot 25]

Picture cleaner and art critic. Merritt, who was from a very humble background, used his spare time to copy pictures in the Bodleian and thus learned the rudiments of art. He came to London in 1846 and cleaned the portrait of Richard II in Westminster Abbey. He subsequently cleaned pictures at the National Portrait Gallery, Hampton Court Palace and Marlborough House. His judgement of old paintings led him to be constantly consulted by the major art galleries. Merritt was acquainted with Gladstone and Ruskin, with whom he corresponded. He was art critic on the *Standard* from 1866, and published an autobiographical romance, *Robert Dalby and his World of Troubles: Being the Early Days of a Connoisseur* (London, Chapman & Hall, 1865). His *Dirt and Pictures Separated in the Works of the Old Masters* (London, Holyoake & Co., 1854) described aspects of painting, conservation and restoration. Merritt was originally buried in Brompton Cemetery, and was subsequently moved to this new grave at Brookwood.

The next ledger-style memorial with a scroll top may be found adjacent to St Denis' Avenue.

2.42. Frederick Augustus Maxse (1833–1900) [plot 25]

Admiral and political writer, and brother of **Sir Henry B.F. Maxse**. Maxse entered the Navy and became a Lieutenant in 1852. He was naval aide-de-camp to Lord Raglan[43] after the Battle of the Alma (1854) and displayed conspicuous gallantry in carrying dispatches. This resulted in his promotion to Commander in 1855. Maxse retired in 1867 and became a Rear-Admiral in 1875. He unsuccessfully contested Southampton in 1868 and Tower Hamlets in 1875, but never entered Parliament. Although a Liberal, Maxse was fiercely opposed to women's suffrage and Home Rule for Ireland. Maxse was a friend of the novelist George Meredith.[44] His novel *Beauchamp's Career* (three vols, London, Chapman & Hall, 1876) has as its main character Nevil Beauchamp, an idealistic naval officer who is based on Maxse. Maxse published many articles, pamphlets and books, his most valuable concerning operations in the Crimean War. His funeral notice stated that a special train would leave the LNC's station at 11.05 a.m., and that 'Ladies will not attend the funeral'.[45]

Adjacent to the junction of St George's and St Cyprian's avenues is another family mausoleum.

2.43. Normand family mausoleum [plot 25]

To the right of this mausoleum is a small memorial commemorating the artists **Ernest Normand** (1857–1923) and **Henrietta Normand, née Rae** (1859–1928). Normand studied at the Royal Academy before continuing his artistic training in Paris. He painted a variety of subjects – landscape, genre, portraits, historical and classical – but felt most successful with his classical paintings. In 1884 he married Henrietta Rae and for many years they lived in Holland Park. Rae entered the Royal Academy schools in 1877 and exhibited from 1881. She specialised in portraits, domestic scenes and classical subjects. One of her commissions was for the huge wall painting *The Charities of Sir Richard Whittington* (completed 1900), which hangs in the Royal Exchange. Her husband executed another of the wall panels depicting *King John Granting Magna Carta*.

All members of the Normand family commemorated and buried here were cremated. They include **George B. Normand** (died 1901), **Mary Ann Normand** (1819–1909), **Georgina Surridge** (*c.* 1846–1928), **William Alfred Surridge** (*c.* 1851–1935), **Richard Lluellyn** 1874–1946), **Rae Prinsep Normand** (*c.* 1886–1954) and **Arthur Normand** (died 1954).

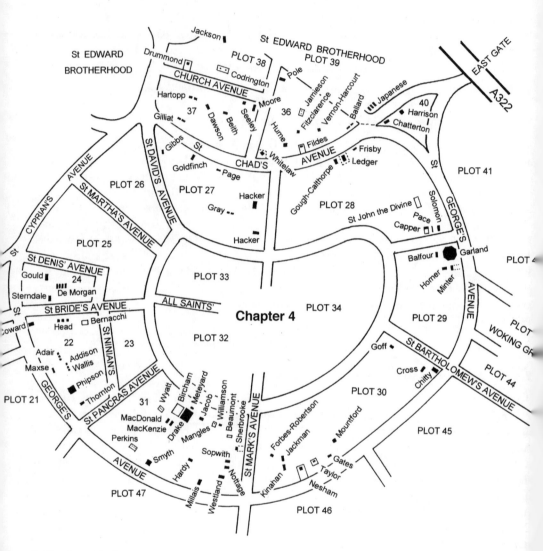

St Chad's and St George's avenues.

Chapter Three

ST CHAD'S AND ST GEORGE'S AVENUES

This route describes a huge circle surrounding the central area of the former Anglican section. Start from the **St Edward Brotherhood** *church, and turn into St Chad's Avenue. The first sequence of memorials lies in the plots to the left of this roadway. Look for the mass of heather near the path.*

3.1. Gilliat family graves [plot 37]

Pilot Officer Simon Howard Gilliat (*c.* 1913–36) was a member of No. 601 (County of London) Squadron, Auxiliary Air Force, otherwise known as the 'Millionaires' Squadron' because of the large number of wealthy young men who flew in it. Gilliat was a stockbroker in the City and joined the squadron in October 1935. On 7 August 1936 he flew to Farnborough (Hants) to collect his brother John and take him to a squadron guest night at Lympne. The aircraft struck telegraph wires on take- off and crashed into an airmen's cookhouse, killing Simon and injuring his brother. **Major John Gilliat** (*c.* 1914–44) of the Irish Guards was one of 121 servicemen and civilians killed on Sunday 18 June 1944 when the Guards Chapel at Wellington Barracks was hit by a V1 flying bomb.

Further into the plot is a low headstone with kerbing, in pink granite.

3.2. John Hay Beith ('Ian Hay') (1876–1952) [plot 37]

Writer under the pseudonym of Ian Hay. Beith was educated at Fettes and St John's College, Cambridge. He became a teacher at Fettes (1901 and 1906–14) and Durham School (1902–6). His first novel, *Pip: A Romance of Youth* (Edinburgh, William Blackwood & Sons, 1907), was a bestseller. It was followed by other light, humorous and very popular books. During the First World War he served with the Argyll & Sutherland Highlanders and then transferred to the Machine Gun Corps. His most famous book, *The First Hundred Thousand, Being the Unofficial Chronicle of a Unit of K(1)* [i.e. Kitchener's First Volunteer Army] (Edinburgh, William Blackwood & Sons, 1915), was written in billets. It was followed by *Carrying On: After the First Hundred Thousand* (Edinburgh, William Blackwood & Sons, 1917) and *The Last Million* [the American Army] (London, Hodder & Stoughton, 1919). During 1916–18 Beith was in America, working in the information bureau of the British War Mission. After the war he successfully translated many of his novels to the stage. Probably the best of these was *Tilly of Bloomsbury: A Comedy in 3 Acts* (London, Samuel French, 1922), based on his novel *Happy-Go-Lucky* (Edinburgh, William Blackwood & Sons, 1913). Beith was an excellent collaborator with other writers, including P.G. Wodehouse[1] but his later novels never approached his pre-war success. Beith travelled extensively. He was Chairman of the Society of Authors (1921–4 and 1935–9) and was on the Council of the League of British Dramatists. Beith was for many years Chairman of the St

Barnabas Pilgrimages, an organisation that arranged trips to the First World War battlefields for those who could otherwise not afford to visit them. He also first coined the phrases 'funny ha-ha' and 'funny peculiar', which appeared in his play *The Housemaster: A Comedy in 3 Acts* (London, Samuel French, 1938).[2]

To the left of this memorial is a badly worn headstone adjacent to a small monkey puzzle tree.

3.3. Rt Hon. George Robert Dawson (1790–1856) [plot 37]

Dawson was educated at Harrow and Christ Church College, Oxford. He was MP for County Londonderry (1815–30), and was the first Orange member who declared for Catholic emancipation; he did so at a public dinner on 12 August 1828.[3] His announcement was followed closely by that of Sir Robert Peel and the Duke of Wellington. Dawson was MP for Harwich (1830–2). He was Under-Secretary of State for the Home Department (1823–8) and was Secretary of the Treasury (1828–30) at the end of the Duke of Wellington's administration. Dawson was brother-in-law to Sir Robert Peel (1788–1850), having married Peel's eldest sister Mary in 1815. Prior to his marriage Dawson was Peel's private secretary. When Peel became Prime Minister in November 1834 Dawson was appointed Secretary of the Admiralty (1834–5). After retirement from public life Dawson accepted the post of Commissioner of the Customs (1841–5) in Peel's government. He was promoted to Deputy Chairman of the Customs in 1846, a post he retained until his death.

To the left of this grave is the next family plot. Two of the headstones have the family crest carved on them.

3.4. Hartopp family[4] graves [plot 37]

Sir Charles Edward Cradock Hartopp, 5th Baronet (1858–1929), was educated at Eton and afterwards joined the Scots Guards. As a Lieutenant he took part in the Egyptian campaign of 1882. Hartopp succeeded his father as 5th Baronet in 1888.

Also buried here is **Sir Frederick Cradock Hartopp,** 7th Baronet (1869–1937). He succeeded his nephew as 7th Baronet in 1930.

George Francis Fleetwood Cradock Hartopp, 8th Baronet (1870–1949), was his brother. He was educated at Wellington College and then joined the London Stock Exchange. He succeeded his brother in 1937.

The next cross ledger memorial is on the extreme right-hand side of plot 37.

3.5. Sir William James Moore (1828–1896) [plot 37]

Surgeon. Moore was educated at Edinburgh University. He was appointed assistant surgeon to the Bombay Army in 1852. Moore served in the Persian War (1856–7), and was appointed Residency Surgeon at Jodhpur in 1862. He later moved to Marwar, and was agency surgeon and superintendent general of dispensaries and vaccination in Rajputana from August 1867. Moore was appointed Deputy Surgeon General in Bombay from 1877 and was Surgeon General from 1885. He retired in 1888 and was appointed Hon. Physician to Queen Victoria (1888–96). He wrote several medical textbooks, including *A Manual of the Diseases of India* (London, Churchill, 1861). His epitaph records that he was cremated at St John's, Woking.

The next Celtic cross memorial is adjacent. It is made of grey granite and faces Church Avenue.

3.6. Harry Govier Seeley (1839–1909) [plot 37]

Geologist and palaeontologist. He was educated privately and at Sidney Sussex College, Cambridge. He described two new species of chalk starfish in 1858. In the following year he was invited by **Professor Adam Sedgwick** to assist arranging rocks and fossils at the Woodwardian Museum, Cambridge. Seeley served as Sedgwick's assistant until 1871. During this period he compiled the *Index to the Fossil Remains of Aves, Ornithosauria and Reptilia, from the Secondary System of Strata arranged in the Woodwardian Museum of the University of Cambridge* (Cambridge, Deighton, Bell & Co., 1869). Seeley moved to London in 1872 to concentrate on teaching, writing and research. He was appointed Professor of Geography at King's College, London in 1876. Seeley formed the London Geological Field Class in 1885 and became Lecturer and Professor of Geology & Mineralogy at the Royal Indian Engineering College, Cooper's Hill, in 1890. He succeeded to the Chair of Geology and Mineralogy at King's College, London, in 1896. His chief work was *Researches on the Fossil Reptilia* (published in ten parts between 1888 and 1896). In 1864 he showed that *pterodactyle* make a transition from living reptiles to existing birds. Seeley also discovered the skeletons of *Pareiasaurus*, *Cynognathus* and other fossils in the Karroo, and these were presented to the Natural History Museum. Seeley also proposed a new classification for dinosaurs since he noticed that all these reptiles had one of two distinctive pelvic designs. Hence he divided dinosaurs into two main orders: *ornithischia* (with a birdlike pelvis) and *saurischia* (with a reptilian pelvis). This classification is still used today. Seeley was elected FRS in 1879, and was the Lyell medallist of the Geological Society in 1885.

Cross over Church Avenue and into plot 38. The next memorial is a Celtic cross set within a large kerbed allotment.

3.7. Dugald Drummond (1840–1912) [plot 38]

Railway engineer. Drummond started an engineering apprenticeship in Glasgow in 1856. He worked under Samuel W. Johnson[5] at the works of the Edinburgh & Glasgow Railway before being appointed foreman (and later Works Manager) at Inverness (1865–70) under William Stroudley.[6] In 1870 he moved with Stroudley to become Locomotive & Carriage Works Manager at Brighton. Drummond was appointed Locomotive Superintendent of the North British Railway in 1875. He drove the first train across the newly completed Tay Bridge on 26 September 1877. The train carried a full complement of Directors of the North British Railway and their guests. The Tay Bridge disaster (1879) also occurred during Drummond's period with the North British, and he attended sessions of the Court of Inquiry. He was responsible for examining and reporting on the train that went down with the bridge.[7] Drummond was Locomotive Superintendent of the Caledonian Railway between 1882 and 1890. He moved to Queensland, Australia, to establish his own engineering works in 1890. This was not a success and he returned to form the Glasgow Railway Engineering Works, building industrial locomotives. Drummond succeeded William Adams[8] as Locomotive Superintendent of the London & South Western Railway in 1895. He organised the removal of the locomotive, carriage and wagon works from Nine Elms to Eastleigh, and developed new main line, suburban and freight locomotives derived from his Scottish designs. His suburban passenger tank engines, the 0-4-4 'M7' class, were for many years the usual motive power used on the Necropolis funeral trains. Drummond supported the L&SWR Servants' Orphanage at Clapham, and was one of the Trustees of the new Home that was opened in Oriental Road, Woking, in 1909. Drummond actively supported the work of the children's home, for the profits from his *Lectures Delivered to the Enginemen and Firemen of the London and South Western Railway Company on the Management of their Engines* (London, Waterlow, 1908) were donated to the Orphanage. The events surrounding his death were dramatic. In early November 1912, and at the age of 73, one of his legs was badly scalded.[9] It had to be amputated, and Drummond died from shock the day after the operation, on 7 November. He died at his home, Morven, South Bank, Surbiton. His funeral train was hauled by his very last locomotive design, the 4-4-0 'D15' class, No. 463, into Brookwood Cemetery on Monday 11 November 1912.

Drummond's memorial was fully restored in November 1994. The Public Affairs Manager of the Co-Operative Funeral Service, Geoffrey Simpson, agreed to undertake the necessary restoration work in return for publicity. On Saturday 29 April 1995 a brief service of rededication was held at the graveside, attended by some of Drummond's grandchildren and great-grandchildren.

Further into the plot is a large grave edged with cast-iron railings.

3.8. Codrington family grave [plot 38]

Sir Henry John Codrington (1808–77) was the third son of Sir Edward Codrington (1770–1851). He too was an Admiral. He entered the Navy in 1823 and was wounded at the Battle of Navarino (20 October 1827). Codrington was promoted to Lieutenant in 1829 and was made Commander in 1831. He was present at the bombardment of Acre (1840), served off the Italian coast (1847–50) and in the Baltic (1854–5). Codrington was promoted to Rear-Admiral in 1857 and to Admiral of the Fleet in 1877.

His brother, **General Sir William John Codrington** (1804–84), was the second son of Sir Edward Codrington. He joined the Army and became an Ensign in 1821. Codrington was promoted to Colonel in 1846 and to Major-General in 1854. He served during the Crimean War where he showed great courage and promptitude at the battles of the Alma and Inkerman. Codrington was Commander-in-Chief at Sebastopol in 1855–6. He was elected MP for Greenwich in 1857, and was Governor of Gibraltar (1859–65).

Just behind this is the next cross ledger memorial.

3.9. The Revd James Jackson (1803–1894) [plot 38]

Jackson was the son of the late James Jackson of Doncaster. He was educated at Brasenose College, Oxford. Jackson was appointed chaplain in the service of the East India Company. Later he became Rector of Lydgate, Suffolk. In 1840 Jackson was appointed vicar of St Sepulchre, London & Middlesex, a position he held for forty-four years. At the time of his death, Jackson was the senior clergyman of the City of London in point of age and ministerial standing. One obituary referred to Jackson's 'courtly manners and devotion to duty'. His memorial records that his wife, Eliza Jackson, née Houlton (1807–77), was buried in Willesden Cemetery.

Return to St Chad's Avenue and locate Goldfinch's headstone with kerbing and footstone. It faces the roadway.

3.10. Lieutenant-General Sir Henry Goldfinch (1781–1854) [plot 27]

The earliest memorial in the cemetery. Goldfinch served with distinction in the Peninsular War (1808–14) and his battle honours are recorded on the headstone. These include Talavera (July 1809), Bussaco (September 1810), Vitoria (June 1813), Nive (December 1813), Orthes (February 1814) and Toulouse (April 1814). He was promoted to Lieutenant-General in the Royal Engineers (1851) and to Colonel Commandant (1854). Goldfinch died in London on 21 November 1854, a week after the cemetery opened to the public. He was buried here on Saturday 25 November and is No. 26 in the burial register. Note the footstone that includes Goldfinch's initials, his year of death and the burial number.

Note the other memorials around Goldfinch's, many of which date from the 1850s. To the left of Goldfinch is another early headstone.

3.11. Emma Page (*c.* 1797–1855) [plot 27]

This memorial commemorates Mrs Page. The epitaph is most interesting, as it records that the memorial was erected by her 'sincere friend' John Lawe of Bowling Street, London, who presumably chose the verse:

> Behold my friend who sleepeth here
> She was kind hearted and sincere
> Her charitable actions are well known
> And needs no record on this stone.

The next memorial, in pink granite, is the first grave fronting the left-hand side of St David's Avenue.

3.12. Sir Benjamin Thomas Brandreth Gibbs (1821–1885) [plot 27]

Gibbs was born in London and was educated at Blemell House, Brompton, and by private tutors. He was Steward of the Yard of the Royal Agricultural Society (1839–42), and subsequently Hon. Director (1843–74) and Vice-President (1871–85). He was Hon. Secretary of the Smithfield Club (1843–85). Gibbs was associated with the agricultural sections of national exhibitions in London (1851 and 1862), Paris (1855, 1867 and 1878), Vienna (1873) and Philadelphia (1875). He was the first person to be knighted for services to agriculture (1878). Gibbs was Secretary of the Fisheries Exhibition, London, in 1883. He wrote *The Smithfield Club: A Condensed History of its Origin and Progress, from its Formation in 1798 up to the Present Time* (London, 1857).

Towards the centre of plot 27 is the following Celtic cross memorial, near to a broken column in pink granite.

3.13. Baroness Eveleen Smith Gray (1841–1918) [plot 27]

Gray married James Maclaren Smith in 1863 (died 1900), who assumed the name of Gray in 1897. On the death of her uncle, the 14th Earl of Moray and 19th Baron Gray, in 1895, the titles were divided, and Mrs Maclaren Smith Gray became the 19th in line to the Barony of Gray. The claim was established in 1896. Her second son, Captain Lonsdale Gray, died of fever in Johannesburg in 1900, as is recorded on the memorial.

Her son, **James Maclaren Stuart Smith Gray**, 20th Baron (1864–1919), who succeeded his mother, is also buried here. He was educated at Pembroke College, Cambridge, and was a Captain of the 5th Battalion Rifle Brigade. He was succeeded by his sister, Ethel Eveleen Gray (1866–1946).

Facing St Mark's Avenue is a prominent memorial with a profile portrait.

3.14. Arthur Hacker (1858–1919) [plot 27]

Painter. The second son of **Edward Hacker**, he studied at the Royal Academy Schools from 1876 and in Paris (1880–1). His first picture to attract attention was *Her Daughter's Legacy*, a scene from rural life, in 1881. Hacker's early work comprises domestic genre. However, towards the end of the 1880s his paintings show changes in the quality of colour and tone, probably influenced by his travels in Spain and North Africa. His figure composition, *Vae Victis* (1890), is an example of this development. It was followed by a number of historical subjects, the best known being *The Annunciation* (1892). Hacker subsequently found inspiration in pastoral scenes (such as *The Gloaming* and *The Cowshed*), and the effects of light and atmosphere in London street scenes (such as *A Wet Night in Piccadilly* of 1911 and *A Matinée Afternoon, Piccadilly*), using soft and misty effects. Hacker also executed a number of fine portraits, all of which show considerable facility of execution. He lived in London all his life, and was found dead on the doorstep of his home in Cromwell Road, South Kensington. His memorial includes a fine profile portrait in bronze. The monument has been recommended for statutory listing by Woking Borough Council.

Further to the left of this grave is the partly incomplete flat ledger memorial with a low headstone.

3.15. Edward Hacker (1812–1905) [plot 27]

Born in Canterbury, Hacker moved to London in 1829. He studied engraving as a pupil of Timothy Englehardt. Hacker was connected with the *Sporting Review* for over forty years, engraving many plates after pictures by Harry Hall,[10] Harrison Weir[11] and John F. Herring.[12] He also engraved several large plates after Aelbert Cuyp,[13] **Richard Ansdell** and John F. Herring, notably the latter's *Three Horses*. Hacker was a friend and contemporary of Samuel Cousins[14] and Henry Ryall,[15] and outlived them and their art by many years. He has been described as 'the last of the line engravers'. He was father of **Arthur Hacker** (see above).

Return to St Chad's Avenue and look for the memorial on the corner of plot 36.

3.16. Dorothy Sa Whitelaw, née Disraeli (1863–1936) [plot 36]

Eldest daughter of Ralph Disraeli (1809–98)[16] and niece of Benjamin Disraeli, Earl of Beaconsfield (1804–81). She married Alexander Whitelaw (1862–1938) in 1886. He was educated at Harrow and Trinity College, Cambridge. Whitelaw served with the Lanarkshire Yeomanry and the Sussex Yeomanry (1885–1909), but he is not buried here. This corner plot measures 25ft × 25ft and the memorial is 5ft high. It is constructed of Hopton wood stone with steps and two planting troughs, all set on a York stone base 8ft × 4ft.

Nearly at the end of this path is a modest headstone with kerbing.

3.17. George Sachaverell Chandos Pole (died 1937) [plot 36]

Pole joined the LNC in early 1896 as a clerk. In 1898 he succeeded **Julian Larkman** as Secretary to the LNC. He continued in this post until his death in 1937, some thirty-eight years' service. At the subsequent board meeting the directors 'stood in silence for a few moments as a token of respect'.[17] Other members of his family are commemorated on adjacent memorials. Pole was succeeded by **Charles Miller**.

Behind the angel to the right of the previous memorial is a double grave with two crosses, one of which is broken.

3.18. Colonel George Jamieson (1843–1920) [plot 36]

Jamieson entered the Consular Service in 1864. He was called to the Bar at the Middle Temple (1880). Jamieson was a Director of the British & Chinese Corporation, the Chinese Central Railways and the Yangtse Valley Company. He was appointed Consul and Judge of the Supreme Court of Shanghai (1891) and was Consul-General (1897–9). The inscription records that his wife, Margaret (*c.* 1849–96), died in Shanghai and was buried in the English cemetery there.

Nearby is a Celtic cross memorial with kerbing, leaning to the left.

3.19. Captain the Hon. George Fitzclarence (1836–1894) [plot 36]

Captain in the Royal Navy. Fitzclarence was the son of George Augustus Frederick Fitzclarence, 1st Earl of Munster, Viscount Fitzclarence and Baron Tewkesbury (1794–1842), who was the illegitimate son of William Henry, Duke of Clarence, later King William IV (1765–1837) and the famous actress Mrs Dorothea Jordan (1761–1816). Thus Captain Fitzclarence's grandfather was King William IV and his great-grandfather was King George III.

Facing St Chad's Avenue is an unusual memorial with two rough columns of different heights.

3.20. Allan Octavian Hume (1829–1912) [plot 36]

Indian civil servant and ornithologist. Hume was the son of Joseph Hume (1777–1855), the radical politician and MP. Hume joined the Bengal Civil Service in 1849. He served as a magistrate in the Etawah district at the time of the Indian Mutiny and was subsequently awarded the CB for services during the Indian Mutiny (1860). Hume was then assigned to the Board of Revenue in the North-Western Provinces. He was appointed Secretary in the Revenue & Agriculture Department of the Indian government in 1870. His views, which favoured greater participation for Indians in their own affairs, created difficulties and he returned to provincial administration. Hume subsequently retired in 1882. He helped found the Indian National Congress that was held in Bombay in 1885, and he continued to support activities and organisations promoting more representational government for Indians. Hume was the first General Secretary of Congress. He was the co-author of a standard work on Indian game birds, *The Game Birds of India, Burmah, and Ceylon* (Calcutta, A. Acton, 1879–81, with coloured plates by different artists). After leaving India in 1894 Hume settled in Upper Norwood. He donated his collection of bird skins and eggs to the British Museum of Natural History in 1885. Hume also founded and endowed the South London Botanical Institute. A sketch of his life and his services to India was published in the *Friends of India Series* (Madras, G. Natesan & Co., 1912).

Close by is the prominent Grecian stele memorial to Fildes.

3.21. Sir (Samuel) Luke Fildes (1844–1927) [plot 36]

Artist. In the late 1860s Fildes submitted drawings for book and magazine articles. His drawing *Houseless and Hungry* appeared in the first issue of *The Graphic*. Through Sir John Millais (1829–96)[18] Fildes met Charles Dickens and was commissioned to illustrate what proved to be his last novel, *The Mystery of Edwin Drood* (1870). After Dickens's death Fildes was invited to stay at Gad's Hill. While there he decided to sketch Dickens's desk and chair in the study, just as they had been left. An engraving of this was published in the Christmas 1870 number of *The Graphic*, and thousands of these prints were sold. Fildes's next great public success was the painting *Applicants for Admission to a Casual Ward*, based on his earlier drawing, which was exhibited in 1874 and sold for £1,250. Sometimes considered a social realist, Fildes also did many subject paintings; these are mainly rural and include many Venetian genre scenes. Examples include *An Al Fresco Toilet* (1889), *A Village Wedding* (1883) and *The Doctor* (1891). The latter painting was an enormous success and was praised by the public and medical profession alike. Fildes sold it to Sir Henry Tate for £3,000. During the 1890s Fildes concentrated on portraits and he gained a large and fashionable clientele. One of these portraits depicts Lord Pirbright (1840–1903) in his peer's robes. He eventually moved into a fine house designed by Richard Norman Shaw at 11 Melbury Road, Kensington. In 1901 he was commissioned to paint a state portrait of King Edward VII. This was followed by portraits of Queen Alexandra (1905) and King George V (1912). He married **Fanny Woods** (1851–1927) in 1874. She was also a painter, and exhibited at the Royal Academy in 1878 and 1883. Her brother, Henry Woods,[19] was another artist! Fildes's memorial has been recommended for statutory listing by Woking Borough Council.

Diagonally to the right is a pink granite Celtic cross leaning to the left.

3.22. Leveson Francis Vernon-Harcourt (1839–1907) [plot 36]

Civil engineer. Educated at Harrow and Balliol College, Oxford. Vernon-Harcourt became a pupil of Sir John Hawkshaw (1811–91) from 1862 to 1865. In 1866–70 he was resident engineer to the new works on the East and West India Docks. He was resident engineer to Alderney harbour (1870–2), and the Rosslare harbour and Wexford Railway (1872–4). In 1882 Vernon-Harcourt became a consulting engineer based in Westminster and was appointed Professor of Civil Engineering at University College London, a post he held until 1905. His professional practice concentrated on docks and harbours, rivers and canals and water supply. He published several textbooks such as *A Treatise on Rivers and Canals* (two vols, Oxford, Clarendon Press, 1882), *Harbours and Docks: Their Physical Features, History, Construction, Equipment and Maintenance* (two vols, Oxford, Clarendon Press, 1885) and *Achievements in Engineering During the Last Half Century* (London, Seeley, 1891). Vernon-Harcourt was involved in many commissions and congresses both at home and abroad, reporting on a wide variety of undertakings.

Adjacent to the entrance to the Serbian section is a pair of headstones.

3.23. Edward Ballard (1820–1897) [plot 36]

Physician and sanitarian. Ballard was appointed Physician of the St Pancras Royal Dispensary and became the first Medical Officer of Health for St Mary, Islington (1856–71). His painstaking research into a local outbreak of typhoid (1870) allowed him to trace its source to an infected milk supply. This was the first investigation of its kind and was published as *On a Localised Outbreak of Typhoid Fever in Islington* (London, Churchill, 1871). Ballard was appointed Medical Inspector of the Local Government Board and to the Medical Department of the Privy Council (1871–92) when he began his study into the nature of summer diarrhoea (published 1888). Ballard married twice, first **Julia Hannah** (died 1866), who is commemorated on the left-hand memorial, and secondly the artist **Emmeline Halse** (died 1923). She designed the unusual memorial to **Henri van Laun**.

The next memorial is on the other side of the gateway to the Serbian section.

3.24. General Sir James Charles Chatterton, 3rd Baronet (1794–1874) [plot 40]

Soldier. Chatterton entered the Army as a Cornet in the 12th Light Dragoons in 1809. After obtaining his commission as a Lieutenant (1811), he served in the Peninsula, Portugal, Spain, Flanders and France (1811–18). According to his epitaph he took part in '37 battles, sieges and engagements besides various skirmishes and minor affairs'. He was present at the battles of Salamanca (July 1812), Vitoria (June 1813), Nivelle (November 1813) and Nive (December 1813), among other actions. He was also present at Quatre Bras (16 June 1815), Waterloo (18 June 1815) and the advance on and capture of Paris (June–July 1815). Chatterton was MP for County Cork (1831–5 and 1849–52). He was High Sheriff of County Cork (1851–2), was a Deputy Lieutenant of the County and City of Cork and a magistrate for Cork, Tipperary and Galway. Chatterton carried the great banner of England at the Duke of Wellington's funeral in 1852. He was a Director of the LNC (1853–74). Chatterton succeeded his brother, Sir William Chatterton, as 3rd Baronet in 1855. He was Colonel of the 5th Lancers (1858–68) and was promoted to General in 1866. At the time of his death Chatterton was one of the Army's oldest Generals. The LNC recorded his passing as follows:

The death of General Sir James Charles Chatterton Bart, GCB, a Director of the London Necropolis Company, having been announced, it is the wish of the Board that the

Secretary make known to the Representatives of the deceased the respect this Company entertains for the memory of their distinguished late Director.[20]

Just inside the entrance to the Serbian section is an interesting group of Japanese graves.

3.25. Japanese graves [plot 39]

Here is a group of Japanese graves along with a modern memorial erected by the Anglo-Japanese Friendship Society in September 1997. The four young men buried here represent some of the first Japanese students sent to Europe and America by the ruler of Japan 'to work for the modernisation of Japan'. This included learning about new technology and culture in order to 'enrich Japan and strengthen soldiers'. Those buried here failed to complete their studies owing to illness and death. Their names are recorded in the Japanese style: family name, given name, then province of birth in brackets.

Arifuko, Jiro (Tokuyama) (*c.* 1844–68) was an officer in the Japanese Army. He came to England with Mori Motoisa to study military matters. He fell ill and died on 13 August 1868 at Highbury, about fifty days after his arrival in this country. Note that his name is mis-spelt in English on the memorial as 'Garifuko'.

Fukuoka, Morito (Tosa) (*c.* 1852–73) was a son of Kenzo Fukuoka of the Lord of Tosa. He came to England in October 1871 and was studying at University College London. His epitaph suggests that he might have converted to Christianity, although this was still forbidden in Japan:

IMBUED WITH MORAL FEELING ADORNED WITH THE GRACES OF MODESTY REFINEMENT AND COURTESY HE LOVED AND EARNESTLY SOUGHT THE TRUTHS OF RELIGION.

Fukuro, Kuhei (Saga) (*c.* 1849–73) came to London in the summer or autumn of 1873 on his way to Japan from Berlin, where he had been studying for about two years. He died from consumption on 2 November 1873 while waiting for a suitable ship to take him home to Japan.

Yamazaki, Kosaburo (Choshu) (*c.* 1844–66) came to London in April 1865 and moved into Mr Cooper's house at 103 Gower Street. He was very short of money as his feudal lord had stopped a money transfer. He caught tuberculosis and died at **Professor Alexander Williamson**'s home in March 1866. Professor Williamson and twelve Japanese students from University College London[21] attended his funeral.

See also **Matzui Kikujiroo** in Chapter 7.

Just inside plot 40 is a pedestal memorial, close to the boundary of the Serbian section.

3.26. Thomas Harrison (1794–1870) [plot 40]

Solicitor, of Walbrook and Gower Street. Harrison's were sometime solicitors to the LNC. Also buried here is his grandson, **Charles Legrew Harrison**, who died in July 1858 aged just 7 months.

*Return to St Chad's. The next memorial is approximately opposite **Fildes**'s grave, and comprises a headstone with kerbing.*

3.27. Flying Officer Ronald Arthur Somerset Gough-Calthorpe, 9th Baron Calthorpe (1924–1945) [plot 28]

Gough-Calthorpe was educated at Stowe and Jesus College, Cambridge. He succeeded his grandfather as 9th Baron Calthorpe in 1940. Calthorpe was killed after the war in a Mustang fighter of No. 64 Squadron which crashed at Blythborough, Suffolk.

His brother, **Peter Waldo Somerset Gough-Calthorpe** (1927–97), succeeded as 10th Baron, served with the Welsh Guards and became an airline pilot with Aer Lingus. He founded Mercury Airlines in 1960. As Peter Somerset he wrote *The Sea Wraith* (London, Collins, 1967) and *A Break in the Clouds* (London, Collins, 1968).

Also buried here is his father, **Hon. Frederick Somerset Gough-Calthorpe** (1892–1935), the famous cricketer. He was educated at Repton and Jesus College, Cambridge. He was a Cambridge Blue in 1912–14 and 1919. Before the First World War he played for Surrey, and later for Warwickshire (1919–30). Five times he scored 1,000 runs in a season, while in 1920 he took 100 wickets. In a cricket career spanning twenty-four years he scored 12,598 runs and took 219 catches. Gough-Calthorpe was a member of A.C. Maclaren's team that toured Australia and New Zealand (1922–3). He also captained the MCC in the West Indies in 1925–6 and 1929–30. He married Rose Mary Dorothy, daughter of **Leveson Vernon-Harcourt**, in 1922.

Immediately adjacent is a large private plot with a grieving figure.

3.28. Edward Ledger (died 1923) [plot 28]

Ledger was educated at the Collegiate and Commercial School at Denmark Hill. He was the proprietor and editor of the theatrical paper *The Era* and *The Era Almanack*. He retired in 1905. Ledger was a keen collector of armour, furniture, silverware and china. His memorial, erected by his widow Ciss, is a scroll-topped tomb surrounded by a low hedge. A mourning figure leans across the monument from the back of the plot.

Just beyond is a pair of headstones facing St Chad's.

3.29. Captain Cyril Hubert Frisby, VC (1885–1961) [plot 28]

Soldier, and member of the London Stock Exchange. Frisby won his VC on 27 September 1918 at the Canal du Nord, near Graincourt in France. He was in command of a company detailed to capture a canal crossing, but when they reached the canal they came under heavy fire from a strong enemy post under the bridge on the far side of the canal. Frisby, with Lance-Corporal T.N. Jackson and two others, climbed down into the canal and succeeded in capturing the post with two machine guns and twelve men. During the course of this attack Frisby was bayoneted in the leg. Having consolidated his position, Frisby gave timely support to a company that had lost all its officers and sergeants. He was one of 100 holders of the VC who formed a guard of honour to the body of the Unknown Warrior in Westminster Abbey on 11 November 1920.

From here follow the path, which now becomes St George's Avenue. The **St Stephen's**, **South Kensington**, *ground (to your left) is covered in Chapter 6. The next allotment lies opposite this section.*

3.30. Sisterhood of St John the Divine [plot 28]

The Sisterhood was a female religious community that acquired a plot here in 1872. The ground reserved was increased in size in 1894 and eventually measured 36ft × 18ft. Note the small marker stone in front of the plot with 'S.J.D.' carved on top. The low memorials mark the graves of members of the Sisterhood. The earliest, that of **Sarah Morris**, dates from March 1878.

The next three memorials face the next path on the right, adjacent to the mausoleum. The first two are Calvary crosses.

3.31. Sir Richard Solomon (1850–1913) [plot 28]

South African statesman. Solomon was born in Cape Town and educated at the Lovedale Mission, Bedford public school and Peterhouse College, Cambridge. He became a lecturer in mathematics at the Royal Naval College, Greenwich, and was called to the Bar at the Inner Temple in 1879. Solomon returned to South Africa to practise at Grahamstown. He took a keen interest in native affairs and served on the Cape Native Law Commission (1882). In 1889 he moved to Kimberley, and was appointed QC in 1893. Solomon was elected to the Cape House of Assembly (1893–4 and 1896–1900) and he was Attorney General of Cape Colony (1898). In supporting Schreiner's policy of punishing Cape rebels, this Government fell in June 1900. Solomon became legal adviser to the Transvaal (1901) and took part in the negotiations resulting in the Peace of Vereeniging (1902). In the same year he was created KCMG and Attorney General of the Transvaal. He was twice acting Lieutenant-Governor of the Transvaal, and in 1906 helped draft the measures by which responsible government was established in the Transvaal. Solomon was the first High Commissioner for the Union of South Africa in London (1910–13).

His brother, **Sir William Henry Solomon** (1852–1930), is buried in the adjacent grave. He was educated at Peterhouse College, Cambridge, and was called to the Bar at the Inner Temple in 1876. Solomon was Judge of the Appellate Division of the Supreme Court of South Africa (1910–27), and was Chief Justice of the Union of South Africa (1927–9).

The next memorial is a wooden graveboard.

3.32. Thomas Richard Pace (1839–1896) [plot 28]

This unusual wooden memorial is known as a graveboard, once common in areas where stone was not readily available. The usual form is a horizontal board running the length of the grave, supported by posts at each end. Graveboards were usually painted white with black lettering and for obvious reasons tended to rot away. Pace's memorial is noteworthy because of the standard of craftsmanship used for the inscription and the Celtic designs used on the posts (which are themselves in the form of Celtic crosses). Although little is known of Pace, his name is among those churchwardens listed on the surviving memorial to **St Antholin's**, **Budge Row**. He served as a churchwarden between 1869 and 1871.

The next memorial is in red brick and terracotta.

3.33. Capper family grave [plot 28]

An interesting memorial with fine terracotta decoration. The inscription panels are also of terracotta and specially made. The memorial commemorates **Eleanor Harriet Capper (Nellie)** (1838–92) and her son **George Lennox Capper** (1857–92), both of whom died in October 1892. Both were cremated and their ashes were buried together here on 20 October. As their epitaph records:

LOVELY AND PLEASANT IN THEIR LIVES,
AND IN THEIR DEATH THEY WERE NOT DIVIDED.

Note the urn on top of the memorial which may be symbolic of cremation. **Walter Kent Capper** (c. 1843–1917) was a hosier. He too was cremated. The memorial may be compared with that of the **De Pothonier** family.[22]

The next grave is behind the mausoleum. It is a large headstone in pink granite.

3.34. Thomas Graham Balfour (1813–1891) [plot 29]

Physician. Born in Edinburgh, Balfour entered the Army Medical Service in 1836. He was involved in compiling the first four volumes of *Statistics of the British Army*, the first ever published in Europe up to this time. Balfour was Assistant Surgeon to the Grenadier Guards (1840–8), and reported on the sanitary state of the Army as secretary to Sidney Herbert's committee (1857–61). He was appointed Deputy Inspector-General in charge of the statistical branch of the Army Medical Department (1859–73). Balfour was elected FRS (1858) and became Surgeon General (1873). He was Hon. Physician to Queen Victoria (1887–91) and was President of the Royal Statistical Society (1888–90).

3.35. Garland family mausoleum [plot 29]

This mausoleum was originally provided for Anna Louise Garland (*c.* 1842–1915). Although she died in August 1915, her body was not placed within the newly completed building until November 1916. A temporary vault may have been used for her coffin while the mausoleum was being constructed. In September 1919 her coffin was moved once again, for the burial registers record that her body was then sent to New York. It is not known where she was finally laid to rest.

Buried within is **Charles Tuller Garland** (*c.* 1875–1921), a well-known American racehorse owner and millionaire. He was an enthusiastic sportsman and was keen on hunting and polo. Garland moved to Britain in the 1890s. His country estate at Moreton Hall, Moreton Morrell, Warwickshire, reputedly cost him £500,000. It was one of the wonders of the county with a private cricket ground, tennis court and polo ground, along with splendid gardens and terraces. In 1914 Garland gave up his American nationality and became a naturalised Englishman. During the First World War he served in the Warwickshire Yeomanry as an ordinary trooper. His best racehorse was probably *Somme Kiss*, a runner-up to *Gainsborough* in the Two Thousand Guineas and winner of the Newmarket Stakes. He also owned *Oatlands*, *Sudden Rise* (which won at Kempton), and *Ardigon* (which won at Epsom). His wife, **Margaret Garland** (*c.* 1881–1918), whom he married in 1903, is also buried within.[23]

The mausoleum was designed by the LNC and is octagonal in plan, accentuated by four pairs of Doric columns on each of its shorter sides. The structure was restored in 1938 at a cost of £50.[24] There is a mausoleum of precisely the same design just inside the entrance to the Eastern Section of Highgate Cemetery to the Dalziel family, although that example is made of pink granite. That was also designed and erected by the LNC, at a cost of £8,477 19s 6d.[25]

To the left of the mausoleum is another interesting memorial in terracotta.

3.36. John Stuart Horner (1855–1923) [plot 29]

Regrettably partly broken, this comprises a delightful standard memorial in terracotta, examples of which may be seen in other burial grounds. The top of the grave space incorporates a low scallop shell formed from the wings of two angels, and about 18in high. The base of the memorial incorporates the inscription panel, which describes Horner as 'of Mells, Somerset'. The kerbing is also in terracotta, while the inscription panel at the foot of the memorial commemorates his wife, **Emily Horner, née Birch** (1861–1952), who subsequently married Dr R.N. Goodman.

The next memorial is directly in front, and extends to St George's Avenue.

3.37. Sara Minter (1865–1926) [plot 29]

The memorial is unusual for including a carving representing a 'pelican in her piety'. The pelican is symbolic of charity and of Jesus Christ, and St Jerome (*c.* 340–420) recorded the story of a pelican restoring its young ones destroyed by serpents and his own salvation by the blood of Christ.[26]

*Continue along St George's Avenue. The plots on your left (including the **Woking ground**) are described in Chapter 6. The next grave is in grey granite, and is located by the junction with St Bartholomew's Avenue.*

3.38. Chitty family graves [plot 30]

Sir Joseph William Chitty (1828–99) was a famous judge and the son of Thomas Edward Chitty (1802–78). Chitty was educated at Eton and Balliol College, Oxford. He was called to the Bar at Lincoln's Inn in 1856. Chitty practised exclusively in the Court of Chancery. He became a QC in 1874 and confined himself to the Rolls Court, where he is said to have made as much as £13,000 a year. In 1880 he was returned as Liberal MP for Oxford. In the following year he was appointed Justice of the High Court, Chancery Division, and was knighted in the same year. Appeals from his judgments were rare, his chief fault being to digress into discussions with counsel, which led to his sobriquet of 'Mr Justice Chatty'. Chitty became a Lord Justice of the Court of Appeal in 1897. His place in the Chancery Division was taken by **Sir E.W. Byrne**. Chitty died at his London home after an attack of influenza.

His grandson, **Lieutenant James Malcolm Chitty** (1898–1917), is commemorated on the same memorial as 'reported to be wounded and missing at Gonnelieu, France on 1 December 1917'. He is also commemorated on panel 2 of the Cambrai Memorial at Louverval, France.

Buried in the adjacent grave is **Sir Thomas Willes Chitty**, 1st Baronet (1855–1930), who was the brother of Sir Joseph. He was educated at Winchester College and was called to the Bar at the Inner Temple in 1877. Chitty joined the North-Eastern Circuit and subsequently became Master of the Supreme Court (1901–20). He edited a number of important legal textbooks including *Chitty's Forms*, *Halsbury's Laws of England*, and *Smith's Leading Cases*.

Behind this, among the rhododendrons, is a carved headstone with an unusually shaped footstone.

3.39. Ann Cross (*c.* 1803–1855) [plot 30]

An interesting early memorial. Little is known about Mrs Cross except what is recorded on this memorial. Note the unusually shaped footstone with the further inscription and reminder: 'Be ye also ready for ye know not the day nor the hour.' The clearance of the rhododendrons from around this stone in 1991–2 subsequently resulted in the foundation of the Brookwood Cemetery Society.

The next memorial is a low headstone near the junction with St Margaret's Avenue.

3.40. Sir Park Goff, 1st Baronet (1870–1939) [plot 30]

Goff was educated at Marlborough College and Trinity College, Oxford. He was called to the Bar at the Inner Temple in 1895. Goff was Gold Staff Officer at the Coronations of King Edward VII and King George V. In 1918 he was elected Conservative MP for Cleveland Division, a seat he held until 1929. During this period he was a member of the British Council of the Olympic Games (1920), Chairman of the House of Commons Committee on the Olympic Games (1923) and President of the Parliamentary Mission to the new Baltic Republics of Estonia, Latvia and Lithuania (1923). In 1931 Goff was returned as Conservative MP for the Chatham Division, Rochester, a seat he held until 1935. He was appointed President of the British Delegation to the Inter-Parliamentary Conference, Constantinople, in 1934.

The next memorial is a cross on a base with kerbing, and is further across the plot.

3.41. Edward William Mountford (1855–1908) [plot 30]

Architect. Mountford was articled to the London firm of Habershon & Pite in 1872, and started his own private independent practice in 1881. He was exceptionally successful in open competitions. His commissions include the Baptist Chapel, Northcote Road, Battersea (1887–9); Battersea Public Library (1888–90); St Andrew's Church, Garratt Lane, Wandsworth (1889–90); Battersea Polytechnic (1890–1); Sheffield Town Hall (1890–7); the Museum and Technical School, Liverpool; Battersea Town Hall (1892–3); St Olave's Grammar School, Southwark (1893); the Northampton Institute, Clerkenwell (1893–8); St Michael's Church, Granville Road and Wimbledon Park Road, Putney (1896–7); and the Central Criminal Courts at the Old Bailey (1900–7). He submitted plans for the Aldwych redevelopment (1900) and was one of eight architects selected to design the new London County Council County Hall (1908). His style developed from the 'free Renaissance' (as at Sheffield) to more conventional classicism (such as the Old Bailey). Mountford was a Fellow of the Royal Institute of British Architects (from 1890), and President of the Architectural Association (1893–5).

Facing St George's is the next headstone.

3.42. Professor Reginald Ruggles Gates (1882–1962) [plot 30]

Botanist, geneticist and anthropologist. Gates was born near Middleton, Nova Scotia. He was educated at Middleton High School and Mount Allison University. Gates became demonstrator in botany at McGill University and was awarded a senior fellowship at the University of Chicago from 1908. He wrote many papers, especially on the genus, for instance *The Mutation Factor in Evolution, with Particular Reference to Oenothera* (London, 1915). Many of his discoveries were years ahead of his time: Gates was the first person to observe the non-disjunction of chromosomes, and he realised that mutation might be of two kinds (that of single genes or of major chromosome rearrangements). Gates moved to England in 1911 and worked at the Imperial College of Science. He was Lecturer in Biology at St Thomas's Hospital (1912–14) and was Associate Professor of Zoology at the University of California (1915–16). Gates was an instructor in aerial gunnery to the Royal Flying Corps between 1917 and 1918. He became Reader in the botany department, King's College, London, in 1919 and was Professor from 1921 to 1942. He was elected FRS in 1931, at the age of 48. At the start of the Second World War the department was evacuated and Gates moved to Harvard as research fellow in botany and anthropology. Gates was also interested in anthropology and human genetics. He was married three times, first to Dr Marie Stopes (in 1911). His third wife, **Laura Greer**, is buried with him at Brookwood.

Nearby is a Calvary cross within a kerbed grave.

3.43. Sir John Taylor (1833–1912) [plot 30]

Architect. Taylor was educated privately and entered the Office of Works in 1859. He was Surveyor of Royal Palaces, Public Buildings & Royal Parks (1866–98). Thereafter he set up a practice as a consulting architect (1898–1908). His designs include the new Bankruptcy Courts and offices in Carey Street, WC; the principal staircase and central exhibition rooms of the National Gallery, Trafalgar Square (*c*. 1885–7); the extension to the Public Records Office, Chancery Lane (1891–6); the new Bow Street Police Court and Station; additions to Marlborough House; the extension to the Patent Office, Southampton Buildings (1901–2); and the new War Office, Whitehall. Taylor was a keen golfer, and was captain of the Royal Wimbledon Golf Club (1883) and of the Home Park Golf Club, Hampton Court (1905–6).

The next grave is a large kerbed plot with Calvary cross fronting St George's Avenue.

3.44. Nesham family grave [plot 30]

This large grave commemorates **Captain Cuthbert Spencer Nesham** (1875–1901), of the

21st Lancers, who served in the Nile Expedition of 1898. He took part in the charge of his regiment at the Battle of Omdurman (2 September 1898), one of the last cavalry charges in British military history. Also attached to the 21st Lancers was the young Winston Churchill, who described the incident in his book of the campaign, *The River War* (two vols, London, Longmans, 1899). Nesham was severely wounded in the attack and, as Churchill wrote, 'Nesham's experience was that of the men who were killed, only that he escaped to describe it.' Nesham subsequently died in Dublin in March 1901. His memorial includes carved elements of his uniform (helmet, sword, sabretache), along with his medals.

Two other members of this military family deserve mention. **Hugh Percy Nesham** (1878–1923), was a Major in the Royal Field Artillery. He fought during the South African War (1900–2) and in the First World War. **Charles Frederick Nesham** (1874–1919), his brother, fought in South Africa with the City Imperial Volunteers and the Imperial Yeomanry (1900–2). He also served during the First World War.

To the left is a pink granite Calvary cross with kerbing.

3.45. Vice-Admiral Richard George Kinahan (*c.* 1836–1911) [plot 30]

Kinahan was the fourth son of the Revd John Kinahan of County Down. He entered the Royal Navy in 1851 and was promoted to Captain in 1877. During the Crimean War he served in the Black Sea and was present at the attack on Sebastopol in October 1854. During the Zulu War (1879) Kinahan commanded the *Orantes*. From 1889 to 1892 he held a good service pension and was in charge of the naval establishment at Bermuda. Kinahan was placed on the retired list in 1892 and promoted to Rear-Admiral. He became Vice-Admiral in 1898 and was Nautical Assessor to the City of London Court from 1905.

The next memorial is immediately behind.

3.46. Arthur Jackman (*c.* 1850–1890) [plot 30]

This attractive cross memorial lies over the first cremated remains to be buried in the cemetery. Arthur Jackman lived in Wimbledon and died on 18 January 1890. He was cremated at Woking on Wednesday 22 January and the ashes were subsequently buried here.[27] Note that the memorial was supplied by Halford Mills of Cambridge Place, Paddington (see front right of kerb).[28]

Nearby is an unusual cigar-shaped stylised cross made of grey granite.

3.47. John Forbes-Robertson (1822–1903) [plot 30]

Art critic. Forbes-Robertson was educated at Marischal College and the University of Aberdeen. While still a student he obtained a position on the literary staff of the *Aberdeen Constitutional* and the *Aberdeen Herald*. Later he moved to London and studied for a while at University College. He toured the United States and the principal art centres of Europe. Returning to London, Forbes-Robertson adopted literature as a profession until about 1891, when advancing blindness prevented him working. His books include *The Great Painters of Christendom from Cimabue to Wilkie* (1877), and lives of Gustave Doré,[29] Rosa Bonheur[30] and others. Forbes-Robertson was the art critic for the *Art Journal*, the *Magazine of Art* and several weekly journals in London and the provinces.

Continue along St George's Avenue. The sections on your left are covered in Chapter 6. Turn right into St Mark's Avenue. The next sequence of graves face this path. The first is a Celtic cross memorial.

3.48. Sir James Westland (1842–1903) [plot 31]

Anglo-Indian financier. Born and educated in Aberdeen, he entered the Marischal College in 1857. Westland joined the Indian Civil Service in 1861 and became an assistant magistrate and collector in the Bengal districts (1862–6). He then became collector of Nuddea and Jessore. Westland was appointed Junior Secretary of the Bengal Secretariat (1869), and was appointed Under-Secretary of the Financial Department of the Government of India (1870). During this time he compiled a *Report on the District of Jessore: its Antiquities, its History and its Commerce* (Calcutta, Bengal Secretariat, 1871). Westland was Accountant-General of Bengal (1873), of the Central Provinces (1873–6), Inspector of Local Offices of Accounts (1877) and Accountant and Comptroller-General (1878). Briefly appointed head of Egyptian Accounts Department (1885), Westland became Secretary of the Indian Finance Department from 1886. He became Finance member of the Viceroy's Council (1893–9). Westland established the gold standard in India and raised the rupee to a fixed value of 1*s* 4*d*.

To the right is a large Celtic cross on a base with kerbing. The cross includes the verse 'God is Love'.

3.49. Charles George Nottage (1853–1894) [plot 31]

Charles Nottage was the only son of the Rt Hon. George Swan Nottage (died 1885), the only Lord Mayor of London who died at the Mansion House during his term of office.[31] Educated at Jesus College, Cambridge, Nottage was called to the Bar at the Inner Temple (1881). He was Captain of the Devon Artillery Militia (1885–94). Under the terms of his will he bequeathed £13,000 to establish The Nottage Institute for instructing yachtsmen and other sailors in the science of navigation. He also left £2,000 for The Nottage Cup for yachting, but this bequest was declared invalid in May 1895. His mother, **Dame Christiana Nottage** (*c.* 1831–1916), is also buried here.

The next memorial is two graves to the right and comprises a Calvary cross with kerbing.

3.50. Thomas Sopwith (1838–1898) [plot 31]

Civil and mining engineer. Sopwith trained as a mining engineer at the W.B. Lead Mines at Allendale, Northumberland, and Weardale, County Durham. He later acquired the lead mines at Linares, Spain, which developed into one of the most important mining and smelting works in Spain. Sopwith was appointed the Managing Director in 1880. His death was caused by a tragic shooting accident when out with his son, Thomas Sopwith (later Sir Thomas, 1888–1989), who became the famous aircraft designer.

Further to the right is an unusual cross memorial.

3.51. Robert Lowe, 1st Viscount Sherbrooke[32] (1811–1892) [plot 31]

Lawyer and politician. Educated at Winchester and Oxford, Lowe became a barrister at Lincoln's Inn in 1842. He worked in Australia from 1842 and served on the Legislative Council for New South Wales (1843–50). On his return to England he became a leader writer for *The Times*. Lowe was elected Liberal MP for Kidderminster (1852–9), Calne (1859–67) and was the first MP for London University (1868–73). He was Joint Secretary of the Board of Control (1852–5) and became a Privy Councillor in 1855. Lowe was Vice-President of the Board of Trade and Paymaster General (1855–8) and was Vice-President of the Committee of Council on Education (1859–64). His best political speeches were made during the Second Reform Bill (1866–7), when he argued the case against broadening the electorate. Lowe promoted the case for 'meritocracy' and his arguments have seldom been bettered. During Gladstone's first

Government he was Chancellor of the Exchequer (1868–73) and Home Secretary (1873–4). During Disraeli's Ministry (1874–80) Lowe criticised the Government over the purchase of the Suez Canal shares in 1875. Disraeli was able to return the compliment in 1876 over the Royal Titles Bill, which made Queen Victoria Empress of India. At a public meeting at East Retford Lowe, unwisely, suggested that at least two former Prime Ministers had resisted regal pressure to change the sovereign's title. Gladstone at once denied that he was one of them, and Disraeli obtained the Queen's permission to state in Parliament that she had never applied pressure in this way. Lowe was forced to make a complete and public apology, and this effectively finished his political career.[33] Lowe was created 1st Viscount Sherbrooke of Warlingham in 1880. He later compiled his memoirs, *Poems of a Life* (London, 1884). There is a memorial bust of Lowe in the Members' porch of St Margaret's Church, Westminster.

Behind this memorial and to the right is a kerbed grave with recumbent cross.

3.52. Dudley John Beaumont (1877–1918) [plot 31]

First husband of Sibyl Mary Collings (1884–1974), later Dame of Sark (1927–74). He met his future wife on a holiday in the Channel Islands in 1899 when he painted a fine miniature portrait. They were married in St James's Church, Piccadilly, in August 1901. The couple eventually settled in Sark from 1913. During the First World War Beaumont served in the Cameroons Campaign (1915), but was sent home owing to ill health. In June 1916 he returned to France, only to be invalided home in less than a year. He was obliged to relinquish his commission in 1917. After the Armistice the couple both caught Spanish 'flu, which raged throughout the world between 1918 and 1919. Beaumont contracted pneumonia and died in November 1918, aged just 41. His funeral service took place in St James's, Piccadilly.

Further across the plot is a headstone with kerbing.

3.53. Professor Alexander William Williamson (1824–1904) [plot 31]

Chemist. Educated at Kensington Grammar School and Heidelberg and Giessen universities. Williamson was appointed Professor of Practical Chemistry at University College London in 1849, and also took the subject of General Chemistry from 1855. He occupied this chair for the next thirty-eight years, becoming a great teacher and researcher. His textbook *Chemistry for Students* (Oxford, Clarendon Press) first appeared in 1868. He retired in 1887 and became Emeritus Professor of Chemistry. Williamson was chosen as the guardian of a small group of Japanese noblemen who came to England from 1863 to work for the modernisation of Japan by learning more about European technology and culture. Of the first five students, three lived in Williamson's own home. Some of the students, who died in this country, are buried in plot 39 (see **Japanese graves** above). Williamson's research work covered the theory of etherification (1850), the theory of the constitution of salts (1852) and the analysis of gases (1864). He was President of the Chemical Society (1863–5 and 1869–71), was elected FRS (1855) and was a founder member of the Society of Telegraph Engineers (afterwards the Institution of Electrical Engineers) in 1872.

To the right of the mausoleum is a Celtic cross within a railed enclosure.

3.54. Ross Lewis Mangles, VC (1833–1905) [plot 31]

Civil servant, and one of only five civilians to be awarded the VC. Mangles was educated at Bath Grammar School and the East India College, Haileybury. He entered the Bengal Civil Service in 1853. Mangles won his VC on 30 July 1857 at Arrah, India. He had volunteered to serve with the force engaged in the relief of the city and, notwithstanding the fact that he had previously been injured, he carried a wounded soldier for several miles across swampy ground. He bound the wounds of the injured man while still under heavy fire (which killed or wounded the whole detachment) and got the casualty safely into a boat. During his career as a civil servant Mangles was variously appointed as Judicial Commissioner of Mysore, Secretary to the government of Bengal and was a member of the Board of Revenue of the Lower Provinces. He retired in 1883. There is another memorial to Mangles in the parish church at Pirbright.

Just to the left is a large headstone.

3.55. Sir George Le Grand Jacob (1805–1881) [plot 31]

Soldier in the Indian Army. Jacob obtained a cadetship in the Indian Infantry in 1820, and was posted as Ensign to the 2nd Regiment Bombay Native Light Infantry in 1821. He quickly gained fluency in Hindustani and in 1833 moved to the East India Military Seminary at Addiscombe. There he translated the *Wonder of the Universe*, but it was never published in his lifetime. Jacob returned to India in 1835 and was appointed political agent in Kattywar (1839–43), Sawat Warnee (1845–51) and Kutch (1851–9). During a period of leave his ship was wrecked on a reef in Torres Straits, and he was saved from cannibals by a passing Dutch ship. Jacob commanded the Native Light Infantry in Persia (1857). After returning to Bombay he suppressed the Mutiny in Kolapore (1857) for which he was especially thanked. His administrative powers were subsequently extended to South Mahratta (1858–9), after which he left India with the rank of Major-General. Jacob was a zealous student of Indian literature and he transcribed many Indian inscriptions. His *Western India Before and During the Mutiny* (London, H.S. King, 1871) was highly commended on its publication.

3.56. Drake family mausoleum [plot 31]

Among those commemorated here is **Sir William Richard Drake** (1817–90). Drake was a lawyer and art connoisseur. He became a partner with **Bircham** & Dalrymple of Bedford Row (1845–8). The firm was later renamed **Bircham & Co.**, and Drake remained with this firm until his death. He specialised in company law and had a particular interest in the formation of public companies. Drake was one of the original members of the Burlington Fine Arts Club (1866), where he met **Francis S. Haden** and **John L. Propert**. Drake was a founder member of the Devonshire Club (1875). He was greatly interested in the Italian arts, which undoubtedly accounts for the style of this mausoleum. He published *Notes on Venetian Ceramics* (London, John Murray, 1868) and *A Descriptive Catalogue of the Etched Work of F.S. Haden* (London, Macmillan, 1880). Drake was involved with the firm of **Salviati & Co.**, mosaic artists, which he helped re-form in 1869 as the Venice & Murano Glass & Mosaic Co. The mosaic frieze above the entrance to the mausoleum was almost certainly undertaken by this firm. (The complete text used to read 'Because I live ye shall live also.'[34]) Drake was also interested in genealogy, and privately published and circulated *Devonshire Notes and Notelets, Principally Genealogical and Heraldic* (London, 1888).

Also buried beneath the mausoleum are **Katharine E. Hornsby-Drake** (*c.* 1888–1903), **Ella Katharine Hornsby-Drake** (*c.* 1860–1930), and **Alfred Western H. Hornsby-Drake** (*c.* 1846–1932). Just to the right of the mausoleum is the separate grave of **Frances Anne Drake** (*c.* 1820–93).

The mausoleum was constructed following the death of Sir Richard Drake's wife, **Dame Katharine Stewart Forbes Drake** (*c.* 1818–80). Arguably this is the most attractive mausoleum anywhere within the cemetery grounds. Its Italianate style closely reflects Sir William Drake's interests in Italian art, ceramics and culture. The rear wall of the mausoleum includes the family crest and motto 'Time Tryeth Truth', while the shallow circular depressions once held bronze plaques with details of his family buried in the vault beneath. Note that the family also purchased a strip of land leading down from the mausoleum and providing a 4ft path to St George's Avenue. Small granite markers were set into the ground marking the boundary of this land; each has a capital 'D' on it, and some can still be seen today. The mausoleum has been recommended for statutory listing by Woking Borough Council.

Immediately to the left is a large kerbed family plot, which contains many separate memorials. Bircham's memorial is at the rear and closest to the mausoleum.

3.57. Samuel Bircham (1838–1923) [plot 31]

Solicitor. Educated at the Revd Boyce's school, Godalming, then at Hatfield, Eton and Oxford. Bircham trained as a solicitor and was articled to his uncle (Mr Dalrymple) of the firm Bircham, Dalrymple & **Drake**; members of each of these families are buried nearby. Bircham's father was solicitor to the London & South Western Railway, and in 1880 or thereabouts, Bircham took over this work. He remained in this post for nearly thirty years. During this period he was involved in many important developments with the railway company, including extensions to Southampton Docks, the quadrupling of the LSWR's main line from Waterloo to Basingstoke, the complete rebuilding of Waterloo station and the consequent negotiations between the LSWR and the LNC for the replacement of the LNC's London terminus. These were onerous duties, undertaken with unfailing energy. His leisure interests included shooting (especially on his Norfolk estate), cricket (he was an Hon. Auditor for the MCC for many years) and scouting (he was a District Commissioner of Scouts). Bircham retired in 1910 and was well known in the Woking district, living at Beech Hill, Mayford. The annual Westfield Fete took place in a field owned by him. He died at his daughter's house, Yarrowfields, Mayford.[35]

Directly behind the mausoleum is the next headstone with kerbing.

3.58. Eliza Meteyard (1816–1879) [plot 31]

Author. Born in Liverpool, Meteyard moved to Shrewsbury in 1818 and then to Thorpe, near Norwich, in 1829. She moved to London in 1842. Meteyard began writing in 1833 by assisting her brother in preparing tithe reports for the eastern counties. She became a regular contributor of fiction to a wide range of magazines including the *People's Journal, Tait's Magazine, Chambers' Journal, Household Words* and *Country Words*, often using the pseudonym Silverpen. Meteyard's first novel was *Struggles for Fame* (three vols, London, 1845), which previously appeared as a series of articles in *Tait's Magazine* in 1840. Her most popular titles were *Mainstone's Housekeeper* (three vols, London, 1860), and *The Lady Herbert's Gentlewoman* (three vols, London, 1862). Meteyard also wrote children's stories between 1850 and 1878. Her important *Life of Sir Josiah Wedgwood* (two vols, London, Hurst & Blackett, 1865–6) was the first of several works dealing with Wedgwood's friends and his products. These include *A Group of Englishmen (1795–1815)* (London, Longmans Green, 1871), a record of the younger Wedgwoods and their friends; *Wedgwood and his Works* (London, Bell & Daldy, 1873); and *The Wedgwood Handbook: A Manual for Collectors* (London, 1875).

The next two memorials are in front of and to the left of the mausoleum.

3.59. Sir Claude Maxwell Macdonald (1852–1915) [plot 31]

Soldier and diplomat. Educated at Uppingham and Sandhurst, Macdonald entered the Army in 1872. He served in the Egyptian campaign (1882) and was subsequently military attaché in Cairo. Macdonald served in the Suakin Expedition (1884–5), and served on the special missions to the Niger Territories (1889) and to Berlin (1890). He was appointed first Commissioner and Consul General to the Oil Rivers Protectorate (1891) and brought the whole area under ordered government. On retirement from the Army in 1896 Macdonald became British Minister at Peking (1896–1900), and secured the leases of Wei Hai Wei, the 'new territories' of Hong Kong and the opening of the West river to trade. During the Boxer Rising (1900) Macdonald commanded the defence of the foreign legations. He successfully did so, withstanding all assaults by the Chinese. He compiled an official report of this defence, *The Siege of the Peking Embassy 1900* (London, HMSO, 1900–1). Later in 1900 Macdonald was moved to Tokyo where he became first British Ambassador (1905). He was involved in the negotiations of the Anglo-Japanese Alliance (1902) and of the Anglo-Japanese Agreement (1905). Macdonald retired in 1912.

3.60. Sir George Sutherland Mackenzie (1844–1910) [plot 31]

Explorer and administrator. Born at Bolarum, India, Mackenzie was educated at Clapham and joined the firm of Gray, Dawes & Co., East India merchants and agents for the British India Steam Navigation Co. In 1866 he was sent by the firm to the Persian Gulf, and was subsequently able to open a trade route from the Gulf into the Persian interior via the Karun river. Mackenzie was a pioneer of Persian exploration. He was a founder member and managing director of the Imperial British East Africa Company (1888), and the area it controlled he named IBEA. Mackenzie was instrumental in developing East Africa by improving the facilities in Mombasa, by sending caravans as far inland as Uganda and by introducing Persian agriculturalists. He returned to England in 1890 and the IBEA charter was surrendered to the British Government in 1895. Mackenzie was Vice-President of the Royal Geographical Society (1901–5).

Further to the left is a kerbed allotment which includes a fine female statue.

3.61. Sir Richard Henry Wyatt (1823–1904) [plot 31]

Lawyer. Wyatt was a JP for the Cinque Ports, Kent and Merionethshire. He was High Sheriff of Merionethshire from 1883. Wyatt was sometime Clerk of the Peace, Lord-Lieutenant of Surrey and a member of Surrey County Council. He was a government parliamentary agent and gave much advice to the LNC on parliamentary matters, including the major alterations to its London terminus in the mid-1870s. Wyatt was knighted for public services in 1883. He was a director of the LNC (1880–1904). Wyatt died from injuries and shock received when he accidentally set his clothes on fire at his home in Broadstairs.

His wife, **Lady Mary Laura Wyatt** (died 1900), is commemorated by the adjacent statue. It is assumed to be a life-size likeness of her.

The plot was selected for the burial of their youngest daughter, **Amy Rudyerd Helpman** (1865–92), who is commemorated on the Celtic Calvary cross to the right of the statue. She was married to **John Henry Helpman** (1858–1912), who is also buried here.

Further across the plot is a headstone with a gable top.

3.62. Dudley Hardy (1867–1922) [plot 31]

Painter, poster artist, cartoonist, watercolourist and illustrator. Born in Sheffield, Hardy was educated at the Boulogne School and University College London. After training with his father T.B. Hardy (a marine painter), Hardy attended a succession of art schools in Europe. In Paris he was introduced to French chalk drawings and poster art, which had a lasting influence on his work and style. He began exhibiting at the Royal Academy from 1884; his first large canvas was

Sans Asile, painted in 1888. During the 1890s he became internationally famous for his posters, especially *The Yellow Girl*, for the weekly magazine *To-Day*, and a colourful series of advertisements for the Gilbert and Sullivan Savoy Operas. His illustrations could be seen in publications such as the *Illustrated London News*, the *Sketch*, *Pictorial World*, *Lady's Pictorial*, *Black and White*, the *Graphic* and *Punch*. Hardy was dubbed the 'English Ceret' after the French artist. He also designed humorous postcards, illustrations and cartoons for many magazines of the period. His paintings included Eastern scenes, studies of Dutch and Breton genre, biblical scenes and seascapes. His essential style was considered to be his spontaneity and the power to set down the passing impressions of his mind.

Facing St George's Avenue, and in the second line of graves, is a stylised Celtic cross with kerbing.

3.63. Sir John Everett Millais, 3rd Baronet (1888–1920) [plot 31]

Grandson of the artist Sir John Everett Millais, 1st Baronet (1829–96). Millais was the only son of Sir Everett Millais, 2nd Baronet (1856–97), and he succeeded to the title in 1897. Millais joined the Royal Navy as a cadet in HMS *Britannia*, and served on HMS *Albemarle* under Captain Jellicoe. Millais retired from the service in 1911 but rejoined on the outbreak of war. He served in HMS *Amethyst* in 1914. Millais retired with the rank of Lieutenant-Commander in 1917. He was a JP for Kent between 1919 and his death.

*The next memorial is the prominent pink granite pedestal directly in line with the **Drake** mausoleum.*

3.64. William Smyth (1845–1899) [plot 31]

Australian businessman and politician. Born in Sydney, Smyth was the son of a hay and corn chandler. He later moved to Weddin Mountain, New South Wales, where a goldfield was discovered, and moved to Gympie in 1868, where gold was also found. Smyth worked in various mines, including the One Mile Mine, before becoming a mine manager. Later he was able to buy gold leases, form companies, buy land and build houses. All this formed the basis of his success. Smyth entered the Queensland Legislative Assembly in 1884, where he officiated for fifteen years and became the authority on mining in the assembly. He was able to introduce a number of reforms in the industry. As a consequence he was dubbed 'Bill, the Miners' Friend'. Smyth travelled to England to recruit mine managers and establish business connections. In Gympie he founded the hospital, school, Masonic Lodge, library and school of arts. Smyth travelled to England in 1899 as the representative of the Queensland Government to the Earl's Court Exhibition in London. Upon arrival he was taken ill. He died as a result of an exploratory operation at the Chelsea Hospital, London. His widow probably never saw his grave again, even though she lived to the age of 93. She died in 1943 and is buried in Brisbane.[36]

Near St George's Avenue are two crosses of Calvary.

3.65. Perkins family grave [plot 31]

General Sir Aeneas Perkins (1834–1901) entered the East India Company Seminary at Addiscombe in 1850. He joined the Bengal Engineers in 1851. Perkins served in the relief of Delhi during the Indian Mutiny (1856), and constructed the 'Perkins' battery' there. He subsequently held various offices in Bengal. Perkins was the field engineer in the Bhutan Expedition (1864) and Executive Engineer at Morshedabad (1865–6). He was transferred to the Darjeeling division in 1866 and was Superintending Engineer to the North West Provinces from 1870. Perkins was Commander of the Royal Engineers of the Kuram Field Force (1878) that facilitated the advance on Kabul. He was present at the battle of Charasiab and the entry into

Kabul (1879). Perkins consolidated the defence of Kabul and was the Commanding Royal Engineer in the march to Kandahar (1880). He became Inspector General of military works (1881), Chief Engineer of the Central Provinces (1883–6) and of the Punjab (1886–9). Perkins commanded the Oudh Division (1890–2) and was promoted to General and Colonel Commandant of the Royal Engineers in 1895. Perkins was a contemporary of Lord Roberts (1832–1914), who wrote of his 'quick perception, unflagging energy, sound judgement, tenacity of purpose, and indomitable pluck'.

From here, cross into plot 22.

3.66. Phipson mausoleum [plot 22]

This mausoleum commemorates the life of **Weatherley Phipson** (1848–1909). Phipson was the son of Thomas Weatherley Phipson QC. Phipson was a barrister, with chambers in Paper Buildings, Temple. By the terms of his will Phipson left specific instructions for his cremation and the erection of this mausoleum to contain his ashes. A sum of £300 was set aside for this purpose from his estate. Therefore, although he died in May 1909, his ashes were not placed within until May 1910, when the building was completed. The interior is of octagonal plan and constructed in red brick, relieved by stone pillars and capitals. The latter form the bases for a series of arches that support the shallow dome and lantern above. Six stone shelves were provided for cinerary urns, but only one (opposite the door) is used. Pevsner describes this building as 'like a miniature Einstein Tower'.[37]

Just behind the mausoleum is a line of graves, facing away from St George's Avenue. One of these is a Calvary cross with kerbing.

3.67. Sir Edward Thornton (1817–1906) [plot 22]

Diplomat. Educated at King's College, London, and Pembroke College, Cambridge. Thornton was attaché at Turin (1842–5) and at Mexico (1845–54), being subsequently promoted to secretary of the legation. He witnessed the occupation of Mexico by the United States in 1847. In 1854 Thornton was appointed chargé d'affaires and Consul-General at Montevideo, and Minister Plenipotentiary at Buenos Aires from 1859. In 1863 he was accredited to the Republic of Paraguay, and in 1865 was sent to Brazil to negotiate for the renewal of diplomatic relations (broken off in 1863), which were shortly restored. In 1867 he became the minister at Washington and remained there for over thirteen years. This was a difficult period since the United States still resented British recognition of the Confederacy during the civil war, and there were outstanding boundary disputes to resolve. Eventually a joint commission was established in February 1871. This resulted in the Treaty of Washington (May 1871) whereby all outstanding claims were referred to arbitration under specific conditions. The eventual settlement did much to mend the bad feeling between the two countries. In 1881 Thornton was appointed ambassador at St Petersburg at a time of Russian expansion towards the Indian frontier. Despite a potentially dangerous incident at Pendjeh on the Afghan frontier (March 1885) a protocol for the settlement of this frontier was agreed in September 1885. As no further embassy became vacant Thornton retired in January 1887, declining the offer of a baronetcy.

Beyond this, and facing St George's Avenue, is a kerbed grave with a gable-topped headstone with much decoration on it.

3.68. Sir Henry Berkeley Fitzhardinge Maxse (1832–1883) [plot 22]

Soldier, and brother of **Admiral Frederick Maxse**. He entered the Army in 1849 and was promoted to Captain in the Coldstream Guards (1854). Maxse served throughout the Crimean

War on the staff of the Earl of Cardigan. He was present at the battles of the Alma and Balaclava (where he was wounded), and at the siege of Sebastopol. Maxse was promoted to Major (1855) and to Lieutenant-Colonel (1863). In the same year Maxse was appointed Lieutenant-Governor of Heligoland, and was later Governor (1864–81). During his period of office a new constitution was agreed (1868), gaming tables abolished (1870) and the island was joined to the mainland by the electric telegraph. Maxse was appointed Governor of Newfoundland in 1881 and died there at St John's in 1883. He published an English edition of Bismarck's *Letters to his Wife and Sisters 1844 to 1870*.

Just to the rear of this is a line of small crosses of Calvary.

3.69. Lieutenant Harold Leigh Wallis (*c*. 1894–1916) [plot 22]

A resident of Caterham, Surrey, Wallis joined the Royal Flying Corps after seeing service with the Royal Field Artillery. He trained at No. 26 Reserve Squadron at Turnhouse near Edinburgh and was killed on his first solo flight in a Maurice Farman Shorthorn trainer. It was suggested that as he was flying low over a railway he may have been startled by a train and lost control of the aircraft.

To the left of the above is a similar modest memorial.

3.70. Revd William Robert Fountaine Addison, VC (1883–1962) [plot 22]

Ordained in 1913, Addison served during the First World War from 1915 to 1918. On 9 April 1916 at Sanna-i-Yat, Mesopotamia, he carried a wounded man to cover, helped several others and attended to their wounds, all under heavy rifle and machine gun fire. His fine example and disregard for personal safety encouraged stretcher bearers to go forward under fire to collect the wounded. For this Addison was awarded the VC. He was one of 100 holders of the VC who formed a guard of honour to the body of the Unknown Warrior in Westminster Abbey on 11 November 1920. After the war Addison was Senior Chaplain at Bulford Camp (1920–3), Aldershot (1923–5), Malta (1925–7), Shanghai (1927) and Shorncliffe (1929–30). He was Chaplain to the Forces at Shoeburyness (1930–1), Tidworth (1931–2) and Bordon (1934–8). He retired in 1938 but returned to Bordon (1939–42).

Diagonally to the left is a sequence of crosses on octagonal bases with kerbing.

3.71. Adair family graves [plot 22]

Charles William Adair (1822–97) was a soldier in the Royal Marine Light Infantry. He served in Syria (1840–1), the Crimea (1854–5), and Japan (1863–6). Adair was ADC to Queen Victoria (1870–7) and was created a KCB in 1882.

His son, **Rear-Admiral Thomas Benjamin Stratton Adair** (1861–1928), entered the Navy in 1874, retiring in 1906. He was a member of the Ordnance Committee (1900–2) and served as Conservative MP for Glasgow Shettleston (1918–22).

His brother, **Brigadier-General Hugh Robert Adair** (1863–1946), entered the Royal Artillery in 1882. He commanded the Humber Garrison (1914–16) and the Thames & Medway Garrison (1916–20).

Towards the rear of the plot is a kerbed grave with two upright stones within it.

3.72. Louis Charles Bernacchi (1876–1942) [plot 22]

Scientist and polar explorer. Born in Tasmania, he moved to England in 1900. He was physicist to the Southern Cross Antarctic Expedition (1898–1900) and also to the National Antarctic

Expedition under Captain R.F. Scott (1901–4). He was awarded the King's Antarctic Medal and the Royal Geographical Medal. He travelled extensively: to British Namaqualand and German South West Africa (1905), to the forests of Peru (1906), to Central Borneo and other remote parts of the world. During the First World War he served as Lieutenant-Commander of the Royal Navy Volunteer Reserve in its anti-submarine division. He wrote many books about his travels, including *To the South Polar Regions: Expedition of 1898–1900* (London, Hurst & Blackett, 1901), an account of the cruise of the *Southern Cross* to the southern Polar regions, an expedition led by Carsten Borchgrevink.[38] He also compiled the *Saga of the 'Discovery'* (London, Blackie & Son, 1938) and completed a biography of Captain Laurence Oates, *A Very Gallant Gentleman* (London, Thornton Butterworth, 1933).

Nearby is a line of granite cross memorials.

3.73. Head family plot [plot 22]

Among those buried here are **Sir Robert Garnett Head**, 3rd Baronet (1845–1907), who was educated at Marlborough College. He married **Florence Julia** (1853–1931) in 1880 and succeeded his father as Baronet in 1887. Head contested Brixton as a Liberal in the 1895 election, but was not elected. There is a memorial tablet commemorating his life in Rochester Cathedral, where he is described as 'In character courageous and sincere, in disposition unselfish and patient, in heart most sympathetic and true.'

    Sir Robert Pollock Somerville Head, 4th Baronet (1884–1924), was a diplomat. He was educated at Wellington College and was nominated an Attaché in the Diplomatic Service in 1905. Head passed the competitive examinations in the following year. He was appointed to Lisbon in 1907, to Madrid later the same year and to Peking in 1911. Promoted to Second Secretary in 1914, he transferred to Vienna in 1914 and to Petrograd later in the same year. He returned to Peking in 1917 and was promoted to First Secretary in 1919. In 1920 he was transferred to Berlin. There is a memorial tablet commemorating his life in Rochester Cathedral.

Adjacent to the junction of St George's with St Bride's Avenue is a flat ledger stone.

3.74. Sir Cecil Allen Coward (1845–1938) [plot 22]

Lawyer. Educated privately, Coward was a student of the Inner Temple from 1865. He was called to the Bar and articled as a solicitor in 1870. Coward was a member of Lord McNaughten's Judicature Committee (1906–8). He was elected to the Council of the Law Society (1910), and was a member of the Royal Commission on Delays in the King's Bench Division (1913). During the First World War he represented the Public Trustee as Controller of Enemy Property under the Trading with the Enemy Acts. Coward was a member of the Royal Commission on the Civil Service (1915) and was President of the Law Society (1927–8). He retired in 1928.

Locate plot 24, near the junction of St George's Avenue with St Cyprian's Avenue. Towards the centre of the plot is a line of memorials, including a fine Grecian-style headstone with two figures.

3.75. De Morgan family graves [plot 24]

William Frend De Morgan (1839–1917) was an artist, inventor and author. The son of Augustus De Morgan (1806–71), he was educated at University College School and University College London. He entered the Academy Schools in 1859 and made acquaintance with the Pre-Raphaelites. De Morgan experimented in the manufacture of stained glass and tiles and established a pottery works in Chelsea from 1871, where he rediscovered the process of making coloured lustres. He joined William Morris at Merton Abbey (1882–8), after which he established his own factory at Fulham. Many of his decorative tile designs were used for decorative panels in steamships and country houses. Examples include the Smoking Room on the P&O liner *Britannia* and the Companion Way on the P&O liner *Arabia*. Use of the tiles in houses was often for fireplaces, using panels either beside or above the fireplace or in the hallway.[39] Examples of these include Cragside, Northumberland (designed by Richard Norman Shaw) and 55–57 Holland Park Road (designed by Halsey Ricardo). De Morgan retired in 1905 and the firm was dissolved in 1907. He then wrote novels, including his bestseller *Joseph Vance: An Ill-Written Autobiography* (London, Heinemann, 1906).

In the same grave is his wife, **Evelyn De Morgan, née Pickering** (1855–1919), who was also an artist. She was the daughter of Percival Pickering QC and Anna Spencer Stanhope, and therefore was the niece of the Pre-Raphaelite painter John Roddam Spencer Stanhope (1829–1908). Evelyn's first main work was *Ariadne at Naxos*, exhibited in 1877. She was quickly established as a highly regarded painter. Evelyn married William in 1887 and at times the sales of her paintings supported them both. One of her major patrons was William Imrie of Liverpool, who alone commissioned twelve paintings. After her husband's death she completed two of his unfinished novels, but it was widely considered that her painting was only a shadow of its former inspiration.

The headstone was designed by Evelyn and sculpted by Sir George Frampton.[40] It includes two figures, representing Grief (left, holding the inverted torch) and Joy (right), and two intertwined hearts at the top of the memorial. The quotation 'Sorrow is only of the earth; the life of the Spirit is joy', is an example of 'automatic writing' taken from one of the letters from angels and quoted in *The Results of an Experiment* (privately printed, London, 1909).[41] During the summer of 1993 the De Morgan Foundation paid for the headstone to be set perpendicular and for the general tidying up of this grave. The memorial has been recommended for statutory listing by Woking Borough Council.

Other memorials of interest adjacent to this grave include **Mary Jane Hales** (*c.* 1852–1926), buried to the right, was for many years nurse to Anna Maria Wilhelmina Stirling (1865–1965),[42] Evelyn's sister, who wrote the poem on this memorial:

Vanished from sight is the love that I knew
Intangible now as the mist and the dew
And the toil and the striving of life and its bliss
And the anguish of death have all ended in this!
Peace from distress and from torturing ill
Here where the sleeper lies silent and still
Peace where the dreamer can know no afright
In the dawning the gloaming, the blackness of night
Peace – where a God has said let there be light!

Stirling spent much of her childhood in the north of England and married **Charles Goodbarne Stirling** (*c.* 1866–1948) in 1901. She wrote from an early age and produced over thirty books during her long life. Stirling's first book, *Fairy Tales for Children*, appeared in 1881. Her first novel, *A Life Awry* (three vols, London, Bliss & Co., 1893), was published under her father's name, Percival Pickering. The book was eventually turned into a play. Under her own name Stirling wrote historical biographies, such as *Coke of Norfolk and his Friends* (London, John Lane, 1907), an account of the life of Thomas William Coke, 1st Earl of Leicester of Holkham;[43] *The Richmond Papers* (London, Heinemann, 1926), based on the correspondence and manuscripts of George Richmond RA and his son Sir William Blake Richmond;[44] and *The Ways of Yesterday* (London, Thornton Butterworth, 1930), being a chronicle of the Way family from 1307 to 1885.

Stirling also wrote the important biography *William de Morgan and his Wife* (London, Thornton Butterworth, 1922). She became an incessant, inquisitive historian, exploring the byways of the past. In 1931 the Stirlings acquired Old Battersea House which they used to form the De Morgan Collection of Pictures and Pottery. To the end of her life she remained able to show visitors around the house. Her book *The Merry Wives of Battersea and Gossip of Three Centuries* (London, Robert Hale, 1956) is her account of all those who had lived in the house, or who visited it. The collection still exists as the De Morgan Centre, based at West Hill Library, Wandsworth. The centre brings together the De Morgan Foundation's extensive collection of the works of William and Evelyn De Morgan, and archive material relating to them and their circle.

Georgina Frederica Mure (1856–1944) was the daughter of **Elizabeth Spencer Stanhope**. She was killed on 12 April 1944 when crossing the railway by the track (instead of the footbridge) at Chilworth station, Surrey.

Rowland Neville Umfreville Pickering (*c.* 1861–1931), buried to the left, was Evelyn De Morgan's brother.

Elizabeth Spencer Stanhope (1836–1920), buried further to the right, was wife of the Pre-Raphaelite artist John Roddam Spencer Stanhope (1829–1908) and Evelyn De Morgan's aunt.

Facing St Bride's Avenue is the next Calvary cross memorial with kerbing.

3.76. Robert Armitage Sterndale (1839–1902) [plot 24]

Colonial administrator. Sterndale was educated privately and went to India in 1856. He volunteered for service during the Indian Mutiny (1857) and helped raise and serve with a body of cavalry in the Central Provinces. He entered the Central Provinces Commission in 1859 and was appointed to the Finance Department from 1864. Sterndale retired from India in 1890. He was Acting Governor of St Helena during 1896. Sterndale was interested in natural history and published several books including *Seonce, or, Camp Life on the Satpura Range: A tale of Indian Adventure* (London, 1877), and *Denizens of the Jungles: A Series of Sketches of Wild Animals* (Calcutta, Thacker, Spink & Co., 1886). His book *The Natural History of the Mammalia of India and Ceylon* (Calcutta, Thacker, Spink & Co., 1884) has become a standard work since it was reissued in abridged form in 1929 and as recently as 1980.

Closer to St George's Avenue is a low hipped ledger stone.

3.77. Robert Freke Gould (1836–1915) [plot 24]

Soldier, barrister and historian of Freemasonry. Gould joined the Army and became a Lieutenant in 1855. He served in Gibraltar, Malta, the Cape of Good Hope, India and China. Gould commanded a company during the North China Campaign (1860) and served on the staff during the Taiping Rebellion (1862). A few years later he left the Army, and in 1868 he qualified as a barrister, working largely on the Western Circuit. Gould first became a Freemason in 1855 and devoted himself to military and Masonic literature from 1858. He was made Master of the Moira Lodge in 1874 and Senior Grand Deacon of England in 1880. Gould's Masonic writings were wide ranging. *The Four Old Lodges: Founders of Modern Freemasonry and Their Descendants* (London, Spencer's Masonic Depot, 1879) is a record of the progress of Freemasonry in England and of the career of every regular Lodge down to the Union of 1813. *The Atholl Lodges* (London, Spencer's Masonic Depot, 1879), is a memorial of the Grand Lodge of England. *The Military Lodges: The Apron and the Sword, or Freemasonry Under Arms* (London, Gale & Polden, 1899) provides an account of Lodges in regiments and ships of war, and of famous soldiers and sailors of all countries who have been Freemasons. Gould's *History of Freemasonry: Its Antiquities, Symbols, Constitutions, Customs &c* (six vols, London, Jack, 1882–7) is regarded as a standard work of reference.

Chapter Four

ST MARGARET'S AVENUE
AND THE 'RING'

*This circuit covers St Margaret's Avenue and the 'Ring', the central areas of the former Anglican sections. Start by the **Columbarium** at the top end of St David's Avenue.*

4.1. The Columbarium [plot 26]

Designed in the classical style, this was the largest mausoleum in the cemetery and was constructed for George Henry, the 5th Earl Cadogan.[1] It was constructed *c.* 1878–80 after the purchase of a plot measuring 32ft × 40ft and costing £640 for the ground. Never used, it was sold back to the LNC by the Earl for £200 in June 1910. Almost immediately afterwards the Board of Directors inspected the vacant mausoleum 'which it is proposed to convert into a Columbarium for the reception of urns'.[2] The interior features a partly glazed dome, with the verse 'Blessed are the Dead which die in the Lord'[3] carved around its base. There is a gallery at entrance level, with a stairway at the back leading to an underground vault. On both levels there are a number of niches or *loculi* for urns. These could be purchased at prices from 5 guineas according to size and position. The additional cost for a cast bronze tablet, including inscription, was £29 15s 6d.[4] The Columbarium has not been used as such for many years and is showing many signs of neglect, damage and vandalism. It has been recommended for statutory listing by Woking Borough Council.

A reminder of its former ownership remains with the adjacent grave of **Charles George Henry Cadogan** (1850–1907), which is just to the right of the entrance. He was the youngest son of the 4th Earl Cadogan,[5] and was originally buried in the mausoleum. After the Columbarium was sold his coffin was removed and buried in this spot just outside.

Behind the Columbarium is the Conolly family grave, which faces towards St Cyprian's Avenue. Commemorated on a plaque within the grave is **Major William Conolly** (1845–1922) whose epitaph records, 'his ashes lie in the Columbarium near by'.

Among the rhododendrons on the other side of St Margaret's Avenue is a very low wide headstone.

4.2. Sir Francis Seymour Haden (1818–1910) [plot 33]

Surgeon, etcher and anti-cremationist. Haden was educated at Derby School, Christ's Hospital and University College London. He continued his medical education at the Sorbonne and Grenoble. Haden became a lecturer on surgical anatomy at Grenoble and was honorary surgeon to the Department of Science and Art (1851–67). He established a large private practice in London, initially in Sloane Street but later in Hertford Street, Mayfair. Haden also undertook more public work, for instance as consulting surgeon of the Chapel Royal, as Vice-President of

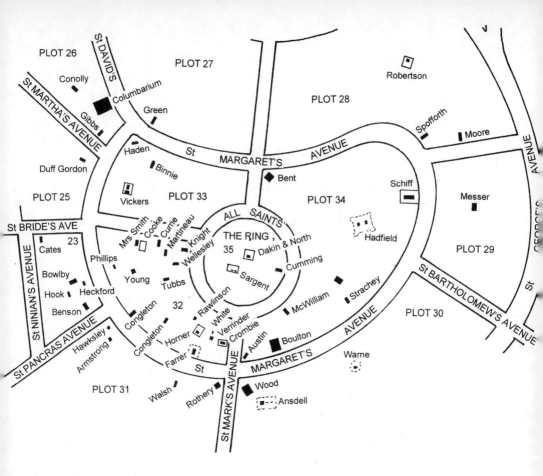

St Margaret's Avenue and the 'Ring'.

the Obstetrical Society of London, and as one of the founders of the Royal Hospital for Incurables (1850). His artistic talents proved a great relaxation from his professional duties. From 1843 Haden devoted most of his time to etching, mainly landscapes. These remain his chief memorial as he executed some 250 etchings throughout his long life. His work was influenced by J.A.M. Whistler,[6] whose half-sister, **Dasha Delano Whistler** (*c.* 1826–1908), he married in 1847. But Whistler's jealousy of Haden led to a fight in a Paris café in 1867 (where Haden was allegedly thrown through a plate glass window) and they never spoke again. Haden founded the Society of Painter-Etchers in 1880 and remained its President until his death. He wrote *The Etched Work of Rembrandt* (London, Macmillan, 1879), which was an introduction to the first chronological exhibition of Rembrandt's etchings held at the Burlington Fine Arts Club in May 1877. It followed on from a catalogue that Haden wrote and was privately printed for members of the Arts Club in 1877. **Sir William Drake**, a fellow member of the Burlington Fine Arts Club,[7] compiled *A Descriptive Catalogue of the Etched Works of F.S. Haden* (London, Macmillan, 1880).

In the 1870s Haden published a series of letters to *The Times* strongly opposing cremation. He pointed out that cremation was wasteful, costly and would unnecessarily pollute the atmosphere. Haden argued that bodies should continue to be buried but in disposable or 'Earth-to-Earth' coffins,[8] whereby the body would be naturally and quickly broken down by the 'resolvent action of the earth upon human remains'. The grave space might then be reused some years after burial. The coffins could be made of wicker or papier mâché since:

All the evils of the present system [of burials] come from the use of solid coffins, which pre-vent the earth having direct access to the body. If we bury a body at Woking in a light paper pulp coffin such as will dissolve as soon as it is placed in the ground, the action of the earth immediately begins, the oxidisation goes on converting the body into harmless products, which pass purified through the porous earth to the atmosphere, and in about three years the body will have entirely disappeared.[9]

These views are still relevant today. Haden's original correspondence was subsequently printed in pamphlet form as *Earth to Earth: An Answer to a Pamphlet on 'Cremation'. Reprinted from* The Times (London, Macmillan, 1875).[10] In January 1876 it was reported that **Julian Larkman** (the secretary) and Mr Diprose (a shareholder) had taken out a patent for such a coffin 'suitable for the object often discussed at this Board & advocated by Mr Haden'. Both had acted without the Board's sanction, but agreed to 'assign the patent & stock in hand . . . and profits already made . . . for £278 18s 11d', while this allotment in the cemetery was presented to Haden for his role in the rise of the 'Earth-to-Earth' coffin.[11] Its cause was taken up with relish by the LNC. The company had already published (in 1875) a leaflet on *The Patent Necropolis Earth-to-Earth Coffins*. Sample coffins were sent to many sanitary and trade exhibitions such as the Manchester & Salford Sanitary Association Exhibition (1877), the Sanitary Institution of Great Britain's exhibition in Leamington (1877) and the Social Congress Exhibition in Sheffield (1878). In 1878 it was agreed to donate a sample 'Earth-to-Earth' to Parkes' Museum of Hygiene, as requested by its curator. The LNC shortly relinquished its patent rights, believing that these coffins should be made as widely available as possible. The enormous interest aroused by these coffins promoted Haden's ideas, provided a sanitary alternative to cremation, allowed for the reuse of graves (hence perpetuity of burial revenues) and promoted burial at Brookwood (where the soil was especially suitable for these coffins). For all these reasons Haden urged that:

In the absence of any amelioration whatever of our present cemeterial system being obtainable, it is plainly to the interest of every class, high and low, to avoid the seething suburban cemeteries and to bury their dead at Woking.[12]

His ideas on more burial reform continued into the 1880s. The LNC issued another of its Sanitary leaflets' on *The Earth-to-Earth Coffin* (London, LNC, 1884), which included the text of an address given by Haden at a conference on 23 July 1884 expressing the desirability of greater simplicity in funerals.[13] Haden developed these ideas further when he published a pamphlet in favour of legislation 'to regulate and insure safe and proper burial' by dealing with the whole subject of cemetery management and reform as follows:

(1) For burial within the earth as the only legal mode of disposing of a dead body.
(2) For a limitation of time beyond which it should be illegal to keep a dead body unburied.
(3) For the illegality of strong coffins, brick graves and vaults, and of all contrivances having for their effect to retard resolution, and to confer on the dead a tenure, practically illim-itable, of the soil which is necessary to the purpose of the living.[14]

The effects of such an Act on the incomes of burial authorities throughout the land can only be guessed at and, needless to say, this proposal was never formally considered by Parliament. When Haden died, he was buried in an 'Earth-to-Earth' coffin here at Brookwood.

Also buried here, and commemorated on the unusual hemisphere monument as 'E.H.', is **Emma Haden** (c. 1794–1881), Haden's mother and an excellent musician. Emma Haden lost her favourite daughter, Emma Bergeron, in 1858. Emma Bergeron died in Paris aged 38, and is buried in Kensal Green Cemetery. There is no evidence that her mother was able to see the body before she was laid to rest. Over a period of more than ten years after her daughter's death, Emma Haden, who was widowed over thirty years earlier, recorded her grief in two commonplace books that have survived. Pat Jalland has used Emma's experience as an example of chronic or abnormal grief experienced by a broken-hearted mother.[15]

Directly opposite is the next memorial.

4.3. Frederick Valentine Green (1853–1953) [plot 27]

Employee of the LNC. He was elected auditor to the LNC in 1887 and was associated with the company for sixty years. Green succeeded **John B. Walker** as Chairman of the LNC in 1943. He resigned as Chairman in May 1947 and was succeeded by Roger B. Pemberton. Owing to ill health he resigned as a director in June 1948. Green died in August 1953 in his 101st year. He is buried with his wife **Isabella Green** (*c.* 1854–1933). Two memorial windows were made in her memory and placed in the large **Anglican chapel**. They were designed by Horace Wilkinson.[16]

Take the left-hand fork of St Margaret's Avenue. On the right, and set back from the path, is a large monument of rough grey granite.

4.4. Sir Alexander Richardson Binnie (1839–1917) [plot 33]

Civil engineer. Binnie worked on various Welsh railways between 1862 and 1866, before his appointment as Executive Engineer of the Public Works Department in India (1867–74). Based at Nagpur, he organised the city's water supply and discovered coal at Warora. A branch of the Great Indian Peninsular Railway was constructed to serve this coalfield. In 1875 Binnie moved to Bradford as its Chief Engineer. He repaired and reconstructed the Stubden, Leeshaw and Leeming reservoirs, and built those at Barden and Thornton Moor. In 1890 he was appointed Chief Engineer to the London County Council. Between 1891 and 1897 Binnie superintended the construction of the Blackwall Tunnel. This was a pioneering engineering project as it was the first time a 'Greathead' shield and compressed air were used together in tunnelling. The Blackwall Tunnel is 4,410ft long, excluding the approaches. He also designed Vauxhall Bridge (1895–1906), reusing the piled footings of the abutments of the previous structure by James Walker (which had been completed in 1816). Binnie designed the Greenwich foot tunnel, with an internal diameter of 11ft (1896–1902), and the Highgate Archway (1897–1900) that replaced Nash's structure of 1812. He was also involved in the work of widening the Strand, including the construction of the Aldwych and Kingsway thoroughfares. He was knighted on the completion of the Blackwall Tunnel in 1897. He ran a private practice from 1901 and reported on matters like the Bann and Lough Neagh drainage (1906), and the water supplies of Malta (1909), Petrograd (1910–11) and Ottowa (1913). Binnie died at his home in Beer, Devon, in 1917.

Continue along St Margaret's Avenue until you reach the large gothic-style memorial at the junction of St Mark's and St Margaret's.

4.5. Bent family memorial [plot 34]

One of the earliest large memorials in the cemetery, and designed in the gothic style. The sad decay is due to the incessant weathering of the Bath stone used in its construction. The memorial is of cruciform plan with a central core built of red brick, faced with Bath stone. From this emerge four decorated roofs supported by columns. The gable ends to each roof are decorated in the style of early fourteenth-century reticulated tracery. The central core of the monument also supports a gothic lantern which is surmounted by a carved cross.

The memorial commemorates the Bent family, who lived at Walton-on-Thames, Surrey, and Hawley Lodge, Farnborough, Hants. Note the decorative letter 'B' which may be seen on the gable ends and the decaying remains of the adjacent carved angels. Among those commemorated are **William Bent** (*c.* 1798–1859) and his wife **Mary** (*c.* 1785–1863), their son **Henry Walter Bent** (1828–78) and his wife **Mary Jane** (1835–1901), and their son **Walter Bernard Bent** (*c.* 1863–1904). This memorial has been recommended for statutory listing by Woking Borough Council.

Continue along St Margaret's Avenue. The next memorial is a tall Calvary cross set within a large family plot towards the centre of plot 28.

4.6. Field Marshal Sir William Robert Robertson (1860–1933) [plot 28]

Robertson was the first person to rise through the ranks from Private to Field Marshal. This remains a unique achievement. He enlisted in the 16th Lancers in 1877 as a Private, and was subsequently gazetted as a 2nd Lieutenant in the 3rd Dragoon Guards in India (1888). Robertson was appointed to the Intelligence Department in 1892 and entered the Staff College in 1896. He was head of the Foreign Section of the Intelligence Department at the War Office (1900–7). Robertson was subsequently promoted to Brigadier-General of the General Staff at Aldershot (1907–10), Commandant of the Staff College (1910–13) and Director of Military Training (1913–14). Robertson was Quartermaster-General, General Headquarters, France (1914–15), Chief of the General Staff and Chief of the Imperial General Staff (CIGS) (1915–18). As CIGS, Robertson's central role was to liaise between the Cabinet and the Army. With Haig, Robertson maintained that the war would be won or lost in France, and he persuaded the British Government to concentrate its resources on the Western Front. Prime Minister Lloyd George was not convinced of the Generals' views, and Robertson was removed from his post in February 1918. In his war memoirs, Lloyd George made a devastating assessment of Robertson and the Generals by stating:

> Had they been men of genius – which they were not – they could have adapted themselves more quickly to the new conditions of war. . . . [Haig] never even saw the ground on which his greatest battles were fought . . . Robertson never saw a battle.[17]

Robertson responded in his own reflections on the war that:

> Certain Ministers still held fast to the belief that victory could never be won – or c prohibitive cost – by straightforward action on the Western Front, and that it sought through lines of indirect attack elsewhere.[18]

Robertson became Commander-in Chief, Home Forces (1918) and of the Army 1919–20). He was created Field Marshal in 1920 and in the following yea memoirs, *From Private to Field Marshal* (London, Constable, 1921).[19] Robertson war memorial in May 1922. He was one of those depicted in **John Singer** *Some Generals of the Great War.*

Return to the path, and look for the low ledger stone in pink granite near the road juncti

4.7. Frederick Robert Spofforth (1853–1926) [plot 28]

Australian cricketer, regarded by many as the greatest ever bowler Spofforth became a bank clerk in the Bank of New South Wales. Cricket Club (1871–2), then the Albert Cricket Club, and in 187 against W.G. Grace's team. Spofforth toured England with the Australian teams of 1878, 1880, 1882, 1884 and 1886. He sprang to fame when he took 10 wickets for 20 runs in Australia's one-day victory over a strong England team at Lord's on 27 May 1878. In 1879 Spofforth took the first 'hat trick' in a Test Match at Melbourne, and later twice obtained 3 wickets in 4 balls. During the 1882 Test at the Oval, England needed 85 runs to win and reached 51 before the third wicket fell, yet Australia went on to win by 7 runs. Spofforth played in 18 Test Matches, taking 94 wickets at an average of 18.41 each. In all his first class matches he took 1,146 wickets for 13.55 each. He continued to play for New South Wales until 1885 when he was appointed Manager of the Moonee Ponds branch of the National Bank of Australia, Melbourne. Spofforth married Phyllis Marsh Cadman, daughter of a wealthy tea merchant, in 1886. They returned to Melbourne, but Spofforth settled in England as a representative for the Star Tea Company from 1888. He developed a great knowledge of botany and horticulture, and planted Australian trees in his English gardens. He died at Ditton Hill Lodge, Long Ditton, Surrey.

Turn left, along the path leading towards St George's Avenue. The next memorial is on the left, a grey granite Celtic cross with kerbing.

4.8. Sir Edward Cecil Moore (1851–1923) [plot 28]

City businessman and Lord Mayor of London. Moore entered his father's accountancy office in 1867, and was made a partner in 1880. He became an Associate of the Institute of Chartered Accountants (1880), a Fellow (1888), Vice-President (1922) and President (1923). Moore practised with his brother, son and other partners at Thames House, Queen Street. He was elected Alderman of the Bishopsgate Ward (1912–23) and was Sheriff of London (1914–15). Moore was a member of the Fruiterers' Company and during his Mastership in 1918 took a prominent part in the creation of the Chamber of Horticulture. He was Lord Mayor of London (1922–3). During his year of office he raised a fund to present the Duke and Duchess of York with a wedding gift, and another for the preservation and restoration of HMS *Victory*. Moore also raised over a quarter of a million pounds for the survivors of the Japanese earthquakes of 1923. He was created a Baronet in 1923.

Return to St Margaret's Avenue. Look for the low headstone near the trees in the plot opposite.

4.9. Lieutenant-Colonel Arthur Albert Messer (1863–1934) [plot 29]

Architect. Messer practised in America between 1888 and 1898 and established a London office from 1898. He designed domestic architecture, partly on the LNC's Hook Heath estate, Weybridge, and elsewhere. He was often assisted by **Cyril Tubbs**, and their designs at Hook Heath include Comeragh Court,[20] High Housen, Hohen Heid, Lingdown, The Links, The ch, Stony Fore and Westward. He also designed (with Cyril Tubbs) the second **Anglican pel** in the cemetery, built between 1908 and 1910. Messer served during the First World partly with the 1st French Cavalry Corps and the 10th French Army. He was missioned in the British Expeditionary Force in 1915 and subsequently worked on the orate of the Graves Registration Unit, forerunner of the Imperial War Graves ission. By the end of 1915 he was Fabian Ware's[21] chief lieutenant in graves registration France. In 1916 Messer was present at the first meeting of the National Committee for of Soldiers' Graves, established by the Prince of Wales. During the same year Messer d in sole charge of the Graves Registration Units on the Western Front. By 1918 he wn surveying and planning office in France, financed by the Red Cross, and was initial arrangements for proper construction work in the military cemeteries. It was suggested the estimate of £10 per grave for the permanent military cemeteries, and overall this proved realistic. He continued links with the Commission after the war and designed some small military cemeteries in Switzerland, Holland and Scandinavia. For many years he lived at Little Widbury, Hook Heath, which he designed.

In the plot opposite is a prominent tomb-style memorial set within a large kerbed enclosure.

4.10. Sir Ernest Frederick Schiff (1840–1918) [plot 34]

Businessman. Schiff was born in Austria on Christmas Day 1840. His father was Leopold Schiff of Trieste. He became the principal partner in the firm of Messrs A.G. Schiff & Co. of Warnford Court EC, a business founded by his brother Alfred that built up a very good continental connection. An able partner, he developed the business considerably. Schiff became a member of the Stock Exchange in 1877. He founded the Schiff Home of Recovery at Cobham in memory of his brother Alfred. In May 1915 he wrote a letter to *The Times* declaring his loyalty to this country and his 'feelings of disgust and abhorrence at the unheard of crimes committed by the enemy'.

To the left and rear of this grave is a large private allotment screened by a conifer hedge.

4.11. Sir Robert Abbott Hadfield (1858–1940) [plot 34]

Metallurgist and industrialist. Hadfield was born in Attercliffe, Sheffield, and was educated at the Collegiate School, Sheffield, before working in his father's steelworks. He experimented with the melting properties of steel and undertook a systematic study of alloys of iron with manganese and silicon, thereby discovering manganese steel (1882), silicon and alloy steels. The manganese steels were useful in crushing and grinding machinery, in tramway and railway crossings, and where resistance to abrasion is needed. Its lack of brittleness meant it was used for helmets in the First World War. The silicon steels had interesting electrical properties, including a high resistance. It proved difficult to roll, and it was some years before it became available commercially, being used especially in electrical transformers. On his father's death in 1888 Hadfield became Chairman and Managing Director of the firm. He was a patient and systematic research worker, often collaborating widely with physicists or other interested parties. Hadfield was a hard worker, being capable of heavy periods of sustained work. Yet he was a model employer, and was one of the first to introduce an eight-hour day, encouraging innovation and providing the means for experimental work. Hadfield supported the 'eight-hour movement' and published a booklet promoting its acceptance, *A Shorter Working Day* (London, Methuen, 1892). Hadfield developed his firm's armaments production and studied the deformation of steel at high velocities, resulting in armour-piercing shells. He was President of the Iron & Steel Institute (1905–7) and of the Faraday Society (1914–20). During his life Hadfield received many honours, including a knighthood (1908), a Baronetcy (1917), and the freedom of the City of London (1917) and of Sheffield (1939). Hadfield published many of his discoveries, including *Alloys of Iron and Tungsten* (London, Iron & Steel Institute, 1903), and *The Work and Position of the Metallurgical Chemist* (London, Griffin & Co., 1921). He died at his home on Kingston Hill, Surrey.

Nearer the path is a round-topped headstone with kerbing.

4.12. Ralph Strachey (1868–1923) [plot 34]

Engineer. The son of Lieutenant-General Sir Richard Strachey, who was long associated with the East Indian Railway. His son owed nothing to this family link. Strachey went to India as assistant engineer to the East Indian Railway in 1890. He rose stage by stage, by conspicuous merit, to become Chief Engineer (1913–20). In this position he showed considerable ability. He retired for family reasons and returned to Britain.

Nearby is an extraordinary and unique memorial.

4.13. Charles Warne (1802–1887) [plot 30]

Archaeologist, who specialised in the prehistoric and ancient remains of Dorset. Warne, with the poet William Barnes,[22] was involved with protecting Maumbury Rings for posterity. The outcry resulted in the statutory protection of Maumbury Rings, on the southern edge of Dorchester, from the route of the proposed Wilts, Somerset & Weymouth Railway (Act of 1845). This was the first antiquity to be saved from injury by a railway as a result of a protest made by local people. Warne published accounts of his archaeological discoveries between 1836 and 1872. Many of these were based on his own research and fieldwork. They include *Dorsetshire: Its Vestiges, Celtic, Roman, Saxon and Danish* (London, D. Sydenham, 1865), *The Celtic Tumuli of Dorset: An Account of Personal and Other Researches in the Sepulchral Mounds of the Durotriges* (London, J. Smith, 1866) and *Ancient Dorset: The Celtic, Roman, Saxon and Danish Antiquities of the County, Including Early Coinage* (Bournemouth, D. Sydenham, 1872). Warne was a Fellow of the Society of Antiquaries (1856). During his lifetime he amassed a large collection of English and Roman coins, which were sold at auction by Sotheby's on 24 May 1889, two years after his death. His unusual memorial is in the form of a stylised barrow or henge: a remarkable design for the Anglican section. The upright stone is made from serpentinite, a rare metamorphic stone from the Lizard.

Continue along St Margaret's Avenue until you reach the classical-style mausoleum to your left.

4.14. Wood family mausoleum [plot 30]

This mausoleum is in the late seventeenth-century English style. Each side elevation comprises a blind arcade of six arched panels that are used for the inscriptions. There are some nice details such as the family crest carved in the pediment above the door. Note also the cherub heads used above each arch on the sides and the swags in the frieze just below the roof. Unfortunately the two stone vases in the niches either side of the door have not survived. The rear wall used to include a large semi-circular frosted window, but this has been vandalised and the opening has been bricked up. Among those commemorated here are:

Lieutenant Andrew Wood (died 1787), who was accidentally drowned while carrying dispatches in an open boat to Lord Cornwallis's fleet.[23]

George Wood (*c*. 1813–92) served in the 2nd Regiment of the Life Guards. He let the Ottershaw Park estate to Lord Belfast in the 1830s. It was finally sold in its entirety to Richard Crawshey in 1841. Wood then moved to Potters Park, Surrey. The original mansion at Ottershaw Park was subsequently replaced by a new one in 1910–11. Two of his infant sons are also buried here.

Lieutenant-General Sir George Hay Wood (*c*. 1750–1824) served in the Bengal Army of the East India Company. He was dubbed the 'Royal Bengal Tiger' and was a friend of Warren Hastings.[24] Wood purchased the Ottershaw Park estate in 1819. At that time it was a Palladian mansion of brick and stone set in landscaped gardens. The estate was entirely self-sufficient with its own stables, wine stores and brewery.

Sir James Athol Wood (1756–1829) was a Rear-Admiral and brother of Sir Mark Wood.[25] He entered the Navy as an Able Seaman in 1774 and was promoted to Lieutenant in 1778. He served in the West Indies (1794) and was captured. Wood was interned in Paris (1794–5), but was exchanged in 1795 and promoted to Commander in 1795. He assisted in the capture of Trinidad, and was promoted to Captain (1797). Wood was in charge of a convoy to the West Indies (1804), stationed in the West Indies (1807–9), attached to the Channel Fleet (1810–12) and the Mediterranean Fleet (1812–15). He was knighted (1809) and became a Rear-Admiral (1821).

Just behind this is a large private allotment containing three memorials and partly screened by conifers.

4.15. Richard Ansdell (1815–1885) [plot 30]

Eminent Victorian artist specialising in sporting, farming and wildlife subjects, most notably in Scotland and Spain (here collaborating with John Phillip[26]). A man of humble beginnings and born in Liverpool, he married a local girl, **Maria Romer** (1819–96). They had eleven children, two of whom are buried in this plot: **Harry Blair Ansdell** (1852–84) and **Rosalie Leech** (1844–1933). He had a vast output of paintings and became very successful as an artist in his lifetime, his paintings often being engraved for the popular market.[27] Joint canvases with fellow artists Thomas Creswick[28] and William Powell Frith[29] were fairly usual. He often carried out commissions for the aristocracy, painting a favourite animal or the 'day's bag' after a shooting expedition. He was particularly known for his wonderful portrayal of dogs. He is also known for his vast canvases of big countryside meetings, comprising crowds of miniature portraits, the *Waterloo Coursing Meeting* (1842) and the *Country Meeting of the Royal Agricultural Society of England* (1842) being two cases in point. Ansdell always escaped to Scotland whenever he could and was a notable sheep farmer in the Highlands where he owned a loch-side mansion. The surrounding countryside was an inspiration for many of his paintings. When his health started to fail he built another mansion near Frimley, Surrey, called Collingwood Tower, where he eventually died in 1885. Ansdell was a member of the Royal Academy in London and President of the Royal Academy in Liverpool. He has a niche in Victorian art and had been somewhat overlooked in recent times because he and Landseer (who enjoyed royal favour) were contemporaries and often painted in the same genre. His pictures are now fetching large sums with the major auction houses and he is getting the recognition he deserves. Ansdell has an area of Lytham St Annes (including a railway station) named after him, and also two streets in Kensington.[30]

Also buried here is Rosalie's husband, **William Leech** (1836–87), and their son **Guy Ansdell Leech** (*c.* 1877–1904).

In the plot opposite is another fine mausoleum.

4.16. Boulton family mausoleum [plot 34]

This is a fine mausoleum in the neoclassical style. The doorcase shows a slight Egyptian influence with its battered sides. Note the fine details such as the egg and dart carving, and the palm and laurel motif above the doorway. The bronze door depicted Christ as the Good Shepherd, but this is no longer visible. Among those buried within are:

Sir Samuel Bagster Boulton (1830–1918), an industrialist. He was Chairman of Burt, Boulton & Haywood Ltd, based in London, Paris, Riga, Selzaette and Bilbao. Boulton was also Chairman of the Dominion Tar & Chemical Company, of the British-Australian Timber Company, and of the London Labour Conciliation & Arbitration Board (1889–1913).

His son, **Sir Harold (Edwin) Boulton** (1859–1935), was an industrialist and lyricist. He was director of his father's firm and of the Baths Club Ltd. Boulton published many volumes of songs and lyrics, including the *Skye Boat Song* and *Glorious Devon!* He also published *Songs of the Four Nations* (London, J. Cramer, 1892), with the musical arrangements by Sir Arthur Somervell.[31] This was a collection of old songs from England, Scotland, Ireland and Wales, many never before published, with the complete words and accompaniment. Boulton was the secretary of the Keats-Shelley Memorial Association (1906–26), and was founder and Chairman of the People's Palace in Mile End Road[32] and of the East London Horticultural Society. Boulton was also founder and President of the Federation of Working Men's Social Clubs (1895–1930) and Director of the Royal Academy of Music (1931).

Sir George Kendall Bushe Power, 7th Baronet of Kilfane (1846–1928), was a tenor. He was a professor of voice production and singing, and sang in Malta and Italy. Power was the original Ralph Rackstraw in *HMS Pinafore* at the Opera Comique (London, May 1878), and the original Frederic in *Pirates of Penzance* at the Opera Comique (London, April 1880). He married Sir Samuel Boulton's daughter **Eva Gertrude** in 1915.

To the left, and adjacent to the junction, is a low ledger in pink granite.

4.17. William Austin (1820–1909) [plot 34]

The son of Edward Austin, a merchant in the City of London; his mother was the third daughter of the political economist David Ricardo (1772–1823). Austin was educated at Hill Top, Birmingham, the school managed by Sir Rowland Hill (1795–1879), and afterwards at Peterhouse College, Cambridge. He was called to the Bar at Lincoln's Inn in 1846 but never practised as a lawyer. Austin interested himself in many public undertakings. Together with William Arthur Wilkinson MP and Charles Gilpin MP he advocated through public meetings and in other ways the construction of the Metropolitan Railway. He was a director of the Metropolitan District Railway, and Chairman of the Metropolitan and St John's Wood Railway. Austin was associated with the formation of the LNC from 1851. Along with his relations and friends, Austin invested some £20,000 in the LNC at this time. He subsequently became one of its directors, served as deputy chairman (1853–70) and succeeded **Sir Thomas Dakin** as chairman (1870–1902). Austin was succeeded by Dakin's son-in-law, **Edward Ford North**.

Diagonally opposite is a fine cross memorial decorated with carved flowers.

4.18. Henry Cadogan Rothery (1817–1888) [plot 31]

Solicitor. From 1842 Rothery worked in the ecclesiastical and admiralty courts. He was one of the original directors of the LNC and Chairman of the Committee of Enquiry, established on 19 July 1853 to investigate 'the state and affairs of the LNC'. The shareholders adopted his subsequent report, issued on 27 September 1853. Rothery, along with John S. Taylor, did much to reform the affairs of the LNC, but felt obliged to resign as a director in April 1854. However, he later served as a director (1871–88).[33] He was legal adviser to the Treasury on the slave trade (1860).

In 1876 Rothery was appointed one of Her Majesty's Commissioners for Wrecks, and was a Commissioner at the time of the Tay Bridge disaster (1879). The Court of Inquiry subsequently produced two reports on the disaster that were published on 5 July 1880.[34] In the first (by Yolland and Barlow) it was not felt necessary to place the blame on any particular person or group of people. The second report was by Rothery, and here he stated bluntly that:

> The bridge was badly designed, badly constructed and badly maintained. For these defects both in the design, the construction and the maintenance, Sir Thomas Bouch is in our opinion [*sic*] mainly to blame. For the faults in design he is entirely responsible. For those of construction he is principally to blame in not having exercised that supervision over the work which would have enabled him to detect and apply a remedy to them. And for the fault of maintenance he is also principally if not entirely to blame in having neglected to maintain such an inspection over the structure as its character imperatively demanded.[35]

This verdict resulted in Bouch's replacement as engineer to the Tay Bridge, and damaged his professional reputation. Bouch died in October 1880, ten months after the disaster and four months after Rothery's report appeared. **James Brunlees**, who had submitted evidence at the inquiry,[36] was initially approached to replace Bouch, but he declined the offer.

In plot 32, opposite, is a large kerbed grave with a hipped ledger stone in granite that faces St Mark's Avenue.

4.19. Lewis Crombie (*c*. 1800–1880) [plot 32]

Crombie was a solicitor working for the firm of **Bircham** & Company. He was for many years in the employ of the London & South Western Railway (LSWR). Crombie was originally appointed as a law clerk in 1852. He was Secretary to the LSWR (1853–62). Succeeded by Frederick Clarke, Crombie remained in the legal department of the LSWR until his retirement.

Behind this grave is a Calvary cross with kerbing.

4.20. George Turner White (*c*. 1853–1899) [plot 32]

Railwayman. White served several years as stationmaster at Exeter Queen Street. He succeeded **Edgar Verrinder** as Superintendent of the Line (1893–99). Note the lettering on the kerbing: 'Erected by officers and staff of the LSWR.' White was succeeded by Sam Fay,[37] who left the Midland & South Western Railway Company to take up his appointment with the LSWR.

Adjacent is a large Calvary cross with carved ivy covering the front of the cross.

4.21. Edgar William Verrinder (*c*. 1837–1893) [plot 32]

Verrinder was in the employ of the LSWR for forty-two years, first as a junior clerk at Woking. His various postings included Wimborne, Farnborough (as senior clerk), stationmaster at Godalming (1859) and Andover (1860). He was superintendent of the North Devon line (1862–5), superintendent of Waterloo station (1865–7), assistant superintendent of the line under Mr W.M. Williams (1867) and became Superintendent of the Line in 1874. From that time Verrinder often took charge of royal trains on the LSWR, particularly supervising Queen Victoria's travel arrangements from Windsor to Gosport. It was after one of these journeys in July 1893 that he was taken ill from diabetes, and died shortly afterwards. His funeral at Brookwood was accompanied by upwards of 3,000 men of the LSWR. Verrinder was succeeded by **George White**.

Behind these graves is a large upright stone with columns. It is set within a large kerbed allotment.

4.22. Leonard Horner (1795–1864) [plot 32]

Geologist and educationalist. Horner studied at Edinburgh University. He was Secretary of the Geological Society (1810) and its President from 1846. Horner organised Whig meetings in Edinburgh (1821–6) and founded the Edinburgh School of Arts (1822) for the instruction of mechanics. He was one of two founders of the Edinburgh Academy. Horner was Warden of London University (1827–31), a Commissioner inquiring into the employment of children in factories (1833) and a Chief Inspector under the Factories Act for twenty-five years. He is buried in a large family grave.

Horner's daughter, **Mary Elizabeth** (1808–73), married Sir Charles Lyell (1797–1875) who, although commemorated here, is buried in Westminster Abbey. Lyell is known as 'the father of modern geology' since his *Principles of Geology* (three vols, London, John Murray, 1830–3) caused a storm. The book overturned the way people thought about geology by piecing together all those arguments that form the basis of modern geology and finally discrediting the 'catastrophic' school of geological thinking. The book went through a total of eleven editions in Lyell's lifetime.

Nearby is the next memorial comprising a Calvary cross with kerbing.

4.23. Sir Henry Creswicke Rawlinson (1810–1895) [plot 32]

Soldier and oriental scholar. Rawlinson entered the East India Company's military service and acquired a good knowledge of Persian and the Indian vernaculars. He served in Persia (1833–9) and was appointed political agent at Kandahar (1840). He distinguished himself in the Afghan War (1842) and became a political agent in Turkish Arabia (1843). In 1844 he was appointed Consul at Baghdad and was Consul-General (1851–5). Rawlinson deciphered the celebrated cuneiform inscription of Darius Hystaspes at Behistun in 1846, and in the same year published his translation as *The Persian Cuneiform Inscription at Behistun, Deciphered and Translated with a Memoir on Persian Cuneiform Inscriptions* (London, John Parker, 1846). He returned to England in 1855 and was MP for Reigate (1858–9) and Frome (1865–8). His other books include *A Commentary on the Cuneiform Inscriptions of Babylonia and Assyria: Including Readings of the Inscription of the Nimrud Obelisk* (London, John Parker, 1850) and, published under the direction of the Trustees of the British Museum, *The Cuneiform Inscriptions of Western Asia* (five vols, London, R. Bowler, 1861–1909). Rawlinson was a member of the India Council (1858–9 and 1868–95), a Trustee of the British Museum (1876–95), President of the Royal Asiatic Society (1878–81) and President of the Royal Geographical Society (1871–2 and 1874–5). He published many valuable papers on his research, including several on cuneiform inscriptions.

Adjacent to this is a large private plot that fronts St Margaret's Avenue.

4.24. Sir Thomas Henry Farrer, 1st Baron Farrer (1819–1899) [plot 32]

Civil servant. Educated at Eton and Balliol College, Oxford. He was called to the Bar at Lincolns Inn in 1844 but ceased to practise in 1848. Farrer moved to the Board of Trade, and in 1850 was made assistant secretary to the marine department. He spent the rest of his career in the civil service, becoming Assistant Secretary to the Board of Trade (1854) and Permanent Secretary from 1865 to 1886. During this period he influenced the development of English commercial legislation, including a memorandum on the Merchant Shipping Law Consolidation Bill, the Merchant Shipping Code (1870), the framing of the Bankruptcy Act (1883), the regulation of railways, and Acts dealing with electric lighting. After he retired from public service Farrer continued to write on economic matters, and helped found the Gold Standard Defence Association (1895). He was a member of the London County Council (1889–98), acting for several years as its vice-chairman. He died at Abinger Hall, Dorking, and was cremated at St John's, Woking.

Also buried here is his first wife, **Frances** (1825–70), their son **Thomas Cecil Farrer**, 2nd Lord Farrer (1859–1940), who was also cremated, and his wife **Evelyn Mary** (1862–98). **Cecil Claude Farrer**, 3rd Lord Farrer (1893–1948), is also buried in this vault. The adjacent graves contain the remains of **Frederick Willis Farrer** (1829–1909) and his wife **Mary** (*c.* 1838–1916); and **Herbert William Farrer** (1861–1912).

The next memorial is on the other side of the path. It is a headstone with kerbing.

4.25. Walter Walsh (1847–1912) [plot 31]

Historian of Protestantism. Walsh devoted his life to Protestant work. He was assistant editor of the *English Churchman* (1884–1900), and editor of the *Protestant Observer* (from 1888). A Fellow of the Royal Historical Society, Walsh founded the Imperial Protestant Federation in 1896, part of a federation of some fifty-six Protestant organisations throughout the British Empire. He was appointed editorial secretary to the Federation in 1905. Walsh published many books and pamphlets on the history of Protestantism, such as *The Secret History of the Oxford Movement* (London, Swan Sonnenschein, 1897; the book went through six editions in two years),

The Ritualists (London, J. Nisbet, 1900), *The Religious Life and Influence of Queen Victoria* (London, Swan Sonnenschein, 1902), *The Jesuits in Great Britain: an Historical Inquiry into their Political Influence* (London, Routledge, 1903) and *The Women Martyrs of the Reformation* (London, The Religious Tract Society, 1905). Somewhat appropriately, his epitaph records that he 'peacefully passed away in St Mary's Church, Spring Grove, Isleworth, on Sunday morning, February 25 1912'.

The next memorial is a large cross ledger stone in pink granite on the other side of the path.

4.26. Parnell family graves (Barons Congleton) [plot 32]

Major General Henry Parnell, 4th Baron Congleton (1839–1906), served with the East Kent Regiment, the Buffs (1855–83). He served in the Crimea (1855) and in the Zulu War (1879), when he commanded the 2nd Battalion of the East Kent Regiment, including the defence of Ekowe. He commanded the Infantry Brigade at Gibraltar (1895–1900) and Malta (1900–1) and retired in 1902. His epitaph notes 'A life of duty well done'.

Henry Bligh Fortescue Parnell, 5th Baron Congleton (1890–1914), is commemorated on the same grave. Educated at Eton and New College, Oxford, he entered the Grenadier Guards. He was mentioned in dispatches for gallant conduct and skilful handling of his platoon against terrific odds on 6 November 1914 during the action of 1st Ypres; he was killed in action four days later. Baron Congleton was the first member of the House of Lords to be killed in the First World War. He is buried in grave E.2 in Zillebeke Churchyard, Belgium, otherwise known as the 'Aristocrats' Cemetery' because of the number of titled men buried there.

William A.D. Parnell (1894–1916), his younger brother, is also commemorated here. A Lieutenant in the Grenadier Guards, he was killed in action on 25 September 1916 during the Battle of the Somme. He is buried in the Guards Cemetery, Lesboeufs, with thirty-nine other men killed on the same day.

To the left of this grave, and further into the plot, is the headstone memorial with kerbing to **Henry William Parnell**, 3rd Baron Congleton (1809–96), who entered the Navy in 1829. He served at the Battle of Navarino (1827) and was promoted to Lieutenant. He retired in 1835. Parnell was Sheriff of Westmeath from 1861. He succeeded his brother in October 1883.

Directly opposite the main Parnell memorial is a small group of Calvary crosses with kerbing. Look for the one with raised lettering.

4.27. Sir George Carlyon Hughes Armstrong (1836–1907) [plot 31]

Journalist and newspaper proprietor. Born at Lucknow, Armstrong was privately educated and became a military cadet with the East India Company. During the Indian Mutiny (1857–8) he was attached to the 59th Bengal Native Infantry, and then as second in command of the Stokes's Pathan Horse. He was dangerously wounded in action near Delhi. After the suppression of the Mutiny Armstrong became Orderly Officer at the East India Company's Military College at Addiscombe, where he remained until it closed in 1861. Armstrong became an agent for the Westminster Conservative Association and was largely credited with the defeat of John Stuart Mill[38] by W.H. Smith[39] at Westminster in November 1868. In 1871 Armstrong was offered the editorship and management of the *Globe* newspaper, then running at a loss. Armstrong, with a natural sense of business and political instinct, made the *Globe* highly profitable and an influential support of Disraelian Toryism. One of his 'scoops' concerned the publication of the terms of the Salisbury-Schouvaloff Treaty in May 1878.[40] These were denied somewhat randomly by the Government, which went on to attempt the prosecution of the poorly paid clerk who sold the text to the newspaper. However, the subsequent publication of the official terms on 14 June vindicated the accuracy of the *Globe*'s coup. In 1882 Armstrong acquired a large interest in the *People*, a Sunday paper very popular with the working classes. He resigned as editor of the *Globe* in 1889, and in 1892 received a baronetcy. Armstrong allowed his second son to take control of the *Globe* from 1899.

The next memorial is nearer the path and comprises a series of irregular stone blocks. No inscription is visible, but Hawksley's grandson's headstone is immediately adjacent to St Pancras's Avenue.

4.28. Thomas Hawksley (1807–1893) [plot 31]

Civil engineer, particularly associated with water supplies to various cities. He was educated at Nottingham Grammar School and was articled to Mr Staveley of Nottingham. Hawksley subsequently became a partner until he left for London in 1852. He provided additional water supplies for Nottingham (1830) and was engineer to the joint water supply companies for Nottingham (1845–80). In conjunction with William Armstrong, Hawksley invented a self-acting valve which automatically closed when water velocity exceeded a certain limit. Hawksley was particularly associated with the water supplies for Liverpool, Sheffield and Leicester. He recommended the Rivington-Pike supply scheme for Liverpool that was completed in 1857. Later further supplies were required, and Hawksley drew up plans for the construction of a masonry dam across the Vyrnwy valley and the creation of an enormous reservoir. He remained engineer of this scheme up to 1885. In Sheffield Hawksley advised on the bursting of the Dale Dike reservoir on 11 March 1864, and prepared plans for additional water supplies for the city. He remained engineer of these works until his death. At Leicester he planned and built the Thornton Park and Bradgate reservoirs. Hawksley was also involved with schemes for the supply of gas and drainage. He was President of the Gas Managers' Association (1864–7) and was one of the experts consulted over London's main drainage (1857). Hawksley was President of the Institution of Civil Engineers (1872–3), of the Institution of Mechanical Engineers (1876–7) and was elected a FRS in 1878.

The next memorial is a large scroll-top ledger stone adjacent to the junction with St Pancras's Avenue.

4.29. Bernard Greenwood Benson (died 1911) [plot 23]

The first airman to be buried at Brookwood and only the third British aviator to die in an aeroplane accident.[41] Benson was studying engineering at the Central Technical Engineering Department of London University and was taking flying lessons at the Valkyrie Flying School at Hendon in his spare time. The Valkyrie monoplane was one of the earliest British designs but it suffered from a lack of stability and was difficult to control. On the evening of 25 May 1911 Benson took off from Hendon, but lost control of the aircraft during his descent and the aircraft crashed onto the airfield. Curiously the cause of death was given as heart failure although whether this occurred before or after the crash is not known.

Further along is a round-topped headstone with kerbing.

4.30. Heckford family grave [plot 23]

Nathaniel Heckford (1842–71) was a surgeon and doctor. He was born in Calcutta and was a student at the London Hospital from 1859. Heckford became consulting surgeon at Broad Street Buildings, City of London, from 1863. He was a licentiate of the Society of Apothecaries from 1867. With the help of his wife, **Sarah Heckford, née Goff** (*c.* 1837–1903), he founded the East London Hospital for Children & Dispensary for Women in January 1868, in a converted warehouse at Ratcliff Cross. Heckford was the resident surgeon there until his death. Charles Dickens was a keen supporter, and published an article about the hospital in *All the Year*

Round (December 1868). Heckford was a good diagnoser and a brilliant surgeon. He was Secretary of the Beaumont Medical Society and author of numerous medical papers. A new children's hospital was opened in Shadwell in 1876. After his death Sarah Heckford moved to Naples, India, then South Africa, where she spent most of the rest of her life and where she eventually died. She wrote *The Story of the East London Hospital for Children* (London, 1887).[42]

In an adjacent grave are buried **Margaret (or Margarite) Macgregor** (*c.* 1849–72), a devoted nurse to the hospital and a great friend of the Heckfords. Buried in the same grave is another nurse from the hospital, **Frances Tolhurst** (*c.* 1847–70).

Behind this is a headstone of pink granite.

4.31. James Clarke Hook (1819–1907) [plot 23]

Painter. Hook studied at the Royal Academy Schools and exhibited from 1839. His early subjects were old-fashioned genre of historical anecdote. He worked and travelled in Ireland and Italy until the 1848 revolutions obliged him to return to Britain. From 1854 he concentrated on English coast scenery, portraiture and subjects from poetry and history. This was partly influenced by his moving to Surrey and visiting Cornwall. His best-known works are *Pamphilus Relating his Story* (1844), *Luff, Boy!* (1859), *The Samphire Gatherer* (1875) and *The Stream* (1885). Hook was a keen radical and Nonconformist, horticulturalist and pomologist. His home at Churt, Surrey, was farmed so that he was virtually self-sufficient.

To the right is a kerbed memorial in white stone.

4.32. Sir Anthony Alfred Bowlby (1855–1929) [plot 23]

Surgeon. The son of Thomas William Bowlby (1817–60), a correspondent for *The Times*. Once qualified, Bowlby worked in various posts at St Bartholomew's Hospital: as Surgical Registrar (1884), Assistant Surgeon (1891) and Surgeon (1893). He served as a surgeon to the Portland Hospital during the Boer War. The hospital was first established at Rondesbosch near Capetown, but it was later moved to Bloemfontein. Bowlby wrote an account of the work of the hospital, his experience of wounds and sickness in South Africa, and described the civilian base hospital in time of war in *A Civilian War Hospital* (London, John Murray, 1901). Bowlby was Surgeon to the Household of King Edward VII (1907) and Surgeon in Ordinary to King George V. During the First World War Bowlby was attached to the 1st London General Hospital, but was shortly appointed Consulting Surgeon to the British Expeditionary Force with the rank of Colonel. His main task at this stage was to organise the casualty clearing stations. Bowlby was Director of Medical Services to the 2nd Army (1915), General Adviser to the Director-General of the Army Medical Service, and finally became Consulting Surgeon to the entire British Army in France. He was an extremely successful medical administrator, for which he achieved the unusual distinction of three knighthoods: KCMG (1915), KCVO (1916) and KCB (1919). Bowlby co-edited *Medical Services: Surgery of the War* (London, HMSO, 1922), and wrote a standard textbook on *Surgical Pathology and Morbid Anatomy* (London, J. & A. Churchill, 1887), which went through seven editions in his lifetime.

The next memorial is near the junction of St Ninian's and St Bride's avenues. It is a headstone with kerbing.

4.33. Arthur Cates (1829–1901) [plot 23]

Architect. Educated at King's College School. In 1846 he entered the office of Sydney Smirke[43] as a pupil. He joined the Architectural Association (1847), was an associate of the Royal Institute of British Architects (1856) and a fellow (1874). Cates was Hon. Secretary to the Architectural

Publication Society (1859–92). In 1870 Cates became architect to the land revenues of the crown under the Commissioners of Woods and Forests. Here he promoted agricultural architecture and education, which are his chief memorials. Cates was Vice-President of the Royal Institute of British Architects (1888–92) and was Chairman of its Board of Examiners (1882–96). Cates was elected the first Chairman of the Tribunal of Appeal under the London Building Act (1894 until his death).

Return to St Margaret's Avenue. On the other side of the path is the next headstone with kerbing and footstone.

4.34. Henry Phillips (1801–1876) [plot 32]

Singer and musician. Phillips appeared as a singing boy at the Haymarket and Drury Lane Theatres, when he was known as 'the singing Roscius' (1810–17). As a baritone, Phillips sang the part of Caspar in the production of *Der Freischultz* (Covent Garden, 1824) and was one of the soloists in the first performance in England of Beethoven's Ninth Symphony (21 March 1825). He became a noted bass singer. Phillips retired in 1863. He was also a singing teacher and composed music to many songs; the most popular was *The Best of all Good Company* (1840). Altogether he composed music for over fifty pieces.

Further in the plot is the next Celtic cross-style memorial.

4.35. Sir Allen William Young (1827–1915) [plot 32]

Sailor and polar explorer. Young joined the Merchant Navy in 1842 and commanded the *Marlborough* (an East Indiaman) and the troopship *Adelaide* during the Crimean War. Young was selected as the navigating officer on McClintock's expedition of 1857–9, searching for Sir John Franklin's missing ships.[44] He took an active part in sledging, travelled over 1,400 miles and discovered 380 miles of new coastline, including the southern and western coasts of Prince of Wales Island and the shores of the Franklin Strait. Young later published an account of these discoveries, based on his own journal, in *The Search for Sir John Franklin* (London, 1875). In 1860 Young commanded the *Fox* on an expedition to survey a route for the North Atlantic telegraph cable via the Faroes, Iceland and Greenland. Young assisted Admiral Osborn in equipping the Euro-Chinese Navy and commanded the *Quantung* during the Taiping Rebellion (1862–4). He commanded the *Pandora*, the first ship to penetrate the Peel Straits, in the North-West Territories (1875). In 1882 Young commanded the whaler *Hope* on the relief expedition to find the explorer Benjamin Leigh Smith. Young rescued him and the crew of the *Eira*, lost in Franz Joseph Sound. He wrote an account of the *Fox* expedition for the *Cornhill Magazine* in 1860, and *The Two Voyages of the Pandora in 1875 and 1876* (London, E. Stanford, 1879). He was knighted in 1877. His inscription is mis-spelt: he is described as 'Artic explorer'.[45]

Further into the plot, within a small hedged enclosure, is the next cross-style memorial.

4.36. Cyril Bazett Tubbs (1858–1927) [plot 32]

Born in Reading, Tubbs trained as an architect, estate agent and surveyor, and joined the LNC in 1887. His first main task was to generally advance the company's interests. These included a survey of the surplus lands the company owned and arranging for suitable land sales on terms advantageous to the LNC. Under his direction these sales were better organised, and Tubbs was largely responsible for the development of the prestigious estate on Hook Heath. He was appointed General Manager (1890–1919), when he also undertook some reorganisation in the cemetery. It was Tubbs who numbered the various plots (like an estate plan) and named the cemetery avenues (like roads on an estate). Tubbs also suggested – as early as 1891 – the construction of a crematorium and **columbarium** within the cemetery. He was also responsible for establishing a nursery and the **Masonry Works** within the cemetery grounds. Tubbs was a director of the LNC (1914–27). During the First World War he served in the Army and was promoted to Captain. As an architect, Tubbs helped design the company's second Westminster Bridge Road station (completed 1902), the second Anglican chapel (with **A.A. Messer**; see **St Edward Brotherhood**) and the **Catholic chapel**. Also with Messer he designed several houses on the LNC's Hook Heath estate, Weybridge, and elsewhere. Those on Hook Heath include Comeragh Court,[46] High Housen, Hohen Heid, Lingdown, The Links, The Patch, Stony Fore and Westward. Tubbs died suddenly at his home, Denhome in Datchet. The Board of Directors recorded the following tribute to him on 13 April 1927:

> Resolved that they [the Directors] desire to express and record their sincere regret at the death of their valued colleague and to place on record their deep sense of the important services rendered by him to the Company during his 40 years connection with its affairs as its Surveyor, General Manager and later as one of its Directors.[47]

Return to St Margaret's Avenue. The next memorial is a grey granite cross with kerbing and is adjacent to the junction with St Martha's.

4.37. Sir Cosmo Duff Gordon (1862–1931) [plot 25]

Businessman and survivor of the *Titanic* disaster. Educated at Eton, Sir Cosmo lived a life of comfort and privilege. He was a first-class fencer and represented Britain at the 1908 Olympic Games. Sir Cosmo and his wife were travelling on the *Titanic* under the assumed names of Mr and Mrs Morgan. Along with his wife's secretary, they occupied lifeboat No. 1. This had only twelve people in it, although the boat was designed for forty. Apart from crew members and the Gordons, only C.E. Henry Stengel of New Jersey was in this lifeboat. Afterwards Sir Cosmo regretted offering every crew member a £5 cheque. However, he claimed at the Court of Inquiry on 17 May 1912 that he had given these out to help the crew buy new clothes once they landed. But the family's near monopoly of the boat, and their failure to rescue other survivors, made the gift look like a payoff to a personal crew. There is little evidence to support this, but the events dogged Sir Cosmo for many years.

Lucy Christiana Sutherland, Lady Duff Gordon (1863–1935), his wife, was a famous fashion designer. Her first shop was at 24 Old Burlington Street and opened as the Maison Lucile. Using the name Lucile for her designs, she pioneered the split skirt and was well known for her picture dresses, tea and ball gowns. Her designs were popular as each one was unique. Lady Duff Gordon also designed stage costumes, for instance for Lily Elsie[48] in *The Merry Widow*. By 1897 larger premises were acquired at 17 Hanover Square and by 1900 the Maison Lucile had become one of the great couture houses in London, with clients ranging from Margot Asquith to the Duchess of York (later Queen Mary). Lady Duff Gordon opened branches of her fashion houses in New York (1909), Paris (1911) and Chicago (1915). The reason for the couple being on the *Titanic* was in order to attend a fashion show in New York. As the great liner sank Lady Duff Gordon remarked to Miss Francatelli, her secretary, 'There is your beautiful nightdress gone'. The *Titanic* disaster gave her and her fashion houses enormous publicity, especially in America. But after the First World War her designs were considered rather *passé* with the 'new look' of the 1920s, and her fashion empire went into steady decline. She ended her days in relative poverty, living in a small house on Hampstead Heath, and published her autobiographical reminiscences, *Discretions and Indiscretions* (London, Jarrolds, 1932). She married James Stuart Wallace, but they were divorced in 1888, and Sir Cosmo Duff Gordon in 1900.

On the other side of the path is a cross ledger memorial.

4.38. Frederick Waymouth Gibbs (1821–1898) [plot 26]

Barrister, author and royal tutor. He was educated at Trinity College, Cambridge, and was a Fellow of the college (1845–53). Gibbs was called to the Bar at Lincoln's Inn in 1848. He was appointed Tutor to the Prince of Wales (1852–8) by Prince Albert. He was made a CB in 1858 on the completion of his duties as royal tutor. Gibbs returned to the law. He was made a Bencher (1882) and appointed QC (1880). He wrote a number of books, including one on the American Civil War, *Recognition: A Chapter from the History of the North American and South American States* (London, William Ridgway, 1863), and *English Law and Irish Tenure* (London, William Ridgway, 1870). A portrait of Gibbs by G.F. Watts[49] was bequeathed to the Prince of Wales.

Cross over to plot 33 and look for the prominent memorial with an eagle.

4.39. Vickers family grave [plot 33]

This large family plot includes a stylised eagle and tomb memorial that may have been designed by Edwin Lutyens.[50] Both memorials have been recommended for statutory listing by Woking Borough Council. Buried here is **Douglas Vickers** (1861–1937), Chairman of the Vickers aircraft manufacturers. He was educated at Marlborough. The Vickers firm originated as a steel-making business based in Sheffield. It gave its name to types of machine guns and to a series of aeroplanes which the firm began to construct from 1911. One of the company's aeroplanes was the first to carry a machine gun (1913). Vickers contested the Brightside Division of Sheffield in both elections of 1910 but was unsuccessful. During the First World War the company produced many types of aircraft for the British and Allied forces. Douglas Vickers was Chairman of Vickers Limited (1918–26)[51] and was Conservative MP for Sheffield Hallam (1918–22).

Commemorated by the stylised eagle memorial is his eldest son, **Oliver Henry Douglas Vickers** (*c.* 1899–1928). He joined the Royal Flying Corps straight from Eton College in 1917, leaving the playing fields of Eton for the killing fields of Flanders. He joined No. 20 Squadron in Flanders in June 1917, flying the FE2d fighter biplane. Vickers was a genuine 'ace' of the First World War. During the space of three months in France he and his observer shot down fifteen German aircraft, including four in the course of one sortie. He returned home in August 1917 and became a flying instructor. After the war he joined the family firm as a special director and technical adviser at the Vickers works at Weybridge. He died of septic pneumonia on 17 June 1928. At his funeral three days later an aeroplane from Weybridge circled the funeral party in a final salute.

Walk over to All Saints' Avenue, which connects St Margaret's Avenue to the 'Ring'. The next headstone is under a rhododendron quite close to St Margaret's.

4.40. Sarah Eleanor Smith (1861–1931) [plot 32]

Widow of Captain E. J. Smith, Captain of the *Titanic*, who was lost at sea as the liner sank on its maiden voyage in April 1912. Mrs Smith was badly injured when she was knocked down by a taxi in London. She died at St Mary Abbot's Hospital, Marloes Road, Kensington, on 28 April 1931. The funeral took place on Friday 1 May and a special funeral train was provided, advertised as leaving the Necropolis station in London at 1.40 p.m. She was buried here, near the grave of her daughter **(Helen) Melville**.

Her husband, Captain Edward John Smith (1853–1912), spent thirty-two years with the White Star Line. He first went to sea as an apprentice on a clipper in 1869. He worked his way up and joined the White Star Line in 1880 as the 4th Officer on the *Celtic*. By 1887 he was Captain of the *Republic*. During the Boer War he commanded troopships to and from South

Africa. Smith became a commodore of the White Star Fleet in 1904 and went on to captain seventeen White Star ships, including the *Olympic* in 1911.[52] By the early 1900s Smith was the Senior Captain of the Line, and he traditionally commanded new ships on their maiden voyages. Due for retirement, Smith was offered the opportunity to take the *Titanic* on what was expected to be an unremarkable transatlantic trip. Smith was a true seaman who once said:

> In a way, a certain amount of wonder never leaves me, especially as I observe from the bridge a vessel plunging up and down in the trough of the sea, fighting her way through and over great waves. A man never outgrows that.[53]

No one really knew what happened to Captain Smith after the *Titanic* sank, although one witness saw him in the water holding a child. There is a statue commemorating his life in Lichfield, sculpted by Kathleen Scott.[54]

The following graves are in the family plot immediately to the left of Mrs Smith's grave.

Cooke family allotment [plot 32]. Among those buried here is **Sir Henry Paget-Cooke** (1861–1923). Paget-Cooke was a solicitor. He was educated at Cheltenham College and admitted as a solicitor in 1886. He joined the firm of Russell-Cooke & Company in 1890, becoming a senior partner in 1903. The firm acted in most of the parliamentary and municipal election petitions from 1890. Paget-Cooke was legal adviser to Princess Beatrice[55] and Governor of the Isle of Wight. He was also legal adviser to the Central Liberal Association.

    Oliver Dayrell Paget Paget-Cooke (1891–1954), only child of the above. Educated at Cheltenham College and Christ Church College, Oxford. During the First World War Paget-Cooke served in the Artists' Rifles, Royal Army Service Corps and as a Lieutenant in the Grenadier Guards. He became a solicitor in 1920 and a senior partner of Russell-Cooke & Company from 1923. Paget-Cooke was Vice-Chairman and Hon. Treasurer of the Princess Beatrice Hospital in Kensington, and was Comptroller of the Household of Princess Beatrice (1933–44).

    Sidney Russell Cooke (1892–1930) was a member of the London Stock Exchange and a director of several companies. He was found shot dead with a double-barrelled gun at his chambers in King's Bench Walk in the Temple. At the inquest it was stated that during the First World War Cooke had suffered from shell-shock. However, this had no bearing on the accident since it appeared he had been cleaning the gun and was leaning over it when it accidentally went off.

    Also commemorated on the headstone is his wife, **(Helen) Melville Cooke, née Smith** (died 1973), whom he married in 1922. She was the daughter of Captain E.J. Smith and **Sarah Eleanor Smith**. Born in Liverpool, she later moved to Southampton with her parents. Known as 'Mel', she married first Captain John Gilbertson, who subsequently died of black water fever on a voyage home from India. She had twins from her marriage with **Sidney Russell Cooke**, Simon (1923–44) and Priscilla (1923–47). 'Mel' had an adventurous life, driving sports cars and becoming a pilot. After her husband's death she moved to Leafield, Oxfordshire, where she died.[56]

Just beyond is a Celtic Calvary cross memorial with kerbing.

4.41. Samuel Currie (1816–1898) [plot 32]

Surgeon. Educated at Edinburgh University. Currie was Assistant Surgeon in the Army from 1836 and Surgeon from 1847. He was appointed Deputy Inspector General of Hospitals from 1859. Currie served in the Sutlej campaign (1846), in China (1860) and was Principal Medical Officer with the Abyssinian Expeditionary Force (1867). He was Surgeon General from 1868, and was Principal Medical Officer for Madras (1870–4), and Bengal (1874–6). Currie retired in 1876. He was Honorary Physician to Queen Victoria (1873–98).

Nearby is another Calvary cross with kerbing.

4.42. Horace R. Martineau, VC (1874–1916) [plot 32]

Martineau is commemorated on the side of his family's grave to the right of All Saints' Avenue. He was awarded the VC for his actions on 26 December 1899 near Mafeking, South Africa, during the action at Game Tree. When the order to retire had been given Sergeant Martineau rescued a corporal who had been struck down near the Boer trenches. He managed to half-drag and half-carry the wounded man to a bush where he attended to his wounds. Although shot in the side, Martineau took no notice and continued to assist the corporal until he was wounded a second time and was forced to give up. Martineau died in Dunedin, New Zealand, and is buried in Anderson's Bay Soldiers Cemetery.

The next memorial is a barrel-topped ledger made of grey granite. It is located beside the junction of All Souls' with the 'Ring'. This area used to be one of the more prestigious sections in the cemetery. Note the planting of monkey puzzle trees surrounding the 'Ring', although the circle of these trees is now incomplete.

4.43. Sir Henry Edmund Knight (1833–1917) [plot 32]

Alderman and Lord Mayor. Knight was educated at the City of London School. He became a member of the Corporation of London for Cripplegate Ward from 1867. Knight was subsequently Alderman of the Cripplegate Wards (1874–1917). He was Sheriff of London & Middlesex (1875). Knight served as Lord Mayor of London (1882–3), and one of his duties was to receive the Prince of Wales when he opened the City of London School on the Embankment. He was also present at the official opening of the Law Courts by Queen Victoria. During Knight's term of office Burnham Beeches was dedicated to the public.[57] On leaving office he was knighted. Knight continued his public work as a member of the Corporation. Earlier in 1917 he was presented with testimonials on the occasion of the fiftieth anniversary of his first election to the Corporation. A memorial service was held at St Giles's, Cripplegate, on 27 November 1917, followed by his funeral at Brookwood.

Further over, but facing the 'Ring', is a Calvary cross with kerbing.

4.44. Sir George Greville Wellesley (1814–1901) [plot 32]

Admiral. Wellesley entered the Navy in 1828 and was commissioned as a Lieutenant in 1838. He took part in the operations of 1840 off the coast of Syria, including the attacks on Caiffa, Jaffa, Tsour and St Jean d'Acre in the frigate *Castor*. In 1841 he was appointed to the frigate *Childers*. As Captain he commanded the *Daedalus* in the Pacific (1849–53). He moved to the *Cornwallis* in 1855 in the Baltic, and commanded a squadron during the bombardment of Sveaborg. His ship was then sent to the North America station, after which he commanded the Indian Navy. Wellesley became a Rear-Admiral (1863) and was Admiral Superintendent at Portsmouth (1865–9). He was Commander-in-Chief North America and West Indies station (1869–70 and 1873–5) and was Commander of the Channel Squadron (1870–1). Wellesley became First Sea Lord in W.H. Smith's Board of Admiralty (1877–9).

In the centre of the 'Ring' is a large kerbed allotment with a large Calvary cross.

4.45. Sir Thomas Dakin (1808–1889) [The 'Ring']

City businessman and Lord Mayor of London. Born in Derbyshire, Dakin was educated at Knutsford Grammar School and London University. Dakin was a partner in the firm of Bryden & Co., wholesale and export druggists. The firm became Dakin Brothers in 1859 and moved to larger premises in 1866. Dakin was a member of the Court of Common Council of the City of London for Candlewick ward (1842), deputy (1853) and Alderman (1861–89). He was Sheriff of London and Middlesex (1864–5) and Lord Mayor of London (1870–1). During his period of office he raised a fund for those besieged in Paris during the Franco-Prussian War and the Paris Commune. Within a month £113,000 was raised, and the fund finally raised £126,000. In February 1871 68 tons of provisions were sent to Paris for distribution. Dakin also raised a large sum for the relief of those affected by a disastrous fire in Chicago, a hurricane in Antigua and a famine in Persia. Dakin was Warden of the Fishmongers Company (1876–8, 1880) and its Prime Warden (1883–4). He was also Master of the Spectacle Makers Company (1876–7). Dakin twice contested a seat in Parliament as a Liberal, but he was never elected as an MP. Dakin was the first Chairman of the LNC (1853–70), and was succeeded by **William Austin**. Dakin died as a result of a fall on the Thames Conservancy steamer on the River Thames on 11 May 1889. He fell awkwardly down a staircase and injured one of his legs. The wound was not at first considered serious, but he subsequently died on 24 May.[58]

Also in this large grave is **Edward Ford North** (*c*. 1842–1927) who married Dakin's daughter **Edith** (died 1917). North was a director of the LNC (1890–1927) and became Vice-Chairman from October 1901. He succeeded **William Austin** as Chairman in September 1902. In February 1906, North purchased 10 acres of the LNC's land for £3,000. The plot was located on Golf Club Road at Hook Heath, and North subsequently built a house there, which he called Comeragh Court. At the subsequent AGM North stated that he and his family intended to live there, thereby showing their faith in the company's estate.[59] Mr Austin felt it was advantageous to have the Chairman holding land that belonged to the company as he would be able to see what was going on in the neighbourhood of Brookwood and Woking. North resigned as Chairman in February 1925, owing to ill health. He had in fact been absent from the Board for a long period. He was succeeded by Colonel Henry George Ricardo.[60]

Behind this allotment is a triple grave with kerbing and two small headstones.

4.46. John Singer Sargent (1856–1925) [The 'Ring']

Painter. Born in Florence of American parents, Sargent began his artistic training in Paris, including a period with the portraitist Carolus-Duran.[61] He exhibited in Paris from 1877, and moved to England in 1884. Although at this stage his portraits attracted attention at exhibitions, Sargent did not enjoy many commissions. His controversial portrait of *Madame X (Madame Pierre Gautreau)*, shown at the 1884 Salon, probably did little to help. Sargent's early years show his 'impressionistic' style (e.g. *Carnation, Lily, Lily, Rose*, 1884–5, first exhibited in 1887). From the 1880s he began to establish himself as a portrait painter, but it was only with the showing of *Gertrude, Lady Agnew of Lochnaw* in 1893 that the public really appreciated Sargent's gift for portraiture. He began to paint an enormous number of innovative and original portraits, and Sargent was soon described as the most fashionable artist since Lawrence.[62] One of these canvases depicts the colonial administrator **Sir Frank Athelstan Swettenham**. After 1900 he tired of 'paughtraiture', since his popularity meant that sitters appeared for whom he felt no empathy and who saw a portrait merely as a status symbol. Initially he compromised by executing charcoal portraits (he called them 'mugs in coke and charcoal'), but by 1906 he confined himself to landscapes, sketches and completing the decoration of the Boston Public Library. Sargent served briefly as an official war artist which resulted in his huge canvas *Gassed* (1918). His *Some Generals of the Great War* includes, among others, **Field Marshal Sir William Robert Robertson**. The epigram on Sargent's memorial, '*laborare est orare*', is the motto of the Benedictines ('to work is to pray').[63] This memorial has been recommended for statutory listing by Woking Borough Council.

On the other side of the 'Ring' is a Celtic cross memorial with kerbing that faces plot 34.

4.47. Admiral Sir Arthur Cumming (1817–1893) [The 'Ring']

Admiral Cumming entered the Royal Naval College at Portsmouth in 1831. He was a mate on the steamer *Cyclops* off Syria in 1840 and assisted in the storming of Sidon. In 1843 Cumming was Commander of the brig *Frolic* off South America, when it met the pirate slaver *Vincedora*. Cumming managed to intercept her retreat and at a critical moment he shot their captain and boarded the slaver. He and his seven men held the crew at bay and the slaver was subsequently escorted to Rio de Janeiro. Cumming was promoted to Commander of the *Rattler* off the west coast of Africa (1849–51). He was promoted to Captain of the *Conflict*, and saw service in the Baltic (1854). Cumming commanded the floating battery *Glatton*, which served in the Black Sea (1855–6). He was commander of the *Emerald* in the Channel Fleet (1859–63). Cumming was made Rear-Admiral (1870) and was Commander-in-Chief in the East Indies (1872–75). He became a Vice-Admiral (1876) and was promoted to Admiral (1880). He retired in 1882.

The next memorial is a Celtic cross on a base with kerbing. The memorial faces the 'Ring'.

4.48. James Ormiston McWilliam (1808–1862) [plot 34]

Medical officer to the Niger Expedition. McWilliam entered the Navy as Assistant Surgeon (1829–36). He was then appointed Surgeon to the *Scout* off the west coast of Africa. McWilliam returned to England in 1839 to improve his medical knowledge. In 1840 he became Senior Surgeon to the *Albert*, which joined the Niger Expedition for geographical and commercial purposes. In September 1841 a fever broke out on the *Albert* and the other two vessels. These were sent back to the coast leaving the *Albert* to continue the voyage. By 4 October it too was forced to return to the coast, being managed for many days by McWilliam and Dr Stanger, the geologist. The rest of the crew were unable to assist. McWilliam returned to England but received no official recognition of his important contribution. He published *A Medical History of the Expedition to the Niger During the Years 1841–2* (London, J. Churchill, 1843), which included an account of the fever and the abrupt termination of the expedition. He subsequently served on a mission to the Cape de Verde islands to report on an outbreak of yellow fever. McWilliam proved that the fever had been imported by the ship *Eclair*, and his official report appeared in 1847. He also reported on the epidemic of yellow fever in Brazil at the end of 1849, which was subsequently published in the *Medical Times* in April 1851. In 1849 he was appointed medical officer to the custom house, a post he held until his death. He was elected FRS in 1848 and was an active member of the Epidemiological Society. McWilliam died after falling downstairs in his home at Trinity Square, Tower Hill.

Chapter Five

THE 'GRIDIRON'

T his is an unofficial and purely descriptive name for these sections of the cemetery. It stretches from **St Cyprian's Avenue** towards the **Glades of Remembrance**, and is the only large area in the cemetery divided into a regular grid pattern.

Start from the junction of St Cyprian's Avenue and St George's Avenue. Locate plot 19 to your right and look for the prominent memorial near the junction.

5.1. Colonel Alan Vincent Gandar Dower (1898–1980) [plot 19]

Soldier and politician. Dower was educated at Sandhurst and Oxford. He served in France during the First World War (1916–17) and was attached to the RAF (1918). Dower was Conservative MP for Stockport (1931–5) and Cumberland (1935–50). He was a member of the Select Committee on Estimates (1938–9). Dower was made a Freeman of the City of London and was a Liveryman of the Barbers Company. His pastimes included hunting, big game shooting and polo.

The next memorial is in a large allotment at the back of the plot edged by a low conifer hedge.

5.2. Sir Nusserwanjee (Ness) Wadia (1873–1952) [plot 19]

The son of the Hon. Nowrosjee Nusserwanjee Wadia, who developed the Wadia group of mills which formed an important section of the Bombay cotton industry. Wadia was educated at St Xavier's College, Bombay. He entered his father's business and trained hard since his father expected him (and his elder brother, Sir Cusrow Wadia[1]) to spend long hours devoted to the affairs of the firm. The Wadia mills developed into an excellent example of commercial efficiency and integrity. Both brothers were held in high esteem and both were great philanthropists. Wadia was a devout Anglican and gave generously to the Bombay diocese and the Indian Church Aid Association. He died in Bombay.

Beyond this plot is a cross memorial within a group of graves at the other side of plot 19.

5.3. Major General Sir Charles Edward Callwell (1859–1928) [plot 19]

Soldier and writer. Callwell entered the Royal Field Artillery in 1878. He worked in the intelligence branch of the War Office (1887–92). On the outbreak of the South African War he was appointed to the staff of Sir Redvers Buller[2] in 1899. Callwell commanded a mobile column in the western Transvaal and Cape Colony (1900–2). He retired in 1909, but returned to active service as Director of Military Operations & Intelligence at the War Office (1914–16). Callwell was promoted to Major-General and was awarded the KCB (1917). As a military writer he

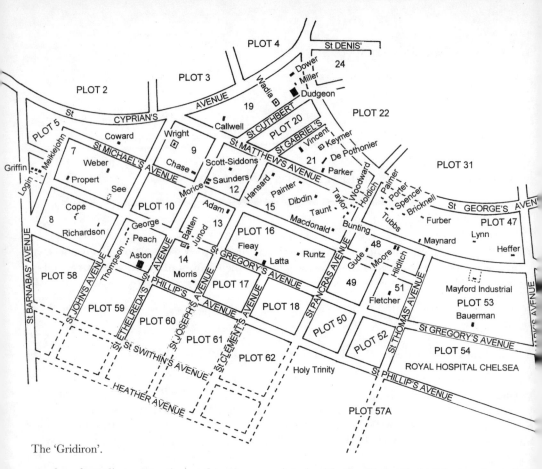

The 'Gridiron'.

produced studies on tactics and topics associated with the First World War, such as *The Dardanelles* (London, Constable, 1919). Callwell wrote military biographies, such as his life of Field-Marshal Sir Henry Wilson (two vols, London, Cassell, 1927; the book includes a preface by Marshal Foch). His other books include *Small Wars: Their Principles & Practice* (London, HMSO, 1896), and *The Tactics of Home Defence* (Edinburgh, William Blackwood & Sons, 1908). Callwell also wrote stories and parodies where his sense of humour came to the fore, such as his *Service Yarns and Memories* (Edinburgh, William Blackwood & Sons, 1912). His *History of the Royal Artillery from the Indian Mutiny to the Great War* was published posthumously (Woolwich, Royal Artillery Institution, 1931) and covered the period 1860–99. It was dedicated by permission to King George V, Commander-in-Chief of the Royal Artillery. The project was completed by Major-General Sir John Headlam[3] with the publication of two further volumes covering the period 1899–1914 (Woolwich, Royal Artillery Institution, 1937) and the campaigns of 1860–1914 (Woolwich, Royal Artillery Institution, 1940).

On the other side of the Wadia allotment is a group of mature trees and shrubs which hides a granite mausoleum.

5.4. Dudgeon family mausoleum [plot 19]

This massive mausoleum built of grey rusticated Scottish granite was completed in 1935. It was built on a plot measuring 24ft × 20ft, which cost £360. The mausoleum itself cost a further £1,345, which included a stained-glass window.[4] Buried within are **Frederick Scheer Dudgeon** (1863–1947), and his wife, **Elizabeth Dudgeon** (1854–1937).

Immediately beside this is an interesting headstone with portrait.

5.5. James Miller (died 1873) [plot 19]

Little is known of Miller's life, but this headstone is included as an interesting example of funerary portraiture. The memorial includes a bas-relief profile portrait of the deceased.

Somewhere in the area adjacent to St Gabriel's Avenue, in plot 20 or 21, is the last resting place of Major-General Beak. Unfortunately the precise location of his grave is not known.

5.6. Major-General Daniel Marcus William Beak, VC (1891–1961) [plot 20 or 21; unmarked]

Born in Southampton, Beak served in the First World War as a Commander in the Royal Naval Volunteer Reserve. His VC was awarded for the period 21 August, 25 August and 4 September 1918, when he led his men and captured four enemy positions under heavy fire at Longest Wood. Four days later, although dazed by a shell fragment, in the absence of the Brigade Commander, Beak reorganised the Brigade under extremely heavy fire and led his men to their objective. When an attack was held up, accompanied by only one runner he succeeded in breaking up a nest of machine guns. His initiative and inspiration contributed very materially to the success of these operations. During the Second World War Beak commanded the 1st Battalion South Lancashire Regiment, Prince of Wales's Volunteers (1939–40). He was appointed General Officer Commanding Malta in 1942 and retired in 1945.

Facing St Gabriel's Avenue is a headstone memorial.

5.7. James Edmund Vincent (1857–1909) [plot 21]

Journalist and author. Vincent was educated at Winchester and Christ Church, Oxford. He entered the Inner Temple in 1881 and was called to the Bar in 1884. Vincent served on the North Wales Circuit and was a reporter for the *Law Times* (1884–9). He joined the staff of *The Times* in 1886 and became its principal descriptive reporter. As a special correspondent he accompanied the Duke and Duchess of York on their colonial tour of 1901. Vincent was editor of *The National Observer* (1894–7), and of *Country Life* (1897–1901). He also wrote on a wide range of subjects, from football to the Welsh land question. Vincent excelled at biography and topography. His *HRH the Duke of Clarence and Avondale: A Memoir* (London, John Murray, 1893) was seen as definitive; and his popular *From Cradle to Crown: His Most Gracious Majesty Edward VII* (London, George Newnes & Co., 1902) was reissued following the King's death in 1910. On topography, Vincent wrote *Highways and Byways in Berkshire* (London, Macmillan & Co., 1906) and completed *The Story of the Thames* (London, Smith, Elder & Co., 1909) in the year he died. There is a brass memorial tablet to Vincent in Bangor Cathedral.

The next memorial is a grey granite Celtic cross with kerbing.

5.8. Sir Daniel Thomas Keymer (1857–1933) [plot 21]

East India and colonial merchant. Keymer was the principal partner of Keymer, Son & Co. of Kingsway; Chairman of D.J. Keymer & Co. of London, Calcutta and Bombay; Managing Director of Keymer, Bagshawe & Co. Ltd of Calcutta; and Managing Director of the Sudan Mercantile Co. Ltd of Port Sudan, Khartoum and Wad Medani. He was agent to the government of Nepal. Keymer was President of the North Hackney Conservative Association and contested Central Hackney in 1923. He was President of the North London Federation and of the North Hackney and Central Hackney branches of the Junior Imperial League. Keymer was a Trustee and Treasurer of the London Diocesan Board of Education and Chairman of the North Hackney branch of the League of Nations Union.

Towards the middle of plot 21 is a wide low headstone in red brick and terracotta.

5.9. De Pothonier family grave [plot 21]

An interesting memorial in brick with terracotta decoration and panels (including the family coat of arms). It may be compared with the **Capper family memorial**. Among those buried here is **Sidney St Arnaud M. de Pothonier** (*c.* 1854–98), who was a stockbroker. He was found dead in his room at 44 Harrington Road, South Kensington, on 28 September 1898. He had been suffering from nerves for at least a year, but refused to seek medical advice. His post-mortem report showed that Mr de Pothonier was probably a chronic alcoholic. The inscription panels are of terracotta and specially made for this grave.[5]

Facing St Matthew's Avenue is a headstone with kerbing. The headstone incorporates a carving of a sailing ship at the top.

5.10. Captain Walter Henry Parker (1869–1935) [plot 21]

Merchant seaman. Born in Birkenhead, Parker was sent to sea in 1882. His first ship, the *Loweswater*, is depicted on the headstone. During one of his voyages on this barque Parker (with some other sailors) was washed overboard. They were saved by circling albatrosses that alerted the *Loweswater* to their whereabouts in the southern ocean. Parker left the *Loweswater* in 1886 and served on a variety of barques and clippers. He obtained his master's certificate in 1892 and joined the Pacific Steam Navigation Company in 1894. Between 1894 and 1899 Parker alternated between mail and cargo steamers, steadily climbing the ladder of promotion. He served as an Acting Lieutenant in the Royal Naval Reserve (RNR) during the Boxer Rising of 1900. Parker joined the Orient Line in 1901, serving on a variety of passenger and mail steamers. During 1904–6 Parker renewed his gunnery training with the RNR and went on to spend nearly a year with the Navy. Afterwards he joined the Royal Mail Steam Packet Company, and in 1906 at the age of 37 was appointed Commander of the *Oraya*. Between 1907 and 1912 Parker sailed largely to the West Indies, South America and China. During the First World War he served in anti-submarine vessels. He was promoted to Commodore of the Atlantic Convoys in 1917, and from then until the end of the war he handled a total of 243 ships and lost none. After the war Parker returned to the South American trade routes, moving to transatlantic routes from 1925, when he commanded the *Ohio*. Parker transferred to the White Star Line in 1927 and was Captain of the *Homeric*, then the largest twin-screw liner in the world (1927–8), and the *Olympic*, then the largest triple-screw liner in the world (1928–9). He retired in 1929 and subsequently wrote his memoirs, *Leaves from an Unwritten Log-book* (London, S. Low, Marston, 1931).

Cross over into plot 15. The next memorial is an obelisk in grey granite, close to St Pancras's Avenue.

5.11. Taylor family grave [plot 15]

W.J. Taylor (1802–85) was a medallist. He is buried with his wife and family, the children being listed on the side of the obelisk in a somewhat unusual way.

Close by is the next headstone memorial.

5.12. Robert Bunting (1810–1893) [plot 15]

This memorial is in a group of family graves. The headstone records that it was placed 'as a mark of the great esteem in which he was held by the firm of James Simpson & Co., Engineers, with whom he was connected for upwards of 60 years'.

Nearby is an unusual gothic obelisk.

5.13. Annie Inglet Starkings Macdonald (died 1915) [plot 15]

The inscription on the base of this obelisk is most unusual as it records not only the date but also the time of death:

> . . . who after a life strenuously & wholly devoted with unsurpassed self-forgetting love to her parents and brothers and sisters passed very tired gently and calmly to rest with God on 24 January 1915 at 11.15am. Her earth garment was laid here on 28 January 1915.

Near the junction of St Pancras's and St Matthew's avenues is an unusual Celtic cross in grey granite.

5.14. Bernard Barham Woodward (1853–1930) [plot 15]

Librarian of the British Museum of Natural History. Woodward was the nephew of Dr Henry Woodward, Keeper of Geology at the British Museum of Natural History. He was an assistant in the British Library at Bloomsbury. When the Trustees of the British Museum decided not to transfer the natural history books to the new museum on Cromwell Road, which would have involved the inclusion of a new reading room, Woodward was given the task of forming a fresh collection for the use of staff and researchers in the departments based there. Woodward catalogued the collection that he formed. His six-volume work, the *Catalogue of the Books, Manuscripts, Maps and Drawings in the British Museum (Natural History)* (London, British Museum, 1903–20), became a well-known work of reference. His own research was on mollusca, on which he published several papers.

Just in front of this is the next grave in grey granite. Unfortunately the memorial is incomplete, but may be identified by Mrs Holdich's details on the surviving base.

5.15. Colonel Sir Thomas Hungerford Holdich (1843–1929) [plot 15]

Anglo-Indian frontier surveyor. Holdich entered the Royal Engineers in 1862 and was sent to India in 1865. He was temporary assistant surveyor to the Bhutan expedition (1865–6), which resulted in his permanent appointment to the Survey Department. He was seconded for survey work during the Abyssinian campaign (1867). For many years he worked in the general area of the North-West Frontier, and was survey officer with the Southern Afghanistan Field Force (from 1878). Later he worked in Baluchistan and Waziristan and other parts of the frontier. He served on the Russo-Afghan Boundary Commission (1884–6) that, largely on Holdich's advice, laid down this frontier. Holdich was Superintendent of Frontier Surveys (1891–8), and in 1895 he was involved once more with the Russo-Afghan border. His work in India came to an end in 1897. Holdich served also on other international boundary disputes, including the Perso-Baluch boundary (1896) and the Argentine-Chile boundary (1902–3). He was a keen watercolour artist and was an ardent geographer; he was President of the Royal Geographical Society (1916–18). Holdich was author of *India* in the *Regions of the World* series (London, Henry Frowde, 1904), *The Indian Borderland 1880–1900* (London, Methuen, 1901), *The Gates of India: Being an Historical Narrative* (London, Macmillan, 1910), and of *Political Frontiers and Boundary Making* (London, Macmillan, 1916). His wife, **Ada Maria Vanrenen** (1850–1937), was daughter of Captain John Heyning Vanrenen of the East India Company. There are several Vanrenens buried in the extensive family plot to the left of this grave.

Behind this is an isolated CWGC headstone.

5.16. Lance Corporal Ernest Edmund (or Edward) Taunt (1895–1914) [plot 15]

Ernest Taunt was born on 9 July 1895 in Toronto, Canada. His father, George Taunt, who came from Oxford, had emigrated to Canada in the early 1890s, where he met and married Charity Pitts, who had emigrated with her parents to Canada as a young girl. They raised four children in Canada, including Ernest. However, their comfortable lifestyle came to an abrupt end when George, who had invested heavily on the Stock Exchange, lost a great deal of money during a period of economic depression in about 1900. George returned to England with his family and settled in London. When old enough to work, Ernest became an employee of the Metropolitan Railway. At the outbreak of the First World War Ernest volunteered for the Army and became a Lance Corporal in a territorial regiment. Ernest was killed on 22 November 1914 while patrolling the London & South Western Railway line near Frimley Green, Surrey. The coroner's verdict at the end of the inquest into his death was that Ernest had died as a result of being hit by a train. The particulars of Ernest's untimely death were reported in the local press:

TERRITORIAL'S TERRIBLE FATE: CUT TO PIECES ON THE LINE

A shocking discovery was made on the London and South Western Railway line at Frimley Green on Sunday night, the decapitated body of Lance-Corporal Ernest Edward Taunt, of the 12th City of London Territorial Regiment, being found on a section of the line between Curzon Bridge and the Canal bridge, Frimley Green.

The inquest was held by Mr Gilbert H. White at the *White Hart* on Tuesday. From the evidence it appeared that the deceased, who was 19 years of age, was a son of Mr G. Taunt, a general merchant, of Cricklewood, and was in charge of the patrol at Deepcut Bridge. On Sunday evening he left the hut to collect some keys from the line for the fire. On returning from Brookwood station along the line later in the evening, Rifleman Turnham, when about 150 yards from the hut, kicked against a soldier's cap, which was ascertained to belong to the deceased. PC Kenward, who examined the line with a number of riflemen, found the deceased's body in a very mangled condition on the Up through line, about 280 yards from the hut. Portions of his equipment were found scattered in various places. Inspector Collins of the London & South Western Railway said that two goods trains passed one another at the spot about 6.23pm. It was possible that the noise of the Down train prevented the deceased hearing the approach of the train from the other direction.

The jury returned a verdict of accidental death, and expressed deep sympathy with the relatives of the deceased; and there were similar expressions on behalf of the officer commanding the regiment, the officers, and non-commissioned officers of No. 1 Company, to which the deceased belonged, and the Railway Company.[6]

The memorial is of interest not only because of this story, but also from the early date of this military burial, which pre-dates the **military cemeteries** by nearly four years. In addition to the grave at Brookwood, Ernest Taunt is also commemorated on the Metropolitan Railway's War Memorial which may be found on platform five at Baker Street underground station.[7]

Adjacent to a pine tree off St Matthew's Avenue is the surviving base of the next grave.

5.17. Charles Dibdin (1849–1910) [plot 15]

Secretary of the Royal National Lifeboat Institution. Dibdin was educated privately and entered the civil service after nomination and examination. He joined the General Post Office in 1866 Dibdin's official connection with the lifeboat movement began in 1870 when he became the Hon. Secretary of the Civil Service Lifeboat Fund, a position he retained until 1906. In 1883 he was appointed Secretary of the Royal National Lifeboat Institution and during the thirty-seven years that he held this office he served the Institution with great enthusiasm, and achieved great results. The remarkable success of the RNLI during this period was largely attributed to Dibdin's efforts. He was awarded the RNLI medal in 1902 and was also a Fellow of the Royal Geographical Society. Dibdin was actively interested in the affairs of the Borough of Holborn, where he lived. He was a borough councillor from 1900 and was elected Alderman in 1903.

Further along the path is a headstone with kerbing. The design includes a seated figure with book.

5.18. John F. Painter (*c.* 1918–1940) [plot 15]

Fighter pilot who was killed on active service on 7 November 1940. His epitaph reads:

Following his chosen duty
He passed beyond the
Sight of men for God
Proved him and found
Him worthy for himself.

The memorial headstone is of Portland stone and cost £26, including the lead lettering, but excluding the additional £3 5s 0d for carving the RAF wings.[8] Note the angel with the book of life, his RAF wings and Churchill's tribute to 'the Few'.

Adjacent to this is a Celtic cross memorial on an octagonal base with kerbing.

5.19. Revd Septimus Cox Holmes Hansard (1823–1895) [plot 15]

Clergyman. Educated at Rugby and University College, Oxford. Hansard became a deacon in 1846 and priest in 1847. He was appointed Curate of Claybrook, near Lutterworth (1846–8); of St Mary's, Marylebone (1848–60); of St George's-in-the-East (1860–1); and of Eversley, Hants (1861). Hansard was Rector of St Matthew, Bethnal Green (1864–95). He was the chief founder of the East London Museum at Bethnal Green, which opened in 1872. This was removed from the Victoria and Albert Museum to its new site in the 1860s. The museum originally contained collections of agricultural products, along with loan collections of art. The museum was the first (partial) home of the Wallace Collection.[9]

Towards the middle of the next plot is a Calvary cross memorial.

5.20. Mary Frances Scott-Siddons (*c.* 1844–1896) [plot 12]

Actress and great-granddaughter of Sarah Siddons (1755–1831). Her first stage appearance was as Juliet in Edinburgh in 1866. Scott-Siddons's London debut was at the Haymarket Theatre playing Rosalind in *As You Like It* in 1867. She toured America in 1868 and in the 1870s, and also toured Australia in the 1870s. Scott-Siddons specialised in classical roles, was popular in the provinces, but was not an overwhelming success in London. She was said to resemble her great-grandmother. She had an excellent voice, a small figure, but poor health. She died near Paris.

Facing St Ethelreda's Avenue is an unusual memorial completely constructed of terracotta.

5.21. Edward Saunders (1848–1910) [plot 12]

Entomologist. Saunders was educated at home, and became the author of many papers on entomology. These appeared in the *Entomologist's Monthly Magazine*, *The Transactions of the Entomological Society* and *The Journal of the Linnaean Society* from 1867. Saunders wrote

The Hemiptera Heteroptera of the British Isles (London, Reeve & Co., 1892), *The Hymenoptera Aculea* *of the British Isles: A Descriptive Account of the Families, Genera, & Species Indigenous to Great Britain &* *Ireland* (London, Reeve & Co., 1896), and *Wild Bees, Wasps and Ants, and Other Stinging Insec* (London, George Routledge & Sons, 1907). The latter was illustrated by his daughter. He wa elected FRS in 1902. Saunders' memorial is made entirely of terracotta and is unique withi the cemetery.

Adjacent to this is a cross ledger in grey granite.

5.22. Revd Francis David Morice (1849–1926) [plot 12]

Educated at Winchester and New College, Oxford. Morice was elected Fellow of Queen College, Oxford, in 1871. He was ordained in 1873 and was assistant master at Rugby Schoo (1874–94). He was known as a sound classical scholar and published a verse translation of *Th Olympian and Pythian Odes of Pindar* (1876) and *Pindar* (1879). Morice was a keen entomologis being President of the Rugby School Natural History Society from 1885. He was interested i bees and wasps and regularly consulted **Edward Saunders**. After retiring, Morice bought house next door to Saunders in Woking, and devoted the rest of his life to studying chrysid European and North American bees and sawflies. He was President of the Entomologica Society (1911–12). Morice was also interested in genealogy and wrote *A Collection of Morice an Morrice Biographies, with Genealogical Trees* (London, Rivingtons, 1923) for private circulation.

Directly opposite is the next memorial. It is a cross of grey granite with the verse 'Christ is risen' carved into th bar of the cross.

5.23. Rt Revd Frederic Henry Chase (1853–1925) [plot 9]

Bishop of Ely. Chase studied at Christ's College, Cambridge, and was ordained in 1876. He wa Lecturer in Theology at Pembroke College (1881–90) and at Christ's College (1893–1901 Cambridge. Chase was appointed Principal of the Cambridge Clergy Training School in 188? a post he retained until 1901. He was President of Queen's College and Norrisian Professor o Divinity at Cambridge (1901–6). Chase was Bishop of Ely from 1905 to 1924. He spent muc time in Convocation and on committees in the revisions of the *Book of Common Prayer*. H published many learned theological books throughout his life, such as *The Lord's Prayer in the Ear Church* (Cambridge, Cambridge University Press, 1891) and *The Creed and the New Testamen* (London, Macmillan, 1920).

The next memorial is a ledger stone within a very large kerbed allotment.

5.24. Brigadier General Wallace Duffield Wright, VC (1875–1953) [plot 9]

Born in Gibraltar, Wright won his VC when he was serving with the Northern Nigeri Regiment. On 26 February 1903 Lieutenant Wright, with only one other officer and forty-fou men, sustained the determined charges of 1,000 horse and 2,000 foot for two hours. When th enemy, after heavy losses, fell back in good order, Wright continued to follow them until the were in full retreat. Wright's personal example, as well as his skilful leadership, contribute largely to the brilliant success of the affair. During the First World War Wright served with th Queen's Own Cameron Highlanders. He commanded the 8th Infantry Brigade (1918–22) an was a member of HM's Bodyguard of Hon. Corps of Gentlemen-at-Arms (1932–50). Durin the Second World War he served with the Home Guard (1940–5).

The next Calvary cross memorial with kerbing faces St Michael's Avenue.

Lieutenant-General Sir Henry Goldfinch, KCB (died 1854), plot 27. The earliest memorial in the cemetery (3.10). *(Anthony Montan)*

Arthur Hacker (died 1919), plot 27. This prominent memorial incorporates a fine bronze profile portrait by an unknown artist (3.14). *(Anthony Montan)*

Sir (Samuel) Luke Fildes (died 1927), plot 36, 1983. A memorial in the style of a Grecian *stele* (3.21). *(Author's collection)*

Edward Ledger (died 1923), plot 28. A scroll-topped tomb supported by a mourning figure. (3.28). *(Anthony Montan)*

Thomas Richard Pace (died 1896), plot 28. This unusual wooden memorial is known as a 'grave-board'. The horizontal board, upon which is carved the epitaph, runs the length of the grave space. This is supported by two wooden upright posts, each one carved in the form of a Celtic cross but with subtle differences in the patterns (3.32). *(Anthony Montan)*

Garland family mausoleum, plot 29, 1980. It was designed and constructed by the LNC, octagonal in plan, with four pairs of columns on each of its shorter sides. A similar mausoleum, also erected by the LNC in the eastern section of Highgate Cemetery, cost nearly £8,500 (3.35). *(Author's collection)*

John Stuart Horner (died 1923), plot 29, 1980. This delightful terracotta memorial comprises the wings and heads of two angels looking down upon the inscription panel. The kerbing is also of terracotta and includes a further inscription panel at the foot of the grave (3.36). *(Author's collection)*

Right: Nesham family memorial, plot 30. It principally commemorates the life of Captain Cuthbert Spencer Nesham (died 1901) of the 21st Lancers, who was severely wounded at the Battle of Omdurman (1898) (3.44). *(Anthony Montan)*

Above: Vice-Admiral Richard George Kinahan (died 1911) and Arthur Jackman (died 1890), plot 30, *c.* 1912. Jackman's otherwise ordinary grave (right) contains the first ashes to be buried at Brookwood (3.45–6). *(Lyndon Davies, Past Images collection)*

Right: Ross Lowis Mangles, VC (died 1905), plot 31. One of only five civilians to be awarded the Victoria Cross (3.54). *(Anthony Montan)*

Drake family mausoleum, plot 31, 1979. This is arguably the most attractive mausoleum in the cemetery. Designed in the Italianate style, it closely reflects Sir William Drake's (died 1890) interests in Italian art and architecture. Five members of his family are buried in the vault beneath, while another, Frances, is buried immediately to the right (3.56). *(Author's collection)*

Lady Mary Laura Wyatt (died 1900), plot 31. This splendid life-size statue is assumed to be a likeness of the deceased, depicted standing and reading a book (3.61). *(Anthony Montan)*

Right: Phipson mausoleum, plot 22. This compact mausoleum is octagonal in plan, with four clerestory windows and a shallow dome. It contains the ashes of Weatherley Phipson (died 1909) (3.66). *(Anthony Montan)*

Below: Sir Henry Berkeley Fitzhardinge Maxse (died 1883), plot 22. This headstone includes a wealth of carved detail and symbolism, along with a shipwreck scene beneath the epitaph (3.68). *(Anthony Montan)*

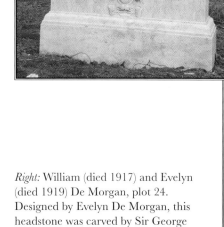

Right: William (died 1917) and Evelyn (died 1919) De Morgan, plot 24. Designed by Evelyn De Morgan, this headstone was carved by Sir George Frampton. The two figures represent Grief (left, holding the inverted torch) and Joy (3.75). *(Anthony Montan)*

The Columbarium, plot 26, *c*. 1979. This classical-style mausoleum is the largest in the cemetery. Originally provided for the 5th Earl Cadogan, it was subsequently sold back to the LNC in 1910 and converted for use as a columbarium (4.1). *(Gerald McKee collection)*

Sir Francis Seymour Haden (died 1910), plot 33. An unusual low marker. Haden promoted the use of disposable or 'earth-to-earth' coffins, especially here in the suitable soil of Brookwood Cemetery (4.2). *(Anthony Montan)*.

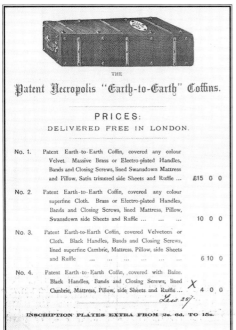

THE

Patent Necropolis "Earth-to-Earth" Coffins.

PRICES:
DELIVERED FREE IN LONDON.

No. 1. Patent Earth-to-Earth Coffin, covered any colour
        Velvet. Massive Brass or Electro-plated Handles,
        Bands and Closing Screws, lined Swansdown Mattress
        and Pillow, Satin trimmed side Sheets and Ruffle ...   £15 0 0

No. 2. Patent Earth-to-Earth Coffin, covered any colour
        superfine Cloth. Brass or Electro-plated Handles,
        Bands and Closing Screws, lined Mattress, Pillow,
        Swansdown side Sheets and Ruffle 10 0 0

No. 3. Patent Earth-to-Earth Coffin, covered Velveteen or
        Cloth. Black Handles, Bands and Closing Screws,
        lined superfine Cambric, Mattress, Pillow, side Sheets
        and Ruffle 6 10 0

No. 4. Patent Earth-to-Earth Coffin, covered with Baize.
        Black Handles, Bands and Closing Screws, lined
        Cambric, Mattress, Pillow, side Sheets and Ruffle ...   4 0 0

INSCRIPTION PLATES EXTRA FROM 2s. 6d. TO 15s.

LNC advertisement and price list for its 'Patent Earth-to-Earth' coffins, *c.* 1877 (4.2). *(Brian Parsons collection)*

Bent family memorial, plot 34, *c.* 1975. One of the earliest large memorials in the cemetery (4.5). *(Author's collection)*

Charles Warne (died 1887), plot 30. An unusual and unique memorial in the consecrated section. Designed to resemble a prehistoric barrow, the upright stone is made of serpentinite (4.13). *(Anthony Montan)*

Wood family mausoleum, plot 30, 1976. Designed in the late seventeenth-century English style, the mausoleum is shown largely in its original form, before vandalism and further decay had left their mark (4.14). *(Author's collection)*

Boulton family mausoleum, plot 34. Designed in the neoclassical style, this mausoleum includes many fine carved details. The bronze door (now bricked over) depicted Christ as the Good Shepherd (4.16). *(Anthony Montan)*

Henry Cadogan Rothery (died 1888), plot 31. Another fine example of the stonemason's art (4.18). *(Anthony Montan)*

Bernard Greenwood Benson (died 1911), plot 23. The third British aviator to die in an aeroplane accident, and the first airman to be buried at Brookwood (4.29). *(Anthony Montan)*

Cyril Bazett Tubbs (died 1927), plot 32, 1979. He had enormous influence on the development of the LNC. (4.36). *(Author's collection)*

Sir Cosmo Duff Gordon (died 1931) and Lady Duff Gordon (died 1935), plot 25. Survivors of the *Titanic* disaster (4.37). *(Anthony Montan)*

Above: John Singer Sargent (died 1925), the Ring (4.46). *(Anthony Montan)*

Above: Oliver Henry Douglas Vickers (died 1928), plot 33. This remarkable headstone commemorates a genuine 'ace' of the First World War (4.39). *(Anthony Montan)*

Right: Sarah Eleanor Smith (died 1931), plot 32. The grave of the widow of Captain Edward John Smith, Captain of the *Titanic* (4.40). *(Anthony Montan)*

Colonel Alan Vincent Gandar Dower (died 1980), plot 19. A prominent family memorial near the junction of St Cyprian's and St George's avenues (5.1). *(Anthony Montan)*

De Pothonier family memorial, plot 21. A wide monument constructed of brick and terracotta. The inscription panels would have been specially made (5.9). *(Anthony Montan)*

Left: James Miller (died 1873), plot 19. An interesting example of funerary portraiture (5.5). *(Anthony Montan)*

Right: Edward Saunders (died 1910), plot 12. A unique terracotta memorial. The upright cross is missing and it is assumed this was also of terracotta (5.21). *(Anthony Montan)*

EDWARD MELLO SAUNDERS

See family memorial, plot 7. This is one of three memorials at Brookwood by Eric Gill, and arguably the finest. Made of Portland stone, it is in the form of a double bedstead, with joined headstones (shown here) and footstones. It was originally completed in 1929, following the death of Henri See (5.29). *(Anthony Montan)*

Sir Arthur Stockdale Cope, RA (died 1940), plot 8. Another unique memorial, commemorating the life of this portrait artist and his family. The surviving monument is incomplete and is missing a bronze decorative feature between the two columns (5.32). *(Anthony Montan)*

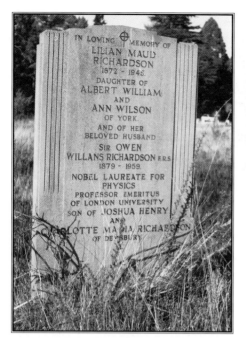

Above left: Sir Owen Willans Richardson, FRS (died 1959), plot 8 (5.33). *(Anthony Montan)*

Above right: Batten family memorial, plot 14. Set within a low stone wall pierced by circular openings, this memorial includes two further stones carved by Eric Gill (5.37). *(Anthony Montan)*

Alice Junod (died 1902), plot 14. Immediately to the left of the Batten grave is the third memorial by Eric Gill, shown here. Completed in May 1902, the stone with its epitaph in French is set within a simple kerb (5.38). *(Anthony Montan)*

Sir Theodore Aston (died 1910) mausoleum, plot 11. Otherwise anonymous, this mausoleum was constructed between 1891 and 1892 and faces St Philip's Avenue (5.40). *(Anthony Montan)*

Royal Hospital Chelsea, plot 54. Designed by Oswald Milne FRIBA, the memorial is built in Portland stone. It was formally unveiled and dedicated at a special ceremony on 27 April 1937 (5.46). *(Anthony Montan)*

Left: John Spencer (died 1865), plot 47. This remarkable memorial commemorates fireman John Spencer who was accidentally killed on the LSWR near Winchester on 11 October 1865. The stone includes a fine carving of a Beattie steam engine of the period. Called *Firebrand*, it is presumed to be the engine Spencer was firing when he lost his life (5.50). *(Anthony Montan)*

Above: Joseph Porter (died 1885), plot 47. Joseph Porter was, according to family legend, the driver of the first train that ran into Brookwood Cemetery on 7 November 1854 (5.50). *(Anthony Montan)*

Left: Ann Matilda Lynn (died 1894), plot 47. Another unusual wooden memorial. The deterioration of the memorial over the years has resulted in much of the inscription being lost (5.51). *(Anthony Montan)*

5.25. Sir [John Charles] Lewis Coward (1852–1930) [plot 5]

Educated at St Paul's School and Corpus Christi College, Cambridge, Coward pursued a legal career, becoming a barrister at Gray's Inn in 1877. He was a member of the Council of Legal Education (1892), a member of the Incorporated Council of Law Reporting (1898–1921), Commissary to the Dean and Chapter of St Paul's Cathedral (1913), Chairman of the Board of Legal Studies (1914–20), Vice-Chairman of the Advice Committee Officers' Families Fund (1914–19), a member of the Aerodromes Committee of the Air Ministry (1917–18) and one of HM's Railway and Canal Commissioners (1921). Coward was also Recorder of Folkestone (1886–1921). On his resignation in 1921 he received the honorary freedom of the borough.

The next three memorials are adjacent to one another at the far end of plot 6. They are described in order from left to right.

5.26. Major-General Sir William Hope Meiklejohn (1845–1909) [plot 6]

Educated at Rugby, he entered the Bengal Infantry in 1861. Meiklejohn served in the Black Mountain Campaign (1868) and the Jowaki Expedition (1877–8). During the Afghan War (1878–80) Meiklejohn took part in the action at Ali Masjid and in the Zaimukt Expedition. He served with the Mahsud Waziri Expedition of 1881, and during the Egyptian Expedition (1882) he was present at the Battle of Tel-el-Kebir. Meiklejohn was employed with the Afghan Boundary Commission (1884–6). He served also with the Waziristan Expedition (1894–5), including the boundary delimitation, and was present at the attack on Camp Wana (1894). Meiklejohn commanded the defence of Malakand in 1897, the Chakdara relief column of the Malakand Field Force (1897) and commanded the 1st Brigade, Malakand Field Force, in action at Landakai (1897). Many of Meiklejohn's actions in the Malakand were described by Churchill in his book *The Story of the Malakand Field Force* (London, Longmans, Green, 1898). Meiklejohn also commanded the 1st Brigade of the Buner Field Force.

5.27. Rear-Admiral Spencer Henry Metcalfe Login (1851–1909) [plot 6]

Educated at Wellington College, Login entered the Royal Navy in 1865. He served in the Ashanti War (1873–4) and Suakin (1884–5). Login was promoted to Lieutenant (1874), to Commander (1888) and Captain (1895). He was sometime Commander of the naval barracks at Portsmouth, where he made much-needed changes to the canteen administration. Login was later president of the committee that reported on victualling and canteen questions that were subsequently incorporated into the regulations of the Fleet (1907). He was made a Rear-Admiral in 1906 and was sometime aide-de-camp to King Edward VII. A keen rugby player, Login played for England in 1875. His funeral took place on 26 January 1909. His coffin was covered with the Union Jack and surmounted with his cocked hat and sword. The mourners included **Major-General Sir William Meiklejohn** and Rear-Admiral Sir John Jellicoe,[10] who represented the First Lord of the Admiralty. Eight petty officers from the naval barracks at Portsmouth, who had served under Login, acted as bearers.

5.28. William Henry Griffin (1812–1900) [plot 6]

Deputy Postmaster General of Canada. Griffin was born in London but spent his entire career with the Canadian Post Office. He was appointed a clerk in 1831, shortly after arriving in Canada, and retired in the summer of 1888. His remarkable record of fifty-seven years' service may well be a record for a Canadian public servant. In 1831 the Canadian Post Office was still part of the imperial civil service. Griffin was Postmaster of Quebec City in 1833 and served as

Post Office Inspector between Kingston and Fredericton from 1835. By 1838 he was also clerk to the Deputy Postmaster General, Thomas Stayner.[11] From 1851 Griffin became Secretary of the Post Office in the Province of Canada under Postmaster General James Morris.[12] During this period the department was transferred to the British North American colonies. In 1857, as part of Post Office reorganisation, Griffin became Deputy Postmaster General. When Canada became a confederation in 1867 the post offices of Canada, Nova Scotia, and New Brunswick came under the new government arrangements, and Griffin was made Deputy Postmaster General of the enlarged postal operations. During his period of office postal services expanded greatly, with a doubling of headquarters staff, and the number of post offices increasing from 3,630 to over 7,600. In recognition of his services Griffin was created CMG in 1890. He returned to England and died at Claygate, Surrey.

Moving on to plot 7, locate the large double headstone and footstone that faces St Gregory's Avenue.

5.29. Henri See (1862–1929) [plot 7]

This is one of three memorials at Brookwood by Eric Gill, and arguably the finest.[13] The monument is made of Portland stone and is in the form of a double bedstead, with joined headstones and footstones. It commemorates **Henri See** (1862–1929) and his wife, **May See** (1880–1940), and was originally completed in 1929. It includes lettering within rectangular recessed panels in the headstones along with the epitaph 'Wherefore they are no more twain but one flesh'[14] below.

Next locate a Calvary cross memorial near St Gregory's Avenue. Part of the inscription is in the bar of the cross.

5.30. John Lumsden Propert (1834–1902) [plot 7]

Physician and art critic. Propert was educated at Marlborough College and King's College Hospital. He then joined his father's medical practice in New Cavendish Street, London. Propert was a fine etcher and connoisseur of art. He was one of the first to revive the taste for miniature paintings in England, although his fine collection of these was sold in 1897. His *History of Miniature Art, With Notes on Collectors and Collections* (London, Macmillan, 1887) was seen as a major contribution to this genre. Propert also compiled the illustrated catalogue of the exhibition of portrait miniatures at the Burlington Fine Arts Club in 1889.[15]

The next memorial is a granite cross on a base facing towards St Michael's Avenue. It is set back from the path.

5.31. Sir Hermann Weber (1823–1918) [plot 7]

Doctor and founder of the science of climatotherapy. Weber was awarded his MD in 1848. Shortly afterwards he moved to England as House Physician at the German Hospital, Dalston. Weber became a member of the Royal College of Physicians in 1855 and was made a Fellow in 1859. He was particularly interested in the treatment of consumption, and was among the first to advise patients to winter in Switzerland. His patients who benefited included five Prime Ministers (Lord Derby, Earl Russell, Lord Salisbury, Lord Rosebery, and Sir H. Campbell-Bannerman). Weber was often consulted by the royal family on the choice of health resorts. He retired in 1903 but continued to take a keen interest in climatotherapy.

Cross over to plot 8 and locate the incomplete memorial with two small towers and a low wall.

5.32 Sir Arthur Stockdale Cope (1857–1940) [plot 8]

Portrait painter. Born in London, the son of Charles West Cope, the historical painter.[16] He was educated at Carey's and the Royal Academy Schools. Cope exhibited at the Royal Academy uninterruptedly from 1876 and later at the Paris Salon. He was made an ARA in 1899 and RA in 1910. Although he painted some landscapes, Cope was almost exclusively a portrait painter of men. He chiefly made his name in royal portraiture, since he was eminently trustworthy and a master of his craft. Cope had 'a sympathetic understanding of how the thing ought to be done in order to satisfy official tastes for a good conventional likeness on the side of reserve in a reasonably good composition. He avoided alike the "grand manner" and the sentimentally domestic.'[17]

His portraits include those of King Edward VII, King George V, King Edward VIII (as Prince of Wales), Kaiser Wilhelm II, the Duke of Cambridge, Lord Roberts and Lord Kitchener. His painting *Some Sea Officers of the War* is probably one of his most accomplished canvases, and was one of three records of the First World War privately commissioned for presentation to the National Portrait Gallery. He married first **Emily Beatrix Hawtayne** (1860–97); and second **Goda Isobel King** (died 1934) in 1906. Also buried here is **Harry Cope**, who died 1 February 1890 aged just 4 days.

In line with this is a modest headstone memorial that faces towards St John's Avenue.

5.33. Sir Owen Willans Richardson (1879–1959) [plot 8]

Physicist. Educated at Batley Grammar School and Trinity College, Cambridge. Richardson carried out research in 'thermionic' emission at the Cavendish Laboratory with Sir Joseph Thomson.[18] This included the maximum electron current which could be drawn by an electric field from a hot filament contained in a vacuum tube. Richardson formulated a general theory of the process which became known as 'Richardson's Law', familiar to physicists and electrical engineers. He used the term 'thermion' (hence thermionics) to describe the emission of electricity by hot bodies. Richardson's contribution to this field of physics resulted in his award of the Nobel Prize for Physics in 1928. He was appointed Professor of Physics at Princeton (1906–14) where he continued his research into electron physics. This covered most phenomena related to thermionic emission and, with A.H. Compton,[19] he was able to verify Einstein's photo-electric law. Richardson predicted a rotational reaction on the magnetisation of iron in 1908, but did not detect the effect. When it was observed by Einstein and de Haas[20] in 1919 it was called the 'Richardson-Einstein-de Haas effect'.[21] Richardson became Wheaton Professor of Physics at King's College, London, from 1914. While there he wrote *The Electron Theory of Matter* (Cambridge, Cambridge University Press, 1914), and *The Emission of Electricity from Hot Bodies* (London, 1916). Richardson was Yarrow Research Professor between 1924 and 1944. He contributed to the analysis of the molecular hydrogen spectrum, and also wrote *Molecular Hydrogen and its Spectrum* (New Haven, Yale University Press, 1934). Richardson was President of the Physical Society (1926–8) and wrote several important books on his theories. He was knighted in 1939.

Almost directly opposite in plot 11 is a group of cross memorials and headstones.

5.34. Sir Edward Maunde Thompson (1840–1929) [plot 11]

Palaeographer and Director of the British Museum. Thompson was born at Clarendon, Jamaica, and was educated at Rugby and University College, Oxford. He joined the British Museum in 1861 and from 1866 was involved in the preparation of the Class Catalogue of all the manuscripts. He was promoted to Assistant Keeper in the Department of Manuscripts in 1871. On the completion of the Class Catalogue Thompson completed the listing of recent accessions (1854–75) in two volumes that were published in 1875 and 1877, with an index volume in 1880. In 1873 Thompson joined Edward Bond[22] in founding the Palaeographical Society. The Society's publications provided students with photo-facsimiles of important classical and medieval manuscripts, thereby laying the foundations of modern palaeography. With G.F. Warner,[23] Thompson published the *Catalogue of Ancient Manuscripts in the British Museum* (London, British Museum, 1881, 1884). It was in two volumes, the first covering Greek manuscripts, the second covering Latin manuscripts. He also wrote the *Handbook of Greek and Latin Palaeography* (London, Paul, Trench, Trubner, 1893). Thompson also edited chronicles and other documents for various societies. He was appointed Keeper in the Department of Manuscripts (from 1878), then Principal Librarian (in 1888) and Director of the British Museum (from 1898). Thompson was an excellent administrator and developed the educational and 'popular' side of the British Museum collections. Objects were more clearly labelled and described, and the exhibitions were better organised. At the same time he promoted the production of catalogues listing the contents of the Museum. He also encouraged excavations abroad, to add to the Museum's collections. Thompson was President of the British Academy (1907–9). He retired in 1909, after which he returned to his writing.

The next two memorials face St John's Avenue and are to the left of the above. The first is a low wide granite headstone with kerbing.

5.35. Lieutenant Crugar Stanley Peach (died 1917) [plot 11]

A resident of Victoria Road in Farnborough, Hants, Peach joined the Royal Flying Corps as an observer after service with the Army. He flew with a reconnaissance squadron in France before returning to England for pilot training with No. 42 Reserve Squadron at Hounslow. Lieutenant Peach was killed when he lost control of his RE8, which spun into the ground at Whitton Park, Twickenham.

To the left is a granite headstone.

5.36. Acting Pilot Officer Geoffrey Clive King George (*c.* 1915–1936) [plot 11]

George was undergoing pilot training at No. 3 Flying Training School at Grantham when his Hawker Audax biplane collided with a Hawker Hart flown by another of the School's pupils. Both pilots were killed when their aircraft crashed near the village of Great Ponton, a few miles south of their airfield.

The next memorial faces St Gregory's Avenue. It is set within its own low-walled enclosure.

5.37. Batten family grave [plot 14]

This family plot includes two stones carved by Eric Gill.[24] At the rear of the enclosure is a stone set into the low wall commemorating **John Winterbotham Batten KC** (1831–1901) and **Sarah Langstaffe Batten** (1835–1908). This stone comprises capital and lower case Roman lettering with long legs for the letters R and K, and was completed in 1902, with additional lettering added in 1909 after Sarah Batten's death. John Batten was a lawyer who was called to the Bar in 1872. According to the burial registers he 'fell dead on [the] railway station at Goring-on-Thames'.

To the right of this stone is another carved by Gill which commemorates **Lindsey Forster Batten** (died 1865) and **Norman Gottfried Batten** (died 1873), 'their eldest and youngest sons buried at Plymouth'. This memorial is of Hopton wood stone and comprises five lines of italic type. It was completed in 1911.

Also buried here is John Batten's third son, **Frederick Eustace Batten** (1865–1918), who was a doctor specialising in nervous and children's diseases. He completed his medical studies at St Bartholomew's Hospital. Batten became a highly skilled pathologist and did much original investigation into the nervous and muscular systems. He subsequently worked at the National Hospital for the Paralysed, Queen Square, London, and at the Hospital for Sick Children, Great Ormond Street. Batten's Disease, a rare hereditary disease of the nervous system, is named after him. Batten wrote many papers for the journal *Brain*. He presented a very comprehensive study of poliomyelitis before the Royal College of Physicians in 1916. This paper was subsequently published in *Brain*, and in book form as *Acute Poliomyelitis: Its Nature and Treatment* (London, John Bale, 1916). He jointly edited *Diseases of Children* (London, E. Arnold, 1913) with Sir Archibald Garrod[25] and Hugh Thursfield.[26] Batten's memorial is just in front of that to his parents.

The next grave is immediately to the left and has a cast-iron hoop at its head.

5.38. Alice Junod (*c.* 1879–1902) [plot 14]

This memorial is another by Eric Gill.[27] It was completed in May 1902. The grave is a simple kerbed design, with a sloping stone with lettering by Gill which is now quite worn:

Oui, la bonté et la gratuité
me suiveront tous les jours de
ma vie et mon habitation sera
dans la maison de l'Eternel
pour de longs jours

The next headstone, which incorporates a fireman's helmet at the top, is on the other side of the plot, adjacent to a pine tree and close to St Philip's Avenue.

5.39. Major Cyril Clarke Boville Morris (1882–1950) [plot 14]

Engineer and fireman. Educated at Haileybury College, Morris became a pupil at the Great Eastern Railway's (GER) locomotive works at Stratford, and for three years was engineer in charge of the GER's motor department. Morris was assistant divisional officer of the London Fire Brigade (1908). He served in France (1914–17), before his appointment as deputy assistant director of transport (1917). Morris was chief officer of the London Fire Brigade (1933–8) and became director of training of the Fire Brigades Division of the Home Office (1939). He was regional controller of the Ministry of Supply for Cambridge (1939–42). In 1939 Morris wrote his autobiography, *Fire! (On the Work of the London and Other Fire Brigades)* (London, Blackie & Son, 1939).[28] His headstone includes a carved fireman's helmet and axe. The grave immediately to the right is of his only daughter, **Elaine Morris**, who died on 12 January 1932, aged 19.

Nearby and facing St Philip's Avenue is a family mausoleum.

5.40. Sir Theodore Aston (1827–1910) [plot 11]

Barrister specialising in the law of patents. The son of Thomas Aston of Handsworth, Birmingham, he was educated at St John's College, Cambridge. Aston was called to the Bar at Lincoln's Inn in November 1853 and joined the Northern Circuit. He was made a QC in 1872. From the 1870s Aston established a commanding practice in patent actions, and was the chief competitor of Mr Webster QC[29] who was one of the first members of the Bar to devote himself to patent law. Aston's reputation was made with actions such as *Plimpton* v. *Malcolmson*, *Plimton* v. *Spiller* and *Patterson* v. *The Gas Light and Coke Company*. He was a clear speaker and reasoner but 'somewhat prolix and tedious'. At the time of his death Aston was the fourth senior KC in Britain. He left over £120,242 in his will.[30] The mausoleum was built in about 1891–2. It is anonymous from the outside, and was constructed on a plot measuring 18ft × 14ft, which cost £100. The mausoleum itself cost a further £288 to construct.[31]

The next memorial is a granite block with kerbing. It can be found adjacent to the junction of St Joseph's and St Michael's Avenues.

5.41. James Adam (1860–1907) [plot 13]

Classical scholar and Platonist. Adam was educated at Aberdeen University and Caius College, Cambridge. He became a classical lecturer at Emmanuel College, Cambridge, and settled into a life of teaching. Adam's lectures were witty and learned. He published his first edition of Platonic dialogue, the *Apologia Socratis*, in 1887 (Cambridge, Cambridge University Press). This was followed by the *Crito* (Cambridge, Cambridge University Press, 1888), the *Euthyphro* (Cambridge, Cambridge University Press, 1890), and the *Protagoras* (Cambridge, Cambridge University Press, 1893). His final version of the *Republic* (Cambridge, Cambridge University Press, 1902) appeared in two volumes and became the standard edition. In 1902 Adam was appointed Gifford Lecturer at Aberdeen, and his lectures delivered there in 1904–5 were very successful. He died there in 1907, and his lectures were posthumously published by his widow in 1908.

The next memorial is a headstone facing towards St Gregory's Avenue. It is set back from the path.

5.42. Frederick Gard Fleay (1831–1909) [plot 16]

Shakespearean scholar. Educated at King's College School and Trinity College, Cambridge, where he was dubbed 'the industrious flea'. Fleay was Vice-Principal of the Oxford Diocesan Training College at Culham (1856–9) and was second master at Leeds Grammar School (1860–6). He became headmaster of Hipperholme Grammar School (1868–72) and at Skipton (1872–6), when he abandoned teaching. Fleay was interested in phonetics and the reform of spelling, and published several books on these subjects. In 1874 he joined the New Shakespeare Society and devoted many years to the elucidation of Shakespearean and Elizabethan drama. These were severely practical works since literary criticism was outside his scope. Instead, Fleay analysed the changes in Shakespeare's metre and phraseology, and applied metrical and linguistic tests to determine the chronology of Shakespeare's works. His books include *A Shakespeare Manual* (London, Macmillan, 1876), *A Chronicle History of the Life and Work of William Shakespeare, Player Poet, and Playmaker* (London, J.C. Nimmo, 1886), and *A Chronicle History of the London Stage 1559–1642* (London, Reeves & Turner, 1890).

The next memorial is a Calvary cross with raised lettering. It may be found further to the right and facing St Gregory's Avenue.

5.43. Professor Robert Latta (1865–1932) [plot 16]

Academic. Educated at the Royal High School and the University of Edinburgh. Latta became assistant and Lecturer in Logic and Metaphysics at St Andrew's University (1892–8). He was Lecturer in Logic and Moral Philosophy at University College Dundee (1898–1900), and was appointed Professor of Moral Philosophy at the University of Aberdeen (1900–2). Latta then became Professor of Logic and Rhetoric at the University of Glasgow (1902–25). His publications include *Leibniz: the Monadology and Other Philosophical Writings* (Oxford, Clarendon Press, 1898), and *The Elements of Logic* (London, Macmillan, 1929).

The next memorial is a rusticated granite Calvary cross. One of its arms is missing.

5.44. Ernest Augustus Runtz (1859–1913) [plot 16]

Architect and surveyor. Born in Hornsey, Runtz was educated at the Kingsland Birkbeck School. In 1876 he was articled to Samuel Walker, Auctioneer, Valuer and Estate Agent, and became an

Associate of the Surveyors' Institution in 1883. At about the same time Runtz became a partner in the firm, which was renamed Walker & Runtz. Developing an interest in architecture, Runtz attended the lectures of Professor Roger Smith[32] at University College London. He studied also under Frederick Barrow FRIBA, and in 1888 passed the qualifying examination for associateship of the Royal Institution of British Architects. His first competitive designs were submitted in 1890 for the Municipal Buildings at Oxford and a scheme for widening London Bridge. Runtz set up his own practice in 1897, making a speciality of theatres and music halls. He designed the Free Library at Stoke Newington (1891); remodelled the Pavilion Theatre, Mile End (1893–4), and the (old) Theatre Royal, Cambridge (1896); and enlarged the Adelphi Theatre (reopening as the Century Theatre); the Cardiff Theatre; the Gaiety Theatre, Aldwych (1902–3, demolished in the late 1950s) and offices for the Anglo-American Oil Company in Queen Anne's Gate (1909). In 1910 the failure of the Birkbeck Building Society & Bank and the London Discount Company left him in financial difficulties. His health deteriorated and he died an undischarged bankrupt in 1913.[33]

The next memorials are in the grove of silver birch trees on the edge of the woodland area to the right of St Philip's Avenue.

5.45. Holy Trinity, Hounslow, reburials [plot 57a]

The earlier church of Holy Trinity, Hounslow, was destroyed by arsonists in June 1943, along with All Saints, Isleworth. A temporary church was built on the site, although it was not until 1953 that reconstruction was considered. Since the insurance fell short of rebuilding costs the only solution was to sell part of the churchyard. A special Act of Parliament was required and the human remains were removed to this area in the late 1950s, the task being completed in 1960. A total of 461 cases of human remains were reburied here, with 186 individual remains that were identifiable at the time. Surviving headstones and memorials were also moved here and these may be located lying flat on the ground (in the case of headstones) or otherwise just placed over the grave (in the case of other memorial designs). No memorial for the unidentified human remains appears to have been erected in this area. The names of all those reburied at Brookwood have been recorded by the West Middlesex Family History Society. The old foundation stone of the church (dated 1828) was re-laid in May 1962 and the new church was consecrated on 18 May 1963.

The next plot is the lawned area at the end of St Philip's Avenue and on the left. The ground is screened by conifers.

5.46. The Royal Hospital, Chelsea [plot 54]

This extensive lawned area is the first burial ground at Brookwood used by the Royal Hospital from 1894. The original burial area was part of the hospital grounds, and the first interment took place in 1692. This allotment was closed in 1854 when an area in Brompton Cemetery was used. During 1893 the Hospital authorities realised that it would be necessary to find a new burial area and a contract was agreed with the LNC for the burial of pensioners at £6 each, inclusive of the rail journey. The area was originally laid out with memorials and headstones in rows, with the appearance of a conventional burial ground.

The first major alteration to this area came in 1937 when the massive central memorial was planned and built. Part of the plot was redesigned, with 818 turves provided, and 1,000 squares of heather planted to create an 8–9ft border beside the plot, along with the planting of four pink thorn trees and two Scots pines. The memorial was designed by Oswald Milne FRIBA[34] and is constructed of Portland stone. It was unveiled and dedicated on 27 April 1937, and serves as a general memorial to all those pensioners buried here. The special ceremony was performed by

General Sir Walter Braithwaite,[35] Governor of the Royal Hospital, and was attended by over 300 pensioners in uniform. The service of dedication was conducted by the Hospital's chaplain, the Revd H.T. Malaher, after which a wreath was laid by the senior captain of invalids, Captain G. Bailey.[36]

The plot was finally altered to its present form in 1954 when the Royal Hospital decided to economise on the maintenance of the plot. It was cleared of memorials (although some survive on the boundary), and an enormous quantity of heather was planted across the ground. The original headstones were replaced by 1,500 stone markers set into the ground at a cost of £750. At the same time more trees were planted.[37] It remains a mystery as to what happened to the stone markers since few if any appear to survive. Subsequently a second burial area at Brookwood was opened, behind the **Canadian Military cemetery**, which is still used. Plot 54 is now used for the burial or scattering of ashes. Some memorials may be found adjacent to St Gregory's Avenue. These are small stones set into the ground where ashes have been buried or scattered.

The following memorials associated with the Royal Hospital Chelsea all face St Gregory's Avenue.

Captain Ludlow (died 1918), of the Grenadier Guards, and Officer of Invalids at the Royal Hospital, is buried with his wife **Jessie Sophia**, and their two sons **Ernest John** (aged 10) and **J. Bernard** (aged 4½). They were killed during an air raid by Gotha bombers on 16 February 1918, when a small force of six planes penetrated the London defences. One aeroplane dropped three large bombs, one of which destroyed their house within the grounds of the Royal Hospital. Their memorial was erected by the officers of the Grenadier Guards 'in affectionate remembrance of a brave and esteemed comrade'.

Major-General Llewellyn Isaac Gethin Morgan-Owen (1879–1960), was Lieutenant-Governor and Secretary of the Royal Hospital (1940–4). He was educated at Arnold House, Llandulas; Shrewsbury School; and at Trinity College, Dublin. He joined the Carnarvon Militia in 1899 and passed into the Army as a university candidate. His active service included the South African War (1900–2) and service with the Northern Nigeria Mounted Infantry (1905–9). During the First World War he served in France, was awarded the DSO at Gallipoli, and saw action in Egypt and Mesopotamia. After the war he served in Waziristan (1920–1) and was subsequently appointed Director of Organisation, India (1927–8). Morgan-Owen went on to command the 160th (South Wales) Infantry Brigade, Territorial Army (1929–31) and the 9th Infantry Brigade (1931–3). He was Colonel of the South Wales Borderers (1931–44) and Major-General in charge of Administration, Eastern Command (1934–8). Morgan-Owen retired in 1938. He served as Commissioner to the Royal Hospital from 1945 to 1958.

Major-General Hugh Clement Sutton (1867–1928), was Lieutenant-Governor of the Royal Hospital between 1923 and 1928. He was educated at Eton and the Royal Military College, Sandhurst. He joined the Coldstream Guards in 1887 and served in South Africa (1899–1902). Afterwards, Sutton was appointed Deputy Assistant Director of Railways. He commanded the 1st Battalion, Coldstream Guards (1910–13) and was Assistant Adjutant General at the War Office (1913–16). During the First World War he served variously as Deputy Assistant Quartermaster General with the British Army in France (1916), Inspector General of Communication to the Home Forces (1917) and Deputy Inspector General of Communication in Mesopotamia (1918–19). After the war he was placed in charge of the administration of the London District (1920) and was Deputy Director of Personal Services at the War Office (1921) after which he was appointed Lieutenant-Governor of the Royal Hospital.

Situated in the far corner of this ground is a group of seventeen **military graves** within a wire enclosure. They commemorate men from various regiments and all pre-date the **military cemetery**. They appear to have died in nearby army camps, although whether this was from wounds sustained on active service or from other causes is not known. The earliest burial is that of **Sergeant E.F. Murray** (died 30 September 1914), of the 10th Battalion, Durham Light Infantry. The last is the memorial to **Private J.R. Carstens** (*c.* 1884–1917) of the 3rd Regiment, South African Infantry.

Beyond this area, looking towards the woodland, it is possible to locate the pathway that leads through part of the **pauper burial grounds**. *For further details see Chapter 6. The next memorial is a granite block with kerbing. It may be found in the plot opposite.*

5.47. Hilary Bauerman (1835–1909) [plot 53]

Metallurgist, mineralogist and geologist. Bauerman entered the Government School of Mines in 1851 and completed his studies at the Bergakademie, Freiburg (1853–5). He was appointed assistant to the Geological Survey of the United Kingdom (1855). He then went to Canada as geologist to the North American Boundary Commission (1858–63). From 1863 he was intermittently employed in searching for mineral deposits and surveying mines in all parts of the world. This employment was by individuals, companies and governments. At the same time Bauerman published many important books and papers on metallurgy and mineralogy. Probably his best-known book is *The Metallurgy of Iron* (London, Virtue, 1868), which includes outlines of the history of iron manufacture, methods of assay, analyses of iron ores and the manufacturing processes for iron and steel. The book reached its sixth edition in 1890. He also wrote a *Text-book of Systematic Mineralogy* (London, Longmans, Green, 1881) and a *Text-book of Descriptive Mineralogy* (London, Longmans, Green, 1884). Later Bauerman turned to teaching. He was appointed Lecturer in Metallurgy at Firth College, Sheffield, in 1883. In 1888 he became Professor of Metallurgy at the Ordnance College at Woolwich. He retired in 1906 and died at Balham. He was cremated at St John's, Woking.

The next memorial is on the other side of plot 53. It comprises a large headstone set within a small allotment.

5.48. Mayford Industrial School for Boys [plot 53]

The Industrial School was a new approach to dealing with destitute and unemployed boys in London. The original school opened in 1867 in Wandsworth and provided accommodation, teaching and training in a suitable craft or trade. By 1871 it had moved to a leased site at Coldharbour Farm, Pyrford. In 1887 a permanent home was acquired at Mayford Farm; this has been administered successively by the London County Council and the Greater London Council. The plot in the cemetery, which faces St Stephen's Avenue, was used for the burial of 'boys who have passed away while at school'. The earliest burial dates from 1898 (**Frederick Daniels**) and the latest recorded on the headstone is that of **Jules Sanderson** (died 1922).[38]

The next memorial is a small cross headstone with kerbing and footstone. It is located towards the centre of plot 51.

5.49. Edna Bessie Fletcher (*c.* 1928–1941) [plot 51]

Edna was the daughter of George and Alice Fletcher. She died suddenly at Woking aged just 13. The footstone includes the following verse:

> Perhaps if we could see
> The beauty of that land
> To which our loved are called
> From you and me
> We'd understand

> Perhaps if we could know
> The reason why they went
> We'd smile and wipe away
> The tears that flow
> And wait – content.

From here, locate plots 47 and 48.

5.50. London & South Western Railway plots [plots 47 and 48]

The LSWR chose Brookwood as a burying ground for its deceased employees, and separate areas were set aside for the burial of the company's officers and servants within the cemetery. Three main areas were used: the 'LSWR 1st class area' (part of plot 47), the 'LSWR 2nd class area' (plot 48) and an area set aside in the former Nonconformist section (see Chapter 8). Other areas were used by more senior staff (especially part of plot 32, see Chapter 4), but were not exclusively reserved for use by the LSWR. About half of plot 47 appears to be devoted to LSWR employees and their families, and probably most of plot 48. However, out of over 200 inscriptions in these areas only thirty-one directly record a link with the railway.

Memorials in plot 47. The earliest memorial in plot 47 appears to be that of **John Spencer** (*c*. 1838–65), a fireman 'who met his death by accident . . . at Winchester on 11 October 1865'. The accident took place on the 7.15 p.m. Up train from Southampton to London. About a quarter of a mile from the Eastleigh side of St Cross tunnel Spencer told the driver, William Watson, that he had a pain in his bowels and would go to the back of the tender to relieve himself. The driver last saw Spencer standing on the tank of the tender, perfectly upright. Spencer was 6ft tall and this meant that he was now taller than the engine's chimney. He was unaware of the approaching bridge close to St Cross tunnel, and was killed instantly by the impact with the bridge. The guard, Henry Jessop, alerted the driver to stop as the train approached Winchester station, since Spencer's body had fallen onto the roof of the guard's van. After arriving at Winchester his body was taken down from the top of the guard's van. A plate-layer discovered Spencer's cap beside the railway. At the inquest Dr Willey, who examined the body at Winchester station, stated the body was still warm. 'There was a wound across the forehead an inch above the eyes, and the skull was fractured right across, and the whole of the brains gone.'[39] The memorial bears a striking carving of a Beattie locomotive of the period called *Firebrand*, presumably the one upon which Spencer lost his life.

Another interesting memorial in this plot is that of **Joseph Porter** (1822–85), whose memorial may be found to the left of Spencer's. Porter was, according to family legend, the driver of the first train that ran into Brookwood Cemetery. This conveyed the directors and shareholders of the LNC from the Necropolis station in London to **South station** for the service of consecration on 7 November 1854. As a boy, Porter was taken by his father to see the Rainhill trials in October 1829. This exciting event, where Stephenson's *Rocket* eventually won the day, appears to have convinced Porter that he must become a railwayman. His first job was as a flag boy when the railway was being laid across Wandsworth Common. By the summer of 1844 he was an engineer, while in the following year he was promoted to engine stoker based at Nine Elms. During this period he befriended the LSWR's Locomotive Superintendent Joseph Beattie.[40] Between 1848 and 1850 Porter was transferred to Dorchester shed, but returned to Battersea in 1850. From 1851 onwards he was an engine driver and probably operated a number of funeral trains into the cemetery. In 1872 Porter transferred to the Locomotive Department at Southampton, and was promoted to Railway Foreman in 1874. Towards the end of his career he became Engine Inspector at Nine Elms. By this time Porter had amassed some forty years' service with the LSWR. Porter married twice, first Elizabeth Young (*c*. 1818–51), and secondly **Elizabeth Susanna Roberts** (*c*. 1820–85).[41]

Among the other railwaymen buried here are **Henry Bricknell** (*c*. 1826–71), who died in 1871 'from injuries received while in the performance of his duty at Clapham Junction'.

The **Furber family** grave commemorates **Edwin Furber** (*c*. 1828–71), 'late an inspector of L&SW Railway Co. who was accidentally killed while in the performance of his duty at Clapham

Junction, 14 August 1871'. In the same grave is his son, **Charles Furber** (*c.* 1857–95), who was stationmaster at Parkstone in Dorset.

George Maynard (*c.* 1844–1916), 'for 50 years in the employ of the L&SWR as signalman, inspector and station master'. Other graves of the Maynard family are nearby.

Joseph Palmer (*c.* 1848–1922), 'for 48 years in the L&SWRly service retiring November 1914 chief inspector Nine Elms goods station'.

George Tubbs (*c.* 1831–90) was a Sergeant in the LSWR Police. He was accidentally killed while on duty at Nine Elms Goods Depot on 8 April 1890. At just after 6 a.m. he was knocked down and run over by a brake van. Both his legs were crushed in the accident. Later he told the surgeon that he was getting on to one of the wagons when his foot or coat caught on one of the point levers and pulled him to the ground. Tubbs was rushed to St Thomas's Hospital, but died during the course of an operation to amputate both his legs below the knee.[42]

Memorials in plot 48. William H. Hilditch (*c.* 1843–1908) was born and bred a railwayman, being the son of the first stationmaster at Esher. He was first employed as a telegraphist by the Electric & International Telegraph Company. In 1856 Hilditch was appointed clerk at Surbiton station, becoming Relieving Agent in 1861. In September 1864 he became stationmaster at Woking, then one of the busiest junctions on the LSWR. In 1877 he was rewarded for his vigilant action during a snowstorm when the failure of a signal very nearly caused a catastrophe. In 1878 Hilditch took general charge of the new Woking–Ascot line, and in April 1880 he was appointed Station Superintendent at Waterloo. For the next twenty-three years he was in charge of a staff of 500 men and a service of 800 trains a day. He retired in September 1903 after forty years' service with the LSWR.

Just to the left of this headstone is that of **Andrew Henry Moore** (*c.* 1857–1909), 'late stationmaster, Wimbledon . . . the last of Sir H.M. Stanley's[43] expedition up the Congo in 1879'. Stanley is buried in the churchyard at Pirbright.

On the other side of this plot is the grave of **William Gude** (*c.* 1852–1938). He worked on the LSWR, latterly as foreman at the Nine Elms Goods Yard. Deeply interested in the welfare of fellow workers and their families, Gude, with six other men and Canon Allen Edwards[44] (then Vicar of All Saints' Church, adjacent to Waterloo station and opposite one of the entrances to the original Necropolis terminus on York Street), founded the London & South Western Railway Servants' Orphanage in Jeffreys Road, Clapham. Gude was involved in its administration and helped in the move out to Woking in July 1909 when the new Orphanage buildings in Oriental Road, Woking, were completed. He retired from the Home's Board of Governors in 1932, when he was presented with an oak chair made by the boys of the Orphanage to mark forty years' work for the Home and its children.

The next memorial is towards the other end of the plot. It is a cross-style memorial made of wood.

5.51. Ann Matilda Lynn (died 1894) [plot 47]

An unusual wooden memorial with lead letters forced into the wood. Unfortunately the wood has deteriorated badly and many of the letters have disappeared.

The next memorial is a headstone with kerbing. It is closer to St Mark's Avenue.

5.52. William Heffer (*c.* 1843–1877) [plot 47]

This headstone records that Heffer was 'run over by a train at the Waterloo Station and died at St Thomas's Hospital' on 15 August 1877.

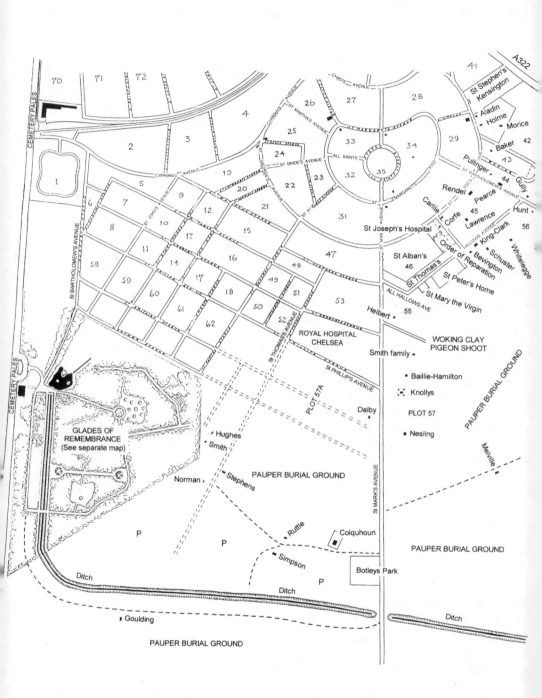

The Glades of Remembrance and the Cemetery Boundary.

Chapter Six

THE GLADES OF REMEMBRANCE
AND THE CEMETERY BOUNDARY

The areas covered by this chapter vary considerably. We start from the entrance to the Glades of Remembrance, and move on to the former pauper burial grounds (now woodland). Then comes a total contrast with the open heath, reminiscent of the original topography before the cemetery was properly laid out and planted. Next we explore plots near the boundary that have many more memorials. The walk finishes by the entrance to the Serbian cemetery, in the centre of the more 'developed' sections of the cemetery grounds. Many of the areas covered in this chapter have very few gravestones, and this reminds us that many parts of the cemetery have been hardly used.

There is a special entrance, with a lay-by, off Cemetery Pales. Start from the entrance gates to the Glades.

6.1. The Glades of Remembrance

The LNC planned these grounds for the reception of cremated remains shortly after the end of the Second World War. Under the terms of the London Necropolis Act (1946)[1] the company intended to open a crematorium directly opposite the present-day entrance to the Glades, with this area available for the reception of ashes. But the LNC never built its crematorium, although the Glades, designed from September 1945, were completed as a partial realisation of these plans. Messrs Milner, White & Sons[2] were used as landscape consultants to advise on the layout. Work proceeded as labour and money became available in the years of austerity that immediately followed the war.[3] The area was originally designated a 'memorial garden', with the name Glades of Remembrance chosen in June 1948. In addition to the £2,000 spent each year to landscape this area, a further £600 was used to create the lake and £150 for the transformer station used for pumping water through to the lake from Lakeside South. The Bishop of Guildford[4] formally dedicated the Glades in 1950, although the first ashes buried here were interred nearly three years before. Most of the land was previously used as a **pauper burial area** (see item 2 below). In some sections it is possible to see the shallow regular depressions in the ground, which are the surviving evidence of these graves. After the Glades were opened it was felt that 'no further developments in the Glades of Remembrance are considered necessary for some long time . . . the maintenance of the existing lay-out will ensure an adequate choice for all enquiries'.[5]

The plan of the Glades shows a sequence of 'glades' with pathways that provide access to the various parts used for the burial or scattering of cremated remains. Each section has its own distinct planting and atmosphere. Near the entrance the main feature is the lake (originally called the Pool of Serenity), with areas north and south. The various glades are called Fern, Maple, Birch and Pine. The two main 'walks' are North and South, and flank the deep drainage channel opposite the lake. Two other areas were named the Sanctuary and the Grove.

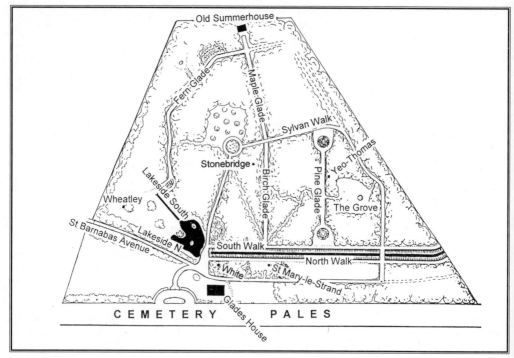

The Glades of Remembrance.

Unfortunately many trees were lost in the great hurricane of 1986 and have never been replaced. This has destroyed much of the original character of the planting.

The Glades were opened and dedicated by the Bishop of Guildford at a special ceremony on the afternoon of Thursday 11 May 1950. Cremated remains are either scattered or buried just below ground level. Small unobtrusive memorials mark the site and no other monuments are allowed. The author Bernard Darwin[6] described the Glades as 'the wildest of wild gardens, lonely and tranquil and cut off from the noisy outer world. . . . Here may be seen landscape gardening at its simplest and so most inconspicuous best.'[7]

Glades House, the whitewashed building just inside the entrance, was originally built as a caretaker's house by Messrs Holford's at a cost of £3,624. The original design of the cottage was to include a thatched roof, but this was changed to tiles. In 1950 Dennis Duffill moved in as the very first Superintendent of the Glades. He married Winifred Dendy, whose parents lived in **North station** between 1948 and 1956. The building is now used as the Cemetery Office.[9] The area beyond the house is used for storing machinery and equipment used by the small cemetery workforce.

Among those whose ashes lie in the Glades is **Ann Isabella Stonebridge** (*c*. 1882–1947). The very first burial of cremated remains in the Glades took place on 19 July 1947. In 1947 this area was referred to as the memorial garden. The tablet set into the ground is rather thicker than is usual, and is located to the left of Birch Glade.[10]

Dennis Yates Wheatley (1897–1977), whose small memorial of pink granite lies beside a tree adjacent to the lake, in the area Lakeside North, was a writer. The son of a wine merchant, he entered the family business in 1914. During the First World War he was commissioned in the Royal Field Artillery, and served with the City of London Brigade until he transferred to the 36th (Ulster) Division in 1917. He was invalided out of the Army in 1919. He took over his father's wine business in 1926–7. It was ruined during the slump of 1929–30, and he sold it off in 1930. His second wife suggested he took up writing. He did so and with immediate success. His first book, *The Forbidden Territory*, has never been out of print since it first appeared in 1933. Some of the characters in this book were used successfully in ten subsequent novels. In *Black August* (1934) the character of Geoffrey Sallust appears; he was also used in further novels. His first thriller set against a background of 'black magic' was *The Devil Rides Out* (1935), but Wheatley had no special knowledge of satanism; he was just a diligent researcher for his novels. During the Second World War he worked with the Joint Planning Staff (the only regular officer to do so) and helped develop warfare scenarios, training schemes and deception measures. The knowledge he gained was invaluable after the war when he returned to writing his adventure stories. In total he wrote over seventy-five books which were translated into over thirty languages. These include three volumes of memoirs, *The Time Has Come* (1977–9), and a posthumous account of his wartime activities, *The Deception Planners* (1980). His epitaph reads 'Prince of thriller writers'.

Edward White (*c.* 1873–1952) was a distinguished landscape architect. Born in Worthing, he came to London and met the well-known civil engineer H.E. Milner to whom he became apprenticed. After being taken into partnership, he married Milner's eldest daughter. The firm gained a reputation with the owners of large estates and local authorities for the 'sympathetic treatment of ground contours and natural features'.[11] He was responsible for the gardens at the new Government Building in Ottawa, Bagshot Park and Drottingholm for the King of Sweden. He also planned the first Chelsea Flower Show, the Royal Horticultural Exhibition of 1912, the gardens at the British Empire Exhibition of 1924 and the British gardens at the Brussels Exhibition. White had a great interest in the cremation movement and for the development of 'gardens of remembrance' where ashes could be scattered or buried. He was responsible for the considerable development of the gardens at Golders Green in 1938, at the West London Crematorium at Kensal Green in 1939, the 'Garden of Rest' at Chipperfield Church, Hertfordshire, and for the Glades of Remembrance at Brookwood.[12] However, his crowning achievement was as architect of the memorial gardens at Stoke Poges. Laid out on land acquired by Sir Noel Mobbs which formed part of Stoke Park, the gardens adjoined St Giles's Church in whose graveyard Thomas Gray wrote his *Elegy in a Country Churchyard*. Dedicated in 1935 and completed in 1937 it has rose gardens, water gardens, rock gardens, formal and informal gardens and an Italian garden with fifty fountains.[13] White also lectured at Cremation Society conferences and contributed to their publications. At the Cremation Society's conference in 1946 White stated:

> The cult of cremation is unlikely to find a more persuasive advocate than a really beautiful garden of remembrance. I emphasise really beautiful. . . . When the first crematorium gardens were made in this country, garden art was at a low ebb. Cemeteries were at their worst, in spite, or perhaps because, of the enormously expensive monuments with which they were cluttered. Compared with such burial grounds, the simple lawns made for the disposal of cremated ashes may have justified their description as 'gardens of rest'. Otherwise the earliest crematorium gardens were primitive and featureless.[14]

For many years he lived at Rowan Bank in York Road, Woking. He was appointed the first President of the British Institute of Landscape Architects (1929), and was presented with the Victoria Medal, the highest award for horticultural work given by the Royal Horticultural Society. White's funeral service took place in the parish church at Sutton Green, followed by cremation at St John's. His memorial stone is near the top of the bank beside the stream.

The memorial to **Forest Frederic Edward Yeo-Thomas**, **GC** ('White Rabbit') (1901–64), may be found on the right-hand side of Pine Glade. Yeo-Thomas was a wartime secret agent. Educated at the Dieppe Naval College and in Paris he served as a dispatch rider with the Americans in 1918. After the First World War he fought in the Polish Army, and was captured by and escaped from the Bolsheviks in 1920. Yeo-Thomas was works manager and secretary of the fashion house of Molyneux between the wars. He joined the RAF in 1939 and was an intelligence officer with No. 308 (Polish) Squadron in 1941 before joining the Special Operations Executive in 1942. He was parachuted into France to organise the French Resistance in 1943. Having gained Churchill's favour, Yeo-Thomas was able to secure more supplies and weapons for the French. He returned to France in 1944 but was arrested, imprisoned and tortured. His various prisons included Frèsnes, Compiègnes, Buchenwald and Rehmsdof. He managed to escape in 1945. Yeo-Thomas has been described as one of the most outstanding workers behind German lines during the Second World War, for which he was variously awarded the George Cross, the Military Cross and bar, the Croix de Guerre and the Polish Cross of Merit. He helped to bring to justice several Nazi war criminals. He returned to Molyneux after the war, but left in 1948 for health reasons. In 1950 he was appointed the Paris representative of the Federation of British Industries. A book about him, *The White Rabbit*, was written by Bruce Marshall in 1952.[15] Yeo-Thomas is also commemorated on a plaque listing members of the RAF who were awarded the George Cross in the church of **St Clement Danes**, London; by a street named after him in Paris; and by a bust in the 16th arrondisement, placed to commemorate the centenary of his birth.

St Mary-le-Strand reburials. To the right of the North Walk, and adjacent to the Critchley-Waring allotment on the bank, may be found the fallen memorial commemorating the reinterment of human remains from St Mary-le-Strand in Russell Court. This burial ground in London was opened in 1723 and was closed in 1853. According to Mrs Holmes this was the graveyard immortalised by Charles Dickens as 'Tom-all-Alones' in *Bleak House*. She described it as '430 square yards. It is probable that few grounds in London were more overcrowded with bodies than this one, which was entirely surrounded by the backs of small houses. When closed in 1853 it was in a very disgusting and unwholesome condition.'[16]

Thereafter the site was used as a rubbish tip until in 1886 the Metropolitan Gardens Association transformed it into a playing ground. In 1897 an application was made to the Consistory Court for a faculty to use part of the disused burial ground as part of the preparations for clearance prior to the construction of the Aldwych. The contract for the exhumation and reburial of human remains by the LNC followed, and the human remains were reburied hereabouts in January 1898.[17]

*The easiest way through the woodland is to follow Lakeside North and join the path that runs through this area. The graves described in the next section are widely scattered. Look out for the regular shallow depressions in the ground, which mark the pauper graves in these plots. Eventually you will emerge at the very end of St Mark's Avenue, adjacent to the deep drainage ditch that should be to your left. Further access is available from the pathway that may be found in the woodland opposite the **Chelsea Hospital** ground. Reference is made to this path in the following section.*

Great care should be taken when walking across these sections as the ground can be very uneven and in places is prone to give way.

6.2. The pauper burial grounds [plots 'P']

The LNC tendered each year for the burial of the poor from several London parishes, and much of the company's business was devoted to the decent burial of paupers in individual graves. It is estimated that at least 80 per cent of the total burials at Brookwood are of paupers, virtually all in unmarked graves. Some parishes, like **St Saviour's**, **Southwark** or **St Anne's**, **Westminster**, set aside distinct burial plots within the cemetery, and these are described in their appropriate sections. Many other parishes left the LNC to allocate burial areas; these were on the western boundaries of the cemetery, closest to Pirbright village. It is quite possible that the drainage ditch and its associated mound was deliberately used as a distinct and definite boundary to the pauper areas, thereby keeping the *hoi polloi* apart from the more wealthy. However, in time it became necessary to use land closer to the main part of the cemetery, and therefore the pauper areas eventually continued on the other side of the drainage channel.

It is now impossible to say whether each parish had separate areas, or whether burials from different parishes followed on from one another. Graves were marked by low mounds, usually with grass or moss growing on them, and probably a wooden marker with the burial number stamped on to a metal strip that was attached to the stake. From some entries in the burial registers it is clear that adults and children were buried in separate areas, unless next of kin made a specific request for an old grave to be reopened. It is also clear from the burial registers that these pauper burial grounds occupied considerable areas, particularly here on the cemetery boundary. Entries like '68th grave from top end of 55th row of adults' or '28th grave from bottom end of 52nd row of children' are fairly typical of those found in the registers. Notes like these would have assisted staff of the LNC when a particular pauper grave had to be identified. Some of the parishes or districts whose poor were buried in this way are **Bermondsey**, **Chiswick**, **St George's**, **Bloomsbury**, **St Giles-in-the-Fields**, **St Luke's**, **Chelsea**, **St Nicholas**, **Deptford** and **St Paul's**, **Deptford**.

Among the anonymous and unmarked pauper graves in this part of the cemetery grounds is that of **Henry Samuel Tabram** (*c.* 1843–90). Tabram was a foreman furniture packer, and was the husband of Martha Tabram (1849–88), one of the alleged victims of Jack the Ripper. Henry and Martha had separated in 1875 because of her heavy drinking. Henry continued to give Martha financial assistance until he discovered that she was living with another man and 'how she was going on'. Martha Tabram was murdered in the early morning of 7 August 1888. Her body was discovered on the first floor landing of George Yard Buildings, Whitechapel, with thirty-nine wounds in her body. Henry identified the body on 14 August 1888. Terry Saxby argues that Henry Tabram was both Martha's murderer and Jack the Ripper. Saxby's theory hinges on there being seven Ripper murders, rather than the canonical five usually described (those of Mary Ann Nichols, Annie Chapman, Elizabeth Stride, Catharine Eddowes and Mary Jane Kelly). The additional murders were those of Emma Elizabeth Smith and Martha Tabram.[18] Henry Tabram died a pauper in the Wandsworth and Clapham Union Workhouse on 17 May 1890. This parish had an agreement with the LNC for the burial of its dead, which is how he came to be buried at Brookwood in an unmarked grave.

Also buried hereabouts is **Corporal William Reynolds**, **VC** (1827–67). Born in London, Reynolds served with the Scots (Fusilier) Guards during the Crimean War. His VC was awarded for his action during the Battle of the Alma on 20 September 1854. At one stage of the battle, the British formation became disordered and Reynolds behaved in a conspicuous manner in rallying the men round the colours. He was presented with his award by Queen Victoria at a general investiture held in Hyde Park on 26 June 1857. Ten years later he died in London and was buried in a pauper's grave in the unidentified 'Bloomsbury ground'.

In some cases the family or relatives of the deceased were subsequently able to purchase the pauper grave, and thereby erect a memorial. If you follow the path that runs beyond **Glades House** you can discover one such headstone, to **Charlotte Goulding** (*c.* 1791–1862). The memorial is now partly obscured by a tree which has grown around it. It records that the memorial was erected 'by her sons and daughters in token respect to her memory, and may God rest her soul'. This headstone may mark part of the **St Luke's**, **Chelsea**, burial area.

Richard Simpson (*c.* 1857–1906), whose headstone with kerbing may be found off a rough pathway near the **Colquhoun family mausoleum**, drowned in the Thames.

His unidentified body was originally buried in an unmarked grave. Later he was identified, the grave was purchased by his relatives and a headstone erected with the epitaph 'found drowned near Blackfriars Bridge August 3rd 1906'. Nearby may be found another headstone with kerbing in memory of **William Ruttle** (1876–1907).

It is also possible to locate an old avenue leading through this part of the pauper burial grounds, which eventually joins St Thomas's Avenue. It is easiest to trace this path from the direction of St Thomas's Avenue, adjacent to the **Royal Hospital Chelsea plot.** *Extreme care should be taken in exploring these areas because of the uneven nature of the ground*. Within plot 57b, and well away from the path, is the isolated headstone of **Winifred C. Hughes** (died 1897), with the tiny Calvary cross with kerbing that marks the grave of **Joseph Barnard Smith** (died 1896) close by. On the other side of the avenue is the kerbed grave of **Frederick John Henry Stephens** (*c.* 1869–1905). Further on, and to the right of the path, may be found the low headstone to **Frederic McBride Norman** (died 1898). Norman came from New Orleans and died in London on 3 November 1898.

Unusually for the pauper areas, the tragedy of an entire family is preserved on the headstone of the **Smith family**, in plot 57 and on the right-hand side of St Mark's Avenue. Access to this grave is easiest after item 9 below, but the memorial is described here as it is another pauper grave. The headstone commemorates **Richard** and **Harriet Smith** and their nine children **Richard** (17), **Alfred** (16), **Harriet** (13), **Harvey** (11), **Walter** (9), **Thomas** (7), the twins **Mary** and **Maria** (5) and **Jessie** (2). They were all killed in the 'awful fire' at 20 Gilbert Street, Bloomsbury, on 28 March 1858. In addition to the Smith family, the four members of the neighbouring Hedger family also perished. The fire started in an adjacent warehouse where minerals (including arsenic) were stored. The tragedy resulted in criticism of the building design, for the family had no means of escape once the fire was discovered and there was no form of fireproofing between the floors. Subsequent Building Acts stipulated that suitable fire escapes should be provided, along with adequate fireproofing. This grave possibly marks part of the burial ground of **St George's**, **Bloomsbury**. It is still not known who paid for the memorial.

Eventually you will emerge at the very end of St Mark's Avenue, adjacent to the deep drainage ditch that should be to your left. The next stage involves the exploration of plots on the left- and right-hand sides of this avenue.

6.3. Botleys Park Hospital and the Brookwood Hospital plot [plot 57a]

This is on the left of the avenue and forms a partial clearing in the trees. **Botleys Park**, near Chobham, was established by Surrey County Council as a 'colony for mental defectives' of all ages in 1932. The need to erect new buildings for the hospital surrounding the eighteenth-century mansion house meant the new institution was not officially opened until June 1939. During the Second World War it was used as a general war hospital. After 1945 it became part of the National Health Service and was more recently made part of the Homewood NHS Trust. **Brookwood Hospital** was opened as the Surrey County Lunatic Asylum in June 1867. At its peak the asylum housed over 1,400 patients (1931). Although it was designed as a self-contained community, all deaths at the asylum usually resulted in the deceased being buried in Brookwood Cemetery. By 1980 the hospital was virtually obsolete as a place to care for the mentally ill. In 1981 the Surrey Area Health Authority announced plans to close the whole complex, and this was completed in 1993.

This plot dates from the late 1930s when part of the area on the right was used for burials from Botleys Park. The allotment is divided into three sections, with two crude paths running between them, each edged with blue bricks. The sides of the plot are partly screened with conifers. Wooden markers were used to indicate each grave, with the burial number stamped on a metal strip that was nailed to the wood. Some simple wooden memorials survive here and there. It is not yet known where burials from Brookwood Hospital took place prior to the late 1930s, and whether another ground remains to be discovered. A small working group from the Brookwood Cemetery Society has begun the sympathetic clearance of this burial ground, and is attempting to log the burials in the whole allotment.

6.4. Colquhoun family mausoleum [plot 57a]

If you follow the crude path just beyond the end of the Botleys Park plot you will see the rear of this family mausoleum. It was almost certainly the earliest mausoleum to be completed in the cemetery (1858) and is somewhat difficult to locate, being effectively hidden in the trees. The architect was J. Johnson, and the mason W. Boulton;[19] these names appear either side of the doorway. This is the most architecturally distinguished mausoleum in the cemetery, and it is possible the building was originally intended to serve as another cemetery chapel. It was purchased by the Colquhoun family and the mausoleum was used as a small family chapel. The structure was last restored in 1924 by Violette Freeman in memory of **Eliza Colquhoun Redhouse**. She also paid £2 2s 0d in 1935 for clearing the ground surrounding the mausoleum and generally putting the area into good order.[20] Drainage has been a continual problem in this area, and there are several references to complaints made by **Sir Patrick Colquhoun** in the Minutes.[21] Some members of the family are buried in the vault beneath the floor of the mausoleum, even though there are small memorials to them outside the building. It is likely that other members of the family are buried in the private ground outside. The whole allotment is enclosed by a low cast-iron fence, with a gateway opposite the entrance to the mausoleum. It seems that some formal planting, possibly comprising an avenue of trees, took place, leading from the private plot towards the main part of the cemetery.

James Colquhoun (1780–1855) was a diplomat, and was Consul General in London for Saxony (1827–55).

Sir Patrick Macchombaich Colquhoun (1815–91) was a diplomat, author and oarsman. Educated at Westminster and Cambridge, he was called to the Bar at the Inner Temple in 1838 and was made a QC in 1868. Colquhoun was Plenipotentiary to the Hansiatic Republics (1840–4). He concluded commercial treaties with Turkey, Persia and Greece (1841–2). Colquhoun was the appointed Aulic Councillor to the King of Saxony (1857), and was a Member of the Supreme Court of Justice in the Ionian Islands (1858). He was knighted (1861), and appointed Chief Justice of the Court (1861–4). On 28 May 1864 the Ionian Islands were ceded to Greece. Colquhoun was a keen oarsman, being Captain of the St John's College Boat Club (1835). He founded the 'Colquhoun sculls' (1836). Colquhoun won the Wingfield sculls and amateur championship of the Thames by sculling from Westminster Bridge to Putney (August 1837). He joined the Leander Boat Club (1844) and was its Secretary (1844–59) and President (1882). Colquhoun published legal and other works. He spoke most of the languages and dialects of Europe. In 1888 he requested that his dog be buried within the family allotment, but the LNC refused permission.[22]

His only child, **Eliza Colquhoun Redhouse** (c. 1843–1923), who married **Sir James William Redhouse** (1811–92) in 1888, is also buried here. Sir James Redhouse was an oriental scholar. Educated at Christ's Hospital, he was a draftsman in the employment of the Ottoman government at Constantinople (1826–30) where he made a careful study of Turkish. In 1830 he went to Russia and returned to England in 1834. Redhouse resumed his employment with the Turkish government from 1838 in the Translations Office, and from 1840 was transferred to the Turkish Admiralty. He was secretary and interpreter to Captain W. Fenwick Williams,[23] the British commissioner arranging a peace between Turkey and Persia (1843–7). From 1847–53 he acted as confidential communicator between the Turkish and British governments. He became Oriental Translator to the Foreign Office from 1854. Redhouse retired in 1857 and devoted most of his time to compiling a great dictionary of the Arabic, Persian and pure Turki languages. Redhouse married first Jane Carruthers in 1836. She died in 1887. He married secondly Eliza Colquhoun in 1888. After his death she subsequently married Colonel George Phillips in 1914. He died in 1918.

Return to St Mark's Avenue and turn left, continuing to walk away from the **Glades of Remembrance**. *Cross the pathway adjacent to the statues commemorating John and Maria Fort, and look for the fence that forms a boundary between the cemetery and what is now open heath. This area is administered by Woking Borough Council and is retained as a rare survival of Surrey heathland. It is from such scenery that the cemetery was laid out and planted (see also the Introduction). Pass through the gate and follow the rough path adjacent to the fence. The next grave is a kerbed memorial to the right of the path.*

6.5. Arthur Melville (1855–1904) [on the heath]

Set in splendid isolation on the edge of the heath is the grave of this Scottish artist. Melville studied at the Edinburgh School of Art, the Royal Scottish Academy and in Paris. It was in Paris (1878–81) that he started to concentrate on watercolours, a medium that revealed his distinctive qualities. Melville travelled extensively in Egypt, Persia and Turkey during 1881–3. He returned to Scotland and strongly influenced the Glasgow artistic movement. During this time he exhibited several oil portraits in Edinburgh (e.g. *The Flower Girl*, 1883) before he settled in London from 1888. Melville later visited Spain (1889–92 and 1904) and Venice (1894). He was a member of the Royal Scottish Academy (1886), the Scottish Water Colour Society, and the Royal Water Colour Society (1900). His misty and distinctive watercolours include *A Moorish Procession* (1893), *The Captured Spy* (1895), *The Blue Night, Venice* (1897) and *Bravo Toro! The Little Bull Fight* (1899). Melville contracted typhoid fever while in Barcelona and died at his home in Witley, Surrey. His funeral arrangements were undertaken by Harrods. Note that the grave is incomplete since the upright stone, which included the inscription, is missing. However, it can be identified as Melville's from the grave number on the kerbing.

Return to St Mark's Avenue and turn right, heading away from the **Glades of Remembrance**. *The next sequence of memorials is in the trees to the right of the path. The first of these has an anchor as part of the design.*

6.6. Arthur Bruce Nesling (died 1920) [plot 57]

Nesling was a Lieutenant-Commander in the Royal Navy. He served with distinction in Crete (1898) and was invalided from the Navy in 1916 after more than two years' arduous service in the First World War.

Nesling's grave also serves as a memorial to two other naval personnel, who are not buried here but are worthy of inclusion in this guide. Note the very apt quotation from Tennyson's Ode on the Death of the Duke of Wellington *at the base of the memorial:*

> Not once or twice in our rough island story
> The path of duty was the way to glory.

Wing-Commander Frank Arthur Brock (1884–1918). Inventor and scientist. Brock's family were the creators of Brock's fireworks, but his knowledge extended well beyond pyrotechnics. His inventiveness was extremely valuable to the Allied cause during the First World War. He worked in naval intelligence where he invented the 'Brock bullet', an explosive bullet for use against Zeppelins. He founded, organised and commanded the Royal Naval Experimental Station at Stratford. Brock also devised the smoke screen (or 'artificial fog') which was used in the attack on Zeebrugge on St George's Day 1918. Brock insisted on taking part in this raid and accompanied the storming party on to the Mole. Thus he lost his life. The Brock factory in London was closed as a mark of respect when the news came through of his untimely death. He is also commemorated on the Memorial to the Missing in Zeebrugge churchyard.

Andrew Yule Catto (died 1939). Sailor, and also commemorated here. Catto served with the Naval Brigade during the South African War (1899–1902). During the First World War he was Inspector of Diving to the Grand Fleet (1914–18).

On the same side of the avenue is the next headstone.

6.7. Sir William Alexander Baillie-Hamilton (1844–1920) [plot 57]

Civil servant. Baillie-Hamilton trained as a barrister, was appointed Secretary to the Colonial Office in 1887, and acted as Private Secretary to the Secretaries of State for the Colonies until 1892. He was appointed Chief Clerk to the Colonial Office in 1896, a post he held until 1909. He was made Officer of Arms of the Order of St Michael and St George in 1901, and Gentleman Usher of the Blue Rod in 1911.

Just beyond this is a prominent white cross set within four conifers.

6.8. Edward George William Tyrwhitt Knollys, 2nd Viscount Knollys (1895–1966) [plot 57]

Businessman and public servant. Son of Francis Knollys, 1st Viscount (1837–1924), the private secretary to King Edward VII (1870–1910) and King George V (1910–13). Born in St James's Palace and educated at Harrow and Oxford. During the First World War he served in the Army and in the Royal Flying Corps. Knollys joined Barclays Bank and worked in Cape Town (1929–32). He was Director of the Employers' Liability Assurance Corporation (1932), Managing Director (1933) and first Chairman of the joint company when it merged with Northern Assurance in 1960. During the Second World War Knollys served as Governor and Commander-in-Chief of Bermuda (1941–3). He was appointed the first full-time Chairman of the British Overseas Airways Corporation (1943–7). He saw the company transformed from an RAF transport command to a successful civil airline business. He became Chairman of **Vickers Ltd** (1956–62), and one result of his term of office was the construction of a new London headquarters at Millbank. Knollys was also Chairman of the English Steel Corporation (1959–65), Chairman of the RAF Benevolent Fund and a Trustee of Churchill College, Cambridge. Knollys was known to his friends as 'Edgey', a nickname taken from his two godfathers, Edward VII and George V.

The next memorial may be found on the opposite side of St Mark's Avenue, at the left-hand edge of the cleared area for green burials beyond plot 54.

6.9. Sir William Bartlett Dalby (1840–1918) [plot 57a]

Surgeon. Educated at Cambridge and St George's Hospital, London. Dalby became a general practitioner in Chester after qualifying but returned to London to study diseases of the ear. His researches and articles made him more widely known, and his opinion was highly regarded. He wrote also on the education of the deaf and dumb by lip reading. He was appointed Aural Surgeon to St George's Hospital (1872–92), the first such appointment. He was knighted in 1886 in recognition of his work with the deaf and dumb and his contribution to the literature of aural disease. He was President of the Medical Society (1894), and later became the first President of the Otological Society.

*Cross St Mark's Avenue into plot 46. Note that it is easiest to visit the **Smith family** grave at this stage.*

6.10. Anonymous grave [plot 46]

Just outside the **St Alban's** plot is this apparently anonymous memorial with a most interesting verse:

> When the great scorer comes
> To write against your name
> He writes not that you won or lost
> But how you played the game.

6.11. St Alban's, Holborn ground [plot 46]

An attractive lych-gate forms the entrance to this ground. St Alban's was a new parish. The church was built and endowed through the generosity of John Gellibrand Hubbard.[24] St Alban's was constructed in an area of appalling destitution, children's brothels, workshops and thieves' kitchens. The new church and clergy house were designed by William Butterfield.[25] It was consecrated on 21 February 1863, and the parish has used Brookwood as a burial ground ever since. The church was badly damaged during the 1941 Blitz, and was restored by Adrian Gilbert Scott[26] between 1959 and 1961. The burial ground retains a secluded air, reminiscent of a country churchyard. A curious feature of the first part of the ground is that the layout is similar to that in a church: the line of priests' graves faces away from the central Calvary cross, while the remainder of the graves all face towards the cross (or 'altar'). The lych-gate was built as a memorial to a parishioner (identified only as 'John' in the carving within the roof) who died in November 1892. Since 1934 members of the church have visited the plot twice a year, when the dead are remembered in an open air mass held at the foot of the great cross.

Among those buried here are **anonymous air raid victims**. In a large kerbed plot in the top corner of the extension to the burial ground is a grave commemorating six unknown persons who were killed in the London Borough of Holborn by air attacks on the capital during the Second World War.

Robert Nisbet Bain (1854–1909). Historical writer and linguist. Bain was privately educated and was for many years a shorthand writer in the office of **Messrs Henry Kimber & Co.**, solicitors. He had a natural aptitude for languages and he became fluent in twenty largely European languages, including Russian, Swedish, Hungarian and Polish. Bain became second-class assistant in the printed books department of the British Museum in 1883 and in due course was promoted to first-class assistant. He wrote much on Scandinavian and Russian history, including *The Daughter of Peter the Great: a History of Russian Diplomacy and of the Russian Court under the Empress Elizabeth Petrovna 1741–62* (London, Constable, 1899) and *Peter III, Emperor of Russia: the Story of a Crisis and a Crime* (London, Constable, 1902). Bain also wrote two volumes in the Cambridge Historical Series: *Scandinavia: a Political History of Denmark, Norway and Sweden from 1513–1900* (Cambridge, Cambridge University Press, 1905) and *Slavonic Europe: a Political History of Poland and Russia from 1447–1796* (Cambridge, Cambridge University Press, 1908). He was also interested in literature and published a *Life of Hans Christian Andersen* (London, Lawrence & Bullen, 1895). Through his translations Bain was largely responsible for introducing the Hungarian novelist Maurus Jokai[27] to the English public. He was a High Churchman, and served for many years as sidesman and attendant at St Alban's.

Sir Gainsford Bruce (1834–1912). Judge under the Benefices Act from 1899. He was educated at Glasgow University and became a barrister in 1859. Bruce was Recorder of Bradford (1877), a QC (1883) and was appointed successively Solicitor-General (1879), Attorney-General (1886) and Chancellor (1887) of the County Palatine of Durham. He was

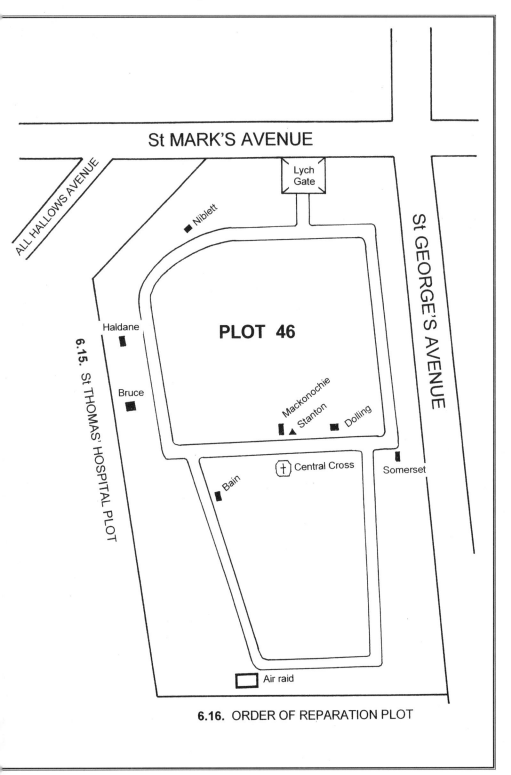

St MARK'S AVENUE

ALL HALLOWS AVENUE

St GEORGE'S AVENUE

Lych Gate

Niblett

PLOT 46

6.15. St THOMAS' HOSPITAL PLOT

Haldane

Bruce

Mackonochie

Stanton

Dolling

Central Cross

Somerset

Bain

Air raid

6.16. ORDER OF REPARATION PLOT

Conservative MP for Finsbury, Holborn Division (1888–92 and 1892). Bruce was appointed Judge of the King's Bench Division of the High Court of Justice (1892–1904). His publications include a life of his father, John Collingwood Bruce[28] (1906).

Revd Robert William Radclyffe Dolling (1851–1902). Divine and social reformer. The son of an Irish land agent, Dolling was educated at Harrow and, for a time, at Cambridge where he did not graduate. He knew both the **Revd Alexander Mackonochie** and the **Revd Arthur Stanton** from his college days, and through them became warden of the south London branch of the St Martin's Postman's League (1879). He entered Salisbury Theological College in 1882 and was ordained in 1883. Dolling became curate of Corscombe, Dorset, and then missionary deacon of St Martin's Mission at Holy Trinity, Stepney. In 1885 he became vicar of the Winchester College Mission of St Agatha's, Landport (now demolished), where for over ten years he did valuable work amid the slums. His mission work was described in his own book, *Ten Years in a Portsmouth Slum* (London, Sonnenschein & Co., 1896). He resigned this living over questions of ritual used in his services. Dolling was then appointed Vicar of St Saviour's, Poplar (1898). He described this parish as 'the great, dullest parish in London', but did his utmost to elevate the 'ten thousand people in one thousand one hundred houses, crouched into forty-four acres, all poor, many out of work', seeking to solve social and municipal problems in the parish. His health failed from March 1901, and he subsequently died in his sister's house in South Kensington. A Dolling Memorial Home for the working girls of Poplar and Landport was opened at Worthing in 1903.

General Sir James Aylmer Lowthrop Haldane (1862–1950). Educated at the Edinburgh Academy, Wimbledon School and the Royal Military College, Sandhurst. Haldane joined the Gordon Highlanders in 1882. He served on the Indian frontier (1894–8). As ADC to General Sir William Lockhart,[29] Haldane was able to ensure the success of the young Winston Churchill's attachment to the Tirah expedition (1897–8), although the campaign was over by the time Churchill was free to travel. They met next in November 1899, during the Boer War. Haldane was serving with the 2nd Battalion, Gordon Highlanders, and was in command of the Chieveley armoured train. This left Estcourt on 15 November 1899 and was ambushed by the Boers near Frere, when part of the train became derailed. Subsequent events laid the foundation of Churchill's public life. Churchill assisted in moving the trucks that were blocking the line and in helping the wounded on to the tender so they might escape to safety. Both Haldane and Churchill were captured and imprisoned in the State Model School in Pretoria. Churchill escaped on 12 December and eventually reached Lourenço Marques (now Maputo) on 22 December. He awoke on 23 December 1899 to worldwide fame. Haldane escaped with Lieutenant Le Mesurier[30] three months later via a secret tunnel, and published a full account in his book *How We Escaped From Pretoria* (Edinburgh, William Blackwood & Sons, 1900).[31] Haldane took part in several subsequent battles in the war. He was military attaché with the Japanese Army during the Russo-Japanese War (1904–5). During the First World War Haldane commanded the 10th Brigade in France (1914), succeeding to the 3rd Division (November 1914) and later commanded the 6th Corps (1917–18). Afterwards he was General Officer Commander-in-Chief in Mesopotamia (1920–2), during which period he suppressed an extensive Arab insurrection. He retired as General in 1925. His other publications include *A Brigade of the Old Army 1914* (London, E. Arnold, 1920), *The Insurrection in Mesopotamia 1920* (Edinburgh, William Blackwood & Sons, 1922), *The Haldanes of Gleneagles* (Edinburgh, William Blackwood & Sons, 1929) and his autobiography *A Soldier's Saga* (Edinburgh, William Blackwood & Sons, 1948).

Revd Alexander Heriot Mackonochie (1825–87). Buried directly in front of the memorial cross is the first Curate of St Alban's. Educated at Wadham College, Oxford, he was ordained in 1849 and worked with Father Charles Lowder[32] as assistant missioner to the St George's Mission from 1856. This was the first modern Anglican mission to the poor of the

East End. It was an outstation of St George-in-the-East under the auspices of the Society of the Holy Cross, with its own chapel in Calvert (now Watts) Street. This in turn was replaced by St Peter's, London Dock, begun 1865–6 but unfinished for many years. Mackonochie was subsequently appointed as Curate to St Alban's in January 1863. He was influential in the formation of this burial ground and saw in its foundation the opportunity to Christianise the burial of the poor within his parish. The area off Brooke Street, where the church was constructed, was one of appalling destitution, and was described by Charles Dickens as 'one of the lowest and worst that improvement has left in the middle of London'. There was no room for the poor to lay out their dead decently at home, therefore Mackonochie provided a mortuary within the church. All this helped accord dignified funerals for the very poor. The care and reverence shown to their dead was something that struck a deep chord in the hearts and minds of the working people of the parish. Mackonochie was a 'ritualist' in that he conducted services with genuflection, chant, incense and the raising of the host above the head. This caused offence to some parishioners. In 1867, under the auspices of the Church Association, a case was pursued against him. On appeal to the Privy Council (1869) practically all points were decided against him. Mackonochie ignored the ruling and was suspended for three months in 1870. He faced further prosecution in 1874 (when he was suspended for six weeks) and again in 1882.[33]

He resigned his living at St Alban's in December 1882 and moved to St Peter's, London Dock, as its third vicar in January 1883. But Mackonochie was obliged to resign this post at the end of the year under threats of further litigation. During this period he began the construction of the clergy house at St Peter's, which he never used as Vicar. He worked unofficially for St Alban's for the rest of his life.

Mackonochie died in December 1887 while out walking the Bishop of Argyll's two dogs (Righ and Speireag) on the moors around Ballachulish. During an atrocious blizzard Mackonochie appears to have lost his way, and, because of the appalling weather, his body was not found for two days, guarded still by the faithful dogs. His body was brought first to Kinloch and thence to the Bishop of Argyll's house in Ballachulish. On Tuesday 20 December 1887 his coffin of plain Scots pine was taken by steamer to Oban, and thence by rail to London. His funeral on Friday 23 December commenced at 10 a.m. with the Office for the Dead, followed at 11 a.m. by a requiem mass. The **Revd R.A.J. Suckling**[34] was the celebrant, and Fathers **Stanton** and Russell were respectively deacon and sub-deacon.

> The next part of the ceremony was the procession through the streets to Waterloo Station. . . . Every shop was closed, and blinds were drawn down, and, as the coffin was brought from the Church and placed in the hearse, every head was bared. Slowly, but in perfect order, and with the helpful concurrence of the police and the vast crowd, the procession was formed.
>
> First came the Crucifer . . . he was supported by two men to relieve him from time to time. Next followed members of the Choir, and after them came some fifty Clergy in cassocks and surplices. Then the hearse, preceded by two Acolytes, bearing lighted tapers in lanterns, cresset fashion. The pall-bearers were the Revs. R.A.J. Suckling, A.H. Stanton, F.F. Russell, G.R. Hogg, H.T. Howes, H.G. Maxwell, E.A. Harris, J.W. Doran, E. Ibbotson, and L.S. Wainwright. Relatives and other principal mourners immediately followed the hearse, and after them came the Parochial Guilds and the general Congregation. . . . Since the days when Puritanism first robbed the Church of her spectacular teaching . . . no such priest's funeral had, probably, been seen in the streets of London. . . . Punctually at one o'clock the solemn cortege started on its way . . . the choir beginning the hymn 'Hark! hark! my soul'. At this time Brooke Street is crowded with spectators.[35]

The procession continued along Brooke Street, High Holborn, Kingsway, the Strand and Waterloo Bridge. At Waterloo a special train, with accommodation for six to eight hundred people, awaited for departure to Brookwood. On arrival at the cemetery the procession was re-formed in the same order as before and made its way to the graveside. The brief service was led by the **Revd A.H. Stanton**, and ended with Father Suckling reading a telegram from the Bishop of Argyll. Members of the Church of England Working Men's Society, at their own request, filled in the grave with earth. There is a fine stained-glass window commemorating Mackonochie in St Peter's, London Dock. It depicts his death in the blizzard along with the two faithful dogs.

Dorothy Niblett (1898–1985). Born in Caterham, Surrey, Miss Niblett moved to the parish of St Alban's in 1955. She became a well-loved and indefatigable parish worker. Miss Niblett was based in St Ursula's Hostel which catered for thirty-four Christian children from all parts of the world. The Hostel also provided a Christmas dinner for the poor and lonely of the parish. In 1979 she was awarded the MBE for her community work. Miss Niblett died in a nursing home in Sussex and her ashes were buried here. She is also commemorated by a memorial tablet under the church tower at St Alban's.

Lady Henry Somerset (Isabel[la] Caroline Somers Cocks) (1851–1921). A prominent advocate of temperance and women's welfare. She married Lord Henry Somerset in 1872. Lady Henry was granted custody of her only child, Henry Somers Somerset, in 1878 and was divorced in 1879.[36] After the suicide of a friend while drunk she took up the cause of temperance. Lady Henry inherited the Somers estates in Eastnor, Reigate and London in 1883. She was President of the British Women's Temperance Association (1890–1903) and of the World's Women's Christian Temperance Union (1898–1906). In 1895 Lady Henry founded the Duxhurst Farm Colony for Inebriate Women near Reigate. This was the first institution of its kind in England, where women 'inebriates' were treated as patients and not as social outcasts. Lady Henry lived at the Priory, Reigate, and was in constant touch with the members of the colony. She went on to open a home for training workhouse children and the 'Children's Village' at Duxhurst, a children's home. She founded *The Women's Signal*, the official paper of the British Women's Temperance Association, in 1894. Her other publications include *Our Village Life* (London, Sampson Low, 1884), a volume of verse and colour illustrations, and *In an Old Garden: Miss Marian's Story* (London, Christian Knowledge Society, 1900). She also wrote an account of the colony at Duxhurst called *Beauty for Ashes* (London, Upcott Gill & Son, 1913), which includes a preface by the Revd E.F. Russell.

Revd Arthur Henry Stanton (1839–1913). Educated at Rugby and Trinity College, Oxford, Stanton went on to Cuddesdon Theological College and then became curate of the newly formed parish of St Alban's (1862). Ordained in the same year, he lived in the clergy house adjoining the church where he lived for the rest of his life. Stanton was a noted and eloquent preacher. When it became widely known that a preacher of an unusual type was at work at St Alban's, invitations to preach came from all quarters. Under the **Revd Alexander Mackonochie**, Stanton also adopted ritualistic views and was also subjected to a number of prosecutions, the last one taking place in 1906. Stanton exercised great spiritual influence within and beyond the parish of St Alban's. His public funeral procession through the streets of London from St Alban's to the Westminster Bridge Road was a striking demonstration of the place he won in the hearts of the people. All the roads along the route were lined by dense crowds. At Brookwood about a thousand people assembled at **South station** for the short walk to the St Alban's burial ground. Among those at the graveside was the **Revd R.A.J. Suckling**, who led the brief final service. After Stanton's death his sermons were published along with his own sermon notes.[37]

Leave the St Alban's plot by the lych-gate and turn left, then left again into All Hallows Avenue. The next memorial is a Calvary cross and is to the right of the path.

6.12. Flight Sub-Lieutenant Alfred Basil Helbert (*c.* 1895–1917) [plot 55]

Helbert is unusual in having a memorial headstone in the original part of the **military cemetery** as well as this memorial in the former Anglican section. The reason for this is at present unknown. Helbert was serving at Felixstowe Naval Air Station in Suffolk when he died very suddenly on 29 August 1917 from the effects of an immersion in the North Sea in October 1916.

The next allotment has a prominent crucifix memorial.

6.13. St Mary the Virgin, Wantage [plot 55]

Originally called St Mary's Convent (or Home), this penitentiary sisterhood was founded by William John Butler (1818–94) on 2 February 1850. Butler was Vicar of Wantage (1846–81) and Warden of St Mary's (1850–94). Butler also knew the **Revd Alexander Mackonochie**. This plot was set aside from September 1920 for the exclusive use of the sisterhood. The first burial appears to be that of **Sister Margaret** (*c.* 1851–1917). The prominent crucifix would have been added to the plot only after it was used exclusively by the convent. The figure of Christ crucified appears to be made of cast-iron. From 1948 interest in the plot was vested in the Society of Servants of Mary, based at the St John's Hostel, Camberwell. The last burial in this plot was that of **Sister Mary Joan (Lillie Mary Thomas)** (*c.* 1915–61).

Just beyond this is an area screened by rhododendrons with its own lych-gate.

6.14. St Peter's Home [plot 55]

St Peter's was a convalescent home in Sandy Lane, Maybury, near Woking, which opened in 1885. It was run by the St Peter Sisterhood, an order of Anglican nuns based in Kilburn. The home was designed for sick women requiring skilled treatment and long periods of nursing. The home was enlarged in the 1890s. The community reserved the burial ground for its exclusive use. The standard memorials used in this plot were marble slabs or tablets. In 1935 these cost £1 2s 6d each (plus the inscription), but by 1956 they cost £2 10s 0d (plus inscription). In the mid-1950s the plot was extended 'as agreed' although no further details are known. It cost £150 for clearing the additional ground required.[38] Unfortunately, because of vandalism virtually all the memorials were removed some years ago, but it continued to be used, especially for the reception of cremated remains. The home closed in 1990.

The next section is on the opposite side of All Hallows Avenue from that of **St Mary the Virgin** *(item 13).*

6.15. St Thomas's Hospital ground [plot 46]

The original St Thomas's was founded in about 1106 in Southwark. The site of the 1709 rebuilt hospital was acquired for the Charing Cross Railway in 1859 and used partly for the site of London Bridge station. The new hospital, off Westminster Bridge, was opened in 1871 and included the Nightingale Training School of Nursing. New wings have been added in more recent years to compensate for the extensive damage during the Second World War. This area was reserved for use by St Thomas's Hospital from February 1919.

Among those buried here is **Marian Agnes Gullan** (1873–1958), a Sister Tutor to the Nightingale Training School for Nurses (1914–35).

Dame Alicia Frances Jane Lloyd Still (1869–1944), Matron of St Thomas's Hospital and Superintendent of the Nightingale Training School (1913–37). She was educated at home and trained as a nurse at the Nightingale Training School. She was appointed Sister at

St Thomas's Hospital, Matron at the Brompton Hospital and Matron at the Middlesex Hospital, before moving back to St Thomas's as Matron. Still was also involved in the wider nursing profession, being a member of the Queen Alexandra's Army Nursing Board and Imperial Nursing Service Committee, President of the Association of Hospital Matrons (1919–37), President of the International Council of Nurses (1933–7), President of the Florence Nightingale International Memorial Foundation and Chairman of the Committee of Management (1934–9), Vice-President of the National Florence Nightingale Memorial Committee and a member of its executive committee. She was awarded the International Florence Nightingale Medal in 1933 and was created DBE in 1934.

Barbara Mortimer Thomas (1908–40), from Sydney, Australia. Her memorial records that she was killed, with five others, 'while on duty at St Thomas's Hospital'.

Continue walking along All Hallows Avenue until you reach the path on your left. Continue along here until you see a crumbling gateway in the rhododendrons to your left.

6.16. The Order of Reparation ground [plot 46]

This religious order was founded by **Father Goulden** in 1869 as the 'Community of Reparation to Jesus in the Blessed Sacrament' to undertake missionary work with the poor in Southwark. The community was originally for men and women, and it reserved this plot for its own use in 1872. Drawings for a 'Chapel, churchyard cross and lych-gate' were approved the same year.[39] The special chapel dedicated to the Order was subsequently built within the allotment, but fell into disrepair. Although the chapel and lych-gate were cleaned and renovated in 1932–3, at a cost of £50, it was probably never repaired again. The building was demolished some years ago, probably sometime in the 1960s. The chapel is believed to have stood in the right-hand corner of the allotment, adjacent to the memorials to **Father Goulden** and others. The standard canopied crosses are made of Portland stone and cost £2 17s 6d each (plus inscription) in the 1930s.[40]

Most of the surviving low stone canopied crosses appear to be concerned with the 'Mission Sisters of St Alphege', who appear to have taken on the role of the Order of Reparation after 1911, when the sisterhood was disbanded and a Mother Superior was appointed. The sisters expanded their work into other areas of London and it appears the convent in Southwark was closed by 1981, but the community continues its work from Windsor. The other, more splendid, monuments in this area commemorate some of the Wardens of the Order and Mission.[41]

The entrance gateway to the plot may still be located (the lych-gate has not survived), along with some of the low crosses that mark the grave spaces in this ground. Adjacent to the site of the chapel is a group of three Celtic cross memorials. The central one commemorates **Father Alfred Benjamin Goulden** (died 1896), the founder of the Order of Reparation and of the St Alphege Mission. Directly opposite these graves is a large cross memorial that seems to record the names of all those buried elsewhere in this allotment, presumably in unmarked graves. The first burial appears to be that of **Sister Agnes** (died 1872), while the last was that of **Sister Lucy** in 1954.

Turn left as you leave the Order of Reparation ground. The next two graves are to the left of the path.

6.17. Corfe family [plot 46]

Charles Carteret Corfe (died 1935) was for many years headmaster of Christ's College, New Zealand.

The **Revd Charles John Corfe** (1843–1921) was educated at All Souls College, Oxford, and was ordained in 1866. He was a naval chaplain (1867–89) and served on HMS *Victor Emanuel* during the Ashanti War (1874). In 1889 he was appointed the first English Bishop in Korea, a post he held until 1904.

Situated on the corner of this path and the junction of St George's Avenue is an area marked by a tall crucifix.

6.18. St Joseph's Hospital [plot 46]

Adjacent to the **Order of Reparation** plot, this allotment is identifiable by an unusual large crucifix with a skull and crossbones underneath. St Joseph's Hospital was based in Kensington Square, London, and the original allotment was set aside in August 1875 for the burial of **Sister Elizabeth (Ann Elizabeth Burbridge)** (*c.* 1836–75). The last death recorded on the base of the cross is that of **Mother Frances** (died November 1909).

The next grave is on the opposite side of the path. It is a grey granite cross set on a base with kerbing.

6.19. Marie Louise Carlile (1861–1951) [plot 45]

Sister of Wilson Carlile,[42] founder of the Church Army. The Church Army was founded in 1882 in the slums of Westminster. Marie agreed to become a 'temporary' helper, yet remained with the Army for the next sixty years. In 1883 Wilson established a training centre for men in Oxford and a similar college was opened for women in west London, off the Edgware Road, during 1887. The women were originally called Church Army Nurses, but this was later changed to the Church Army Sisters. By 1937 some 3,000 women were accepted for training, of which 2,000 were commissioned as Sisters. The work originally centred around missionary work in the slums and gradually developed to include bible studies, church history and assisting the local clergy. In 1891 a 'laundry house' was opened where inmates did laundry to help raise money to run the home. The first Medical Mission opened in 1894 with a doctor who gave free advice and dispensed medicines for 1*d* a time. Other work included Mission Vans, which allowed the Sisters to visit country areas and prisons, the Holiday Homes, which provided seaside havens for poor mothers and sick children, and the Sunset Homes for the elderly and infirm. Marie retired to a Sunset Home in Coley Avenue, Woking, in 1947. She died there in 1951.[43] Her brother's ashes are buried in St Paul's Cathedral.

The next memorials may be found towards the centre of the same plot. Look for the group of three headstones; the central one is slightly taller and more distinctive than the others.

6.20. Lawrence family graves [plot 45]

Lieutenant-Colonel George Aubrey Kennedy Lawrence (c. 1892–1917) was a member of a well-known military family and lies in the family plot next to the grave of his father, **Major-General William Alexander Lawrence**. He transferred to the Royal Flying Corps from the Artillery in 1915 and became a reconnaissance and bomber pilot; he made many long-range raids behind the lines for which he was awarded the DSO in November 1915. Lawrence later commanded No. 70 Squadron in France. He returned to England in December 1916 and was appointed Assistant Commandant at the Central Flying School at Upavon. On 28 January 1917 he took off in a Vickers ES1 fighter for a test flight but, being unfamiliar with the aircraft, he stalled and it crashed into the ground.

    Humphrey Richard Locke Lawrence (c. 1888–1915), his brother, is also commemorated on the memorial. He was drowned off Crete on 30 December 1915 when his troopship, the SS *Persia*, was sunk by a U-boat.

    Major-General William Alexander Lawrence (1843–1924) entered the Army in 1861. He served with distinction during the Afghan War (1878–80), and was promoted to Major-General in 1897. He retired in 1902.

Further into the plot, and facing towards St George's Avenue, is a large family grave with a wide low headstone fronted with ledger memorials.

6.21. Sir Alexander Meadows Rendel (1829–1918) [plot 45]

Civil engineer. Rendel was born in Plymouth into an engineering family. His father was James Meadows Rendel,[44] who trained under Thomas Telford and who specialised in constructing docks and tunnels. Rendel was educated at the King's School, Canterbury, and Trinity College, Cambridge. He became an assistant to his father, whose death in 1856 compelled him to take over the practice. Rendel was engineer to the London Dock Company and designed the Royal Albert Dock (1875–80), which was unusual for its early use of electric light. He also designed the Albert Dock (1863–7) and Edinburgh Dock (1874–81) for the Leith Harbour authorities. Rendel was also associated with the design and construction of many railways in the Indian subcontinent. He reorganised the East India Railway Company so that it was the first railway in India to show an operating profit. This attracted the attention of the India Office so that in 1872 he was appointed consulting engineer to the Indian State Railways. Rendel was responsible for designing many bridges in India. These include the Lansdowne Bridge over the River Indus at Sukkur, opened in 1889 and the largest cantilever bridge in the world at that time, with a clear span of 790ft from the tower centres. Another of Rendel's designs was the Hardinge Bridge over the River Ganges, which opened in 1917 and comprised fifteen girder spans of 345ft and three land spans of 75ft at either end. Rendel also operated a successful engineering practice in London, known latterly as Rendel, Palmer & Tritton.[45] His wife, **Eliza Hobson**, who died in 1916, was the eldest daughter of Captain William Hobson, the first Governor of New Zealand.

From here, return to All Hallows Avenue. The next sequence of graves may be found in the plot opposite. The first is in a small plot of twin headstones with kerbing.

6.22. 2nd Lieutenant Colin Corry Bevington (*c.* 1900–1918) [plot 56]

Bevington was a direct entrant to the RAF and had only recently gained his 'wings' when he was killed while flying a Sopwith Camel of No. 72 Training Squadron at Beverley in East Yorkshire. Over 400 pilots were accidentally killed while flying Camels during the First World War. Bevington had been educated at Rugby School and was a native of Pyrford, near Woking. He now lies next to his parents.

Further to the left is a Commonwealth War Graves Commission headstone.

6.23. Pilot Officer Cuthbert King-Clark (died 1940) [plot 56]

King-Clark was commissioned into the RAF on the day that war broke out. He was a navigator on Blenheim night fighters with No. 23 Squadron at Wittering and was killed during an attack on a Heinkel He111. King-Clark was badly wounded and unconscious, so the Blenheim's pilot clipped on his parachute and pushed him out of the escape hatch as the aircraft was going down in a spin. Unfortunately King-Clark was hit by a propeller blade and was killed instantly. The Heinkel eventually crashed near Cambridge. The kerbing of his grave includes the inscription 'So he passed over and all the trumpets sounded for him'.

Further into the plot and behind a plot enclosed by conifers is the next grave.

6.24. Professor Sir Arthur Schuster (1851–1934) [plot 56]

Mathematical physicist. Born at Frankfurt, Schuster was educated at Frankfurt Gymnasium Geneva, Owens College, Manchester, and Heidelberg. He was naturalised in 1875. In the same year he led an expedition organised by the Royal Society to observe the total eclipse of the sun in Siam. He took part in similar expeditions in 1878, 1882 and 1886. Schuster was based at the

Cavendish Laboratory, Cambridge (1876–81), working with James Clerk-Maxwell[46] and John W. Strutt (3rd Baron Rayleigh)[47] on the determination of the ohm in absolute measure. He was appointed Professor of Applied Mathematics at Owens College, Manchester (1881–88), and Professor of Physics (1888–1907). Schuster's particular interests were spectroscopy, electricity in gases, magnetism, optics and the mathematical theory of periodicity. He obtained the first photograph of the spectrum of solar corona in 1882; he was the first to show that an electric current flows through a gas by means of gaseous ions; and he was the first to show that the ratio e/m can be obtained by deflecting cathode rays in a magnetic field. While still in Manchester Schuster was actively involved in the scheme to replace the old Victoria University with three separate universities in Manchester, Liverpool and Leeds; this was achieved in 1903. He also designed the new physical laboratories in Coupland Street that opened in 1900. Schuster held various appointments with the Royal Society after his election in 1879, culminating as Secretary (1912–19) and Vice-President (1919–24). He was President of the British Association (1915) and Secretary to the International Research Council (1919–28). He was knighted in 1920. Schuster was one of the first to use the 'safety bicycle' and to take up motoring. His publications include *An Introduction to the Theory of Optics* (London, E. Arnold, 1904), and *Britain's Heritage of Science* (London, Constable, 1917). His *Biographical Fragments* (London, Macmillan, 1932) records some impressions of times and places, and of the personality of scientific men of a past generation. Schuster's memorial slab, which includes a portrait, is of Roman stone and was specially carved by an unknown craftsman.[48]

Further into the plot is the following headstone with kerbing.

5.25. Sir (Benjamin) Arthur Whitelegge (1852–1933) [plot 56]

Whitelegge studied medicine at University College London, graduating in 1874. He was appointed Medical Officer of Health for Nottingham (1884), and for the West Riding of Yorkshire (1889). In 1894 he became Chief Sanitary Officer of the West Riding Rivers Board, and was invited to become Lecturer on Hygiene & Public Health at the Charing Cross Hospital Medical School. In 1896 he was appointed HM Chief Inspector of Factories & Workshops, a post he retained for twenty-one years until his retirement in 1917. During this time he reorganised the department so as to secure uniformity of administration. For instance, in 1896 there were five separate inspectors for Derbyshire; under Whitelegge's administration definite districts were assigned to each inspector following wherever possible the county boundaries. Districts were grouped into clearly defined divisions, each under a superintending inspector to whom the more junior staff were directly responsible. His reports on various subjects were brilliantly composed and written. Whitelegge also introduced technical inspectors (medical, electrical and engineering) within his reorganised department. He wrote the textbook *Hygiene & Public Health* (London, Cassell, 1890), which eventually went through a total of seventeen editions. He married **Fanny Marian Horsley**, a daughter of the painter John Callcott Horsley RA (1817–1903).

Return to All Hallows Avenue and turn right, continuing to the end of the path. Turn right at the junction, into St Bartholomew's Avenue. The next headstone is on the right of the path.

5.26. Alfred William Hunt (1830–1896) [plot 56]

Landscape painter. Son of the painter Andrew Hunt,[49] Alfred Hunt was educated at the Liverpool Collegiate School and Corpus Christi, Oxford. He was a member of the Liverpool Academy from 1850. Hunt first exhibited at the Royal Academy in 1854 with *Wastdale Head from Styhead Pass, Cumberland*. In 1856 his painting *Llyn Idwal, Carnarvonshire* attracted the notice of

John Ruskin. Further landscapes followed, influenced by the Pre-Raphaelites, but these did not find favour with the Royal Academy. He began to turn to watercolours and in 1864 he was elected a member of the Old Water Colour Society. Until 1870 he worked only in this medium, completing several hundred pieces, as he was a rapid (though careful) worker. Hunt used Turner's system of hatching and scraping out. He painted subjects in the north-east of England (especially Durham), on the Thames, in Scotland, Wales and throughout Europe. Hunt was a Trustee of the Royal Water Colour Society (1879–96) and Deputy President (1888). From 1865 he lived in London, and eventually settled at 1 Tor Villas, Campden Hill, a house previously owned by **James Clarke Hook** and Holman Hunt.

His wife, **Margaret Raine** (1831–1912), was a successful novelist. She was the original of Tennyson's *Margaret*. It was through her literary connections that during the early 1880s Oscar Wilde cultivated the family's friendship. Wilde invited her and her daughter to contribute to *Woman's World*, but neither did so. Her novels include *Under Seal of Confession* (London, Sampson Low, 1874; written under the pseudonym Averil Beaumont), *The Leaden Casket* (London, Chatto & Windus, 1880) and a translation of Grimm's folk tales. With her daughter **Violet Hunt** she co-wrote *The Governess* (London, Chatto & Windus, 1912), which included a preface by Ford Madox Ford.[50]

Their daughter, **(Isobel) Violet Hunt** (1862–1942), was also a novelist, although it was intended that she should be a painter. In the early 1880s Oscar Wilde (who was then a neighbour) considered marrying her. In November 1880 Wilde sent her *Libertatis Sacra Fames*, his first 'political' poem. In the following year he sent her a copy of his collected *Poems*. Violet wrote short pieces for magazines and her first novel, *The Maiden's Progress: a Novel in Dialogue* (London, Eyre & Spottiswood), appeared in 1894. In *The Celebrity at Home* (London, Chapman & Hall, 1904) she described her youthful experiences with the artistic and fashionable milieu, which her parents knew so well, with biting satire. In 1908 she met Ford Madox Ford and they began a passionate relationship, which lasted until they separated after the First World War. They settled at South Lodge, the London house that Violet bought in 1908. This became a centre for new writers and artists, and also a base for her strong support for women's suffrage and the changing role of women in society.[51] Her subsequent novel, *The Flurried Years* (London, Hurst & Blackett, 1926), was her attempt at explaining their relationship; in fact it made the rift more bitter. It also contains interesting accounts of the famous people she met.[52] Her last book, *The Wife of Rossetti her Life and Death* (London, John Lane, 1932), was also controversial, for she alleged that Dante Gabriel Rossetti caused Elizabeth Siddal's death through neglect.

Beyond this grave, and on the same side of the path, is a rough track leading towards the heath. Follow this for a short way to find the next memorial, which is a low irregular stone set within a plot edged with small stone blocks.

6.27. Flight Lieutenant Richard Carew Reynell (*c.* 1912–1940) [plot 56]

Reynell was an Australian who came to England in 1929. Following two years at Oxford he joined the RAF in 1931 and flew Hawker Fury fighters with No. 43 Squadron at Tangmere. In January 1937 he joined the Hawker Aircraft Company as a test pilot, flying Hurricane fighters from Brooklands (at Weybridge) and Langley. Reynell was a first-class aerobatic pilot and remained with Hawkers during the first year of the war test flying and delivering new Hurricanes. On 26 August 1940 he was attached to his old squadron for operational experience. He shot down a Messerschmidt Bf109 at West Hythe, Kent, on 2 September. Five days later his Hurricane was damaged by German fighters during a dogfight over South London. Reynell baled out but his parachute failed to open. He fell near Greyladies while his aircraft crashed at Crown Point, Blackheath.

The next grave is further to the right, and is partly hidden in the heather.

6.28. Flying Officer Kenneth Gordon Seth-Smith (*c.* 1914–1942) [plot 56]

Friend and fellow test pilot with **Richard Reynell**. He joined Hawkers in the mid-1930s but retained his military rank under the Reserve of Air Force Officers scheme. Like Reynell he was heavily involved in the testing of Hurricanes at Langley and Brooklands, but later transferred to the Typhoon fighter that Hawker hoped would supersede the Hurricane. During a test flight in a Typhoon on 11 August 1942 the aircraft's tail broke off over Staines Reservoir and the plane crashed near Thorpe Park. Following this accident Hawkers discovered the cause of the Typhoon's tail problem and modified the aircraft, which went on to be a most successful ground attack fighter.

Return to St Bartholomew's Avenue. The next sequence of graves is on the other side of the path. The first of these is a headstone with kerbing quite near the path.

6.29. Flight Lieutenant Henry Michael Moody (*c.* 1899–1931) [plot 44]

Moody joined the Royal Flying Corps as an air mechanic in 1916 and was later commissioned. He became a pilot and flew Sopwith Camels with No. 45 Squadron in France and Italy, and finished the war credited with eight victories. After the war he remained in the RAF and served at Cranwell, Flowerdown and in India. On 30 March 1931 Moody was posted to the Headquarters of Fighting Area Command at Uxbridge where his duties included piloting senior officers on their tours of inspection. On 23 April he was flying Air Vice-Marshal F.V. Holt[53] in a de Havilland Moth when his aircraft was struck by a Siskin fighter of No. 43 Squadron, which was flying past as part of a formation salute. Both occupants of the Moth died instantly when the aircraft crashed at Selhurst Park, near Goodwood, Sussex.

Nearby is a large family plot surrounded by a cast-iron railing.

6.30. Freshfield family allotment [plot 44]

Douglas William Freshfield (1845–1934) was a mountain explorer and geographer. Educated at Eton and University College, Oxford, he developed a passion for mountain travel from frequent trips to the Alps as a boy. Freshfield made at least twenty first ascents, mainly in the Italian Alps. He also travelled in the Near East, and explored the (then) largely unknown area of the Caucasus in 1868, 1887 and 1889. Some of his discoveries were described in his book *The Exploration of the Caucasus* (London, E. Arnold,1896, with illustrations by Vittorio Sella). In 1899 he explored the unmapped areas of Sikkim and Nepal, which was recorded in his book *Round Kangchenjunga: a Narrative of Mountain Travel and Exploration* (London, E. Arnold, 1903). Freshfield was keenly interested in the advancement of geography and was President of the Royal Geographical Society (1914–17). He was a strong supporter of the Geographical Association. Freshfield was editor of the *Alpine Journal* (1872–80), and President of the Alpine Club (1893–5).

Commemorated on the huge upright stone panel at the rear of the plot is his only son, **Henry Douglas Freshfield** (1877–91), who died on 16 May 1891 after only three days' illness. The huge stone memorial is an astonishing *tour de force*, with its profile portrait of the deceased and the two cherubs leaning on upturned torches underneath. It was designed and carved by Edward Onslow Ford.[54] This memorial has been recommended for listing by Woking Borough Council.

Further along the path is a cross memorial, near the junction with All Hallows Avenue.

6.31. William Court Gully, 1st Viscount Selby (1835–1909) [plot 44]

Speaker of the House of Commons between 1895 and 1905. The son of James Manby Gully,[55] he was educated privately and at Trinity College, Cambridge. Called to the Bar at the Inner Temple in 1860, Gully established a good practice, especially in commercial cases. He was appointed QC in 1877. In 1892 Gully was elected Liberal MP for Carlisle and, in 1895, on the retirement of Mr Speaker Peel,[56] he was elected the new Speaker by eleven votes. His period of office was noted for its dignity, courtesy and impartiality. However, he lost the confidence of the Irish Nationalist Party after he ordered the forcible removal of their members from the House of Commons on 5 March 1901. He resigned as Speaker in March 1905, owing to ill health. He was made 1st Viscount Selby in the same year. He continued to attend debates in the House of Lords, however, and chaired a number of Royal Commissions. He was taken seriously ill while staying near Lake Como, and died at Sutton Place, Seaford. His best portrait is reckoned to be that by Sir George Reid, which hangs in the Speaker's House.

The next memorials are in the adjacent plots.

6.32. Woking ground [plots 42, 43 and 44]

These plots form the Anglican burial areas for the parish of Woking. Most of the burials for the town are concentrated in these plots, although there is a separate area for Nonconformists (see Chapter 7). It is not known where parishioners of Woking were buried before these areas were set aside for the Borough's use from November 1903 (when the official agreement was sealed). Possibly the churchyards at Old Woking and St John's were used, and certainly other areas within Brookwood Cemetery. At one stage the Council tried to purchase land at Maybury for use as a burial ground, but the LNC refused to sell land for this purpose.[57]

Winifred Beatrice Baker (*c.* 1900–12) [plot 43]. Winifred was a pupil at Goldsworth School. She was found strangled in a passageway between 201 and 203 Walton Road, Woking, on 5 December 1912. She had left the Mission Hall in Walton Road after a drill of the Nightingale Scouts with two friends. When they reached the corner of the street a man approached them saying their teacher needed to see one of them. Winnie agreed to go with him. It is believed that her killer was never traced. The memorial was placed here on the first anniversary of her death by public subscription. Her twin sister, **Enid Baker** (*c.* 1900–85), is buried in the same grave.

William Mills (*c.* 1869–1914) [plot 43]. Mills lived in Walton Road, Woking. In 1914 he was an out of work bricklayer's labourer. He drowned himself in the Basingstoke Canal on 6 May 1914. Two days later he was buried in an unmarked '2nd class grave', almost certainly located towards the centre of plot 43.

Joyce Pearce (1915–85) [plot 44]. Teacher and founder of the Ockenden Venture. Born in Woking, Joyce was educated at the Woking County School for Girls and at Lady Margaret Hall, Oxford. She taught history at Mitcham Girl's Grammar School before returning to Woking and founding the Ockenden Venture. In 1951 she brought seventeen young orphans from the wretched refugee camps in Germany for the temporary opportunity of proper schooling and a happy community life. During their stay they visited St George's Chapel, Windsor. Canon Venables[58] was asked by one of the children what was the significance of two ladies holding anchors beside a cracked globe on Lord Linlithgow's shield. In tears he replied that the figures signified Hope: 'If all the world should crack, still Hope remains.' The children gained so much from their visit to this country that over the next decade or more nearly 1,000 children came to Britain to build a new future from the misery of the Second World War. They were housed initially in Joyce's rambling house Ockenden, in White Rose Lane. More houses were acquired and opened in the country to provide a safe haven for those who had been driven from their own homes. Over the years the Ockenden Venture has accommodated refugees from every continent and nearly every conflict. Joyce Pearce died, after several months' illness, on 15 July 1985, shortly before the Venture's thirtieth birthday. Now called Ockenden International, the charity continues to work with refugees and displaced people all over the world. Her plaque rests in a large family grave.[59]

Also buried here is **Henry Dafter Quartermaine** (*c.* 1869–1941), who was Joyce's grandfather. He was a garage owner, plumber, fire brigade officer and entertainments entrepreneur. In 1903 he opened Woking's first cinema, the Central Halls Cinema, at 54 Chertsey Road. He was the only councillor to serve two terms as Chairman (1925–6 and 1930–2).

Also buried here is **Mabel (Mary) Pearce** (1892–1976), the elder daughter of Henry Quartermaine and Joyce's mother. She was a VAD nurse during the First World War and a Commandant in the British Red Cross in the Second World War. Joyce's father, **Albert (Vic) Pearce** (*c.* 1887–1948), is also buried here. He ran a radio shop in Woking above which Joyce was born. A plaque now commemorates her birthplace. Albert played football for Woking and was a well-known local sportsman. He was a Lieutenant in the Woking Home Guard during the Second World War.

In the same grave are the ashes of **Margaret Dixon** (*c.* 1907–2000) who was also involved in the formation and foundation of the Ockenden Venture, along with Joyce Pearce and **Ruth Hicks**. She was a geography teacher at Mitcham Grammar School and worked for Ockenden for much of her life. She ran the hostel at Donington Hall, Leicestershire, between 1959 and 1966, and afterwards The Abbey at Sutton Courtenay, Oxfordshire. Latterly she acted as a Trustee of the Ockenden Venture, and was consulted on all issues regarding the charity.

The graves immediately around the Quartermaines' also have links with Ockenden. One of the graves in front commemorates **Hilda Ruth Hicks** (1900–86), a cousin of Mary Pearce. She was Deputy Head at Woking County School for Girls before becoming Head at Greenfield School, where the Ockenden refugees were educated free. The unusual verse

> In heaven shalt thou receive, at length,
> The guerdon of thine earthly strength
> And dauntless hand

is from Longfellow's poem *Coplas de Manrique*.[60]

To the left of this grave is that of **Czeslaw Chmielinski** (1921–86), who was brought to England as a young man by Sue Ryder from a German labour camp. He lived with **Mary Pearce** and **Ruth Hicks** and ran the Claremont Stores, Ockenden's small grocery shop in Claremont Avenue.

To the left is the **Melka family**, who were invited to England by Joyce to help her with the Polish people already here. They also assisted in organising the paperwork necessary for the young refugees to return to their parents for holidays. The grave commemorates **Sylwia Melka** (1919–71) and **Tadeusz Michal Melka** (1912–79).

Frederick Pullinger (1852–1923) [plot 44]. Woking shopkeeper who moved to Woking in the 1880s, at about the time he married **Fanny Jones Robinson** (*c.* 1858–1931). For many years they ran a pastrycook and family baker's store at 10 Chertsey Road. Some of their children are buried in adjacent graves: **Edith Maud Drewitt** (1885–1939), and **Dorothy Emily Pain** 1889–1975). Shopkeeping was very much a family speciality, for Frederick's brother George inherited a stationery shop in 109 West Street, Farnham, in 1887. This remained in the family until the 1980s and is still known as Pullingers today.[61]

From here, continue to the end of St Bartholomew's Avenue, and turn right along the 'main' St George's Avenue. The next graves are on the right of this road. Set a little way into the plot is a Calvary cross memorial with kerbing that faces the cemetery wall.

6.33. John Charles Morice (died 1898) [plot 42]

Surgeon. Born in Chelsea, he entered the Indian Army in 1856. Morice served during the Indian Mutiny (1857–9) and was present at the siege and relief of Lucknow. He also served in the Harara campaign (1868) and in the Sudan (1885). He retired shortly afterwards owing to failing health.

Facing the avenue is a headstone in pink granite.

6.34. James Ronald Holme (1863–1932) [plot 42]

This interesting memorial includes a clock face without hands, along with the following inscription:

James Ronald Holme
Born 7 March 1863
Went to the Summerland
17 March 1932.

Further to the left is a large upright block of granite with a Celtic cross carved into the top.

6.35. Alexis Theodorovich Aladin (1873–1927) [plot 42]

Russian politician. Aladin came to England as an exile in 1901–2 and left for Russia in 1905 to contest the elections for the First Duma, becoming prominent in Russian politics when he was elected a member in 1906. He formed and led the Peasants' Party. Aladin was one of the most brilliant and respected members of the Duma. He was sent to England as a delegate from the Duma to a peace conference in London. While he was in this country the Duma was dissolved. The most prominent left-wing members fled to Viborg and issued the Viborg Manifesto against the Tsar. They were banished, Aladin included, even though he had been no party to the document, which he considered ill-advised. He remained in this country until 1917, when he returned to Russia at some risk to himself. Aladin hoped to have some influence in saving his country; instead he was captured and imprisoned by the Bolsheviks. He managed to escape, and joined Generals Denikin[62] and Wrangel[63] in the Crimea (1917–20) during the ensuing civil war. Aladin subsequently returned to this country. He hated the worship of materialism that formed part of the Bolshevik creed, believing it would destroy all that was best in Russian life. Aladin believed the future of Russia lay with the peasants, and had an undying faith in the recovery of his country and in the cooperation between Russia and Britain for which he worked so hard.

Further to the left is an attractive lych-gate.

6.36. St Stephen's, South Kensington [plot 41]

This burial ground was opened in about 1910. Like the **St Alban's**, **Holborn** plot, a lych-gate forms the entrance to the allotment. Once again this was erected as a memorial to a parishioner. The wording inside the lych-gate reads 'Erected to the glory of God in affectionate memory of **John Edward Hubbard** by intimate friends 1917.' The central memorial cross, with part of the requiem mass carved in Latin, is used as an altar when members of the parish visit in the summer.

To the right of the central memorial is the Allen family grave.

Sir Walter Macarthur Allen (1870–1943). Commander-in-Chief of the Metropolitan Special Constabulary (1925–43). He was educated at Trinity Hall, Cambridge, and was called to the Bar at the Inner Temple in 1896. Allen subsequently joined the Metropolitan Police and became Assistant Staff Officer of the Metropolitan Special Constabulary (1914). He was Director of Supplies (1915–17) and Staff Officer (1918–24).

His son, **Geoffrey Thornton Macarthur Allen** (*c.* 1898–1940), was killed at Dunkirk on 30 May 1940.

Sir George (Gubby) Oswald Browning Allen (1902–89), his second son, represented England in twenty-five Test Matches. He was educated at Eton and Trinity College, Cambridge. He was a member of the London Stock Exchange (1933–72). Allen was in the Eton XI (1919–21) and was a Cambridge Blue (1922–3). He was Captain of England in the Test Matches against India (1936), Australia (1936–7) and the West Indies (1948). Allen was Chairman of the England Selection Committee (1955–61), Chairman of the MCC Cricket Subcommittee (1956–63), President of the MCC (1963–4) and Treasurer of the MCC (1964–76). He was a member of the Cricket Council (1968–82) and was Hon. Vice-President of the National Cricket Association (1985). Allen was knighted in 1986. The Q stand at Lords is named after him.

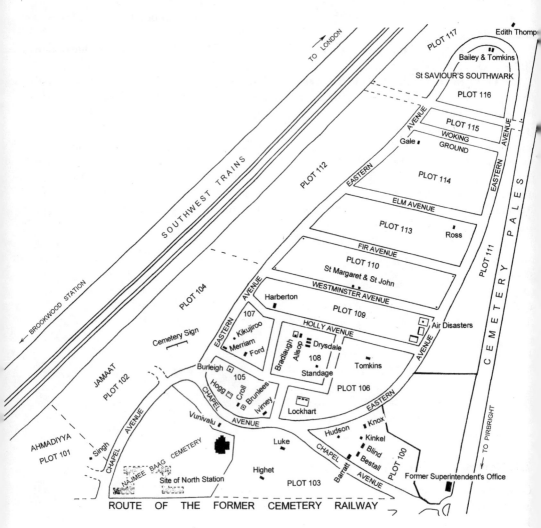

The eastern part of the former Nonconformist section.

Chapter Seven

THE EASTERN PART OF THE FORMER NONCONFORMIST SECTION

The remaining chapters cover those sections of the cemetery on the other side of **Cemetery Pales**. These are the former Nonconformist or unconsecrated parts of the cemetery, reserved for all those who did not desire or qualify to have the rites of the Church of England read at the burial service. Therefore the graves in this section of the cemetery cover all other religions, those of no particular religion and also atheists. This part of the cemetery is rather smaller than the Anglican equivalent. It comprises about 180 acres (including the **military cemeteries**), or just under a third of the total area of Brookwood Cemetery.

This area of the cemetery is similar to its equivalent in the former Anglican section (see Chapter 1) in that it covers a roughly triangular area to the east of the former cemetery railway. The principal route across this section is Eastern Avenue, which describes a loop through this part of the grounds. All the graves described here are to one side or another of this road. However, unlike its Anglican equivalent there is no splendid avenue of redwoods, although there is one particularly fine specimen near to the **cemetery sign**. Another change is in the avenue names. We move from saints to mere descriptive titles: Chapel Avenue, Holly Avenue (albeit no holly!), Westminster Avenue and so on. Another feature of this section is that it is flanked on one side by the main railway line, which provides a constant reminder of the cemetery's former links with London.

7.1. Cemetery Pales

Cemetery Pales is the name of the road that runs from the West Hill Golf Club (on the A322) and Pirbright village. This right of way already existed when the LNC laid out its cemetery in 1854, but the road was not named at that time. It is not known when the name Cemetery Pales was first used, since the road was otherwise called the Pirbright Road or Aldershot Road. The term 'pales' doubtless refers back to the original wooden fencing or paling that was required by the LNC's Act of Parliament of 1852 to enclose the cemetery grounds. The paling was constructed on top of an earth mound, the two elements producing a barrier nearly 8ft high.[1] The earth mound was partly used as foundations for the new walls at the turn of the century. It is possible to see some remnants of the old mounds, minus the wooden fence, on the western boundaries of the cemetery. Examples may be seen in the boundary area well beyond the **Glades of Remembrance**, or its equivalent in the Nonconformist **pauper sections**. The existing brick and pebble-dashed cemetery walls were erected about 1902–3. The cost of this was largely met from the compensation paid to the LNC by the LSWR for the inconvenience caused by moving to new station premises in London.

7.2. Former Superintendent's offices off Cemetery Pales [adjacent to plot 100]

This site by the cemetery entrance has changed much over the years, serving variously as the Parsonage House, the Superintendent's office, and considerably altered and enlarged in modern times. The development of this area will be described in chronological order of its main uses.

The Parsonage House. The core of the original structure is the building closest to the cemetery entrance with the chimney-stacks. It was designed by Sydney Smirke, architect to the LNC, in 1854–5.[2] The cost of building the 'Stables, Parsonage House & Cottages' was £2,970, with the contract awarded to Messrs Nicholsons. The stables were to be completed by 1 December 1854 with the house and cottages by the end of January 1855.[3] It was originally occupied by, or put at the disposal of, the company's chaplains, the Revd Henry Atcheson (Church of England) and the **Revd Robert Le Maire** (Nonconformist). But it was not popular with the chaplains. In 1857 the directors referred to the 'neglected state' of the house and garden and reminded Atcheson that he 'should be in constant residence in accordance with his intentions at his appointment'. Atcheson resigned in 1861 and was succeeded by the Revd F. Owsten, who lived in the house.[4] As far as is known he continued living there until the early 1880s. He must have moved out by the summer of 1885 since the house was then offered for use by the LNC's secretary, **Julian Larkman**, at a rent of £25 per year.[5]

The Superintendent's office. It is likely that at most Larkman only occupied the Parsonage House for a short time, since on the appointment of **George Barratt** as Superintendent he was offered use of the house.[6] Thereafter, with its strategic location within the cemetery grounds, this became the centre of operation for all work within the cemetery, including digging and maintaining graves, maintaining buildings and structures throughout the grounds, planting and so on. In 1887 Mr Barratt supervised some twenty-eight staff, comprising:

> The Superintendent
> Three Clergymen
> Three Gravediggers
> Nineteen Gardeners, Labourers and Assistants, who help in conducting the funerals and are otherwise engaged in planting and keeping private graves in order, fixing stones, repairs to buildings, &c., &c.
> Two females at Refreshment Rooms.[7]

A fine Frith's postcard of the office in 1898 shows the gateway to the Nonconformist section and a number of signs variously declaring:

> The Gates are locked at 5p.m. in Winter, 8p.m. in Summer, or at Dusk
> Dogs and Perambulators are NOT ADMITTED
> VISITORS are requested to keep on the PATHS and not to touch the FLOWERS

Various buildings were added to this area over the years. In addition to the stables and cottage adjacent to the office, further outbuildings such as workshops, stores and garage accommodation were constructed at various times, along with heated and unheated greenhouses and frames (see below). When Mr Barratt died in 1927 he was succeeded by Mr Harry Greaves who also lived in the office, probably until the 1950s. After the Second World War the premises became the headquarters of the LNC from 29 July 1946, until the cemetery office moved from here to the **Glades of Remembrance** in 1976.

The Original Masonry Works. The original **Masonry Works** was also located in this general area adjacent to the Superintendent's offices. After the opening of the cemetery, the LNC

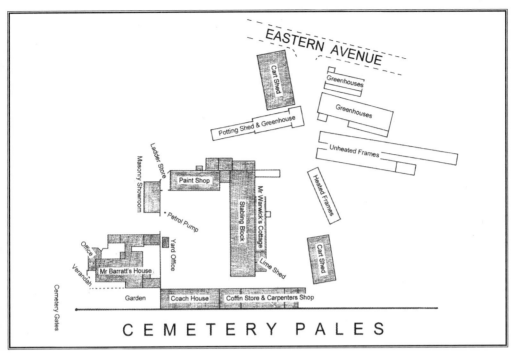

The Superintendent's office area, 1926.

allowed independent masons to occupy land for statuary and masonry work, the first mason being Mr W. Boulton of Guildford. He was given permission to occupy sufficient land (presumably near here) for the exclusive purpose of his trade. Any buildings and workshops were to be erected at his expense and subject to the approval of the LNC.[8] This type of arrangement probably continued until about 1888 when the LNC decided to operate its own premises within the cemetery. Located beside the Superintendent's offices and opened in 1889, a full range of work was undertaken. The showroom appears to have comprised a greenhouse where various memorial designs could be inspected.[9] In the early twentieth century it was decided that these premises were too cramped, and therefore a new site was selected just inside the entrance to the Anglican section.

The Greenhouses. The first greenhouse in this area was ordered at the end of 1855 and cost £91 7s 4d. It is not clear where this stood in relation to the Parsonage House. Later, the original **Masonry Works** was established near to the cemetery wall, and the earliest showroom for monumental masonry was a small greenhouse. It was completed in May 1891. Further greenhouses were ordered in 1905 and 1909.[10]

Modern Times. The major changes to this site are a direct consequence of the 1975 Brookwood Cemetery Act.[11] The Superintendent's office remained here until the site (including the various outbuildings and surviving greenhouses) was sold off. Consequently this area is not, strictly speaking, part of the cemetery grounds. After this sale the outbuildings were demolished and a new single-storey wing was added at right angles to Cemetery Pales, with a small private car park between the two wings. A larger car park was provided on the cleared land beyond, where the outbuildings used to stand. From the late 1970s to 1994 the offices were occupied by Wootton Jeffreys, transport consultants. Latterly the premises were shared with Sherwood Software. Both firms had left by the end of 1994. In November 1998 the site was developed further, with the larger car park occupied by a more extensive (and intrusive) office development. A new entrance into Cemetery Pales was constructed, involving the destruction of a substantial part of the old cemetery wall, along with a new car park. Mature trees were wantonly destroyed and those remaining on the boundary of this development are clearly dying as a direct consequence of this building work.[12] Fortunately the original buildings adjacent to **Cemetery Pales** remain, although its decorative tiled roof was replaced with modern tiles, and a brick wall was built around most of the site in keeping with the design of the rest of this development. The former Superintendent's office is now privately owned and occupied.

Take the right-hand fork into Chapel Avenue. The first grave in this section is a grey granite Celtic cross on the right, just set back from the path.

7.3. Alfred Edmeades Bestall (1892–1985) [plot 100]

For thirty years the illustrator of Rupert Bear. Born in Mandalay, the son of a Methodist missionary, Bestall attended school in Colwyn Bay and won a scholarship to the Birmingham College of Arts and Crafts. Later he studied at the Central School of Arts and Crafts in London. During the First World War he joined the Army Service Corps and served as a driver in Flanders. From this time he began to submit drawings to periodicals such as *Punch* and *The Tatler*. He also drew illustrations for books by Enid Blyton and A.A. Milne. In 1935 Bestall was invited to take over the Rupert Bear strip when its originator, Mary Tourtel, had to retire owing to failing eyesight. He not only had to draw the cartoons but to think up the stories as well. In total Bestall developed and wrote over 270 Rupert adventures, and remained the regular artist and author until his official retirement in 1965. He started the Rupert annuals in 1936, introduced the familiar rhyming couplets, devised new friends for Rupert and developed more science-fiction-type storylines. Bestall ensured that Rupert always behaved correctly, and was never involved in wartime situations. During the Second World War Bestall served as an air raid warden, and the cartoon only failed to appear on just two dates in 1940. In 1948 Mary Tourtel died, and Bestall was able to sign the stories himself. He retired in 1963 but continued to contribute material for the annuals up to 1983. Sir Hugh Casson[13] once described Rupert as 'a quiet corner of British genius', and this tribute appears on the grave. This memorial has been recommended for listing by Woking Borough Council.

Also buried here is his father, **Albert Henry Arthur Bestall** (1863–1936), for thirty years a missionary in Burma. His mother, **Rebecca Bestall** (1864–1964), was just over 100 years old when she died. The rustic grey Cornish granite memorial cross and kerbing cost £34, plus £3 15s 0d for carving 'IHS' in relief on the cross, and £7 7s 0d for ninety-eight lead letters.

The next two memorials are just behind the Bestall family grave. The first is a headstone with kerbing.

7.4. Blind family grave [plot 100]

Karl Blind (1826–1907) was a political refugee and author. He was actively involved in political agitation. Born in Mannheim, Blind was educated at the Lyceum, Mannheim, and at Karlsruhe. In 1846 he was arrested for treason for writing an article, and although he was acquitted on trial he was dismissed from Heidelberg University. Blind continued his studies at Bonn. He was imprisoned for distributing a treasonable pamphlet at Durkheim. In March 1848 he took part in the democratic rising at Karlsruhe, and was present at meetings of the Frankfurt *Vorparlament*. Blind also joined the republican rising near Lake Constance in April 1848. Banished by the Baden government, he fled to Alsace. For his part in the June rising in Paris, he was imprisoned at Strasbourg and taken to the Swiss frontier. Blind took part in the rising at Staufen in September 1848 and was imprisoned at Wehr. Released by revolutionaries in May 1849, he helped establish the Baden provisional government in June 1849. Sent on a political mission to Paris, he was exiled permanently from France in 1849 and was conducted to the Belgian frontier. He was exiled from Belgium in 1852, and decided to settle in unrevolutionary Hampstead. Blind devoted the rest of his life to the championing of nationalist and democratic causes in all countries. His house became a meeting place for political refugees from Europe including Mazzini, Ledru-Rollin, Louis Blanc, Karl Marx and the **Kinkels**.[15] He tried to promote the independence of Schleswig-Holstein, Poland, Greece, the Boers (from 1878) and of Egypt (after 1882). Apart from his political writings, he wrote on history and on German and Indian mythology. He was cremated at Golders Green, and his ashes buried with those of his wife. The epitaph in German may be translated as 'Liberty, democracy and nationalism were the guiding lights of his life'.

Friederike Blind (1819–97) was the widow of a merchant banker named Cohen. She married Karl Blind in 1849. Friederike joined her husband into exile in Belgium (1852) and moved with him to England. She supported his work in promoting nationalism and in entertaining political refugees from the continent. They had one son (Rudolph) who became an artist, and a daughter, Ottilie. From her previous marriage Friederike had one daughter called Mathilde (1847–96) who was a poet and a champion of women's rights.

Behind this, in the trees, is a large pedestal memorial with a portrait.

7.5. Johanna Kinkel, née Mockel (1810–1858) [plot 100]

German pianist, choral composer, poet, writer and composer. Kinkel married the poet (Johann) Gottfried Kinkel (1815–82) in 1843. The composer Felix Mendelssohn[16] encouraged her to pursue a musical career and she became a pupil of Karl Boehmer and William Taubert. From 1840 she was involved with chamber and vocal ensembles and salon performances. During the 1848 revolutionary uprisings her husband was arrested and condemned to death. He managed to escape from Spandau prison and the family fled to London. Kinkel became a choir director, and continued to write music, librettos, poetry and essays. She committed suicide on 15 November 1858. The pedestal-style memorial has a bas-relief profile head, apparently by Philippe Grass, carved on the front of the base.[17] There used to be a carved harp and wreath on top of the memorial, but these became unsafe and have been removed. Kinkel's essays about music, especially on Chopin, are still valued today. Her husband, who was examiner in German at the University of London (1851–66), subsequently remarried and moved to Zurich where he died in 1882. The grave also contains one of Johanna's children, **Johanna** (1845–63), and one infant from (presumably) her husband's second marriage, **Marie** (18 January to 12 February 1861).[18]

Return to Chapel Avenue. The next headstone memorial with kerbing fronts the road and is next to a holly tree.

7.6. George Barratt (*c.* 1852–1927) [plot 100]

Cemetery Superintendent between 1886 and 1927. Barratt joined the LNC in 1864, and worked for the company for the rest of his life – a period of over sixty years. He succeeded **Stephen Standage** as Superintendent in October 1886, at a salary of 27s a week. Barratt was probably the first Superintendent to live in the **Superintendent's office**. Much respected, in the early years of this century he was in charge of about 100 men divided into various departments: the garages and chauffeurs under Mr Taylor, coffin making under Mr Fry, the greenhouses under **Mr Edmund Boylett** and masonry under Mr Clack. In March 1914 he was presented with a gold watch and chain to commemorate fifty years' continuous service to the LNC. At the same time his salary was increased to £4 a week. Ten years later, in March 1924, he was presented with a cheque for £60 and a silver salver to mark his sixty years' service with the LNC. Barratt died in December 1927 and the Board of Directors recorded his death in January 1928:

Mr Barratt's death on 28 December was reported and the Directors recorded their deep regret at the loss of such an old and valued servant who entered the Company's service 63 years ago and was for 41 years Superintendent at the Cemetery.[19]

Like so many of the LNC's employees, he chose to be buried in the cemetery he had served for so long. He was buried free of charge by the LNC as a further mark of respect.

The next memorial is set further back into the plot and comprises a broken column on a pedestal.

7.7. W.T. Vashti Hudson (*c.* 1841–1859) [plot 100]

This memorial records that Mr Hudson's 'sudden death was caused by falling down the hold of a ship lying in the London Docks, March 14 1859', and the following verse:

> Great God on what a slender thread
> Hang everlasting things
> In the midst of life
> We are in death.

Cross Chapel Avenue and find the rough path opposite the junction with Eastern Avenue. The next headstone is made of black marble with gilt lettering.

7.8. Luke family grave [plot 103]

Among those commemorated here are **William Joseph Luke** (1862–1934), shipyard director. Luke worked for John Brown & Company Ltd of Clydebank, the firm that constructed the *Lusitania* among many other ships.

    Charles Sneed Williams (1883–1964). American artist. Born at Evansville, Indiana, Williams studied at the Allan-Fraser Art College, Arbroath (1902–5). He married **Elsie Luke** (1886–1976) in 1912. Williams specialised in portraits and landscapes. His paintings were shown at major exhibitions in Europe and America. He held one-man exhibitions in London, Paris, New York and Chicago. During the First World War he served with the American forces, and was an air raid warden in London (1939–41). Williams organised the Anglo-American Brains Trust via the British Army & Navy Education Department (1942–5). Six large murals by Williams may be seen in St Andrew's Episcopal Church at Louisville, Kentucky.

Further along this path is the next memorial.

7.9. Sir Robert Swan Highet (1859–1934) [plot 103]

Railway civil engineer. Highet was chief engineer to the East Indian Railway (1903–12), General Manager (1912–19) and President of the Indian Railway Conference Association (1918). He was subsequently made Chairman of the East Indian Railway Company. Highet was knighted in 1916.

Return to Chapel Avenue and cross into plot 106. The next grave is in a group of three Celtic crosses, adjacent to a yew tree.

7.10. William Ewart Lockhart (1846–1900) [plot 106]

Scottish painter. The illegitimate son of Ann Lockhart and a farm labourer Thomas Ewart, he was educated at Annan Parish School and in Glasgow. In 1860 Lockhart secured a place at the Trustees Academy in Edinburgh. In 1861 he had two paintings accepted by the Royal Scottish

Academy Annual Exhibition – a remarkable achievement for a boy of 15. Owing to his somewhat delicate health he tended to spend each winter abroad, usually in Spain, Majorca or Italy. Some of his greatest paintings were inspired by Spain, by the people and cities he visited, or by literature and legends such as those of El Cid and Don Quixote. His hard work as an artist and the increasing popularity of his paintings ensured the prosperity of his family. His painting *The Cid*, exhibited in 1882 and the painting that really made his name, earned him £2,000 when it was purchased. This was the largest sum he was ever paid for a picture. Lockhart painted with great skill in both oils and watercolours. He was also commissioned to paint illustrations that were published as engravings in special editions of the works of writers such as Sir Walter Scott, Robert Burns and Robert Louis Stevenson. While in Edinburgh he concentrated on landscapes, genre and portraits. He helped found the Scottish Society of Painters in Watercolours (1878) and was made a full member of the Royal Scottish Academy in the same year. In 1884 he decided to move to London. He was a driving force behind the 1886 Edinburgh International Festival and had the honour of conducting Queen Victoria around the exhibition. From this, Lockhart received the commission to paint *The Jubilee Celebration in Westminster Abbey* (1887). This was the greatest triumph of his career and was a monumental work, measuring 8ft × 10ft and containing some 278 portraits (including that of the artist and his wife!). This painting still hangs in Buckingham Palace. It remains one of the last royal commissions to record a great state occasion and is probably the finest. The painting marked a watershed in Lockhart's life, and he became a popular choice for portraiture. But his output declined and it was felt that his health never really recovered from the strain of this particular commission. He received the Jubilee Medal from Queen Victoria for his services but no knighthood, which bitterly disappointed him. Although Lockhart and his family benefited from the commission he never really recovered from this disappointment and his health deteriorated. He died in the Bethlehem Hospital, London, in February 1900. The fine memorial cross, with its lock and heart symbol at the base, was erected as a mark of esteem by his friends in the same year.[20]

His second daughter, **Adelaide Mary Lockhart** (1872–1935), had a brief career as a flower painter, and assisted her father with the preparatory work for the Jubilee painting. She married Ferdinand Goudsmit in 1896, and she wrote a book, *Et Nos in Arctis* (1913), based on their voyage to Spitzbergen.

William Douglas Lockhart (1884–1954), Lockhart's only son, studied civil engineering. He became a Major in the Royal Engineers during the First World War, and was awarded the OBE in 1951 for his work as senior inspector in the Ministry of Town and Country Planning.

Join Eastern Avenue, and look for the flat stone set back from the path, next to a grave with a cast-iron chain.

7.11. Dr Robert Knox (1791–1862) [plot 100]

Anatomist, and one of Burke and Hare's best customers. Knox began his medical studies at Edinburgh University in 1810, graduating in 1815. He became Assistant Surgeon in the Army (1815–20), where he gained surgical experience after Waterloo and also in South Africa (1817–20). He furthered his medical studies in Paris and was then appointed a private anatomy lecturer in Edinburgh (1825). Knox was a brilliant lecturer, and his student intake of over 500 in 1828–9 broke all previous records. He was an enthusiast of practical dissection and so it was vital to have an adequate supply of 'subjects' or human bodies for dissection. The supply of these was inadequate, and Knox was not alone in requiring more 'subjects'. The 'resurrectionists' or body snatchers assisted this supply. Near the end of 1827 Knox was provided with a new source. Two Irish immigrants, William Burke and William Hare, needed to dispose of the body of a pensioner who had died in Hare's lodging house owing money. By chance they were directed to Dr Knox's house, and were offered £7 10s 0d for the body. Together they eased another sixteen people into the afterlife, but became careless when they murdered the well-known 'Daft Jamie' and the prostitute Mary Paterson. So when a body was discovered in Knox's rooms, both Burke and Hare were arrested. They were tried at Christmas 1828. Hare turned King's Evidence and Burke was subsequently hanged. Knox was popularly considered just as guilty because he never questioned how the corpses were acquired. He was burnt in effigy portrayed as King Richard III. Although a medical committee of investigation cleared Knox of any complicity in the murders, the number of students he attracted fell steadily because of his association with Burke and Hare. By 1842 he could get no students at all and in 1844 he left Edinburgh. He tried to get various posts in Glasgow and elsewhere, but discovered that lecturing and writing on ethnology (the science of race) were sound means of maintaining his family. His researches, however, have led him to be described as the 'founder of British racism'. In 1856 Knox was appointed pathological anatomist to the Royal Marsden Cancer Hospital at Brompton. He was buried at Brookwood for he had been attracted to the heather and wild flowers there as they reminded him of his native Scotland. His original grave comprised just the flat ledger stone. The Royal College of Surgeons of Edinburgh placed the small granite memorial stone here in May 1966. This memorial has been recommended for statutory listing by Woking Borough Council.

Cross into plot 106 and locate the next headstone.

7.12. Charles Tomkins (*c.* 1843–1899) [plot 106]

Railwayman. Tomkins was latterly stationmaster at Brookwood and would have supervised the operation of the funeral trains into and out of the cemetery grounds, along with those serving Bisley Camp (from 1890). He lived in the stationmaster's house that still stands opposite the Brookwood Hotel on the other side of the main railway line to the cemetery.

At the junction of Holly and Eastern avenues may be found three large plots commemorating three separate air crashes.

7.13. Air disasters [plot 109][21]

Brookwood was – and remains – large enough to accommodate mass graves. These are usually plots containing human remains removed from old London churchyards (for which see Chapter 1), but this section includes three large plots containing the dead from three separate air disasters. They are described in order, from left to right.

Barcelona (1959). This accident took place on 19 August 1959 when a thirty-four seat Dakota, chartered from Transair by the National Union of Students, crashed into the Montseny mountains, north of Barcelona. The aircraft had just taken off from Barcelona airport on its return flight to Britain. There were no survivors among the twenty-nine passengers and three crew. All the passengers were students returning from holidays in Spain. Local villagers raised the alarm, but when detachments of the Civil Guard located the wreckage the remains of the aeroplane were almost totally burned out. The dead were carried from the crash site for three miles down steep and winding paths to the village of Santa Fe and thence to Barcelona. Twenty-seven of the thirty-two dead were subsequently buried here during a special funeral service that took place on Friday 28 August 1959.

The investigation into the accident by the Spanish authorities could offer no explanation for the aircraft captain's actions in flying under Visual Flight Rules into cloud at a height insufficient to clear local terrain. The Spanish accident report was highly controversial, and on 16 May 1960 questions were asked in the House of Commons on behalf of relatives of the deceased, during which the report was described as 'extremely brief' and 'shockingly inadequate'.[22]

Perpignan (1967). The second disaster took place on 3 June 1967 when a DC-4 airliner belonging to Air Ferry crashed into Mount Canigou, south-west of Perpignan. The aircraft was on the first leg of a fifteen-day package holiday organised by Lyons Tours Ltd. It remains a mystery why the plane was so far off course when it crashed as the pilot had contacted the control tower just minutes before the crash and had not reported anything amiss. All eighty-eight people on board were killed instantly; of these, twenty-two were subsequently buried here. This accident made front-page news because it coincided with news of another: on the morning of 4 June an Argonaut airliner crashed at Stockport, killing seventy-two out of the eighty-four people on board. *The Times* referred to a 'black weekend' for British aviation. So shocking was the news of this double disaster that the Pope sent a message to the Queen and Government expressing his profound sympathy to the bereaved.

Post-mortem examinations on the pilot and co-pilot found high levels of carbon monoxide and, although not proven conclusively, it is thought that fumes escaping from a faulty cockpit heater had gradually intoxicated the crew, thereby reducing their level of awareness and concentration. At the last moment the crew may have realised their dilemma as the aircraft banked steeply to avoid high ground ahead, but its wing struck the crest of a ridge and broke away. The bodies of the British victims were flown back to Gatwick in two transport planes on 8 June.[23]

Fernhurst (1967). The third accident took place on the night of 4 November 1967 when an Iberian Airlines Caravelle jet crashed into the Blackdown Hills near Fernhurst, Sussex. The plane was less than eighteen months old and was *en route* to Heathrow from Malaga. All thirty-seven passengers and crew were killed, among whom were twenty-five Britons, including the actress June Thorburn, and the Vice-President of Coventry City Football Club, **John Clarkson**. Sixteen British and (somewhat strangely) two Spanish passengers, along with one of the Spanish stewardesses (**Miss Araceli Casanova**), were subsequently buried here.

The accident remains a mystery since there was no explosion or sudden descent prior to the crash. Despite a lengthy investigation no definite cause could be given for the crew's continued descent through their assigned altitude. One theory is that they may have misread the altimeter, which was of a type using a combination of pointers and shaded windows that was not easy to interpret at a glance. As the Caravelle was flying in the dark and mostly above a low-lying bank of cloud, the crew would have had no visual clues that they were too low until the last moment.

The funeral service took place on Thursday 16 November. The plot measures 30ft × 20ft and extra labour was required to prepare the site and to help refill the area afterwards. Additional attendants were needed to receive and lower the coffins. Owing to the numbers of mourners attending the service, a marquee was provided along with a public address system.[24]

Continue walking along Eastern Avenue and locate Elm Avenue. The next memorial is a prominent upright stone in grey granite with a profile portrait on it.

7.14. William Stewart Ross ('Saladin') (1844–1906) [plot 113]

Prominent agnostic, radical journalist, writer, poet and publisher. Born at Kirkbean, Ross was educated at Glasgow University. Although it was intended he should join the Church, Ross moved to London to concentrate on literature and journalism. His early writings were verse and fiction. He moved into educational works and was successful enough to establish his own publishing business, William Stewart & Company, in 1872. Ross also became interested in secularism, and was associated with the *National Reformer*, published by **Charles Bradlaugh** and Mrs Besant.[25] However, Ross broke all links with them after Bradlaugh's publication of Dr Knowlton's pamphlet promoting birth control in 1876. Ross then supported the secularist themes put forward by George Holyoake[26] and Charles Watts, and used these as a basis for criticising Bradlaugh and Besant. From 1882 Ross co-edited the *Secular Review* with Watts, and became sole editor when Watts emigrated in 1884. In 1889 the paper was renamed the *Agnostic Journal*. Ross used the pen name 'Saladin' for his articles in this periodical. But secularism was only part of Ross's life. His educational books include a *Practical Text-book of Grammatical Analysis* (1870) and a *History of Scotland* (1872). He was a poet of the 'romantic' school begun by Sir Walter Scott. Ross's major poetical works include *The Harp of the Valley* (1868), *Lays of Romance and Chivalry* (1882) and *Isuare and Other Poems* (1894). Ross is buried a respectable distance from his old adversary Charles Bradlaugh. His large memorial includes a profile portrait, his pen name Saladin and the epitaph 'A champion of mental freedom; a foe to superstition and mendacity'.

Move on to plots 114 and 115.

7.15. Woking ground [plots 114 and 115]

These plots form the Nonconformist burial areas for the parish of Woking. Most of the burials are concentrated at this side of the ground. There is a separate area for Anglican burials (see Chapter 6). It is not known where parishioners of Woking were buried before these areas were set aside for the Borough's use from November 1903 (when the official agreement was sealed). Possibly the churchyards at Old Woking and St John's were used, and certainly other areas within Brookwood Cemetery.

On the far side of this plot is a headstone commemorating **Edith Mary Gale** (*c.* 1870–82), daughter of Alfred Augustus and Clara Esther Gale of Woking. Edith was accidentally killed while 'crossing the railway near Woking' on 19 January 1882. She was just 12 years old.

The boundary of the St Saviour's burial ground is marked by a partial line of monkey puzzle trees.

7.16. St Saviour's, Southwark [plots 116 and 117]

St Saviour's was the first metropolitan parish to use Brookwood as a burial ground. Two areas were set aside for the use of the parish: plots 116–17 (2 acres here in the Nonconformist section), and plots 88–90 (3 acres in the Anglican section, see Chapter 1, which provides further background notes on the parish). Gateways in the cemetery wall allowed pedestrian access between both plots. The boundaries of the plots are still marked by pairs of cast-iron bollards and by the line of monkey puzzle trees which was probably planted at the request of the burial board. The parish used these plots from November 1854 to *c.* 1920 and it is estimated that upwards of 20,000 people were buried in these areas. Most of the ground is planted. The majority of those interred here were paupers, buried in unmarked graves, but a number of memorials survive.

The first burial at Brookwood was hereabouts (plot 116 or 117), on 13 November 1854. The stillborn twin boys of **Mr and Mrs Hore** of the parish were the very first to be buried at Brookwood, although the exact spot is unmarked.

Thomas Bailey (*c.* 1796–82) [plot 116]. Bailey was one of the original members of the St Saviour's burial board. His memorial also records the names of his children, virtually all of whom died young: **Sarah** (*c.* 1820–40), **Elizabeth** (1823–24), **Ann** (born and died 1825), **George** (1829–32), **Emma** (*c.* 1833–57), and **Mrs Eliza Cue** (*c.* 1826–70).

Benjamin A. Tomkins (*c.* 1800–1871) [plot 116]. This grave also faces Eastern Avenue and is near to Bailey's. Tomkins was another member of the St Saviour's burial board.

The next grave is a ledger stone in grey granite, set well back from the avenue.

7.17. Mrs Edith Jessie Thompson (1893–1923) and others [plot 117]

This memorial records the names of four women who were executed at Holloway Prison in London. It covers virtually the entire history of judicial executions at Holloway as a women's prison. The bodies were removed from Holloway on the night of 31 March–1 April 1971 because of the complete rebuilding of the prison.

Mrs Thompson was executed because her lover, Frederick Bywaters (1902–23), murdered her husband. At the subsequent trial at the Old Bailey both were found guilty, the Crown somehow 'proving' her complicity through her surviving letters to Bywaters. The Solicitor General misled the jury when he stated in court that Edith Thompson's correspondence contained the 'undoubted evidence of a preconcerted meeting between Mrs Thompson and Bywaters at *the* place', meaning the place where Percy Thompson was murdered. But there is no such evidence in the letters, although the jury could not know this because only half the correspondence was submitted in court. The jury had to assume either that the Solicitor General was lying or that explicit conspiracy to murder was spelled out in one of the withheld letters.

The judge also failed to set the record straight in a summing up that was notoriously unfair to Mrs Thompson. Innocent of murder, she was hanged for adultery. A million people signed a petition for the reprieve of Edith Thompson and Frederick Bywaters but it failed to stop the executions. Both were hanged at the same time on 9 January 1923, she at Holloway and he at Pentonville. Almost immediately rumours began circulating about the nature of Mrs Thompson's execution, resulting in the suspicion that she may have been pregnant. It is odd that her weight increased between the date she was sentenced to death and the day she died, even though she ate very little during her last two weeks in prison and virtually nothing in the four days before she died.

The permanent memorial was placed here in October 1993 by a number of interested parties including Professor René Weis (Mrs Thompson's biographer[27]), Patricks of Farnham (who donated virtually the entire cost of the stone), Mr Ramadan Guney (owner of the cemetery, who waived all cemetery fees) and other interested parties. A special service of dedication took place to mark the completion of the memorial on 13 November 1993. It was led by the Revd Barry Arscott, Vicar of St Barnabas Church, Manor Park. This is the church where Mrs Thompson was married in 1916. During the service, the Revd Arscott declared:

> We place and dedicate this stone first, because it would be what Edith Thompson's family would have wanted, and because we want to acknowledge and recognise Edith Thompson alongside all the departed. No-one should be treated as they never were. Secondly, we have this ceremony because the way in which she died and the injustice of that should never be forgotten. John Donne, the poet, said that 'Any man's death diminishes me', and it is true that when someone whom we love dies, part of us dies too. But in the case of this particular death we may well say that Edith Thompson's death diminished humanity.[28]

A film about Mrs Thompson's life and death was made by Winchester Films. Natasha Little played Mrs Thompson, and Ioan Gruffudd played Freddy Bywaters. Called *Another Life*, it was released in the spring of 2001. The campaign to clear Mrs Thompson's name continues and has now been referred to the Criminal Cases Review Commission.

Mrs Styllou Pantopiou Christofi (*c.* 1901–54) was found guilty of murdering her daughter-in-law, Mrs Hella Dorothea Christofis, on the night of 28 July 1954. Mrs Christofi appears to have developed a fanatical and jealous hatred of Hella, and struck her from behind with a cast-iron ashplate from the kitchen stove. Afterwards she tried to burn the body in the backyard of her house at 11 South Hill Park, London. She was discovered and arrested. Mrs Christofi was almost certainly insane (something she denied at her trial), and was unable to speak a word of English (she was illiterate even in her native Greek). Efforts were made in Parliament to prevent the hanging. But the Home Secretary, Major G. Lloyd-George,[29] was determined that the law should take its course and she was hanged at Holloway on the morning of 15 December 1954. Although Mrs Christofi was the penultimate woman to be hanged in Britain there were no mass demonstrations outside Holloway Prison on the morning she died. After her execution many MPs expressed their disquiet at the Home Secretary's failure to recommend a reprieve after the prison doctor had declared Mrs Christofi insane. The Home Secretary reported to Parliament on 20 December that:

> It would be contrary to long-established practice, and, I think, open to considerable objection, to disclose any advice tendered to the Home Secretary in a case of this kind by the trial Judge, or to disclose the terms of the medical report submitted by the statutory inquiry, and I am not prepared to make these documents available.[30]

Amelia Sach (*c.* 1874–1903) and **Annie Walters** (*c.* 1849–1903) were the first women to be executed at Holloway Prison after it became a female gaol in 1902. Annie Walters was arrested with a dead male child in her arms. Aged about four days, he had been born on 15 November 1902 to a Miss Galley. Amelia Sach was arrested and charged with conspiring with Annie Walters to commit the murder. Sach ran a small 'nursing home' where the 'adoption' of unwanted infants could be arranged and paid for. This was a common practice at the time, more usually referred to as 'baby farming'. It arose from the need for working mothers to have their young children looked after during working hours, and that of unmarried mothers who could not care for their illegitimate offspring. 'Baby farming' provided 'nurses' (sometimes vicious, sometimes criminal) who were entrusted to care for the child in return for a fee. In general these fees were low, and many babies either died from neglect or were simply dumped in the streets. Despite legislation, little could be done without also addressing the appalling social conditions and the isolation of unmarried mothers at this time.[31] At the conclusion of their trial Sach and Walters were found guilty. Despite a recommendation for mercy by the jury (because the accused were female), both women were hanged at 9 a.m. on 3 February 1903.[32] The coroner, Dr F.J. Waldo,[33] performed the double inquest actually on the scaffold while their coffins stood across the drop. He was also present twenty years later for Mrs Thompson's inquest.

Follow Eastern Avenue around plots 116 and 117, and emerge from the rhododendrons on the railway side of Eastern Avenue. Continue walking along this road until you reach plot 110, marked by low stones at each corner of the plot.

7.18. St Margaret & St John, Westminster [plot 110]

Like **St Anne's**, **Westminster**, two plots were provided for this parish, one for Anglicans (plots 70–1, see Chapter 1) and one for Nonconformists (plot 110). Both plots have pairs of fine granite obelisks that mark each burial ground, and both pairs survive. They appear to have been erected in 1896, the date given on the side of the left-hand obelisk. Each one commemorates the members of the parish burial board in 1855 and 1896. It is interesting to note that only one member was still on the board in 1896, William Lewis Josephs. The plot was opened in April 1855. In this area there are no surviving memorials. However, unlike the plots in the Anglican section, the four boundary markers survive: these are the low white stones in each corner of the plot that undoubtedly date from the opening of the ground in 1855.

Continue along Eastern Avenue until you reach the next junction, with Holly Avenue on your left. Turn up this path. The next chest-style memorial is to the left of the path.

7.19. Pomeroy family grave (Viscounts Harberton) [plot 109]

James Spencer Pomeroy, 6th Viscount Harberton (1836–1912), was the third son of the 5th Viscount and succeeded to the title in 1862. He was educated at Trinity College, Cambridge, graduating in 1859 with a first in the Classical Tripos. He retained an enthusiasm for the classics throughout his life, and wrote several books reflecting this interest.

He married **Florence Wallace Legge** (1843–1911) in 1861. Lady Harberton was the leader of the 'rational dress' movement, and was founder and President of the Rational Dress Society. This group was established at a meeting in Westminster Town Hall, chaired by Constance Lloyd (Mrs Oscar Wilde).[34] During the meeting Lady Harberton declared:

> What can be the true state of intelligence of a creature which deliberately loads itself with quantities of useless material round its legs, in spite of discomfort and danger, without any object in view beyond the abject copying of one another? And then, in order to correct the ugliness of such a dress, squeezes in its body until the vital functions can only be carried on imperfectly?

She wrote a book promoting this cause, *Reasons for Reform in Dress*, in 1885.[35] Lady Harberton was refused entry to a number of establishments owing to her 'inappropriate' manner of dress. On 27 October 1898, wearing a jacket and a pair of long knickerbockers (women's attire then considered outrageous, along with the divided skirt), she rode on a bicycle to the Hautboy Hotel in Ockham, Surrey. She was refused refreshment. Lady Harberton complained to the Cyclists Touring Club (CTC), claiming that the landlady of the hotel had broken the law in refusing food to a traveller and that an agreement with the CTC to serve meals to cyclists at beneficial rates had been broken. The CTC supported Lady Harberton and the case went to trial as *Regina* v. *Sprague* in April 1899. However, she lost the case when the landlady's lawyer managed to convince the jury that the law had not been broken.

Ralph Legge Pomeroy, 8th Viscount Harberton (1869–1956), was educated at Charterhouse and Balliol College, Oxford. He then joined the Army. Pomeroy was a Major with the 5th Dragoon Guards during the South African War (1899–1902), where he was severely wounded. He was a Major with the 4th Reserve Dragoons during the First World War. Pomeroy compiled *The Story of a Regiment of Horse* (1924), a regimental history of the 5th Dragoon Guards from 1685 to 1922.[36] He succeeded as the 8th Viscount in 1944.

Henry Ralph Martyn Pomeroy, 9th Viscount Harberton (1908–80), is also buried here. Educated at Eton, he succeeded his father as 9th Viscount in 1956.

The next memorial is further along the path and on the right. It is surrounded by a yew hedge.

7.20. Charles Bradlaugh (1833–1891) [plot 108]

One of the most controversial public figures of nineteenth-century Britain, championing such unpopular ideas as birth control, atheism, republicanism, reform, peace and anti-imperialism. Bradlaugh was born at Hoxton and enlisted in the Army in 1850. He obtained a discharge in 1853, gained employment in a law office and subsequently took over the common law department in the practice. From 1860 he contributed articles to the *National Reformer*, the journal of the Secular Society, under the pen name 'Iconoclast'. In 1862 he became the paper's editor and proprietor, and used this opportunity to promote his own ideas.

In 1876 he set up the Freethought Publishing Company with Mrs Annie Besant[37] in order to publish an edition of Dr Knowlton's *The Fruits of Philosophy* – a booklet advocating birth control.[38] They were found guilty of publishing 'a dirty, filthy book', but the case was dismissed on appeal in 1878. The trials provided a useful advertisement for birth control, and this is one element that contributed to the declining birth rate towards the end of the nineteenth century. Another important effect was the foundation of the Malthusian League by **Charles Robert Drysdale** in 1877, largely due to Bradlaugh's support and enthusiasm.

In April 1880 Bradlaugh was elected Liberal MP for Northampton. On 3 May he requested to affirm (rather than swear) the oath. The Speaker, on his own authority, refused permission and the matter was referred to a Select Committee. It decided by a majority of one against Bradlaugh. When he attempted to swear the oath (20 May) there was uproar in the House of Commons. He was subsequently unseated and a by-election took place. Bradlaugh was duly re-elected on 9 April 1881. He continued to be re-elected as MP, and each time he was denied the right to take his seat in the House of Commons. The dispute was resolved only with the new Parliament when, in January 1886, the new Speaker refused to interfere with Bradlaugh's right to take his seat. Bradlaugh subsequently secured an Act legalising affirmation in Parliament (1888), and he served as MP for Northampton until his death.

His funeral was as unconventional as his life. There was a total absence of customary black mourning dress (the sole exception being Mrs Besant), and no service of any sort took place. The mourners included the young David Lloyd George (later Prime Minister) and John Morley (Gladstone's great friend and biographer). Most of London's resident Indian population attended because Bradlaugh was sympathetic to the cause of Indian self-government. He was unofficially known as the MP for India. Among this group was the young Mohandas Gandhi, and he witnessed another bizarre aspect of this funeral. As Gandhi was returning from the graveside and awaiting a return train to London he overheard a heated argument taking place between a 'champion atheist' (quite possibly **William S. Ross**) and one of the clergymen present. All this probably took place on or near the platform of **North station**.

The memorial in the cemetery was the first to be completed after Bradlaugh's death. It consisted of a bronze bust by Mr F. Verheyden on a red granite pedestal. It was erected at a cost of £225, and the money was subscribed absolutely spontaneously, without a single appeal or word of request. Unfortunately the memorial as it survives is incomplete. During the night of 12–13 September 1938 the bust was mysteriously removed. The incident was timed to embarrass delegates of the International Congress of the World Union of Freethinkers, then convening in London, who were due to inspect the memorial later on 13 September. It must have taken at least two men to remove the bust, but no trace of it has ever been found.[39]

The next headstone with kerbing is immediately to the left of Bradlaugh's.

7.21. Thomas Allsop (1795–1880) [plot 108]

Stockbroker, author and 'disciple' of the poet and philosopher, Samuel Taylor Coleridge.[40] Educated at Wirksworth Grammar School, Allsop then moved to London to his uncle's silk mercery establishment in 1812. Allsop eventually left for the stock market where he promoted railway projects. In 1818 he heard Coleridge lecture, and Allsop sent a number of letters that prompted Coleridge to meet him. From this grew a deep friendship which lasted until Coleridge's death. Allsop then published his *Letters, Conversations and Recollections of Samuel Taylor Coleridge* (1836). Through Coleridge, Allsop knew also Charles Lamb,[41] William Hazlitt,[42] Barry Cornwall[43] and other eminent men of the period. When Feargus O'Connor,[44] a prominent Chartist, was elected MP for Nottingham (1847), Allsop gave him his property qualification (then necessary by law), so that Chartism might be represented in Parliament. Sceptical of the value of the clergy, Allsop once advertised for a house in the country 'where no church or clergyman was to be found within 5 miles'. He deplored the rise to power of Napoleon III and showed sympathy for the Italian Felice Orsini,[45] who attempted the assassination of the Emperor in January 1858. It transpired that Allsop had ordered the shells used in the attempted assassination from Birmingham, but as he gave his name and address openly it appears that he believed the shells were to be used to improve a French or Italian gun. Allsop also believed that there was a duty to testify the obligation due at the burial of someone who had done something for mankind. When Allsop died at Exmouth, he was subsequently buried here so that his friend George Jacob Holyoake,[46] to whom he had left his personal papers, might speak at his graveside. This could be done only on unconsecrated ground.

The next group of graves is adjacent to Allsop's, beside a large rhododendron.

7.22. Drysdale family grave [plot 108]

Founders and supporters of the Malthusian League (1877–1952). This was the first organisation to advocate birth control as a solution to the problems of poverty and overpopulation. All its presidents are buried here.

Charles Robert Drysdale (1829–1907), doctor and engineer. As an engineer, Drysdale took part in the building of Brunel's SS *Great Eastern* (while employed by Scott Russell & Co.) and was also involved in railway surveying in Switzerland and Spain. He was subsequently appointed Senior Physician to the Metropolitan Hospital, London. Drysdale founded the Malthusian League in 1877 in the wake of the controversy arising from **Charles Bradlaugh**'s publication of *The Fruits of Philosophy* (1876). He was the first President of the League (to 1907), and was known as the 'Malthusian King'.

Dr Alice Vickery Drysdale (1844–1929) was a doctor and promoter of birth control. Born at Swinbridge, Devon, she began her medical studies when her family moved to London. She became the first woman to qualify as a chemist of the Pharmaceutical Society of Great Britain. In the early 1870s she studied midwifery and diseases of women at the London Women's Medical College, and it was here that she met her husband. In 1876 she was one of the witnesses for the defence in the Bradlaugh-Besant trial. In June 1880 she became one of only five women in England with a medical degree when she was enrolled as a member of the Royal College of Physicians of Ireland. She had an extensive private practice in London and did much work for the sick and poor in London. At the same time she worked alongside her husband in promoting the Malthusian League, as one of its Vice-Presidents. She founded the Women's branch of the International Neo-Malthusian League in 1904. She succeeded her husband as President of the League (1907–21) and made few changes to its format and activities. When she resigned in 1921 she was succeeded by her son, **Charles Vickery Drysdale**.

Charles Vickery Drysdale (1874–1961), their only son, was an electrical engineer, physicist and social philosopher. Educated privately and at Finsbury Technical College and the Central Technical College, South Kensington, his first post was as scientific assistant to Nalder Brothers & Co. In 1896 he became associate head of the Applied Physics and Electrical Engineering Department of the Northampton Institute in London. Drysdale developed an interest in the design of electrical measuring instruments. From 1910 he supervised their manufacture with Messrs H. Tinsley & Co. He developed the AC potentiometer, the polyphase wattmeter and a phase-shifting transformer. In 1918 he moved to the Admiralty Experimental Station at Harwich. Drysdale developed a cable system designed to allow a ship to steer along a cable on the seabed. He moved with the Experimental Station to Shandon in 1920 and was appointed its scientific director. He was appointed its first superintendent when it moved to Teddington in 1921. In 1929 he was put in charge of scientific research at the Admiralty. He retired in 1934. In 1907 he and his wife became co-secretaries of the Malthusian League. He replaced his mother as President in 1921, a position he retained until the League was dissolved in 1952.

Bessie Ingman Drysdale (1871–1950), his wife, was a teacher and Malthusian. She taught at Stockwell College. Drysdale inaugurated the Walworth Women's Welfare Centre & Birth Control Clinic in November 1921, which was second only to Marie Stopes's Mothers' Clinic that had opened the previous March.

On the adjacent memorial their only daughter, **Eva Drysdale** (*c.* 1901–14), is commemorated. The niche used to contain a fine bust of Eva but, regrettably, this has been stolen.

Follow the path running towards Chapel Avenue. The next memorial is in the form of a miniature granite obelisk.

7.23. Stephen Standage (*c.* 1827–1888) [plot 108]

Cemetery Superintendent between 1870 and 1886. In 1854 two superintendents were appointed, living in each of the cemetery stations: George Bupell (consecrated side, **South station**) and James Bailey (Nonconformist side, **North station**). Sometime prior to 1861 Mr Bailey (who came from Yorkshire) became the sole Superintendent, and probably moved from North station into one of the cottages in the cemetery. Standage was the third Superintendent, succeeding Mr Bailey in August 1870.[47] He was replaced by **George Barratt**. Note that the style of this memorial is very similar to the obelisks that mark the burial ground of **St Margaret and St John**, **Westminster**.

Follow the same path as it turns sharply to the right. The next memorial is made of pink granite and is towards the end of this path and on the right.

7.24. PC David Fleming Ford (*c.* 1907–1929) [plot 107]

PC Ford was killed when he fell through a plate glass roof during a burglar hunt in the LNC's private station in the Westminster Bridge Road on 14 March 1929. His funeral procession from Kennington Road to the station was watched by thousands of people. Senior members of the detective and uniformed forces marched in the procession along with constables from several divisions, inspectors and sergeants from various parts of the Metropolitan Police, and officers and men from PC Ford's own 'L' Division. The Metropolitan Police Pipers Band accompanied the procession through the streets. Owing to the circumstances of PC Ford's death the LNC waived all funeral charges. The officers and men of the 'Met' paid for the memorial, which includes PC Ford's own badge in the Metropolitan Police Force carved into the headstone.

Diagonally opposite is the next grave. It is a Calvary cross within a double-kerbed allotment.

7.25. Bennet Burleigh (1839–1914) [plot 105]

War correspondent for the *Daily Telegraph*. Born in Glasgow, Burleigh fought in the American Civil War for the confederacy. After helping 2,500 confederate soldiers escape from a prison on Johnson's Island, he was apprehended on Canadian territory and stood trial for extradition in Montreal as demanded by the United States. Extradited to Ohio, and again tried, he managed to escape before a verdict was reached. Twice during the continuing civil war he was sentenced to death, but Burleigh managed somehow to evade execution. Burleigh was the Central News correspondent during the Egyptian campaign (1882) and was present at the Battle of Tel-el-Kebir. The quality of his reporting of these events led him to be engaged by the *Daily Telegraph*, and he remained with this newspaper until his death. He covered the advance of the desert column from Korti to Metamneh during 1884–5 and was present at the battles of Abu Klea (which included a famous account of the death of Colonel Burnaby[48]), Abu Kru and Gubat. A week after the action at Gubat the news came through that Khartoum had fallen and that the relief expedition had failed to reach the city in time. The other campaigns he reported included the Ashanti expedition, the war in Madagascar between the French and the Hovas, and the Atbara expedition. He covered the Egyptian campaign of 1896–8, and was present at the Battle of Omdurman. During the Boer War (1899–1902) he was present at the battles of Glencoe, Elandslaagte, Farquhar's Farm and the relief of Ladysmith.[49] During the Russo-Japanese War (1904–5) he followed the Japanese advance into Manchuria. He also reported the Italian campaign in Tripoli (1911) and the fighting between Turkey and the Balkan states. The *Daily Telegraph* described him as exemplifying:

> the new era of war reporting, corresponding by telegraph . . . with unsurpassed skill, accuracy and judgement. In him there passes away one of the most intrepid and most brilliant journalists of his time.[50]

It was said that he had probably seen more of the warfare of the previous half-century than any other living man. The 5ft 6in rustic grey Cornish granite cross was added later.[51]

The next memorial is diagonally opposite and on the junction with Eastern Avenue. It is a headstone with footstone and sunken kerbing.

7.26. Charles W. Merriam (*c.* 1831–1855) [plot 107]

Merriam came from Chippena, Canada. Six days after his arrival in England he died, aged just 24. This memorial was 'erected as a mark of esteem by a few of his fellow passengers from Sydney, New South Wales'. Note that the footstone includes the burial number (887).

Further to the left is a narrow upright stone on a small base.

7.27. Matzui Kikujiroo (died 1868) [plot 107]

This unusual memorial commemorates Matzui Kikujiroo of Jedo in Japan. He was a member of the Imperial Japanese troupe that was then performing in London. Fellow members of the troupe erected the memorial in his memory.[52]

7.28. Cemetery sign [plot 104]

Adjacent to the shrubberies off Eastern Avenue is the iron framework that used to support the letters BROOKWOOD CEMETERY. The sign was for the convenience of railway passengers passing by on the main line. The ironwork is somewhat dilapidated and many of the wooden letters have rotted away.

Rejoin Chapel Avenue and turn left. The Hogg family grave is under the large yew tree opposite the chapel.

7.29. Robert Hogg (1818–1897) [plot 105]

Horticulturalist and writer. Born at Duns, Hogg was educated privately and at Edinburgh University. His father ran a business supplying forest trees and agricultural seeds. In 1836 he moved to London and found work with the nursery of John Ronalds. He travelled extensively on the continent before returning to London and becoming a partner in the Brompton Park Nursery (1845–51). The nursery closed in 1852 and part of the site was subsequently used for the Victoria and Albert Museum. In 1854 Hogg helped found the British Pomological Society, which eventually merged with the Fruit Committee of the Horticultural Society in 1858. He was co-editor of the *Cottage Gardener* (1855–61) and of the *Journal of Horticulture* (1861–81, with G.W. Johnson[53]). Hogg was made a Fellow of the Linnaean Society in 1861. His many books include *The Vegetable Kingdom* (1858), *The Fruit Manual* (1860) and *Wild Flowers of Great Britain* (1863–80, with G.W. Johnson).

This memorial is almost certainly the oldest in the Nonconformist section, originally commemorating Hogg's infant son, **Charles Milligan Hogg** (1852–4), who died on 5 December 1854 aged just 2 years and 4 months. Note that on the top left-hand side of the headstone is carved the name of the mason, 'Arch. Ritchie, Edinburgh'.

In the adjacent grave, commemorating Mrs Hogg's family, the Milligans, lie the mortal remains of **Robert Howes** (*c.* 1800–66), 'upwards of 40 years their faithful servant'.

To the right is a low-hipped ledger memorial in pink granite.

7.30. Colonel Angus Alexander Croll (1811–1887) [plot 105]

Civil engineer and promoter of electric telegraphy. Born in Perth, Croll moved to London and established a successful engineering practice. He was particularly interested in the gas industry, and his connection with the Great Central Gas Company and similar undertakings allowed him to secure special privileges for the metropolitan gas companies. Croll also promoted cheap telegraphic messages. As Chairman of the United Kingdom Electric Telegraph Company he pioneered the extension of telegraphy throughout Britain and overseas. In 1871 he was presented with a testimonial and silver plate as public recognition of his services in this sphere. Croll was honorary Colonel of the 2nd Tower Hamlets Regiment of Engineer Volunteers. He was one of the original directors of the LNC (1854–7).

Immediately to the right is an unusual obelisk surrounded by a low railing.

7.31. Sir James Brunlees (1816–1892) [plot 105]

One of the most outstanding civil engineers of his time. Born at Kelso, he was educated at Edinburgh University. In 1838 he was appointed assistant engineer to Alexander Adie on the Bolton & Preston Railway. He later worked with Joseph Locke[54] on the Caledonian Railway on the route from Beattock to Carstairs, Glasgow and Edinburgh. John Hawkshaw[55] made him acting engineer on the Lancashire & Yorkshire Railway (1844–50). Brunlees' subsequent appointments included engineer to the Londonderry & Coleraine Railway (1850) and of the Ulverston & Lancaster Railway (1851). In 1855 he was invited to undertake the construction of the Sao Paulo Railway. On its completion in 1873 he was awarded the Brazilian Order of the Rose by the Emperor of Brazil. His other major works include the Solway Junction Railway (1865–9), including the Solway viaduct; the Mont Cenis Railway (1865–8), which provided the first rail link between France and Italy (it was closed in 1871 when the Mont Cenis tunnel was completed); the Clifton Extension Railway; the Minas & Rio Railway; the Port Alegre Railway; the Central Uruguay & Bolivar Railway; and the Southport & Cheshire Lines Extension Railway. He was also involved in the construction of tunnels, docks and piers. He was engineer to the Mersey Railway, including the 1,300-yard tunnel under the river, and with Hawkshaw he was joint engineer to the Channel Tunnel Company (1872–86). He built the docks at Avonmouth (1868–77), King's Lynn and Whitehaven. He constructed the piers at Southport, Llandudno, New Brighton and Southend. Brunlees was appointed an independent assessor of the workmanship on the Tay Bridge in April 1880, when he noted that 'the quality of the wrought iron throughout the work is good'. He saw no evidence that the train had left the rails before the bridge collapsed, and believed that excessive wind force was the immediate cause of the tragedy. He was asked to become the new engineer of the Tay Bridge, but declined (July 1880).[56] Brunlees was Vice-President of the Institution of Civil Engineers (1878) and President (1882–3). He was knighted on 8 May 1886 at the opening of the Mersey Railway.

Further to the right is a flat ledger stone with a small cross.

7.32. Joseph Ivimey (1803–1878) [plot 105]

London solicitor. Ivimey was one of the promoters of the Anti-Corn Law League, and was solicitor to the London District of the League (1839–46). The League was formed by a number of businessmen who believed in Free Trade and that the Corn Laws benefited landowners at everyone else's expense. The Corn Laws were repealed in June 1846, resulting in a divided Conservative Party and the end of Sir Robert Peel's political career. Ivimey was also involved with the Necropolis project, and served as a director from its formation until his death.

On the other side of Chapel Avenue is a large plot within a wire fence.

7.33. Dawoodi-Bohra Najmee Baag cemetery [adjacent to plot 103]

This Muslim community comprises the followers of His Holiness Dr Syedna Mohammad Burhanuddin. It is an Ismaili sect of the western or *mustali* grouping, dating from 1095. Bohra Muslims are Indian Muslims who have been converted from Hinduism. This area of the cemetery is one of several that were sold off as a consequence of the 1975 Brookwood Cemetery Act (see the Introduction for further details).

The building within the enclosure is the former **Nonconformist chapel**, designed by the LNC's architect Sydney Smirke, and constructed for the opening of the cemetery in 1854. As originally constructed, it was described as:

> built in the Tudor style of architecture, and remarkable for [its] singularly neat appearance . . . [with a] small tower and spire, loop windows, open pointed roofs, open stained pewing and neat Gothic pulpit. . . . The floors are paved with blue and red Staffordshire tiles, and bear a resemblance to tessellated pavement.[57]

Since it was located on a slight hill, the bell tower was a noticeable feature from the main railway line and other parts of the cemetery. The area surrounding the chapel also became known generally as 'chapel hill'. Since the site was sold the building has been altered and extended. Owing to the poor state of the chapel the bell tower was dismantled (although its square base can still be seen), and the original roof slates replaced by tiles. Two new extensions have been added to the building and the windows have been altered.

Also within the plot is the surviving platform of **North station**, which served this part of the cemetery grounds. It is best seen from the other side of the allotment, where a gateway usually allows access on to the platform area. The stations were described as follows in 1854:

> The stations are constructed with peculiar neatness, and are situated at a very convenient distance from the chapels. They comprise first class and general reception rooms, apartments for the officials, and first and second class refreshment rooms. The latter have semi-circular counters formed of marble. Attached to each station is a courtyard of small dimensions for the conveniences of the *attachés* of the company. The south, or Church of England station, is situated about half a mile from the South-Western main line . . .[58]

In 1854 the station was occupied by the Superintendent for the Nonconformist section, James Bailey, who had accommodation adjacent to the refreshment rooms. However, by 1861 he had become the sole Cemetery Superintendent and it is assumed he was given accommodation in one of the cottages within the cemetery grounds. Thereafter the station was used as accommodation for one of the cemetery porters, Richard Lee, who lived there with his mother Ann (who died in 1865). By 1871 Richard Lee was living there with his wife Charlotte. Ten years later the records show that the station was occupied by **Robert** and **Caroline Spooner** and their son **Robert**. The Spooners remained in the station until about 1892, when they moved to **South station** following the dismissal of Walter Parker. The subsequent occupants of the station are not known until Mr and Mrs Stonard, who ran the refreshment room from 1928 to 1941. Gwen Spencer, the Stonards' daughter, remembers:

In the early days we had no running hot water, although there was a big coal fire range to cook on. My mother catered for funeral parties, sometimes up to and over 100 people, with teas, coffee, sandwiches and cakes, which were all homemade. The ham was home cooked, with whole gammons cooked in a large iron pot for several hours. The charge was 2d per sandwich and the little fairy cakes were 1d each.

As well as catering for mourners, who mostly came down from London by train, we also had local people who walked through the cemetery calling in for afternoon tea. Of course the bar was an added attraction, as it had a full licence and kept to pub opening hours, much to the delight of the locals.

Across the back of North station were our living quarters with the bar in the middle. We had to go through the bar to the bedrooms. Down the sides were four waiting rooms with toilets between, men one side, women the other. We had to use these toilets and it wasn't very pleasant having to go out in the cold and rain, but in those days millions of people had to do the same.

Behind North station on top of the hill was the chapel, which my father used to clean. Every day at 8 a.m. and again at 5 p.m. he would ring the bell for the staff to start and finish work. As well as looking after North station, my father was part of the undertaking service and towards the end of the 1930s the men were issued with a top hat and tails uniform, complete with wing collars on their shirts.[59]

There is another short gap in our knowledge of the occupants of North station until Mr and Mrs Dendy, who ran the refreshment rooms from 1948 to 1956, when they retired. By this time the railway track had been removed but the station was otherwise unaltered, except being renamed the North Bar. Their son remembers:

There was no electric light or gas at the North Bar. Lighting was by oil lamps and the cooking was done on a range – my mother loved cooking with it. . . . On average my mother catered for about three funeral parties a week, with sometimes as many as sixty people. At this time the cemetery chapels were in constant use (depending on the religion) and I believe the hand biers were still being used at funerals. My father would prepare the chapels for the services required. The refreshment bar was a very civilised place for mourners to adjourn to for a welcome drink and something to eat before their return journey. The undertaker made arrangements with the Necropolis Company so that the cost of refreshments was included on the bill for the funeral. . . .

I was married from [the North Bar] in 1950 [and] we stayed there for about six months before getting our own house. We occupied a large room at one end of the Bar. I used to wake up some nights with my hair standing on end, and the feeling that someone was standing beside me. It was uncanny. At the time I never told my wife, but one day she met me from work looking somewhat upset. She told me she was working in the room when it felt as if someone was standing beside her. She just dropped her tools and ran. She also told me that she had sometimes woken at night and felt there was someone there. We discovered that our room had been used as a temporary mortuary for American soldiers who were removed from the military cemetery and being sent back to America.[60]

After the Dendys retired in 1956 the station remained empty until it was demolished sometime in the 1960s owing to dry rot. The remains of the platform may still be seen. It was unusual in having steps at each end of the platform, rather than the customary ramps. It was also rather shorter than the platform at **South station**.

The next grave is close to Chapel Avenue and in front of the Dawoodi-Bohra section.

7.34. [Ratu] Ravuama [Catanaivalu] Vunivalu (1921–1964) [plot 103]

Fijian patriot and parliamentarian. This memorial is a splendid example of the catholicism of the cemetery. Vunivalu was educated at Auckland University and St John's College, Cambridge. He joined the Fijian civil service in 1938 as a clerk in the Training Secretariat. Vunivalu was a temporary clerk and interpreter at the Supreme and Lower Courts (1940–3), served in the Public Relations Office (1942–5) and was Supreme Court interpreter (1943–5). Between 1945 and 1949 he studied in New Zealand and the United Kingdom on scholarship grants. Vunivalu was appointed Chief Inspector of the Cooperative Department (1950) becoming its Assistant Registrar (1951–6). In 1956 he transferred to the Education Department and moved into the Colonial Service from 1960. Vunivalu was a member of the Legislative Council of Fiji (1959–64) and was one of eight signatories to the 'Wakaya Letter'. This document was drafted at a Great Council of Chiefs held at Wakaya in January 1963 and asserted the principles of Fijian sovereignty. It became the main negotiating factor for Fijian independence in the 1960s. Vunivalu also wrote a standard history of Fiji, *The Colony of Fiji: a Handbook* (6th edn., 1957). He died in London while on leave, aged just 42 years. His epitaph reads 'Fijian scholar, politician and soldier; a fearless upholder of Fijian rights'. The Fijian epitaph *Keimami nanomi koya tiko* may be translated as 'We will always remember you'.[61]

Follow Chapel Avenue around to the left. The entrance to the next ground is signposted from the road.

7.35. Ahmadiyya burial ground [plot 101]

This Islamic plot was opened for the Ahmadiyyas in 1975, and forms one of several areas in the cemetery that were sold off as a consequence of the 1975 Brookwood Cemetery Act (see the Introduction for further details). The sect developed as a religious reform movement in 1889 in India by Mirza Ghulam Ahmad (1839–1908), who claimed to be the Messiah or *Mahdi*. Considered to be outside the mainstream of Islam, the Ahmadiyyas have undertaken missionary work in Europe and Africa. The reopening of the Woking Mosque in 1913 by Kamal ud din Kwaja (1870–1932) was an example of their missionary work. It included the Woking Muslim Mission that made Woking a centre of British Islam in the 1920s and 1930s.

Just to the right of the entrance to this ground is a pedestal memorial with an urn on top. This commemorates **Roop Sing** (*c*. 1869–1887). Sing was born at Bulana, India. He was a Rajput of the Ponwar family. He came to England with Mahraj Sir Pertab Sing and died of 'malarious fever' within a fortnight of his arrival, on 11 May 1887.

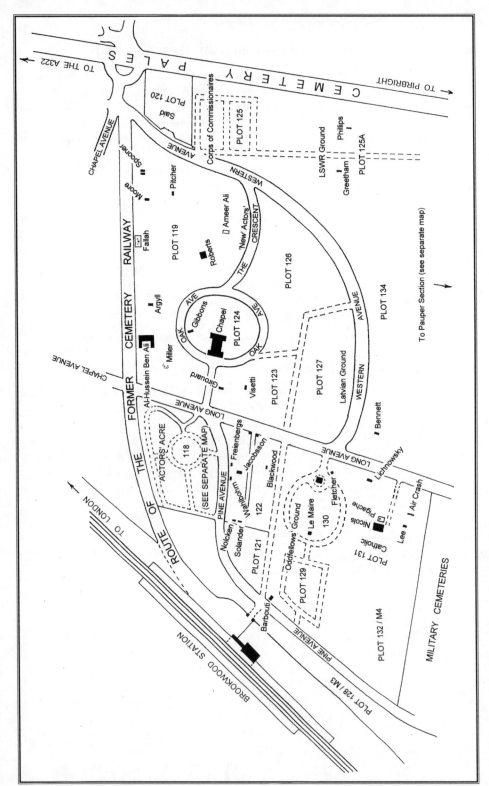

The western part of the former Nonconformist section.

Chapter Eight

THE WESTERN PART OF THE FORMER NONCONFORMIST SECTION

W e turn next to the area between the route of the former cemetery railway and the military cemeteries (which are covered in the following chapter). This section of the cemetery is distinguished by the various allotments set aside for the use of various churches, guilds or other organisations, some of which are still in use to this day. The area is divided by **Long Avenue**, which stretches from the site of **North station** right through to the **military cemeteries**. This avenue is one of the longest in the cemetery, and reminds us of the original plans of the LNC. These included the construction of cemetery avenues up to 3 miles long, stretching from hereabouts to Hook Heath, and the intended 'national mausoleum' church. The view down Long Avenue, with its splendid planting of redwoods, reminds us what might have been.

8.1. Said family allotment [plot 120]

This area is one of several that were disposed of as a consequence of the 1975 Brookwood Cemetery Act.[1] The extensive walled plot contains three recent burials. The first was that of **Karim Wafic Said** (1971–81), killed accidentally in Riyadh; also **Racha Rida Said** (1938–81), wife of Muhammed Munzer Mudarres, and **Kherien Manicne Rida Said**, who died in 1998. The ground has been extensively landscaped and planted.

This plot occupies the site of the former Nonconformist burial ground of **St Anne's, Westminster**. St Anne's is situated off Wardour Street in Soho and was built in 1677–86 to the designs of either Wren or William Talman. The original tower was replaced by S.P. Cockerell in 1801–3. King George II worshipped at this church when he was Prince of Wales. The church, with the exception of the curious tower, was destroyed in 1940 during the Blitz. In recent years some rebuilding has taken place to provide accommodation for the Soho Housing Association and the Soho Society, along with a museum and chapel.

Under the terms of the Metropolitan Interments Act (1852)[2] the Government was empowered to close down overcrowded burial grounds in London, and metropolitan parishes were enabled to elect burial boards to arrange for the decent interment of their dead. St Anne's received an Order to close its churchyard on 25 August 1853. By this time it was estimated that some 10,000 burials had taken place there, and consequently the churchyard was some 6ft above the pavement. The first meeting of the St Anne's burial board took place on 20 July 1854.[3] Eventually two areas at Brookwood were acquired for the exclusive use of St Anne's: plot 1 in the former Anglican section (originally 2 acres, see Chapter 2), and this one in the Nonconformist section, comprising 1 acre. The agreement with the LNC was dated 26 April 1855 and was to last for 999 years. It is not known what burial ground the parish used during the intervening period 1853–5 but, like **St Saviour's**, **Southwark**, Victoria Park Cemetery may have been used.[4]

Both plots at Brookwood had pairs of 10ft high cast-iron obelisks, but only the pair in plot 1 survives. These were made by Messrs Cottain & Hallow of Oxford Street for £54, and were painted to resemble stone. The boundaries of the plots were planted by Messrs Donald & Sons for £50.[5] Most of the burials here were of paupers, whose graves were unmarked. Burial at Brookwood was never popular with those parishioners who could afford to be buried elsewhere. There are no surviving memorials from the parish in this plot. The parish burial board inspected the plots annually until 1900, when the board was dissolved under the London Government Act (1899). Thereafter the Borough of Paddington maintained the plots until about 1921. Meanwhile in 1892 the churchyard in London was laid out as a garden by the Metropolitan Public Gardens Association and maintained by the Strand District Board of Works as a recreation ground. In 1903 part of the churchyard was cleared when Wardour Street was widened. The human remains were transferred to Brookwood in a large plot measuring 56ft × 20ft, but so far its location has not been traced.[6] The only remaining evidence of its former usage is the small white boundary marker stone at the corner of the plot, immediately beyond the wall and facing plot 125.

The next headstone with kerbing may be found directly opposite.

8.2. Mary Pitcher (*c.* 1808–1856) [plot 119]

A fascinating early headstone. Mary was the wife of Richard Pitcher, a genealogist. Her epitaph includes the following touching verse:

Married was I
9 children had I
3 infants died, 6 survived I
Lord be pleased to give them health
Untill [*sic*] you call them to I

The next pair of graves face towards Railway Avenue.

8.3. Spooner family grave [plot 119]

This is a double grave enclosed by kerbing. Commemorated on the left-hand headstone are **Robert Spooner** (*c.* 1829–1914) and his wife **Caroline** (*c.* 1831–93). Robert came from Woking and worked as a gardener in the cemetery. By 1881 he and his wife were living in **North station**, with Caroline in charge of the refreshment room. Towards the end of 1892 the Spooners moved to **South station** following the dismissal of Walter Parker. Their son **Robert Spooner** (died 1913) is buried in the right-hand grave. He became an under-gardener in the cemetery and married Emily in 1891. They had two sons, Charles and Albert.

Just beyond the walled Said plot is the next burial area.

8.4. The Corps of Commissionaires burial ground [plot 125]

The Corps of Commissionaires was established in 1859 by Captain Sir Edward Walter[7] for the employment of ex-soldiers and sailors. It was subsequently extended to include the air and police forces, the fire service and the merchant navy. The central granite obelisk commemorates Walter and his life, although he is not buried here but at Bearwood in Berkshire. The ground was opened sometime after the foundation of the Corps. The records show that 111 burials have taken place in this ground by 1908. Originally simple wooden markers were used as memorials and these have long since rotted away. From time to time the Corps allowed the plot to become overgrown. Subsequent clearance work meant that some markers and memorials were lost. Among those buried here are two holders of the Victoria Cross:

Lance-Corporal James Hollowell, **VC** (1823–1876) [grave marker]. Hollowell's award was made during the Indian Mutiny, when he was serving as a Private with the 78th Regiment. On 26 September 1857 at Lucknow he was shut up and besieged in one of the houses. During the day he encouraged nine other men who were in low spirits to keep going 'in a most admirable manner'. Hollowell's persuasion prevailed and they made a successful defence of the burning house despite the enemy firing through four of its windows. Hollowell was buried in the Corps of Commissionaires plot, but the exact location of his grave is unknown since no permanent memorial appears to have been placed, and any marker on the grave has since been lost. In the autumn of 2000 a permanent marker to his memory was placed next to that of **William Kenny**. The headstone is a standard Commonwealth War Graves Commission design and includes the Victoria Cross carved into the stone.

Sergeant William Kenny, **VC** (1880–1936) [grave marker]. Kenny was awarded the VC as Drum Major in the Gordon Highlanders. He was with the 2nd Battalion when they took part in the first Battle of Ypres. He was awarded his VC for conspicuous bravery on 23 October 1914 near Ypres, when he rescued wounded men under very heavy fire in a 'most fearless manner', and for twice previously saving machine guns by carrying them out of action. On numerous occasions Drummer Kenny conveyed urgent messages under dangerous circumstances over fire-swept ground. Kenny was presented with his medal by King George V at a ceremony held on Glasgow Green on 15 May 1915.

Kenny was discharged in 1923 having achieved the rank of Sergeant. He joined the Corps of Commissionaires in London. His military bearing and distinctive moustache made him a popular figure with shoppers in Bond Street, where he was affectionately known as 'Paddy'. Kenny died aged 55 in 1936, and was buried somewhere in this plot. However, no permanent memorial appears to have been placed, and any marker on the grave has since been lost. On Saturday 20 March 1999 a service was arranged by Kenny's old regiment, the Gordon Highlanders, and held in this ground to mark the placing of a permanent marker to his memory. The headstone is a standard Commonwealth War Graves Commission design and includes the Victoria Cross carved into the stone.

The next area is just beyond, and is partly defined by the old pathway that runs through this section towards the woodland.

.5. London & South Western Railway ground [plot 125a]

The LSWR Company chose Brookwood as a burying ground for its deceased employees, and separate areas were set aside for the burial of the company's officers and servants within the cemetery. Three main areas used were the 'LSWR 1st class area' (plot 47, see Chapter 5), the 'LSWR 2nd class area' (plot 48, see Chapter 5) and this area set aside in the former Nonconformist section. Other areas were used by more senior staff (especially part of plot 32, see Chapter 4), but were not exclusively reserved for the LSWR.

The Nonconformist area has very few identifiable LSWR memorials, but those that may be found here include: **James Greetham**, 'who lost his life on the LSWR, 4 September 1896'; and **William Phillips** (c. 1830–88), a locomotive inspector.

Also buried here, but in an unmarked grave, is **John Stamp** (c. 1858–1911), a constable in the LSWR police. On 14 July 1911 he was on duty at Esher station in connection with race traffic for Sandown Park:

The day was an extremely hot one, and shortly after 3pm Inspector Barnett told the men to take a rest and be in readiness for the return traffic. The Inspector and PC John Stamp went into the Sandown Park Race Club's ground to rest under some trees, and just as Stamp was sitting down he fell forward into Inspector Barnett's arms, and although medical assistance was at once obtained, Stamp was found to be dead. An inquest was held in the Village Hall on 17th July, when it was shown that death was due to a syncope caused by the deceased condition of the heart, and the Jury returned a verdict accordingly. The funeral took place at the Brookwood Necropolis on the 18th.[8]

From here, a poorly defined path leads towards the woodland and the former pauper areas in this section of the cemetery grounds. Most of this land is now privately owned, and access from here is not possible. If you wish to explore these areas, access is easiest from Pirbright village. You can walk up **Cemetery Pales** *and gain access to these areas from where the boundary wall commences. All directions given here are from the Pirbright end of the cemetery. The graves described below are rather scattered. Look out for the regular shallow depressions in the ground that mark the pauper graves in this section.*

As noted in the section on pauper burials in Chapter 6, great care should be taken when exploring these areas as the ground can be very uneven and in places is liable to give way.

8.6. Pauper burial grounds [plots P]

The LNC tendered each year for the burial of the poor from several London parishes, and much of the company's business was devoted to the proper burial of paupers in individual graves. It is estimated that some 80 per cent of the total burials at Brookwood were of paupers, virtually all in unmarked graves. Some parishes, such as **St Saviour's**, **Southwark**, or **St Anne's**, **Westminster**, set aside distinct burial plots within the cemetery and these are described in their appropriate sections. Many other parishes left the LNC to allocate burial areas, and these were on the western boundaries of the cemetery, closest to Pirbright village.

It is now impossible to say whether each parish had separate areas, or whether burials from different parishes followed on from one another. Graves were marked by low mounds, usually with moss or grass growing on them, along with a wooden marker with the burial number stamped on to a metal strip that was attached to the stake. From some entries in the burial registers it is clear that adults and children were buried in separate areas, unless next of kin made a specific request for an old grave to be re-opened. It is also clear from the burial register that these pauper burial grounds occupied considerable areas, particularly here on the cemetery boundary. Entries like '68th grave from top end of 55th row of adults' or '28th grave from bottom end of 52nd row of children' are fairly typical of those found in the registers. Notes like these would have assisted staff of the LNC when a particular pauper grave had to be identified for some reason. Some of the parishes or districts whose poor were buried in this way are **Bermondsey, Chiswick, St George's, Bloomsbury, St Giles-in-the-Fields, St Luke's, Chelsea, St Nicholas', Deptford** and **St Paul's, Deptford**.

Among the anonymous pauper graves in this part of the cemetery grounds is that of **George William Martin** (1828–81), a composer. Martin became a chorister at St Paul's Cathedral and was one of the choir boys at Queen Victoria's coronation in Westminster Abbey in 1838. He became Professor of Music at the Normal College for Army Schoolmasters and was resident master at St John's Training College, Battersea (1845–53). Martin was the first organist at Christ Church, Battersea, when it opened in 1849. He founded the National Choral Society in 1860 and edited and published a number of cheap editions of the works of the great masters. For the tercentenary of Shakespeare's birth (1864) he organised a choir of 1,000 for *Macbeth*. H

'Sentinel pine', Pine Glade, in the Glades of Remembrance, 1950. This is a typical view of one of the glades as originally laid out (6.1). *(Brian Parsons collection)*

Colquhoun family mausoleum, plot 57a: the earliest and most architecturally distinguished mausoleum at Brookwood. It was designed by John Johnson and the mason was W. Boulton of Guildford (almost certainly the original mason to the LNC). This engraving shows the astonishing carving that decorates the front of the mausoleum. It includes an elaborately carved and decorated gothic arch and at least five carved figures, culminating in the figure of Christ just under the roof (6.4). *(Brian Parsons collection)*

Arthur Melville (died 1904), on the heath, *c.* 1910. This photograph shows the memorial in its original condition with an upright stone that incorporates the inscription. Today only the kerbing survives, which is anonymous save for the grave number (6.5). *(Lyndon Davies, Past Images collection)*

Entrance to the burial ground of St Alban the Martyr, Holborn, plot 46, *c.* 1910. This is one of four lych-gates in the cemetery, and the finest (6.11). *(Author's collection)*

The Revd Alexander Heriot Mackonochie (died 1887) and the Revd Arthur Henry Stanton (died 1913), plot 46. These memorials may be found directly in front of the Calvary cross in the centre of the St Alban's plot (6.11). *(Anthony Montan)*

Above: St Peter's Home allotment, plot 55. This lych-gate forms the entrance to this burial ground, which served the convalescent home in Maybury (6.14). *(Anthony Montan)*

Freshfield family allotment, plot 44. The large upright memorial was designed and carved by Edward Onslow Ford (6.30). *(Anthony Montan)*

St Stephen's, South Kensington, burial ground, plot 41 (6.36). *(Anthony Montan)*

Entrance to the Nonconformist section, *c.* 1900. Through the gateway can be seen Chapel Avenue and the bell tower of the Nonconformist chapel. To the right is the Superintendent's cottage (7.2). *(Reproduced by permission of Surrey History Service)*

Aerial view of the Superintendent's office area, *c.* 1970. This shows the office complex and Masonry Works in its final form just before the site was sold off under the 1975 Brookwood Cemetery Act (7.2). *(Jenny Graveson collection)*

Alfred Edmeades Bestall (died 1985), plot 100. Alfred Bestall was for thirty years the illustrator of Rupert Bear (7.3). *(Anthony Montan)*

Johanna Kinkel (died 1858), plot 100. The portrait is by Philippe Grass (7.5). *(Anthony Montan)*

Dr Robert Knox (died 1862), plot 100. The famous anatomist, and one of Burke and Hare's best customers (7.11). *(Anthony Montan)*

William Stewart Ross (died 1906), plot 113. Includes a profile portrait in bronze (7.14). *(Anthony Montan)*

Mrs Edith Jessie Thompson (executed 1923) and others, plot 117. Mrs Thompson was executed for the murder of her husband following a trial that was notoriously unfair to her. This permanent memorial was placed over the grave in October 1993 by a number of interested people. The names of the other executed women appear around the base: Amelia Sach and Annie Walters (executed together in 1903), and Mrs Styllou Christofi (executed 1954) (7.17). *(Author's collection)*

Eva Drysdale (died 1914), plot 108, 1979. This bust used to stand in the niche commemorating the only daughter of Charles Vickery Drysdale and Bessie Ingman Drysdale. Regrettably it was stolen some years ago (7.22). *(Author's collection)*

Charles Bradlaugh (died 1891), plot 108, *c.* 1900. This view shows Bradlaugh's memorial in its original state, complete with the bronze bust by Francis Verheyden and the bronze wreath beneath. It is possible to identify virtually all the surrounding memorials today (7.20). *(Reproduced by permission of Surrey History Service)*

Sir James Brunlees (died 1892), plot 105. One of the most outstanding civil engineers of his time (7.31). *(Anthony Montan)*

Ravuama Vunivalu (died 1964). Fijian parliamentarian and patriot. He died in London and is buried here far from his homeland (7.34). *(Anthony Montan)*

The former Nonconformist chapel, adjacent to plot 105, 1979. It was designed by Sydney Smirke in the Tudor style as the sister chapel to that in the Anglican section. This photograph was taken just before the chapel and the surrounding area was sold off as the Najmee Baag (Muslim) Cemetery, a consequence of the 1975 Brookwood Cemetery Act. At this time the chapel was in an appalling state of repair, but the bell tower was still in place (7.33). *(Author's collection)*

North station, *c.* 1907. North station faced the Roman Catholic section (plot 119). This postcard view shows part of the station and a funeral train approaching on its return journey to London (7.33). *(Author's collection)*

The Corps of Commissionaires allotment, plot 125. A general view of this burial ground, looking towards Cemetery Pales from Western Avenue. Note the large grey granite obelisk which commemorates Captain Sir Edward Walter, founder of the Corps (8.4). *(Anthony Montan)*

Nicols' family mausoleum, plot 131, *c.* 1979. This buttressed mausoleum is built in the style of a private chapel. It was constructed to contain the mortal remains of Daniel Nicols (died 1897), founder of London's Café Royal (8.9). *(Author's collection)*

Left: Oddfellows' burial ground, plot 130. This picture shows the obelisk commemorating the inauguration of the ground on 14 October 1861 (8.10). *(Anthony Montan)*

Below: Thomas Blackwood (died 1847) plot 122: another memorial that pre-dates the opening of the cemetery. Blackwood was a Swedish engineer (8.13). *(Anthony Montan)*

Left: Daniel Charles Solander (died 1782), plot 122: the Swedish botanist who accompanied Joseph Banks on Captain Cook's voyage in the *Endeavour* (1768–71) (8.13). *(Anthony Montan)*

John William Anson (died 1881), plot 118. Anson was instrumental in the opening of the Actors' Acre at Brookwood in June 1858 (8.14). *(Anthony Montan)*

Sir Percy Girouard (died 1932), plot 123. His headstone incorporates a circular inset depicting Christ crucified, alpha and omega, and the PX (or *chi-rho*) (8.18). *(Anthony Montan)*

The former Catholic chapel, plot 124, 1980. Built in 1899 by Harris & Company, the chapel was designed by Cyril Tubbs. In recent years it was hardly used until gutted by fire in 1989. It was subsequently restored by Mr Guney as the only inter-denominational chapel within the cemetery. This view shows the chapel in its original form (8.16). *(Brian Parsons collection)*

Polish Military Cemetery. This memorial faces Long Avenue and depicts the Polish eagle within a recess. It also serves as an altar during memorial services held here (9.4). *(Anthony Montan)*

Czechoslovakian Military Cemetery. This large monument serves as a general memorial to all Czechoslovakian servicemen and women who lost their lives during the Second World War (9.5). *(Anthony Montan)*

Royal Air Force Shelter and memorial. Designed by (Sir) Edward Maufe, the shelter is constructed of Portland stone with York paving in front. It includes a vaulted cloister with three arches, flanked by two curved wing walls. The shelter was completed in 1947 (9.8). *(Anthony Montan)*

The British Military Cemetery, *c.* 1925. This early view of the recently completed original military cemetery shows the Cross of Sacrifice to the right and the various national plots in front. In the distance may be seen the records and reception lodge of the Brookwood American Cemetery (9.10). *(Lyndon Davies, Past Images collection)*

Lieutenant Roger Douglas (died 1919), plot 4 Row H Grave 1. Lieutenant Douglas and Lieutenant J.S. Leslie Ross (buried in plot 4 Row J Grave 1) were killed on 13 November 1919 when their aircraft crashed on the first leg of the England to Australia air race. They were buried with full military honours in separate graves at Brookwood on 17 November 1919. This picture shows the wreaths for Lieutenant Douglas shortly after the funerals had taken place. Note the original wooden crosses painted white: these were used to mark the grave spaces before the permanent headstones were provided (9.10). *(Lyndon Davies, Past Images collection)*

American Memorial Chapel. Designed in the neoclassical style by Egerton Swartwout, John R. Pope and Harry B. Cresswell. The chapel commemorates 563 American servicemen, all of whom were either lost or buried at sea. Regular memorial services are still held here, as shown in the photograph (9.11). *(Anthony Montan)*

American Memorial Chapel, interior. Opposite the entrance is the altar. High up in the wall are six of the eighteen stained-glass windows designed by Reginald Hallward. Above the altar is the dedication 'With God is Their Reward'. Either side of the altar can be seen some of the memorial panels listing the names of the missing, along with the flags of the Allies (9.11). *(Anthony Montan)*

The Brookwood (Russia) Memorial, commemorating those who died in Russia during both world wars. Completed in 1983, it stands on the site of part of the 1942–4 extension to the Brookwood American Cemetery (9.13). *(Anthony Montan)*

Parsee (Zoroastrian) burial ground, *c.* 1907. This postcard view shows part of the mausoleum commemorating the life of Nowrosjee N. Wadia (died 1899) on the left. The main entrance to this area is to the right of the picture. The photograph was taken behind the mausoleum to Jamsetji Tata, looking towards the old Muslim burial ground (9.18). *(Brian Parsons collection)*

The Tata family mausoleums. Shown here is the unique trio of family mausoleums. From left to right they commemorate Sir Dorabji Tata (died 1932) and his wife Mehrbai, Lady Tata (died 1931), Jamsetji Tata (died 1904) and Ratan Tata (died 1918) (9.18). *(Anthony Montan)*

Turkish Air Force burial ground, plot 128/M1. This allotment includes fourteen members of the Turkish Air Force who were killed during the Second World War. In the far corner is the grave of Arif Bey (died 1836) and, just to the left, the small stone commemorating the fifteen victims of the Gatwick air crash of 17 February 1959 (9.21). *(Anthony Montan)*

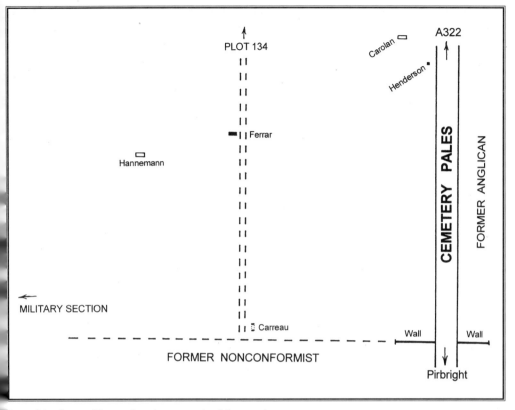

Part of the former Nonconformist pauper burial ground.

composition was largely in madrigals and part-songs, including *Is She Not Beautiful?* (1845, a prize glee), and the tune 'Leominster', associated with the hymn *A Few More Years Shall Roll*. Because of drink, Martin sank from a position of musical influence to one of destitution. He died at Bolingbroke House Hospital, Wandsworth, and was buried in a pauper's grave.

Another anonymous grave in this section contains the body of **John Lynch** (*c*. 1832–66), a Fenian.[9] Lynch was a former publican who became a legal clerk and lodged in Cork City. He became involved with the Cork City Fenians and attended seditious meetings in public houses, took part in military drill and lectures and was present outside the city when 400 Fenians were inspected by an American envoy. Lynch was convicted on the word of an informer, John Warner, who stated that Lynch was an 'A' (or colonel) in the Fenian organisation in Cork. Lynch was found to own an old shotgun and sword, and was convicted of treason and felony by Judge Keogh on 14 December 1865. During his trial letters to his girlfriend Bridget Noonan were used in evidence. They revealed his expectation of a Fenian rising and also his sense of humour. Evidence was also submitted concerning Lynch's weak chest and constitution. Overall the evidence used to convict him was fairly weak for a sentence of ten years' penal servitude: he appears to have been convicted largely on the evidence given by the informer who caused his arrest.

Lynch was first sent to Pentonville. In December 1865, owing to a chest infection, he was moved to the hospital at Woking prison. Other inmates at Woking included O'Donovan Rossa, Captain Richard O'Sullivan Burje, Captain Timothy Deasy, Brian Dillon and the writer Charles Kickham.[10] Here is a description of Lynch's experience at Woking Prison by John Creasy:

John Lynch was sentenced by an extraordinary tribunal in December 1865 and died at Woking Prison in April 1866 [*sic*]. Whatever may be the cause to which the jury has attributed his death, I confirm, and am able to furnish proof, that his death was accelerated by the cruelty of the prison warders.

To be imprisoned in the heart of winter in a cold cell for twenty-three hours out of twenty-four, insufficiently clad, sleeping on a hard board with a log of wood as a pillow and two worn blankets weighing barely ten pounds as one's only protection against the excessive cold, deprived through an inexpressibly fine stroke of cruelty of even covering our frozen limbs with our clothes which we were forced to put outside our cell door, given unhealthy, meagre nourishment, having no exercise apart from a daily walk lasting three-quarters of an hour in a cage about 20ft long by 6ft wide designed for the worst type of criminals: such privation and suffering would break even an iron constitution. So it is not surprising that a person as delicate as Lynch should succumb to it almost immediately. On arrival at the prison Lynch asked for permission to keep his flannels on. His request was rudely refused. 'If you refuse I shall be dead in three months' he replied on that occasion. Ah, little did I suspect that his words would come true. I could not imagine that Ireland was to lose one of her most devoted, ardent and noble sons so soon, and that I myself was to lose a tried and trusted friend.

At the beginning of March I noticed that my friend was looking very ill and one day I took advantage of the gaoler's brief absence to ask him about his health. He replied that he was dying, that he had consulted the doctor several times, but that the latter had not paid the slightest attention to his complaints. His cough was so violent that although my cell was a long distance from his, I could hear it day and night resounding along the empty corridors. One jailer even told me, 'Number 7's time will soon be up – he should have been in hospital a month ago. I've often seen ordinary prisoners there looking a hundred times healthier than him.'

One day in April I looked out of my cell and saw a skeleton-like figure dragging itself along with difficulty and leaning on the bars for support, with a deathly pale face, glazed eyes and hollow cheeks. It was Lynch. I could not believe it was him until he looked at me, smiled and pointed to the ground as if to say: 'I'm finished.' This was the last time I saw Lynch.[11]

Lynch died in Woking Prison on 2 June 1866, aged just 34. He was subsequently buried in the Catholic section of this pauper ground on 6 June. Lynch is commemorated on the National Monument in Cork City.[12]

Also buried in this area is **James Ward** (died 1879), a rescued slave. Ward was rescued from an Arab slave dhow in the Indian Ocean by HMS *Spiteful*. Dubbed 'Mumbo Jumbo' by the crew, he was adopted by an Edinburgh family who had him baptised James Ward in 1870. Ward eventually moved to London as painter-cum-decorator. He died after falling from a ladder near Piccadilly in October 1879.

In some cases the family or relatives of the deceased were subsequently able to purchase the pauper grave and thereby erect a permanent memorial. If you follow the line of the cemetery boundary you will find a headstone just to the right of this. It commemorates **Dr Ludger Carreau** (*c.* 1839–79), 'late of Canada'. Adjacent to the grave is the remains of one of the access paths that led into this area from the main part of the cemetery. Continue along this track until you find the remains of a kerbed memorial to your left. This commemorates **Placido Ferrar** (1835–96), and was 'erected by his loving daughter'. Nearby, and further into this plot, is the headstone with kerbing and footstone commemorating **Hector Louis Charles Hanneman** (1841–98); regrettably the remainder of the inscription is entirely illegible. More difficult to locate, being close to the cemetery wall, is the kerbed memorial to '**J.P.C.**' who died on 10 December 1921. This commemorates **Joseph P. Carolan** (*c.* 1851–1921) who died in the Westminster Infirmary. Adjacent to this grave, and closer to the wall, are the remains of the granite memorial to **William Henry Henderson** (*c.* 1860–1923), who also died in the Westminster Infirmary.

Continue along Western Avenue. The next section is to the right of the path.

8.7. Latvian ground [plot 127]

The Latvian ground was opened in 1952 as recorded on the small monument situated near the left-hand entrance to the plot. This part of the ground contains a large central monument with inscription and cross and forms the original part of the Latvian cemetery. To the right of this section is a prominent gateway erected in memory of **Ilze Rotbachs** and the Latvian Evangelical Lutheran Church.

The next headstone may be found on the other side of the main path.

8.8. Bennett family grave [plot 134]

John Bennett (*c.* 1815–94) was an author and publisher. His books include *Night and Day, or Better Late Than Never* (London, 1858); *Tom Fox, or the Revelations of a Detective* (London, 1860); *The Life and Career of a London Errand Boy* (London, 1865); *My Wife's Earnings, a Tale of the Married Women's Property Act* (London, 1873); *John Bull's Daughters* (London, 1876) and *Simon Peter and Pio Nono at the Gates of Heaven* (London, 1879).

    Mary Bennett (*c.* 1813–1899), his wife, was also a writer. She wrote historical novels including *The Gipsy Bride, or the Miser's Daughter* (London, 1841); *Madge Gordon, or the Mistletoe Bough* (London, 1843); *The Cottage Girl, or the Marriage-Day* (London, 1853); *The Orphan's Sisters, or the Lover's Secret* (London, 1860); *Stella* (London, 1864) and *Elinor Clare, or the Haunted Oak* (London, 1867).

    Bennett was also a pioneer of the Field Lane Mission. Based in Vine Street, Clerkenwell, the mission was established in 1842 to assist the destitute and homeless. The charity maintained destitute children and adults and provided dinners to ragged children who would otherwise starve. The mission maintained a servants' training home, so that work could be found for some of those the charity assisted, and it ran an industrial school for girls and boys that was based in Hampstead. Its work continues to this day, although it has been renamed the Field Lane Foundation, providing care and opportunity for elderly and physically disabled people and homeless families.

*Continue to the T junction and turn left. The next plot is to your right, immediately before the **military cemeteries**.*

8.9. The original Catholic ground [plot 131]

This is the earliest Roman Catholic burying ground at Brookwood. The one-acre plot was set aside for Catholics under the terms of an agreement dated 27 April 1859. The ground was consecrated by the Roman Catholic Bishop of Southwark and, at the time, was the only consecrated ground in his diocese near London. Since then it has been considerably enlarged by the 'new' Catholic grounds (see below); nevertheless this area is still used. Among the graves in this section are:

    Air-crash victims.[13] This low memorial has a headstone comprising three panels. The right-hand panel commemorates 'those who lost their lives in the air-crash of 5 October 1945 when returning to their liberated country Czechoslovakia'. The centre panel lists the names of thirteen of the victims, while the left-hand panel repeats the inscription in Czechoslovakian. The accident took place when a Liberator aircraft crashed in flames at Elvetham, Hants, shortly after taking off. The plane was carrying eighteen Czechoslovakian citizens back to their own country, and was one of several arranged for the repatriation of Czech citizens from Britain. There was a crew of five, also Czechoslovakian. Of the twenty-three victims, thirteen were subsequently buried here at Brookwood. The dead included **Miss Marina Paulinyova**, Vice-Chairman of the Czechoslovakian Red Cross in London, eight other women and five children. The official flight list included twenty-two names and the identity of the last was thought to be the wife of one of the flight crew. As a result of this tragedy the repatriation by air of Czechoslovakian citizens was stopped, and the journeys were made by sea to Ostend, continuing by rail across Belgium and Germany.[14]

Frederick George Lee (1832–1902). Theological writer. Educated at Thame Grammar School and St Edmund Hall, Oxford, Lee was ordained in 1854. He was assistant minister of Berkeley Chapel, London (1858–9) at the time of the ritualist riots. Lee showed sympathy with **Father Mackonochie** and others by preaching and taking part in services at St George-in-the-East. He then moved to St John's, Aberdeen, before returning to London in 1867 as vicar of All Saints', Lambeth. This church was opposite one of the entrances to the LNC's original London terminus. Lee was its final incumbent as the church was acquired by the LSWR on 1 November 1899 and subsequently demolished prior to the complete rebuilding of Waterloo station. Lee had advanced High Church views. He founded the Association for Promoting the Union of Christendom in 1857, with the object of uniting the Churches of Rome, England and Russia. Lee also founded the Order of Corporate Reunion, which aimed to restore to the Church of England valid orders supposedly lost at the Reformation. He was also a writer of history, archaeology, theology and poetry, as well as being an active journalist. Lee was sometime editor of the *Church News*, the *Church Herald* and the *Penny Post*, and a leader writer for *John Bull*. Lee was received into the Catholic Church in 1901. His name does not appear on the headstone, but it may be identified by his wife's name, **Elvira Louisa**, who had previously joined the Catholic Church and who died in 1890.

Princess Mechtilde Lichnowsky, née Arco-Zinneberg (1879–1958). Austrian authoress. The daughter of Count Arco and the great-granddaughter of the Austrian empress, Maria Theresa. She married Prince Charles Max Lichnowsky, the German Ambassador to London (1912–14), in 1904.[15] Together they travelled widely in pre-First World War Europe and Egypt. Her first success was the travelogue *Gods, Kings and Animals in Egypt* (Leipzig, 1913).[16] Her prose, plays and essays are all eloquent discussions of the decline of an aristocratic European culture. After her husband's death in 1928 she subsequently married Major Ralph Harding Peto in 1937 (who died in 1945). In 1946 she published *Conversations with Sybaris*, which was a devastating critique of Nazi ideology.[17] She died in poverty.

Nicols' family mausoleum. This is one of the few surviving mausolea in the former Nonconformist sections of the cemetery, most being situated in the former Anglican sections. It has been recommended for statutory listing by Woking Borough Council. Buried within this fine building are:

Daniel Thevenon Nicols (1833–97), the founder of London's Café Royal. He was born in Paris and was originally a coachbuilder. His French name was Daniel Nicolas Thevenon, but it was subsequently anglicised to Daniel Thevenon Nicols. He and his wife **Celestine** then purchased and operated a successful wine business from about 1852; it was sold at a profit in 1862. They decided to move to England and established the first Café Royal at 15 Glasshouse Street in 1863. The business expanded into two other premises in Regent Street and Air Street but the main restaurant became centred on Regent Street. They also owned the land upon which the Empire Theatre, Leicester Square, was subsequently built. Nicols built a country house just outside Surbiton. Called Regent House, it was set within a large estate that lay between the present Park Road and Berrylands Road across to the railway. A deer park was subsequently added to his domain. When Daniel Nicols died he left a vast fortune that was estimated at £600,000. The mausoleum was constructed for the reception of his mortal remains, and his body lay in a temporary vault while it was completed. His Surbiton estate was eventually sold off and the area is now known as Berrylands.

Celestine Nicols, née Lacoste (*c.* 1832–1916), his wife, outlived the rest of her immediate family. After Daniel's death the management of the Café Royal was entrusted to Celestine and her son-in-law **Georges Pigache**. But Georges died in 1898 and so the running of the restaurant remained with Celestine until her death.

Emma Josephine Pilet (*c.* 1856–1912) was their daughter, and also rests within.

Georges Alexandre Pigache (*c.* 1851–98) was **Emma**'s first husband. He assisted in the management of the Café Royal. The decoration of the Café Royal, with its 'N' surrounded by a laurel wreath and surmounted by an imperial crown, is down to Georges Pigache. Daniel Nicols would have removed this imperial symbol, had not his son-in-law explained that the 'N' stood not for Napoleon but for Nicols! Georges had a particular interest in the catering arrangements and the kitchens; consequently he acquired a large girth. Every day, when he commuted from Surbiton to London, three burly porters eased him into and out of his railway carriage. When he died he was placed in a specially constructed coffin. The banisters had to be removed from the staircase before the casket could be borne downstairs. Georges is buried to the right of the mausoleum, because his coffin was too large to go inside! [18]

There are poignant reminders that infant deaths touched even the richest of families. Also buried here are **Juliette Pigache** (1893–96), 'our dearly loved child, for ever mourned and so missed', and **Blanche Pigache** (*c.* 1878–97).

The next section is to the right of the Catholic ground.

8.10. The Oddfellows' burial ground [plot 130]

The Independent Order of Oddfellows (Manchester Unity), a benevolent and fraternal association founded in the eighteenth century, reserved this plot in the cemetery under an agreement dated April 1859. This allowed for the burial of deceased members of the various lodges of the Metropolitan District of the Society. The prominent central obelisk commemorates the inauguration of the plot, which took place on 14 October 1861. The carving deserves close attention: note the arms of the Order, the symbolism used (the eye of truth, the cross keys, the beehive representing industry, the hourglass and the hand pointing heavenwards), and the inverted torches (representing mortality) on each corner of the base. Note that the plot actually extended up to Pine Avenue (adjacent to **Brookwood station**), and further memorials identifiable as deceased Oddfellows may be found there.

Among those buried at the Long Avenue end of the plot is **Thomas Fletcher** (*c.* 1797–1877). Initiated in the Salopian Lodge, Shrewsbury, in about 1826. Fletcher then moved to London where he joined the St Olave's Lodge in 1836. His memorial records that Fletcher had '50 years of continued usefulness to the Order'. The monument was erected by fellow members of the South London District.

Revd Robert George Le Maire (*c.* 1793–1872). This unusual gothic-style obelisk memorial commemorates the LNC's first Nonconformist Chaplain. Le Maire was employed at a salary of £2 a week[19] and undertook the majority of burial services in this part of the cemetery from its opening on 13 November 1854 until his death. The inscription panel on the left records that the memorial was erected by the Oddfellows' friendly society, 'as a mark of affection and esteem'.

From here, take the path on the right-hand side of the Oddfellows' ground and turn left, approachin
Brookwood station. *The next grave is opposite the entrance to the station.*

8.11. Professor Dr Ihsan Barbouti (1927–1990) [plot 129]

Barbouti was a London-based Iraqi architect and businessman. He built the Rabta Chemica
complex in Libya using his German-based company, thereby breaking UN sanctions. The plan
was destroyed by the Americans in 1990; it has probably since been rebuilt elsewhere. Tw
weeks after a warrant was issued for his arrest Barbouti died of a heart attack. He had previousl
faked his death and reappeared, and there has been speculation that his grave at Brookwood i
empty.

8.12. Brookwood station

When the cemetery opened on 13 November 1854 it was not served by any station on the mai
line. Access to the cemetery – by relatives and friends of the deceased, or other visitors – wa
limited to the daily funeral train, or by hiring suitable transport from Woking. This station
originally called Brookwood (Necropolis), was opened on 1 June 1864. The costs of it
construction were largely met by the LNC, which also provided the land. It was enlarged i
1890 and virtually rebuilt in 1903 when the main line was quadrupled: the old Down platform
(on the cemetery side) was demolished to provide room for the two new main lines. A new
platform with waiting rooms was provided on the cemetery side, while the buildings on the U
(or Brookwood) side were altered and extended. Railway services operated by South West Train
still use this station, the journey time to London Waterloo being about forty-five minutes. Th
area just outside the station entrance is where the private railway line entered the cemeter
grounds. The gateway to the right of the entrance, erected after the First World War, was paic
for by the War Office at the time when the original **military cemetery** was being laid out.

Turn right, away from the station, following Pine Avenue. At the junction with Long Avenue, turn right and int
the Swedish section.

8.13. Swedish ground [plot 122]

This plot dates from 1857 and forms the burial ground of the Swedish Congregation in London
The Swedish Congregation dates back to 1710, and its first London church was built in
Wapping in 1728. The present church in Harcourt Street, Marylebone, was built in 1911. A
separate Swedish Seaman's Church was established in the mid-nineteenth century.
    The section is screened from Long Avenue by large banks of rhododendrons and mature
trees. Two stone obelisks mark the entrance: one has the inscription in English, the other in
Swedish. The interior of the ground is delightful: trees and shrubs screen the plot from othe
parts of the cemetery and there is an avenue of silver birches down the centre of the ground
Among the many interesting memorials here are:
    Thomas Blackwood (*c.* 1820–47). Swedish engineer who died at Greenwich. His memoria
includes a fine carved portrait of the deceased, along with a beam engine. This suggests tha
Blackwood may have been involved in the mining industry. His body would have been removec
here from the Swedish Church in London after the opening of the ground.
    Captain Fricis Freienbergs (1892–1941). Captain of the SS *Katvaldis*, who died on the
North Sea in November 1941. His unusual memorial is shaped like a lighthouse.
    Dr Per Jacobsson (1894–1963). Economist. Jacobsson was born at Tanum, Sweden, anc
took his first examinations in economics before the First World War. In 1917 he was appointec
assistant secretary of the Swedish Commission on Economic Defence Preparedness. Jacobsson

joined the Secretariat of the League of Nations in 1920 and remained there until 1928. He returned to Sweden and became the economic adviser to the Bank for International Settlements in Basle. While there, Jacobsson could network with Europe's leading central bankers. His handling of the economic department was unrivalled and the annual reports of the Bank were seen as model financial papers. In 1956 Jacobsson became the Chairman of the International Monetary Fund, one of the world's leading financial institutions. He transformed the IMF from an automatic dollar provider into a broadly based support for all currencies. His skills were proven at the end of 1961 when he managed to achieve a compromise between the United States and Europe, thereby avoiding a major international financial crisis. Jacobsson married **Violet Mary Nye** (1889–1979) of Farnham, Surrey, in 1921; one of Jacobsson's sons-in-law is Sir Roger Bannister.

Gustavus Adam Baron von Nolcken (1739–1812). Swedish Envoy extraordinary and plenipotentiary to the Court of St James's. He read the eulogy at **Solander**'s funeral in the Swedish Church in London in 1782. His body was exhumed from the Swedish Church, Princes Square, and was reburied here with his wife on 19 February 1913.

Professor Carl Wahlbohm (1810–58). Professor at Konsterna, Stockholm. This is an interesting early memorial with the cross contained within a circle.

Daniel Charles Solander (1733–82). Botanist. Solander was born at Norrland, Sweden, and became a pupil of Carl von Linné (otherwise known as Carolus Linnaeus). He moved to England in 1760 and was instrumental in introducing the Linnaean system to this country.[20] In 1763 he was appointed assistant librarian cataloguing the natural history collections at the British Museum. Solander accompanied Joseph Banks[21] on Captain James Cook's voyage in the *Endeavour* (1768–71) at a salary of £400. During this voyage Solander had a narrow escape from death by sleeping in the snow on Tierra del Fuego. Solander was the first Swede to circumnavigate the globe and one of the earliest Europeans to visit and study the south-west Pacific. Solander also accompanied Banks on his expedition to Iceland (1772). He acted as secretary and librarian to Banks (1772–3) and was Keeper of the Natural History Department of the British Museum (1773–82). He died at Banks's house in Soho Square, London. Solander published very little. He edited Linné's *Elementa Botanica* (Upsala, 1756), but his death prevented the publication of his descriptions of the plants collected on the voyages of the *Endeavour*. However, his manuscripts survive in the British Museum and these valuable notes have been extensively exploited by botanists ever since. Solander was originally buried in London. His body was exhumed from the Swedish Church, Princes Square, and reburied here on 19 February 1913. The memorial was thoroughly cleaned in November 1954 at a cost of £5 10s 0d.[22]

Leave the Swedish ground and turn left. The next section is immediately opposite Pine Avenue.

8.14. The Actors' Acre [plot 118]

This area was reserved for use by the Dramatic, Equestrian & Musical Sick Fund, founded in 1855 by **John William Anson**. The plot was opened subsequent to an agreement dated 2 June 1858. An important factor in choosing Brookwood was that funerals could take place on Sundays, which was not then a common practice. This was more convenient for members of the theatrical profession as they found it distressing to attend a family funeral during the week and then have to play in the theatre the same evening. A special service to inaugurate the ground took place on Wednesday 9 June 1858, led by the Revd Horace Roberts. A total of 569 burials have been identified so far, the earliest being in July 1857 and the latest in July 1984. The Brookwood Cemetery Society has started to map some of the previously unmarked graves in this plot, and some of these are now marked by the low white posts in various parts of the ground. The selection used for this section concentrates on those with a surviving memorial.[23]

John William Anson (1817–81). Actor, born William John Rust. His debut was at the Theatre Royal, Bath, in 1842. Anson was Manager of the Dundee, Perth, Montrose and Inverness Theatrical Companies (1848–53) and was based at Astley's between 1853 and 1859. He became treasurer and acting manager of the Adelphi (1858–78). Anson founded the Dramatic, Equestrian & Musical Sick Fund (1855). Associated with this, Anson was also instrumental in founding the Royal Dramatic College at Maybury, near Woking (1859), and inaugurating this burial ground in the cemetery. Anson is buried within the enclosed family plot opposite his memorial. The obelisk opposite commemorates his wife, **Barbara Rust Anson, née Johnson** (1827–57). She died from tuberculosis and was one of the first people to be buried in the Actors' Acre.

Alexander Brown (*c*. 1801–68). He worked in the offices of Anson's Fund and was loved by everyone for his kindness. Brown was a descendant of Rob Roy McGregor, and **J.W. Anson**'s uncle by marriage.

Llewellyn Cadwaladr (*c*. 1860–1909). Singer. He appeared in many performances of the Gilbert & Sullivan Savoy Operas. He sang with the D'Oyly Carte Company on tour (1879–95). In 1881 he made his debut in America at the Standard Theatre, New York, in *Patience*, singing the Duke. The production was the greatest financial success the house ever knew, taking $100,000. His grave has a white marker, with the burial number 163,543.

William Berry Clarkson (*c*. 1861–1934). Wigmaker and costumier, by special appointment to Queen Victoria and King Edward VII. He took over his father's business in 1875 and for fifty years was perruquier to the theatres of London and many international stars, including both Sarah Bernhardt[24] and Adelina Patti.[25] His father, **William Henry Clarkson** (*c*. 1820–78), is buried nearby. He was a wigmaker to the legal and theatrical professions from 1833. Clarkson is also commemorated by a blue plaque on the building in Wardour Street where his business premises used to be.

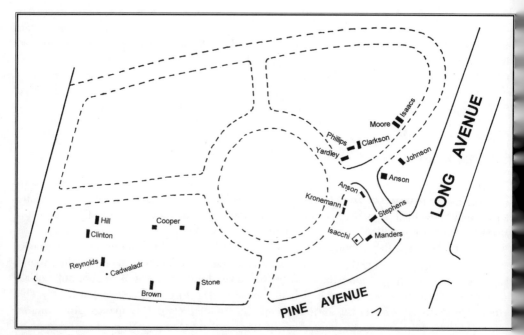

The Actors' Acre.

John Wade Clinton (*c.* 1804–80). A resident of the Royal Dramatic College at Maybury. He was the author of the catalogue of pictures and theatrical ephemera that belonged to the College.

Frederick Fox Cooper (1806–79). Playwright, newspaper proprietor and dramatic critic. His plays include stage versions of several of Charles Dickens's novels and short stories. He was often imprisoned for debt while managing theatres. There are at least twenty members of his family from four generations buried in the Actors' Acre.

Reynard Cooper (*c.* 1857–92). Grandson of the above and son of Harwood Cooper, who was an actor at the Adelphi Theatre. Reynard Cooper was also known as **'Rene Renad'**. He died aged 35 when he accidentally poisoned himself with cyanide of potassium, which he thought was lavender water.

Ellen Hill, née Shaw (died 1866). Actress and wife of William John Hill, the composer. She acted with 'Master Betty' and Charles Kean, and was a leading actress at the minor theatres.

Rebecca Isaacs (1828–77). A singer, who first appeared on stage at the City Theatre, London, in 1835. She travelled with the Distins as a singer under the name 'Miss Zuchelli' (1838). She acted at Drury Lane, taking the leading roles in English operas (1846), and was Directress of Operas at the Strand Theatre (1852–3 and 1855). Her voice was a soprano of great compass and sweetness. Her husband, **Thomas Roberts** (*c.* 1831–76), was a dental surgeon and acting manager of the Princess's Theatre.

Rebecca Francisco Isacchi (*c.* 1819–72). Probably the equestrienne 'Madame Francisco'. Her second husband was **Francis Thomas Francisco Isacchi** (*c.* 1826–82), an equestrian. He and his brothers, John and Louis, appeared with their father at Astley's Amphitheatre as 'The Francisco family'. The brothers appeared with Cooke's and Hengler's Circuses until John's death in 1862, following an accident.

Samuel Johnson (1830–1900). Actor, and a brother of **Barbara Anson**. He was born in Ayrshire, the son of a local actor and manager of several theatres. Johnson first appeared on stage at the Maryport Theatre, Cumberland, in 1844 as Bartolo in *The Wife*. In 1853 Johnson became a partner with John Coleman in the management of the Theatre Royal, Sheffield. In 1855 he moved to the Lyceum Theatre, Sunderland. His London debut took place at the Lyceum in 1859 in the Savage Club burlesque of *The Forty Thieves*. Johnson toured many provincial theatres and stayed at the Theatre Royal, Dublin, for the entire period 1864–74. From 1878 and for the next twenty years, Johnson was an esteemed member of Sir Henry Irving's company at the Lyceum Theatre. (Johnson had been at the Lyceum in September 1856 when Irving made his first stage appearance.) His last appearance was as Maître Van Spennen in *The Black Tulip* at the Haymarket on 28 October 1899. Johnson was secretary of the Lyceum Benevolent Fund, a well-known Freemason, and was Master of the St Asaph Lodge.

Ludwig Christian Kronemann (1863–99). A Danish acrobat who died aged 36 following an accident during a performance at the Empire Theatre, Leicester Square, London. His family now live in America, and they paid for this memorial to be placed in the Actors' Acre. The exact site of his grave has only recently been identified, and it is intended to move the memorial in due course.

Thomas Manders (1797–1859). Manders originally worked in the one pound note department at the Bank of England until the post was abolished in 1821. He adopted a theatrical career as a 'richly humorous actor of comic parts' and spent sixteen years at the Queen's Theatre. He was sometime landlord of the Sun Tavern in Long Acre and the Marquis of Granby in Knightsbridge. His wife, **Louisa Manders** (1801–80), suffered several accidents during her long career as an actress, including a fall from the flies at Sadler's Wells Theatre in 1834. Later she was celebrated for playing old women.

Daking William Carter Moore (1797–1870). The son of Carter Moore, a solicitor, and father of the Revd Carter Moore, Curate of Woking and Honorary Chaplain of the Royal Dramatic College.

Richard Empson Phillips (died 1872). The stage manager and Chairman of the Dramatic, Equestrian & Musical Sick Fund. His father, **Richard Randall Empson Phillips**, was the first person to be buried in the Actors' Acre, on 18 July 1857.

Alfred E. Reynolds (died 1879). For many years connected with the York circuit both as an actor and treasurer. He died in the Royal Dramatic College at Maybury.

Mrs Jane ('Grannie') Stephens (c. 1813–96). Mrs Stephens first appeared on stage at the Olympic Theatre in 1840. She enjoyed a long and distinguished career, during which she was considered the best actress of 'old women's parts' – hence her nickname of 'Grannie'. She was cremated at St John's, Woking.

Philip Stone (c. 1781–1863). Property man at the Theatre Royal, Drury Lane, at the time of the great actresses Sarah Siddons and Mrs Jordan. *The Era* reported that, 'though he never raised a laugh before the curtain, he, by his quaint manner, caused many a hearty one behind it'. A small man with a pronounced lisp, he also ran a shop selling savoury relishes, hot sheep's-heads and baked potatoes in Old Drury Lane. Stone died in the Workhouse.

William Yardley (1849–1900). Amateur actor, drama critic and cricketer. Yardley was born in Bombay and was educated at Rugby and Cambridge. He trained as a barrister but was also one of the greatest amateur cricketers of his time. Yardley played for Cambridge University, and was the first person to score a century in a university match (in 1870), a feat he repeated two years later when he scored 103 against Oxford; this record remained unbroken for another fifty-three years. Yardley played for Kent (1868–77) and was a brilliant batsman. He wrote successful pantomimes and burlesques for the Gaiety and Drury Lane theatres, including *Little Jack Shepherd* and *The Passport*. Yardley was the drama critic for the *Pink 'Un*, and wrote a regular column in the *Sporting Times*.

Leave the Actors' Acre and turn right, looking down Long Avenue.

8.15. Long Avenue

Long Avenue stretches from the site of **North station** (just behind), right through to the **military cemeteries**. It is one of the longest in the cemetery, and reminds us of the original plans of the LNC for Brookwood. Drawings for the use of further parts of the company's estate for burial purposes include several long avenues up to 3 miles long, stretching from hereabouts towards Hook Heath, running parallel with the main railway and lined throughout with trees. At Hook Hill the avenues would have converged on the intended 'national mausoleum' church, forming a focal point for the London Necropolis. This view down Long Avenue, with its splendid planting of redwoods, reminds us of what might have been.

Turn left, into Oak Avenue. The areas around the chapel form the 'new' Catholic grounds.

8.16. Former Catholic chapel [plot 124]

This chapel was built in 1899 by Harris & Company, whose tender was £715 plus £44 for the seating.[26] The architect was probably **Cyril Tubbs**. The chapel was dedicated to the Holy Souls, and was consecrated by the Revd Francis Bourne, Bishop of Southwark,[27] on 6 November 1899. It stands in the centre of the new Catholic plots. The chapel was derelict when it was gutted by fire in about March 1989. It was subsequently rebuilt, however, and serves as the only inter-denominational chapel within the cemetery grounds. The next graves are all located in the sections surrounding this chapel.

8.17. Caroll Gibbons (1903–1954) [plot 124]

Pianist and dance band leader. Born in Clinton, Massachusetts, Gibbons sailed to England on board the RMS *Olympic* in 1924 with Rudy Vallee, who had been invited to play in the Savoy

Havana Band as saxophonist. On hearing Gibbons's captivating piano playing, the entertainments manager for the Savoy Hotels Group immediately engaged him as pianist for the Boston Orchestra at the Berkeley Hotel. From there Gibbons quickly moved on as leader of the 'Savoy Sylveans' and then the 'Savoy Orpheans'. The band was instantly recognisable, with Gibbons's magical piano playing. From 1932 he began recording under his own name. Through the radio he became a household name, playing popular tunes such as *A Nightingale Sang In Berkeley Square* (recorded June 1940), *Dancing In The Dark* (recorded January 1932) and *I'm Going To Get Lit Up* (recorded April 1943). His signature tune was *On the Air*. His last recording was made on 1 April 1950 and marked the end of a remarkable twenty-five-year recording career. Fortunately most of these are preserved and may still be enjoyed today.

8.18. Sir (Edouard) Percy (Cranwill) Girouard (1867–1932) [plot 123]

Canadian railway engineer and colonial administrator. Girouard was born in Montreal and was commissioned in the Royal Engineers in 1888. He served in the Dongola expeditionary force (1896) and was awarded the DSO. Girouard constructed and managed the Nile Railway whereby the reconquest of the Sudan was accomplished by Kitchener (1896–8). Churchill referred to his enormous efforts and achievements in his book of the campaign: 'Nothing was forgotten. Every want was provided for; every difficulty was foreseen; every requisite was noted.'[28] Girouard was subsequently made Director of the South African Railways (1899–1902). He was appointed High Commissioner (1907) and Governor (1908–9) of Northern Nigeria, and later became Governor of the British East African Protectorate (1909–12). Girouard joined the Board of Armstrong Whitworth & Company in 1912. Lloyd George appointed him Director General of Munitions Supply (1915–17). One of his first tasks was to investigate the regional organisation of munitions firms. Lloyd George later described Girouard as:

> a man of great natural gifts and accomplishments, and he was credited with possessing a resourcefulness which approximated to the genius of purposeful action. In addition to that he was a man of considerable charm, with a pleasant sense of humour fortified by much interesting and entertaining reminiscence. I discovered that he had a gift of persuasive speech which was invaluable at the meetings we held in London and in the provinces to stimulate co-operation. Although he was primarily a railway man and his success had been achieved in that sphere, his association with Armstrong's had furnished him with experience in the manufacture of every kind of munition of war.[29]

8.19. Charles G. Miller (c. 1891–1961) [plot 119]

Employee of the LNC. In 1937 Miller succeeded **George Pole** as Secretary, and in turn succeeded **John B. Walker** as Managing Director in 1943. He retained this post until the LNC ceased to exist as an independent company in 1959–60. In this position Miller was the driving force behind the LNC's post-war plans and reorganisation, following the effective destruction of the company's main London office in the Westminster Bridge Road. He therefore planned the transfer of the company's London station to the Southern Railway, established the new office at 123 Westminster Bridge Road, supervised the transfer of the LNC's headquarters from London to Brookwood, and planned the several post-war alterations within the cemetery, including the removal of the cemetery railway and in its place the creation of a pathway through the Nonconformist section. Miller also saw the need for the LNC to fully embrace cremation by opening the **Glades of Remembrance**, and was closely involved with both private Acts of Parliament in two major attempts to open a crematorium within the cemetery. At the same time Miller continued to expand the LNC's network of local offices in London and the south-east through the acquisition of businesses such as Messrs Hatt and Frederick Paine.[30]

8.20. Margaret, Duchess of Argyll (1912–1993) [plot 119]

One of the most photographed and publicised society beauties of the twentieth century. The daughter of George Whigham, she married first the American stockbroker and golfer **Charles Sweeny** (see below) in 1933. She was immortalised in Cole Porter's song 'You're the Top', which he wrote especially for her. She remained in London during the war, assisting her husband in forming the Eagle squadrons of American pilots. Divorced in 1947, she then married Ian Douglas Campbell, 11th Duke of Argyll, in 1951.[31] They were involved in a sensational divorce case (1959–63) which attracted huge media interest. In 1975 she published her memoirs, *Forget Not: the Autobiography of Margaret, Duchess of Argyll* (London, W.H. Allen, 1975). The Duchess died in St George's Nursing Home, Pimlico, in July 1993. Although her will expressed her wish to be buried near Inverary Castle (the Argyll family home), this was denied and she was buried with her first husband.

Charles Sweeny (1909–93),[32] her first husband, was an American stockbroker and an excellent golfer. Sweeny also founded the American Eagle squadrons, manned by American volunteer pilots. During the 1930s he was one of the most eligible bachelors in London. He married Margaret Whigham (later Duchess of Argyll) in 1933. In 1939 he helped import American guns, rifles and armoured cars, which were used to form the 1st American Motorised Squadron. After the fall of France, Sweeny suggested the idea of an American volunteer air unit, and the Government agreed that new squadrons could be formed from American volunteer pilots. It should be remembered that at this stage of the war America was still neutral, therefore these pilots were clandestinely recruited in the United States by Sweeny's uncle, Colonel Charles Sweeny, through the Clayton Knight Committee. Many of these pilots came from California, where flying was very popular. The first Eagle squadron was No. 71, formed on 19 September 1940, followed by No. 121 Squadron (formed 14 May 1941) and finally No. 133 Squadron (formed 1 August 1941). In his autobiography Sweeny claims there was to have been a fourth, but twelve of the pilots were drowned during a U-boat attack on the convoy. Although the remaining ten pilots reached England the new squadron was never formed. When America entered the war in December 1941, the three Eagle squadrons were decommissioned and the pilots transferred to the 4th Fighter Group of the United States Army Air Force (29 September 1942).[33] Sweeny and his wife divorced in 1947. He married Aarden Snead in 1958, but they were divorced in 1966. Sweeny attended the unveiling of the memorial to the Eagle squadrons in Grosvenor Square, London, on 12 May 1986.

8.21. Albert Visetti (1846–1928) [plot 123]

Musician. Born in Dalmatia, Visetti gained musical scholarships from the Austrian and Italian governments. He entered the Milan Conservatoire and made friends with Bioto. Visetti was later engaged as a conductor at Nice before moving to Paris. The composer Daniel Auber[34] introduced Visetti to the court of Napoleon III. While in Paris he composed an opera, *Le Trois Mousquetaires*, after meeting Dumas *père* who wrote the libretto. Visetti moved to England in May 1870 and became a champion of British music and musicians. He was naturalised and became one of the foremost professors of singing in the country. Visetti was musical adviser to the soprano Adelina Patti for five years, and wrote *La Diva* especially for her. Among his pupils were John Boland, Lillian Burgess, Jamieson Dodds, Parry Jones, Phyllis Lett, Kirkby Lunn and Agnes Nicholls (Lady Harty). Visetti was one of the professorial staff at the National Training School of Music (later the Royal College of Music). He was Director and Conductor of the Bath Philharmonic Society and wrote two cantatas for the society. Visetti also wrote and translated several books, including a life of Giovanni Palestrina and a biography of Verdi. By marriage, Visetti became stepfather to the novelist Radclyffe Hall. Visetti's death in 1928 was ill-timed for Hall since the arrangements for his funeral occurred at the same time as the publication of *The Well of Loneliness*.[35]

Cross the Catholic area and locate the large mausoleum facing Railway Avenue.

8.22. His Highness Sharif Al-Hussein Ben Ali (*c.* 1919–1998) [plot 119]

This beautiful mausoleum celebrates the life of His Highness Sharif Al-Hussein Ben Ali, who was a member of the Iraqi royal family. He was a cousin of King Faisal II (born 1935, regency 1935–53, deposed and assassinated in 1958), while his father was Prince of Mecca until 1908 and an uncle of King Faisal I (born 1885, reigned 1921–35). The family fled Iraq in 1958 and lived in Lebanon and Britain. His Highness Sharif Al-Hussein Ben Ali married Princess Badia, daughter of King Ali bin Hussein I and aunt of King Faisal II. Their son, Al-Sharif Bin Ali Bin Al-Hussein (born 1956), is the current leader of the Constitutional Monarchy Movement in Iraq.

The building was designed by **Rula Al-Chorbachi** and is the newest mausoleum in the cemetery. It is constructed of Portland stone and includes a gilded dome and beautifully executed script along each side. The setting has only recently been completed by the addition of a surrounding balustrade of reconstituted stone.

Leave the Catholic area and turn right, along Railway Avenue. The next memorial is about halfway down the path and is screened by a low brick wall.

8.23. Dr Reza Fallah (1909–1982) [plot 119]

Oil expert. Graduated from Birmingham University (1932) and obtained his Ph.D. in petroleum technology (1934). Fallah became an influential figure in the Iranian oil industry in the days of the Shah. After the Anglo-Iranian oil dispute (1950), when the Abadan refinery was nationalised, it was Fallah who reactivated the refinery under Iranian control and it became known as 'Fallah's flame'. Subsequently Deputy Managing Director of the National Iranian Oil Company, he exercised considerable authority as the Shah's oil adviser, especially during the 1970s. After the Iranian revolution of 1979 Fallah lived mostly in Britain. He died at his home in Datchet in 1982.

Return to the main part of plot 119. The next memorial is near to the Crescent.

8.24. Stanley Hugh Coryton Roberts (1889–1957) [plot 119]

An outstanding figure in technical education, training and invention in Britain. Roberts founded the British School of Motoring in 1909, and was its first Chairman. Increasingly convinced that this country could maintain its position in the world only by training more people in science and technology, Roberts established the Automobile College in 1923. This was followed by the College of Aeronautical & Automobile Engineering, established at Chelsea in 1924. The young Alec Issigonis[36] was a student there. Roberts was also a great inventor, which extended into gramophones. He invented the Vestone gramophone with its special quality of sound reproduction, and through his experiments met and befriended **Caroll Gibbons**.

The next plot is to the right of this grave, and adjacent to the path.

8.25. The 'New' Actors' Acre [plot 119]

This area adjacent to the Crescent forms an extension to the original **Actors' Acre** in plot 118. It appears to have come into use from December 1931, presumably because the original ground was virtually full. Once again, most of the forty-nine graves identified so far in this area are unmarked, and there are virtually no memorials.

One of those buried here in an unmarked grave is **Rose Norrys** (*c.* 1864–1946). Born in America of Irish parents, her background is obscure. Norrys was highly literate, and she wrote two stories for Christmas editions of *The Theatre*. Her first stage appearances were probably in

1881 in London. During 1882–4 she toured America with Charles Wyndham's Criterion Company, playing in a number of farces. Norrys had considerable success as an actress after she moved from addresses in Covent Garden to High Street, Kensington (from 1888), and to Cheyne Row, Chelsea (from 1890). She had an extraordinary range of roles, some of which may have provided a diversion from her major characters. Norrys was an accomplished comedienne and enjoyed challenging interpretations of the woman on stage. In 1895 she was found wandering the streets and spending nights in Hyde Park. She was eventually sent to the Colney Hatch Asylum suffering from a form of schizophrenia. *The Era* launched a fund to assist her, instigated by its editor, **Edward Ledger**. Tragically, Norrys spent the rest of her life in institutions not knowing who she was. The Actors' Benevolent Fund paid for her funeral.

Behind this area is a private plot, screened by a low conifer hedge.

8.26. Ameer Ali family grave [plot 119]

Among those buried in this small family plot is **Rt Hon. [Syed] Al Razawi Ameer Ali** (1846–1928), an Indian jurist and Islamic leader. His judicial career was largely spent in India. Ameer Ali was the first Muslim to take an MA in Calcutta. He founded the Muslim League, the first Muslim political organisation in India, in 1877. Ameer Ali was one of three Indian judges of the Governor General's Council (1883–5), and was Judge of HM High Court of Judicature, Bengal (1890–1904). He retired and settled in England in 1904. Ameer Ali was the first Indian member of the Privy Council (1909). He founded the British Red Crescent Society and was for several years Chairman of the Woking Mosque Committee, and a keen supporter of the scheme to establish the London Mosque. He wrote many works on history, law and Islam. His first Islamic publication appeared when he was only 24.

    Sir Torick Ameer Ali (1891–1975) was also a judge. Ameer Ali was educated at Marlborough and Christ Church College, Oxford, and was called to the Bar at the Inner Temple. He was Puisne Judge of the High Court, Calcutta (1931–44), Judge of the Federal Court (1943) and was Acting Chief Justice of Bengal (1944). Ameer Ali was adviser to the Secretary of State for India (1944).

    [Syed] Waris Ameer Ali (1886–1975) was a civil servant and administrator. Educated at Wellington College and Balliol College, Oxford, he joined the Indian civil service and served in the United Provinces of Agra and Oudh. He was later appointed District & Sessions Judge of Gonda-cum-Bahraich in Oudh. He retired in 1929. Ameer Ali served as War Services Adviser to the High Commissioner for India (1939–45). He was a member of the India Rifle Team at Bisley (1930–38).

Beyond the rhododendrons is a line of graves beside Railway Avenue. The next grave is towards the right-hand end of these.

8.27. Thomas Ivor Moore (1858–1917) [plot 119]

Civil engineer and Fellow of the Imperial Institute, London. Moore lived in Woking for many years and was a magistrate, Chairman of the Higher Education Committee for Woking and a member of the Wesleyan Church. As recorded on his memorial, Moore was killed during an air raid on London on 13 June 1917. This involved fourteen Gotha aeroplanes that bombed the City and the East End. The raid killed 162 people and wounded another 432. Of these, eighteen children were killed and thirty injured when a bomb hit a school.[37] Liverpool Street station was also hit. The total of 594 dead and injured was the highest for any individual air raid during the whole of the First World War. The raid caused a panic demand for strengthening the air defences of London, so the War Cabinet ordered the return of a fighter squadron from France. **Thomas Moore** (died 1946), his son, was a Colonel in the Royal Tank Regiment.

Chapter Nine

THE MILITARY AND MUSLIM SECTIONS

This chapter covers the western extremity of the Nonconformist side of the cemetery. The military cemeteries take up most of this area and, at 37 acres, they comprise the largest Commonwealth war cemetery in the United Kingdom. The military sections date from 1917, but some earlier 'civilian' sections were formed many years before. They are described in the appropriate numbered items below. To the north of the military cemeteries are the Parsee and Muslim grounds, both the first of their kind in the United Kingdom and both featuring many interesting burials. The main boundaries between the military and Muslim areas are marked first by a screen of rhododendrons and pines and secondly by a wire fence, which is principally there to protect the plants within the military sections from deer and rabbits.

9.1. Annexe to the Czechoslovakian Military Cemetery

Just outside the boundary fence to the Commonwealth War Graves Commission (CWGC) sections and on the left-hand side of **Long Avenue** is the 'annexe' to the **Czechoslovakian Military Cemetery**. The annexe is owned not by the CWGC but by the Czechoslovakian Ex-Servicemen's Association. The distinctively shaped headstones are similar but not identical to the Czechoslovakian section.

Here may be found the grave of **Eduard M. Prchal** (1911–84), the pilot of General Wladyslaw Sikorski's[1] Liberator aircraft, which crashed shortly after taking off from Gibraltar on 4 July 1943. A portion of Prchal's ashes was scattered over the English Channel; the remainder were buried here.

Karel Jan Staller (1896–1975). The designer of the Bren gun. This was designed by Staller in Brno in 1937. The Bren gun was gas-operated and air-cooled with a distinctive banana-shaped magazine, and was developed into one of the most widely used machine guns of its type. The name Bren is an acronym of **Br**no and **En**field, where the British adaptation was made. The British produced it as a .303 calibre, and the gun had a long life even after the Second World War.

Colonel Judr Pavel Svoboda (1916–93). Czech patriot. Svoboda escaped to Syria and joined the Czech Army, fighting in France (1940). Evacuated to England, he joined the RAF. During this time he lectured on conditions in the German concentration camps, for he had been interned during 1938. Shot down in December 1941, he was sent to a POW camp and tried to escape three times. The last attempt was successful and he joined the Czech patriot forces. He was recaptured but managed to escape. After the war he returned with his family to Czechoslovakia until communist persecution led to the family fleeing. They eventually settled in England, although Svoboda was unable to rejoin the RAF on health grounds.[2]

Ivo Tonder (1913–95). Born in Prague, Tonder trained in the Czechoslovakian Air Force. After the Nazis invaded Czechoslovakia (1939) Tonder fled the country and joined the French

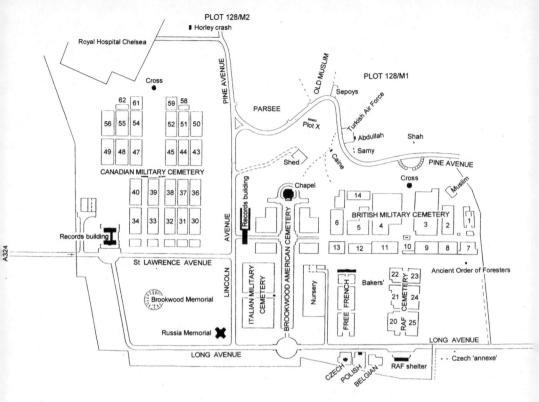

The Military and Muslim sections.

Foreign Legion. He later transferred to the Free Czech Forces based in Agde, France. After the collapse of France Tonder made his way to Spain and thence to England. He joined the second Czech Squadron (No. 312) of the RAF. Tonder took part in the latter stages of the Battle of Britain. During 1941 he took part in the offensive fighter sweeps over occupied France. In June 1942 he was shot down over the Channel and was captured. Tonder was sent to Stalag Luft III at Sagan in Silesia. He was among the seventy-six prisoners of war who took part in the 'Great Escape' of 24–25 March 1944. Tonder was finally recaptured having reached Czechoslovakia, was interrogated by the Gestapo and kept for eight months in solitary confinement in Prague. Eventually Tonder was sentenced to death and sent to Colditz to await execution; the prison was liberated before the sentence could be carried out. After the war he returned to Czechoslovakia, but subsequently moved to England where he finally died aged 82.

In front of the annexe are some graves that face directly on to Long Avenue.

9.2. Lieutenant-Colonel John Ormsby Evelyn (Joe) Vandeleur (1903–1988)

Born in Nowshera on the North West Frontier, Vandeleur was educated at Cheltenham College and the Royal Military College, Sandhurst. He was commissioned into the Irish Guards in 1924. Vandeleur was seconded to the Sudan Defence Force (1928–31), which had a lasting influence on him. He also served in Egypt, attached to the 1st Battalion in Palestine. Vandeleur commanded the 3rd Battalion from 1941, and in 1944 took charge of the reorganised Irish Guards Battle Group. The Group successfully moved through Belgium, taking the Escault Canal crossing, which became known as 'Joe's Bridge'. During Operation Market Garden, Vandeleur was given the task of leading the advance of 30 Corps to link up with the airborne troops at Arnhem. They were hampered by ditches, streams, canals, narrow roads and German resistance. The advance failed by 8 miles to relieve the remnants of the Airborne Division. In the film *A Bridge Too Far*, Vandeleur is played by Michael Caine. Vandeleur commanded the Irish Guards (1946–8), and retired with the rank of Brigadier (1951).

Enter the military section through the wooden gate. The Belgian section is just beyond the RAF shelter and on the left of the path.

9.3. Belgian Military Cemetery

This section dates from 1949 when the Belgian Government instructed the LNC to carry out exhumations of Belgian service personnel previously buried in various churchyards and burial grounds throughout the United Kingdom for repatriation or re-interment in this new plot.[3] Note the distinctively shaped headstones that feature the Belgian lion rampant on a shield at the top of each stone. The memorial at the front of the plot was added in 1996.

9.4. Polish Military Cemetery

The Polish ground includes a prominent memorial facing Long Avenue. It depicts the Polish eagle displayed and also serves as an altar during memorial services. The headstones have an arched top, and show the Polish eagle on a shield in the middle of each stone.

9.5. Czechoslovakian Military Cemetery

The large monument in this plot serves as a general memorial to all Czechoslovakian servicemen and women killed in the Second World War, whose bodies were buried in various cemeteries and churchyards throughout the United Kingdom. There are forty-five Czech airmen buried here. In addition there are three others buried in the main **RAF cemetery**. Distinctively shaped memorials mark each grave space. Two Battle of Britain pilots may be found here:

Sergeant Jan Chalupa (1919–40) [row D, grave 10]. A fighter pilot serving with No. 310 Squadron based at Duxford. Chalupa's Hurricane crashed near Ely on Wednesday 16 October 1940 during a routine training flight. The cause of the accident remains a mystery. He was originally buried at Royston and was removed to Brookwood in November 1948.

Pilot Officer Emil Fechtner, DFC (1916–40) [row E, grave 1]. Born at Prague. After retraining in Hurricanes he was posted to No. 310 Squadron. On 26 August 1940 he was made leader of Green Section, and up to 7 September he shot down four enemy planes. Fechtner was awarded the DFC on 28 October. The next afternoon he took off to cover Maidstone. While forming into a 'wing' patrol he collided with **Pilot Officer Jaroslav Maly**'s[4] Hurricane. Maly was only slightly injured; Fechtner was killed. He was buried in Royston churchyard and removed to this plot in November 1948.[5]

Directly opposite is the Free French area.

9.6. Free French Military Cemetery

The entrance to this section is marked by two crosses of Lorraine. The site of this military cemetery was previously used as part of the 1942–4 extension to the **Brookwood American Cemetery**. Three plots, designated letters K, L and M, occupied the whole of this area. The Americans were exhumed during 1948 and the area was reused for the Free French. At the far end of the Free French section is a large memorial with a bronze figure representing either victory or liberty. It was unveiled by Lord Alexander of Tunis,[6] Minister of Defence, at a special service that took place on 15 November 1953. Also present was the French Minister of

Ex-Servicemen, M. Mutter, who paid tribute to the courage of the Free French who gave their lives in the cause of peace. Mr Randolph Churchill[7] represented his father (then Prime Minister), who sent a message praising the men who had fought for France and the cause of peace but who did not live to see their country liberated. His message concluded with the words 'It is fitting that their memorial should be cherished in these islands'.[8] Note the different styles of memorial: the traditional cross, the headstones with the Star of David, and the 'moorish arch' style of headstone, which remind us of the colonial elements of the Free French forces.

9.7. Bakers' ground [plot 133a]

This plot is adjacent to the **Free French** and the **Royal Air Force cemetery**. It was established sometime during the nineteenth century. Two memorials may be located here. The first is a headstone memorial with kerbing. **Robert Blair** (c. 1814–80) [plot 133a] was a baker, whose epitaph records that '. . . being maimed of an arm for half his life his kindly distinction and genial manners endeared him to a large circle of friends who erected this tablet to perpetuate his memory.'

The other memorial is a Calvary cross and is located on the left-hand side of the RAF ground. **John Jenkins** (c. 1840–1923) [RAF ground] was General Secretary of the Amalgamated Union of Operative Bakers & Confectioners.

The RAF ground is opposite the shelter on Long Avenue.

9.8. Royal Air Force Cemetery

This forms an extension to the original **British Military Cemetery** and accommodates casualties from the RAF. The area appears to have been laid out during 1947 since the LNC sealed a grant of allotment to the War Graves Commission in October of that year. This provided for the shelter (to the north-west of Long Avenue) and for burials (to the south-east), along with the spaces in between which were to be maintained as grass walkways.[9] The splendid shelter, on the other side of Long Avenue, serves as a further memorial to these servicemen and servicewomen. It was designed by Edward Maufe[10] and was completed in 1947. It comprises a vaulted cloister with three arches at the front, flanked by two curved wing walls. The shelter is constructed of Portland stone with York stone paving. The RAF badge and motto on top of the shelter were carved by Esmonde Burton. Copies of the Registers and a visitors' book may be found inside the shelter. Please sign the book, as the number of signatures indicates the level of interest in visiting the war graves section. There are many memorials of interest here, including:

Flight Lieutenant Hugh Richard Aden Beresford (1915–40) [RAF plot 24, row D, grave 14]. A fighter pilot during the Battle of Britain, who served with No. 257 Squadron. He was shot down on 7 June 1940 and was reported as missing. In 1971 the crash site was identified and the BBC recorded a complete investigation of the area for one of its *Inside Story* documentaries. This proved a fascinating decision, as the archaeological group conducting the search unearthed not only the wreckage of the Hurricane but also the pilot's remains. Beresford was buried here at Brookwood with full military honours on 16 November 1979, while the headstone was erected over the grave in March 1980.

Flight Lieutenant Philip Meyer Davis (c. 1905–42) [RAF plot 23, row A, grave 12]. Davis came from San Mateo in California. He was the adopted son and nephew of Lady Davis of Montreal. He served in the Eagle squadrons, founded by **Charles Sweeny**. These squadrons were manned by American pilots at a time when the United States was still neutral. His memorial is an example of one with no religious symbol.[11]

Pilot Officer G.J. Drake (c. 1920–40) [RAF plot 22, row E, grave 2]. Drake came from South Africa and was a fighter pilot during the Battle of Britain, serving with No. 607

Squadron. He was shot down near Goudhurst, Kent, on 9 September 1940. As Drake's body was not found at the time he was commemorated on the RAF Memorial at Runnymede (panel 8). However, the crash site of his Hurricane was excavated in May 1972; the complete airframe was recovered, along with the pilot's remains. Drake's body was buried here with full military honours on 22 November 1972.

Pilot Officer William Richard Driver (*c*. 1919–41) [RAF plot 20, row B, grave 18]. Careful study of this memorial shows that Driver came from the USA. He was born in Tunica, Mississippi, and flew with the RAF. He served with No. 71 Squadron, which was the first of three Eagle squadrons, founded by **Charles Sweeny**. These squadrons were manned by American pilots. Driver served and died with the RAF when America was still neutral and had yet to enter the Second World War. His epitaph is worthy of note: 'He volunteered for Britain and died that we might know a safer world.'

Sergeant Edward J. Egan (*c*. 1921–40) [RAF plot 24, row D, grave 16]. Egan served with No. 501 Squadron based at Kenley. His Hurricane was shot down in flames by a Messerschmitt Bf109 in a surprise attack over Ashford during the afternoon of 17 September 1940. The plane crashed in Daniels Wood, near Bethersden, Kent. As his body was not found, Egan was posted as missing and was commemorated on the RAF Memorial at Runnymede (panel 14). However, the crash site was excavated in September 1976 and part of the aircraft and the pilot's remains were recovered. Although the inquest found the remains to be that of Egan, the Ministry of Defence insisted on further proof of identity. Therefore when Egan was buried here in early 1977 his original headstone recorded him as an unknown aviator. The crash site was re-excavated in November 1978 and the aircraft manufacturer's plate was recovered, which confirmed beyond any doubt that the aircraft was that of Sergeant Egan. Thus the headstone seen today replaced the original memorial.

Sergeant Pilot John Hugh Mortimer Ellis (*c*. 1919–40) [RAF plot 20, row E, grave 3]. Ellis entered the RAF Volunteer Reserve in 1938 and was called into full-time service on the outbreak of war. He joined No. 85 Squadron at Debden on 24 May 1940. Ellis was shot down in his Hurricane on 1 September 1940 and was posted as missing. Part of his remains were buried in the grave of an unknown airman at St Mary Cray, south London. Because of a wartime error another part of his body was discovered the next day but was buried in an adjacent grave. But the dates on the two headstones (11 September and 12 October) do not bear this out. When parts of the aircraft were unearthed in 1992 further investigation proved that both 'unknown' airmen were in fact Sergeant Ellis. He was buried with full military honours on 1 October 1993. Although the coroner was minded to order the exhumation of the 1940 grave, he deferred to the wishes of the CWGC and it was left undisturbed.

Ken Farnes (1911–41) [RAF plot 21, row A, grave 11]. Cambridge, Essex and England cricketer. Farnes was born in Leytonstone, Essex, and attended the Royal Liberty School in Romford and Cambridge University. Farnes made the most of his fine physique (he was 6ft 4in tall) and bowled as fast as anyone in modern times. He started playing for Essex in 1930, and received his Cambridge Blue in 1931. He first appeared for England against Australia in 1934 at Nottingham, dismissing ten batsmen for 179 runs. He played fifteen Tests for England and took sixty wickets, and was Wisden Cricketer of the Year for 1939. Farnes was killed in an experimental night landing on 20 October 1941. Note especially the inscription, chosen by his family: 'He died as he lived, playing the game.' His old school has a memorial stained-glass window commemorating his life.

Fitzgerald brothers [RAF plot 21, row A, grave 3]. An unusual double grave containing **Sergeant Joseph Gerald Fitzgerald** (*c*. 1922–41) of the RAF (Volunteer Reserve), who died 25 September 1941 aged 19. He is buried with his brother **Leslie Fitzgerald** (*c*. 1912–41), who died 31 March 1941, aged 29.

Sergeant John Stanley Gilders (1920–41) [RAF plot 20, row E, grave 15]. The most recent interment in the RAF ground. Gilders flew with No. 72 Squadron during the Battle of Britain and was attached to No. 41 Squadron when his Spitfire was shot down during a dogfight over Kent. The official report stated that Gilders had baled out over the Channel and drowned. In fact the impact of the crash buried his plane some 16ft into the ground. The crash site was identified in 1991 as a field at Chilham Beeches, near Canterbury. The aircraft was excavated in April 1994 with permission of the landowner, and Sergeant Gilders' remains were recovered. The Ministry of Defence charged the aircraft archaeologist with removing 'military remains' without their permission. However, Sergeant Gilders' family protested and the Coroner subsequently ignored the Ministry of Defence's claim. Sergeant Gilders was buried here with full military honours on 11 May 1995.

Flight Lieutenant Andrew (Andy) Mamedoff (1912–41) [RAF plot 21, row A, grave 7]. Mamedoff was one of the first American pilots to come to Europe and join the first Eagle squadron. He was also one of seven 'official' Americans to see combat experience during the Battle of Britain. Mamedoff was originally contracted to fight for Finland in March 1940. With Finland defeated, he went to France. Mamedoff arrived in Paris in mid-May, only to discover the *Armée de l'Air* was not interested in American pilots. He managed to escape from France on the last ship from St Jean de Luz, the *Baron Nairn*. Arriving in England, Mamedoff – with Eugene 'Red' Tobin and Vernon 'Shorty' Keough[12] – had some difficulty joining the RAF since this violated the American Neutrality Acts. All three stood to lose their American citizenship. However, with the help of an MP they were signed up and sent to No. 7 Operational Training Unit at Hawarden, Cheshire, in July 1940. They were posted to No. 609 (West Riding) Squadron in Dorset on 8 August, but were not allowed to fly combat duties until 16 August. On 19 September Mamedoff was transferred to the first Eagle squadron, No. 71, at Church Fenton, Lincolnshire. He stayed with No. 71 until transferred to the third Eagle squadron, No. 133, on 1 August 1941. Mamedoff was killed during No. 133's transfer to Eglinton, Londonderry. On 8 October 1941, while landing in poor weather to refuel on the Isle of Man, a portion of his 'B' Flight hit a mountain. Tragically, Mamedoff had only recently married an English girl, Alys Craven.

Squadron Leader Stanley Thomas Meares, **DFC** (*c.* 1916–41) [RAF plot 24, row A, grave 20]. Meares came from Ash Vale in Surrey, and commanded No. 71 Squadron, the first of three Eagle squadrons. These squadrons were manned by American pilots at a time when the United States was still neutral.

The Foresters' plot is reached by walking through the pine trees that flank the RAF section.

9.9. Ancient Order of Foresters burial ground [plot 133]

The Ancient Order of Foresters is a benevolent self-help group or friendly society. The name 'forester' grew out of the belief that worthy craftsmen felt it was their duty to support their brethren in need or want as they walked through the forests of this life. The Foresters' ground was inaugurated by the South London District on Monday 15 June 1863 for the burial of deceased members (and their relatives) of the various Courts of the South London District of the Order. Despite the thousands of members of the South London District, it appears that very few were buried here.

The dominant memorial of a broken red granite column commemorates **Edward Victor Robbins** (*c.* 1845–1903) who assisted the running of his Court, his District and his Sanctuary. He was also involved in the Foresters' London Asylum at Bexley Heath and with the Widows' and Orphans' Fund. At the unveiling of his memorial, in September 1904, the following eulogy was given by Brother **Alfred Chapman**:

Dear Friends, we are assembled to do honour to the memory of Brother Edward Victor Robbins, who was a very dear friend of most of us, and an earnest worker in the cause of thrift – more especially Friendly Society thrift – and other good movements affecting his fellow men. His influence was felt and recognised by his Court and Sanctuary, by the Ancient Order of Shepherds (of which he was a Past High Pastor) and by the South London District of which he was District Sub Chief Ranger at the time of his death, and it is certain he would have passed District Honours many years since if his business engagements had permitted attendance at the District Meetings. As Trustee of the Lambeth Savings Bank he did good public service, and everywhere he made a host of friends. He was one of Nature's gentlemen; always courteous, considerate, kind, genial, painstaking and brotherly. He never made a noise, yet exercised a wide influence and always for what was best and truest. We regret his loss; we cherish his memory; and we hope that many will be inspired to emulate his bright example. As one who enjoyed his friendship and goodwill for more than thirty years it is my honour now to unveil this memorial to his memory – the memory of a good and worthy man.[13]

Also buried here, but in an unmarked grave, is **Alfred Chapman** (1840–1912). He was a bootmaker, and was completely self-taught, having learned to read at Sunday school. In 1861 he obtained a job with a gum and drug works in London. Chapman then became a clerk in the County Court at Lambeth, where he stayed for the rest of his working life. At about the same time he joined a Foresters' Court in the South London District. Later he became the District Secretary and the Order's Parliamentary Agent. Chapman took up issues such as old age pensions, shop legislation and the need for unemployment benefit. He even visited Germany in about 1900 to see how they were dealing with a tuberculosis epidemic.

Return to the main military ground.

9.10. The British Military Cemetery

These plots form the oldest part of the military sections. The LNC made an offer of a military burial ground to the War Office and Admiralty in August 1914: 'The Directors would be glad to place at the service of the War Office & Admiralty an area of about an acre of ground in their Cemetery at Brookwood . . . for the free interment of soldiers & sailors who have returned from the front wounded & may subsequently die.'[14]

This offer was politely declined. The reason was almost certainly that no government agency was then set up to deal with the war dead, for the Imperial War Graves Commission (IWGC) only received its Royal Charter in May 1917. Therefore it was not until March 1917 that the LNC was contacted again and an interim agreement was signed, dated 11 July 1917. In June 1918 Captain Goulden RE attended a board meeting to display a contour model of the proposed 5- or 6-acre 'soldiers' cemetery', which would incorporate a 'national memorial' and a new entrance to the cemetery at the north. Colonel B.R. Ward,[15] Chief Engineer, London District, as secretary to the Brookwood Memorial Committee, then wrote:

> . . . an improved entrance from the north . . . is one of the most important items in the scheme & one which we should hope to put in hand at an early date. Any concession made by your Company would of course be subject to existing contracts and also of course subject to reasonable safeguards as to your rights as owners of the cemetery. . . . You will observe the positions of the proposed graves are arranged so that a fitting harmony may exist, and one admitting of a suitable development & inclusion of proposed enrichment by commemorative features. At the same time the method of indicating by numbers the order of

interments is introduced to prevent awkwardly shaped groups being formed should the whole space allotted not be required by the Dominions, on account of cessation of hostilities. I should be obliged if you will signify formally . . . the willingness of the Board to accept this plan so that I may direct sappers to peg out & number the plots at once. . . .[16]

The land set aside amounted to about 3½ acres and was formally granted to the IWGC for £2,542 10s 0d in September 1921. This provided for 'a permanent and last resting place for British Dominion and Colonial Soldiers who have died from wounds inflicted or accident occurring or disease contracted while on active service . . . and a cemetery for the interment of such deceased Imperial troops as may be determined by the Imperial War Graves Commission.'[17]

The cemetery would be called the 'British Military Cemetery', and the IWGC would be given a free hand in the layout, design and structures within this ground. The IWGC also undertook to construct a separate entrance to the new military cemetery, adjacent to **Brookwood station**. The new area was used for the burial of soldiers, sailors and nurses who died in the London Military District. Apart from the United Kingdom (602 burials in plots 5, 6, 12 and 13), the following Commonwealth countries are also represented by individual sections: Australia (352 burials in plots 4 and 11), Canada (311 burials in plots 3 and 9), New Zealand (148 burials in plots 2 and 8), South Africa (148 burials in plots 1 and 7), Newfoundland (15 burials in plot 10) and the British West Indies (2 burials in plots 6 and 13). Some of these sections were subsequently extended to include casualties from the Second World War as follows: United Kingdom (880), Canada (over 100: most were buried in the separate **Canadian Military Cemetery**), Australia (95), New Zealand (82), South Africa (3) and India (8).

The military cemeteries are administered separately by the Commonwealth War Graves Commission (CWGC) and similar organisations from other countries. Over 5,075 casualties from both world wars are buried in the CWGC sections. This total includes 1,601 burials from the First World War and 3,474 from the Second World War (including the separate Canadian section). In addition there are 468 American war dead, the dead from other nationalities represented here and other casualties buried elsewhere in the grounds of Brookwood Cemetery. Then there are those servicemen and servicewomen with no known graves who are commemorated on the **Brookwood Memorial** (3,500 casualties from the Second World War), the **Brookwood (Russia) Memorial** (662 casualties from both world wars) and the Memorial Chapel in the **Brookwood American Cemetery** that commemorates 563 servicemen from the First World War.

The design and layout of this section are typical of that used by the CWGC throughout the world. Note the cross of sacrifice (designed by Reginald Blomfield[18]) at the far end of the plot, with its bronze Crusader's sword. Near the front of the cemetery is the stone of remembrance (designed by Edwin Lutyens[19]), inscribed with the words 'Their name liveth for evermore'. All the headstones are of a uniform size and design. At the top of each one is the national emblem, or the service or regimental badge. This is followed by the rank, name, unit, date of death and age (if known). Next comes the appropriate religious emblem (if requested). Lastly, at the bottom (and in most cases) is an inscription chosen by relatives.

Among those commemorated in these sections are **Lieutenant Roger Douglas** (1894–1919) [Mil. plot 4, row H, grave 1] and **Lieutenant J.S. Leslie Ross** (1895–1919) [Mil. plot 4, row J, grave 1]. Douglas and Ross were both killed on 13 November 1919 when their aircraft *Endeavour* crashed near Surbiton on the first leg of their bid to win the England–Australia air race and a prize of £10,000. Their aircraft was a single-engine Alliance biplane, specially designed for long-range flying. Eyewitnesses reported that after taking off from Hounslow at 11.33 a.m. the aircraft appeared to go into a spin, then straightened out before spinning and crashing into an apple orchard near Surbiton Cemetery. Both were killed instantly. They were buried here with full military honours on 17 November 1919.

Flying Officer Robert Edwards (died 1940) [Mil. plot 3, row C, grave 1a]. Edwards was a fighter pilot serving with No. 1 (Royal Canadian Air Force) Squadron based at Northolt. At about 3.30 p.m. on 26 August 1940 his Hurricane was shot down in an attack on a Dornier 215 over North Weald. The aircraft crashed near The Hydes, Little Bardfield, Thaxted, killing the pilot.

Flight Sub-Lieutenant A.B. Helbert (c. 1895–1917) [Mil. plot 6, near hedge]. This special marker is a curiosity. Set at right angles to the rest of the memorials in this section and separated from them, it appears at first to be a standard CWGC headstone. However, careful study of the inscription shows that it reads 'buried in Brookwood Cemetery'. Helbert is not in fact buried in the military section, but in his family grave in plot 55 (see Chapter 6). The reason why Helbert should be commemorated in this unique way is still a mystery.

Lieutenant Walter Hyatt Jamieson (died 1918) [Mil. plot 3, row E, grave 8]. Jamieson had previously served with the 1st Battalion Central Ontario Regiment. He died of pneumonia on 28 October 1918 when he was attached to the RAF as a Balloon Officer. This is one example of the CWGC putting the wrong emblem on the headstone.

Corporal 'George Mitchell' (c. 1895–1918) [Mil. plot 13, row A, grave 10a]. 'George Mitchell' was the assumed name of **Ronald Wiggins** of East Sheen. He was serving on board the aircraft carrier HMS *Argus* when he died on the last day of the First World War, 11 November 1918, probably from the 'flu epidemic.

The **Muslim section** is located in the north-eastern part of this area, and is set at an angle to the main areas. This group of twenty-four graves contains the bodies of Muslims who were originally buried in the Horsell Common Muslim Military Cemetery. They were removed here in 1969 after that cemetery fell into disrepair.

Flying Officer O.J. Peterson (1916–40) [Mil. plot 3, row K, grave 1a]. Peterson was a fighter pilot serving with No. 1 (Royal Canadian Air Force) Squadron based at Northolt. At about 9.15 a.m. on 27 September 1940 his Hurricane was shot down over Hever during a dogfight with Junkers 88s and Messerschmidt Bf110s over north Kent. Peterson was killed and his Hurricane was destroyed.

Flying Officer Ross Smither (c. 1910–40) [Mil. plot 3, row H, grave 1]. A Canadian fighter pilot who was shot down by Messerschmidt Bf 109s in combat over Tunbridge Wells just after midday on 15 September 1940. Smither was killed and his Hurricane was a write-off.

Lieutenant Frank William Henry Thomas (c. 1896–1918) [Mil. plot 6, row A, grave 2]. Born at Zeerust, Transvaal, Thomas was a pilot with No. 47 Squadron based on the Salonikan Front in northern Greece. Thomas was wounded in his Armstrong Whitworth FK3 near Monastir on 20 August 1917 and was evacuated to England, where he eventually died of his wounds at the 3rd London General Hospital on 5 January 1918. His burial here represents why the Military Cemetery was established.

Note that there is a separate **Canadian Military Cemetery**.

The American section is the next large area adjacent to the military section. There is a side entrance from the left-hand path leading off from the stone of remembrance.

9.11. The Brookwood American Cemetery

This is the only military cemetery in Britain for American casualties during the First World War. It covers about 4½ acres of cemetery land that was sold to the American Government for £5,500 under a special grant in September 1922. The LNC later submitted estimates for the construction of the cemetery that amounted to £8,851 by October 1923 (this presumably excluded the cost of building the Memorial Chapel).[20] The cemetery is the final resting place of

468 American servicemen, including 41 unknown. Most of these casualties were seriously wounded men who had been brought back to Britain where they subsequently died of their wounds. The bodies were brought here from various temporary sites throughout the British Isles after the Armistice in 1918. The Memorial Chapel commemorates a further 563 servicemen all of whom were either lost or buried at sea. It was – until the Second World War – the only one of its kind in Britain. The victims of the SS *Tuscania*, a British troopship sunk by a U-boat off the west coast of Scotland on 5 February 1918, are commemorated here, either listed in the Memorial Chapel as 'Missing in Action' or as some of the forty-one 'unknowns' buried here. These men were the first American troops to be killed while on their way to Europe, and a stone tower with a commemorative plaque was erected on the Isle of Islay in their memory. The cemetery and its Memorial Chapel in neoclassical style were designed by Egerton Swartwout,[21] John Russell Pope[22] and Harry B. Creswell.[23] The stained-glass windows in the Memorial Chapel were designed by Reginald Hallward[24] of London, and incorporate the regimental insignia of the American Army. There are eighteen windows in total, occupying three sides of the chapel. Reginald Hallward also carried out the decoration of the memorial altar and of the cross above it. The Memorial Chapel is built of Portland stone without and Ham Hill stone within. The contractors were Messrs Holloway Brothers and the work was carried out under the direction of Harry Creswell. Pevsner was very enthusiastic about this section, noting, 'magnificent landscaping for the American [Cemetery] . . . It is bursting with *panache*, which is an odd word to use of a cemetery: the quality that makes U.S. Neo-Colonial so much better than our own Neo-Georgian.'[25]

The cemetery was completed in 1929, although the formal ceremony of dedication did not take place until 15 August 1937, some twenty years after the first American troops marched through London *en route* to Wellington Barracks. The service was attended by several hundred guests and visitors, 314 of whom travelled from Waterloo by train. Catering was provided for 305 people, and there were British troops and a military band of 225 officers and other ranks. The ceremony was presided over by the American Ambassador, Mr R.W. Bingham,[26] while the British Government was represented by the First Lord of the Admiralty, Mr A.D. Cooper.[27] During the service Mr Bingham spoke of the ideals for which the Americans had given their lives so that democracy should not perish, and that 'they live here in a land which is free'.[28] The cemetery is laid out like a garden backed by fir trees. Note the central memorial flagpole that flies the stars and stripes, and the fine lawns of Kentucky bluegrass.

During the Second World War this cemetery was extended for the burial of members of the American armed forces who died in England. Burials commenced from 8 April 1942 and by 31 August 1944 (when burials at Brookwood ceased) over 3,600 bodies had been laid to rest in plots surrounding the original Brookwood American Cemetery. As the original four plots were designated A to D, the new plots continued in sequence from E to S, although the letters I and J were not used in order to avoid any possible misreading or misunderstanding of these plot numbers. The new areas were located as follows: allotments E and G were on the site of what is now the **Italian Military Cemetery**; sections F and H were on the site of what is now the CWGC nursery and garages; plots K, L and M were located where the **Free French** section now is; and the remaining six areas (designated letters N to S) were where the **Brookwood (Russia) Memorial** now stands, stretching towards the site of the **Brookwood Memorial**. From September 1944 the burial of American servicemen took place at Madingley, near Cambridge, and the plots at Brookwood were evacuated during the period January–May 1948. This work was performed under the authority of the Office of Quartermaster General, Washington, and by the American authorities. The cases containing human remains were for repatriation to America or for re-interment at Madingley.[29] An isolated 'plot x' (behind the chapel) was used for the burial of eighteen American servicemen who were executed at Shepton

Mallet prison for various offences during the Second World War. These graves were unmarked, and after the Second World War seventeen bodies were transferred to a 'dishonoured' plot in the American Military Cemetery at Oisne-Aisne (Fère-en-Tardenois) in France.[30] The other body, that of Private David Cobb (*c.* 1922–43), was returned to America, for his family had requested his body be returned only ten days after his execution on 12 March 1943.[31] The adjacent Records and Reception Lodge includes a fine visitors' room, where the registers may be consulted. The resident American Superintendent will be happy to answer any questions, and please remember to sign the visitors' book. The Memorial Chapel, flagpole and the entrance walls on Long Avenue are all Grade II listed structures.

Follow the path to the rear of the Memorial Chapel and find the pair of marble headstones close to the boundary fence with Pine Avenue.

William Sproston Caine (1842–1903) [rear of Brookwood American Cemetery]. Politician and promoter of temperance. Educated privately, Caine entered his father's metal merchandising business in 1861 and became a partner from 1864. He moved from Cheshire to Liverpool in 1871 and, with public affairs taking up more of his time, he retired from the firm in 1878. As a Baptist, Caine developed a taste for preaching and philanthropy. The temperance movement absorbed much of his spare time and he became President of the Liverpool Temperance and Band of Hope Union. From this he established the Popular Control and Licence Reform Association. Caine was elected the Vice-President of the United Kingdom Alliance from 1873. He was also President of the Baptist Total Abstinence Society, the Congregational Temperance League and of the National Temperance Federation. Caine was elected radical MP for Scarborough (1880–5) and urged on the House of Commons his views on temperance. He seconded Henry Labouchere's motion of dissent from Gladstone's proposal for a national memorial to Lord Beaconsfield (May 1881) and was subsequently appointed Civil Lord of the Admiralty (1884–5). He was returned as Liberal MP for Barrow-in-Furness (1886–90). He opposed Gladstone's policy of Home Rule for Ireland, helping form the Liberal Unionist party, which helped defeat the first Home Rule Bill. Caine became chief Liberal Unionist whip after the 1886 election, but his radical and extreme temperance views meant his alliance with the Conservatives did not last, and he vacated his seat in 1890. He subsequently rejoined the Liberals and was elected Liberal MP for East Bradford (1892–5), and supported Gladstone's second Home Rule Bill of 1893. He lost his seat during the 1895 election but was returned as Liberal MP for Camborne (1900–3). Caine was sympathetic to increased self-government for India and was a delegate to the 1890 Indian National Congress at Calcutta. He published widely, including a series of letters in the *Pall Mall Gazette* on 'Young India', a life of his father-in-law, *Hugh Stowell Brown, his Autobiography, his Commonplace Book and Extracts from his Sermons and Addresses: a Memorial Volume* (1887), *A Trip Round the World in 1887–8* (1888), and *Picturesque India: a Handbook for European Travellers* (1890). Caine was forthright in his views but good-humoured. He was dubbed the 'genial ruffian' by his political comrades. John Newton wrote a biography of Caine, published in 1907.[32]

Leave the American section via the Records and Reception building. Turn left along Lincoln Avenue. The Italian section is on the left of the road.

9.12. Italian Military Cemetery

During the Second World War this section formed part of the extension to the **Brookwood American Cemetery**. The additional plots designated letters E and G occupied the whole of this section. It was subsequently used as a concentration cemetery for Italian prisoners of war who died in Britain.

The next memorial is on the opposite side of the road.

9.13. Brookwood (Russia) memorial

The site of this memorial was also used as part of the 1942–4 extension to the **Brookwood American Cemetery**. Six plots, designated letters N to S, occupied the whole of this section and stretched towards the **Brookwood Memorial**. The Brookwood (Russia) memorial commemorates 662 sailors, soldiers and airmen of the forces of the British Commonwealth who died in Russia during both world wars. It was constructed because many of the CWGC cemeteries in Russia were very difficult to visit, although in recent years all travelling restrictions within Russia have been virtually eradicated. The memorial was completed in 1983.

Among those commemorated on this memorial are **Sergeant Samuel George Pearse**, **VC** (1897–1919) [panel 3, column 2]. Sergeant Pearse was born at Penarth, but his family moved to Australia where they acquired a property near Mildura. Pearse undertook two years' service in the militia before enlisting in the Australian Imperial Force in 1915. He joined the 7th Battalion at Gallipoli in December 1915. In the summer of 1916 he transferred to the 2nd Machine Gun Company. In September 1917 he was awarded the Military Medal for his courage during the fighting near Ypres, where he crept forward and threw grenades into a German position, forcing the enemy to retreat. He was wounded in action in May 1918. He joined the 1st Machine Gun Battalion in December 1918. Pearse volunteered for the North Russia Relief Force in 1919, enlisting with the 45th Battalion, the Royal Fusiliers. He was posthumously awarded the VC for his gallantry against an enemy battery position north of Emtsa (North Russia) on 29 August 1919. During this action Pearse cut his way through enemy barbed wire under heavy machine-gun and rifle fire, and cleared a way for troops to enter the battery. He then charged a blockhouse that was impeding the advance and was causing casualties, and killed the occupants with bombs. Shortly afterwards he was killed, but owing to his action the position was captured with few casualties. Pearse is buried in the Archangel Allied Cemetery, special memorial B, grave 107.

Major James Valentine (1887–1917) [panel 2, column 3]. Valentine came from London and trained as a motor mechanic. He was one of the most daring and skilful drivers on the road. In 1910 he began flying from Brooklands, and was employed as a pilot in Paris in 1911. In the same year he was the only British competitor in the European Circuit from Paris to Reims, Utrecht, Amsterdam, Brussels, Calais, Shoreham, Hendon and back to Paris. Also in 1911 he took part in the *Daily Mail*'s 'Circuit of Britain', and was one of only four to complete the race. In 1914 he joined the Royal Flying Corps and was placed in charge of the British aviation depot in Paris. He was also sent on special missions to Italy and Russia. He died in Kiev on 7 August 1917 after one of these special operations.

9.14. The Brookwood Memorial

Designed by Ralph Hobday, this large circular colonnade of Portland stone has inscribed on twenty-eight green slate panels the names of 3,500 men and women of the land forces of the British Commonwealth 'to whom the fortune of war denied a known and honoured grave'. This includes the Norway campaign (1940), members of raiding parties that set out from Britain and never returned, and special agents or workers with Allied resistance movements. A separate panel commemorates the loss at sea of 639 members of the African Pioneer Corps, whose names are recorded individually on memorials in Lesotho and Botswana. Queen Elizabeth II unveiled the Brookwood Memorial at a special service on 25 October 1958. The invited guests included relatives, ambassadors, high commissioners, members of the Commonwealth forces, and ex-services organisations. During the unveiling the Queen said: 'Had those whom we now commemorate not stood fast in the face of tyranny, our Commonwealth and all that it represents would have perished. Let us give thanks to God that such men and women lived and died, and by their death preserved for us our heritage of freedom.'[33]

This important memorial has been recommended for statutory listing by Woking Borough Council. Among the thousands of names on the panels are **Ernest James Harman Kemp** (1923–44) [panel 3, column 2]. Kemp represents one of thirty-six servicemen who were executed during the Second World War. Born at Gillingham, Kent, he was a railway porter at New Cross until he joined the Royal Artillery. He was found guilty of the murder of Leading Aircraftwoman (Iris) Miriam Deeley on the night of 12–13 February 1944. His trial took place at the Old Bailey in April and he was condemned to death. His execution took place at Wandsworth Prison on 6 June 1944. Miriam Deeley's body was subsequently buried in the City of London Cemetery, Manor Park, where a standard CWGC headstone marks her grave.[34] Kemp is not the only serviceman guilty of murder represented on the Brookwood Memorial. The Ministry of Defence view is that any serviceman or woman who died between 3 September 1939 and 31 December 1947, from whatever cause, would be referred to the CWGC for commemoration. The CWGC play no part in this decision as they act solely under instructions issued via the Ministry of Defence.[35]

Violette Szabo, **GC** (1921–45) [panel 26, column 3]. The widow of a French officer killed in North Africa, and the first British-born woman to be awarded the George Cross. Szabo volunteered to work with the French section of the Special Operations Executive in early 1944 and did much of her training at Christmas Pie near Normandy, Surrey. Szabo was twice parachuted into occupied France and did valuable work for the French Resistance immediately prior to D-Day. On her second mission she was captured and sent to Ravensbruck concentration camp. She was tortured but refused to speak. Sometime in January 1945 she was shot. Szabo was posthumously awarded the George Cross (7 December 1946). She is also commemorated on the First Aid Nursing Yeomanry memorial plaque located at St Paul's Church, Wilton Place, Knightsbridge. In 1956 R.J. Minney wrote a book about her life called *Carve Her Name With Pride*.[36] In 1958 it was made into a film with the same title. Virginia McKenna starred as Szabo.[37]

Captain Jenkin Robert Oswald Thompson, **GC** (died 1944) [panel 18, column 1]. Thompson was one of the Army's seagoing soldiers, being a member of the Royal Army Medical Corps. He spent most of the war serving on hospital ships. Thompson was killed in January 1944 off the coast of Anzio, when the hospital ship *St David* was bombed and started to sink. He organised parties of men to evacuate the wounded, and every patient save one was carried to safety. Thompson went below to try and free the sole remaining trapped patient. As he was doing so the ship sank and claimed both their lives.

From the Brookwood Memorial cross St Lawrence Avenue and enter the Canadian ground.

9.15. Canadian Military Cemetery

This section includes Brookwood's second cross of sacrifice and stone of remembrance; note also the avenue of maples. The cross of sacrifice was unveiled by Field-Marshal Lord Alexander of Tunis on 28 June 1953, during a special service of dedication led by Canon V.J. Pike.[38] Lord Alexander was patron of the Canadian Veterans Association of the UK, which was represented by a large parade. Over 2,000 Canadian casualties from the Second World War are buried here, including 43 casualties from the Dieppe raid (18–19 August 1942). The adjacent records and reception building (Beaver House), designed by Edward Maufe[39] in 1947, was built at the expense of the Canadian Government as a gift to the CWGC and as a further memorial. It was erected by the Royal Canadian Engineers and consists of a visitors' room, waiting room and offices. It is constructed of Portland stone with a roof of Cornish slates. The Canadian crest of the maple leaf with the lion and imperial crown, set in the centre of the pediment that faces the burial grounds, was carved by Esmonde Burton. The sculpted beaver which may be seen above the entrance to the building was carved by one of the Royal Canadian Engineers. Inside the reception room are the coats of arms of Canada and the three Canadian armed forces, painted by Eleanor Esmonde-White.[40]

Among those buried here are **Private Edmund Philip Baines** (*c.* 1912–44) [plot 48, row E, grave 9]. Baines served with the Royal Canadian Infantry Corps and was killed in April 1944. This is another example of a double burial, as the memorial records that his son, **Geoffrey Edmund Baines**, who died 28 January 1945 aged 8 months, shares the same grave.

Corporal James Hendry, **GC** (*c.* 1912–41) [plot 31, row F, grave 9]. Hendry was killed by an underground explosion at Loch Laggan on 13 June 1941. The excavation work was associated with the construction of a vitally needed aluminium plant, and the No. 1 Tunnelling Company of the Royal Canadian Engineers was sent in to assist. On the day of the explosion Corporal Hendry was in charge of an underground working party. A fire broke out in the magazine, and Hendry ordered his men and civilians nearby to take cover. Having satisfied himself that everyone else was safe, he attempted to get the fire under control. But he never reached the magazine, as a violent explosion shook the hillside. Hendry and one other man were killed and two others injured; but the casualties would have been far heavier had Corporal Hendry not acted as he did.

Private Teddy Manywounds (died 1942) [plot 36, row F, grave 5]. This interesting headstone commemorates a Canadian Indian. His epitaph reads 'died in the service of the Great White Father'.

Sergeant John Rennie, GC (*c.* 1920–43) [plot 47, row D, grave 8]. Rennie was killed in a training accident at Slough, near Thetford, on 20 November 1943. He was instructing recruits in throwing grenades from a trench when one bungled the throw and the grenade rolled back. Rennie ran to pick it up, and as he did so it exploded. His body shielded the blast from three other men who were standing only 5 yards away.

Flying Officer J.W. Watson & crew [plot 51, row F, graves 3–9]. This line of graves commemorates the entire crew of Lancaster RF150 QB-W ('Willie') of No. 424 'Tiger' Squadron, Royal Canadian Air Force. On 4 April 1945 this aircraft was part of a force of thirteen bombers attacking a synthetic oil plant at Merseburg. The target was heavily defended, and it is believed that 'Willie' suffered from fire on board. Despite the plane making its way back to England, an attempted emergency landing at Booker airfield, near High Wycombe, failed. During a second circuit of the airfield the bomber's wing tip struck a water tower and the aircraft spun into nearby woods killing all on board. The entire crew were buried here on Friday 13 April 1945: **Flying Officer Watson, Pilot Officer E.T. Ashdown** (flight engineer), **Pilot Officer S.J.O. Robinson** (air gunner), **Pilot Officer S. Thomson** (wireless operator & gunner), **Pilot Officer C.N. Armstrong** (air bombardier), **Flying Officer J. Rochford** (navigator) and **Flight Sergeant C.K. Howes** (air gunner).[41]

*Note that there are further Canadian burials in the **British Military Cemetery**.*

There is a rough path adjacent to the cross of sacrifice that leads through the trees at the back of the Canadian plot and leads into the Chelsea Pensioners' ground.

9.16. Royal Hospital, Chelsea

This is the current plot used for the burial of pensioners from the Royal Hospital. The original ground used by the Royal Hospital from 1894 is in plot 54, off St Mark's Avenue (see Chapter 5).

This plot behind the **Canadian Military Cemetery** came into use from 1962. The headstones are in the CWGC style, but with distinctively shaped tops. The inscription at the foot of each memorial gives details of when the soldier first entered the Royal Hospital. The earliest burial is that of **Corporal W. Hayes** (died 1962) of the Royal Irish Regiment. He was an in-pensioner at the Royal Hospital from 24 July 1951, and died on 3 July 1962. His grave is on the left-hand side of the central lawn and closest to the circular driveway near the entrance to the plot.

Leave the Chelsea plot by the gateway adjacent to the small turning circle. The next memorial is a large grave with a black marble headstone.

9.17. Horley air crash [plot 128/M2]

This large memorial is dedicated to the memories of six Afghan victims of the Ariana Afghan Airlines air crash at Horley in January 1969. For many years the burial place was marked only by a small wooden post with the interment number stamped on to a metal plate attached to the stake. Annette Bolt, a family friend of a relative of one of the victims, mounted a campaign to have a permanent memorial erected to their memory. SCI (UK), one of the largest funeral companies in this country, heard of the campaign and agreed to donate the entire memorial. A special service of dedication took place on 14 May 1999 to mark the placing of the stone. Unlike other air crash memorials in the cemetery (see Chapters 7 and 8), none of the victims is named on the memorial.

Return to the main path and continue walking along it until you reach the plot with the three large mausolea adjacent to the path.

9.18. Parsee or Zoroastrian burial ground [plot 128/M2]

This is the only Parsee or Zoroastrian burial ground in Europe. Zoroastrianism is the major ancient, pre-Islamic religion of Iran. Founded by the Iranian prophet and reformer Zoroaster in the sixth century BC, this religion, containing both monotheistic and dualistic features, influenced the other major world religions: Judaism, Christianity and Islam. Zoroastrianism survives in Iran in isolated areas but also, more prosperously, with the Parsees (or Parsis) of India, descendants of immigrants who went there from Iran sometime after the Muslim conquest. In modern times a few adherents have transported the religion into the West.

The ground at Brookwood was opened in November 1862 as a direct consequence of the first recorded death of a Parsee in Britain, that of **D.H. Hakim**. Zoroastrians may not be buried in a Christian cemetery, therefore the London Zoroastrian Association, formed in 1861 and the first Asian religious association founded in this country, came to an agreement with the LNC for a burial ground at Brookwood. The two small pink obelisks mark the original entrance to the ground. There used to be a boundary hedge screening the plot.[42] The whole burial ground has been recommended for statutory listing by Woking Borough Council.

Among those buried here is **Bapsybanoo, Dowager Marchioness of Winchester** (1902–95). Born in Bombay, the daughter of the Most Revd Khurshedji Pavry, High Priest of the Parsees in India, she was an educated and cosmopolitan lady. At the age of 50 she became the third wife of 'Monty', the 16th Marquis of Winchester, then in his 90th year.[43] Despite this marriage he continued his affair with Mrs Valentine Fleming (mother of the novelist Ian Fleming), and Bapsy started six years of litigation with her. After the death of the Marquis she remained in London, somewhat shunned by the establishment. Bapsy had a flamboyant style and demanded free tickets to public events for herself and her brother. She erected her headstone before her death in Bombay. Her ashes are now back in Britain.

Sir Mancherjee Merwanjee Bhownagree (1851–1933). Called to the Bar in London, Bhownagree returned to India as a Judicial Councillor and introduced many legal reforms. From 1891 he settled in London and became Britain's second Indian-born MP, serving as the Conservative member for Bethnal Green (1895–1906). He fought for the cause of Indians in South Africa after meeting with Gandhi, yet retained strong pro-British views – which earned him the nickname 'Bow and agree'. He became Chairman of the Zoroastrian Association (owners of this plot) in 1891 and dominated its activities, especially after he became President in 1908. Bhownagree was present at the opening of the Zoroastrian Temple here in June 1901, when he paid tribute to **Nowrosjee Nusserwanji Wadia**, whose wife had bequeathed the temple in his memory.

D.H. Hakim (died 1862). This memorial marks the grave of the first recorded death of a Parsee in Britain, and the reason for the opening of this burial ground. Hakim worked for Muncherji Hormusji Cama, one of the founders of the London Zoroastrian Association. He died in London on 3 November 1862.

Dr Rustomjee Naserwanjee Khory (1839–1904). Khory studied medicine in Bombay, Brussels and London. He published the *Bombay Materia Medica and their Therapeutics* (1887), the first systematic and scientific catalogue and description of the drugs and remedies used by Vayids or Hakims. This received much critical acclaim. A second edition was published with the help of Dr N.N. Katrak.

Dastur Dr Sohrab Hormusji Kutar (1912–94). Kutar trained as a doctor in Poona. He served in the Royal Army Medical Corps during the Second World War. He was a Parsee priest from 1938, and became the only recognised High Priest outside the Indian subcontinent. He held this post up to his death and officiated at many funerals in the Parsee ground at Brookwood. His wife became President of the Zoroastrian Association of Europe.

Dr Cawas C. Lalcaca (1862–1909). Lalcaca was an Indian Parsee doctor. A resident in Shanghai, he was Surgeon-Major and the Principal Medical Officer of the volunteers of the British settlement. He also acted as leader of the Parsee community there. He was shot in the mêlée following the assassination of Sir William Hutt Curzon Wyllie[44] at the Imperial Institute on 1 July 1909. The assassin was arrested and was brought to trial twenty-two days later, found guilty, and was executed after a further twenty-five days. Lalcaca's memorial includes the following tribute:

> To save a life and guard from shame his land
> He rushed to foil th' uplifted felon hand
> True self-forgetful in his love and brave
> His all he ventured and his all he gave.

Hon. Sir Homi Mehta (1871–1948). Born in Bombay and with humble origins, Mehta worked at the Bombay Mint. He moved to England and gained experience in the cotton industry. Mehta returned to Bombay and slowly gained control of a number of mills. Later he acquired silk factories, insurance companies, chemical and sugar enterprises. In 1930 Mehta was elected to the Council of State at New Delhi. In 1941 he accepted the Presidency of the Bombay National Democratic Union, and worked hard to support the war effort. Mehta was killed on 15 April 1948 when a Pan-American Constellation airliner crashed at Shannon Airport, Ireland. The plane was on a routine flight from Karachi to New York and appeared to strike a stone wall near the airport as it was landing. Thirty people were killed, although one passenger had a miraculous escape by falling through a hole in the aircraft before it burst into flames.

Sir Nowroji Bapuji Saklatvala (1875–1938). Worked with **Dorabji Tata** in the formation and development of the Indian iron and steel industry. On the death of Dorabji he

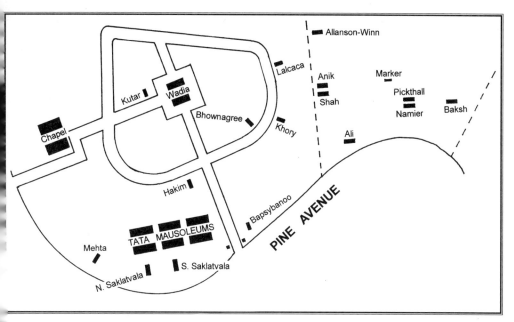

The Parsee and Old Muslim grounds.

became Chairman of the Tata Corporation and extended it into new areas. He travelled extensively and died of heart failure at Aix-les-Bains, just after completing a world tour.

Shapurji Saklatvala (1874–1936). The son of a Bombay merchant and **J.N. Tata**'s sister, Jerbai. He worked for the Tata companies in India where he developed an interest in social welfare, living with his workers and improving their wages. Later he moved to Britain and became involved with politics. He helped found the Communist Party of Great Britain. Elected Labour MP for North Battersea (1922–3), Saklatvala became the first Communist MP in Britain 1924–9), also representing North Battersea. He continued his political activities and was a popular lecturer and speaker, being critical of social inequality and of British rule in India.

Sir Dorabji Jamseti Tata (1859–1932). Buried in the left-hand mausoleum. He was the eldest son of **J.N. Tata** who took over the firm on the death of his father and built on the solid foundations already in place. Educated in India and England, he then gained experience in many of the Tata group companies. By the time of his death the company was employing over 20,000 people and was the largest industrial concern in India. He set up many charitable trusts in India and England, notably the Tata Trust (1932) for charitable endowments irrespective of caste or creed. He died in Bavaria at the age of 73.

In the same mausoleum rests **Mehrbai, Lady Dorabji Tata** (1879–1931), the daughter of Hormasji Jehangir Bhaba, a distinguished educationalist. She married Dorabji Tata in 1898. She was well educated and worked tirelessly for charitable causes and women's welfare. Her mausoleum is the most ornate of the Tata group, and her husband had it especially designed for the reception of her mortal remains. However, he never lived to see it completed, for he joined her here a year after her death.

The mausoleum was designed by Gilbert Bayes[45] and was constructed by the LNC under the supervision of Mr E.J. Baker, an independent surveyor. The walls are all of selected Portland stone 1ft 1½in thick, battening to 9in. The adjacent paving, steps and balustrading are also of Portland stone, the paving slabs being 3in thick and the steps 6in thick. The roof is made of 'selected well-seasoned first-quality fir to be well creosoted'. The roof is covered with terracotta glazed tiles of the same design as the adjacent **Wadia** mausoleum. The floor is 5in thick reinforced concrete covered by Portland stone paving slabs 3in thick. Inside, the walls include an inset dado of 2in Doulton ware strips which are set flush with the walls. The tomb is of bronze, set on a solid Sicilian marble plinth. The headstone is also of Sicilian marble. The various carvings were all supplied directly by the designer and sculptor. The total cost of the mausoleum was £2,359 18s 0d.[46]

Jamsetji Nasarwanji Tata (1839–1904). The man who industrialised India. Born in Gujerat, into a Parsee priestly caste, he moved to Bombay. Tata set up a business in Hong Kong (1859) and in 1869 bought a bankrupt cotton mill, returned it to profit and sold it. He subsequently purchased other mills, introduced improvements and laid the foundations of his fortune. In 1892 Tata sent his first students to Britain for training, and later established his own training institute in India. He prospected for iron and coal, the work being led by his son **Dorabji Tata**. This formed the basis of the Indian steel industry. He also helped develop Bombay and became interested in hydroelectric power for the region. His legacy was a modern cotton industry, an iron and steel industry, a hydroelectric industry and a world-class industrial and scientific training institution.

Ratan Tata (1871–1918). The youngest son of **J.N. Tata**, he also worked in the family firm. He married Suzanne Brier who became a Parsee. A keen Anglophile, he lived in Twickenham and helped extend the Parsee burial ground at Brookwood. He was a lavish supporter of the Indian Salvation Army. Tata suffered from poor health and died in St Ives at the age of 47.

Nowrosjee Nusserwanji Wadia (1849–99). His early training in the Lancashire cotton industry enabled Wadia to help modernise the Bombay cotton mills. He was instrumental in the introduction of modern techniques to the manufacturing and dyeing industries there. Wadia was a supporter of educational and Parsee charities. He died in Bournemouth at the age of 52. In addition to his vast tomb in the centre of the Parsee ground, his wife funded the building of the adjacent fire temple; both were formally opened on 26 June 1901 at a service also attended by **Edward Ford North**.[47]

The Muslim ground is the next plot.

9.19. Old Muslim ground [plot 128/M1]

This ground dates back to the end of the nineteenth century, making it the oldest Muslim burial ground in the country. It was originally set aside as a plot reserved for use by the Oriental Institute. **Dr G.W. Leitner** applied to the LNC for two allotments, 'one for Hindoos the other for Muhammadans', measuring 27ft × 24ft, enclosed by a line of shrubs and costing £5 5s 0d per year per plot to maintain.[48] Note that the original marker stone survives in the middle of the allotment. This stone records how 'Muhammadans' should be buried in the plot:

> The graves of Muhammadans are so dug as to allow the body to lie with its face towards Mecca (see direction of Kibla stone). The graves should be 4ft deep with a side recess at the bottom for the body. Nothing should press on the body when placed in the recess which is then closed with unburnt bricks. The grave is then filled with earth and a mound raised over it.

None of the burials here has any direct connection with the Institute, probably because of the short period that it was open. The plots may have remained unused until another agreement was sealed for the exclusive use of this area for 'Muhammadans' in June 1914. That contract reserved this section of the cemetery 'for the exclusive right of Mahomedans only'.[49] There are many graves of interest in this section, some of which are described here.

Abdullah Yusuf Ali (1872–1953). Educated in India and at Cambridge, Ali was called to the Bar at Lincoln's Inn. He joined the Indian civil service, working as a magistrate, judge and then holding various secretarial posts in government ministries. Ali retired early owing to ill health and family anxieties, and then took up an academic career. He published many works covering the law, Indian history, ethnic arts, morality and Islam. Ali is still remembered for his translation of the Koran into English in the 1930s, which is still in print.

Rt Hon. Rowland George Allanson-Winn, 5th Baron Headley (1855–1935). Educated at Westminster School and Trinity College, Cambridge, he worked as an engineer in Ireland and Kashmir, where he was involved in the construction of the Baramula to Srinagar road. Headley announced his conversion to Islam in the House of Lords (1913) and was the first peer to perform the *Hadj*, or pilgrimage to Mecca, with Kamal-ud-Din (July 1923). Three times offered the throne of Albania, he declined each time as there was no salary attached: 'the only thing that goes with it is trouble and the almost certainty of assassination'. Representatives of the Turkish embassy and the Albanian and Persian legations attended his funeral.

Mulla Abdeali Shaikh Mahomed Ali Anik (1860–1939). Born in Surat, Anik moved to London and established a merchant's business in 1901, after years in Singapore, China and Japan. One of the first Bohra-Mohamedans to establish a business in Britain, Anik was an active Freemason, Honorary Treasurer of the British Red Crescent Society and London Mosque Fund.

Mian Qadar Baksh (1878–1927). Pioneer of the leather industry. Baksh was educated in England, Japan and America. He established leather and match factories in Kabul (1911–27). Baksh helped establish new industries and opportunities in Afghanistan, and died in London while on a purchase mission for his government.

Clara Sophia Namier (1890–1945). First wife of the historian Sir Lewis Namier.[50] They parted in 1921 and she moved to America. During the Second World War she returned to England, and worked as a maid in the Randolph Hotel. She fell seriously ill in 1943 and subsequently died in 1945. According to the historian A.J.P. Taylor, Clara remained a mystery to Namier. She was undoubtedly Russian, speaking and teaching the language beautifully, but at some point she converted to Islam. Six women from the Woking Mosque prepared her body for burial.[51]

Muhammad Marmaduke William Pickthall (1875–1936). The son of a High Church Anglican who converted to Islam in 1917. Pickthall travelled extensively in the Near East, but despite this and his extensive linguistic abilities he failed to gain entrance to the Levant Consular Service. He was considered a security risk during the First World War, and was not offered a Near Eastern post. Pickthall published his first novel in 1898 and the first of his nine Near Eastern novels, *Saïd the Fisherman*, in 1903. *Saïd* was a critical and commercial success and became required reading for Consular staff posted to the East. In addition to these novels he wrote a series of Suffolk novels, political and religious works. His translation of and commentary on the Koran (1930) remains in print to this day.

Aga Shamsudin Shah (1875–1910). Born in Bombay, the son of Aga Jangi Shah, a brother-in-law of the Aga Khan. Shah's marriage took place as a joint ceremony with the Aga Khan when the latter married his sister. The ceremony took place in Poona, with 25,000 guests, lasting sixteen days. He died of an apoplectic seizure in London, aged just 35.

The next section is adjacent to the Muslim ground.

9.20. Indian sepoys [plot 128/M1].

These graves, set at an angle to Pine Avenue, date from the early years of the First World War, before the Indians were fighting regularly on the Western Front. First surveyed by the Imperial

War Graves Commission in 1920, the headstones were probably erected by private subscription. The majority of the deaths occurred in special Indian Military Hospitals in Brighton and Brockenhurst.

*Follow Pine Avenue around the back of the **Brookwood American Cemetery**. A low conifer hedge screens the next section.*

9.21. Turkish Air Force allotment [plot 128/M1]

This ground contains fourteen members of the Turkish Air Force who were killed during the Second World War. It is assumed they were unofficially serving the Allied cause since the inscriptions are suitably diplomatic, such as 'shot down by German aircraft'.

Arif Bey (1816–36). A young Turkish officer who was sent to England by Sultan Mahmoud II (ruled 1808–39) to receive military instruction at Woolwich. Bey travelled to England via Syria, Palestine, Libya, Gibraltar and France. He died on 10 August 1836, probably after being thrown from his horse. It is possible that he was the Sultan's son. His original burial took place in ground adjoining the depot close to the Royal Engineers' barracks. Bey's body was placed in a brick grave with a plain but solid monument erected over it. This was surrounded by iron chains supported by four upturned cannon. His mortal remains were removed to Brookwood on 13 April 1962, owing to the redevelopment of the site at Woolwich. Unfortunately the original tomb did not survive and Bey has just a flat ledger stone over his new grave, with the ironic epitaph 'Let no man disturb the remains of the stranger!!' Clearly the cannon and iron chains accompanied him to Brookwood, as they still surround his memorial.

Gatwick air crash (1959). A small stone at the rear of this plot commemorates fifteen victims of an air crash near Gatwick airport on 17 February 1959. This was at the time of the British withdrawal from Cyprus and negotiations between the Greeks and Turks about a new constitution. The Turkish delegation was on board a flight from Istanbul via Rome to Heathrow, but fog caused its diversion to Gatwick. The plane crashed about 3 miles from the airport at Jordanswood. Several ministers, politicians and officials were killed, although the Turkish Prime Minister survived. A Turkish Cypriot day of mourning was declared. Fourteen coffins were returned to Ankara by RAF transport, and were buried at the Mosque of Haji Bayram in Old Ankara on 23 February.

Directly behind the Turkish plot is the following headstone.

9.22. Dr Shaikh Mohammed Abdullah (1899–1956) [plot 128/M1]

Abdullah was born in the Punjab and educated there and in Germany. For some years he was in charge of the mosque in Berlin. In 1946 he was appointed Imam of the Shah Jehan Mosque, Woking, and remained there until his death. Abdullah had performed the *Hadj* and was one of the principal spiritual leaders of Islam in Britain.

Adjacent to the Turkish plot are two distinctive headstones with ledgers.

9.23. Prince Samy (1885–1961) [plot 128/M1]

Nephew of the last Sultan of Turkey, Abdul Hamid II (ruled 1876–1909). After the Young Turks forced the Sultan to restore the constitution and summon a parliament (1908), he was deposed and exiled in 1909. Prince Samy was also exiled, and lived mainly in Britain.

Further along Pine Avenue is a simple headstone.

9.24. Idries Shah (1924–1996) [plot 128/M1]

Afghani oriental scholar, novelist and teacher. Shah was born in India. He wrote many works which introduced Sufi thought to the West, influencing Doris Lessing[52] among others. His books were an unconventional mixture of jokes, anecdotes, questions, precepts and illuminations inspired by Sufi wisdom and psychology. He wrote over thirty publications, the most famous being *The Way of the Sufi* (London, 1968). In 1974 a special conference was held in London to commemorate Shah's services to Sufi studies. His epitaph reads:

> Do not look at my outward shape
> But take what is in my hand.

To the left of Pine Avenue is a low headstone of black marble screened by a low conifer hedge.

9.25. Said bin Taimar, Sultan of Oman (died 1972) [plot 128/M3]

Sultan of Oman (1932–70). He succeeded his father, who abdicated in 1932. Internal problems during his reign resulted in serious oil exploration not taking place until 1954, with exports not starting until 1967. A prudent traditional monarch, he allowed only 10km of metalled roads to be constructed during his reign and there were few motor cars. Bicycles and transistor radios were banned as manifestations of an unacceptable world. He became a virtual recluse, remaining in his palace at Salalah and not visiting the north of his country at all after 1958. A bloodless rebellion in 1970 resulted in the Sultan being flown to this country, where he died in exile. He was succeeded by his son, Qaboos bin Said (born 1940).

Further along Pine Avenue and to the left of the path is a headstone in black marble with kerbing.

9.26. Prince Soltan Hamid Mirza Kadjar (1918–1988) [plot 128/M3]

Prince Hamid was the grandson of Mohammad Ali Shah Qajar (reigned 1907–9), the nephew of the last Qajar Shah of Iran (Ahmad Mirza, reigned from 1909, and deposed in 1925) and the son of Crown Prince Mohammad Hassan Mirza (the last Qajar Crown Prince). Prince Hamid was sent to England to study and attended the Merchant Marine Academy, where he gained scholastic and nautical qualifications in 1936. Prince Hamid then joined the Royal Mail Steam Packet Company as a cadet. He later worked for the Mobil Oil Company. In 1941 the British considered restoring him to the Iranian throne, but the idea was dropped owing to Russian opposition and his poor command of Farsi. In 1942 he volunteered for the Royal Navy, adopting the pseudonym 'David Drummond' and gaining promotion to the rank of Lieutenant-Commander. After the war he worked for Mobil Oil in London and later for the Iranian Oil Consortium. He retired in 1979 and lived in London until his death. His memoirs were published in English in 1996.

Appendix A

MISSING PERSONS

This section lists brief details of those persons known to be buried at Brookwood. However, at the time of writing precise locations have not been found. Further information on any of these would be welcome.

A.1. Hon. George Charles Agar (1780–1856)

Educated at Westminster and Christ Church, Oxford. He entered the Army as an Ensign in the Foot Guards in 1804. He served as a Lieutenant between 1809 and 1811, when he retired. Agar was elected FRS in 1832. He died at Ropley House, Alresford, Hants. His grave is described as 'near church', which suggests he was buried in plot 27, 37 or 38, but no trace of it has been found. It is possible his grave is one of the anonymous flat ledger stones in plot 27 or 37.

A.2. Charles Edward Austin (c. 1820–1893)

Businessman and Director of the LNC (1871–93). Probably related to **William Austin**. On his death the Board of Directors recorded: '[their] desire to convey to Mrs C. Austin their sincere sympathy with her in this her deep hour of sorrow for the loss she has sustained in the death of their colleague her late husband who had been an energetic member of the Board since February 1871.'[1]

His grave is probably in plot 28 opposite the East Gate, but no trace of a memorial to him has so far been found.

A.3. Walter Baker Clode (1856–1937)

Judge. Educated at Winchester College and Oriel College, Oxford. He was called to the Bar at the Inner Temple in 1881. For many years Clode worked on the North-Eastern Circuit. He was President of the Railway Rates Tribunal (1922–32) and Master of the Merchant Taylors' Company (1904). Clode became a Bencher of the Inner Temple in 1920. His publications include *The Law and Practice of Petition of Right under the Petition of Rights Act* (1860), *The Law Relating to Tenement Houses and Flats* (1889) and *The Law Relating to the Assessment and Valuation of Railways and Stations for Rating Purposes* (1899).

A.4. Sir James Parker Deane (1812–1902)

Judge. Educated at Winchester and St John's College, Oxford. Deane entered the Inner Temple (1837) and became a member of the College of Advocates (1839). He was called to the Bar (1839) and appointed a QC (1858). Deane was Legal Adviser to Sir Charles Napier (1786–1860), the Commander of the British Fleet in the Baltic. Deane was present at the bombardment of Bomarsund and formed part of the landing party. Deane worked in the Courts of Probate and Divorce and obtained a large practice. His most conspicuous appearances were in the ecclesiastical courts, and there were few Church cases of importance for which he was not retained. One of these was *Martin v. **Revd A.H. Mackonochie*** (1867–82). In 1868 Deane was made Chancellor of the Diocese of Salisbury and in the same year was made Advocate General to the Admiralty. In 1872 Deane was appointed Vicar General of Canterbury. Between 1872 and 1886 Deane was Legal Adviser to the Foreign Office, and prepared the British case in the arbitration between Great Britain and Portugal over territory adjacent to Delagoa Bay. He also advised the Government over the *Alabama* incident (1871–2).[2] Deane and Dr T.H. Tristram were the last of the 'civilians' trained in the 'Doctors' Commons', and described in Dickens's *David Copperfield*.[3] Deane's grave is described as being 'near the church', but so far has not been identified.

A.5. Benjamin Leopold Farjeon (1838–1903)

Novelist. At the age of 14 he joined the *Nonconformist* newspaper. His unwillingness to conform to the Jewish faith resulted in his embarking for Australia in 1855, where he went to the goldfields of Victoria and New Zealand. Farjeon settled in Dunedin and became a journalist. He assisted in the *Otago Daily Times*, the first daily paper in New Zealand. He soon turned to writing novels, including *Christopher Congleton* and *Grif* (1866, also published in London in 1870). In 1868 he returned to England where he spent the rest of his life producing Dickensian-type novels and mysteries. These include *London's Heart* (1873), *The Duchess of Rosemary Lane* (1876), *Great Porter Square* (1884) and *Devlin and the Barber* (1888). Farjeon was cremated and his ashes were buried at Brookwood.

A.6. Sir Frederick Mitchell Hodgson (1851–1925)

Colonial administrator. Hodgson was based in the Secretary's Office of the Post Office Department (1868–82) and was appointed Postmaster General of British Guiana (1882–8). He served as Colonial Secretary of the Gold Coast (1888–98) and administered the government on several occasions. He was successively Governor of the Gold Coast (1898–1900), Governor and Commander-in-Chief of Barbados (1900–4) and Governor of British Guiana (1904–11). His wife, **Mary Alice Young** (dates not known), was the author of *The Siege of Kumassi* (1901).

A.7. Charles Lucas (1808–1869)

Composer. Born in Salisbury, Lucas became a chorister at the cathedral. In 1830 he joined Queen Adelaide's private band and was music preceptor to Prince George (later Duke of Cambridge, 1819–1904) and the Princess of Saxe-Weimar. Lucas was conductor at the Royal Academy of Music from 1832 and organist of the **Hanover Chapel**, **Regent Street**, from 1839. He was Principal of the Royal Academy of Music (1859–66). Lucas composed three symphonies, string quartets, anthems, songs and an opera *(The Regicide)*.

A.8. John Ayrton Paris (1785–1856)

Physician. Studied at Caius College, Cambridge, and Edinburgh. Physician to the Westminster Hospital (1809–13) and then practised in Penzance (1814–17). During his time there Paris founded and was First Secretary of the Royal Geological Society of Cornwall (1814–17). He returned to London in 1817 where he continued to practise until his death. He lectured at the Royal College of Physicians on *materia medica* (1819 –26). Paris was made Harveian orator (1833) and was President of the Royal College of Physicians (1844–56). He published many medical works, principally his *Pharmacologia*, which was first published in 1812 and reached its ninth edition in 1843. This book made him £5,000. His other books include *A Guide to Mount's Bay and the Land's End* (1815) and a life of Sir Humphry Davy (1831). His grave is described as 'rear of **Colquhoun**', but no trace of it has been found, unless it is the (now demolished) mausoleum in that locality, marked only by a large ledger stone.

Appendix B

PRINCIPAL STAFF OF THE LONDON NECROPOLIS COMPANY

Chairmen

Sir Thomas Dakin	1853–1870
William Austin	1870–1902
Edward Ford North	1902–1925
Lt-Col H. G. Ricardo	1925–1940
John Baker Walker	1940–1943
Frederick V. Green	1943–1947
Roger B. Pemberton	1947–1959?

General Managers/Managing Directors

Cyril B. Tubbs	1890–1919
John Baker Walker	1919–1943
Charles G. Miller	1943–1959?

Secretaries

Richard Churchill	1850–1870
Julian Larkman	1870–1897
George S. C. Pole	1898–1937
Charles G. Miller	1937–1943
H.C. Christopherson	1943–1945
Arthur F. Green	1945–1953?
George W. Lambert	1953?–1954?
E. J. Jennerway	1954?–1959?

Cemetery Superintendents

George Bupell	1854–?
James Bailey	1854–1870
Stephen Standage	1870–1886
George Barratt	1886–1927
Mr Harry L. Greaves	1928–?

Appendix C

THE BROOKWOOD CEMETERY SOCIETY

The Brookwood Cemetery Society was established in April 1992 to promote a wider interest in the Cemetery and its history. The Society's aims include:

- ensuring the long-term future of the Cemetery,
- assisting with maintenance, clearance and renovation work,
- ensuring that the Cemetery remains a valuable haven for a wide variety of flora and fauna,
- helping relatives locate graves in the Cemetery.

The Brookwood Cemetery Society organises a regular programme of events during the year. This includes regular guided walks through the grounds, usually on the first Sunday in the month, and also at other times; an annual Open Day, usually held in August; regular clearance sessions in the grounds; Society Lectures by visiting speakers which cover some aspect of the history of cemeteries or undertaking, or about people buried at Brookwood. The Society also arranges occasional visits to other cemeteries, graveyards and crematoria. In addition, members of the Brookwood Cemetery Society give talks to local organisations about the Cemetery and the work of the Society; it also publishes leaflets and booklets on the Cemetery.

Membership is open to anyone interested in the work of the Society. Benefits of membership include:

- access to information on the burial registers, 1854–1976,
- a regular Newsletter (*The Brookwood Express*) giving up-to-date information about the Society's activities and news about the Cemetery,
- the opportunity to assist in recording details of those buried at Brookwood,
- reduced admission to Society Lectures.

If you would like to know more about the Society and our forthcoming activities, visit our website at http://www.tbcs.org.uk.

NOTES

FOREWORD

1. St Antholin, Watling Street, in 1875, St John Clerkenwell, St Magnus the Martyr, St Martin Ludgate Hill and St Botolph without Aldersgate in 1894, All Hallows the Great & Less, Upper Thames Street, in 1896, St Michael Wood Street and the Hanover Chapel in 1897, St Mildred Bread Street and Charterhouse in 1898, St George the Martyr, Southwark, in 1899 and St Clement Danes in 1900.

PREFACE

1. Most people seem surprised that the main responsibility for maintaining memorials is the family's. Grants for private burial plots issued by the LNC clearly stated that 'any monument to be erected on such Allotment shall be subject to the approval of the Officers of the said Company, and shall be kept in repair *at the expense of the Allottee*' (my italics).
2. For instance, see the Introduction of this guide. Even forty years ago people were prepared to pay for the maintenance and upkeep of family graves and monuments. Today this practice has all but disappeared (except among certain communities such as the Muslims and Catholics), with cemeteries consequently appearing grossly neglected and overgrown.
3. Why? One of the LNC's brochures suggested: 'This, however, is not the place to use too freely the names of the great Dead; the privacy of Brookwood has often influenced its choice as a place of burial, and there is no intention of committing an indiscretion that might give unintentional pain.' *The London Necropolis* (London, LNC, *c.* 1904), pp. 22–3.
4. A revised second edition of the introductory guide was published by the Society in 2002.
5. John M. Clarke, *The Brookwood Necropolis Railway* (3rd edn, Oxford, Oakwood Press, 1995).
6. James S. Curl, *The Victorian Celebration of Death* (Newton Abbot, David & Charles, 1972), p. 156.

INTRODUCTION

1. *Census of Great Britain 1851* (London, 1851); *Fourth* [and *Fourteenth*] *Annual Report of the Registrar-General* (London, 1842 [and 1855]); *A Supplementary Report on the Results of a Special Inquiry into the Practice of Interments in Towns* (Parliamentary Papers, 1843, vol. XII).
2. See for instance G.A. Walker, *Gatherings from Grave Yards* (London, Longmans, 1839, also reprinted New York, Arno Press, 1977), *passim*.
3. The scheme is outlined in the *Report on a General Scheme for Extramural Sepulture* (Parliamentary Papers, 1850, vol. XXI); see also Chris Brooks, *Mortal Remains* (Exeter, Wheaton, 1989), pp. 45–7.
4. 'An Act to Make Better Provision for the Interment of the Dead in and near the Metropolis' (13 & 14 Vict., c. lii).
5. The Metropolitan Interments Amendment Act ('An Act to Amend the Laws Concerning the Burial of the Dead in the Metropolis', 15 & 16 Vict., c. 85). This Act repealed the 1850 legislation and allowed vestries to elect burial boards to set up new parochial burial grounds either by building new

cemeteries or arranging burials in an existing one. See Chris Brooks, *Mortal Remains* (Exeter, Wheaton, 1989), pp. 47–54, which also discusses later burial Acts of the nineteenth century.

6. Sir Richard Broun (1801–58). Miscellaneous writer and projector of a number of schemes, and the compilation of pamphlets, articles and letters regarding them. His main enterprises were a plan for direct intercourse between Europe and Asia via British North America (1833); the attempted revival of supposed privileges of baronets (1835); a plan for an Anglo-Canadian Company (1852); the revival of the Order of Knights Hospitallers of St John of Jerusalem and the Venerable Langue of England (1856); and the London Necropolis (1849–50). Benjamin Disraeli lampooned him as Sir Vavasour Firebrace in his novel *Sybil* (1845).

7. Little is known of Richard Sprye. He was described as 'gentleman' of 37 Great George Street, Westminster, during the provisional stages of the LNC's registration. He may have been a merchant, and undoubtedly knew several of the London businessmen who subsequently acquired shares in the LNC.

8. There was a general meeting with the inhabitants of Woking at the end of 1849, for which see the *County Chronicle & Surrey Herald*, 19 December 1849. Many other meetings took place to gain publicity and support for this plan. See also Sir R. Broun, *Extramural Sepulture: Synopsis of the London Necropolis and National Mausoleum at Woking* (London, Trelawney Saunders, 1851). Hereafter cited as *Synopsis*.

9. Broun, *Synopsis*, pp. 7–8, 9–10.

10. Sir James Caleb Anderson, John Gardiner, Charles Robert Thompson and William James Voules. Anderson (1792–1861) was an inventor and experimentalist, especially in steam coaches, steamboats and engines. Thompson (dates not known) was a wine merchant and East India agent. He traded under the name of C.R. Thompson & Company, Old Broad Street. Thompson was declared bankrupt in January 1856. He was acquainted with Richard Sprye, since one of his assets was Sprye's claim on the LNC valued at £2,740 (*Daily News*, 30 January 1856). Voules (dates not known) was sometime Poor Law Commissioner. He was 'nominated' deputy chairman at the end of 1850, and effectively acted as chairman of the LNC until his resignation caused by the investigations of the LNC's committee of inquiry (for which see below).

11. Sir Richard Broun, *Metropolitan Extramural Sepulture: London Necropolis and National Mausoleum Company. Letter to the Right Honourable Lord Palmerston, with a copy of a Letter to Messrs Rothery, Dakin and others* (London, Pelham Richardson, 1854), pp. 3, 13. Hereafter cited as *Letter to Palmerston*. Broun and Sprye were also to retain 500 acres of the LNC's estate for their own, non-cemetery, use.

12. These included Consulting Engineer, Captain William S. Moorsom (1804–63); Architect, Henry R. Abraham (see n. 24); Solicitors, Messrs Coombe & Nickoll; Secretary, Richard Churchill and office clerk, **Julian Larkman**.

13. A provisional contract was reached with Lord Onslow on 27 April 1852, who was to receive £38,000 for Woking Common (Onslow Collection, Surrey History Centre). Arthur George Onslow, 3rd Earl Onslow (1777–1870). Educated at Harrow, styled Viscount Cranley between 1814 and 1827, when he succeeded the 2nd Earl. He appears to have led an unremarkable life.

14. The various deeds were required, since the officers of the LNC chose the device of the 'unincorporated company', using the law of Chancery, prior to its formation under a private Act of Parliament. Broun and Sprye often referred to themselves as the 'Sole Projectors of the Necropolis and Founders of the Company and two of its largest Shareholders'.

15. Preamble to the London Necropolis & National Mausoleum Act 1852 (15 & 16 Vict., c. cxlix).

16. For instance, Broun, *Letter to Palmerston*, pp. ii, 1–5.

17. Sir Richard Broun, *Extramural Interment and the Metropolitan Sanitary Association: Letter to the Prime Minister and the Chief Commissioner of Woods and Forests* (London, Trelawney Saunders, 1852), p.12.

18. Henry Drummond (1786–1860). Politician, MP for Plympton Earls (1810–13) and for West Surrey (1847–60). Helped found the Continental Society (1819). Founded the Professorship of Political Economy at Oxford (1825). Helped found the Irvingite Sect (1826).

19. *Hansard*, vol. CXIX, cols 925–6, 928, 930.

20. The actual figure awarded was £15,000. 'Turbary' (otherwise 'turbaries' or 'common of turbary') is the legal right to cut peat or turf for fuel on a common.

21. Alan Crosby, *A History of Woking* (Chichester, Phillimore, 1982), p. 56.

22. Broun, *Letter to Palmerston*, pp. 14–15.

23. Drummond asked for a single example where a railway company had purchased over 2,000 acres and used only 400.

24. Henry Robert Abraham (1804–77). Architect and surveyor, son of Robert Abraham (1774–1850). Some of his London buildings included the Library of the Middle Temple, and 188–191 and 184 Strand. All have since been demolished.

25. Clause XVI: 'That the Company shall not, without the Sanction and Authority of Parliament, sell any Lands which they may acquire under the Authority of this Act. . . . '.

26. Minutes of Evidence of the Select Committee of the House of Commons, Group DD, 1852, vol. 40.

27. Clause XIV.

28. G.A. Sekon, *The London & South Western Railway: Half a Century of Progress* (London, 1896), p. 33.

29. Cemetery Clauses Act 1847 (10 & 11 Vict., c. cxv). The figure of 6s 2d was undoubtedly chosen since it was the same fee paid to Anglican clergymen under the Metropolitan Interments Act 1850; the Bishop of London (Charles James Blomfield) was a keen supporter of the Necropolis bill.

30. *Hansard*, vol. CXXI, cols 891–3. Ebrington was referring to the Metropolitan Interments Amendment Act which was also proceeding through Parliament. See n. 5 above.

31. Clause XXXI.

32. *Hansard*, vol. CXXII, cols 190–2.

33. London Necropolis & National Mausoleum Act 1852 (15 & 16 Vict., c. cxlix).

34. Broun, *Letter to Palmerston*, pp. 13–16. Compare Broun's figures to those cited in the LNC's first annual report, below.

35. Captain Moorsom to Richard Churchill, 29 June 1853. Abraham was requested to stop all work for the LNC at the end of April 1853 (Churchill to Abraham, 27 April 1853). The LNC then began an action for negligence (Minutes of the LNC Board of Directors [hereafter 'Minutes'], 26 July 1853). Abraham sued the company for non-payment of his fees. The case was heard at Croydon Assizes on 28 July 1853, where Abraham claimed £7,000 compensation (*The Times*, 9 August 1853). The matter went to arbitration, and on 24 March 1854 Abraham was awarded £3,159 plus costs.

36. Other problems included no general shareholders' meetings, no annual reports and no proper auditing of the accounts. *The Times* reported the lack of share capital on 15 November 1853, catching the attention of a wider public.

37. *The Times*, 17 June, 3 and 23 November 1852. For more on Thompson, see n. 10.

38. Minutes, 17 May 1853.

39. Minutes, 19 July 1853; John S. Taylor to the Committee of Enquiry, 20 July 1853. The committee comprised **Colonel Chatterton**, John Jones, Captain C.R. Knight, F. Parker and **Henry C. Rothery**.

40. The original trustees were replaced by Sir James Duke MP, Archibald Hastie MP, John B. Smith and William Arthur Wilkinson MP. Duke (1792–1873) was a coal factor and insurance broker in London (1819–48), Alderman of Farringdon Without (1840–73), Lord Mayor of London (1848–9) and MP for Boston (1837–49); he was a keen supporter of the LNC's bill during its passage through Parliament. Hastie (1791–1857) was a coachbuilder and East India agent in London, director of the East India Docks and its chief manager, and MP for Paisley (1836–57). Wilkinson (1794–1865) was a member of the London Stock Exchange (1816–46); Chairman of the London & Croydon Railway (1839–46), MP for Lambeth (1852–7) and promoted the construction of the Metropolitan Railway with **William Austin**, Charles Gilpin MP and others. Nothing further has been traced on John Smith. A letter dated 18 May 1853 from the LNC's original solicitors, Messrs Coombe & Nickoll, implies Mr Voules's 'fees' may have been used to clear his debts elsewhere.

41. Minutes, 27 September 1853.

42. Consulting Engineer, Sir William Cubitt; Engineer, Joseph Cubitt; Architect, Sydney Smirke; Auditors, Alfred H. Shadwell, William Wing and Edmund Harding; Bankers, Messrs Currie & Co.; Solicitors, Messrs Harrison; Secretary, Richard Churchill.

43. The initial board comprised **William Austin**, the Hon. Francis Henry Fitzhardinge Berkeley MP, **Colonel J.C. Chatterton**, **Alexander A. Croll**, **Thomas Dakin**, William Frederick Augustus Delane, the Rt Revd Samuel Hinds, **Joseph Ivimey**, John Jones, T. Hacket Massey, **Henry C. Rothery** and Horace Wilkinson. Of these, Berkeley (1794–1870) was a politician, MP for Bristol (1837–70) and leader of the ballot question in the House of Commons (1837–70). Delane (1794–1857) was financial manager of *The Times*; manager of the *Morning Chronicle* to 1847, treasurer of the county courts of Kent and part of Surrey (1847–57) and author of several legal works. Nothing has been traced on the other directors.

44. Sir William Cubitt (1785–1861). Civil engineer, inventor of the self-regulating windmill sail (1807), and the treadmill (1818). Constructed many docks and railways including the Oxford Canal, Cardiff Docks, Middlesbrough Docks and the South Eastern Railway. FRS (1830), President of the Institution of Civil Engineers (1850–1) and knighted in 1851.

45. Sir William Cubitt to the Chairman and Board of Directors, 3 February 1854.

46. *[First] Annual Report of the Directors*, 7 February 1854.

47. Sir William Tite (1798–1873). Architect, famous for London's Royal Exchange (1841–4) and many railway stations, including Nine Elms (1838), Carlisle (1847–8), Perth (1848) and Windsor (1851). At this time Tite was architect to the LSWR. He was architect to the South Metropolitan Cemetery at Norwood (1836–7), where he designed both the layout and the chapels. Tite is buried at Norwood.

48. John M. Clarke, *The Brookwood Necropolis Railway* (3rd edn, Oxford, Oakwood Press, 1995), ch. 2.

49. Accounts and estimates of the total size of the London Necropolis vary in a similar way to estimates of the size of the estate purchased from Lord Onslow. Figures for the cemetery vary between 400 and 500 acres, probably because the initial area laid out was 400 acres but later extended. For reasons of consistency I have used 500 acres throughout this book.

50. Alan Crosby, *A History of Woking* (Chichester, Phillimore, 1982), pp. 16–21, 57–9. The commoners of these 'waste' lands were compensated for the loss of access to these areas under the Woking Commoners Act 1854 (17 & 18 Vict., c. ix). Their claims were settled by a jury, which awarded them £15,000, payable by the LNC, which was finally distributed in 1857.

51. George Bourne [i.e. George Sturt], *William Smith: Potter and Farmer 1790–1858* (London, Chatto & Windus, 1920), p. 1.

52. Minutes, 22 March and 8 May 1854. This may not be the complete cost since the *Builder* cited £2,958 14s 8d for fencing (8 March 1856).

53. Minutes, 14 June; 12 July; 2 and 17 August 1854; 17 and 22 August 1855.

54. In all cases the modern avenue names have been used, although it is likely that most of the roads were un-named at this time.

55. Minutes 12 July, 11 and 18 October 1854; 1 February 1855. The *Builder* cited £8,802 19s 0d for drainage, and £3,048 14s 0d for 'planting and road-making' (8 March 1856).

56. Sydney Smirke (1798–1877). Architect, and brother of Sir Robert Smirke (1781–1867, who designed the British Museum). Smirke designed the Bazaar in Oxford Street (1834), completed the restoration of the Temple Church, London (1841), the dome and portico to the Imperial War Museum (1843–5), the Conservative Club, St James's (1845–56, with George Basevi), the Carlton Club, Pall Mall (1845–56), St John the Baptist, Loughton, Essex (1846), the Athenaeum, Bury, Lancashire (1846–7), the round reading room of the British Museum (1854–7), twice restored the Savoy Chapel, and completed the exhibition galleries at Burlington House (1870). Smirke was elected to the Royal Academy in 1859, was Professor of Architecture at the Royal Academy (1861–5) and founded the Architects' Benevolent Society in 1852.

57. Minutes of Evidence of the Select Committee of the House of Lords, 1852, vol. 4; Minutes of Evidence of the Select Committee of the House of Commons, Group DD, 1852, vol. 40. Several designs by Abraham also exist, for instance, the engraving published in the *Illustrated London News*, 18 December 1852.

58. The contract for the construction of the chapels and stations at Brookwood was awarded to Messrs Lucas for £6,040 (Minutes, 12 April 1854).

59. Sydney Smirke to Richard Churchill, 8 March 1854. None of the plans or drawings referred to appear to have survived.

60. Presumed to be the landscape gardener, William Broderick Thomas (1811–98). He made alterations to the gardens at Buckingham Palace and designed the gardens at Sandringham House. Thomas also designed the gardens at Benenden, Kent; Bestwood Lodge, Nottingham; Felbrigg Hall, Cromer; Hemsted House, Kent; and Overstone Park, Northampton. He designed the great parterre at Baronscourt, County Tyrone, and made improvements at Powerscourt, County Wicklow. See Ray Desmond, *Dictionary of British & Irish Botanists and Horticulturalists* (London, Taylor & Francis, 1994).

61. Minutes, 12 April 1854.

62. Donald appears to have run into financial difficulties from 1863 when his property was assigned to Tannton & Broom as creditors for about £2,700. The sale of his stock was postponed until after Donald's death in May 1866. Donald had also leased land from the LNC adjacent to the LSWR and the Bagshot Road. The collapse of his business affected the LNC since he also owed them money. Richard Churchill, its first Secretary, helped Donald financially, apparently using company funds. As a consequence Churchill was obliged to resign his position (17 May 1870). He was replaced by **Julian Larkman**. (Minutes, 22 January, 12 and 18 February, 13 April, 18 May 1870.)

63. Anon., 'Extramural Interments: Woking Cemetery', in *The Leisure Hour*, vol. V, 1856, p. 347.

64. Minutes, 8 May, 30 October 1854; 18 April, 29 August 1855. The *Builder* cited £3,048 14s 0d for 'planting and road-making' (8 March 1856). Donald was also a shareholder in the LNC, and was listed with ten £25 shares in July 1857.

65. Minutes, 4 March 1857.

66. W. Botting Hemsley, *A New and Complete Index to the Botanical Magazine from its Commencement in 1787 to the end of 1904, including . . . a History of the Magazine* (London, Lovell, Reeve & Co., 1906), p. xli; Anthea Taigel and Tom Williamson, *Parks and Gardens* (London, B.T. Batsford, 1993), pp. 97–8.

67. Not in height, or diameter, but the two combined, resulting in the highest volume of timber for its size.

68. This overall scheme followed many of the suggestions contained in J.C. Loudon's *On the Laying Out, Planting and Managing of Cemeteries, and on the Improvement of Churchyards* (London, Longman Brown Green, 1843).

69. For more on Mount Auburn Cemetery see Stanley French, 'The Cemetery as a Cultural Institution: the Establishment of Mount Auburn and the "Rural Cemetery" Movement' in D.E. Stannard, *Death in America* (Philadelphia, University of Pennsylvania Press, 1975).

70. Anon., 'Extramural Interments: Woking Cemetery', in *The Leisure Hour*, vol. V, 1856, p. 347.

71. *War Graves: How the Cemeteries Abroad will be Designed* (London, HMSO, 1918). Sir Frederick Kenyon (1863–1952), an adviser to the IWGC, was then Director of the British Museum.

72. *The Times*, 2 September 1920, describing the IWGC's first completed war cemetery at Forceville.

73. This practice evolved from that of Edward Milner (1819–84), a former assistant to Joseph Paxton. Edward White (c. 1873–1952) was a distinguished landscape architect who was a supporter of cremation and was particularly interested in designing gardens attached to crematoria.

74. Edward White, 'Crematorium Gardens', in P.H. Jones (ed.), *Cremation in Great Britain* (3rd edn, London, The Cremation Society, 1945). These cemetery styles – and others – are also discussed in G. Jellicoe *et al.*, *The Oxford Companion to Gardens* (Oxford, Oxford University Press, 1986), pp. 101–4.

75. Ian Nairn and Nikolaus Pevsner, *The Buildings of England: Surrey* (2nd edn, revised by Bridget Cherry, London, Penguin, 1971), p. 120.

76. Dr John Sutherland (1808–91). Sanitary reformer, Inspector to the General Board of Health from 1848. Later sent by Lord Palmerston to investigate the sanitary condition of British troops in the Crimea, and subsequently undertook a number of sanitary reforms in the Army.

77. Letter of Dr John Sutherland to the LNC, 21 February 1855.

78. *The Times*, 8 November 1854.

79. The Rt. Revd Charles Richard Sumner (1790–1874). Chaplain to George IV (1823–5), Prebendary of Canterbury Cathedral (1825–7) and Bishop of Llandaff (1826–7), Bishop of Winchester (1827–69), during which he made ten visitations and issued two Conspectuses of his Diocese.

80. *The Times*, 8 November 1854; the *Surrey Standard*, 11 November 1854.

81. *The Times*, 14 November 1854; the *Spectator*, 14 November 1854.

82. Minutes, 20 October 1854.

83. The Metropolitan Interments Amendment Act ('An Act to Amend the Laws Concerning the Burial of the Dead in the Metropolis', 15 & 16 Vict., c. 85); and see n. 5.

84. Minutes, *passim*.

85. The company discussed its financial position and loans on 6, 29 May; 5 July; 8, 11 October 1854 (Minutes). See also Smirke's letter of 8 March 1854 above. The 1852 Act identified certain land for compulsory purchase. This was a further drain on company funds since thirty-one plots, amounting to 130 acres, had been acquired at a cost of over £8,600. See *Daily News*, 15 February 1856.

86. Several estimates exist, including figures quoted in *Builder* (8 March 1856), that suggests a figure of about £110,000. However, the sum of £151,592 10s 7d was cited at the LNC's annual general meeting for 1856, 'a sum exceeding the actual amount of share capital'. See *Daily News*, 15 February 1856.

87. Draft 'Proof of Mr Richard Churchill' and draft 'Petition to Sir George Grey'. The reason why Palmerston did not extend this requirement to existing cemeteries is not clear. Undoubtedly it would have led to difficulties with most (if not all) of the existing private cemetery companies.

88. London Necropolis & National Mausoleum Amendment Act 1855 (18 & 19 Vict., c. clxiii).

89. Minutes, *passim*.

90. Anon., 'The Great Cemetery at Woking' in *Illustrated London News*, 26 April 1856. An engraving of the cemetery accompanied this article. It appears elsewhere as plate 1.

91. The distinction between the three main classes of grave was as follows. A '3rd-class' grave was one allocated to those buried at the expense of the parish and located in a designated area of the cemetery. The grave was rarely purchased by the family (so that a permanent memorial could be erected), although some examples are described under **pauper graves**. A '2nd-class' grave could be selected with some choice of location, but the standard fee of £1 excluded the right to erect a permanent memorial (which was 10s extra). If no permanent memorial was placed, the company reserved the right to reuse the grave space at some future date. A '1st-class' or 'private' grave could be located virtually anywhere in the cemetery, although 'special' positions (designated by the LNC) were charged extra. A permanent memorial was expected to be placed over '1st-class' graves in due course. Prices ranged from £2 10s 0d for a standard 9ft × 4ft plot, to £5 5s 0d and upwards for a similar grave in a 'special' position.

92. Anon., 'Extramural Interments: Woking Cemetery', in *The Leisure Hour*, vol. V, 1856, p. 348.

93. Dottridge Brothers were based on East Road, City Road, N1.

94. John M. Clarke, *The Brookwood Necropolis Railway* (3rd edn, Oxford, Oakwood Press, 1995), appendix 2.

95. *Era*, 30 March 1907. The 'National Burial Device' was a new apparatus for lowering coffins into graves. It has been described as follows: 'This is an exceedingly ingenious contrivance. An oblong frame is laid over the top of the grave, and across from side to side run webbing bands, which are wound and unwound on rollers in the frame. The coffin is placed upon the webbing, and the simple touching of a wheel sets the mechanism in motion, and the weight of the coffin takes it down as slowly or as rapidly as it is desired. When the coffin reaches the bottom the web bands are automatically detached and wound back in position by a simple process. The whole contrivance folds double, so as to be easily portable, and is placed in position in a moment. For the device it is claimed that coffins

are much more reverently and safely lowered by its use, and in addition the bearers can leave directly the coffin is placed on the webbing, so that the mourners alone need stand by the grave, and there is no tripping over the lengths of webbing which are an inevitable accompaniment to the old process.' See *Undertakers' Journal*, 31 January 1902, pp. 18–20. I am grateful to Brian Parsons for drawing my attention to this article.

96. *Era*, 30 March 1907.

97. See John M. Clarke, *The Brookwood Necropolis Railway* (3rd edn, Oxford, Oakwood Press, 1995), especially ch. 4.

98. Sir Henry Thompson (1820–1904), surgeon, studied and practised at University College Hospital, London. He invented a technique for crushing gall-stones without cutting, and performed this operation on King Leopold I (1863) and Napoleon III (1873). Thompson helped found the Cremation Society and the company which erected Golders Green Crematorium in 1902. He was a keen amateur artist, astronomer, novelist, horticulturalist, photographer and collector of Oriental porcelain. See Zachary Cope, *The Versatile Victorian, Being the Life of Sir Henry Thompson, Bt. 1820–1904* (London, Harvey Blythe, 1951).

99. *The Times*, 15 January 1879.

100. *The Times*, 31 January 1879; *Surrey Advertiser & County Times*, 1 February 1879. The deputation presented the Home Secretary with a memorial against the crematorium signed by 853 persons.

101. Sir H. Thompson, *Modern Cremation: Its History and Practice* (2nd edn, London, Kegan Paul, 1891), pp. 5–20.

102. In the words of one of its brochures the 'Earth-to-Earth' coffin 'is peculiarly suited to the process of natural interment, facilitating the free resolvent action of the earth upon human remains. Its construction is simple as it is salutary. Possessing the apparent strength, solidity, and other qualities of a Solid Coffin, it yet differs in this important respect, namely: that while the latter interferes with the natural dissolution of the body, the former promotes its disintegration and absorption, thus effectually carrying out the sanitary principle of "Earth-to-Earth" burial.' The coffins continued to be developed further to include veneers of various woods and different shapes. They were increasingly used for pauper burials and samples of a new design with joints were sent to various parishes for inspection in the summer of 1890 (Minutes of the Committee Appointed to Reconsider the Price Lists, 17 June; 8, 15 and 28 July 1890).

103. Reissued later in 1875 with additional material including 'a plea for a change of system in our Burial of the Dead'. Sir Henry Thompson later responded to Haden's claims by enquiring 'How the system of placing a diseased or any other body in a mere basket for the express purpose of ensuring contact at once with every channel by which its contents may escape, can be advocated for sanitary purposes or by any sanitary authority, I am unable to conceive.' Sir H. Thompson, *Modern Cremation: Its History and Practice* (2nd edn, London, Kegan Paul, 1891), pp. 111–12.

104. Minutes 2, 16 March; 27 April 1876.

105. *The Times*, 15 January 1879.

106. *The London Necropolis & National Mausoleum (Woking Cemetery), Brookwood, Surrey* (London, LNC, 1887), pp. 10–11.

107. Minutes, 2 May 1888; *Circular to Shareholders* dated 1 December 1888.

108. Minutes, 7 December 1887; 1 February 1888; 17 April, 21 May 1889.

109. Minutes, 28 July 1891.

110. Minutes of the Committee Appointed to Reconsider the Price Lists, 28 January 1890.

111. Minutes, February–April 1890; 28 June, July 1891. Also based on information supplied by Brian Parsons and Stephen White.

112. Jackman's epitaph does not mention that he was cremated. The first to do so is **Isabella Hirst Knight** (died 1891). By this time a total of 177 cremations had taken place at Woking. Cremation became increasingly popular after 1945, but not before.

113. A perishable coffin patented by the LNC, see n. 102.

114. *The Times*, 28 July 1892, p.6; 4 August 1892, p. 6.

115. *The London Necropolis* (London, LNC, *c*. 1902), pp. 18–20.

116. London Necropolis & National Mausoleum Amendment Act 1864 (27 & 28 Vict., c. lxii).

117. Minutes, 27 November 1867.

118. Minutes, *passim*; cemetery burial registers.

119. London Necropolis & National Mausoleum Amendment Act 1869 (32 Vict., c. iii).

120. Even the passage of the 1869 Act led to further financial difficulties since the LNC disputed the bill of costs with its solicitors Harrisons & Co. Consequently Harrisons lost the LNC's account but, in doing so, Richard Churchill was removed from office as secretary (Minutes, 1868–70, *passim*).

121. *Annual Report of the Directors*, 1870 and 1887.

122. *The London Necropolis* (London, LNC, *c*. 1904), p. 42.

123. Minutes, *passim*.

124. This might also be seen as a desperate attempt by the Chairman to encourage other members of the board and shareholders to do likewise. However, land sales continued on a piecemeal basis. North's house was Comeragh Court on Golf Club Road.

125. These windows were removed when the St Edward Brotherhood adapted the building for its own services after 1982.

126. Colonel Bernard Rowland Ward (1863–1933). Royal Engineer, Colonel (1909), retired (1919). He wrote several books on military engineering. I have failed to trace any information on Captain Goulden. An excellent guide to the IWGC, the CWGC and its cemeteries is Phillip Longworth, *The Unending Vigil: A History of the Commonwealth War Graves Commission 1917–1984* (London, Leo Cooper, 1984).

127. Egerton Swartwout (1870–1943). Architect, practised in New York. Works include US State Post Office and Court House (Denver); George Washington Memorial Building (Washington); Mary Baker Eddy Memorial (Cambridge, Mass.); Elkes Memorial Building (Chicago); US National St Mihiel Monument, Montsee (France); Home Club (New York); New Haven City Hall; and the Baily Memorial Foundation (Brooklyn). Swartwout also wrote a number of monographs and articles on architectural subjects.

128. John Russell Pope (1874–1937). Architect, ran his own practice from 1900. Works include Scottish Rite Temple (Washington DC); Plattsburg City Hall, Richard (Va.) Terminal Station; additions to the Metropolitan Museum, New York; American Battle Monument, Montfaucon (France); mausoleum for William B. Leeds, Woodlawn Cemetery, New York; Baltimore Museum of Art; additions to the British Museum and Tate Gallery. Russell reputedly designed more monumental buildings than any other architect of his generation.

129. Harry Bulkeley Creswell (1869–1960). Architect and author, private practice from 1900. Works include domestic buildings; churches at Rugby and Coventry; the Law Courts and Law Offices, Sierra Leone; College of Agriculture, Mauritius; New Parthenon Room, British Museum. Wrote novels and children's stories.

130. *The Times*, 16 August 1937. In 1937 the American chapel at Brookwood was the only one of its kind in the United Kingdom.

131. Lieutenant-Colonel Henry George Ricardo (1860–1940). Soldier and administrator. He joined the Royal Artillery and served during the First World War. Ricardo was awarded the DSO in 1917. He was a director of the LNC from 1904. Ricardo was twice married: first to Adela Lucy Cobbold in 1885 (who died in 1921), and secondly to Sybil Agnes Hoare in 1923. Although there is a Ricardo family allotment in plot 28, facing towards the East Gate, Ricardo is not apparently buried in the cemetery. He is the only Chairman of the LNC not buried at Brookwood.

132. Public Records Office J 107/43, BT 58/109/COS/3911.

133. Minutes, 13 April 1927.

134. Minutes, 12 January 1928.

135. Extracted from Ledger Books, 23–27.

136. The families concerned were **Braine**, **Dudgeon**, **Glorney** and **Tata**.

137. Extracted from Ledger Books, 23–5 and 32.

138. George Sydenham Clarke (1848–1933). Administrator, lecturer at the Royal Indian Engineering College (1871–80), secretary to the Colonial Defence Committee (1885–92), superintendent of the Royal Carriage Department, Woolwich Arsenal (1894–1901), Governor of Victoria (1901–3) and Bombay (1907–13).

139. Edward Stuart Talbot (1844–1934). Vicar of Leeds (1889–95), Bishop successively of Rochester (1895–1905), Southwark (1905–11) and Winchester (1911–23).

140. A.R. Hope-Moncrieff, *Surrey* (3rd edn, London, Black, 1934), pp. 213–14.

141. LNC Ledger Book, 25; *The Times*, 28 April 1937.

142. Minutes, 7 April 1943.

143. Minutes, 12 September, 14 November 1945; 10 April, 10 July, 11 December 1946; 12 March 1947. In 1950 the chief London branches were situated at 123 Westminster Bridge Road (adjacent to the site of the old station) and 82 Kensington High Street.

144. Minutes, 12 September 1945, 16 April 1947 (when £500 was allocated for these alterations).

145. *The Times*, 27 October 1958.

146. London Necropolis Act 1946 (9 & 10 Geo. 6, c. xviii). It is interesting to speculate why the LNC sought parliamentary approval, since the crematoria at St John's, Woking (opened 1885); at Golders Green, London (opened 1902); the Birmingham Crematorium (opened 1903); the Hendon Park Crematorium (opened 1922) and the South London Crematorium, Streatham Park (opened 1936), were all established without private Acts of Parliament. It is possible the 1946 Act was required owing to the proximity of the crematorium at St John's, Woking. The 1956 Act (see below) may have been required since it dealt with properties on consecrated ground. I am grateful to Brian Parsons for these suggestions.

147. Minutes, 12 September, 12 December 1945. Work proceeded on the Glades as labour and money became available. About £2,000 a year was spent on the project. It should be noted the Glades were laid out on part of the former **pauper burial ground**.

148. Bernard Darwin, *The Glades of Remembrance, Brookwood* ([Brookwood?], LNC, *c.* 1950), p. 4.

149. Entry 211,981 in the Burial Register, and No. 1 for the Glades of Remembrance Register.

150. Minutes, 11 October 1950.

151. London Necropolis Act 1956 (4 & 5 Eliz. 2, c. lxviii)

152. Public Records Office, TS 58/300.

153. Minutes, 10 July, 14 August, 9 October, 13 November, 11 December 1946; 11 February 1947. There is a very useful history of Frederick Paine, Funeral Directors, in Brian Parsons, *The London Way of Death* (Stroud, Sutton Publishing, 2001).

154. Land sales had continued to decline from the mid-1930s to an annual average of just over 2 acres, although the LNC still retained about 260 acres to dispose of at this time. Minutes, *passim*.

155. *The Times*, 3, 9, 14 May, 4, 29 June, 4, 14 July, 20 December 1955.

156. The original lease for Woking Golf Course ran from December 1892 to December 1897, but was destined to continue for nearly eighty years. It appears both the Woking and West Hill golf courses were offered for auction by the LNC in September 1961. However, it was not until 1972 that the Alliance Property Company (which presumably had retained the remaining non-cemetery properties of the LNC) sold the freehold to the Woking Golf Club for £145,000. See James Connelly, *A Temple of Golf: A History of Woking Golf Club 1893–1993* (Woking, Woking Golf Club Estates, 1992), especially ch. 15.

157. London Necropolis & National Mausoleum Amendment Act 1869 (32 Vict., c. iii), section 2.

158. The sale to the West Hill Golf Club did not proceed at this time. At one stage Brookwood Estates was pursuing a parallel policy of developing housing on part of the golf course, and was forced to withdraw this proposal when the Minister of Housing refused to grant planning permission (*The*

Times, 22 December 1955; 30 January 1957). The course was offered for auction in September 1961, but the writer does not know when it was finally sold.

159. The second plot of land was opposite the East Gate; it partly fronted the A322 and Heath House Lane. It comprised about 7 acres but, as it remains undeveloped, it is not clear if this was actually sold.

160. *The Times*, 14 October, 20 December 1955; 12 January 1956; 8 November 1957.

161. Sir Harold (Vaughan) Kenyon (1875–1959), of J.H. Kenyon, Funeral Directors. Member of Kensington Borough Council from 1908 (Alderman 1933, Mayor 1931–4), member of Paddington Council from 1910 (Alderman 1915, Mayor 1920–4 and 1935–7) and made Freeman of the City of London in 1919. Kenyon served on or chaired many committees or boards dealing with the administration of London, along with charitable institutions. He was President of the Metropolitan Mayors' Association in 1958, and sometime member of the National Council for the Disposition of the Dead. Kenyon was a director of the LNC (1943–59). He is buried in St Marylebone Cemetery.

162. *The Times*, 24 December 1957; 18 December 1958; 7, 14 January 1959.

163. *The Times*, 26 September 1960.

164. *The Times*, 22 August 1972.

165. Great Southern Group PLC, prospectus of 24 September 1986.

166. During the period 1854–1974 the LNC had on average disposed of 12½ acres a year, assuming the total available for sale was 1,500 acres (the remaining 700 acres comprising the cemetery and the outlying heaths). However, it should be remembered that in the early years the LNC succeeded in selling some large plots amounting to 281 acres, and therefore the overall average is somewhat misleading.

167. Maximillian Investments had but two directors and shareholders: Mr M.R. Lewinsohn (aged 28) and Mr D.G. Neville, see Dundonian Limited *Proposed Acquisition of Brookwood Cemetery*, 26 February 1976. The cost of the purchase was reported in *The Times*, 6 July 1974. The Great Southern Group was acquired by Service Corporation International (SCI) in 1994, see Brian Parsons, *The London Way of Death* (Stroud, Sutton Publishing, 2001), p. 116. The exhumation business, Necropolis, finally closed in 2002.

168. Brookwood Cemetery Act 1975 (c. xxxv).

169. *The Times*, 6 July 1974.

170. *The Times*, 6 July, 6 August 1974.

171. By this time the offices were also partly occupied by Sherwood Software, who vacated the premises at the end of 1994. Several planning applications followed for the redevelopment of the site, for which see below.

172. Dundonian Limited, *Proposed Acquisition of Brookwood Cemetery*, 26 February 1976; *The Times*, 11 August 1988.

173. Brookwood Cemetery Act 1975 (c. xxxv), preamble, paragraph 6.

174. Father Alexis, 'The St Edward Brotherhood', *Necropolis News* 1996, 2 (1), p. 10.

175. 'Brookwood Cemetery lies in a very shallow valley. It is underlain by the Bracklesham beds, a mixture of sand, clays and silt which is not a good aquifer . . . [therefore] this land tends to be on the wet side. There is a small stream rising in the western end of the grounds and another stream rising in the West Hill area, not far away, which indicates seepage.' David Banks, a hydrogeologist from Reading, quoted in *Surrey Mail*, 13 May 1989; *Daily Telegraph*, 15 May 1989.

176. It is highly regrettable that Woking Borough Council remains largely unsupportive of Mr Guney's work at Brookwood.

177. Further information on Brookwood Cemetery Limited, the company that manages the cemetery, may be found at www.brookwoodcemetery.com.

178. The work of the Brookwood Cemetery Society has been recorded in its regular newsletter, *The Brookwood Express*, first published in May 1992. Further information on the Society may be found at www.tbcs.org.uk.

179. These have been designed by David Cowley. Each replica is constructed, painted and lettered by Cowley, with the Society bearing the cost of the materials. Each signpost is supported on a single

wooden post and stands about 2ft tall. The post incorporates the initials of the Society. The first six signs were erected in October 1999 starting – appropriately enough – with St David's Avenue. Since then over fifty signs have been placed throughout the cemetery. However, with over sixty named avenues within the cemetery this project will take some years to complete.

180. The De Morgan Foundation has an extensive collection of the works of William and Evelyn De Morgan. It is now part of the De Morgan Centre, based at West Hill Library, Wandsworth, which incorporates the Foundation and archive material relating to the De Morgans and their circle.

181. Why this official indifference? Brookwood Cemetery is listed as Grade II in the English Heritage National Register of Historic Parks and Gardens (ref. GD 2282) and surely deserves some form of national funding to assist its restoration and maintenance.

182. *House of Commons, Select Committee on the Environment, Transport & Regional Affairs. 8th Report [on] Cemeteries HC-91-I, HC-91-II*, 21 March 2001.

183. *The Government Reply to the 8th Report from the Environment, Transport and Regional Affairs Committee Session 2000–2001 HC91 Cemeteries*, October 2001 (Cm 5281).

184. *Quality of Life Capital: Overview Report*, March 2001. Published jointly by the agencies mentioned above, a copy of the report may be found at www.qualityoflifecapital.org.uk. 'Quality of Life Capital' is a tool for maximising environmental, economic and social benefits as part of any land use, planning or management decision.

185. Published by the Stationery Office, 29 November 2000 (Cm 4911). This is the first urban white paper for twenty years, and sets out the Government's policies to bring about a renaissance in all urban areas.

186. Brenda Wilson, *Home Office Research into Cemeteries and Their Management, Case Study 3: Brookwood Cemetery Ltd, Private Company, English Suburbs* (2002), p. 8. The full report may be viewed at www.tbcs.org.uk/homeoffice.htm.

187. *Surrey Mail*, 1 July 1989.

188. Thus bringing about one of the fears voiced by local residents at the time of the Brookwood Cemetery Act (1975). Several planning applications were submitted to Woking Borough Council from 1994 for the redevelopment of this site. Some of these, submitted by First Choice Estates, included plans for an estate of five-bedroomed houses.

189. *Woking News & Mail*, 7 May 1998; *Woking Review*, 16 May 1998. I leave it to the interested visitor to form his or her own opinion about this so-called enhancement. The council has taken no action over the destruction of mature trees during the construction of these offices, nor does it appear interested in the fate of the mature trees now dying on the perimeter of this development.

190. *Woking News & Mail*, 12 June 2003.

CHAPTER ONE

1. *Surrey Standard*, 11 November 1854.

2. 4 & 5 Eliz. 2, c. lxviii.

3. The directors accepted the need for this chapel by a Minute dated 16 July 1907. The plans were agreed on 10 March 1908. Although Mr Drowley's estimate was accepted, Mr Hughes was awarded the contract (19 May 1908).

4. Minutes, 12 January 1909. A sum of up to £85 was allowed for these items.

5. Prices were to range from £5 5s 0d upwards depending on size and stone used (Minutes, 11 January 1910). The first stained-glass memorial window was placed by Mrs Darbyshire (Minutes, 7 December 1920). **Mr F. V. Green** had two windows made in the memory of his wife **Isabella Green**. They were designed by Horace Wilkinson (Minutes, 14 December 1933).

6. The organ was situated where the shrine of **St Edward the Martyr** now is, and this extension may have been built to accommodate the new organ (Minutes, 9 December 1926). The organ was removed when the **St Edward Brotherhood** acquired the site. In 1984 it was installed in the church of St Michael & All Angels, Borehamwood.

7. *Surrey Standard*, 11 November 1854.

8. The circumstances of his dismissal are not clear, but two years previously Mr Parker was reprimanded by **Julian Larkman** following a complaint made by a Mr Henwood for Parker's refusal to serve him with refreshments. (Minutes, 23 September 1890; 18 October 1892).

9. Father Alexis 'The Enshrinement of the Sacred Relics of Saint Edward the Martyr' in *The Shepherd*, 1984 V (1), pp. 4–5. *The Shepherd* is an Orthodox Christian pastoral magazine published monthly by the St Edward Brotherhood.

10. LNC Ledger Book, 24.

11. Louis Comfort Tiffany (1848–1933). Trading under the name of Louis C. Tiffany & Associated Artists, the company worked mainly with glass and fabrics. Tiffany's firm continued to produce glass until 1938.

12. LNC Ledger Book, 23.

13. Mrs Knight was the third person whose ashes are buried at Brookwood. From the Burial Registers we can tell that Isabella Knight was cremated on 14 February 1891 and that her ashes were buried on the same day. Her funeral cost a total of £45 18s 2d, which included £5 5s 0d for the grave plot and £19 19s 0d for the coffin, removal to the crematorium, and crematory fee.

14. Sir H. Thompson, *Modern Cremation: its History and Practice* (2nd edn, London, Kegan Paul, 1891), p. 21.

15. Edmund Lyons, 1st Baron Lyons (1790–1858). Entered the Navy in 1801, Captain (1814), commanded the frigate *Blonde* in the Mediterranean (1828), Minister and plenipotentiary at Athens (1835–49), Minister to the Swiss Confederation (1849–51), Minister at Stockholm (1851–3), Rear Admiral (1850), Vice-Admiral (1857), second in command of the Mediterranean Fleet (1853), Commander-in-Chief (1855–8). Practical commander of the fleet during the Crimean War (1853–5). Created Baron Lyons of Christchurch (1856).

16. For more on this tragedy, see John Ovenden and David Shayer, *The Wreck of the Stella: Titanic of the Channel Islands* (St Peter's Port, Guernsey Museums & Galleries, 1999).

17. Sir Henry Bartle Edward Frere, 1st Baronet (1815–84). Statesman, Chief Commissioner of Sind (1850–9). During the Indian Mutiny he sent nearly all his armed forces to relieve the Punjab. Governor of Bombay (1862–7). President of the Geographical Society (1873) and of the Asiatic Society (1872). Sent to Zanzibar to negotiate the suppression of the slave trade (1872). Accompanied the Prince of Wales to India (1875). Governor of the Cape and first High Commissioner of South Africa (1877–9).

18. Sir George Christopher Molesworth Birdwood (1832–1917). Anglo-Indian official and author. On the Bombay Medical Staff (1854–68); worked in the revenue and statistics department of the India Office (1871–1902). A prolific writer on Indian art, flora and history.

19. Matthew Parker (1504–75). Ordained (1527), Chaplain to Anne Boleyn (1535), Master of Corpus Christi College, Cambridge (1544). Supported the cause of Lady Jane Grey. Deprived of his living by Queen Mary, he lived in concealment. Appointed Archbishop of Canterbury by Queen Elizabeth and consecrated in 1559. Published the 'Bishop's Bible' (1563–8).

20. Frederick Sleigh Roberts, 1st Earl (1832–1914). Field Marshal. Served during the Indian Mutiny, during which he won the VC. Commanded a division and then the force sent to Kandahar during the Afghan War (1878–80), including the march from Kabul to Kandahar which pacified Afghanistan. Commander-in-Chief of the Madras Army (1881–5), of India (1885–93) and Ireland (1895–9). Commander-in-Chief in South Africa (1899–1900), capturing Pretoria and achieving the annexation of the Transvaal.

21. His Highness the Aga Khan (born 1936). Educated in Switzerland and Harvard University. Succeeded his grandfather as the 49th hereditary Imam of the Shia Imami Ismaili Muslims in 1957. His chief concern is the well-being of all Muslims, since Ismailis now live in twenty-five countries, all of which have seen major political and economic changes.

22. Minutes, 13 December 1854. The arrangement did not last long since the company was not happy with the way he ran his business. A lasting reminder of his presence in the cemetery seems to be the **Colquhoun mausoleum**, presumably completed before his dismissal in October 1855.

23. The original Masonry Works opened in 1889, since this is when the first Ledger Book (recording orders for statuary and masonry work) began (Minutes, 17 April 1889). Unfortunately the earliest Ledger Books have not survived. The original masonry showroom was not opened until May 1891 at a cost of about £70 (Minutes of the Committee Appointed to Reconsider the Price Lists, 10 March, 7 and 28 April 1891).

24. Minutes, 26 April 1904. Harris & Company tendered £885 to build the works. The equipment was to cost £1,250. A new saw for cutting stone was ordered in November 1920.

25. John M. Clarke, *The Brookwood Necropolis Railway* (3rd edn, Oxford, Oakwood Press, 1995), pp. 87–8.

26. Minutes, 10 November 1938.

27. Minutes, 21 June 1944.

28. See the Introduction for more details of the 1975 Act.

29. Presumably since this was so close. Typewritten reminiscences of driver Bill Mullins, who drove the funeral train in the late 1920s.

30. William Henry Randoll Blacking FSA, FRIBA (1889–1958), architect. Commenced practice in Guildford (1919), and Salisbury (1932). He undertook work in many cathedrals and numerous parish churches and designed the churches at Litton, Derbyshire, and St Alban's, Northampton.

31. LNC Ledger Book, 24.

32. Minutes, 13 February, 3 November 1891. The mausoleum cost £419 in stone and materials, and £360 to build.

33. LNC Ledger Book, 32.

34. Sir Benjamin Baker (1840–1907). Civil engineer and business partner of Sir John Fowler from 1875. With Fowler he helped construct the Metropolitan Railway (1861) and District Railway (1869); they were consulting engineers for the City & South London Railway (1890), Central London Railway (1900) and the Bakerloo line. Constructed the Forth Railway Bridge (1882–90) and designed the Aswan dam, Egypt (1898–1902).

35. Sir John Fowler, 1st Baronet (1817–98). Civil engineer. Engaged on the London Brighton & South Coast Railway, consulting engineer in London from 1844, designed the Pimlico Railway Bridge (1860) and the Metropolitan Railway (from 1853). Formed partnership with Sir Benjamin Baker (1875). Constructed the Forth Railway Bridge (1882–90).

36. Sir Reginald Blomfield (1856–1942). Architect. Restored many houses, including Chequers; designed the cross of sacrifice, the Menin Gate Memorial (Ypres) and several war cemeteries for the Imperial War Graves Commission; designed Lady Margaret Hall, Oxford; Lambeth Bridge and the Regent Street quadrant.

37. LNC Ledger Book, 23.

38. Frederick William Hulme (1816–84). Landscape painter and art teacher. He often painted the scenery of the Surrey countryside, including several canvases depicting Woking Common, such as *Near Woking, Surrey* (1858).

39. Shirley Hibberd (1825–90), journalist and horticultural writer. Edited *Floral World* (1858–75) and *Gardener's Magazine* (1861–90).

40. *Wisden Cricketers' Almanack* 1878, p. 289. According to the information contained in this obituary the coffin plate read 'Thomas Humphrey, died September 3rd, 1878, aged 38' which, as the writer pointed out, must have been incorrect. He notes that other inaccurate accounts described Humphrey as born on 16 January 1838 and aged 40. Humphrey's immediate cause of death was congestion of the lungs. His funeral costs amounted to £6 16s 2d, with the grave space costing £2 10s 0d.

41. The Revd Henry Aylmer Skelton (1884–1959). Curate of Chertsey (1910–13); Vicar of St Barnabas, Epsom (1913–16); Vicar of Mentmore and chaplain to Lord Rosebery (1916–21); assistant priest at St Mary's Cathedral, Auckland, New Zealand (1921–3); Rector of North Yorke's Peninsular Mission, South Australia (1923–4); Rector of Toddington, Bedfordshire (1924–7); Sub-Dean of St Alban's (1927–36); Archdeacon of St Alban's (1936–42); Suffragen Bishop of Bedford (1939–42); Bishop of Lincoln (1942–6).

42. Francis Giles (1787–1847). Civil engineer. Planned and constructed much of the Newcastle & Carlisle Railway and the London & South Western Railway; built the Warwick Bridge, Cumberland.

43. Victoria Park Cemetery was opened in about 1845 off Usk Street, Bethnal Green, and near the Mile End Road. Mrs Holmes described it as 'a space of 11½ acres, and by far the largest of the private venture burial-grounds. In this ground it was stated that, on every Sunday in the year 1856, 130 bodies were interred' (Mrs Basil Holmes, *The London Burial Grounds* (London, T. Fisher Unwin, 1896), p. 202). After years of negotiation it was acquired by the Metropolitan Public Gardens Association and transformed into a small park. It was opened by the Duke of York in July 1894 as Meath Gardens. Victoria Park Cemetery should not be confused with Victoria Park, which is close by.

44. Barry Devonshire and Frank Lawer, 'St Saviour's Southwark' in *Necropolis News* 1995, 1(5), pp. 15–24.

45. The details for Southwark pauper funerals were probably followed by other parishes and boroughs. It is fortunate that a lot of the administrative papers covering these arrangements survive in the Southwark Local Studies Library.

46. Mrs Holmes understood this burial ground to be at least 250 years old and 'crowded to excess'. Nevertheless two schools were built in it. Mrs Basil Holmes, *The London Burial Grounds* (London, T. Fisher Unwin, 1896), p. 309.

47. Ibid., p.179.

48. LNC Ledger Book, 27.

49. LNC Ledger Book, 24.

50. *The Undertakers' Journal*, 15 December 1903, p. 259.

51. Vyvyan Beresford Holland (1886–1967). Second son of Oscar Wilde. Practised as a barrister until the First World War. Served in the Interpreters' Corps, later in the Royal Field Artillery and in 1916 to the Staff of 3rd Corps. Between the wars he travelled and wrote. During the Second World War he served with the BBC and was a sergeant in the Home Guard. His autobiography, *Son of Oscar Wilde*, appeared in 1954.

52. *The Complete Letters of Oscar Wilde* appeared in 1962 edited by Rupert Hart-Davis. A new edition was published by Fourth Estate in 2000.

53. West was not always so liberal or sympathetic. In December 1922 she described the condemned **Edith Thompson** as 'a shocking little piece of rubbish. . . . I am not asking for sympathy for Edith Thompson. She is a poor, flimsy, silly, mischievous little thing.' (*Reynolds News*, 17 December 1922).

54. The history of the Tiller Girls may be found in Doremy Vernon's *Tiller's Girls* (London, Robson Books, 1988).

55. LNC Ledger Book, 24. The work cost £6 15s 0d.

56. Sir (Francis) Osbert Sacheverell Sitwell, 5th Baronet (1892–1969). Writer. Served with the Grenadier Guards (1912–19). Published many novels, poems, short stories and travel writings. Wrote a five-volume autobiography, *Left Hand, Right Hand* (1944–50).

57. *The Times*, 25 September 1963.

58. Minutes, 7 April 1943.

59. Arthur Reed Ropes, stage name Adrian Ross (1859–1933). Author. Produced the comic opera *Faddimir* in 1899. Wrote lyrics and collaborated in libretti of over thirty plays including *In Town*, *The Messenger Boy*, *The Merry Widow*, *The Girl in the Train* and *The Toymaker of Nuremberg*. He also wrote poetry, on history and edited many French books.

60. Percy Greenbank (1878–1968). Author and lyric writer. Wrote for *Punch*, the *Sketch* and the *Tatler*, but after 1899 wrote exclusively for stage works. He wrote lyrics for more than thirty plays including *The Messenger Boy*, *Blue Moon*, *The Belle of Brittany*, *Tina*, *The Girl for the Boy*, and *Cupid and the Cutlets*.

61. Lionel Monckton (1862–1924). Composer, especially of popular songs. Musical critic of the *Daily Telegraph*.

62. Sir Emile Littler (1903–85). Theatrical impresario, producer, author and company director. His theatrical productions include *Victoria Regina*, *Song of Norway*, *Annie Get Your Gun*, *110 in the Shade* and *The Maid of the Mountains*. President of the Society of West End Theatre Managers (1964–7 and 1969–70).

CHAPTER TWO

1. The Metropolitan Interments Amendment Act ('An Act to Amend the Laws Concerning the Burial of the Dead in the Metropolis'), 15 & 16 Vict., c. 85.

2. The members of the Board were George Allen (Clerk of the Board), Samuel Bonsor, James Chatfield, William Cox, **Joseph George**, Henry Grant, Richard Jeffreys, James Reeves and Joseph Rogers.

3. Victoria Park Cemetery was opened in about 1845 off Usk Street, Bethnal Green, and near the Mile End Road. Mrs Holmes described it as 'a space of 11½ acres, and by far the largest of the private venture burial-grounds. In this ground it was stated that, on every Sunday in the year 1856, 130 bodies were interred.' (Mrs Basil Holmes, *The London Burial Grounds* (London, T. Fisher Unwin, 1896), p. 202). After years of negotiation it was acquired by the Metropolitan Public Gardens Association and transformed into a small park. It was opened by the Duke of York in July 1894 as Meath Gardens. Victoria Park Cemetery should not be confused with Victoria Park, which is close by.

4. See the Introduction for more on Robert Donald.

5. The memorial cost £82 12s 0d (Minutes, 18 August 1903). Mrs Basil Holmes, *The Burial Grounds of London* (London, T. Fisher Unwin, 1896), p. 286.

6. See the Introduction for more on Robert Donald and Churchill's resignation.

7. Minutes 2, 16 March, 27 April 1876.

8. *The Times*, 15 January 1879.

9. *The Times*, 31 January 1879; *Surrey Advertiser & County Times*, 1 February 1879. The deputation consisted of the Hon. Francis Scott (Chairman of the Visiting Committee, Brookwood Asylum), Mr W.F. Harrison (Deputy Chairman of Quarter Sessions and Visiting Justice of the Brookwood and Wandsworth Asylums), Mr W. Wainwright (Visiting Justice), Dr Bruchfield (Medical Superintendent of the Brookwood Asylum), Mr Percival, Mr T. Scott (owner of property nearby), Mr Jackman (owner of property nearby), Mr Stanley Percival (owner of 'The Hermitage', a property adjoining the site), Mr Larkman, the Revd O'Leary (Roman Catholic chaplain, Woking Prison) and the Revd J. Oliphant (Vicar of Woking). The deputation presented the Home Secretary with a memorial against the crematorium signed by 853 persons.

10. Minutes, 29 July 1885.

11. Minutes, 2 May 1888; *Circular to Shareholders* dated 1 December 1888.

12. Mohammad Reza Pahlavi (1919–80). Shah of Persia (Iran). He succeeded after the abdication of his father in 1941. His marriages to Princess Fawzia and Soraya Esfandiari ended in divorce since they failed to produce a male heir. His third wife, Farah Diba, produced two sons, Crown Prince Reza and Ali Reza, along with two daughters. His reign ended with the new government formed by Ayatollah Khomeini, and the Shah was exiled.

13. Thomas Andrew Walker (1828–89). Civil engineer and contractor. Engaged on various railway contracts with Thomas Brassey, including several in Canada. As an independent contractor he surveyed lines in Russia and Egypt. Works in England include the extension of the Metropolitan and Metropolitan District Railways, the East London Railway from the Thames to Shoreditch, the completion of the Severn Tunnel, the Barry Docks and railway, Preston Docks and the Manchester Ship Canal.

14. Sir Leslie Edmond Percy Riggs Falkiner of Annemount, Cork (1866–1917). Educated in France and for a time at Marlborough College. He then joined the Merchant Navy. Sir Leslie succeeded his father as the 7th Baronet in 1894, the same year he married Elaine. He subsequently married Elaine's good friend, Mary Orde-Powlett (died 1948), in April 1902. They had three sons and one daughter. Initially they lived at Pleystowe House, Surrey, but subsequently moved to Burghley Park, Stamford, Lincolnshire. Sir Leslie is buried at Stamford.

15. Based on Ecclesiastes 12:6–7.

16. I am grateful to Mrs V. Brown and Mr D. Brown for additional information on Elaine Falkiner.

17. An auction catalogue of these collections may exist, but I have been unable to locate any details. An exhibition catalogue of Leitner's collections of coins, sculptures and rare manuscripts exists for the Vienna Universal Exhibition of 1873.

18. Sir Eric Campbell Geddes (1875–1937). Engineer, politician and administrator. Deputy director general of munitions supply (1915–16), director general of transportation to the British Expeditionary Force (1916–17), director general of military transportation in all theatres of war (1916–17), MP for Cambridge (1917–22), First Lord of the Admiralty (1917–18), Minister of Transport (1919–21). Chairman of Imperial Airways and the Dunlop Rubber Company.

19. Total output of machine guns rose from 6,102 in 1915 to 33,507 in 1916.

20. David Lloyd George, *War Memoirs* (two vols, London, Odhams, 1938), especially pp. 371–4.

21. Horace Brand Farquhar, 1st Earl Farquhar (1844–1923). Politician. Partner in Sir Samuel Scott & Co., bankers; Member of the London County Council (1889–1901); MP for West Marylebone (1895–8); Master of the Household of King Edward VII (1901–7) and Extra Lord-in-Waiting (1907–10). Lord-in-Waiting to King George V (1910–15) and Lord Steward of the Household (1915–22). Created Viscount (1917) and Earl (1922).

22. Sir Derek Keppel (1863–1944). Equerry-in-Ordinary to the Duke of York and Prince of Wales (1893–1910), and to King George V (1910–12), Master of the King's Household (1912–36) and to King Edward VIII (1936). Extra Equerry to King George VI (1936–44).

23. Sir William Withey Gull (1816–90). Medical tutor and lecturer at Guy's Hospital. Fellow of the Royal Society (1869). Physician-in-Ordinary to Queen Victoria and the Prince of Wales. Suffered from poor health after a stroke in 1887.

24. Sir William Jenner (1815–98). Physician-in-Ordinary to Queen Victoria and the Prince of Wales. President of the Royal College of Physicians (1881–8).

25. The very first murder to take place on a British train, on 9 September 1864, near Old Ford on the North London Railway. As a consequence of this murder small windows were introduced in the partitions between railway compartments by several railway companies. These windows became known as 'Muller's lights'.

26. Arthur Orton (1834–98) was a butcher claiming to be Sir Roger Tichbourne, a missing heir to a considerable fortune. Orton lost an action to establish the claim in 1872 and was convicted of perjury in 1874, serving ten years' imprisonment. One of **Richard Ansdell**'s engravings, *The Trapped Fox*, was used as the basis of a political cartoon concerning this case. Orton is depicted as the fox, ensnared by the trap called perjury.

27. This arose from Ruskin's description of Whistler and his *Nocturne in Black and Gold: the Falling Rocket* as 'a coxcomb [asking] two hundred guineas for flinging a pot of paint in the public's face'. At the libel trial Whistler won the case but was awarded damages of one farthing.

28. Strictly speaking his proper name was John Wolfe Wolfe-Barry, but the customary style of his name is used here.

29. Sir John Hawkshaw (1811–91). Civil engineer. Engineer to the Manchester & Leeds Railway (1845), consulting engineer in London from 1850. Built the railways at Cannon Street and Charing Cross, with bridges over the Thames; also the East London Railway, the Severn Tunnel and (with W.H. Barlow) the Clifton suspension bridge. Reported favourably on the proposed site of the Suez Canal (1863).

30. LNC Ledger Book, 25.

31. Other members of the **Cradock Hartopp** family are buried in plot 37, for which see Chapter 3.

32. The sculpture was probably commissioned in 1895 and paid for from the large sum of money left Lord Edward by Laura Thistlethwayte (1831–94). At about the same time Lord Edward commissioned a new entrance porch to St Gabriel's Church, Warwick Square, London. Mrs Thistlethwayte was Gladstone's 'Dear Spirit'. She was thought to be the occasional mistress of

Gladstone and many others. She may have begun a relationship with Lord Edward in the hope of an introduction into court circles, although there is no evidence for this.

33. The entire plot measures 24ft × 29ft 6in. The original grave for Lady Matilda cost £36 for a plot measuring 9ft × 8ft.

34. Sir John Clayton Cowell (1832–94). Educated at Woolwich, 2nd Lieutenant, Royal Engineers (1850). Served in the Baltic during the war with Russia (1854–5) and in the Crimea (1855). Retired with the honorary rank of Major-General in 1879. Governor to Prince Alfred (1856–65) and Prince Leopold (1865–6). Master of Queen Victoria's Household (1866–94), Lieutenant-Governor of Windsor Castle (1892–4).

35. General Sir Godfrey Clerk (1835–1908). Served with the Rifle Brigade during the Indian Mutiny and on the North-West Frontier. Adjutant-General to the Madras Army (1880–5) and Deputy Adjutant-General to the Forces (1887–92). Lieutenant of the Tower of London (1897–1900). Groom-in-Waiting to Queen Victoria (1897–1901) and to King Edward VII (1901–2).

36. Lieutenant-Colonel Sir William Henry Peregrine Carington (1845–1914). Served with the Grenadier Guards. MP for Wycombe (1868–83), Secretary to the Lord Great Chamberlain (1871–96), Groom-in-Waiting to Queen Victoria (1880–2), Equerry to Queen Victoria (1882–1901).

37. *The Times*, 12 and 15 July 1907. See also Barry St-John Neville (ed.), *Life at the Court of Queen Victoria, 1861–1901: Illustrated from the Collection of Lord Edward Pelham-Clinton, Master of the Household, with Selections from the Journals of Queen Victoria* (Stroud, Sutton Publishing, 1997).

38. It is a curious fact that this mausoleum faced directly on to the cemetery railway and therefore a funeral train passed by twice daily for many years.

39. Sir Ian Standish Monteith Hamilton (1853–1947). Entered the Army in 1872, Major-General and knighted in 1900. Chief of Staff to Lord Kitchener (1901–2), General (1914), Commander of the Central Force (1914–15). Commanded the Expeditionary Force to Gallipoli (1915), after which he received no further military command.

40. William Crawford (1788–1847). Inspector of Prisons and Secretary of the Society for the Improvement of Prison Discipline. Visited America to report on their prisons and the merits of the rival 'silent' and 'separate' systems of prison discipline (1834–5). Appointed one of the first Inspectors of Prisons (1835).

41. The Revd Whitworth Russell (1795–1847). Vicar of Chiddingly and sometime chaplain of Millbank Prison. Appointed one of the first Inspectors of Prisons (1835).

42. Jebb's personal papers, correspondence and papers concerning his work on prisons and transportation are held in the London School of Economics. Brixton Prison, which dates from 1819, is located on Jebb Avenue.

43. Lord Fitzroy James Henry Somerset, 1st Baron Raglan (1788–1855). Soldier. Fought during the Peninsular War and wounded at the Battle of Waterloo. Military secretary at Horse Guards (1827–52); succeeded the Duke of Wellington as Commander-in-Chief of the forces (1852). Commander of the British forces during the early stages of the Crimean War (1854–5). Strongly criticised for the charge of the Light Brigade at Balaclava (1854). Died after the failure of the assault on Sebastopol (1855). Arguably the scapegoat for mismanagement during the winter of 1854–5.

44. George Meredith (1828–1909). Novelist and poet. He contributed poems to *Household Words* and *Chambers' Journal* and also wrote for *Fraser's Magazine, Ipswich Journal, Fortnightly Review* and *Once a Week*. His early novels did not bring much financial reward, and he depended on his journalism. Although his growing output of novels found favour with discerning readers, he did not achieve wide popularity until *Diana of the Crossways* (1885). He is chiefly celebrated for *The Egoist* (1879), while *Poems and Lyrics of the Joy of Earth* (1883) probably contains his best poetry. By the time of his death Meredith had been writing for fifty years and was a revered man of letters.

45. *Daily News*, 29 June 1900.

CHAPTER THREE

1. Sir Pelham Greville Wodehouse (1881–1975). English novelist and writer of more than 100 books. These fall into three main groups: his school stories, including *The Pothunters* (1902); the American period, including *Psmith, Journalist* (1915) and *The Indiscretions of Archie* (1921); and his country house period where characters like Lord Emsworth, Bertie Wooster and Jeeves abound.

2. *Brewer's Dictionary of Phrase & Fable* revised by Adrian Room (millennium edn, London, Cassell, 1999), p. 473.

3. The achievement of full civil and political rights for Roman Catholics. The Test Act (1673) required holders of public office to receive Anglican sacrament and reject the doctrine of transubstantiation. Daniel O'Connell founded the Catholic Association in 1823 to press for full emancipation. Wellington and Peel were opposed to emancipation, but feared a civil war in Ireland if the Test Act was not repealed. This was achieved in 1828, and a Catholic Emancipation Act followed in 1829.

4. **Matilda Jane Pelham-Clinton**, third daughter of the 3rd Baronet, is buried in plot 4. See Chapter 2.

5. Samuel Waite Johnson (1831–1912). Locomotive engineer. Acting locomotive superintendent, Manchester Sheffield & Lincolnshire Railway (1859); locomotive superintendent, Edinburgh & Glasgow Railway (1864) and of the Great Eastern Railway (1866) and the Midland Railway (1873–1903).

6. William Stroudley (1833–89). Locomotive engineer. Manager of the Cowlairs works of the Edinburgh & Glasgow Railway (1861), locomotive superintendent of the Highland Railway (1865) and of the London Brighton & South Coast Railway (1870–89).

7. A contributory factor to the disaster may have been that trains running over the Tay Bridge were exceeding the 25mph speed limit set down by the Board of Trade Inspector, Major-General C.S. Hutchinson. However, at the inquiry Drummond was never questioned about the top speed of the North British Railway's engines. See also **Henry C. Rothery** and John Thomas, *The Tay Bridge Disaster: New Light on the 1879 Tragedy* (Newton Abbot, David & Charles, 1972).

8. William Adams (1823–1904). Locomotive engineer. Initially worked on marine engines in Blackwall, Marseilles, Genoa and Sardinia. Locomotive superintendent of the North London Railway (1853), of the Great Eastern Railway (1873) and of the LSWR (1878–95).

9. There are two versions of how the scald was sustained. One story states it was an accident on an engine footplate, the other that it was caused by an (overly) hot mustard bath.

10. Harry Hall (1814–82). Artist specialising in horse portraits and other animal subjects. He was one of the most sought after painters of this genre after the death of John Frederick Herring in 1865.

11. Harrison William Weir (1824–1906). Artist, author and cat lover. Weir was a wood engraver for the *Illustrated London News* from its first issue and illustrated many books on natural history. He wrote and illustrated *Every Day in the Country* (1883) and *Our Cats and All About Them* (1889). He was the first President and Show Manager of the National Cat Club (1887).

12. John Frederick Herring (1795–1865). Animal painter, who depicted winners of the St Leger for thirty-two years, along with many other sporting subjects.

13. Aelbert Cuyp (1620–91). Dutch painter and draughtsman. Cuyp specialised in landscapes and animals.

14. Samuel Cousins (1801–87). Mezzotint engraver. His subjects included portraiture and dogs.

15. Henry Thomas Ryall (1811–67). Engraver. Ryall was appointed honorary engraver to Queen Victoria for engraving Charles R. Leslie's *The Christening of the Princess Royal*. He also executed plates after works by Landseer and others.

16. Ralph Disraeli, brother of Benjamin Disraeli, was for many years the Deputy Clerk of Parliament. He has been described as 'a conscientious and dull public servant'. It is interesting to note that his son, Coningsby Ralph Disraeli (1867–1936), died the same year as Dorothy Sa. Coningsby had no children and so was the last of the male line. The Hughenden estate was sold, and in 1949 it was acquired by the National Trust.

17. Minutes, 21 January 1937.

18. Millais's grandson, **Sir John E. Millais**, is buried in plot 31, see below.

19. Henry Woods (1846–1921). Painter. Worked initially for illustrated periodicals and was one of the original staff of the *Graphic*. He lived and worked in Venice from 1876. Exhibited at the Royal Academy and the Royal Academy of Venice.

20. Minutes, 22 January 1874.

21. The very first (five) Japanese students to study at University College London had arrived there in 1863, and represented some of the earliest ever to study in the West.

22. The burial of Mrs Capper and her son cost £20 0s 10d including the cost of a grave plot 9ft × 8ft (£17 6s 6d), but excluding the funeral and cremation fees. Walter Capper's funeral was undertaken by the LNC and cost a total of £41. This included the 'incineration fee' (£5), the 'cinerary urn & plate' (£1 5s 0d), and opening and re-closing the grave (£5 5s 0d).

23. *Stratford Upon Avon Herald*, 11 January 1918, 17 June 1921. I am grateful to Mr David Owen for drawing my attention to these sources. Mr Garland was unable to attend his wife's funeral through illness.

24. LNC Ledger Book, 26.

25. Minutes, 5 September 1929.

26. See the Notes on Using this Guide for further information on symbolism used on memorials.

27. The Burial Registers show that the funeral costs amounted to £15 9s 8d of which £11 11s 0d was for the grave plot. It is likely that Halford Mills dealt with the undertaking aspects of this funeral.

28. Halford Lupton Mills (*c*. 1843–1931). Funeral director. Mills worked for the Reformed Funeral Company at 1 Langham Place from 1872. In 1880 he bought the business and opened a branch at 31 Cambridge Place which became the main office. He strongly favoured 'reformed funerals' (that is, simpler and less expensive funerals), and was an early enthusiast of embalming and cremation. I am grateful to Brian Parsons for providing further information on Halford Mills.

29. Gustave Doré (1832–83). French painter and book illustrator.

30. Rosa Bonheur (1822–99). French animal painter.

31. George Nottage was taken ill at Brighton at Easter, and died on 11 April 1885 in the Mansion House. It was at first proposed to bury him in Kensal Green Cemetery. Nottage had the great bell of St Paul's Cathedral tolled for him and he was buried in the crypt of St Paul's, where a remarkable brass depicts him in full mayoral robes. In her will **Lady Nottage** requested to be buried with her husband, but the cathedral authorities were unable to comply with her wish. One Lady Mayoress has died in the Mansion House, Lady Pryke, in 1925.

32. For an account of his funeral see the Introduction.

33. Lowe never again held office or the respect of the House of Commons. Disraeli rarely bore grudges, but at the end of his life admitted Lowe was the one person in London with whom he would not shake hands.

34. See John 14:19.

35. Curiously Bircham was born in the year that the London & Southampton Railway reached Woking Common, and died in the year that the Railways Act (1921) created the Southern Railway.

36. I am grateful to Cynthia White, Smyth's great-great-niece, for further biographical information.

37. Ian Nairn and Nikolaus Pevsner, *The Buildings of England: Surrey* (2nd edn, revised by Bridget Cherry, London, Penguin, 1972), p. 120.

38. Carsten Egebarg Borchgrevink (1864–1934). Norwegian explorer. Emigrated to Australia in 1888. Worked as a surveyor and teacher. Ascended Mt. Lindsay in 1890. Travelled to the Antarctic on a whaler in 1894. Led the 1898–1900 Antarctic expedition. Investigated the volcanic conditions of the West Indies in 1902.

39. Or just a few tiles for the fireplace surround. In March 1887 Charles Dodgson (Lewis Carroll) purchased a number of De Morgan's red tiles for his fireplace in Oxford. They were interpreted for his child visitors as the Lory, the Dodo, the Fawn, the Gryphon and the Eaglet, and they survive as a firescreen. See Mavis Batey, *Alice's Adventures in Oxford* (London, Pitkin, 1980), pp. 14–15.

40. Sir George James Frampton (1860–1928). Sculptor and craftsman, enthusiast of the 'Arts and Crafts' movement. His works include several statues of Queen Victoria, Peter Pan in Kensington Gardens (1912) and Edith Cavell in St Martin's Place (1920).

41. 'Automatic writing' is one manifestation of spiritualism. William and Evelyn both investigated automatic writing and produced their book, *Results of an Experiment*, in 1909. See also Mark Hamilton's book *Rare Spirit: a Life of William De Morgan 1839–1917* (London, Constable, 1997), ch. 7.

42. Unfortunately Mrs Stirling does not appear to be buried here with her husband. She was cremated at the South London Crematorium in Streatham, and her ashes appear to have been scattered there, rather than at Brookwood. However, her story is particularly relevant to the De Morgans and so is included here.

43. Thomas William Coke (1752–1842). Travelled extensively and succeeded to his patrimony in 1776. MP for Norfolk (1776–1806 and 1807–32). Bred Southdown sheep and Devon cattle, and improved the Suffolk breed of pigs. First grew wheat in West Norfolk from 1787.

44. Painters. George Richmond (1809–96) exhibited at the Royal Academy from 1825. Specialised in portraiture and later sculpture. He achieved worldwide fame through his watercolour of William Wilberforce. His son, Sir William Blake Richmond (1842–1921), was also a successful portrait painter. He was Slade Professor of Fine Art at Oxford (1879–83). He undertook mosaic decorations (in the diagonal apses and chancel) in St Paul's Cathedral.

CHAPTER FOUR

1. George Henry Cadogan, 5th Earl (1840–1915). Conservative statesman, Under-Secretary of State for War (1875) and for the Colonies (1878), Lord Privy Seal (1886–92) and Lord Lieutenant of Ireland (1895–1902). His youngest son, Alexander (1884–1968), became Permanent Under-Secretary of State at the Foreign Office (1938–46).

2. Minutes, 11 October 1878; 3 August 1909; 28 June 1910.

3. Revelation 14: 13.

4. LNC Ledger Book, 24.

5. Henry Charles Cadogan, 4th Earl (1812–73). Soldier and politician. Colonel of the 3rd Middlesex militia (1841–73), MP for Reading (1841–7) and Dover (1852–7). Succeeded as 4th Earl in 1864. Captain of the Yeoman of the Guard (1866–8).

6. James Abbott McNeil Whistler (1834–1903). Painter and etcher. Moved to London in 1859 and subsequently exhibited at the Royal Academy. His libel action against John Ruskin (1879) bankrupted him (see also under **John H. Parry**) and he moved to Venice. Whistler later returned to London and had an enormous influence on contemporary art. His best-known works include *Portrait of my Mother*, his *Nocturnes*, *The Blue Girl* and the *Yellow Buskin*.

7. **John L. Propert** was another member.

8. In the words of one of its brochures the 'Earth-to-Earth' coffin 'is peculiarly suited to the process of natural interment, facilitating the free resolvent action of the earth upon human remains. Its construction is simple as it is salutary. Possessing the apparent strength, solidity, and other qualities of a Solid Coffin, it yet differs in this important respect, namely: that while the latter interferes with the natural dissolution of the body, the former promotes its disintegration and absorption, thus effectually carrying out the sanitary principle of "Earth-to-Earth" burial.' The coffins continued to be developed further to include veneers of various woods and different shapes. They were increasingly used for pauper burials and samples of a new design with joints were sent to various parishes for inspection in the summer of 1890 (Minutes of the Committee Appointed to Reconsider the Price Lists, 17 June; 8, 15 and 28 July 1890).

9. *The Undertakers' & Funeral Directors' Journal & Monumental Mason's Review*, 23 February 1891. Haden conducted experiments to show that animals as large as calves, buried at a depth of 4ft, were completely dissolved in the earth within four and a half years. This may be compared with the

Cremation Society's first use of Professor Gorini's apparatus at Woking in 1879, when the body of a horse was successfully cremated in less than two hours.

10. Reissued later in 1875 with additional material including 'a plea for a change of system in our Burial of the Dead'. Sir Henry Thompson, the President of the Cremation Society, later responded to Haden's claims by enquiring 'How the system of placing a diseased or any other body in a mere basket for the express purpose of ensuring contact at once with every channel by which its contents may escape, can be advocated for sanitary purposes or by any sanitary authority, I am unable to conceive.' Sir H. Thompson, *Modern Cremation: its History and Practice* (2nd edn, London, Kegan Paul, 1891), pp. 111–12.

11. Minutes 2, 16 March; 27 April 1876.

12. Quoted in several LNC brochures at the end of the nineteenth century.

13. The LNC published a series of 'Sanitary leaflets' promoting the merits of funeral reform, sanitary burials, and its own cemetery. At least seven were published during the course of the 1880s, as follows: (1) *The Plan and Purport of the 'Earth-to-Earth' Coffin*, (2) *Effective and Non-Effective Burial*, (3) *The 'Earth-to-Earth' Question*, (4) *The Funerals of the Future*, (5) *Cremation or Inhumation*, (6) *A Serious Peril to Health* and (7) *Burial of the Dead Without Danger to the Living*.

14. Francis Seymour Haden, *The Disposal of the Dead: a Plea for Legislation, and a Protest Against Cremation* (London, Bemrose & Sons, 1888), pp. 13–14. See also *The Undertakers' & Funeral Directors' Journal & Monumental Mason's Review*, 22 August 1891, p. xi.

15. See Pat Jalland, *Death in the Victorian Family* (Oxford, Oxford University Press, 1996), especially chapter 16. The book includes a portrait of Emma Haden in mourning dress, *c*. 1858.

16. Minutes, 14 December 1933. All these memorial windows were removed when the **St Edward Brotherhood** adapted the building for their own services after 1982.

17. David Lloyd George, *War Memoirs* (two vols, London, Odhams, 1938), p. 2038.

18. Field Marshal Sir William Robertson, *Soldiers and Statesmen 1914–1918* (two vols, London, Cassell, 1926), p. 239.

19. Robertson's military correspondence, between December 1915 and February 1918, was edited by David Woodward for the Army Records Society in 1989.

20. The home of **Edward F. North**.

21. Sir Fabian Ware (1869–1949). Originator of the Imperial War Graves Commission. Ware served with the Red Cross in France (1914–16) from which he created the Graves Registration Service, and became the Director-General of the Graves Registration and Inquiries Service (1916–19). He was Vice-Chairman of the Imperial War Graves Commission (1917–48), making it an imperial executive organisation.

22. William Barnes (1801–86). Known as the 'Dorsetshire poet'. His poetry includes *Poems in Dorset Dialect* (1844), *Hwomely Rhymes* (1858) and his collected poems in Dorset dialect (1879).

23. Sir William Cornwallis (1744–1819). Admiral. Entered the Navy in 1755 and in constant service between 1755 and 1787, taking part in many actions. Commander-in Chief, East India water (1789–93), Rear-Admiral (1793), Vice-Admiral (1794) and Admiral (1799). He commanded the Channel Fleet (1801 and 1803–6).

24. Warren Hastings (1732–1818). Governor-General of India. Member of the Bengal Council (1761), of the Madras Council (1768), Governor of Bengal (1771) and created the first Governor-General in 1773. Impeached for corruption and cruelty in 1788. His trial before the House of Lords lasted for 145 days (1788–95). It ended with his acquittal.

25. Sir Mark Wood (1747–1829). 1st Baronet Wood. Colonel of the Bengal Engineers. Returned to England in 1793 and was MP for Milborne Port, Somerset (1794), Newark (1796) and Gatton, Surrey (1802–18).

26. John Phillip (1817–67). Subject and portrait painter. He exhibited at the Royal Academy from 1838, painting chiefly portraits and Scottish subjects. However, the style of his painting changed following a visit to Seville (1851) and his later work was strongly influenced by Velasquez.

27. One of these, *The Trapped Fox*, was used as the basis of a political cartoon concerning the Tichbourne claimant, Arthur Orton. See **John H. Parry**.

28. Thomas Creswick (1811–69). Landscape painter. Exhibited for more than thirty years at the Royal Academy and the Suffolk Street Gallery.

29. William Powell Frith (1819–1909). Artist. Exhibited at the Royal Academy from 1840. He specialised in subject pictures such as *Ramsgate Sands* (1853), *Derby Day* (1858) and *The Railway Station* (1862).

30. I am grateful to Sarah Kellam for additional biographical information on Richard Ansdell. By an extraordinary coincidence Ansdell's former London home in St Alban's Grove, Kensington, was bombed on the same night that the LNC's Westminster Bridge Road station was largely destroyed, 16–17 April 1941.

31. Sir Arthur Somervell (1863–1937). Composer and teacher at the Royal College of Music (1894–1901). From 1901 he was Inspector of Music to the Board of Education and Scottish Education Department. A prolific composer, including the song-cycle *Maud*, *A Shropshire Lad* (1904) and *Highland Concerto* (1921).

32. The Queen's Hall of the People's Palace was burned down in 1931. It was subsequently rebuilt and now forms part of Queen Mary and Westfield College.

33. See the Introduction for more on the Committee of Enquiry.

34. The Court of Inquiry also comprised Colonel William Yolland, Chief Inspector of Railways, and William Henry Barlow, President of the Institution of Civil Engineers. The Court first sat on 3 January 1880 and ended on 8 May 1880. During this period it sat for twenty-five non-consecutive days in Dundee and London. John Thomas, *The Tay Bridge Disaster: New Light on the 1879 Tragedy* (Newton Abbot, David & Charles, 1972).

35. To be fair to Sir Thomas Bouch, when the bridge was inspected by Major-General C.S. Hutchinson he declared the bridge safe to use and reported that 'the ironwork has been well put together both in the columns and girders'.

36. **Dugald Drummond**, then Locomotive Superintendent of the North British Railway, also submitted evidence.

37. Sir Sam Fay (1856–1953). Railway general manager. Joined the LSWR in 1872. Secretary, then General Manager of the Midland & South Western Railway (1892–9); Superintendent of the Line at Waterloo (1899–1902); General Manager of the Great Central Railway (1902–22).

38. John Stuart Mill (1806–73). Philosopher. Formed the Utilitarian Society (1823–6), helped found the Speculative Society (1826). Published his influential *Political Economy* in 1848. MP for Westminster (1865–8), after which he returned to literary pursuits.

39. William Henry Smith (1825–91). Statesman. Entered his father's news agency business in 1841, and developed it enormously by securing a railway bookstall monopoly. MP for Westminster from 1868. First Lord of the Admiralty (1877), First Lord of the Treasury and leader of the House of Commons (1886).

40. The embarrassment caused was partly because the terms had been agreed by Britain and Russia before the Congress of Berlin met (the Treaty of Berlin was signed in July 1878), and partly because Britain had agreed not to make an issue out of the port of Batum (which the Russians later turned into a fortified base).

41. The first was Charles S. Rolls (1877–1910), of Rolls-Royce fame.

42. The East London Hospital for Children was later renamed the Princess Elizabeth of York Hospital for Children. It was merged with the Queen Elizabeth Hospital for Children, Hackney, in 1942.

43. Sydney Smirke (1798–1877). Architect to the LNC. See the Introduction for more on his life and work.

44. Sir John Franklin (1786–1847) was another Arctic explorer who discovered the north-west passage, the Arctic sea route from the Atlantic to Pacific Oceans. Franklin led two major expeditions, in 1819–22 and in 1825–7. During 1845, in command of the *Erebus* and *Terror*, he again sought the passage but, together with all other members of his expedition, perished on the voyage.

45. See also **Louis C. Bernacchi**.

46. The home of **Edward F. North**.

47. Minutes, 13 April 1927.

48. Lily Elsie (1886–1962). Musical comedy actress. She mimicked many vaudeville celebrities such as Vesta Tilley and Sir Harry Lauder. Enormously successful in *The Merry Widow* (1907), *The Dollar Princess* (1909) and *The Count of Luxembourg* (1911).

49. George Frederic Watts (1817–1904). Painter and sculptor. Famous for his portraits of eminent contemporaries and his allegorical works (such as *Time and Oblivion, Love and Death*). Watts also painted distinguished landscapes and executed monumental sculpture.

50. Sir Edwin Landseer Lutyens (1869–1944). Architect. Built many superb country houses; consulting architect, Hampstead Garden Suburb (1908–9); joint architect for New Delhi (1913–30); designed the Cenotaph (1919); and many war memorials, including that to the missing of the Somme at Thiepval; designed Britannic House, Finsbury Circus (1920–2); the British Embassy, Washington (1926–9) and Campion Hall, Oxford (1934).

51. See **Edward Knollys** for a later Chairman of Vickers Ltd.

52. See also **Captain Walter Parker**.

53. Walter Lord, *A Night to Remember* (London, Penguin, 1978), p. 119.

54. Edith Agnes Kathleen Kennet (Lady Kennet), otherwise Kathleen Scott (1878–1947). Sculptor. Influenced by her friend Rodin. Married Robert Falcon Scott (1908) and secondly Edward Hilton Young, later Baron Kennet, in 1922. Executed many portrait busts and statues. Her sitters included Asquith, Lloyd George and Neville Chamberlain. The statue of Captain Smith was unveiled in July 1914, after Smith's native town of Hanley had rejected it.

55. Princess Mary Victoria Feodore Beatrice (1857–1944). Fifth daughter and constant companion of Queen Victoria. She transcribed and edited her mother's diaries after her death, destroying the originals. Governor of the Isle of Wight (1896–1944).

56. It appears that she was buried or cremated in Oxfordshire, but her details are included here to complete the story of the Smith family.

57. Burnham Beeches, Buckinghamshire, is a remnant of ancient forest. It was purchased by the City of London in 1879 and was dedicated to public use from 3 October 1883.

58. I am grateful to Margaret Dyson for further biographical information on Dakin.

59. This might also be seen as a desperate attempt by the Chairman to encourage other members of the Board and shareholders to do likewise. However land sales continued on a piecemeal basis. See the Introduction for further discussion of the LNC's estate.

60. Lieutenant-Colonel Henry George Ricardo (1860–1940). Soldier and administrator. He joined the Royal Artillery and served during the First World War. Ricardo was awarded the DSO in 1917. He had been a Director of the LNC from 1904. Ricardo was twice married: first to Adela Lucy Cobbold in 1885 (who died in 1921) and secondly to Sybil Agnes Hoare in 1923. After his death, in December 1940, he was succeeded by **John B. Walker**. Although there is a Ricardo family allotment in plot 28 facing towards the East Gate, Ricardo is apparently not buried in the cemetery.

61. Carolus-Duran, properly Charles Auguste Emile Durnad (1838–1917). French portrait artist, strongly influenced by Velasquez and the Spanish school.

62. Sir Thomas Lawrence (1769–1830). Portrait painter. From the age of twelve he had his own studio in Bath. His full-length portrait of Queen Charlotte (1789) is remarkable and is one of his best works. He was President of the Royal Academy from 1820. Lawrence was the favoured portrait painter of his time and had a huge European practice.

63. Sargent once joked that his epitaph should be 'a little something wrong with the mouth' after one of his female clients complained about the treatment of her mouth in a portrait. Sargent replied 'Perhaps, madam, we should leave it out altogether.'

CHAPTER FIVE

1. Sir Cusrow Wadia (1869–1950). Indian businessman. Educated at King's College, London. Chairman of Indian Cables & Radio Telegraph Company Ltd, and of the Century Manufacturing Company Ltd.

2. Sir Redvers Henry Buller (1839–1908). General. Awarded the VC in 1879 for bravery during the frontier wars in the Cape. Present at the Battle of Tel-el-Kebir and knighted (1882). Initiated important reforms as quartermaster general from 1887. Adjutant general (1890–7). His command of the Army during the early stages of the Boer War was unsuccessful and included the defeats at Colenso and Spion Kop. Replaced by Lord Roberts in 1900.

3. Major-General Sir John Emerson Headlam (1864–1946). Soldier. Entered Army in 1883, Instructor at the School of Gunnery (1892–7), headquarters staff in South Africa (1900–2), served in the First World War, retired in 1921. Colonel Commandant of the Royal Artillery (1928–34).

4. LNC Ledger Book, 24.

5. The design for this memorial was formally approved in 1890 (see Minutes, 7 October 1890).

6. *Surrey Advertiser*, 28 November 1914.

7. I am very grateful to Mrs Wendy Cook for supplying further information on the life of Ernest Taunt.

8. LNC Ledger Book, 27.

9. After the First World War the agricultural collections were removed and the museum became an art collection with a children's section. It was renamed the Bethnal Green Museum of Childhood in 1974.

10. John Rushworth Jellicoe, 1st Earl Jellicoe (1859–1935). Admiral of the Fleet. With Lord Fisher at the Admiralty (1889–92). Commander of the *Victoria* and *Ramillies*; Captain (1897); director of naval ordinance (1905–7); Rear-Admiral (1907); Controller and Third Sea Lord (1908–10); Second Sea Lord (1912–14); Commander-in-Chief, Grand Fleet (1914–16); First Sea Lord (1916–17); Admiral of the Fleet (1919); Earl (1925).

11. Thomas Allen Stayner (1788–1868). Soldier and Deputy Postmaster General. Appointed Postmaster General of Upper and Lower Canada (1827), and began to lobby for the right to control the postal service. He was unpopular with the British administrators for opening additional post offices (seen as an unnecessary expense), and also with the Canadian Assembly for the charges levied on newspapers (which he was allowed to retain until removed by law in 1844). He retired in 1851 as the Province of Canada assumed full responsibility for its postal services.

12. James Morris (1798–1865). Politician, merchant and banker. Engaged in mercantile and banking activities from 1836. Representative for Leeds, Toronto (1837–44). Appointed to the Legislative Council (1844). First Canadian Postmaster General (1851), when the Canadian government assumed responsibility for its postal service. Morris arranged for the designs of the first Canadian postage stamps, and negotiated the terms of a postal treaty with the United States. He standardised postage at 5¢, and began the policy of establishing post offices as widely as possible. Speaker of the Legislative Council (1853–4 and 1858). Receiver General (1862–3).

13. Arthur Eric Rowton Gill (1882–1940) was a sculptor, engraver, writer and typographer. Apart from an enormous output of stone and wood carvings, engravings, and new type designs, he wrote a number of books concerned with his crafts. Information on these memorials is partly taken from David Peace, *Eric Gill: the Inscriptions, a Descriptive Catalogue* (London, The Herbert Press, 1994). The book also lists a fourth memorial for Brookwood, commemorating Ernest Syrett (died 1906) and Marian Syrett (died 1923). However, no entry for the Syretts has been traced in the burial registers. Coincidentally, the other memorials by Gill are also covered by this chapter: see the **Batten family grave** and **Alice Junod**.

14. Matthew 19: 6.

15. **Sir William Drake** and **Francis S. Haden** were also members of the Burlington Fine Arts Club.

16. Charles West Cope (1811–90). Cope obtained a prize of £300 in competition for decoration in the Houses of Parliament (1843), and was one of six painters commissioned in 1844 to prepare decorations for the House of Lords, where he executed several frescoes. These include *Edward III*

Conferring the Order of the Garter on the Black Prince (1848) and *Prince Henry Acknowledging the Authority of Chief Justice Gascoyne* (1849). These pictures flank William Dyce's *The Baptism of King Ethelbert* over the throne in the House of Lords. Cope executed many paintings and frescoes illustrating incidents in history and romance. He was Professor of Painting to the Royal Academy (1867–75).

17. *The Times*, 6 July 1940.

18. Sir Joseph John Thomson (1856–1940). Physicist. Educated at Manchester and Trinity College, Cambridge. Cavendish Professor of Experimental Physics (1894–1919), Master of Trinity (1918–40), Professor of Natural Philosophy, Royal Institution (1905–20), President of the Royal Society (1915–20) and of the British Association (1909), Nobel Prize (1908). Made the Cavendish Laboratory the greatest research school in experimental physics.

19. Arthur Holly Compton (1892–1962). American physicist. Professor of Physics, University of Chicago (1923–5), Nobel Prize for Physics, 1927, Director of the American plutonium research project (1942–5), Chancellor of the University of Washington (1945–53). Compton made several discoveries on X-rays, directed the development of the first atomic chain reaction and of the first quantity production of plutonium.

20. Wander Johannes de Haas (1878–1960). Dutch physicist. Worked in Berlin, Haarlem, and was Professor of Physics at the Technical University, Delft. With Einstein he won the Baumgartner Prize of the Vienna Academy (1916).

21. The reverse effect, observed in 1914 by S.J. Barnett, was called the 'Richardson-Barnett effect'.

22. Sir Edward Augustus Bond (1815–98). Principal Librarian of the British Museum. He joined the British Museum in 1838, appointed Egerton Librarian (1850), Keeper of Manuscripts (1866) Principal Librarian (1878–88). Replaced the manuscript catalogues with printed catalogues in the printed book department and adopted sliding press for books.

23. Sir George Frederic Warner (1845–1936). Palaeographer and scholar. Entered the department of manuscripts at the British Museum in 1871, Assistant Keeper (1888), Keeper and Egerton Librarian (1904–11). Interested in palaeography and illuminated manuscripts.

24. For more on Gill see n. 13 to this chapter.

25. Sir Archibald Edward Garrod (1857–1936). Physician and biochemist. Assistant physician at St Bartholomew's Hospital (1903), full physician (1912), consulting physician to the Mediterranean forces (1915–19), Regius Professor of Medicine at Oxford (1920–7), Fellow of the Royal Society (1910).

26. (James) Hugh Thursfield (1869–1944). Physician. Educated at Trinity College, Oxford, and St Bartholomew's Hospital. Held various posts in the Medical School and Hospital of St Bartholomew's Latterly Consulting Physician to St Bartholomew's Hospital and the Hospital for Sick Children, Great Ormond Street.

27. For more on Gill see n. 13 to this chapter.

28. Major Morris's papers, chiefly legal and patent documents on the improvements in carburettors, are held in the Library at Imperial College.

29. Thomas Webster (1810–75). Barrister. Educated at Trinity College, Cambridge. Called to the Bar at Lincoln's Inn (1841). Became a leading authority in patent law.

30. *The Times*, 27 October, 22 November 1910.

31. Minutes, 30 June 1891.

32. Thomas Roger Smith (1830–1903). Architect. Ran his own practice from 1863. Fellow of the Royal Institute of British Architects (1863), Professor of Architecture, University College London (from 1879). His works include the Elphinstone College and Post Office, Bombay; country houses in Oxford, East Grinstead, Maidenhead and Stevenage; and laboratories and Technical School at University College London.

33. For more on Runtz's life see Joan Ronald, 'Ernest Augustus Runtz' in *Necropolis News* 2000, 3 (5), pp 5–10.

34. Oswald Partridge Milne (1881–1968). Architect. Articled to Sir Arthur Blomfield; started practice in London (1905); works include many country houses, school buildings (including Christ's Hospital, Cheltenham College, Blundell's and Highgate), the new building for Claridge's Hotel and the Christian Science Church in Putney.

35. General Sir Walter Pipon Braithwaite (1865–1945). Entered Army (1886), served in Burma (1886–7), South Africa (1899–1902) and during the First World War. Governor of the Royal Hospital, Chelsea (1931–8).

36. LNC Ledger Book, 25; *The Times*, 28 April 1937.

37. LNC Ledger Book, 32.

38. It is possible this plot comprises reburials from an earlier burial ground. The grant for this plot appears to date from 1929 when an area 27ft × 16ft was granted to the London County Council (Minutes, 9 May 1929).

39. *Hampshire Chronicle*, 14 October 1865.

40. Joseph Hamilton Beattie (1804–71). Locomotive engineer. Originally apprenticed as an architect. Worked under Joseph Locke on the Grand Junction Railway (1835) and on the London & Southampton Railway (1837). Later he took charge of the carriage and wagon stock. Succeeded J.V. Gooch as locomotive superintendent (1850). Designed the new workshops at Nine Elms (1863–4).

41. I am very grateful to Sheila Heasman for further information on her great-grandfather. See also *The Brookwood Express*, No. 45 (2001).

42. *South London Chronicle*, 12 April 1890. See also Ian Devine and Chris Bartlett, 'London and South Western Railway burial ground' in *Necropolis News* 2000, 3 (2), pp. 6–7.

43. Sir Henry Morton Stanley (1841–1904). Explorer, administrator and journalist. Born in Wales, he emigrated to America (1859) and became a naturalised American. Served in the American Civil War on both sides. A brilliant journalist, Stanley was sent by the *New York Herald* to search for the explorer David Livingstone. In November 1871 he located Livingstone at Ujiji. Between 1874 and 1877 Stanley crossed Africa from Zanzibar to the Atlantic, tracing the course of the River Congo. Helped establish for Belgium the Congo Free State (now Zaire). Crossed central Africa from west to east (1887–9) and helped lay the foundations of what became Uganda and Kenya. Re-naturalised as a British subject, he became MP for North Lambeth (1895–1900). Granted a state funeral in Westminster Abbey, his body was then removed to Pirbright via the LNC's private funeral train.

44. The Revd Canon Allen Edwards (1844–1917). Educated at Corpus Christi College, Cambridge, Vicar of All Saints' & St Augustine's, South Lambeth (1874), member of the London School Board (1891), Rural Dean of Kennington (1891), Canon of the Collegiate Church, Southwark (1897–1905), Proctor in Convocation for the Diocese of Rochester (1900–5), Proctor in Convocation for the Diocese of Southwark (1905).

CHAPTER SIX

1. London Necropolis Act 1946 (9 & 10 Geo. 6, c. xviii). See also the Introduction for further information on the two attempts to build a crematorium within the cemetery, and on the Glades.

2. This practice evolved from that of Edward Milner (1819–84), a former assistant to Joseph Paxton. **Edward White** was a distinguished landscape architect.

3. It seems the LNC allocated on average £2,000 a year to landscape and develop its 'memorial garden' (e.g. Minutes, 11 February 1947).

4. The Rt Revd Henry Colville Montgomery Campbell (1887–1970). Vicar, St Saviour's, Poplar (1917–19); Rector of West Hackney (1919–26), Hornsey (1926–33) and St George's, Hanover Square (1933–40); Suffragen Bishop of Willesden (1940–2) and Kensington (1942–9); Bishop of Guildford (1949–56); Bishop of London (1956–61).

5. Minutes, 11 October 1950.

6. Bernard Richard Meirion Darwin (1876–1961). Essayist and sports writer, grandson of Charles Darwin. Educated at Trinity College, Cambridge; called to the Bar at the Inner Temple (1903), but decided to write full-time. Golf correspondent for *The Times* (1907–53) and to *Country Life* (1907–61). He made golf reporting a branch of literary journalism. Captain of Woking Golf Club (1908–9) and captain of the British golf team in the first Walker Cup (1922). Editor of the first two editions of the *Oxford Dictionary of Quotations* (Oxford, Oxford University Press, 1941 and 1953). President of Woking Golf Club (1946–61).

7. Bernard Darwin, *The Glades of Remembrance, Brookwood* ([Brookwood?], LNC, *c.* 1950), p. 4.

8. George Dendy, 'Last Orders Please! Memories of Brookwood Cemetery' in *Necropolis News* 1995, 1 (5), p. 8. In the same article Mr Dendy refers to his sister often being woken in the night by the sound of a child crying and sobbing, which she found very distressing. Mr Duffill made enquiries but nothing came to light, although one or two of the builders told him they had also heard the crying. Mr and Mrs Duffill moved from the Glades in about 1958.

9. The original **Superintendent's office** was more centrally located off **Cemetery Pales**.

10. Entry 211,981 in the Burial Register, and No. 1 for the Glades of Remembrance Register.

11. *Pharos* (1952), 18 (2), p. 9. I am very grateful to Brian Parsons for providing further information on the life of Edward White.

12. For Golders Green see P.C. Jupp and H.J. Grainger (eds), *Golders Green Crematorium 1902–2002* (London, London Cremation Company, 2002), chapter 5. For Kensal Green see James Stevens Curl (ed.), *Kensal Green Cemetery* (Chichester, Phillimore, 2001), p. 295. For Chipperfield see *Pharos* (1949), 15 (1), pp. 6–7 and 15 (2), pp. 10–11.

13. *Pharos* (1936), 1 (4), pp. 14–17 and (1936) 2 (3), p. 16. Edward White 'Crematorium Gardens' in P.H. Jones (ed.), *Cremation in Great Britain* (3rd edn, London, The Cremation Society, 1945), pp. 124–7. The Stoke Poges memorial gardens were privately owned and managed until they were acquired by South Bucks District Council in 1971. The gardens – now Grade II on the English Heritage Register of Historic Parks and Gardens – were refurbished in 2003 and are a unique survival of gardens from this period.

14. Paper presented by White at the Cremation Society's Conference, 19 July 1946.

15. Bruce Marshall, *The White Rabbit* (London, Evans Brothers, 1952). More recently Mark Seaman has written the biography *Bravest of the Brave: the True Story of Wing Commander Tommy Yeo-Thomas, SOE Special Agent, Codename 'the White Rabbit'* (London, Michael O'Mara, 1997).

16. Mrs Basil Holmes, *The London Burial Grounds* (London, T. Fischer Unwin, 1896), p. 286. She also mentions '6 gravestones against the wall' of the playground, but whether these were ever removed to Brookwood is unknown.

17. *The Times*, 23 July 1897; Minutes, 18 October 1898.

18. Saxby's book describing this theory in more detail has yet to be published.

19. Probably the original mason to the LNC, see the **Masonry Works**.

20. LNC Ledger Book, 24.

21. For instance 15 and 22 July 1890.

22. Minutes, 27 May 1888.

23. General Sir William Fenwick Williams (1800–83). Educated at Woolwich and entered the Royal Artillery. British commissioner for settlement of the Turkish–Persian boundary (1848), British commissioner with the Turkish Army in Anatolia (1854); held Kars against the Russians and won the Battle of Kars (1855), but was compelled to capitulate. General-Commandant of the Woolwich Garrison (1856–9), MP for Calne (1856–9), Governor of Nova Scotia (1865), Governor-General and Commander-in-Chief of Gibraltar (1870–6), Constable of the Tower of London (1881).

24. John Gellibrand Hubbard, 1st Baron Addington (1805–89). Director of the Bank of England (1838), Chairman of the Public Works Loan Commission (1853–89), Conservative MP for Buckingham (1859–68) and London (1874–87), created Baron Addington in 1887.

25. William Butterfield (1814–1900). Architect. Other works include the chapel of Balliol College, Oxford (1856–7); All Saints', Margaret Street, London (1859); the new buildings at Merton College, Oxford (1864); school buildings at Rugby (1875) and Keble College, Oxford (1876).

26. Adrian Gilbert Scott (1882–1963). Architect. Other works include: Cairo Cathedral; Farnborough Hill Convent and Chapel, Hampshire; Church of Our Lady and St Joseph, Poplar, London; St Anthony's Church, Manchester; Church of Our Lady of Victories, Kensington, London; Church of St Rose of Lima, Birmingham; with his brother Sir Giles Gilbert Scott, he rebuilt the House of Commons after the Second World War..

27. Maurus Jokai (1825–1904). Hungarian novelist. Active partisan of the Hungarian struggle for independence in 1848. Wrote dramas, humorous essays, poems, novels and romances. Jokai also edited several newspapers.

28. John Collingwood Bruce (1805–92). Antiquary. Proprietor of the Percy Street Academy, Newcastle-upon-Tyne (1834–63), Fellow of the Society of Antiquaries (1852), Secretary and Vice-President of the Society of Antiquaries of Newcastle (1846).

29. General Sir William Stephen Alexander Lockhart (1841–1900). Served in the Indian Mutiny (1858–9), the Bhutan campaigns (1864–6) and the Abyssinian expedition (1867–8). Quartermaster-General in northern Afghanistan (1878–80), Brigadier-General during the Burmese War (1886–7), commanded the Punjab Frontier Force (1890–5), commanded the Tirah expedition (1897), Commander-in-Chief, India (1898).

30. Lieutenant Frederick Neil Le Mesurier (1875–1915), of the Dublin Fusiliers.

31. Churchill's account appeared at the time in the national and international press. He also recorded an account of his escape in his autobiography *My Early Life* (London, Thornton Butterworth, 1930). There are some major differences between Churchill's account of his escape and Haldane's version, as recorded in his diary. See Randolph S. Churchill, *Winston S. Churchill: Vol. 1: Youth* (London, Heinemann, 1966), pp. 497–502.

32. Charles Fuge Lowder (1820–80). Educated at Exeter College, Oxford. Joined the mission at St George's-in-the-East (1856); built the new church at St Peter's, London Docks, consecrated in 1866; published accounts of his ministry at St George's. Widely known as 'Father Lowder'.

33. **Sir James P. Deane**, who was involved in the prosecution of these ecclesiastical cases, is referred to in **Appendix A**.

34. The **Revd Robert Alfred John Suckling** (1842–1917), who succeeded Mackonochie as the second Vicar of St Alban's in December 1882. Educated at St Edmund Hall, Oxford. Curate of Rowde (1865–8); Rector of Barsham, Suffolk (1868–80); Vicar of St Peter's, London Dock (1880–2). He was Vicar at St Alban's until 1916, and is buried to the right of Mackonochie's grave.

35. *St Alban's Parish Magazine*, No. 49, January 1888, pp. 8–10.

36. There were rumours that Lord Henry was homosexual, for he lived abroad for the rest of his life. See David Cannadine, *The Decline and Fall of the British Aristocracy* (London, Papermac, 1996), p. 381.

37. See also G.W.E. Russell, *Arthur Stanton: a Memoir* (London, Longmans, Green & Co., 1917), an excellent biography.

38. LNC Ledger Book, 24, 32.

39. Minutes, 22 August 1872.

40. LNC Ledger Book, 23, 24.

41. Further information on the community was published by Ian Devine in *Necropolis News* 2001, 3 (5), pp. 7–10.

42. Wilson Carlile (1847–1942). Founder of the Church Army. Curate at St Mary Abbots, Kensington (1880–2). Sought contact with the working classes and founded the Church Army (1882) as a lay society within the Church of England. Established training colleges for men (1884) and women (1887). Rector of St Mary-at-Hill (1891–1926); Prebendary, St Paul's Cathedral (1906–42).

43. This Sunset Home was the Church Army's very first, and was previously Wilson Carlile's home. It was subsequently renamed Marie Carlile House. Despite these important connections with the movement, and amid some local (and national) controversy, the Church Army closed it in December 2000.

44. James Meadows Rendel (1799–1856). Engineer. Surveyor under Thomas Telford (1757–1834). Set up business in Plymouth, constructed harbours, canals and docks. His works include Torquay breakwater (1836), Birkenhead Docks and Portland harbour.

45. The practice still exists. Other designs include Chelsea Bridge (1934–7), Waterloo Bridge (1937–42) and the Thames Barrier (1974–82).

46. James Clerk-Maxwell (1831–79). First Professor of Experimental Physics at Cambridge University. Professor of Natural Philosophy at Aberdeen (1856–60) and King's College, London (1860–5); elected to the new chair at Cambridge (1871). Investigated the kinetic theory of gases, the theory of colours in relation to colour blindness, theories on electricity and magnetism, and electromagnetic waves.

47. John William Strutt, 3rd Baron Rayleigh (1842–1919). Mathematician and physicist. Educated at Trinity College, Cambridge. Cavendish Professor of Experimental Physics at Cambridge (1879–84); directed research on the re-determination of electrical units in absolute measure; Secretary of the Royal Society (1885–96); discovered argon with Sir William Ramsay (1894); carried out important research into physical optics; an original recipient of the Order of Merit (1902); Nobel prize (1904); Chancellor of Cambridge University (1908).

48. LNC Ledger Book, 24. The slab cost £23 15s 0d.

49. Andrew Hunt (1790–1861). Landscape painter.

50. Ford Madox Ford (1873–1939). Novelist and critic. His works include *Rossetti* (1902), *The Fifth Queen* historical trilogy (1906–8), the Tietjens series of war novels (1924–8; the first was called *Some Do Not*). He changed his name from Hueffer to Ford in 1919. Ford founded the *English Review* (1908) and *Transatlantic Review* (1924). He left his first wife in 1909 and was imprisoned for ten days in Brixton for refusing to pay her an allowance. After 1922 Ford lived in France and America.

51. Douglas Goldring later wrote a book based on this period: *South Lodge: Reminiscences of Violet Hunt, Ford Madox Ford and the English Review Circle* (London, Constable, 1943).

52. The book includes a recollection of Oscar Wilde after his trip to America in 1882. Violet described him as 'a slightly stuttering, slightly lisping, long-limbed boy . . . and talking-talking'.

53. Air Vice-Marshal Felton Vesey Holt (1886–1931). Entered the Army in 1905, Captain (1914), acting Brigadier-General (1918–19), Air Commodore (1925), Director of Technical Development at the Air Ministry (1928–31), Air Vice-Marshal (1931), Air Officer Commanding Fighting Area, Air Defence of Great Britain (1931).

54. Edward Onslow Ford (1852–1901). Sculptor. His works include statues of Rowland Hill (1881), Henry Irving as Hamlet (1883), General Gordon (1890), the Shelley Memorial at Oxford (1892) and the Queen Victoria Memorial at Manchester (1901).

55. James Manby Gully (1808–83). Physician. Practised in London and afterwards in Malvern, where he and James Wilson pioneered the hydropathic treatment of disease. The novelist Charles Reade based his 'Dr Gullson' in *It is Never too Late to Mend* (1856) on Gully.

56. Arthur Wellesley Peel, 1st Viscount Peel (1829–1912). Speaker of the House of Commons (1884–95). Youngest son of Sir Robert Peel. MP for Warwick (1865–85) and Warwick and Leamington (1885–95). First Speaker to use the power of closure to outmanoeuvre the Irish policy of obstruction. Viscount (1895).

57. Minutes, 13 October, 10 November 1903.

58. The Revd Canon Edward Malcolm Venables (1884–1957). Educated at Magdalen College, Oxford. Assistant Master of Packwood Haugh (1907–11) and Felstead School (1912–17), Master at Harrow (1917), Housemaster (1922–42) and Chaplain (1926–32). Rector of Wootton Courtenay, Somerset (1943–5), Canon of St George's Chapel, Windsor (from 1948).

59. For more on the Ockenden Venture see Pamela Watkin, *Joyce's Ockenden* (Woking, Broadmead Press, 1993).

60. I am very grateful to Lynne Cowley for providing the source of this quotation.

61. I am grateful to Jenny Mukerji for further information on the Pullinger family graves.

62. General Anton Ivanovich Denikin (1872–1947). Entered the Army in 1887. Served in the Russo-Japanese War (1904–5). Deputy Chief of Staff (1917), Commander of the Western Front (1917) and of the South Western Front (1917), Commander-in-Chief of the South (1918–19). Escaped from Russia and lived first in Constantinople, then France. Moved to the United States in 1945.

63. General Peter Nikolaevich Wrangel (1878–1928). Served in the Russo-Japanese War (1904–5) and the First World War. Joined the anti-Bolshevik forces of General Denikin (1918). Assumed the command of the anti-Bolshevik forces in southern Russia (1920). Launched an offensive against the Bolsheviks (1920), resulting in the loss of British support, and the necessity of evacuating his forces from the Crimea. Exiled to Belgium.

CHAPTER SEVEN

1. London Necropolis & National Mausoleum Act 1852 (15 & 16 Vict., c. cxlix) clause V: 'That the Cemetery shall be enclosed by Walls, Iron Railings, or substantial Wooden Fences of the Height of Eight Feet at the least.'

2. See the Introduction for more on Sydney Smirke.

3. Minutes, 6 September 1854. It is not clear where the four cottages were built, but they probably included the pair off Long Avenue (now privately owned and with very restricted access from the cemetery), another adjacent to the Parsonage House, and one opposite the East Gate on the Bagshot Road (A322). There were two Cemetery Superintendents appointed in 1854, George Bupell (consecrated) and James Bailey (unconsecrated), each of whom lived in one of the cemetery stations. At some stage James Bailey was appointed sole Superintendent and may have been accommodated in another cemetery cottage, along with his successor, **Stephen Standage**.

4. Minutes, 7 January 1857; 12 June, 26 June 1861.

5. Minutes, 29 July 1885.

6. Minutes, 6 October 1886. Julian Larkman subsequently lived in Brookwood Lodge on Heath House Road.

7. Report of Messrs Slater & Sons, 29 March 1887. There were five staff in London comprising the secretary, an office clerk, two assistants for the undertaking business, and a station porter. In 1854 the staff at the cemetery comprised two gatekeepers and eighteen porters (Minutes, 20 October 1854).

8. Minutes, 13 December 1854. The arrangement did not last long since the company was not happy with the way he ran his business. A lasting reminder of his presence at the cemetery seems to be the **Colquhoun mausoleum**, presumably completed before his dismissal in October 1855.

9. The original Masonry Works opened in 1889, since this is when the first Ledger Book (recording orders for statuary and masonry work) began (Minutes, 17 April 1889). Unfortunately the earliest Ledger Books have not survived. The original masonry showroom was not opened until May 1891 at a cost of about £70 (Minutes of the Committee Appointed to Reconsider the Price Lists, 10 March, 7 and 28 April 1891).

10. Minutes, 28 November 1855; 24 October 1905; 18 May 1909.

11. Brookwood Cemetery Act 1975 (c. xxxv). See the Introduction for more on this Act.

12. It is hard to understand how this intrusive office development complies with Woking Borough Council's creation of the Brookwood Cemetery Conservation Area in 1989. It also conflicts with the cemetery landscape being a Grade II listed historic park and garden. The council could have refused planning permission for these offices, but decided otherwise.

13. Sir Hugh Casson (1910–99). Architect. Educated at St John's College, Cambridge. In private practice as an architect from 1937; senior partner of Casson, Conder & Partners (1946). Director of

Architecture for the Festival of Britain. Professor of Environmental Design, Royal College of Art (1953–75); planning adviser to several local authorities after the Second World War; President of the Royal Academy (1976–84); Provost of the Royal College of Art (1980–6).

14. LNC Ledger Book, 24. The total cost was £45 2s 0d. For an explanation of 'IHS' see the section on symbolism in Notes on Using this Guide.

15. Giuseppe Mazzini (1805–72). Italian patriot and a leader of the Risorgimento. From London he planned the attempted risings in Mantua (1852), Milan (1853), Genoa (1857) and Leghorn (1857). Alexandre Auguste Ledru-Rollin (1807–74), French politician, republican and democratic agitator. As presidential candidate he lost to Napoleon III and in June 1849 attempted an insurrection. He fled to England and returned to France in 1870. Jean Joseph Louis Blanc (1811–92), French socialist statesman and historian. A member of the 1848 provisional government, he was forced into exile later that year. In London he completed his *Histoire de la Révolution* (1862), and returned to France in 1870.

16. Felix Mendelssohn (1809–47). German composer, pianist, organist and conductor. His works include *Midsummer Night's Dream* (overture, 1826), the *Hebrides Overture* (1829), and his oratorio *Elijah* (1846).

17. Philippe Grass (1801–76). Studied at the Ecole des Beaux Arts, Paris. Studied under Ohmacht and Bosio. Exhibited at the Paris Salon (1831–73). Specialised in marble portrait busts of contemporaries, statue and genre groups in bronze, portrait reliefs and medallions.

18. For more on Johanna Kinkel and other political refugees see Rosemary Ashton, *Little Germany: Exile and Asylum in Victorian England* (Oxford, Oxford University Press, 1986). The revolutionaries described here are only a few of those whose funerals were undertaken by the LNC. For instance, the company arranged the obsequies of Friedrich Engels (1820–95), the joint-founder (with Karl Marx) of modern communism. About eighty people attended his funeral service in the LNC's private station on 10 August 1895. Afterwards his body was conveyed by rail for cremation at St John's, Woking, where only a handful of people attended. The LNC also arranged the funeral of Eleanor Marx (1855–98), the youngest daughter of Karl Marx, who had committed suicide on 31 March. Her funeral took place on 5 April 1898 at the Necropolis station, where a large number of mourners assembled. Many of the friends present travelled down to Woking, where her body was cremated.

19. Minutes, 12 January 1928.

20. See Margery A. Wilkins, *By Royal Command: William Ewart Lockhart RSA RSW* (Annan, The Friends of Annandale & Eskdale Museums, 1998).

21. Other air disasters are described in Chapters 8 and 9.

22. *The Times*, 20, 21, 26 August 1959.

23. *The Times*, 5, 6, 9 June 1967.

24. *The Times*, 6, 7 November 1967. The funeral cost a total of £631 14s 6d, which included £357 for the large plot. Another victim of this disaster, Elizabeth Luff (c. 1947–67) is buried in Ship Lane Cemetery, Farnborough, Hants.

25. Mrs Annie Besant (1847–1933). English theosophist. Separated from her husband in 1873. Vice-President of the National Secular Society from 1874. Worked closely with **Charles Bradlaugh**. From 1889 she developed an interest in theosophy and went to India. President of the Indian National Congress (1917–23).

26. George Jacob Holyoake (1817–1906). Social reformer, the founder of secularism. Joined the Birmingham Reform League (1831); Chartist (1832) and present during the Birmingham Chartist riots (1839); sentenced to six months' imprisonment for blasphemy (1842). Invented secularism, and explained it further in a pamphlet published in 1854. Started the *Secular Review* (1876).

27. René Weis, *Criminal Justice: the True Story of Edith Thompson* (rev. edn, London, Penguin Books, 2001).

28. 'Service of Dedication of the Memorial to Mrs Edith Thompson and others' in *Necropolis News* 1994, 1 (3), p. 16.

29. Major Gwilym Lloyd-George, 1st Viscount Tenby (1894–1967). Politician. Son of the wartime Prime Minister David Lloyd George. Served in the First World War. MP for Pembrokeshire (1922–4 and 1929–50), Parliamentary Secretary to the Board of Trade (1939–41) and the Ministry of Food

(1941–2); Minister of Fuel and Power (1942–45), MP for Newcastle-upon-Tyne North (1951–7), Minister of Food (1951–4), Home Secretary (1954–7).

30. *The Times*, 16 and 21 December 1954.

31. See Leslie Housden, *The Prevention of Cruelty to Children* (London, Jonathan Cape, 1955), which includes a chapter on baby farming. This section draws attention to the similar case of Margaret Waters and Sarah Ellis in 1870, although only Waters went to the gallows.

32. *The Times*, 16, 17, 31 January 1903; 4 February 1903.

33. Dr Frederick Joseph Waldo (1852–1933). Educated at St John's College, Cambridge, and St Bartholomew's Hospital. Called to the Bar at the Middle Temple (1896). First Medical Officer of Health for the Inner and Middle Temples; Coroner for the City of London and Southwark (1901–32); Secretary of the Coroners' Society of England and Wales and President (1915–16).

34. Constance Mary Lloyd, Mrs Oscar Wilde (1859–98). She married Oscar Wilde in 1884 and had two sons. While Wilde was in prison she changed her name to Holland and left England.

35. Lady Harberton, *Reasons for Reform in Dress* (London, Hutchings & Crowsley, 1885).

36. Ralph Legge Pomeroy, *The Story of a Regiment of Horse: Being the Regimental History from 1685 to 1922 of the 5th Princess Charlotte of Wales' Dragoon Guards* (2 vols, London, W. Blackwood & Sons, 1924).

37. See n. 25.

38. Charles Knowlton (1800–50), *The Fruits of Philosophy; or, the Private Companion of Young Married People* (London, J. Watson, 1841). The pamphlet was originally published in America and several editions pre-date the Bradlaugh-Besant trial. Many subsequent editions appeared with a commentary by **Charles Drysdale**.

39. *Evening News*, 13 September 1938. But this is not the full story. LNC Ledger Book, No. 26 (8 May 1939) shows an entry for 'Reboring for dowel and refixing on its pedestal the bronze bust of Charles Bradlaugh £4 5s 0d', so the bust must have been found shortly after this incident. What its subsequent fate was remains a mystery.

40. Samuel Taylor Coleridge (1772–1834). Poet. Contributed verses to the *Morning Chronicle* (1793–5), and co-wrote the play *The Fall of Robespierre* with Robert Southey (1794). Published his first volume of *Poems* (1796). Moved to Somerset in 1797 and met William and Dorothy Wordsworth. Their joint work *Lyrical Ballads* (1798) opens with Coleridge's *The Ancient Mariner* and ends with Wordsworth's *Tintern Abbey*. They visited Germany together (1798–9). Moved to Keswick (1800), living close to the Wordsworths and Southey. Secretary to the Governor of Malta (1804–6). Broke with the Wordsworths in 1810 and moved to London, where he wrote and lectured. His play *Remorse* (1813) was performed at Drury Lane. His critical writing of this period is regarded as some of the finest in English.

41. Charles Lamb (1775–1834). Essayist at India House (1792–1825). First poems published in 1795. His first major success was *Tales from Shakespeare* (1807), co-written with his eldest sister Mary. Other collaborations followed. In 1818 he published his *Works of Charles Lamb*, collating his scattered verse and prose in two volumes. Joined *London Magazine* (1820). Published his *Essays of Elia* (1823) and *The Last Essays of Elia* (1833).

42. William Hazlitt (1778–1830). Essayist. Met Coleridge in 1796 and encouraged to write *Principles of Human Action* (1805), *Free Thoughts on Public Affairs* (1806) and *Reply to Malthus* (1807). Wrote for *Morning Chronicle* and *Edinburgh Review*. Lectured at the Surrey Institute on the English poets, comic writers and Elizabethan dramatic literature (1818–21); all the lectures were subsequently published. A master of epigram, invective and withering irony. His *Life of Napoleon Bonaparte* appeared between 1828 and 1830.

43. Barry Cornwall, pseudonym of Bryan Waller Procter (1787–1874). Poet. Trained as a solicitor. Contributed poetry to the *Literary Gazette* from 1815. Called to the Bar in 1831, Metropolitan Commissioner of Lunacy (1832–61). His works included *Dramatic Scenes* (1819), *English Songs* (1832), the tragedy *Mirandola* (1821) and memoirs of Charles Kean (1835) and Charles Lamb (1866).

44. Feargus Edward O'Connor (1794–1855). Irish Chartist leader. MP for County Cork (1832–5). Devoted himself to the English working classes; hugely popular. His Leeds newspaper, *Northern Star*,

became the official organ of Chartism. Founded the National Land Company to buy estates and let them to subscribers by ballot (1846). MP for Nottingham (1847–52). Presented the enormous Chartist petition in London (April 1848). Pronounced insane in June 1852.

45. Felice Orsini (1819–58). Italian revolutionary. The son of a conspirator, he was initiated into several secret societies. Elected to the Roman Constituent Assembly (1848). Took part in the defence of Rome and Venice. Exiled to England by the Sardinian government (1853). Joined the Young Italy movement and became close friends with Giuseppe Mazzini (see n. 15). Returned to Italy in 1854. Arrested, he escaped to England in 1856. Regarding Emperor Napoleon III as an obstacle to Italian unity, he went to Paris to assassinate him. On 14 January 1858 Orsini and three others threw bombs under Napoleon's carriage, killing ten people and injuring 156 others. Both the Emperor and Empress were unharmed. Orsini and another conspirator were guillotined.

46. See n. 26.

47. Minutes, 31 August 1870.

48. Frederick Gustavus Burnaby (1842–85). Soldier and journalist. Cornet in the Royal Horse Guards (1859). Reputedly the strongest and tallest man in the Army. Correspondent for *The Times* at the Carlist camp, Spain (1874). Commanded the 5th Turkish brigade at the Battle of Tashkean (1877). Made nineteen balloon ascents; crossed the English Channel by balloon (1882). Volunteered to serve in Egypt in the expedition to relieve General Gordon (1884). Killed by a spear wound at the Battle of Abu Klea (17 January 1885).

49. Burleigh was the only war correspondent in Ladysmith who decided to leave before the siege took effect. He left in the last train on 2 November 1899.

50. *Daily Telegraph*, 18 June 1914.

51. LNC Ledger Book, No. 24. With additional lettering, it cost £21 6s 11d.

52. See also the section on other **Japanese graves** in Chapter 3.

53. George William Johnson (1802–86). Academic, horticulturalist and writer. Worked in his father's salt works. Experimented in gardening and the manufacture of manures. Called to the Bar at Gray's Inn (1836), Professor of Moral & Political Economy at the Hindu College, Calcutta (1839–42). Owner of the Fairfax MS, published as the *Fairfax Correspondence* (1848–67); edited the *Gardener's Almanack* (1844–66) and co-editor of *Journal of Horticulture* (1861–81). Wrote many other books on horticulture.

54. Joseph Locke (1805–60). Civil engineer. Assisted George Stephenson in constructing the Liverpool & Manchester Railway. Constructed various lines in Britain, France, Spain and Germany (1832–52), including part of the London & Southampton Railway. Fellow of the Royal Society (1838), MP for Honiton (1847–60), President of the Institution of Civil Engineers (1858 and 1859).

55. Sir John Hawkshaw (1811–91). Civil engineer. Engineer to the Manchester & Leeds Railway (1845); consulting engineer in London from 1850. Built the railways at Cannon Street and Charing Cross, with bridges over the Thames; also the East London Railway, the Severn Tunnel and (with W.H. Barlow) the Clifton suspension bridge. Reported favourably on the proposed site of the Suez Canal (1863).

56. For more on the Tay Bridge disaster see under **Henry C. Rothery** and **Dugald Drummond**.

57. *Surrey Standard*, 11 November 1854.

58. Ibid.

59. Memories of Mrs Gwen Spencer.

60. George Dendy 'Last Orders Please! Memories of Brookwood Cemetery' in *Necropolis News* 1995, 1 (5), pp. 6–7. Mr Dendy's recollection of the use of North station as a temporary mortuary is quite correct, for which see under the **Brookwood American Cemetery**. During the Second World War North station was prepared for use as an emergency mortuary, for which see Minutes, 14 October 1942.

61. I am indebted to the Fijian Ambassador to London, His Excellency Filimone Jitoko, for supplying information from the *Fijian Who's Who*. His Excellency visited the grave in August 1999.

CHAPTER EIGHT

1. See the Introduction for more information on this Act.

2. The Metropolitan Interments Amendment Act ('An Act to Amend the Laws Concerning the Burial of the Dead in the Metropolis'), 15 & 16 Vict., c. 85.

3. The members of the Board were George Allen (Clerk of the Board), Samuel Bonsor, James Chatfield, William Cox, **Joseph George**, Henry Grant, Richard Jeffreys, James Reeves and Joseph Rogers.

4. Victoria Park Cemetery was opened in about 1845 off Usk Street, Bethnal Green, and near the Mile End Road. Mrs Holmes described it as 'a space of 11½ acres, and by far the largest of the private venture burial-grounds. In this ground it was stated that, on every Sunday in the year 1856, 130 bodies were interred' (Mrs Basil Holmes, *The London Burial Grounds* (London, T. Fisher Unwin, 1896), p. 202). After years of negotiation it was acquired by the Metropolitan Public Gardens Association and transformed into a small park. It was opened by the Duke of York in July 1894 as Meath Gardens. Victoria Park Cemetery should not be confused with Victoria Park, which is close by.

5. See the Introduction for more on Robert Donald.

6. The memorial cost £82 12s 0d (Minutes, 18 August 1903). Mrs Basil Holmes, *The London Burial Grounds* (London, T. Fischer Unwin, 1896), p. 286.

7. Captain Sir Edward Walter (1823–1904). Founder and Commanding Officer of the Corps of Commissionaires. Entered the 44th Regiment (1843), Captain (1847), moved to the 8th Hussars (1848), retired (1853). Founded the Corps of Commissionaires (1859). In 1884 a Testimonial from the officers of the Army and Navy was presented to him in acknowledgement of his services.

8. *South Western Gazette*, 1 August 1911. I am grateful to Terry Stamp for further information on his grandfather's life.

9. The Fenians (or Fenian Society) were an Irish revolutionary society committed to the establishment of an independent republic of Ireland. The group was formed by James Stephens (1825–1901) in New York in 1858. The organisation continued to exist into the early twentieth century, when it was eclipsed by the IRA.

10. Jeremiah O'Donovan Rossa (1831–1915) was the business manager of the *Irish People* (1863–5). He was arrested in 1865 with O'Leary, Kickham and others, and sentenced to penal servitude for life. There was an amnesty in 1871 on condition he left Ireland and Rossa emigrated to America. He edited the *United Irishman* and published his *Prison Life* (1874) and *Rossa's Recollections 1838–1898* (1898). Rossa died in New York and is buried in Glasnevin Cemetery, Dublin. Captain Richard O'Sullivan Burje (dates not known) was retired from the 15th Regiment of the American Army. Captain Timothy Deasy (dates not known) was late of the 9th Massachusetts Infantry Volunteers. Brian Dillon (died 1871) was another Irish patriot. He was a law clerk and also from Cork. Dillon died shortly after his release from Woking Prison. Charles Joseph Kickham (1828–82) was a Fenian and author. Aged 13, he was involved in a gunpowder explosion which impaired his sight and hearing. He joined the Fenians in 1860. Kickham was a contributor to the *Irish People*. Arrested in 1865, he was tried and sentenced to penal servitude for fourteen years. Kickham was released after four years owing to poor health. He wrote popular ballads and the fine novel *Knocknagrow, or the Homes of Tipperary* (1879).

11. This was one of several letters smuggled out of English prisons and used by Jenny Marx (1844–83) to draw attention to these prisoners and the conditions they had to endure. Since these articles would have been deemed seditious by the English authorities, she published them under the pseudonym 'J. Williams' in the French newspaper *La Marseillaise*. The publication of these letters in a major Parisian paper eventually resulted in most of the Irish political prisoners being freed. The letters were first fully translated into English by Progress Publishers in 1970. Jenny Marx Longuet was a journalist and the first daughter of Karl and Jenny Marx. She married Charles Longuet, a former member of the Paris Commune, in 1872. She died shortly before her father in 1883. There is a more direct link between the LNC and the Marx family, for the company arranged the funeral of Eleanor Marx (1855–98),

the youngest daughter of Karl Marx, who had committed suicide on 31 March. Her funeral took place on 5 April 1898 at the Necropolis station, followed by her cremation at St John's, Woking.

12. I am grateful to Charles McLauchlan of the Hibernian Association & Institute for information on John Lynch.

13. Other air crashes are described in Chapters 8 and 9.

14. *The Times*, 8 October 1945.

15. Prince Charles Max Lichnowsky (1860–1928). German diplomat. Born at Kreuzenort into an illustrious Polish family. Sometime Officer in the Life Guard Hussars, he became an attaché of the German Embassy in London from 1885. He was posted to Stockholm, Constantinople, Dresden, Bucharest and Vienna. Ambassador to London (1912–14), desiring to improve Anglo-German relations. In his *My Mission to London 1912–1918* (London, Cassell, 1918) he charged Germany with deliberately destroying the chance of peace. He was obliged to resign his Ambassadorial rank and was prohibited from writing articles for the press.

16. Published in German as *Götter, Könige und Tiere in Ägypten* (Leipzig, 1913).

17. Published in German as *Gespräche in Sybaris: Tragödie einer Stadt in 21 Dialogen* (Vienna, Gallus-Verlag, 1946).

18. See Guy Deghy and Keith Waterhouse, *Café Royal: Ninety Years of Bohemia* (London, Hutchinson, 1955).

19. Minutes, 10 November 1854.

20. Carolus Linnaeus (Carl von Linné) (1707–78). Swedish naturalist and physician, the founder of the modern scientific nomenclature for plants and animals.

21. Sir Joseph Banks (1744–1820). Botanist. Made a voyage to Newfoundland in 1766, collecting plant specimens. Between 1768 and 1771 he accompanied Captain Cook's expedition around the world. Banks visited the Hebrides and Iceland (1772). Fellow of the Royal Society (1766) and its President (1778–1820). Founded the African Association. Through Banks the bread-fruit was transferred from Tahiti to the West Indies. His collections and library are preserved in the British Museum.

22. LNC Ledger Book, 32.

23. Virtually all of the research for the Actors' Acre (and into other actors and actresses buried at Brookwood) has been undertaken by Jennie Bisset, and I am grateful for her help in this section. The Brookwood Cemetery Society has published two of her articles on this plot in *Necropolis News* 2001, 3 (4), pp. 17–22, and 2001, 3 (5), pp. 11–15.

24. Sarah Bernhardt (1844–1923). French actress and the greatest tragédienne of her day. She had a leg amputated in 1915 but did not abandon the stage. Willy Clarkson provided her with a false leg so she could continue acting.

25. Adelina Patti (1843–1919). Italian-born singer, the daughter of a Sicilian tenor. Her soprano voice was unusually high, rich and ringing.

26. Minutes, 16 May 1899.

27. His Eminence Cardinal Francis Alphonsus Bourne (1861–1935). Ordained (1884), Rector of Southwark Diocesan Seminary (1889), Domestic Prelate to Pope Leo XIII (1895), Titular Bishop of Epiphania and Coadjutor to the Bishop of Southwark (1896), Bishop of Southwark (1897–1903), Archbishop of Westminster (1903–35), Cardinal (1911).

28. See Winston S. Churchill, *The River War* (London, Longmans Green, 1899), chapter 8.

29. David Lloyd George, *War Memoirs* (two vol. edn, London, Odhams, 1938) p. 152.

30. For more detailed information on these postwar changes, see the Introduction.

31. Ian Douglas Campbell, 11th Duke of Argyll (1903–73). Served during the Second World War, and was captured. Succeeded his cousin as 11th Duke in 1949. The Duke was married four times: in 1927 to Hon. Janet Aitken (divorced 1934), in 1935 to Hon. Louise Vannick (divorced 1951), in 1951 to Margaret Whigham (marriage dissolved in 1963) and lastly in 1963 to Mrs Mathilda Mortimer.

32. These are the dates from Sweeny's autobiography, *Sweeny* (Canterbury, Harrop Press, 1990). The headstone states 1910–93.

33. See Chapter 9 for more on the Eagle squadrons.

34. Daniel Francois Esprit Auber (1782–1871). French composer of operas, including *Masaniello* (1828) and *Fra Diavolo* (1830).

35. Marguerite Radclyffe Hall (1886–1943). Writer. Initially wrote lyric poems, but turned to writing novels from 1924. Her books include *The Forge* (1924) and *Adam's Breed* (1926). She is chiefly remembered for *The Well of Loneliness* (1928), which embodies a sympathetic approach to lesbianism. Its subject matter resulted in a trial for obscenity and the book was banned. It was not republished in England until 1949.

36. Sir Alexander Arnold Constantine Issigonis (1906–88). Car designer. Born in Smyrna, he settled in Britain in 1923, studying at Battersea Polytechnic. A period as a sports driver in the 1930s and 1940s familiarised him with all aspects of car design. He enjoyed a long and successful association with Morris (later BMC) with the Morris Minor (produced 1948–71) and the revolutionary Mini (launched in 1971).

37. There is a memorial over the communal grave of these children in the East London Cemetery.

CHAPTER NINE

1. General Wladyslaw Sikorski (1881–1943). Polish general and statesman. Prime Minister of Poland (1922–3). Sikorski led the Polish government in exile (1939–43).

2. See 'Colonel Judr Pavel Svoboda 1916–1993' in *Necropolis News* 1995, 1 (5), pp. 12–14. The article reproduces Dr Karel Machachek's eulogy given at Svoboda's funeral and was reproduced with permission of his widow, Mrs Ellen Svoboda.

3. Minutes, 13 July 1949.

4. **Jaroslav Maly** (1905–41) was later promoted to Wing Commander. He was killed in June 1941 and is buried in the main **RAF cemetery** (plot 20 row B grave 1).

5. For a full list of all the graves in this section visit http://www.geocities.com/Pentagon/4540/Map.html

6. Harold Rupert Leofric George Alexander, Earl Alexander of Tunis (1891–1969). Field Marshal in the Second World War. Organised the retreat from Dunkirk (1940), commanded in North Africa (1943), Sicily and Italy (1944–5), Governor General of Canada (1946–52), Minister of Defence (1952–4).

7. Randolph Frederick Edward Spencer Churchill (1911–68). Journalist. Served in the Second World War in North Africa, Italy, and as an intelligence officer on the general staff. MP for Preston (1940–5). A forthright commentator on public affairs, he wrote the first two volumes of the multi-volume biography of his father.

8. *The Times*, 16 November 1953.

9. Minutes, 8 October 1947.

10. Sir Edward Maufe (1883–1974). Architect. Chief architect to the CWGC (1943–69). His works include Guildford Cathedral, the Runnymede Memorial, the Magna Carta Memorial and buildings for Trinity and St John's Colleges, Cambridge.

11. More information on **Charles Sweeny** and the Eagle squadrons may be found in Chapter 8. The other known members of the Eagle squadrons represented at Brookwood are Paul Roger Anderson (plot 20 row A grave 18), Roger Hall Atkinson (plot 21 row A grave 10), Charles Sewell Barrell (plot 21 row A grave 2), Lawrence Albert Chatterton (plot 21 row A grave 13), Ben Perry De Haven (plot 24 row B grave 6), **William Richard Driver** (plot 20 row B grave 18), William Burness Inabinet (plot 24 row A grave 1), Hugh Harrison McCall (plot 21 row A grave 8), James Leland McGinnis (plot 25 row A grave 11), **Andrew Mamedoff** (plot 21 row A grave 7), Gilbert Inland Omens (plot 24 row B grave 5), Ross Orden Scarborough (plot 24 row A grave 19), Walter Gordon Soares (plot 21 row A grave 1), Roy Neal Stout (plot 21 row A grave 8), Kenneth Samson Taylor (plot 20 row B grave 19), Jack Wesley Weir (plot 25 row B grave 15) and William Joseph White (plot 24 row A grave 17).

12. Eugene Quimby Tobin (*c.* 1917–41) came from California. He was killed in action on 7 September 1941 and is buried in the Boulogne Eastern Cemetery on the Pas de Calais (plot 13 row A grave 10).

Vernon Charles Keough (c. 1912–41) came from New York and was a professional parachute jumper. At only 4ft 10in tall he had to sit on two cushions in order to see over the instrument panel on Spitfires. He was killed on active service on 15 February 1941 and is commemorated on the Runnymede Memorial (panel 33).

13. Audrey Fisk, 'Humble heroes: the Ancient Order of Foresters' in *Necropolis News* 1998, 2 (5), pp. 17–18.

14. Minutes, 25 August 1914.

15. Colonel Bernard Rowland Ward (1863–1933). Royal Engineers, Colonel (1909), retired (1919). Wrote several books on military engineering.

16. Col. Ward to the LNC, 1 July 1918.

17. Minutes, 13 September 1921.

18. Sir Reginald Blomfield (1856–1942). Architect. Restored many houses, including Chequers; designed the cross of sacrifice, the Menin Gate Memorial at Ypres and several war cemeteries for the IWGC; designed Lady Margaret Hall, Oxford, Lambeth Bridge and the Regent Street quadrant.

19. Sir Edwin Landseer Lutyens (1869–1944). Architect. Built many superb country houses; consulting architect for Hampstead Garden Suburb (1908–9); joint architect for New Delhi (1913–30); designed the Cenotaph (1919) and many war memorials, including that to the missing of the Somme at Thiepval; designed Britannic House, Finsbury Circus (1920–2); the British Embassy, Washington (1926–9) and Campion Hall, Oxford (1934).

20. Minutes, 12 September 1922; 8 May, 10 December 1923.

21. Egerton Swartwout (1870–1943). Architect. Practised in New York. Works include US State Post Office and Court House (Denver), George Washington Memorial Building (Washington), Mary Baker Eddy Memorial (Cambridge, Mass.), Elkes Memorial Building (Chicago), US National St Mihiel Monument, Montsee (France), Home Club (New York), New Haven City Hall and the Baily Memorial Foundation (Brooklyn). Swartwout also wrote a number of monographs and articles on architectural subjects.

22. John Russell Pope (1874–1937). Architect. Ran his own practice from 1900. Works include Scottish Rite Temple (Washington DC); Plattsburg City Hall (Richard, Va.), Terminal Station; additions to the Metropolitan Museum, New York; American Battle Monument, Montfaucon (France); mausoleum for William B. Leeds, Woodlawn Cemetery, New York; Baltimore Museum of Art; additions to the British Museum and Tate Gallery. Russell reputedly designed more monumental buildings than any other architect of his generation.

23. Harry Bulkeley Creswell (1869–1960). Architect and author. Private practice from 1900. Works include domestic buildings; churches at Rugby and Coventry; the Law Courts and Law Offices, Sierra Leone; College of Agriculture, Mauritius; New Parthenon Room, British Museum. Wrote novels and children's stories.

24. Reginald Hallward (1858–1948). Painter, decorator, illustrator and designer of stained glass. His works include the decoration of Oldham Parish Church; Holy Trinity Church, Bury; a series of nave windows in St Ethelreda's Church, Fulham, and principal windows at Cobham, Kent, Ealing and Tilbury. Hallward also designed the windows for the American Memorial Chapel at Suresnes, Paris, and executed designs for war memorials in England, France and Belgium. He also wrote a number of children's books, poetry and works on art.

25. Ian Nairn and Nikolaus Pevsner, *The Buildings of England: Surrey* (2nd edn, revised by Bridget Cherry, London, Penguin, 1971), p. 120. A full description of the Memorial Chapel appeared in the *Architects' Journal*, 17 September 1930.

26. Robert Worth Bingham (1871–1937). American Ambassador to London (1933–7).

27. Sir Alfred Duff Cooper, 1st Viscount Norwich (1890–1954). Politician and diplomat. Served in the Grenadier Guards during the First World War. MP for Oldham (1924–9) and St George's, Westminster (1931–45), Financial Secretary to the War Office (1928–9 and 1931–4) and to the Treasury (1934–5), Secretary of State for War (1935–7) and First Lord of the Admiralty (1937–8).

Resigned over the Munich agreement (1938). Minister of Information (1940–2), Ambassador to France (1944–7).

28. *The Times*, 16 August 1937; LNC Ledger Book, 26.

29. Minutes, 14 April, 10 June 1948.

30. The full story of 'plot x' is told in 'The US prison at Shepton Mallet' in *After the Battle* no. 59 (1988), pp. 28–51. This fascinating article also includes a useful reference plan of the American Military Cemetery showing all the additional plots used during the period 1942–4.

31. For a detailed account of Private Cobb's trial and execution, see Prof. J. Robert Lilly, 'US military executions' in *After the Battle* no. 90 (1995), pp. 50–3.

32. John Newton, *W.S. Caine: A Biography* (London, J. Nisbet, 1907). The book includes an introduction by Alexander McLaren and an appreciation by Sir Charles W. Dilke.

33. *The Times*, 27 October 1958.

34. Plot 261, grave 111,455.

35. Thus following on from practice dating from the First World War. A fundamental principle of the CWGC is that all servicemen and women should be treated equally in death, with no distinction as to rank or the manner of the person's passing. The Brookwood Memorial is one of several war memorials where the name of a person executed may be inscribed next to someone who fell in the service of their country. The same is also true in several military cemeteries. For a more detailed account of the discussion surrounding these principles, see Cathryn Corns and John Hughes-Wilson, *Blindfold and Alone: British Military Executions in the Great War* (London, Cassell, 2001), chapters 21 and 37. For more information on Kemp's case, see 'D-Day's most ignominious casualty' in *After the Battle* no. 45 (1988), pp. 44–53.

36. A more recent biography has been written by Susan Ottaway, *Violette Szabo: the Life That I Have* (Barnsley, Leo Cooper, 2002).

37. Virginia McKenna (born 1931). Graduated at the Central School of Speech Training & Dramatic Art. Her stage debut was in 1950, and her screen debut in 1952 *(The Second Mrs Tanqueray)*. Her other films include *Born Free* (1966), *Ring of Bright Water* (1969) and *Swallows and Amazons* (1974). She has also made many television appearances.

38. Revd Victor Joseph Pike (1907–86). Served as chaplain to various garrisons including Aldershot, Gibraltar and Woolwich (1932–9); served as chaplain to the 43rd and 11th Divisions, the 5th Corps and the 8th Army (1940–5); Chaplain-General to the Forces (1951–60), Chaplain to the Queen (1953–60).

39. See n. 10 above.

40. Eleanor Esmonde-White (born 1914). South African painter and graphic artist. In partnership with Le Roux Smith Le Roux she painted impressive murals for the Cunard liner *Queen Elizabeth 2*, and for a number of buildings including South Africa House in London. She also designed the tapestry depicting Orpheus at the Nico Theatre, Cape Town.

41. See David King and Peter White, 'The strongest, bravest and best' in *After the Battle* no. 67 (1990), pp. 22–5.

42. For more information see John R. Hinnells, *Zoroastrians in Britain* (Oxford, Clarendon Press, 1996).

43. Henry William Montagu Paulet, 16th Marquess of Winchester (1862–1962). Succeeded his brother (1899). Chairman of Hampshire County Council (1904–9), President of the Territorial Association (1909–19). Captain of the Hampshire Carabineers in France (1915–17). Married first Charlotte Garnett (1892), secondly Caroline Marks (1925: she died in 1949) and thirdly Bapsy Pavry in 1952.

44. Lt-Col Sir William Hutt Curzon Wyllie (1848–1909). Served in the Indian Army (1866–79), joined the Political Department (1879), served in Afghan War (1879–80), Governor-General's Agent in central India and Rajputana, Political Aide-de-camp to the Secretary of State for India from 1901.

45. Gilbert Bayes (1872–1952). Sculptor. Works include the Great Seal of King George V, figures of Sir Charles Barry and Sir W. Chambers for the Victoria and Albert Museum, the bronze equestrian statues of war and peace for the National Art Gallery, Sydney, the King's Police Medal, the Gold

Medal given by the Royal Geographical Society to Captain Scott and Sir Ernest Shackleton, the great clock and the 'Queen of Time' at Selfridge's, the Sports Frieze at Lords and the London Fire Brigade Memorial and other sculpture at its headquarters on the Albert Embankment.

46. 'Estimate of works required in connection with Mausoleum' dated 10 August 1932 in LNC Ledger Book, 23.

47. Minutes, 9 July 1901.

48. Minutes, 8 October 1884.

49. Minutes, 23 June 1914.

50. Sir Lewis Bernstein Namier (1888–1960). Historian. Educated at Balliol College, Oxford. Served in the First World War. Lecturer in Modern History at Balliol College, Oxford (1920–1); Professor of Modern History, Manchester University (1931–53). Member of the editorial board for *The History of Parliament*. In 1947 he married Julia de Beausobre.

51. A.J.P. Taylor, *A Personal History* (London, Hodder and Stoughton, 1983), pp. 217–18.

52. Doris Lessing (born 1919). Novelist. Her first novel, *The Grass is Singing*, appeared in 1950 and was made into a film in 1981. She has published over fifty novels, short stories and other works.

APPENDIX A

1. Minutes, 11 April 1893.

2. This warship was completed in 1862 for the Confederate States, then at war with the Northern States. It was eventually captured in 1864 having inflicted considerable damage on Northern shipping. Gladstone accepted the case for arbitration in 1871. The international tribunal awarded the USA $15,500,000 compensation in 1872.

3. The Doctors' Commons was a society or college of English lawyers. It was founded in 1768 with its headquarters near St Paul's Cathedral. Its members had the sole right of appearing in Ecclesiastical, Probate and Admiralty courts. Proctors, equivalent to solicitors, were attached to the Commons. The college was dissolved in 1857 and the buildings were demolished in 1867.

BIBLIOGRAPHY

(I) PRIMARY SOURCES

(A) RECORDS OF THE LNC

Miscellaneous surviving records of the company including minute books, copies of agreements, draft agreements, letters, reports, receipt books, burial registers, ledger books, brochures, etc. Consulted at the Cemetery Office, Brookwood Cemetery (1978–79). Some of this material is now held at the Surrey History Centre, Woking.

(B) PARLIAMENTARY RECORDS

a. Minutes of evidence of the Select Committee of the House of Lords, 1852, Vol. 4.
b. Minutes of evidence of the Select Committee of the House of Commons, group DD 1852, Vol. 40.

(C) PRINTED PARLIAMENTARY PAPERS AND ACTS OF PARLIAMENT

1842 Vol. X: *Report from the Select Committee on the Improvement of Health in Towns: Effect of the Interment of Bodies in Towns*

1843 Vol. XII: *A Supplementary Report on the Results of a Special Inquiry into the Practice of Interments in Towns*

1850 Vol. II: *A Bill for Promoting Extramural Interments*

1850 Vol. XXI: *Report on a General Scheme for Extramural Sepulture*

1850: *Metropolitan Interments Act* (13 & 14 Vict., c. lii)

1852: *London Necropolis & National Mausoleum Act* (15 & 16 Vict., c. cxlix)

1852: *Metropolitan Interments Amendment Act* (15 & 16 Vict., c. lxxxv)

1854: *Woking Commoners Act* (17 & 18 Vict., c. ix)

1855: *London Necropolis & National Mausoleum Amendment Act* (18 & 19 Vict., c. clxiii)

1864: *London Necropolis & National Mausoleum Amendment Act* (27 & 28 Vict., c. lxii)

1869: *London Necropolis & National Mausoleum Amendment Act* (32 Vict., c. iii)

1946: *London Necropolis Act* (9 & 10 Geo. 6, c. xviii)

1956: *London Necropolis Act* (4 & 5 Eliz. 2, c. lxviii)

1975: *The Brookwood Cemetery Act 1975* (c. xxxv)

2000: *Our Towns and Cities the Future: Delivering an Urban Renaissance* (Cm 4911)

2001: *House of Commons, Select Committee on the Environment, Transport & Regional Affairs. 8th Report [on] Cemeteries.* (HC 91-I, HC 91-II)

2001: *The Government Reply to the 8th Report from the Environment, Transport & Regional Affairs Committee Session 2000–2001 HC91 Cemeteries* (Cm 5281)

(D) BOOKS, PAMPHLETS, ETC.

Anon., *Extramural Burial: the Three Schemes* (London, 1850); this pamphlet is probably by Sir R. Broun

Anon., *The London Necropolis & National Mausoleum (Woking Cemetery), Brookwood, Surrey* (London, LNC, 1887)

Anon., *The London Necropolis* (London, LNC, *c.* 1899)

Anon., *The London Necropolis* (London, LNC, *c.* 1902)

Anon., *The London Necropolis* (London, LNC, *c.* 1904)

Broun, Sir R. *Extramural Interment and the Metropolitan Sanitary Association: Letter to the Prime Minister and the Chief Commissioner of Woods and Forests* (London, Trelawney Saunders, 1852)

——, *Extramural Sepulture: Synopsis of the London Necropolis and National Mausoleum at Woking* (London, Trelawney Saunders, 1851)

——, *Metropolitan Extramural Sepulture: London Necropolis and National Mausoleum Company. Letter to the Right Honourable Lord Palmerston, with a copy of a Letter to Messrs Rothery, Dakin and others* (London, Pelham Richardson, 1854)

Darwin, B., *The Glades of Remembrance, Brookwood* ([Brookwood?], LNC, *c.* 1950)

Loudon, J.C., *On the Laying Out, Planting, and Managing of Cemeteries, and on the Improvement of Churchyards* (London, Longman Brown Green, 1843; also reprinted Redhill, Ivelet Books, 1981)

Walker, G.A., *Gatherings from Grave Yards* (London, Longman, 1839; also reprinted New York, Arno Press, 1977)

——, *Practical Suggestions for the Establishment of National Cemeteries* (London, 1849)

(E) NEWSPAPERS AND PERIODICALS CONSULTED

Builder

County Chronicle & Surrey Herald

Daily News

Daily Telegraph

Era

Evening News

Globe

Illustrated London News

Leisure Hour

South Western Gazette

Spectator

Surrey Advertiser

Surrey Mail

Surrey Standard

Surrey Times

The Times

Undertakers' Journal

Westminster Review

Woking News & Mail

Woking Review

(II) OTHER SOURCES

(A) BOOKS

Adams, Steven, *The Arts & Crafts Movement* (London, Grange Books, 1997)

Anon., *The Dictionary of National Biography* (Oxford, Oxford University Press, various dates)

Anon., *Who Was Who* (London, A. & C. Black, various dates)

Ariès, Philippe, *The Hour of our Death* (London, Penguin, 1981)

Ashton, Rosemary, *Little Germany: Exile and Asylum in Victorian England* (Oxford, Oxford University Press, 1986)

Bindman, David (ed.), *The Thames & Hudson Encyclopaedia of British Art* (London, Thames & Hudson, 1985)

Boase, Frederic, *Modern English Biography* (London, Frank Cass & Co., 1965)

Brooks, Chris, *Mortal Remains: the History and Present State of the Victorian and Edwardian Cemetery* (Exeter, Wheaton/The Victorian Society, 1989)

Caine, Philip D., *American Pilots in the RAF: the WWII Eagle Squadrons* (Washington, Brassey's, 1998)

Camp, John, *Holloway Prison: the Place and the People* (Newton Abbot, David & Charles, 1974)

Clarke, John M., *The Brookwood Necropolis Railway* (3rd edn, Oxford, Oakwood Press, 1995)

——. *Cemeteries in Conflict: the Disposal of the Dead in Nineteenth Century London 1849–1854* (unpublished BA dissertation, University of Cambridge, 1982)

——. *An Introduction to Brookwood Cemetery* (Brookwood, The Brookwood Cemetery Society, 1992)

——. *An Introduction to Brookwood Cemetery* (revised and updated 2nd edn, Brookwood, The Brookwood Cemetery Society, 2002)

Clout, Hugh (ed.), *The Times London History Atlas* (London, Times Books, 1991)

Cobb, Gerald, *The Old Churches of London* (2nd edn, London, B.T. Batsford, 1942)

Copper, Basil, *Necropolis* (Wisconsin, Arkham House Publishers, Inc., 1980; also London, Sphere Books, 1981)

Countryside Agency (*et al.*), *Quality of Life Capital: Overview Report* (London, The Countryside Agency, 2001)

Crystal, David, *The Cambridge Biographical Encyclopaedia* (Cambridge, Cambridge University Press, 1994)

Curl, James S., *A Celebration of Death* (London, Constable, 1980)

——. *Death and Architecture* (revised and updated edn of the above; Stroud, Sutton Publishing, 2002)

——. *Kensal Green Cemetery* (ed.), (Chichester, Phillimore, 2001)

——. *The Victorian Celebration of Death* (Newton Abbot, David & Charles, 1972)

——. *The Victorian Celebration of Death* (revised and updated edn, Stroud, Sutton Publishing, 2000)

Dixon, Roger, *Victorian Architecture* (London, Thames & Hudson, 1978)

Drabble, Margaret (ed.), *The Oxford Companion to English Literature* (5th edn, Oxford, Oxford University Press, 1985)

Gilbert, Martin, *First World War* (London, HarperCollins, 1994)

Hackman, Harvey, *Wates's Book of London Churchyards* (London, Collins, 1981)

Harvey, David, *Monuments to Courage: Victoria Cross Headstones & Memorials* ([Bahrain?], Kevin & Kay Patience, 1999)

Hayward, Arthur L., *The Dickens Encyclopaedia* (London, The Folio Society, 1989)

Hobson, Chris, *Airmen Died in the Great War, 1914–1918: the Roll of Honour of the British and Commonwealth Air Services of the First World War* ([Colchester?], Hayward & Son, 1995)

Holmes, Mrs Basil, *The London Burial Grounds* (London, T. Fischer Unwin, 1896)

Hyde, Ralph, *The A to Z of Victorian London* (London, The London Topographical Society, 1987)

Jalland, Pat, *Death in the Victorian Family* (Oxford, Oxford University Press, 1996)

Jellicoe, G. *et al.*, *The Oxford Companion to Gardens* (Oxford, Oxford University Press, 1986)

Johnson, David A., *The Battle of Britain and the American Factor July–October 1940* (Pennsylvania, Combined Publishing, 1998)

Jones, P. Herbert & Noble, G.A. (eds), *Cremation in Great Britain* (2nd edn, London, The Cremation Society, 1931)

Jupp, Peter C. & Howarth, G. (eds), *The Changing Face of Death: Historical Accounts of Death and Disposal* (London, Macmillan, 1997)

—— and Gittings, C. (eds), *Death in England: an Illustrated History* (Manchester, Manchester University Press, 1999)

—— and Grainger, H.J. (eds), *Golders Green Crematorium 1902–2002* (London, London Cremation Company, 2002)

Kennedy, Michael, *The Concise Oxford Dictionary of Music* (4th edn, Oxford, Oxford University Press, 1996)

Kent, William, *An Encyclopaedia of London* (rev. edn, London, J. Dent, 1951)

——. *My Lord Mayor* (London, Herbert Jenkins, 1947)

Kenyon, J.P. (ed.), *The Wordsworth Dictionary of British History* (Ware, Wordsworth, 1994)

Kenyon Report, *War Graves: How the Cemeteries Abroad will be Designed* (London, HMSO, 1918)

Litten, Julian, *The English Way of Death: the Common Funeral since 1450* (London, Robert Hale, 1991)

Lloyd George, David, *War Memoirs* (two vol. edn, London, Odhams Press, 1938)

Longworth, Philip, *The Unending Vigil: A History of the Commonwealth War Graves Commission 1917–1984* (London, Leo Cooper, 1985)

Magnusson, M. (ed.), *Chambers Biographical Dictionary* (5th edn, Edinburgh, Chambers, 1990)

Marshall, John, *A Biographical Dictionary of Railway Engineers* (Newton Abbot, David & Charles, 1978)

May, Trevor, *The Victorian Undertaker* (Princes Risborough, Shire Publications, 1996)

Meller, Hugh, *London Cemeteries: an Illustrated Guide and Gazetteer* (3rd edn, Aldershot, Ashgate, 1994)

Middlebrook, M. & M., *The Somme Battlefields: a Comprehensive Guide from Crecy to the Two World Wars* (London, Viking, 1991)

Morley, John, *Death, Heaven and the Victorians* (London, Studio Vista, 1971)

Mukerji, Jenny, *Brookwood Cemetery: a Necropolis for Victorian London* (unpublished BA dissertation, University of Surrey, 1999)

Muthesius, Stefan and Faidman, Clifton (eds), *The Faber Book of Anecdotes* (London, Faber & Faber, 1985)

Nairn, Ian and Pevsner, Nikolaus, *The Buildings of England: Surrey* (2nd edn, revised by Bridget Cherry, London, Penguin, 1971)

Palmer, Alan, *The Penguin Dictionary of Modern History 1789–1945* (2nd edn, London, Penguin, 1983)

Parsons, Brian, *The London Way of Death* (Stroud, Sutton Publishing, 2001)

Peace, David, *Eric Gill: the Inscriptions, a Descriptive Catalogue* (London, The Herbert Press, 1994)

Pearson, Lynn F., *Mausoleums* (Princes Risborough, Shire Books, 2002)

Pevsner, Nikolaus, *The Buildings of England: London,* rev. Bridget Cherry (London, Penguin, various dates)

Pickles, J.D., *The Victorian Cemetery: an Illustrated Exhibition* (Cambridge, [Cambridge University Press], 1993)

Richardson, Ruth, *Death, Dissection and the Destitute* (London, Penguin Books, 1988)

Russell, G.W.E., *Saint Alban the Martyr, Holborn: A History of Fifty Years* (London, George Allen & Unwin, 1916)

Sekon, G.A., *The London & South Western Railway: Half a Century of Railway Progress* (London, 1896; also reprinted Weston-super-Mare, Avon Anglia, 1989)

Small, Ken, *The Forgotten Dead* (London, Bloomsbury, 1988)

Taigel, A. and Williamson, T., *Parks and Gardens* (London, B. T. Batsford, 1993)

Thompson, Sir Henry, *Modern Cremation: its History and Practice* (2nd edn, London, Kegan Paul, 1891)

Treuherz, Julian, *Victorian Painting* (London, Thames & Hudson, 1993)

Weinreib, Ben & Hibbert, Christopher, *The London Encyclopaedia* (London, Macmillan, 1983)

Weis, René, *Criminal Justice: the True Story of Edith Thompson* (rev. edn, London, Penguin, 2001)

Whiteman, J.R.& S.E., *Victorian Woking* (Guildford, Surrey Archaeological Society, no date)

Wilkins, Margery A., *By Royal Command: William Ewart Lockhart RSA RSW* (Annan, The Friends of Annandale & Eskdale Museums, 1998)

Williams, R.A., *The London & South Western Railway, Volume 1: the Formative Years* (Newton Abbot, David & Charles, 1968)

Willson, E.J., *Nurserymen to the World: the Nursery Gardens of Woking and North-West Surrey and Plants Introduced by Them* (London, E.J. Willson, 1989)

Wilson, Brenda, *Home Office Research into Cemeteries and their Management, Case Study 3: Brookwood Cemetery Ltd, Private Company, English Suburbs* (London, Home Office, 2002)

Young, E. & W., *Old London Churches* (London, Faber & Faber, 1956)

(B) ARTICLES

Alexis, Fr. 'The Enshrinement of the Sacred Relics of Saint Edward the Martyr' in *The Shepherd* 1984, V (1), pp. 2–7

——. 'The St Edward Brotherhood' in *Necropolis News* 1996, 2 (1), pp. 3–13

Anon., 'The American Memorial Chapel, Brookwood' in *Architects' Journal* 1930, pp. 403–8

Anon., 'The US Prison at Shepton Mallet' in *After the Battle* 1988, no. 59, pp. 28–51

Bisset, Jennie, 'Actors' Acre: Burial Ground of the Dramatic, Equestrian and Musical Sick Fund Association' in *Necropolis News* 2001, 3 (3), pp. 17–22; and 2001, 3 (2), pp. 11–15

Clarke, John M., 'Brookwood Cemetery: Midst Surrey Pines' in *Genealogists' Magazine* 2001, Vol. 27, pp. 29–32

——. 'Brookwood Necropolis Railway' in *South Western Circular* 1981–2, Vol. 5, pp. 118–144

——. 'The Development of London's Cemeteries: a Brief Survey' in *Genealogists' Magazine* 1998, Vol. 26, pp. 9–13.

——. 'Necropolis Line: Comments' in *South Western Circular* 1983–5, Vol. 6, pp. 196–200

——. *Necropolis Trail No. 1: the Cemetery Railway* (The Brookwood Cemetery Society, 1993)

——. *Necropolis Trail No. 2: the Military Cemeteries* (The Brookwood Cemetery Society, 1994)

——. *Necropolis Trail No. 3: The Anglican Section I* (The Brookwood Cemetery Society, 1995)

——. *Necropolis Trail No. 4: The Anglican Section II* (The Brookwood Cemetery Society, 1995)

——. *Necropolis Trail No. 5: The Nonconformist Section I* (The Brookwood Cemetery Society, 1995)

——. *Necropolis Trail No. 6: The Nonconformist Section II* (The Brookwood Cemetery Society, 1996)

——. 'Service of Dedication of the Memorial to Mrs Edith Thompson and Others' in *Necropolis News* 1994, 1 (3), pp. 15–18

——. 'Staff of the L&SWR Co. buried at Brookwood' in *South Western Circular* 1986–8, Vol. 7, pp. 56–65

——. 'Two Railway Funerals' in *South Western Circular* 1981–2, Vol. 5, pp. 260–61

Dendy, George, 'Last Orders Please! Memories of Brookwood Cemetery' in *Necropolis News* 1995, 1 (5), pp. 6–8

Devine, Ian, 'The Community of Reparation to Jesus in the Blessed Sacrament' in *Necropolis News* 2001, Vol. 3, pp. 7–10

Fisk, Audrey, 'Humble Heroes: the Ancient Order of Foresters' in *Necropolis News* 1998, 2 (5), pp. 5–20

French, Stanley, 'The Cemetery as a Cultural Institution: the Establishment of Mount Auburn Cemetery and the "Rural Cemetery" Movement' in D.E. Stannard (ed.), *Death in America* (Philadelphia, University of Pennsylvania Press, 1975)

Harvey, David, *Necropolis Trail No. 8: The Victoria Cross* (The Brookwood Cemetery Society, 1999)

Hobson, Chris, *Necropolis Trail No. 7: Airmen (Anglican Section)* (The Brookwood Cemetery Society, 1998)

King, David and White, Peter, 'The Strongest, Bravest and Best' in *After the Battle* 1990, no. 67, pp. 22–5

Lilly, J. Robert, 'US Military Executions' in *After the Battle* 1995, no. 90, pp. 50–3

Machachek, Karel, 'Colonel Judr Pavel Svoboda 1916–1993' in *Necropolis News* 1995, 1 (5), pp. 12–14

Parsons, Brian, 'From Welbeck to Woking: William Garstin Funeral Director and the Early Cremations at Woking Crematorium' (forthcoming)

Ronald, Joan, 'Ernest Augustus Runtz' in *Necropolis News* 2000, 3 (5), pp. 5–10.

White, Edward, 'Crematorium Gardens' in P.H. Jones (ed.), *Cremation in Great Britain* (3rd edn, London, The Cremation Society, 1945)

Wilkinson, T.W., 'Burying London' in George R. Sims (ed.), *Living London* (London, Cassell, 1901–3; also reprinted in 4 vols as *Edwardian London*, London, The Village Press, 1990)

INDEX

Note: numbers in parentheses refer to main chapter entries, denoting a brief biography and/or a description of the memorial or structure.